JON E. LEWIS is an historian and writer. His many books include *The Mammoth Book of True War Stories*, *The Mammoth Book of War Letters and Diaries*, *The Mammoth Book of How It Happened: World War I* and *The Mammoth Book of How It Happened: World War II*.

Also available

The Mammoth Book of 20th Century Science Fiction, vol. 2
The Mammoth Book of Best British Mysteries
The Mammoth Book of Best Horror Comics
The Mammoth Book of the Best of Best New SF
The Mammoth Book of Best New Horror 19
The Mammoth Book of Best New Manga 3
The Mammoth Book of Best New SF 21
The Mammoth Book of Best War Comics
The Mammoth Book of Bikers
The Mammoth Book of Boys' Own Stuff
The Mammoth Book of Brain Teasers
The Mammoth Book of Brain Workouts
The Mammoth Book of Comic Fantasy
The Mammoth Book of Comic Quotes
The Mammoth Book of Cover-Ups
The Mammoth Book of Crime Comics
The Mammoth Book of the Deep
The Mammoth Book of Dickensian Whodunnits
The Mammoth Book of Egyptian Whodunnits
The Mammoth Book of Fast Puzzles
The Mammoth Book of Funniest Cartoons of All Time
The Mammoth Book of Great Inventions
The Mammoth Book of Hard Men
The Mammoth Book of Historical Whodunnits
The Mammoth Book of How It Happened: America
The Mammoth Book of How It Happened: In Britain
The Mammoth Book of Illustrated True Crime
The Mammoth Book of Inside the Elite Forces
The Mammoth Book of Jacobean Whodunnits
The Mammoth Book of King Arthur
The Mammoth Book of Limericks
The Mammoth Book of Maneaters
The Mammoth Book of Martial Arts
The Mammoth Book of Men O' War
The Mammoth Book of Modern Battles
The Mammoth Book of Modern Ghost Stories
The Mammoth Book of Monsters
The Mammoth Book of Mountain Disasters
The Mammoth Book of New Sherlock Holmes
The Mammoth Book of New Terror
The Mammoth Book of On the Road
The Mammoth Book of Pirates
The Mammoth Book of Poker
The Mammoth Book of Prophecies
The Mammoth Book of Tattoos
The Mammoth Book of Roaring Twenties Whodunnits
The Mammoth Book of Sex, Drugs and Rock 'N' Roll
The Mammoth Book of Short Spy Novels
The Mammoth Book of Sorcerers' Tales
The Mammoth Book of The Beatles
The Mammoth Book of The Mafia
The Mammoth Book of True Hauntings
The Mammoth Book of True War Stories
The Mammoth Book of Unsolved Crimes
The Mammoth Book of Vintage Whodunnits
The Mammoth Book of Wild Journeys
The Mammoth Book of Zombie Comics

THE MAMMOTH BOOK OF

Modern
Battles

Edited and with an Introduction
by Jon E. Lewis

ROBINSON

RUNNING PRESS
PHILADELPHIA · LONDON

ROBINSON

Originally published as *The Mammoth Book of Battles* by Constable & Robinson, 1999

This revised and updated edition first published in the UK by Robinson,
an imprint of Constable & Robinson Ltd, 2009

Reprinted by Robinson in 2017

5 7 9 10 8 6 4

Copyright © Jon E. Lewis, 1999, 2009

The moral right of the author has been asserted.

All rights reserved.
No part of this publication may be reproduced, stored in a retrieval system, or transmitted,
in any form, or by any means, without the prior permission in writing of the publisher, nor be
otherwise circulated in any form of binding or cover other than that in which it is published and
without a similar condition including this condition being imposed on the subsequent purchaser.

A CIP catalogue record for this book
is available from the British Library.

UK ISBN: 978-1-84529-885-2

Robinson
An imprint of
Little, Brown Book Group
Carmelite House
50 Victoria Embankment
London EC4Y 0DZ

An Hachette UK Company
www.hachette.co.uk

www.littlebrown.co.uk

First published in the United States in 2009 by Running Press Book Publishers
A member of the Perseus Books Group

All rights reserved under the Pan-American and International Copyright Conventions

*This book may not be reproduced in whole or in part, in any form or by any means, electronic or
mechanical, including photocopy, recording, or by any information storage and retrieval system
now known or hereafter invented, without permission from the publishers*

Books published by Running Press are available at special discounts for bulk purchases in the
United States by corporations, institutions and other organizations. For more information, please
contact the Special Markets Department at the Perseus Books Group, 2300 Chestnut Street, Suite 200,
Philadelphia, PA 19103, or call (800) 810-4145, ext. 5000, or email special.markets@perseusbooks.com.

US Library of Congress number: 2009920313
US ISBN 978-0-7624-3625-5

10 9 8 7 6 5 4 3 2 1
Digit on the right indicates the number of this printing

Running Press Book Publishers
2300 Chestnut Street
Philadelphia, PA 19103-4371
Visit us on the web!
www.runningpress.com

Printed and bound in Great Britain by CPI Group (UK) Ltd., Croydon CR0 4YY

Papers used by Robinson are from well-managed forests and other responsible sources

MIX
Paper from
responsible sources
FSC
www.fsc.org   FSC® C104740

Contents

List of Maps

Acknowledgments

The editor has made every effort to locate all persons having any rights in the selections appearing in this anthology and to secure permission from the holders of such rights. Any queries regarding the use of material should be addressed to the editor c/o the publishers.

Parts of this work previously appeared in the partwork *War Monthly*, unless otherwise stated all material is copyright © Marshall Cavendish Partworks Ltd.

Introduction copyright © 2009 Jon E. Lewis.

"Spion Kop" is an extract from *Great Military Battles* by Howard Green. Copyright © 1971 Leo Cooper Ltd. Reprinted by permission of the publishers.

"Tsushima" is an extract from *Great Battles of the 20th Century*, edited by Barrie Pitt. Copyright © 1977 Phoebus Publishing and BPC Publishing Ltd.

"The Marne" by Robert B. Asprey is reprinted from *Great Military Battles*, ed. Cyril Falls, Spring Books, 1969. Copyright © 1964 George Weidenfeld & Nicolson Ltd.

"Megiddo" by Basil Liddell Hart is an extract from *The Real*

War, Faber & Faber, 1930. Copyright © 1930 Sir Basil Liddell Hart.

"Battle of Britain 1940" by Christopher Dowling was first published in *Decisive Battles of the Twentieth Century*, edited by Noble Frankland and Christopher Dowling, Sidgwick & Jackson, 1976. Copyright © 1976 Dr Christopher Dowling. Reprinted by kind permission of the author.

"Dunkirk" by Peter Young is reprinted from *The British Army 1642–1970*, William Kimber, 1967. Copyright © 1967 William Kimber & Co Ltd.

"Stalingrad" by E. D. Smith is reprinted from *Decisive Battles of Hitler's War*, ed. Antony Preston, New Burlington Books, 1977. Copyright © 1977 Quarto Ltd.

"Midway" by Donald Macintyre is reprinted from *History of the Second World War*, ed. Basil Liddell Hart, Macdonald & Co (Publishers) Ltd, 1989.

"The Battle of the Atlantic" by Herbert A. Werner is an extract from *Iron Coffins*, Da Capo Press, 1998. Copyright © 1969 Herbert A. Werner.

"Ardennes" is an extract from *World War 1939–45: A Short History* by Peter Young. Copyright © 1966 Brigadier Peter Young. Reprinted by kind permission of Mrs Mary Delion and London Management and Representation Ltd.

"El Alamein" is an extract from *Decisive Battles of the Western World* by J. F. C. Fuller, Vol III. Copyright © 1974 J. F. C. Fuller. Reprinted by permission of David Higham Associates.

"Imjin River" by A. H. Farrar Hockley and E. L. Capel is an extract from *Cap of Honour* by David Scott Daniell. Copyright © 1951 David Scott Daniell and 1975 The Gloucestershire Regiment.

"Hamburger Hill" is an extract from *Vietnam: The Decisive Battles* by John Pimlott, Marshall Editions, 1990. Copyright © Marshall Editions Developments Ltd 1990. Reprinted by permission of Marshall Editions Developments Ltd.

"Jerusalem" by Ashley Brown was first published in *The Elite: Special Forces of the World*, Marshall Cavendish 1987. Copyright © 1987 Marshall Cavendish Ltd. Reprinted by permission of Marshall Cavendish Ltd.

"Wireless Ridge" is an extract from *2 Para Falklands* by Maj-Gen John Frost, Buchan & Enright Publishers Ltd. Copyright © 1983 by Maj-Gen John Frost.

"Desert Storm" by Jon E. Lewis, copyright © 1995 Jon E. Lewis.

"Tora Bora" by Johnny Verey. Copyright © 2008 Johnny Verey.

Introduction

If war is not an inevitable part of human nature, it is an enduring one. The profession of arms is man's oldest, and the moments in the last three millennia when peace has existed across the globe have been few. It is a startling fact that in only one year since 1945 has a British soldier not been killed in the line of duty. (That year was 1969). The timespan covered by this book, the twentieth century and the first decade of the twenty-first, differs only from previous epochs in that it has been more war torn; it has also been the epoch in which warfare has, courtesy of technological advance, achieved Armageddon-like destructive capability.

Modern warfare is not quite synonymous with the period from 1900 to the present: the industrialization of slaughter began with the American Civil War in the 1860s, when entire ranks of close-pressed troops were felled by the Gatling gun. This was but a portent, however, and the mechanics and methods of mass slaughter would only truly proliferate in the following century. The replacement of cavalry by artillery, the invention of the aircraft, the tank, the ballistic missile and the atomic bomb are peculiar to this age of violence and have taking the killing power of armies into realms unimaginable by those who fought at Agincourt, or even Gettysburg and Bull Run. Technology has given humankind original and powerful means to kill; technology has also changed the strategy and tactics of warfare. This is most clearly seen in the addition of airpower to land campaigns, such as the Wehrmacht's Blitzkrieg and the US armed forces' Air Land Battle Doctrine in the Gulf War. And, as the Scud and Cruise missile exchanges in the Persian Gulf proved – if proof was needed – developments in electronics, robotics, satellite and computer technology have resulted in the automation of war. War by remote control is no longer science fiction.

So far, however, no modern war has been won without the small but necessary contribution of the foot soldier, the seaman and the pilot. And I would say that the mental and emotional strain on that service man over the last century or so has become greater. War is increasingly unendurable because it is increasingly far removed from anything the combatant undergoes in ordinary, civilian life. Most of the post-1950s generations have no experience of war beyond distant images on television screens, leaving the soldier, together with his (and sometimes her) naval and air force peers, isolated from society. War, as the general said, is hell. But hell does not remain behind on the battlefield. It lives on in the mind of survivors.

This book is a collection of decisive battles from the modern era, engagements which have changed the course of history. Some are directly decisive, such as the naval battle of Tsushima (1905), which saw the spectacular sinking of the Russian fleet, or El Alamein (1942), which witnessed the effective destruction of Rommel's Afrika Korps, while others are indirectly so. The battle of the Marne (1914) seemed to merely halt the German army; in retrospect, the failure of the Germans to deal France a knock-out blow meant they were fighting a war they had little, if any, chance of winning thereafter. Neither do decisive battles have to be titanic clashes of arms: Dien Bien Phu (1953) was a relatively small engagement, but the shock of losing broke the morale of the French army and people, and ended France's reign as a colonial power in the Far East. Similarly the battle of Admin Box (1944), which should perhaps more properly catalogued as a "skirmish" in military annals, had a galvanizing effect on the British army in Burma, because it showed that the Tommy could beat "the Jap". Most of the forty-five battles described on the following pages are by a distinguished company of military historians, but I have not forgotten that the experience of a battle – as distinct from its analytical hows and whys – is best communicated by one who fought in it. Accordingly, a number of the accounts are by soldier participants.

This is the last age in which the human factor, the courage of the frontline combatant and the tactics of the battlefield commander, will be of supreme importance and the last age in which armed men and women will make history.

So then, soldier/sailor/airman, a salute. This book is dedicated to those who fought and fell in the battles it describes.

1
The Boer War

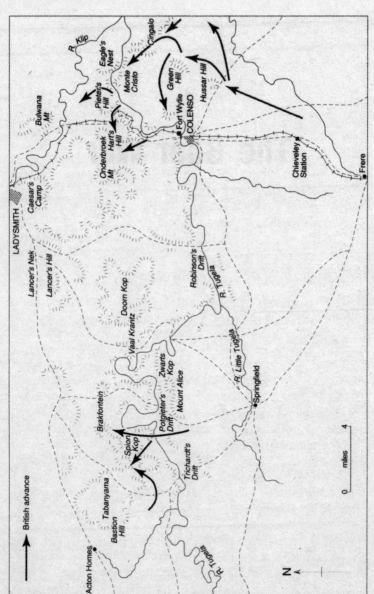

1.1 Spion Kop

Spion Kop (1900)

Howard Green

Occasioned by the discovery of vast reserves of gold and diamonds in an area of South Africa outside British jurisdiction, the Anglo-Boer War (1899–1902) began as an exercise in imperial humiliation, with the volunteer Boer army scoring impressive successes over Queen Victoria's regular. Not the least of the Boers' successes was at Lady-smith, where Sir George White and 12,000 troops were besieged on 2 November 1899. In an effort to relieve Ladysmith (and the similarly surrounded garrisons at Mafeking and Kimberley), the British government dis-patched two divisions and appointed General Sir Redvers Buller the supreme commander in Natal. Buller – who had won a VC in the Zulu Wars – was a vastly experienced soldier but, like other commanders in the British army, his experience was limited to fighting poorly armed "natives". The Boers were white, Dutch-speaking farmers who had used their mineral wealth to buy state-of-the-art arms. The had also pioneered a highly mobile style of "commando" warfare whose pièce de résistance was the ambush. On the approach to Ladysmith, Buller's force was caught in a bloody trap at Colenso on 15 December 1899, losing ten out of twelve field guns and over 1,000 men killed, wounded or taken prisoner. Depressed by this defeat, Buller abandoned

effective control over his army to Major-General Sir
Charles Warren, who let it blunder towards Ladysmith
without any clear tactical course to follow through the hills
to the town's south. One of these hills was Spion Kop,
towering 1,500 feet above the Tugela River.

On the late evening of 23 January, the Lancashire Brigade of
Royal Lancasters, Lancashire Fusiliers, South Lancashires and
Thorneycroft's Mounted Infantry left camp, and started to
climb the hill, the most formidable, and the highest in the
whole range, 1,500 ft above the river. The night was dark, a fine
drizzle was falling and the going very difficult. Moreover, the
Brigade Commander, Major-General Woodgate, an ex-Royal
Lancasters CO, was 55 years of age and in poor health. The
operation bore many similarities to the disaster of Majuba, 19
years earlier.

Spion Kop has three very steep sides, with one convenient
and less acute shoulder up which the brigade climbed. Towards
the end of the climb the hill flattens out considerably, the top
being a shallow inverted saucer. At the farther (northern) end
the high ground runs away into a long narrow saddle, terminat-
ing in a pronounced knoll. To the east and 200 ft below the main
hill, and quite separate from it, rises another small feature, Aloe
Knoll.

Advancing on a two-battalion front, the Royal Lancasters
on the left and the Lancashire Fusiliers on the right followed
by Thorneycroft's Mounted Infantry and led by the Brigade
Commander in person, the brigade reached the first "flatten-
ing out" without incident after climbing for most of the night.
Owing to their weight and the noise inseparable from carrying
them, many of the picks and shovels were dumped, but the
men were still encumbered with greatcoats and ammunition,
though not with rations or water. At about 6 a.m. the thick
dawn mist gave the impression that the summit had been
reached, the only Boer encountered had been bayoneted and
the men ordered to give three cheers to indicate success to
Warren below.

An hour or so later the mist suddenly lifted to disclose the summit 200 yards further on up the hill. The ensuing movement on to the hilltop in the now broad sunlight warned the main enemy force on the far side of the hill and on the plain below of the occupation, and they immediately started to climb the Aloe Knoll and the north-western end of the main feature at the end of the saddle. From the former they were soon able to accurately enfilade the shallow trench being built on the summit by the Lancashire Fusiliers on the right, while the Royal Lancasters, prolonging the line to the left, came under accurate though frontal fire from the knoll at the far end of the saddle. From Tabanyama Hill, 3,000 yards to their left front across the intervening valley, an enemy battery enfiladed both battalions.

The extreme rockiness of the hill precluded any serious trench digging although both battalions scraped together some skeleton forms of breastwork two feet high. The picks left behind would now have come in useful, although the Lancashire Fusiliers could only have protected themselves from the accurate enfilade fire from Aloe Knoll by changing direction through 90 degrees. Even then it is doubtful whether much entrenching could have been done under this fire.

Thorneycroft's Mounted Infantry passed through the two battalions and tried to reach the far end of the inverted saucer, but were prevented from doing so by the fire from the north-west knoll. A few men from the two left-hand companies of the Royal Lancasters managed to crawl forward individually, around the left (outer) flank of the MI, meeting some success but also meeting enemy scouts who had crept up along the saddle on to the far segment of the saucer. Attempting to relieve this complete hold-up, the South Lancashires were ordered forward to support. They too were quickly pinned down before reaching the three forward battalions. About an hour after the two forward battalions had commenced their trench digging, General Woodgate was mortally wounded, standing at the right of the Lancashire Fusiliers trench – the nearest man to Aloe Knoll. He was carried down the hill and died in hospital some days later.

Woodgate left chaos behind him in the command on the hill and Colonel Crofton, CO of the Royal Lancasters, as the senior officer present, assumed command. Losing his head he sent a panic signal to Warren below: "Reinforce at once or all is lost. General dead." Buller intercepted this message before it reached Warren and he rode over with his usual advice, suggesting that an officer more vigorous than Crofton should be appointed. Warren chose Thorneycroft, and as he was junior to Crofton heliographed to him his promotion to Brigadier-General. The news of his promotion reached Thorneycroft later but he neglected to tell Crofton.

Later in the day Warren sent up the Middlesex to the summit, and the Scottish Rifles to work round the right flank, in order to relieve the pressure on the Lancashire Fusiliers. They were unsuccessful, however, and not only added to the general confusion on the hill, but also further confused the problem of command. Colonel Hill of the Middlesex was senior to both Crofton and Thorneycroft.

When Hill arrived he assumed command at the eastern end of the summit, while Thorneycroft was commanding with vigour at the other end. They did not meet for several hours. The commander of the brigade to which the Middlesex and Scottish Rifles belonged, Major-General Talbot-Coke, felt that he too should ascend the hill to see his two battalions and was then, of course, the senior officer present. However, he did not attempt to take command and the delicate point as to who was in fact the commander on the hilltop was never settled.

During the afternoon the CO of the 60th Rifles (from yet another brigade), acting on his own initiative and without orders from any superior officer, moved his regiment far out to its right and, climbing a long low ridge, came up behind the Boers on Aloe Knoll, causing them considerable casualties from long-range fire. The Boers, seeing the British were in front of and now apparently behind them, were about to leave the Knoll, when General Buller rode up to Warren and demanded to know who had ordered the 60th on its lone though effective mission. On hearing that the CO had done so without orders Buller immediately and peremptorily ordered the battallion to withdraw, on the grounds that he would not tolerate such independence, almost amounting to impertinence:

At dusk the problem of who in fact was in command on the hilltop became acute. General Talbot-Coke advised Colonel Hill, whom both believed to be in charge, to retire to the plain during the night. Thorneycroft at the other end of the hill had now run into Crofton. Both felt that they should stay for some time yet and therefore sent a heliograph message to Warren for orders. Warren had by now heard from Hill, advising retirement, yet Thorneycroft was, as far as Warren knew, in command. However, Warren took Hill's advice and ordered withdrawal. As the left-hand units were on their way down they met Hill, who, having by now changed his mind, ordered them back. Thorneycroft came along and met Hill and, after a considerable wrangle, the latter had to admit that Thorneycroft as a Brigadier-General was the senior. The withdrawal continued.

And so the British left their objective leaving 300 dead behind them. Probably at about the same time, the Boers, quite certain that the British troops were immovable, withdrew too, and for several hours Spion Kop remained unoccupied. At dawn next day a Boer scout, finding the hill empty, signalled to his commander below and the hill was reoccupied.

It must be remembered that Woodgate's brigade did not capture Spion Kop. It took possession of it on finding it untenanted after the climb – and there remained unmolested for some hours. Had the Lancashire Fusiliers only advanced another 300 yards over the top to the far rim, they would have reached the edge of the plateau and so seen the Boers leave their laager on the plain below when commencing their climb. To assault such a slope against the fire of the defending British infantry was an impossible task for the enemy, no matter how mediocre the British shooting. But Woodgate did not see the obvious advantage he held.

Amongst the might-have-beens that are found in every account of every defeat must appear Warren's failure during the day to visit the hilltop where seven of his battalions, parts of his three brigades, were closely in action. A firm grip of the situation taken there must have shown a general with dominance how the battle could be controlled. The *junta* of five or six colonels on the site was quite incapable of doing so.

By 4 a.m. the next morning the last battalion had left Spion Kop, and rejoined the camp at Spearman's. When it was all over Buller moved Warren's command away to the east again, and out of range of Boer guns.

After Spion Kop a curious psychological change came over the Boers along the Tugela. They knew they had successfully invaded Natal, had surrounded and were now successfully besieging behind them a garrison of 8,000 British soldiers, had won resounding victories at Colenso and Spion Kop, all in less than three months. Their morale should indeed have been high. But it wasn't.

Many of them felt they had done enough and that their farms and families were now again top priority. Many applied for, and got, leave for "private affairs" and went back to Transvaal. Others, more fearful, wondered whether they had not taken on too much. They felt that their invasion of friendly territory and then the defeats of their enemy would sooner or later bring retribution on them from the ever-growing and professional British Army. These Boers did not apply for leave. They quietly left their comrades in the hours of darkness and also rode back to Transvaal. By the time the next British advance took place there were only 4,000 Boers to face Buller's 20,000 British soldiers.

The battle of Spion Kop not only affected the morale of the Boers. It proved to be a sledge-hammer blow to the insouciant confidence of Victorian Britain. Football fans in Liverpool, in ironic reference to the battle, nicknamed the high-terraced end of the local stadium "the Kop".

Paradoxically, the loss of arrogance proved to be Britain's salvation. After its maulings by modern weaponry and tactics at Spion Kop and elsewhere in South Africa, the British army woke up to the need for good shooting and battlefield flexibility. Consequently, the British Expeditionary Force of 1914 was probably the best-trained force

*ever put into the field by Britain. So accurate and fast,
indeed, was the Tommy's rate of fire with a Lee Enfield
rifle in the initial – and key – battles of the First World
War that the Germans were convinced that they were
facing men with machine guns.*

2
The Russo-Japanese War

Tsushima (1905)

C. P. Campbell

The great sea battle that was fought on 27 May 1905 in the straits dividing Tsushima island from Japan ended with the complete destruction of a first-class European battle squadron by the navy of a country with only 50 years of modern industrial and organizational experience. In those 50 years warship design had progressed from wooden sailing-ships firing cannon broadsides to steel steam-powered battleships, equipped with wireless, fire-control systems and mounting guns capable of engagement at ranges over five miles. When the battle came it was a clash of design ideas and tactical doctrines, but above all of two different social systems' will to win. As the Japanese commander, Admiral Togo, wrote after the battle, "The *Mikasa* [Togo's flagship] and the 11 others of the main force had taken years of work to design and build, and yet they were used for only half an hour of decisive battle. We studied the art of war and trained ourselves in it, but it was put to use for only that short period. Though the decisive battle took such a short time, it required 10 years of preparation."

On 30 January 1902 Japan announced the conclusion of an alliance with Great Britain. The Royal Navy's tactical doctrines and British shipbuilding practice had already permeated the thinking of those directing Japan's emergence as a world naval power. Japan's transformation from a medieval to a modern state had proceeded at breakneck speed. They had imported 200 years of Europe's industrial revolution wholesale, but in choosing their military mentors – Germany for the army, and Britain for the navy – they had chosen well. There had even been a modern naval action for Japan to test and show her efficiency at sea.

In 1894 the Chinese Empire seemed on the verge of breaking up. Korea and the vast Manchurian hinterland were tempting targets for Japanese military ambition. The Japanese successfully convoyed a large army to Korea in August, 1894, until the Chinese Admiral Ting sought battle off the mouth of the Yalu River.

When the time came, however, the contest was not so clear; Admiral Ting adopted outdated tactics, throwing away his advantage in gunpower, and the Japanese Admiral Ito decided the action by out-manoeuvring and encircling the Chinese line of battle. Four Chinese ships were sunk by gunfire and one by collision, but their battleships proved the value of armour against hits from smaller guns. Ito's flagship, the *Matsushima*, was hit three times by 12-in and once by 10-in shells, causing great damage and over a hundred casualties. Both fleets retired, but Japan was left in command of the Yellow Sea and free to continue her military adventure in Korea.

The prize of the Liaoutang Peninsula, with the ice-free port, Port Arthur, at its base, was snatched away when the European powers put on diplomatic pressure to "protect" China. The wound to Japanese pride was deepened when, as soon as Port Arthur had been returned to China, Russia bullied the ailing Empire into allowing the Trans-Siberian Railway to be completed to Vladivostok across Manchuria. By March 1898 the Russians were in Port Arthur itself and developing an ice-free naval base to complement Vladivostok, 300 miles to the north. The Japanese, however, had already started a programme of naval expansion which would bring their fleet up to six new battleships, six armoured cruisers, and eight light cruisers by 1903.

Russia watched with alarm, and commenced production in Baltic yards of eight battleships. In contrast to the Anglophile Japanese, these ships were strongly influenced by French

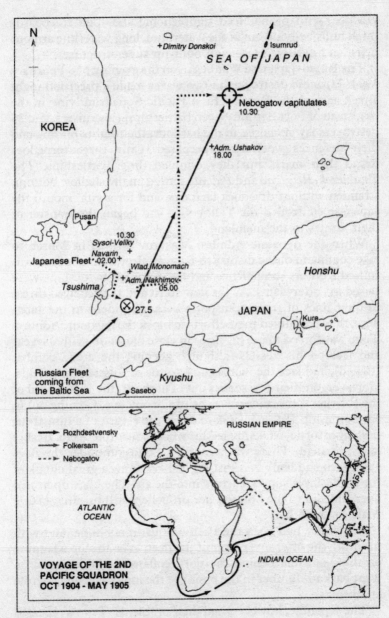

2.1 The Battle of Tsushima

practice, with pronounced tumblehome and high freeboards (high hulls bellying out at the waterline), long waterline armour belts, and massive masts and built-up superstructures.

The Russo-Japanese War began on the evening of 8 February 1904. Japanese destroyers in two waves made a precision night attack against the Russian First Pacific Squadron lying in the roadstead of Port Arthur. Seven battleships, six cruisers, and 25 destroyers lay anchored in the harbour, their lights blazing and their defences woefully ill-prepared. Only three torpedoes found their mark, but they crippled three battleships. The *Tsarevitch*, *Retzivan* and *Pallada* settled on the shallow bottom, stranded without dry-dock facilities, and for a vital month the Japanese controlled the Yellow Sea and began the transfer of their armies to the mainland.

When the dynamic Admiral Makarov arrived in March to take command of the dispirited Russian fleet, the squadron was roused from its somnolence and the damaged battleships were raised in coffer-dams. As the new spirit and the renewed threat to their lines of troop transports became evident to the Japanese, they redoubled their efforts to block the harbour. Admiral Togo was forced to use his ships in close blockade, with its wear and tear on his vessels (although keeping the crews combat trained), and face the increasing hazards of Russian minefields. However, on their few sorties out of harbour, the lack of skill of the Russian commanders was painfully obvious. Coming out in the battleship *Petropavlovsk* to cover the return of a disastrous destroyer sortie, Makarov led his whole squadron over a freshly laid minefield. There was a muffled explosion under the flagship, then suddenly two vast explosions threw a great chunk of the battleship's superstructure into the air. The big ship heeled over and slid to the bottom, her propellers still turning, taking Makarov with her.

His ability had been the Pacific Squadron's hope, and with his death the offensive power of the fleet, even to stop a landing on the peninsula behind the port, collapsed. "The squadron went back to slumber in the basins of the inner harbour," wrote an observer.

The Japanese, however, had their problems. Togo's repeated attempts to block the harbour with suicide assault blockships had failed. The battleships *Habuse* and *Yashima* were claimed by mines. The Vladivostok cruisers were harrying troop transports. It was clear that the Russians were gathering a fleet in the Baltic to come to the aid of embattled Port Arthur, and Togo was still forced to keep his fleet concentrated should the new if reluctant Russian commander, Admiral Vitgeft, attempt a breakout.

It was not Togo, however, who had to make the first move. Vitgeft received direct orders from the Tsar to take the squadron to Vladivostok and, led by minesweepers, the fleet left harbour on 10 August 1904. There was little hope aboard the Russian ships and already Japanese scouts were signalling the news of the attempted break-out to Togo's battle-squadron, now steaming north to engage. Togo had hoped the Russian fleet could be kept inside harbour where it would be destroyed or captured by the besieging army. Now his Combined Fleet, the entire battleship strength of Japan, would have to accept battle, with the threat of the Baltic Fleet still to come. He could afford to lose no more ships.

The Japanese purpose would be served by barring the way out, if not destroying the Pacific Squadron in battle. Suitably the opposing heavy squadrons opened fire at extreme range, with the Russian gunnery surprisingly accurate. As the long daylight action continued and the opposing fleets manoeuvred for the best position, the Japanese were taking serious punishment. Mutual destruction would bring Togo a tactical victory but would lose him the strategic object.

Then suddenly, with darkness beginning to fall, two 12-in shells struck the Russian flagship *Tsarevitch*, killing every man on the bridge. Of Vitgeft only a bloody piece of one leg remained, and the battleship lurched out of control, turning the battle-line into a milling throng. After minutes of utter disorder, Admiral Prince Uhtomski, flying signals from the bridge-rails of *Pereviet* (the signalling masts had been shot away), led the squadron back to Port Arthur as *Retzivan* and *Pobieda* put up a gallant rear-guard. Japanese destroyers closed in for the kill, but in the darkness the Russian stragglers managed to regain the harbour they had so recently left. The crippled *Tsarevitch*, hit by over 15 12-in shells, was interned in German Kiau-Chow, and two cruisers suffered similar fates. The sortie had been a fiasco, but until the hit on *Tsarevitch* the Russians had held their station. With their leadership gone, their fighting ability collapsed. The Vladivostok squadron was brought to action on 14 August, but again this resulted in a Russian defeat. The cruiser *Rurik* was sunk and the cruiser *Gromoboi* ran aground. All that was left was the cruiser *Rossiya* and three Russian admirals, unable to reach Port Arthur, where the leaderless Russian battleships had retired to lick their wounds.

The humiliations in the East made the dispatch of reinforcements inevitable. The Russian confidence of 1904 that the "yellow monkeys" would be crushed had been shattered by Admiral Togo Heiacho and his British-built battleships. In the Baltic a force of new first-class battleships were under construction, while older cruisers and battleships were undergoing refits. If Port Arthur held out, and a powerful new fleet could come to the rescue, Japan might still be denied her mainland ambitions.

The man appointed to command this "Second Pacific Squadron", Rear-Admiral Zinovei Petrovitch Rozhdestvenski, faced immense problems in even getting his ships ready for sea. Food and clothing had to be procured for the fleet's 12,000 seamen, and machinery prepared for an ordeal beyond any design endurance. In the brief periods of manoeuvres nothing had gone right, with ships colliding and wildly inaccurate gunnery. The overriding problem, however, was coal. Great Britain, with her virtual monopoly of high-grade smokeless Welsh coal, had declared it contraband, but not before the Japanese had built up large stockpiles. The Royal Navy's dominance in the world's oceans was maintained by a strategic chain of coaling stations. Russia had none and only a fitful access to "neutral" French and German colonial ports. The Baltic Fleet would have to cover 19,000 miles of sea, round the Cape and across the Indian Ocean, consuming 17,000 tons of coal per 1,000 miles. The bunkering capacity of the most modern Russian battleship was 1,063 tons. The solution was a fleet of 60 German colliers dispatched in succession to meet the slow-moving fleet at prearranged rendezvous between Libau in the Baltic and Port Arthur on the other side of the globe.

On 15 October 1904 Rozhdestvenski raised his flag on *Kniaz Suvorov* and, with flags waving and bands playing, the fleet steamed out of Libau to avenge the humiliations in the East. It comprised seven battleships – the recently completed *Suvorov, Aleksandr III, Borodino, Orel* and *Oslyaba*, and the *Sissoi Veliki* and *Navarin*, with two armoured cruisers, *Admiral Nakimoff* and *Dmitri Donskoi*, four light cruisers, *Aurora, Svietlana, Zhemtchug* and *Almaz*, plus seven destroyers and nine transports. The modern battleships mounted four 12-in and seven 6-in guns in paired turrets and had complete waterline armour belts 10 inches thick. The pronounced tumblehome and built-up superstructures, following French design practice, made them bad seakeepers. The overloading of coal and stores added to the miseries of the voyage.

Once at sea, the morale and incompetence of the fleet was revealed to the world when fantastic rumours of a Japanese torpedo attack were taken seriously. To the men on the bridges who remembered the surprise night attack on Port Arthur, however, an attack from British bases did not seem that fantastic. In the North Sea the repair ship *Kamchatka* lost contact with the main fleet, and her frantic signals of sighting torpedo-boats (in fact a Swedish steamer) reached the line of battleships just as they ran into British trawlers working off the Dogger Bank. Wild alarm seized the Russians and equally wild gunnery tore into the trawlers. The voyage had opened in fiasco, and meanwhile Britain seemed on the brink of war.

At Tangier the fleet divided. Admiral Velkerzam was ordered to take the older shallow-draught ships through the Suez Canal and rendezvous at Nossi Bé on the northern tip of Madagascar. At a halting pace the main squadron crawled around the coast of Africa. Ships got lost. Engines broke down. Sailors went mad in the heat, cursing the back-breaking ritual of coaling from the faithful German colliers. Inside the ships coal was piled everywhere, "not up to the neck but over the ears", as an officer wrote, blinding and choking, but, worst of all, making any combat training impossible.

At Nossi Bé the divided squadron rejoined and learned the news that Port Arthur had fallen. Worse still, the coaling arrangements had broken down and the fleet was stuck. All the Russian Admiralty could do was dispatch a "Third Pacific Squadron" under the command of Rear-Admiral Nebogatov. The fleet did manage an epic crossing of the Indian Ocean, coaling at sea from lighters, until on 9 May, off the coast of French Indo-China, Nebogatov's 'tubs' caught up to further embarrass Rozhdestvenski.

On 23 May the Russians coaled off the China coast for what was going to be the last time. The force heading into the battle-zone was organized in four divisions. The first, led by Rozh-destvenski's flagship *Suvorov*, comprised the battleships *Alek-sandr II, Borodino*, and *Orel*. The Second Division was commanded by Admiral Velkerzam aboard the *Oslyaba*. The unfortunate admiral had succumbed to a tropical disease on the day of the last coaling, but Rozhdestvenski kept this informa-tion from the fleet. The *Sissoi Veliki, Navarin*, and *Admiral Nakhimoff* followed the dead admiral's flagship. In *Nicolai I* Nebogatov led the Third Division, *Apraxin, Seniavin* and *Ushakoff*, while Admiral Enquist, in the *Oleg*, commanded the eight cruisers.

On board the *Mikasa*, flagship of the Combined Fleet lying in the anchorage of Masan on the Korean mainland, Togo directed the operations to meet Rozhdestvenski's ships, now heading for Vladivostok. The most likely route, the Tsushima Strait separ-ating the island of that name from Japan, was divided into boxes, each patrolled by Japanese cruisers. The Tsugau Strait and the northern route around the top of Japan itself was left thinly protected, but it was a gamble that would pay off. The Russian crews prayed for fog to conceal the seven miles of the ships under their black smoke haze until they reached the safety of Vladivostok, which now seemed like the promised land. But for Rozhdestvenski merely to evade Togo and take refuge in another Port Arthur might merely repeat the fate of the First Pacific Squadron. The Russian admiral had at least to inflict some damage on the enemy, so the squadron's speed was adjusted so that it would enter the zone of maximum danger at daylight on 27 May 1905.

A Japanese armed merchant cruiser, the *Shinano Maru*, made the first contact at 0330. The wireless message reached Togo in the *Mikasa* – "The enemy sighted in section 203, he seems to be heading for the eastern channel." Ninety minutes later Togo led the battleships of the First Division out of Masan, the *Mikasa, Shikishima, Fuji,* and *Asahi,* the armoured cruisers *Kasuga* and *Nisshin.* Vice-Admiral Kanimura led the Second Division, the armoured cruisers *Izumo, Azuma, Tokira, Yagumo,* and *Iwate.* The cruisers *Naniwa, Takachino, Tsushima* and *Akashi* made up the Third Division. Every ship was fuelled and armed for maximum combat efficiency and able to make 18 knots, in contrast to the worn-out Russian ships' nine or ten. Togo's fleet could bring to action 16 12-in guns, and 112 8-in and 6-in guns. The Russians had 26 12-in, 10-in and 121 8-in and 6-in. Any disparity in gunpower mattered little, however; it was how the rivals used their gunpower that would decide the battle.

Togo's operations officer, Commander Akiyama, had set a seven-stage trap for the Russians to sail into. The battle would open with torpedo and destroyer attacks and the third phase would be the direct fleet engagement. The remaining stages envisaged the piecemeal destruction of any survivors who might break through towards Vladivostok. The Russian fleet was detected too late for torpedo attacks, but shadowing cruisers forced Rozhdestvenski into weakening his formation. Fearing an attack, he ordered a manoeuvre designed to give him the advantage of crossing the "T" of the main Japanese force that must be waiting somewhere ahead. When the shadowing cruisers disappeared, the Russian admiral ordered the First and Second Battleship Divisions to make an eight-point turn to starboard to bring the ships in line abreast. As *Suvorov* began the turn, the Japanese cruisers reappeared and the order to the Second Division was contradicted. The Russian captains could not execute the change with any kind of precision and, as Nebogatov wrote, "The enemy continued to turn to port and lay parallel to our mob, since this is the only word to describe our formation." Thus the Russians were suddenly steaming towards Togo's battlefleet at a closing speed of 24 knots in a ragged battle formation exposed on the port side.

It was not Togo's intention to make a north–south broadside pass which, although it might damage the weaker Russian ships, would leave them travelling in the direction of Vladivostok. At 1355 the Japanese line swung to port, following the *Mikasa* in

line ahead. Rozhdestvenski meanwhile had ordered the First
Division to increase speed and come out from behind the
weaker line to his left and take up battle formation in one line
ahead. Then, as Togo reached the chosen position, the battle
ensigns were unfurled, and in a breathtaking manœuvre the
whole Japanese line swung round 180 degrees, turning in
succession, with the *Mikasa* leading. At the moment of the
turn they were helpless targets, but only the lighter Russian
shells were making hits. Coming out of their turn, one after the
other, the Japanese ships opened a slow deliberate fire at a range
from 5,000 to 6,000 yards. Then they put on speed, sprinting
north-east at 15 knots across the head of the labouring Russian
column. The classic manœuvre that the pirates of the Inland
Sea had known for centuries, crossing the "T", had been
achieved.

As the Japanese gunners found the range, the leading Russian
ships were subjected to a fearful battering. *Suvorov* and *Oslyaba*
were soon set ablaze, while, on board, stunned Russian seamen
struggled with primitive damage-control procedures. At 1455
Suvorov fell out of line on fire. At 1505 *Oslyaba* sank, throwing
the following ships into chaos. *Aleksandr III* turned to port to
escape under the smoke haze and slip behind the stern of the
Japanese line, all steaming in perfect formation at 15 knots, all
guns in action. As they looped back to intercept them, only the
Suvorov was left in sight, still fighting back with one remaining
12-in gun and a few remaining 12-pounders. From the shattered bridge the severely wounded Rozhdestvenski was carried
to a gun turret.

An hour later the missing Russian main body was resighted
and forced to turn away south-east as Togo's ships poured fire
into them at a range of 1,000 yards. *Aleksandr III* was forced out
of formation until, at 1800, it capsized and sank. The *Orel* was
raked with fire and the *Borodino* burned until her exploding
magazines ripped the ship apart. At the same time the gallant
Suvorov was being finished off with torpedoes. The agony of
the battleships could not relieve the cruisers *Oleg* and *Zhemtchug*, set ablaze, and the sinking of several auxiliary ships.

At darkness, with Vladivostok still 300 miles away, Admiral
Nebogatov, in the old *Nicolai I*, attempted to achieve some sort

of order from the decimated survivors of the First and Second Divisions and his still largely intact Third Division. The gathering darkness, however, brought the torpedo-boats. Pressing home vicious attacks at ranges under 300 yards, the Japanese sank *Navarin* and *Sissoi Veliki*. Admiral Enquist, in the *Oleg*, led *Zhemtchug* and *Aurora* away from the slaughter out by the southern exit of the Tsushima Strait, but the cruisers *Admiral Nakhimoff* and *Monomakh* were scuttled on the island of Tsushima itself.

At dawn the next day Nebogatov's shattered fleet was found again by the Japanese battlefleet. The tragic Rozhdestvenski lay critically wounded in the destroyer *Bedovi*. By 1115 the Japanese had formed a great circle around the Russian ships. There was no other choice. A white tablecloth was run up on *Nicolai I*, but Togo did not cease fire until the Russians had stopped their engines. Victory was complete when the unconscious Admiral Rozhdestvenski was carried into captivity. Of the 12 Russian ships that had made up the battle-line, eight had been sunk and four captured. Four cruisers had been sunk, three scuttled and Enquist's three escaped to the Philippines and were interned in Manilla. One cruiser, the *Almaz*, and two destroyers reached Vladivostok. The Russians lost 4,830 men killed, 7,000 prisoners and more interned. The Japanese lost three torpedo-boats, 117 killed and 585 wounded.

What had happened? How had two battlefleets – on paper, at least, evenly matched – met and fought with such an uneven outcome? The reports of the British naval attachés who had gone into action with the Japanese fleet were eagerly studied, and they indicated several things: that Russian gunnery had been surprisingly accurate at long range but had rapidly deteriorated as soon as the Russian ships themselves took damage; high-explosive shells had caused the most damage, and a high proportion of Russian shells found their target but failed to explode; that shells, not torpedoes, were the deciders; that both sides had fought bravely, but that the Japanese were vastly more competent than their opponents. All this was true, and the reports strongly influenced naval thinking up to the start of the First World War and beyond, however, the Second Pacific Squadron had been disadvantaged from the very start.

The ships were worn out by the voyage from across the world. Of the men themselves, many were sick. Ironically, after the repeated stops and the backbreaking task of coaling, the Russians had gone into action with too much, some of it stacked on the decks in bags. The Japanese, taking the advice of a Royal Navy report by Admiral Fisher, had actually dumped coal, losing weight to fighting trim and giving them the crucial speed advantage which allowed Togo's in succession turn and the foiling of Russian evasive manoeuvres. The Japanese had concentrated fire on the Russian flagships, and as soon as they had been battered out of line, their squadrons' formation and fighting qualities fell to pieces.

Finally, the initiative and competence of the Japanese commanders and seamen was something that could not be quantified in the reports drafted by naval attachés. As they had closed for action, Admiral Togo had been urged to take cover as he stood on the exposed bridge. He shook his head. "I am getting on for sixty, and this old body of mine is no longer worth caring for. But you are all young men with futures before you, so take care of yourselves and continue living in order to serve your country." The Imperial Japanese Navy was a curious mixture of Royal Navy traditions of understatement and Oriental determination to triumph. Togo had signalled to the fleet: "The rise and fall of the Empire depends upon the result of this engagement. Do your utmost, every one of you."

3
The First World War

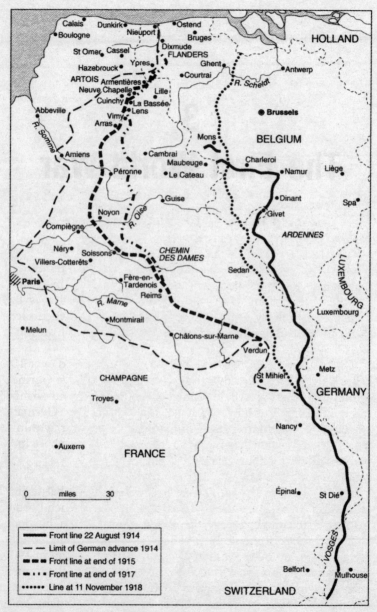

3.1 The Western Front, 1914–18

The Marne (1914)

Robert B. Asprey

The first battle of the Marne changed history as men thought to make it and war as men thought to fight it. This vast, incredibly complex action fought from 5–10 September 1914 was the climax of a military campaign begun on 4 August when Germany invaded Belgium in the first great offensive of the First World War.

The major front of the Battle of the Marne covered over 125 miles – from north-east of Paris to Verdun – with five German armies fighting six Allied armies, and another four armies engaged from Verdum south to the Alps. The Germans marched to the Marne expecting to finish the war within a week; five days later they began a retreat to trenches where they would remain for four years.

What went wrong?

The opening of the western war saw a German battle line stretching almost from the Swiss Alps along the French border through Luxembourg past the Belgian and Dutch borders, some 475 miles of mountains, valleys, hills, and plains. Under a plan drawn up by the military *maestro* Schlieffen and in 1905 bequeathed to his weak successor, Moltke, a small German army was holding the Russians in the east; two armies were defending Alsace-Lorraine up to Metz-Diedenhofen; and, stretching from this fortified bastion, five other armies, Germany's best, poised to wheel scythe-like through neutral Belgium into northern France, then sweep down west of Paris on to the French armies – a gargantuan development designed for swift, total victory.

To counter a German invasion the French army, under General Joffre, evolved Plan XVII, a monument to the doctrine of the *offensive à outrance* – the all-out offensive – that held the French army in its tactical grip. Plan XVII called for strengthened covering forces to fight a defensive action along the northeastern frontier until the thirteenth day of mobilization. Then two right-wing armies would attack into Lorraine and two centre armies would strike east of Metz. Joffre's left army, commanded by Lanrezac and buttressed by Sir John French's British Expeditionary Force, would attack either into Belgium or straight ahead towards Metz, depending on the route of the German invasion. Simultaneously Russia would send two armies into eastern Germany.

The French army commander did not dream that the enemy could muster sufficient strength for a sweep from the north. His error and that of most of his staff and commanders stemmed from the completely mistaken but enduring belief that German reserve corps and divisions were employed behind and separate from their regular forces – the conventional method discarded years before by Germany.

On 20 August the French dream became a nightmare when the disastrous Battle of the Frontiers began. In four days Joffre's armies, one after the other, met the enemy and were beaten. By 24 August the battle was over, a fantastic Allied defeat with casualties estimated as high as 300,000, with all the armies in retreat to the Marne.

A good many commanders would have given up. Joffre did not. He sensed that his armies were beaten, but not broken. He knew his terrain and he knew the staying power of artillery, particularly the French 75 mm cannon, the most advanced artillery piece of the day. On 24 August he revealed the secret of the Battle of the Marne to the Minister of War:

We are therefore compelled to resort to the defensive . . .
our object must be to last out as long as possible, trying to

wear the enemy out, and to resume the offensive when the
time comes . . .

From 24 August to 5 September the French and British
retreated, the British stopping to fight the bitter action of
Le Cateau, the French the vicious fight at Guise-Saint
Quentin. Time and again Joffre attempted to halt the retreat,
to reorganize and strike back. Time and again the advancing
grey hordes of enemy upset his plans; time and again he faced
disaster from the recalcitrant commanders, Sir John French
and General Lanrezac, who seemingly loathed each other
more than the enemy. He could not persuade Sir John to
hold up his withdrawal; he had to threaten Lanrezac into
fighting at Guise. Yet with stolid calm he continued to face
each crisis as it arose, patching here, plugging there. Evil days
these, but patience is said to be its own reward, and Joffre was
to find this true.

For while Joffre roamed the battlefield like a frustrated
Napoleon, his finger on the precise pulse of his people, his
German counterpart was trying to fight a battle from hundreds
of miles away. Reports of great victories pouring into Moltke's
headquarters, first at Coblenz, later at Luxembourg, lulled him
into a false optimism that was to cost him victory and deprive
him of command. During those weeks Moltke reduced the
strong right wing demanded by Schlieffen from seventeen to
less than twelve corps. No longer could he wheel west of Paris.
But with the fantastic victories claimed by his commanders and
with the victory of Tannenberg in Prussia, no longer did this
seem necessary. At the end of August, with Kluck encountering
only slight resistance, with the British (in Kluck's mind) obviously defeated, the main French strength, Moltke supposed,
lay in front of his centre armies. If Rupprecht could break
through on the left and Bülow and Kluck on the right, Moltke
would win a classic envelopment battle. Kluck already had
suggested a change of direction and Moltke now approved:
Bülow to march towards Rheims, Kluck toward Compiègne-
Noyon.

This was what Kluck wanted and he now pushed his tired
army recklessly to the south. When Moltke, suddenly worried

by reported French troop movements from east to west, ordered him to "follow in echelon behind the Second Army" where he would be responsible for the flank protection of the force, Kluck refused the order. Demonstrating the selfish independence that characterized the German commanders, he continued to push his advance across the Marne.

By 5 August Moltke realized the true situation and ordered the two right wing armies to "remain facing the eastern front of Paris, to act offensively against any operations of the enemy from Paris . . ." Convinced of Moltke's confusion, Kluck decided to let his army reach the day's objective *south* of the Marne, but did order one corps to halt where it stood in the north.

Learning of Kluck's change of direction on 31 August, Joffre followed his subsequent advance with the keenest interest. His patching and plugging had given him two new forces, Maunoury's Sixth Army north of Paris and Foch's Ninth Army in the centre. A visit from the British Secretary of State for War, Lord Kitchener, had also slowed Sir John's withdrawal and Joffre further appeased the British commander by relieving Lanrezac in favour of the dashing Franchet d'Esperey. Trusting that his right and centre armies could hold, Joffre decided to send the Sixth Army against Kluck's right while the BEF and Fifth Army attacked north.

In moving to the jump-off line on 5 September, Maunoury struck Kluck's rear corps commanded by Gronau, who that evening withdrew some six miles to a better defensive position. Kluck did not learn of the action until late in the evening. By then one of Moltke's staff officers, Lieutenant-Colonel Hentsch, sat in Kluck's headquarters giving the aloof Army Commander for the first time a realistic picture of the overall situation, in short that all the victories claimed by all the German commanders had been grossly exaggerated and the French army was still very much alive. Kluck now began feeding back a corps to Gronau with plans to send back another on the following day. He would keep one corps in the south until Bülow's army could wheel south-west to screen Paris by extending Kluck's left flank. Simultaneously Moltke's centre armies were attacking to the south-east to open the way for

Rupprecht's Sixth Army, struggling since 4 September to push in from the east.

On 6 September Maunoury continued his advance but soon ran into Gronau's new line stretching from Vincy south to the Marne, where the first elements of Linsingen's corps were arriving. Throughout the day the battle roared with one side gaining here, one side there, a vicious but inconclusive fight that left the battlefield strewn with dead and wounded. To the south the BEF moved forward with maddening slowness despite slight opposition. D'Esperey's advance ran into Kluck's two corps on the left while on the right he sent a corps to help Foch whose Ninth Army was caught by Bülow's wheeling movement. Although this slowed d'Esperey's advance, it also disrupted Bülow's movement, an accomplishment whose importance would grow with the hours.

Joffre's centre formed his most vulnerable area, for on Foch's right only a single cavalry division screened the twelve-mile wide Gap of Mailly, and on Langle's right the five-mile Gap of Revigny separated him from Sarrail. Only very hard fighting elsewhere on this line prevented the enemy from exploiting these gaps that would remain a threat until plugged by two corps marching in from the east.

To Joffre the day gave a slight tactical edge to the enemy, a strategic edge to himself. He was about to be rewarded hugely, if unknowingly, for Bülow, using Kluck's two corps on his right, decided to complete his own wheeling movement on 7 September. But now Kluck, seriously worried about the battle north of the Marne, ordered *these same two corps* to retire ten to twelve miles behind the Petit Morin River. This meant that the gap already existing between Bülow's right and Kluck's left would be considerably widened. To worsen matters, Kluck early on 7 September forced Bülow to send the two corps north.

Here was a decision of paramount importance to the entire battle, a decision made by Kluck and Bülow with no reference to Moltke, and with not even a very clear idea of the enemy's intentions. By transferring these two corps north, the German commanders extended a gap already insufficiently guarded by tired cavalry divisions inadequately supported by Jäger battalions. Coming up from the south, pointed precisely at this gap, was not only the entire British army but, on its right, Conneau's cavalry corps and d'Esperey's Fifth Army.

Joffre correctly recognized this as the key to the battle and in the ensuing days his every moment went to holding in the north, centre, and east while pushing up from the south. It was not easy to hold. Everyone wanted more divisions, troops that Joffre did not possess. When Sarrail complained of his weak left Joffre told him to pull in his right from Verdun, that the bastion could temporarily hold on its own. When Castelnau proposed to withdraw from the Grand Couronné at Nancy, Joffre ordered him to stay where he was. To help Maunoury he brought a division from the east. When it reached Paris on 7 September that city's military governor, the doughty old soldier Galliéni, collected a thousand taxicabs to convoy two regiments to the front – and "Galliéni's taxicabs" became a household phrase in the history of war.

Joffre was commanding, Moltke was not. Convinced finally that a dangerous gap existed between his right wing armies, Moltke called a staff meeting on 8 September. Someone suggested sending Hentsch to visit the front and determine the true situation. Moltke agreed and gave the staff officer oral orders that are still surrounded in controversy. Allegedly, Moltke told Hentsch that if a retreat were necessary he should influence the movement so as to close the gap between these armies, that is the First Army should withdraw to the line Soisson-Fismes, the Second Army to a line behind the Vesle River.

At Second Army headquarters, Bülow, no longer the victor but a tired old man, told Hentsch:

> As a result of all that we have been through and of the hard combats of the last few days, the Second Army has naturally lost a considerable part of its combat value. It is no longer capable of forcing a decisive victory. As a result of the transfer of two army corps from the left to the right wing of the First Army, a gap has been created which forms an immediate danger to the inner wings of both the First and Second Armies. I am informed that enemy columns, brigades or divisions [the BEF and d'Esperey's Fifth Army], are on the march into this breach, and I have

no reserves left to attack the enemy or to hold him off . . .
It should therefore be considered whether it would not be
better, viewing the situation as a whole, to avert the danger
by a voluntary concentric retreat of the First and Second
Armies.

Their meeting was still going on when a corps commander
telephoned to report the loss of Marchais-en-Brie to a French
night attack. Montmirail could no longer be defended. Bülow
now ordered his right-wing commanders to begin withdrawing
to a line some six miles east, which once more widened the gap
between the two armies.

Although Hentsch did not again see Bülow, he left the next
morning convinced that Bülow was going to retire. At First
Army headquarters he explained the bleak situation to Kluck's
chief of staff, Kuhl. His pessimism was soon rewarded by the
arrival of Bülow's message, ". . . Second Army begins retirement".

Satisfied that even if Kluck rolled up Maunoury's left he was
in no condition to exploit the victory, Hentsch now repeated
Moltke's instructions for the First Army to withdraw to the line
Soissons-Fismes, where its left would join Bülow's right. Kluck
later agreed. In mid-afternoon of 9 September First Army units
received orders to break off the action and join a general retreat.
Two days later Moltke ordered a retreat along the line.

No one on the French side quite realized what had happened.
Not sure of a victory to exploit, Joffre issued conservative
orders for 10 September. By that evening he knew the battle
was won. After issuing vigorous pursuit orders for the following
day he wrote, "to confirm and exploit this success, the advance
must be pursued energetically, leaving the enemy no respite;
victory is now in the legs of the infantry".

The legs of the infantry were either too tired or too confused
to conform, nor did low weather followed by high winds and
cold, drenching rain help. The pursuit dragged and despite
Joffre's best efforts continued to drag. By 12 September Germany's right wing was trickling into prepared defences behind
the Aisne. At 1.15 a.m. on 15 September Joffre telegraphed his
commanders: "It seems as if the enemy is once more going to

accept battle in prepared positions north of the Aisne. In consequence it is no longer a question of pursuit but of methodical attack".

These were momentous words, for they rang down the curtain on a stage of hopes. Act One of the great war drama – the campaign of the Marne – was played out. Gone now on either side were any pretensions to swift, crushing victory. Gone now on either side were any illusions of the glory and romance of modern war.

The French won the campaign, but there was little to applaud in the victory. France put her casualties for August and September at 329,000. Britain recorded 12,733. The Germans did not publish their figures, which were appalling. Wounded filled the hospitals in both countries; dead covered the fields of France; tons of matériel and guns had been lost.

Now there would be a pause between the acts, a shifting of human scenery along the stage from the Alps to the English Channel. Then the curtain would rise again. In Act II there would be no more mobile warfare. This time the play would take place in trenches. This time the act would last four years.

Gallipoli (1915)

Nigel Bagnall

The order to "fall in" came ringing down to the men of the 10th Australian Battalion resting on the lower decks of HM battleship *Prince of Wales*. They were approaching the Gallipoli peninsula. There was only a dim glow from the stars as the men calmly assembled and formed into dark, shapeless groups. Between these were the smaller Naval beach parties, whose duty it was to put the men ashore. After the final breathless orders, the Australian and New Zealand Army Corps (ANZACs) clambered down the improvised ladders and ship's gangways into the waiting barges.

The expedition was made for a number of reasons. The Russians were asking Britain for aid against the invading Turks. At this time the British War Cabinet were alarmed at the seemingly endless war of bloody attrition in France. Alternative strategies were needed. And an attack on the Turks would help the Russians, make new British Allies in the Balkans and raise home morale. The War Cabinet were unsure about the attack but it was First Lord of the Admiralty Winston S. Churchill's enthusiasm that convinced them. But although the concept was bold, it was marred by indecision, delay and bad planning. Time was lost and with it the chance of surprise and success.

By March 1915 the Turks were alerted to possible British intentions after a failure by the Fleet to force past the Turkish

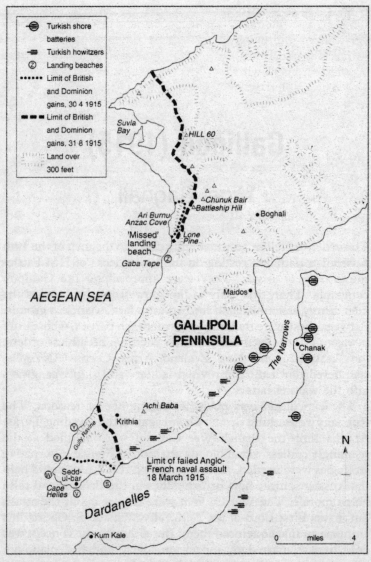

Legend:
- Turkish shore batteries
- Turkish howitzers
- ⓩ Landing beaches
- •••••• Limit of British and Dominion gains, 30 4 1915
- ▬▬▬ Limit of British and Dominion gains, 31 8 1915
- Land over 300 feet

Suvla Bay

△ HILL 60

△ Chunuk Bair
△ Battleship Hill

Ari Burnu
Anzac Cove

• Boghali

'Missed' landing beach

Lone Pine

Gaba Tepe ⓩ

AEGEAN SEA

Maidos •

GALLIPOLI PENINSULA

The Narrows

• Chanak

Achi Baba

Ⓨ

Gully Ravine

• Krithia

Ⓧ

Limit of failed Anglo-French naval assault 18 March 1915

Ⓦ

Sedd-ul-bar

Ⓢ

Cape Helles Ⓥ

Dardanelles

N ↑

0   miles   4

• Kum Kale

3.2 Gallipoli

forts and minefields defending the Dardanelles. This unmistakable warning had been realized by the Turks, who, under their energetic German commander, Marshal Liman von Sanders, began improving their defenses.

The Turkish Fifth Army were to defend the Dardanelles, a 50-mile peninsula with mountainous cliffs falling down into the sea. The ground was rugged and scrub-covered, with little cultivation. All landing sites were dominated by Turkish defenses. Three of their six divisions were on the peninsula, two on the Asiatic mainland and one astride the narrow isthmus of Bulair.

Reports of the preparations for the expedition reached the Turks from their agents. They secretly watched the gathering concentrations of shipping, troops and stores at Alexandria and the island of Lemnos. Exactly where the enemy planned to land remained a mystery. Fearing the effects of the supporting naval bombardment, von Sanders had ordered each division to remain concentrated – maintaining only the minimum forces necessary near the coastline. His defences were to be mobile. With this in mind, he exercised his 60,000 troops with forced marches, developed the paths and bridle tracks on the peninsula into roads, and assembled barges at specially chosen harbors. At the same time, the field fortifications were strengthened by all means possible – mainly by night. Stores were not plentiful, so considerable improvisation was necessary. Torpedo heads were used as mines. Wire and posts were taken from fences enclosing the cultivated areas, and pressed into service as assorted obstacles – both above and below the water line.

General Sir Ian Hamilton, Commander of the 78,000-strong BEF, planned to make two converging attacks at the southern end of the peninsula. The first would be by the British 29th Division. They were to make five separate but simultaneous landings on small beaches near Cape Helles. The ANZACs were to mount the second attack near Gaba Tebe. It was hoped that these separate actions would link up to roll the Turks back along the whole length of the peninsula. Two diversionary operations were also planned. The French contingent would land near the ruins of Troy on the Asiatic mainland, while the

Royal Naval Division in transports accompanied by warships, feinted at Bulair.

Late on the afternoon of 24 April the armada, assembled in Mudros Bay, set sail. At 1000 on the 25th the three battleships and seven destroyers carrying the 3rd Australian Brigade, which formed the assault wave, stopped short of the peninsula. The final preparations for disembarkation were completed. Each of the battleships had towed astern three steam pinnaces – in addition to her own. These now took in tow the ships' boats which had already been lowered. Once alongside, they waited to receive the assembled troops.

Thanks to the rigorous rehearsals there was no confusion. As the midshipman in the stern reported each boat full, the officer in charge ordered 'Cast off and drift astern.' The boats fell behind until arrested by the hawsers connecting them. Once in position the battleships moved slowly towards the shore, each ship trailing four tows. At about 0430, the ships came into line. They were about 3,000 yards from the coast. The signal was given for the tows to cast off and make for the beach. Like so many snakes, they slowly forged their way ahead packed with men – gunwales almost flush with the water. Behind them, until the water became too shallow, the warships followed to cover the final approach. Thirty minutes after the tows had left the battleships, the seven destroyers moved forward right behind them ready to disembark their troops twenty minutes later in a second wave.

General Sir William Birdwood, commander of the ANZACs, planned to land 4,000 men of the 1st Australian Division in three successive waves, on a front of about 2,000 yards. The essence of his plan was speed and surprise. There would be no preliminary naval bombardment. Once ashore, the troops were to strike rapidly inland for some 2,000 yards and secure three prominent hill features. Having captured these, the main body would be passed through and the advance extended over comparatively easy ground for a further 3,000 to 4,000 yards. This was to be the limit of the first day's objectives.

Exactly what happened next remains in dispute. Some blame a northerly current, others a last-minute and largely unknown change of plan, while a Turkish source attributes it to deception on their part. They claim that they found and moved a previously positioned British marker buoy – causing the battleships to anchor too far north. Whatever the cause, instead of approaching the shore over a 2,000-yard front just south of the Ari Burnu promontory, the boats crowded together in the direction of the promontory itself.

This error became apparent to some of the troops and naval officers in the landing boats. But it was too late for the majority to do more than hope to reach the beach before the Turks saw them. Fifty yards from the water line the pinnaces cast off and the boats were rowed in by the sailors until grounding on the shelving beach. During this final approach they were seen. The Turks opened fire from the high ground. Scrambling out of the boats – often into several feet of water – the Australians struggled to the shore and rushed across the beach to take cover where they could. After quickly reorganizing and discarding their heavy packs, they charged the Turkish trenches on the foreshore and bayoneted the enemy. Then, heaving themselves up the steep, broken slope by the roots and branches of trees or shrubs, they doggedly pressed inland as ordered.

Not all the men were so lucky. Some of the packed boats were hit by Turkish machine-gun fire and their occupants suffered severely. Other boats ran aground at the foot of sheer cliffs. The troops were forced to move along the beach until they could find an exit. One effect of this was that the sheer cliffs protected them from Turkish guns. It caused confusion and delay, however, sub-units became hopelessly mixed, and objectives impossible to identify.

But by 0600 the Australians had secured the first ridge and began to infiltrate the second. On the left flank the greatly outnumbered Turkish survivors were falling back in disorder. Waves of Australians were landing unhindered. Some 4,000 men were already ashore and the advance inland gathered strength. By 0700 small groups of Australians had reached the third ridge. Looking down, they could see the Dardanelles only three miles away. Success appeared within reach. But the situation was to change.

The Australians' progress was delayed and then halted by the growing confusion on the beach. As a result of landing on a beach only a few hundred yards long instead of one of 2,000, the confusion and delay in bringing ashore the two follow-up brigades was immense. The control organization ashore had all but collapsed. Wounded were beginning to flow back in an ever-increasing stream and choked the beach from where many of them could not be moved. Others were loaded into boats which were meant to land further reinforcements. The one hospital ship was soon full. Successive waves of troops were landing in an increasingly chaotic manner and – on coming ashore – could be given no precise orders in the absence of any clear knowledge as to what the situation was inland.

The beach itself soon became a scene of confusion. Heaps of hastily dumped ammunition and stores lay around. Among these lay the dead. Overhead the sky was rent with the flash of shrapnel, and the air hummed with bullets. Fortunately, most of the Turkish fire was wild and casualties were not heavy. The same sanctuary was not available farther out to sea where fountains of water were thrown up around the tows operating to and from the ships.

The New Zealand Brigade was part of the reinforcements. They were given the job of lengthening the line to the left of the Australian 1st Division. The transports with their field guns on board were delayed in the face of the Turkish guns, and the New Zealanders were to feel the full bitterness of being subjected to enemy shellfire with no means of retaliation. Eventually some support was given by an Indian Mountain Battery which skilfully maneuvered themselves into seemingly inaccessible vantage points. Unloading, they would fire a dozen or so shots and be down the gully and up to a new position before the Turks could find them.

Of greater impact than even the chaos on the beach was perhaps the arrival of 34-year-old Mustafa Kemal Pasha, Commander of the Turkish 19th Division. Like all able commanders, he contrived to arrive at the critical part of the front when most needed. Alerted by the sound of gunfire from Gaba Tepe where the Australians had first landed, he at once alerted the 19th Division and at 0630 received orders to send one battalion to the heights of Ari Burnu, where the leading Australians were reported to have arrived. Kemal instinctively sensed that a major threat had developed. Far more than one battalion would be needed.

Disregarding orders, he gave instructions for the whole division to move to the coast and he himself led the first regiment which was ready towards the threatened key ridge. On arrival, he ordered the men to rest after their forced march over broken ground while he continued on his way, accompanied only by his ADC, a second officer and an orderly. Then he saw some Turkish troops fleeing towards him. Confronting them he demanded to know why they were running away. The reason was clear enough. Their ammunition was exhausted and the Australians were close behind. This explanation did not satisfy Kemal. He ordered them to fix bayonets and lie down and take up firing positions as the leading Australians came into view. The Australians did the same and unwittingly lost the initiative to the Turks.

Then Kemal ordered an officer to bring up his resting regiment at the double. They soon arrived at the position. The small band of Australians – isolated and unable to resist the ever-increasing weight of Turkish fire – withdrew to the next ridge. It was held by their countrymen. But they were widely dispersed and largely uncoordinated.

From about 1000 the Turks started to push against the Australians' left flank and filter round the seaward slopes of Baby 700 – the main hill feature held by their leading troops. A little later the second Turkish regiment started to arrive. The Turks mounted a series of savage counter-attacks. Baby 700 was lost but retaken again by two companies newly arrived from the beaches.

By now the Turks were arriving in increasing numbers and Baby 700 changed hands no fewer than five times before the Australians were finally driven off. The Australians and the New Zealanders, who had joined them during the afternoon, were suffering heavy casualties. No more than scattered and mixed up elements of seven battalions were trying to stem the advance of most of the Turkish 19th Division which were attacking in massed waves. Silhouetted against the sinking sun, they screamed "Allah" as they advanced. They were cut down *en masse* but successive waves continued the frenzied attacks over the corpses of their fellows.

Neither side were taking prisoners. Groups of ANZACs were cut off and could not repel the Turkish charges any longer. They died where they fought. The firing line was indeterminable. Isolated groups of Australians and New Zealanders clung grimly to a number of key features as night fell and a steady drizzle set in. In the tangled gullies, when not actually fighting, men dug for their lives until, trumpets blowing and still calling on "Allah!" the Turks again surged forward. One New Zealander remembers how they would counter these attacks by running forward themselves "cursing in loud round English and very bad Arabic." Many strange duels were fought that night. One Turkish rush was stemmed by a small band commanded by a corporal armed with nothing more effective than a pick-handle.

Not only the fighting men showed such tenaciousness. From the firing line it took two and a half hours to get a wounded man back onto the beach. Ignoring both bullets and shells, carefully threading their way down the twisting tracks made ever more treacherous by the endless rain, the stretcher bearers and doctors worked unstintingly. Only the most severe cases could be dealt with on the crowded beaches. Many a man, when asked whether he was badly hurt, replied quietly that "he was all right," then died uncomplaining.

Shortly after 2200 General Birdwood came ashore at the request of his two Australian and New Zealand divisional commanders. He found a demoralized force, tired and shaken by the day's events and disorganized by the confusion on the beach. But he was taken aback when it was proposed that there should be an immediate evacuation. Tired themselves, neither the divisional commanders nor their brigadiers believed their men could resist the renewed Turkish counter-attack. They all believed this would be mounted in overwhelming strength by fresh troops at daybreak. With no reinforcements to replace their own exhausted and fragmented units, there seemed no alternative but to evacuate and save what they could. Reluctantly Birdwood agreed. He dictated a message to Hamilton recommending that re-embarkation should start immediately.

In response to this totally unexpected proposal, Hamilton held a conference with his principal advisors. Among them was

Rear-Admiral C. F. Thursby, his naval commander. The Admiral was emphatically opposed to evacuation. He did not regard it as being administratively feasible. The men were tired and disorganized and it was a dark and stormy night. Control on the crowded beaches would be virtually impossible. Under such conditions the losses could be dreadful. Hamilton needed no further persuasion. His instructions were explicit and ended with the exhortation: "You have got through the difficult business, now you have only to dig, dig, dig, until you are safe."

Admiral Thursby was given the job of delivering the message. He landed on the right of the ANZAC position. Here he saw for himself the chaos and suffering which had provoked such despair among the commanders. They felt too much was being demanded of their men. However, he found Birdwood cheerful, though not exactly hopeful, and the two divisional commanders more inclined to stay and fight it out.

What had not been allowed for was the courage and resolution of the troops. Had the order to evacuate been given it is probable that it would have been received with incredulity – possibly even contempt. In the succeeding days' fighting the few orders to withdraw which were given were usually queried and as frequently countermanded.

Although it was known that their own landing and that of the British at Helles should converge, it was as well that neither Birdwood nor his men counted on getting any early help as a result of this plan. The initial British landing had resulted in appalling casualties. The survivors were fighting as grimly as the ANZACs themselves to maintain their positions ashore.

Preceded by a naval bombardment, the British 29th Division had begun to land at five beaches in the vicinity of Cape Helles shortly after the Australians had got ashore at Ari Burnu. The landings at "V" beach by the 88th Brigade were intended to be the most important. An old ruined fort dominated the beach but it was hoped that the Turkish defenders – dug in along the cliff edges as well as concealed in the fort itself – would be largely accounted for by the Navy's guns. The plan was to run the *River Clyde* – an old collier turned "Trojan Horse" specially adapted for landing troops – as close to the beach as possible and bridge the intervening water gap with two lighters. At the same time, other troops would be landed by boat.

Because of a strong current which had delayed their arrival, there was a long interval between the lifting of the naval bombardment and the landings. This allowed the Turkish defenders to recover and take up their positions. When the *River Clyde* gently grounded, the 2,000 men of the Dublin and Munster Fusiliers and the Hampshire Regiment began to cross the improvised causeway. But as they did so, whole platoons were shot down as they raced into the withering Turkish fire. Those in the boats fared no better. The Turks had laid wire below the water and along the beach. Holding their fire until the packed boats became entangled and crowded together on the obstacles, they devastated the leading wave. There were few survivors. A handful of men managed to cross the beach and shelter under the cliffs. Others, who had been ordered to stay below and cease the senseless slaughter, remained aboard the *River Clyde*. With the brigade commander dead, any further attempt to land at "V" beach was suspended until nightfall.

Farther north on "W" beach the Lancashire Fusiliers suffered similar carnage. The naval bombardment had little impact on either the defenders or their defenses. Holding their fire until the last possible moment the Turks reduced the Fusiliers to a handful as they struggled through the water and wire entanglements and tried to cross the open beaches. One officer, who died later, described the scene he saw as he looked behind.

There was one soldier between me and the wire, and a whole line in a row on the edge of the sands. The sea behind was absolutely crimson, and you could hear the groans through the rattle of musketry. A few were firing. I signalled to them to advance. I shouted to the soldier behind me to signal, but he shouted back that he was shot through the chest. I then perceived they were all hit.

In spite of their appalling losses and suffering, the Fusiliers re-formed into a thin line and began to assault the cliffs. Six VCs were won on that desperate morning, but it is unlikely that the survivors would have had the strength to dislodge the Turks had not one of the companies been landed unopposed under a promontory slightly farther to the north. From here the Fusiliers scrambled up onto the high ground and, after being reinforced, extended this foothold to relieve the survivors on the beach. On the other three subsidiary beaches – "X", "Y" and "S" – only light opposition had been encountered and the few troops assigned established themselves ashore without great difficulty.

The Turks had fought resolutely. Of the 9,000 men who had been disembarked onto the five beaches, 3,000 had been killed or wounded and the survivors had secured little more than precarious toeholds. Only "W" and "V" beaches were linked together after dark. The troops who had been kept on board the *River Clyde* were landed and helped extend the bridgehead to make contact with those advancing south from "W" beach.

The landing of the French regiment on the Asiatic mainland near the site of Troy occurred after a preliminary bombardment from French warships at about 1000. There appears to have been some delay and confusion. But by the afternoon the whole force was ashore after encountering only light opposition. The Turkish units in this area initially showed little of the tenacious determination which had been displayed on the peninsula. Progress was easier for the French. Later, however, they were unable to advance farther. After withstanding a series of Turkish counter-attacks during the night, they were withdrawn the following day to reinforce the right flank of the British line on the European side of the straits. "V" beach was handed over to them as their base.

None of these details was known to the ANZACs. Most of them only had time to concern themselves with their own immediate difficulties. After the close-quarters fighting during the earlier part of the night, exhaustion and confusion forced a lull. There was still continuous firing. Here and there the front would flare into angry violence. Generally, however, both sides had reached the limit of exertion. They concentrated on holding on to what they had. Some reinforcements came ashore during the night. The Wellington Regiment were disembarked and sent straight up Plugge's Plateau – a prominent feature behind the firing line. Here the sappers were already hard at work preparing a second and last line of defense. Behind this position no organized resistance would be possible.

Most of the 4th Australian Brigade was also landed but arrived in a very irregular order. Some elements came from one ship and some from another. As each platoon or company came ashore it was immediately sent under the senior officer present to the right flank where the 1st Australian Division was particularly hard pressed. In this manner units became further mixed up.

Elsewhere, the gunners labored through the night to prepare positions and improve access routes for the guns which it was hoped would be disembarked urgently. Stores and supplies poured ashore onto the congested beach. Movement was further hampered by the darkness and the running sea. It was therefore not until daylight on the 26th that the first howitzer was landed. It went into action shortly afterwards. The gun's arrival did not significantly affect the situation, but its steady, reverberating fire acted as a tonic to the hard-pressed infantrymen.

After a night of feverish activity, bitter fighting and at one time near despair, the expected Turkish dawn attack never materialized. Instead, a series of piecemeal assaults took place. These were fiercely mounted but containable because they were neither overwhelming nor sustained. The Turks had themselves suffered heavily. Further reinforcements were slow in arriving, co-ordination was difficult and the situation no clearer to them than to their enemy. The front started to stabilize. Shell scrapes became trenches, outposts became firm strongpoints, the firing was incessant. But it became possible for the troops to snatch a few moments of sleep, eat and adjust to their condition.

However immediately welcome this stabilization of the front may have been to Birdwood and his senior commanders after their earlier anxieties, it represented the first small step towards reproducing the stalemate of Western Front trench warfare which the Dardanelles expedition had been intended to break. As the days turned into weeks and then months, the deadlock became firm. The ANZACs could not materially extend their positions beyond where they had been established during the first night's fighting. The Turks had suffered the most dreadful losses as a result of repeatedly attempting to dislodge them.

In the five weeks since the expedition had begun the British and Dominion troops had suffered almost 40,000 casualties, and the French a further 20,000. Hospitals throughout the Middle East were crammed with the wounded and sick. Large numbers had been shipped back to England. The toll of sickness had arisen alarmingly. All that had been gained was a 6,000-yard-deep front across the peninsula. In the wearing heat of a Mediterranean summer swarms of flies and vultures feasted on the unburied dead that littered the battlefield and invaded every sanctuary of the living. Disease became rife, especially in the crowded conditions at ANZAC, from where an ever-increasing number of sick were having to be evacuated daily. Many of those who remained were gaunt and weak – they were barely recognizable as the same robust, exuberant men who had so recently terrorized Cairo.

After heavy deliberations, it was decided by the War Cabinet that a great endeavor would be made to break the deadlock with large reinforcements. Three separate attacks would be mounted at the same time. First, a new landing would be made due north of the ANZAC position by two British divisions at Suvla Bay. Secondly, the ANZACs would break out and link up with the Sulva Bay landings. Finally, at Helles a holding attack would be mounted to stop the Turks switching reinforcements to the north. Including reserves available either at sea or on the adjacent Aegean islands, the Allies had some 120,000 men. Against this the Turks had an approximately equal number. About 100,000 of these were on the peninsula.

Despite great courage and impressive fighting skill by British, Dominion and Indian troops, by the end of August it was clear that the operation had failed. With certain notable exceptions the inertia of the senior commanders and the rawness of many of the troops at Suvla resulted in an over-cautious advance inland. This allowed the Turks to move their reserves to the threatened area and stem all further progress. About 1,000 men had been lost on the day of the landings. Nearly 8,000 were killed or wounded during the two days following. Another bridgehead had been established but it only served to strain the expedition's administrative resources even more and increase the need for reinforcements to maintain units at fighting strength. A break-out seemed as unrealizable at Suvla as it had proved to be at ANZAC and Helles. The weeks and months dragged on. With the approach of winter, storms added to the supply difficulties. Piers and barges were pounded and smashed on the beaches. Inland, the trenches were flooded and tracks washed away or blocked – preventing ration parties from getting forward. No sooner had the storms abated than a November blizzard swept the peninsula. The battlefields were blanketed in snow and ice. Blankets were frozen solid, weapons jammed and a lull in the fighting was enforced while men struggled to survive in the savage cold. Frostbite increased the sick-rate and deaths occurred amongst the already physically exhausted troops on both sides. One morning at stand-to, 30 men of a British battalion were found frozen to death on the fire-steps of their trenches.

Inevitably – but after much conflicting advice and painful debate – the decision to evacuate the entire peninsula was taken. Planning for such a possibility had already been put in hand. Clear, carefully considered instuctions were issued to selected officers. Unless anything unforeseen happened, the evacuation would be conducted in three stages. All surplus men, equipment and animals would begin to be withdrawn immediately. Then the force would be progressively reduced by formed units between 13 and 18 December. Finally, on the nights of 19 and 20 December the last rearguard would be withdrawn.

If the evacuation was to be undertaken successfully the highest degree of security and deception was essential. Losses of up to 40 per cent were already being expected in some quarters. Every night the outgoing barges were jammed full. But as it grew light a show of landing troops would be made. By day stores and ammunition which could not be evacuated were prepared for destruction, barricades were erected in all the principal communication trenches and a final covering position to be manned by machine-gunners was prepared.

Smoothly and methodically the evacuation continued. Only 3,000 volunteer "Diehards" were left in each of the three divisions to hold the bridgeheads for the last 24 hours on 19

December. About 1,500 of them manned the forward trenches moving from position to position to keep up the usual pattern of fire. Others marched uphill where they could be heard and even seen to impersonate reinforcements, kept the cooking fires burning and maintained the atmosphere of general activity. To accustom the Turks to complete inactivity, periods of total silence had been imposed at irregular intervals during the preceding weeks.

Soon after dusk on the last night the rearguard started to thin out. The guns opened fire for the last time before they too were withdrawn or destroyed when this was not possible. Midnight came and the firing died down on both sides – as was usual. At 0145 the silence was broken on the New Zealand sector when the duty machine-gunner fired three rapid bursts. This was the signal for the brigade's machine-guns to withdraw. At 0200 the already sparsely populated trenches were further depleted as the infantry started to thin out. Individuals slipped away from their positions to form a shadowy stream as they flowed into the main communication trenches from the web of forward posts and trenches.

Those left behind stared into the darkness. They watched fearfully for any signs of Turkish suspicions being aroused, before it was time for they themselves to withdraw. Not all the positions could be abandoned at the same time. Those farthest from the beaches were vacated at 0130. Others, covering the more direct and short approaches, were held until 0315.

As the last of the men were being checked through the control posts manned by staff officers, a huge mine which had been tunnelled under the forward Turkish trenches was detonated. Its deafening roar abruptly shattered the silence and tension of the last few hours. The Turks took this as a signal for an all-out attack and opened fire along the entire front. They kept this up with unrelenting vigor until long after the last of 83,000 soldiers had been safely embarked from both Suvla and ANZAC. As dawn broke the Turks realized at last that their enemy had vanished. With a mixture of disbelief and awesome relief, they left their trenches to work their way down to the abandoned piles of stores and equipment lying burning and broken along the beaches.

Against all expectation of being able to surprise the Turks again, the evacuation of 35,000 men from Helles was equally successfully carried out on the night of 8 January. This was in spite of a Turkish attack taking place when the front line had already been withdrawn.

Few military expeditions create such controversy – even today – as does Gallipoli. But whether or not it was ill-conceived, hesitant in its implementation, a sad saga of "might-have-beens", it remains an epic of heroism. Its tragedy was that it was all for nothing, but, as one New Zealander wrote, "It was not our wasted energy and sweat that really grieved us. In our hearts it was to know that we were leaving our dead comrades behind. That is what every man had in his mind."

Suez (1915)

Anthony Burton

In the 1973 Yom Kippur War both the Egyptians and the Israelis crossed the Suez Canal. They were not the first to do so – some 50 years before them a Turkish army had marched across the forbidding wastes of Sinai and put men on the western bank of the Canal.

In the middle of January 1915 a Turkish Expeditionary Force of 25,000 men left its base at Beersheba and prepared to cross the Sinai peninsula. Its goal was the Suez Canal – a vital link in Britain's Imperial chain. Djemal Pasha, Commander-in-Chief of the Turkish force, despite his arrogant proclamation as he left Constantinople for the front – 'I shall not return until I have conquered Egypt' – should have been under no illusions as to the magnitude of his task.

On the far bank of the Canal there was a British force much stronger than the Turks. Its base was only a few miles to the rear. The Turkish troops would find it difficult to carry sufficient stores across Sinai to maintain an offensive for more than a few days. Yet Djemal considered that the political situation was promising. Agents of the German Baron Oppenheim were busy stirring up a rebellion in Cairo which was timed to break out at the approach of the army of another Islamic Power. In the west of Egypt the Senussi tribes were revolting against the British. Djemal Pasha hoped that the infidels would soon find themselves faced with a holy war, a *jihad*, in their very midst. He had, he believed, already scored a propaganda triumph by the insulting messages he had sent to the British generals, inviting them to come out and fight in the open. Understandably, the British had ignored these suggestions and remained behind their Canal defenses.

They did not commit the error of underestimating their enemy. The contemporary issue of *War Illustrated* (13 March 1915) said: "Whatever may be thought of his intelligence and skill, the ordinary Turkish soldier is at least no coward. He can usually die as bravely and stubbornly as men of any race."

If German agents and the promise of a Turkish invasion could succeed in inciting rebellion in Cairo then Djemal could hope to repeat the exploits of Sultan Selim, the first Turkish conqueror of Egypt in 1517. Even if the hoped-for risings did not materialize, the Turks still reckoned on being able to seize a portion of the Canal and hold it long enough to destroy or block it. At the very least they would be able to sink some of the ships which would be trapped *en route* by the advance. Their hulks would take weeks, perhaps months, to shift. So Djemal took with him nine batteries of field artillery and one 150 mm (5.9 in) howitzer battery – supplemented by a quantity of mines – to attack the British shipping.

The Turks possessed one other advantage. They had with them as adviser the true architect of the advance to the Canal, the Bavarian Colonel Kress von Kressenstein – "a most excellent and efficient Officer", wrote the German General Liman von Sanders. Von Kressenstein's forte was desert warfare.

The German Major Fischer saw to it that the problem of watering man and beast on the trek were overcome. Nature also helped the passage. The winter of 1914 had been exceptionally wet and the force was to find a number of springs and pools of water as it marched towards the Canal and the waiting British. Fischer had charge of 5,000 water-carrying camels. A similar number were loaded with stores and ammunition.

British Intelligence knew of the impending assault but the short range of their available aircraft made early discovery of the direction of the attack difficult. The defenders only had three Maurice Farmans, two Henri Farmans, one BE2a and seven

French seaplanes at their disposal. Therefore, Djemal and Kress believed that an element of surprise might be achieved by avoiding the traditional coastal route, which would be under the guns of the British and French navies. Instead they decided to strike across the center of Sinai at the section of the Canal between Lake Timsah and the Great Bitter Lake. This approach would provide the possibility of access to Ismailia. He who controlled that town controlled the Canal. Here were the sluices which would enable the water supply to be cut off from its whole length.

Of the three possible routes – the central, the coastal strip and the Akaba–Nekhl–Suez line – that chosen was the worst watered. Also, none of the routes was at that time more than a camel track. However, the central approach via Jifjaffa had the advantages of reasonably firm going and immunity from British naval attack.

To confuse his enemy, Djemal sent out two diversionary columns, one in the north against Kantara, the other to his south towards Kubri. Guided by local Bedouin tribesmen, the main Turkish force crossed central Sinai in two contingents, patiently laying brushwood tracks when the surface deteriorated into areas of sand dunes – sometimes several square miles in extent. It is a tribute to German organization and Turkish doggedness that the force crossed Sinai in ten days without losing a single man or animal. By the end of January the Turks were poised before their objective. Djemal then issued a flowery exhortation:

"Warriors! Behind you lie the vast deserts; before you is the craven enemy; behind him the rich land of Egypt, which is waiting impatiently for you. If you falter, death will overtake. Before you Paradise lies."

After this rhetorical flourish Djemal gave his orders and the Turks moved forward.

On the right flank, in the north, a weak force of irregulars and Bedouin was sent with some Turkish infantry detachments to mount a feint attack on Kantara. In the south, a pack battery accompanied the 69th Regiment, 23rd Division, as it moved towards Kubri while in the center 20,000 of the best Turkish troops prepared for the attack. Kress von Kressenstein was with the first group of the central force while his fellow German, Colonel von Frankenberg und Proschlitz, accompanied Djemal Pasha and the crack 10th Division in the second contingent.

By now the British were ready for them. Small raids against Kubri (27 January) and Kantara (29th) did not disguise the Turkish intention to thrust at the center. Spies as well as aerial reconnaissance confirmed that the attack would concentrate on that sector. Accordingly, Major General A. Wilson, GOC Canal Defenses, reinforced Serapeum with the 2nd Rajputs.

Thirty thousand troops, mainly Indian, now awaited the attack along the line of the Canal. The 10th and 11th Indian Divisions were supported by the Imperial Service Cavalry Brigade and the Bikanir Camel Corps. Behind them the 42nd (East Lancashire) Division, Australian and New Zealand contingents and some Yeomanry units lay in reserve. The total overall strength was 70,000 men, but not all were fully trained. The defenders were short of artillery. There were only three batteries of Indian mountain artillery and a battery of Egyptian artillery available in the threatened sector. This deficiency was made up for by stationing British and French warships in the Canal. Eight were eventually used in this role. The most powerful of these were HMS *Ocean*, a *Canopus*-class pre-Dreadnought battleship of 12,950 tons (four 12-in, 12 6-in and 12 12-pounder guns) and HMS *Swiftsure* (formerly the Chilean Navy battleship *Constitution*, bought by the Royal Navy in 1909), 11,800 tons, armed with four 10-in, 14 7.5-in and 14 14-pounders. Other vessels involved included the *Eclipse*-class second-class cruiser HMS *Minerva* (5,600 tons), the sloop HMS *Clio*, the armed merchantman *Himalaya* and the Royal Indian Marine armed troopship *Hardinge*. *D'Entrecasteaux*, the French cruiser, and the coastguard ship *Requin* were also to be involved. The latter, together with the *Hardinge*, was destined to play an important part in the action on the central sector.

The attack began on the night of 3 February. It was cloudy and the waiting British strained their eyes into a darkness made more impenetrable by the blown sand which stung their faces and against which they had to wrap their rifles for protection. Three posts on the east bank, Tussum, Serapeum and Deversoir – two companies in each – watched for a sign of the Turkish advance. Behind them on the west bank 11 smaller posts, each manned by two platoons, covered the opposite shore – and waited. Among the 62nd Punjabis was a 30-year-old subaltern who was to achieve fame in the Second World War. The defense of the Canal was his first experience of action ('I remember the first bullet that went over my head, which made me duck damn quickly'). His name was Claude John Eyre Auchinleck.

At 0325 Arab irregulars – calling themselves the 'Champions of Islam' – disobeyed orders and gave away their positions south of Tussum by calling loudly upon Allah and cursing the infidel. After sporadic firing on both sides there was once again silence. A little after 0400, the clouds cleared and the moonlight illuminated hundreds of the attackers struggling down to the water's edge, carrying rafts and pontoons. At 0420 this party was engaged by an Egyptian artillery battery and by rifle fire and driven back. Immediately after this, larger groups appeared to the north, near Tussum. These troops tried manfully to launch their cumbersome craft – galvanized iron pontoons and rafts of kerosene tins in a simple wooden frame. Over their heads fierce fire raged between defenders and their own supporting infantry. Three boatloads succeeded in crossing the Canal but were attacked by a bayonet charge from the 62nd Punjabis and the 128th Pioneers. As Auchinleck laconically remarked, "We were on the west bank and they came over and our men charged down the bank and put a bayonet into them – that was all." In these engagements every Turkish soldier on the west bank was either killed or captured. At the same time as the Tussum incident the Turks launched a half-hearted attack on the Ismailia ferry post.

In the weary dawn the cost of the attack became clear. Turkish dead lay among their abandoned rafts and pontoons on the east bank. The defenders of the east bank outposts sallied forth from their perimeters. More troops crossed the Canal to support them and put paid to any surviving Turk from the eastern margins of the waterway. A torpedo boat was sent north from Deversoir to destroy any pontoons still intact.

But these British counter-attacks were halted by the appearance of a superior Turkish force. Artillery duels between the

ships anchored in the Canal and the Turkish batteries continued throughout the rest of the day.

Here the Turkish artillery was efficient. Two batteries of
field artillery and the 150 mm howitzer battery succeeded in
hitting the outgunned 6,520-ton *Hardinge*, armed only with six
4.7-in guns. She was forced to break off action at 0845. A duel
now began between the *Requin* and the Turkish battery. At first
the Turks had the better of it, but at 0900 their position was
betrayed by a puff of smoke. Their range was estimated and
their howitzers silenced. *Requin* and the cruiser *D'Entrecasteaux*
– ordered up to replace the *Hardinge* – now concentrated their
fire on the assumed position of the main Turkish force. Artillery
engagements were fought elsewhere on the front, particularly
between HMS *Clio*'s six 4-in and two Turkish field guns which
had scored some direct hits on El Ferdan railway station. At
1030 these too were silenced.

Next day, to the surprise of the watching British and Indian
troops, the Turks began to retreat. Djemal had in fact ordered it
on the evening of the 3rd. The speed of the withdrawal, which
both Kress and Djemal believed to be necessary, left some of the
Turkish troops behind. These were duly attacked and captured
before they could escape from their trenches facing the Canal.
The remainder of the Turkish army escaped without incident
since the British were neither physically nor psychologically
prepared for pursuit. Djemal fell back to Beersheba, leaving
Kress in the desert with three infantry battalions and a squadron of cavalry with two mountain batteries to support. Kress's
orders were to exploit his mobility to keep the enemy occupied,
to hamper shipping movements and slow down preparations for
any British advance across Sinai.

British casualties numbered only 32 killed and 130
wounded. Enemy losses were heavier. Kress gives figures
of 192 killed, 371 wounded and 727 missing, a total of
1,290 – but the true numbers were higher, since the Turks
did not record the casualties of their irregulars. British
archives show that they buried 238 of the enemy dead and
captured 716 prisoners. One of the dead was the German
Staff Officer who had been in charge of the crossing, Captain
von dem Hagen.

While Turkish expectations of a rising in their favor were certainly over-optimistic, their less ambitious plan of seizing a section of the Canal for a few days was more realizable. Therefore, their failure to come anywhere near to achieving this objective is puzzling.

Kress claimed that the sandstorm delayed his preparations, that the force lacked the training necessary for a night crossing of the Canal under enemy guns and, finally, that the use of an Arab, rather than a Turkish division was an error – the former's loyalty being suspect. While the first two of these reasons may have some plausibility the third does not bear examination. It would indeed have been more sensible to have used the 10th Division in the first place, instead of holding it in reserve to pass through the Arab 23rd (Homs) and the 25th (Damascus) Divisions after they had made an initial breach in the British defenses. The assertion, made by General Liman von Sanders among others, that Arab units went over to the British is certainly untrue. On the contrary, the crossing was bravely attempted against an entrenched enemy who had prepared the ground – even to the extent of putting range markers out in the desert – and had excellent fields of fire. The warships were the eventual victors of their clash with the Turkish artillery. The reluctance of the Turkish troops to press their attacks later on the morning of the 3rd must be attributed to the warships' shelling accuracy, not least with their 12-pounders and smaller quick-firing guns.

Djemal Pasha and Kress von Kressenstein argued later that the raid had in any case been worth the effort. It had demonstrated the vulnerability of the Canal and had floored British assumptions as to the numbers of men who could cross the Sinai peninsula. In 1906 the British War Office had estimated that, in view of the water situation, the largest force that could cross would be 5,000 men and 2,000 camels. Technically, the expedition had been impressive and this demonstration of German/Turkish expertise made necessary the continuation of a huge British presence – first to defend and then to move out from the area of the Canal. One British commentator, Major-General Sir M. G. E. Bowman-Manifold, is generous in his praise for the Turkish achievement.

The Turkish effort deserves admiration. To bring thousands of men, artillery and pontoon train across 140 miles of desert was creditable; to assault a front defended potentially by 70,000 men and the heavy metal of ships' armament, was audacious: to depart again with artillery and baggage intact, and a loss of not 10 per cent of infantry was clear gain and left the defenders with little to boast of.

Troops occupied in Egypt – and the next time the Canal was threatened, early in 1916, 400,000 troops were massed to oppose any expedition – were at least kept out of the European theater. This, to von Kressenstein, was reason enough for the original attack. Djemal had escaped without serious loss, while the British were to pay dearly for letting Kress von Kressenstein escape them. It is difficult to avoid the impression that the British were much too cautious in their counter-attack, even allowing for the fact that their reconnaissance capabilities were reduced by damage to the French seaplanes.

Djemal and Kress had twisted the lion's tail – and got away with it. There was little glory in the affair. But what there was must, on the Turkish side, go to those who crossed the Canal. Nearly 60 years before the SAMs and the Phantoms, the T62s and the Centurions, a few infantrymen struggled over the one hundred yards of the Canal, paddling rafts made of kerosene tins.

Verdun (1916)

Brenda Ralph Lewis

In choosing Verdun as the main German objective for 1916, General Erich von Faikenhayn, Chief of the German General Staff and Minister for War, pre-dated the jibe that the British would fight to the last man in the armies of their allies. Falkenhayn reasoned that, for the British, the European fronts in the First World War represented nothing more than a sideshow, with the Russian, Italian and French armies as their whipping boys. The Italians and Russians, Falkenhayn believed, were already foundering on their own ineptitude. Only France remained.

"France has almost arrived at the end of her military effort." Falkenhayn wrote to the German Kaiser Wilhelm II in December 1915.

> If we succeeded in opening the eyes of her people to the fact that in a military sense they have nothing more to hope for . . . breaking point would be reached, and England's best sword knocked out of her hand . . . Behind the French sector on the Western Front, there are objectives for the retention of which the French General Staff would be compelled to throw in every man they have. If they do so, the forces of France will bleed to death, as there can be no question of a voluntary withdrawal.

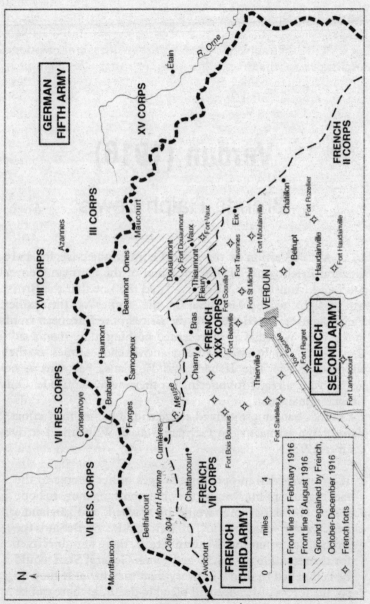

N

GERMAN
FIFTH ARMY

XV CORPS

III CORPS

XVIII CORPS

VII RES. CORPS

VI RES. CORPS

FRENCH
THIRD ARMY

FRENCH
VII CORPS

FRENCH
XXX CORPS

FRENCH
SECOND ARMY

FRENCH
II CORPS

• Étain

R. Orne

• Azannes

• Beaumont
• Ornes

Maucourt

Douaumont
Fort Douaumont
Thiaumont
Vaux
Fleury
Fort Vaux

Eix
Fort Tavannes
Fort Moulainville
Châtillon
Fort Rozelier

• Haumont
• Samogneux

• Brabant
• Consenvoye
• Forges

• Bras
Charny

Fort Souville
Fort St Michel
Fort Belleville

Belrupt
• Haudainville
Fort Haudainville

Cumières
Mort Homme
Côte 304

• Béthincourt
• Chattancourt

• Montfaucon

• Avocourt

VERDUN

Thierville

Voie Sacrée
Fort Regret

Fort Sartelles

Fort Landrecourt

R. Meuse

Fort Bois Bourrus

3.3 Verdun, 1916

---- Front line 21 February 1916
- - - Front line 8 August 1916
▨ Ground regained by French,
  October–December 1916
✧ French forts

0   4
miles

The objective Falkenhayn chose to put France in this moral and military dilemma was the massively fortified town of Verdun, on the canalized river Meuse. Verdun fitted Falkenhayn's bill admirably. It had immense historic and emotional significance for the French and formed the northern linchpin of the double defense line of fortifications built to protect France's eastern frontier after the Franco-Prussian War of 1870–1. Mount an assault here, with enough threatening potential, Falkenhayn reckoned, and the French Army would be inextricably lured to Verdun and mangled to extinction by the Germans. The mangle would be provided by a series of limited, but attritionist advances, intensively supported by artillery and spiced with surprise.

Falkenhayn's proposals appealed to the Kaiser and to his son, Crown Prince Wilhelm, whose Fifth Army had been pounding away at Verdun with little success since 1914. But the prince and his Chief of Staff, General Schmidt von Knobelsdorf, seemed to see the Verdun campaign more in terms of shattering the French with a bombardment than of bleeding them dry by attrition. Wilhelm, who wanted to attack on both sides of the Meuse, not on the right bank only, as Falkenhayn proposed, stated the campaign's purpose as "capturing the fortress of Verdun by precipitate methods". Compared with this fierce phraseology, Falkenhayn's notion of "an offensive in the Meuse area in the direction of Verdun" seemed enigmatic. Despite the suitably malevolent code-name of Operation *Gericht* (Judgement) given to his offensive, Falkenhayn's essentially half-hearted approach to it planted the seeds of ultimate German failure at Verdun. Basically, that failure was rooted in Falkenhayn's timid choice of too narrow a front for the initial attack and also in his extreme parsimony in doling out reserves.

Although Crown Prince Wilhelm and others seemed to suspect this outcome, preparations for the campaign went ahead as Falkenhayn had originally planned. It did so at a pace remarkable for those leisurely times. Weeks, rather than the usual months, divided Falkenhayn's preliminary consultations with the Kaiser at Potsdam on or about 20 December 1915 from the issue of final orders on 27 January 1916 and the projected attack date of 12 February.

During this period, the Germans amassed in the forests that surrounded Verdun a massive force of 140,000 men and over 1,200 guns – 850 of them in the front line – together with 2.5 million shells brought by 1,300 munitions trains, and an air arm of 168 aircraft as well as observation balloons. A superlative standard of secrecy was achieved by deft camouflage of the guns, by the building of underground galleries to house the troops instead of the more usual, give-away "jump-off" trenches, and by dawn-to-dusk air patrols to prevent French pilots from casting spying eyes over the area.

These gargantuan preparations were, however, being directed against a military mammoth whose teeth had been drawn. By early 1916, Verdun's much-vaunted impregnability had been seriously weakened. It had been "declassed" as a fortress the previous summer and all but a few of its guns and garrison had been removed. This was primarily the work of General Joseph J. C. Joffre, C-in-C of the French Army, who, with others, had presumed from the relatively easy fall in 1914 of the Belgian fortresses at Liège and Namur that this form of defense was redundant so far as modern warfare was concerned. Between August and October 1915, therefore, Verdun was denuded of over 50 complete batteries of guns and 128,000 rounds of ammunition. These were parcelled out to other Allied sectors where artillery was short. The stripping process was still going on at the end of January 1916, by which time the 60-odd Verdun forts possessed fewer than 300 guns with insufficient ammunition.

The result was that on the eve of the German offensive, the French defenses at Verdun were perilously weak, from the trench-works, dugouts and machine-gun posts to the communications network and barbed-wire fences. Far-sighted men who protested at the headlong disarmament of Verdun did so in vain. One of them, General Coutanceau, was sacked as Governor of Verdun and replaced in the autumn of 1915 by the ageing and apparently more tractable General Herr. Another, Colonel Emile Driant, commander of 56th and 59th *Chasseur* Battalions of 72nd Division, 30th Corps, warned as early as 22 August 1915: "The sledge-hammer blow will be delivered on the line Verdun–Nancy." After his opinion reached the ears of

Joffre, Driant was sharply reprimanded in December for arousing baseless fears. Gen. Herr quickly realized that Coutanceau's alarm had been perfectly justified, and that he was in dire need of reinforcements to prepare the defense line Joffre had ordered at Verdun. But Herr's pleadings did little to penetrate the cloud of smugness that swirled about the question of defending Verdun. This mood remained impervious for some weeks, despite information from German deserters about troop movements and cancelled leave and other glimpses at the dire truth.

The very last moment had almost arrived before a glimmer of sense started to seep through. On 24 January General Nöel de Castelnau, Joffre's Chief of Staff, ordered a rush completion of the first and second trench lines on the right bank of the Meuse, and a new line in between.

On 12 February, two new divisions arrived at Verdun – much to Herr's heartfelt relief – to bring French strength up to 34 battalions against 72 German. Had the German attack begun on 12 February as planned, it would doubtless have smashed through the weak French defenses to score a stunning steam-roller victory.

As it was, 12 February was not a day of savage battle, but of snow-blizzards and dense mist which afforded less than 1,100 yards visibility. The Verdun area was said to "enjoy" some of France's filthiest weather. For a week it lived up to its reputation with snow, more snow, rain-squalls and gales.

Not until 21 February – just before 0715 – did a massive shell, almost as high as a man, burst from one of the two German 15-in (380 mm) naval guns and roar over the 20 miles that separated its camouflaged position from Verdun. There, it exploded in the courtyard of the Bishop's Palace. At this signal, a murderous artillery bombardment erupted from the German lines and a tornado of fire – including poison gas shells – began to flay the French positions along a six-mile front. The earth convulsed and the air filled with flames, fumes and a holocaust of shrapnel and steel which, the Germans clearly hoped, would destroy every living thing within range. The bombardment hammered on and on until about 1200, when it paused so that German observers could see where – if anywhere – pockets of French defenders survived. Then the artillery began afresh,

smashing trenches, shelters, barbed wire, trees and men until
the whole area from Malancourt to Eparges had become a
corpse-littered desert.

Between 1500 and 1600, the barrage intensified as a prelude
to the first German infantry advance along a 4.5-mile front from
Bois d'Haumont to Herbebois. The advance began at 1645
when small patrol groups came out over the 656 to 1,203 yards
of No Man's Land in waves 87.5 yards apart. Their purpose was
to discover where French resistance might still exist and to
pinpoint it to the artillery – which would then finish off the
surviving defenders. This tentative approach, the result of
Falkenhayn's excessive caution, was not to the taste of the
belligerent General von Zwehl, commander of 7 Reserve Corps
of Westphalians. Von Zwehl, whose position lay opposite Bois
d'Haumont, paid brief lip-service to Falkenhayn's orders by
sending out probing patrols first, but only a short while elapsed
before he ordered his fighting stormtroopers to follow them.
The Westphalians surged into the Bois d'Haumont, overran the
first line of French trenches and within five hours had seized the
whole wood.

To the right of the Bois d'Haumont lay the equally devastated
Bois des Caures. Here, 80,000 shells had fallen within one
500,000-square-yard area. In this shattered wasteland, the
advance patrols of the German 18 Corps expected to find
nothing but mounds of shattered bodies in the mud. Instead,
they were faced with a fierce challenge from Colonel Driant's
Chasseurs. Of the original 1,200 men under Driant's command,
fewer than half had survived the artillery bombardment. Now,
these survivors poured machine-gun and rifle fire at the infiltrating Germans from the concrete redoubts and small strongholds which Driant had cunningly scattered through the trees.

Similarly ferocious isolated resistance was occurring all
along the front, causing the Germans more delay and more
casualties – 600 by midnight – than they had reckoned
possible. By nightfall on 21 February, the only hole decisively
punched in the French line was in the Bois d'Haumont, where
Gen. Zwehl's Westphalians were now solidly entrenched.
Elsewhere, the Germans had captured most of the French
forward trenches, but were held up when darkness put an end

to the first day's fighting which had yielded only 3,000 prisoners.

On the next two days, the Germans attacked with far greater force and much more initiative. On 22 February they blasted the village of Haumont, on the edge of the wood, with shellfire and flushed out the remaining French defenders with bombs and flamethrowers. That same day, the Bois de Ville was overwhelmed and in the Bois des Caures, which the Germans enveloped on both sides, Col. Driant ordered his *Chasseurs* to withdraw to Beaumont, about half a mile behind the wood. Only 118 *Chasseurs* managed to escape. Driant was not among them. On 23 February, the Germans saturated Samogneux with a hail of gunfire, captured Wavrille and Herbebois, and out-flanked the village of Brabant, which the French evacuated. Next day – 24 February – despite their inch-by-inch resistance, the pace of disaster accelerated for the French with 10,000 taken prisoner, the final fall of their first defense line and the collapse of their second position in a matter of hours.

The Germans were now in possession of Beaumont, the Bois de Fosses, the Bois des Caurieres and part of the way along La Vauche ravine which led to Douaumont.

Incredibly enough, at first the magnitude of the disaster did not sink in at Joffre's HQ at Chantilly, where the Staff had persuaded themselves that the German attack was a mere diversion. "Papa" Joffre, who had long believed a serious German offensive was more likely in the Oise valley, Rheims or Champagne, maintained his customary imperturbability to such an extent that at 2300 on 24 February, he was fast asleep when General de Castelnau came hammering on his bedroom door bearing bad news from the front. Armed with "full powers" from Joffre, who then went calmly back to bed, de Castelnau raced overnight to Verdun.

At about the time he arrived there, early on 25 February, a 10-man patrol of 24th Brandenburg Regiment of 3 Corps walked into Fort Douaumont and took possession of it and its three guns while the French garrison of 56 reserve artillery-men slept. This farcical episode, which German propaganda exaggerated into a hard-fought victory, shocked the French into melancholic despair and realization of the true state of affairs. At Chantilly, many officers openly advocated abandoning Verdun.

There, de Castelnau drew the conclusion that the French right flank should be drawn back and that the line of forts must be held at all costs. Above all, the French must retain the right bank of the Meuse, where de Castelnau felt that a decisive defense could, and must, be anchored on the ridges. The hapless Gen. Herr was replaced forthwith by 60-year-old General Henri Philippe Pétain. De Castelnau cannibalized Pétain's Second Army with the Third Army to form for him a new Second Army.

Pétain took over responsibility for the defense of Verdun at 2400 on 25 February, after arriving that afternoon to find Herr's HQ at Dugny, south of Verdun, in a chaos of panic and recrimination. Pétain, however, judged the situation to be far less hopeless than it seemed, even though the loss of Fort Douaumont and its unparalleled observation point was a serious blow. He decided that the surviving Verdun forts should be strongly re-garrisoned to form the principal bulwarks of a new defense. Pétain mapped out new lines of resistance on both banks of the Meuse and gave orders for a barrage position to be established through Avocourt, Fort de Marre, Verdun's NE outskirts and Fort du Rozellier. The line Bras–Douaumont was divided into four sectors – the Woevre, Woevre–Douaumont, astride the Meuse, and the left bank of the Meuse. Each sector was entrusted to fresh troops of the 20th ("Iron") Corps. Their main job was to delay the German advance with constant counter-attacks.

Pétain saw to it that the four commands were supplied with fresh artillery as it arrived along the Bar-le-Duc road – which was soon rechristened "Sacred Way". Three thousand Territorials labored unceasingly to keep its unmetalled surface in constant repair so that it could stand up to punishingly heavy use by convoys of lorries – 6,000 of them in a single day. Along *La Voie Sacrée* came badly needed reinforcements to replace the 25,000 men the French had lost by 26 February – five fresh Corps of them by 29 February. Already, Pétain was topping up his stock of artillery from the 388 field guns and 244 heavy guns that were at Verdun on 21 February towards the peak it reached a few weeks later of 1,100 field guns, 225 80–105 mm guns and 590 heavy guns. He also set the 59th Division to work building new defensive positions.

His injection of new strategy, new blood, new supplies and new hope into the Verdun defense soon began to disconcert the Germans. In any case, their impetus was gradually grinding down. On 29 February, their advance came to an exhausted halt after the last of their initial energy had been expended in three days of violent attacks against Douaumont, Hardaumont and Bois de la Caillette.

At that juncture, apart from their own mood of 'grievous pessimism', the most damaging factor for the Germans was the French artillery sited on the left bank of the Meuse. Here, more and more Germans came under fire the farther along the right bank they advanced. The solution was obvious, as Pétain had long feared and Crown Prince Wilhelm and Gen. von Knobelsdorf had long urged. On 6 March, after a blistering two-day artillery barrage, the German 6 Reserve and 10 Reserve Corps, partly pushed across the flooded Meuse and in a swirling snowstorm, attacked along the left bank. A parallel prong of this new onslaught was planned to strike along the right bank towards Fort Vaux, whose gunners had been savaging the German left flank.

Despite a plastering from French artillery in the Bois Bourrus, the Germans sped along the left bank and swept through the villages of Forges and Regneville – ending by nightfall in possession of Height 265 on the Côte de l'Oie. This ridge was of crucial importance, since it led through the adjacent Bois des Corbeaux towards the long mound known as Mort Homme. Mort Homme possessed double peaks and offered two advantages to the Germans. First it sheltered a particularly active battery of French field guns, and secondly, from its heights there stretched a magnificent all-round vista of the surrounding countryside. This gave whoever possessed it a prize observation point.

But Mort Homme soon lived up to its grisly name. After storming the Bois des Corbeaux on 7 March and losing it to a determined French counter-attack next day, the Germans prepared another attempt on Mort Homme on 9 March – this time from the direction of Béthincourt in the NW. They seized the Bois des Corbeaux a second time, but at such a crippling cost that they could not continue.

Results were depressingly similar on the right bank of the Meuse, where the German effort faded out beneath the walls of Fort Vaux. Difficulties of ammunition supply had made the attack there limp two days behind the left bank assault. With that, the parallel effect of the German offensive was ruined.

Inexorably, perhaps inevitably, the fighting around Verdun was acquiring that quality of slog and slaughter, and of lives thrown away for petty, short-lived gains that was so familiar a characteristic of fighting in the First World War.

Both Pétain and, in his own way, von Falkenhayn, were devotees of attrition by gunpower rather than manpower, but between March and May, the struggle at Verdun, like some Frankenstein's monster renouncing its master, assumed a will of its own and reversed this preference. German casualties mounted from 81,607 at the end of March to 120,000 by the end of April, and the French from 89,000 to 133,000, as the two sides battered each other for possession of Mort Homme. By the end of May, when the Germans had at last taken this vital position, their losses had overtaken their enemy's. On the right bank of the Meuse, in the same three months, the fighting swung to and fro over the "Deadly Quadrilateral" – an area south of Fort Douaumont – to the tune of maniacal, endless artillery barrages, never resolving itself decisively in favor of one side or the other.

The process greatly weakened both contestants. Mutinous behavior and defeatist gossip became more common in the French ranks and French officers tacitly condoned this mood. More and more Germans, many of them terrified, clumsy 18-year-old boys were becoming sickly from exhaustion, the din of the guns and the filth in which they were forced to live.

Ennervation and dismay affected the heads as well as the bodies of the two opposing war efforts. By 21 April, Crown Prince Wilhelm had made up his mind that the whole Verdun campaign was a bloody failure and ought to be terminated. "A decisive success at Verdun could only be assured at the price of heavy sacrifices, out of all proportion to the desired gains," he wrote. These sentiments were echoed by Gen. Pétain, who was being nagged by Joffre to mount an aggressive counter-offensive. Pétain baulked at the increase in human sacrifice which that implied and clung to the principle of patient, stolid defense. Pétain was in a difficult position. Verdun had already become a national symbol of implacable resistance to the Germans, and Pétain himself a national idol. On the other hand, Verdun was threatening to gobble up the whole French Army and it certainly presented a serious drain on the manpower being reserved by Joffre for the coming Anglo-French offensive on the Somme.

For both sides at Verdun, these falterings at the top opened the way for men more ruthlessly determined to escalate the fighting onto even more brutal levels. On 19 April, Pétain was made Commander of Army Group Center, a position which placed him in remote rather than direct control of operations. His place as commander of Second Army was taken by General Robert Georges Nivelle, whose freebooter style of warfare had caught Joffre's attention during his series of audacious, if expensive, attacks along the right bank of the Meuse. Nivelle took over on 1 May, and arrived at headquarters at Souilly with the brash announcement: "We have the formula!" He was also responsible for a quotation attributed sometimes to Pétain: "*Ils ne passeront pas!*"

Nivelle's formula displayed itself in all its gory wastefulness on 22/23 May, when General Charles Mangin staged a flamboyant attack on Fort Douaumont. After a five-day bombardment, which barely chipped the fort's defenses, Mangin's troops streamed out of their jump-off trenches straight into a hurricane of deadly German gunfire. Within minutes, the French 129th Regiment had only 45 men left. One battalion had vanished. The remnants of the 129th charged the fort and set up a machine-gun post in one casemate against which the defending Germans flung themselves in a matching mood of suicidal madness. Out of 160 *Jägers*, *Leibgrenadiers* and men of the German 20th Regiment who attempted to overcome the French nest, only 50 returned to the fort alive. By the evening of 22 May, Fort Douaumont was in French hands, but the Germans staged violent counter-attacks, capping their onslaught with eight massive doses of explosive lobbed from a mine-thrower 80 yards distant. One thousand French were taken prisoner, and only a pathetic scattering of their comrades managed to stagger away from the fort.

This bloody fiasco ripped a 500-yard gap in the French lines and greatly weakened their strength on the right bank of the Meuse. Together with the fact that German possession of Mort Homme largely nullified French firepower on the Bois Borrus ridge, the self-destructive strife at Fort Douaumont gave great encouragement to the so-called "May Cup" offensive which the Germans planned for early June.

The inspiration behind "May Cup" was Gen. von Knobelsdorf, who had temporarily eclipsed Crown Prince Wilhelm. As Nivelle's new opposite number, von Knobelsdorf soon displayed an equally implacable resolve to overcome the enemy by brute force. "May Cup" comprised a powerful thrust on the right bank of the Meuse by five divisions on under half the 21 February attack frontage. Its purpose was to lift Verdun's last veil – Fort Vaux, Thiaumont, the Fleury ridge and Fort Souville.

On 1 June, the Germans crossed the Vaux ravine and after a frenzied contest forced Major Sylvain Raynal – commander of Fort Vaux – to surrender on 7 June. By 8 June, Gen. Nivelle had mounted six unsuccessful relief attempts, at appalling cost. He was stopped from making a seventh attempt only when Pétain expressly forbade it. Elsewhere – notably round the Ouvrage de Thiaumont – the fighting brought both sides terrible losses. The French alone were losing 4,000 men per division in a single action. By 12 June, Nivelle's fresh reserves amounted to only one brigade – not more than 2,000 men.

With the Germans now poised to take Fort Souville – the very last major fortress protecting Verdun – ultimate disaster seemed imminent for the French. Eleventh-hour salvation came in the form of two Allied offensives in other theaters of war. On 4 June, on the Eastern Front, the Russian General Alexei A. Brusilov threw 40 divisions at the Austrian line in Galicia, in a surprise attack that flattened its defenders. The Russians took 400,000 prisoners. To shore up his war effort, now threatened with total collapse, Field Marshal Conrad von Hötzendorf, the

Austrian C-in-C, begged Falkenhayn to send in German reinforcements. Grudgingly, Falkenhayn detached three divisions from the Western Front. Meanwhile, the French had
been doing some pleading on their own account. In May and
June, Joffre, de Castelnau, Pétain and French Prime Minister
Aristide Briant had all begged General Sir Douglas Haig, the
British C-in-C, to advance the Somme offensive from its
projected starting date of mid-August. Haig at last complied
on 24 June, and that day the week-long preliminary bombardment began.

At this juncture, a German 30,000-man assault on Fort
Souville, which had begun with phosgene – "Green Cross" –
gas attacks on 22 June had already crumpled. Despite its
horrifying effects on everything that lived and breathed, the
novel phosgene barrage was neither intense nor prolonged
enough to sufficiently paralyze the power of the French artillery. This shortfall, together with German failure to attack on a
wide enough front, their recent loss of air superiority to the
French, their shrinking store of manpower and the ravages
thirst was wreaking in their lines, combined to scuttle the
German push against Fort Souville on 22 June. July and August
saw increasingly puny attempts by the Germans to snatch the
prize that had come so tantalizingly close, but all ended in
failure and exhaustion. German morale was at its lowest. On 3
September, the German offensive finally faded in a weak
paroxysm of effort. Verdun proper came to an end.

For the Germans, this miserable curtain-fall on the drama of
Verdun was assisted by the fact that after 24 June, the exigen-
cies of the fighting elsewhere denied them new supplies of
ammunition and, after 1 July, men.

All that remained was for the French to rearm, reinforce their
troops and counter-attack to regain what they had lost. By 24
August 1917, after a brilliant series of campaigns masterminded
by Pétain, Nivelle and Mangin, the only mark on the map to
show the Germans had ever occupied anything in the area of
Verdun denoted the village of Beaumont.

During this counter-offensive, the formerly maligned forts
reinstated themselves as powerful weapons of defence. As the
French recaptured them, they found how relatively little they

had suffered from the massive artillery pounding they had received. This discovery made forts fashionable among French military strategists once more. It did so most notably, and later mortally for France, in the mind of André Maginot, Minister for War from November 1929 to January 1931 and in that time sponsor of the Maginot Line of fortifications.

Of course, fortress-like durability was given neither to the 66 French and 43.5 German divisions which fought at Verdun between February and June 1916, nor to the terrain they so bitterly disputed for so long. Both suffered permanent scars. The land around Verdun, raked over again and again by saturation shelling – over 12 million rounds from the French artillery alone – became a ravaged, infertile lunar-like waste-land. By 1917, the soil of Verdun was thickly sown with dead flesh and irrigated by spilled blood, having claimed more than 1.25 million casualties. Between February and December 1916, the French had lost 377,231 men and the Germans about 337,000 in a scything down of their ranks. In these circumstances, the Western Front ceased to be a sideshow for the British – if it had ever been so. They were forced to assume the star role in the Allied war effort which the French had formerly played. A repetition of Verdun was simply inconceivable.

Vimy Ridge (1917)

Brenda Ralph Lewis

Four divisions of the Canadian Corps, with the 5th British Division in support, began their assault on Vimy Ridge on 9 April 1917. This six-mile hogsbacked pleat in the plains near Arras in NE France possessed an almost legendary reputation for impregnability. French forces had battered incessantly against it in 1914 and 1915, only to gain the Lorette Spur next to the Ridge and part of the slopes. They gained it in the typically wasteful and bloody style of the First World War with the loss of 150,000 men. In 1916, when the British took over from them, they, too, employed the same dismally ineffective tactics of repeated shelling, mining, raiding and skirmishing by night. The British, like the French, lost men by the thousand – 2,500 in the three days 23–26 May alone.

The slaughter of all these men, like that of millions of others on the Western Front, achieved absolutely nothing from a strategic point of view. For while the Germans remained firmly entrenched in their warren of tunnels and deep dugouts, and while they stayed strongly in possession of the crest of Vimy Ridge, which dominated the Lens–Douai Plain, they were able to keep their opponents' position in Arras, six miles away, in a constantly precarious condition.

The apparent unshakeable hold of the Germans on Vimy Ridge also maintained the Allied High Command in a mood of

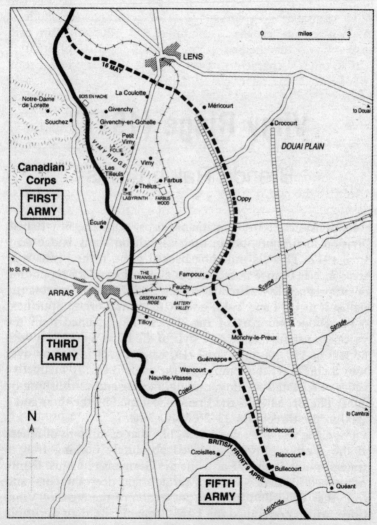

3.4 Vimy Ridge and the Battles of Arras, April–May 1917

fuming frustration. These were men to whom territory gained equalled success, no matter what the cost, and territory lost (or like Vimy Ridge, not captured), spelled failure. It was this rigid mentality – divorced from the realities of modern, mechanized warfare and untempered by humanitarian considerations – that helped account for the quality of attrition that so quickly characterized hostilities on the Western Front. Among the firmest exponents of attrition and the mass assault by thousands of human lemmings, was Marshal Joseph Joffre, C-in-C of the French Armies on the Front between 1914 and 1916. Joffre's methods were so successful in killing off his own troops that in 1916 he stated they could stand just one more great battle, after which France's pool of men of military age would virtually dry up.

But by the end of 1916 the French were no longer able to countenance the wholesale slaughter of their men for the sake of a few patches of gain, or, more commonly, for none at all. In 1916 alone, a year of almost unmitigated failure on the Western Front, the inconclusive battles of the Somme (1 July to 15 November) and Verdun (21 February to 24 August) had taken more than 500,000 French lives and left thousands of survivors gassed, crippled, blinded and otherwise ruined.

French patience and trust in Joffre finally ran out and he was relieved of his command. He was replaced on 12 December 1916, by General Robert Georges Nivelle. He had won instant popularity in the public imagination by masterminding two successful French counter-attacks at Verdun. Nivelle appeared to have a more mobile and more promising concept of warfare. The enemy was to be violently and repeatedly hammered by masses of artillery and assaulted by vast numbers of infantry. Nivelle's ideas seemed to herald the decisive victory for which the French now thirsted. As 1917 began, the impression mushroomed that the hour had found the man and the man could produce with one stunning strike the longed-for miracle of a complete and permanent rupture of the German lines.

In this atmosphere, the plan Nivelle conceived – that the French should mount an offensive along a 50-mile front between Soissons and Champagne – was as much of a public relations venture as a battle campaign. To draw the German reserves away from the French sector, the British were to attack along the Hindenburg Line, which was held by the German Sixth Army under General Freiherr von Falkenhausen. The Hindenburg Line skirted Queant and Bullecourt in the south, crossed Telegraph Hill, part of Vimy Ridge, and ended at the Railway Triangle about two miles east of Arras. It was intended that the British Third Army, under General Sir Edmund H. Allenby, would break through the line and advance south-eastwards towards Cambrai. At the same time, the British First Army, of which the Canadian Corps formed part, would advance towards Douai to the north-east. During these offensives – the battles of Arras which began on 9 April and cost 150,000 casualties – the Third Army succeeded in puncturing the Hindenburg Line with a dent 11 miles long and 3.7 miles deep. But, although Monchy-le-Preux and Hill 102 were also gained, the British effort round Arras fell short of most of its other objectives.

The onslaught on Vimy Ridge, on the other hand, was a brilliant success. The Ridge, which ran NW to SE from south of Givenchy to the edge of Farbus Wood, was the northernmost part of the British front. It was a depressing wasteland. The continuous struggle staged there since 1914 had pulverized it into a quagmire of mud and waterlogged pot-holes and trenches, scattered with the rotting flesh and stripped bones of thousands of unburied dead, numerous rats, lice, bugs and nits, the jagged debris of countless shells, bombs and bullets, torn-up fragments of barbed wire and corrugated iron and the empty cans and litter that were the junk of everyday living.

Early in 1917, the Canadian Corps began to replace the British on this derelict compost heap. It was assumed on both sides that they would repeat the melancholy mixture as before, and do no more than wage fruitless running warfare resulting in heavy losses. The five regiments of the German Sixth Army, who were occupying the Ridge, together with their commanders, were confident that this was the case. The German reading of the situation was well founded. The mediocre performance Allied troops had so far made in the war convinced them that incompetence was inherent in the Allied war effort. Any attack – on Vimy Ridge or anywhere else – was bound to fail.

Therefore, it was in complacent mood and without undue alarm that the Germans fended off occasional Canadian raiding of their lines and observed the quickening pace of the British build-up around the Ridge in late 1916 and early 1917. During that winter, the British dug thousands of feet of new tunnels in the chalk of Vimy Ridge, together with caves capable of housing men by the hundreds. In March, 1917, piles of ammunition and supplies were stockpiled in the area, the roads leading to it and from it bustled with activity, fresh wire barricades were erected and strongpoints reinforced. Early in April, the Allied artillery bombardment, which had been more or less continuous in the months before, suddenly intensified. The Germans' former superior firepower began to be overwhelmed. The number of rounds fired rose sharply – doubling the Allied expenditure in March and rising to a peak of 90,000 rounds on 5 April: this was three times the number pumped out by the Germans in reply. The bombardment flattened several German trenches and smashed huge gaps in the wire. Each hammering was followed up with British and Canadian forays, made in greater strength than before, to discover the damage caused.

Despite all this, the Germans concluded only that some time soon, some strenuous effort – bigger than a raid, but not so powerful and much more limited than a "Big Push" – was about to be made. But they believed that they could deal with anything their enemies would throw at them. In this complacent mood, General von Falkenhausen not only failed to move up the best part of his reserves, but kept them so far back that they had little chance to intervene should the coming battle put the front line under impossible pressure. The men of von Falkenhausen's First Guards Reserve Division and 18th Infantry Division were in fact, still 12.5 miles behind the lines on 9 April. What was more, von Falkenhausen did not order his artillery to the rear, where they might have mounted a defence in depth, until the Canadian attack was imminent. To make the Germans' plight worse their sluggish supply system failed to deliver rations and reinforcements. They also suffered from an ammunition shortage.

The magnitude of the threat to the Germans on Vimy Ridge was considerably greater than they imagined. For one thing, their Canadian opponents possessed qualities unusual in ordinary soldiers of the First World War. The nature of Canadian society encouraged tenacity and toughness to a far higher degree than did the rigid class societies of Europe. Similarly, the plan of battle for Vimy Ridge was not the sort the Germans' experience so far had led them to expect. Though it was a set-piece offensive, it contained the uncommon element of surprise. The preliminary artillery barrage was to be much briefer than the usual days or even weeks. It would last only three minutes before the Canadians went "over the top" and would creep forward at the rate of about 33 yards per minute. The infantry would march behind at a careful synchronized pace. At the same time, 150 Vickers machine-guns would thicken up the barrage and spray the ground 40 yards ahead of the advance, while HE and gas shells saturated the German positions and mortars spread a smokescreen in selected sectors. The overall effect would be to provide the infantry with a devastating artillery umbrella to get them to the German front line long before they were expected.

On the night of 8/9 April, the first attack wave of Canadian troops – 15,000 men – stood packed shoulder to shoulder in the jump-off trenches in freezing and unseasonable weather. They were weighted down with full battle kit, extra ammunition and rations and – as was all too familiar – were standing knee-deep in freezing, muddy water. At 0530, a large gun coughed out a throaty signal from nearby Mont St Eloi. Immediately, 1,000 Allied guns, the heaviest of them 15-in howitzers, responded with a huge concerted roar. The air was rent with shells that whooshed over the heads of the men hunched in the jump-off trenches. The barrage speared out over No Man's Land ripping apart the semi-darkness blanketing the German front line with a flickering, flashing curtain of light. At the same time, counter-battery fire thundered down upon the German gun emplacements, and to add to the cacophony, two large mines were detonated in the German lines, tearing massive holes in the wire.

After three minutes, the guns of the "creeping barrage" lengthened their range and the bombardment leapt 100 yards ahead. The deluge of shells pounded its way foward as the Canadians scrambled out of the trenches and moved over the mud-wastes that led up the slopes of Vimy Ridge. Their rate of advance – drummed into them by intensive training – was the same as that of the barrage. Some of the most heavily laden troops had trouble keeping up even with this crawling pace. It was snowing fairly heavily and the sticky mud beneath their feet made the Canadians slither and slide. The eight MK 1 "Female" tanks, armed with machine-guns, which were moving forward with 2nd Division, soon lumbered to a complete halt – their tracks quite unable to grip the near-liquid sludge beneath them. Three of the tanks were wrecked by German gunfire.

Overhead and in front of them, the advancing Canadians could see amber-coloured flares leaping up into the gradually lightening sky as the Germans fired desperate signals for immediate artillery support. They signalled largely in vain. The best part of the German heavy artillery – accurately plotted earlier by Allied sound ranging or aerial photography – had been neutralized or destroyed. Those guns further back which were still intact were not in communication with their beleaguered front line, and could not lay down fire where it was needed. All that the German guns were able to do was to fire at the known position of the Canadian front line, which the initial attack wave had already left.

Only the German machine-guns, which were strongly emplaced almost flush with the ground, were able to retaliate to any advantage. Their answering fire streamed out among the Canadians. Many fell dead in the mud. Even if they were not mown down in neat rows – as had happened during infantry advances on the Somme and elsewhere – the Canadians suffered considerable losses. For example, the 7th Battalion of the 1st Division, which lost half its men during the battle of Vimy Ridge, lost most of them to machine-gun fire in the first half-mile of their advance.

The deadly machine-gun nests could only be silenced by close personal onslaught. This tactic was extremely dangerous and likely to be fatal to the attacker. Two Victoria Crosses won at Vimy Ridge – both awarded posthumously – went to a 1st Division private who crawled up to the gun-slit of a machine-gun and slammed a hand grenade inside, and to a 2nd Division lance-sergeant who charged another nest single-handed and bayoneted the crew.

If the machine-gunners on the Ridge were able to defend themselves adequately, the German infantry were the exact opposite. The preliminary barrage, which had been directed with punishing accuracy from Forward Observation Posts, observer balloons and aircraft of the Royal Flying Corps, had smashed the German trenches to near-oblivion along with many of their deep dugouts – most of them unwisely placed in the first 700 yards of the front line. This bombardment had buried hundreds of Germans alive in the dugouts and those who managed to survive were taken completely by surprise. They had not expected an attack to arrive for hours, perhaps days. Several were taken prisoner while sitting down to breakfast. Others were captured in their beds or skulking sockless, shirtless and otherwise half-dressed in tunnels, shafts and dugouts. The shock of surprise was quickly followed by terror, as the Germans realized that the roarings and shudderings they could hear and feel close by were caused by Canadians tossing Mills bombs into neighbouring dugouts.

Germans who had been surprised underground, but who managed to avoid capture, rushed down their tunnels to the rear in a frantic effort to escape, carrying the dire news of disaster to gun-crews in the German artillery area of Farbus Wood. There was immediate panic and those crews able to began to pull out across the Douai Plain. The demoralization the Canadians achieved by swiftness and surprise proved a valuable, even economic, weapon in their armoury. One German machine-gun crew which opened fire a few hundred yards ahead of troops of the 31st Battalion of 3rd Division gave themselves up as soon as a Canadian fired a Mills bomb at them from his .303 rifle. Another lone Canadian, a member of the

29th (British Columbia) Battalion of the same division, achieved even easier success while reconnoitring in Farbus Wood. A short burst of bullets from his rifle, fired in the general direction of a German howitzer crew, resulted in the instant evacuation of their position.

By 1100 – after five and a half hours of battle – the German defences were in almost total disarray. Some scattered spots on the front, in the areas covered by the 2nd and 3rd Canadian Divisions, were still held by the Bavarian 79th Reserve Infantry Division, but the Germans' centre had been pushed well over the crest of Vimy Ridge. The German left wing had fallen back as far as Intermediate Position No. 11, which coincided roughly with the Canadians' "Brown Line". The overall picture now was that the most important parts of Vimy Ridge, including Telegraph Hill and its south-eastern contour, were in Canadian hands. Also, men of the 1st Division were swarming through Farbus Wood. There, they were performing an unprecedented function for Allied troops in the First World War – capturing German guns, several of them the much-dreaded 5.9-in howitzers.

The dictum that 'artillary conquers, infantry occupies' had for once come true – and much faster than anyone had forseen.

However, the rapid and spectacular success of the 1st, 2nd and 3rd Divisions and most of the 4th Division was not being matched on Hill 145, a vital part of the 4th Division's area. Hill 145 (475 ft), the highest point of Vimy Ridge, lay in the centre of the 4th Division's operation and was the objective of its 11th Brigade, under Brigadier V. W. Odlum. Opposing the 11th Brigade was the Reserve Infantry Regiment No. 261, a unit of the Bavarian 79th Division. The Germans were dug into strong defences – the normal three forward trenches, with a strong tunnel, the *Munchener-Lager*, between trenches two and three. On the crest and reverse slope of Hill 145 lay a twin-trench system which included the deep defences of the *Obere Hangstellung*, the *Untere Hangstellung*, a reserves' double tunnel, and a large encampment, the *Hanseaten-Lager*. This defence system was basically no different from those faced by the other three Canadian divisions, and the method of attack used by them was the same as on Hill 145. There was, nevertheless, one crucial difference, and a difference ironically created by a Canadian commanding officer.

Before the battle began, the CO of the 87th (Montreal) Battalion of the 4th Division had requested that the artillery barrage should leave intact and undamaged a German trench of the second line, which he wished to capture and exploit. The CO seemed confident of seizing the trench – only 150 yards from the Canadian jump-off trenches – before its defenders had time to emerge from their deep tunnels and fight back. In these circumstances, the CO's request was granted. Unfortunately, in keeping this trench sacrosanct, the CO had also preserved unharmed several machine-gun nests and infantry sections of the German 5th Company of 261st Regiment. This factor, combined with German reserve machine-guns farther back on Hill 145, and the peculiarly stubborn fighting qualities of the 5th Company, brought the Canadians near to disaster.

Machine-gun fire, rifle fire and hand grenades were unleashed from the undamaged trench, slaughtering half the advancing Canadians in minutes, and producing piles of khaki corpses in front of the German position. All around them, shell-holes full of water were stained a deep red.

Despite their appalling losses, the Canadians managed to overwhelm the left wing of Regiment No. 261 and the opposition they faced narrowed down to the centre. Here, the Germans scrambled from their tunnels and viciously counter-attacked. Soon, the fighting degenerated into confusion and discernible lines of Canadians and Germans disappeared. The battle dissolved into small close-quarter skirmishes, fought by groups of isolated men. Battered battalions of the ill-fated 11th Brigade, together with neighbouring units of the 12th Brigade, on their left, broke up into scattered remnants. Of the 11th Brigade battalions, the 54th on the left flank was rapidly reduced to about 90 men, the 102nd to not many more and the manpower of the 87th was scythed in half. As for the 12th Brigade, "A" Company of its 78th Battalion lost all its officers, either killed or badly wounded, and out of the 700 men the battalion sent into the battle, only 199 reported at the first roll call afterwards.

The 11th Brigade Commander, Brigadier V. W. Odlum, was distraught. Reports reaching him were non-existent or scanty. As far as he could tell, the 54th, 102nd and 87th Battalions had gone up Hill 145 and disappeared. Of the 30 scouts Odlum had sent out to reconnoitre and report, only one had returned. And he brought dismal news that the Germans were still holding their Second Line on the left of the 11th Brigade's front. The major part of Hill 145 was still in German hands long after the battle plan had specified that it should have been wrested from them.

At 1450 Brigadier Odlum summoned officers of the 85th Battalion, Lieutenant-Colonel J. Warden commanding, to urgent consultations at Tottenham Tunnel, the communications trench that served as 11th Brigade HQ. The result of this anxious get-together was orders for the 85th, which consisted mainly of untried men, to prepare to take Hill 145. A covering artillery bombardment was promised but, in the event, failed to materialize.

At 1745 the 85th Battalion began to advance without the comfort and reassurance of covering fire. They ran straight into a barrage of German machine-guns. Bullets whipped through the Canadian ranks. Many men fell to the ground but the advance was not halted. Several men of the 85th had been trained in the tricky job of firing Mills bombs from rifles. This daunting marriage of two weapons had a terrifying effect on the Germans. Corporal H. M. Curll, of the 85th's "C" Company, fired a Mills bomb to within five yards of one machine-gun crew, producing instant surrender. Curll's initiative was followed by other rifle-bombers and by the time "C" Company got within 50 yards of the Germans' Second Line five crews had leapt from their gun positions and fled.

At nightfall on 9 April, troops of the 85th Battalion were passing over the crest of Hill 145. Isolated Germans in scattered positions on the Hill were still resisting, but their main defence effort had been effectively quelled. At 1600 on 10 April, under cover of an artillery barrage, the 44th and 50th Battalions of the 10th Brigade (4th Division) crossed over the north of Hill 145 and down the reverse slope to the *Untere Hangstellung*. A few hours later, as night closed in, Hill 145 was in Canadian hands and the "Southern Operation", the main part of the Vimy Ridge offensive, was over. The cost had been 3,000 Canadians killed, over 4,000 wounded, and the reward, 4,000 German prisoners taken and unknown numbers killed.

The hiatus on Hill 145 had, however, put the timetable out by about 48 hours. The 44th and 50th Battalions had originally been detailed to spend 10 April carrying out the "Northern Operation" to take the wooded knoll – known as the "Pimple" – commanding the Souchez Valley. Because of the rescue operation on Hill 145, the attack on the "Pimple" which was made with very heavy artillery support, did not start until 0530 on 12 April.

The weather, which had alternated between squalls of snow, hail, sleet and rain, leaden skies and brief glimpses of bright sunshine since 9 April, was now decisively in favour of the Canadians. It was snowing as the 44th and 50th Battalions, together with the 46th Battalion, struggled towards the German positions on the "Pimple", sunk up to their knees in gluey sludge. Fortunately for them, the freezing wind was blowing the snow straight at the Germans, and their machine-gunners were so blinded and bemused by it that the Canadians were upon them before they had a chance to mount an effective defence. The ensuing fight was vicious and the result never in serious doubt. By 0900, after three and a half hours, the Canadians had taken the "Pimple" and had completed the capture of Vimy Ridge. Their toll of casualties was now climbing towards the final figure of 10,000 which was officially acknowledged on 14 April. The Canadians had lost one tenth of the men they put into the battle. In human terms, this is a chilling toll, but in cold statistics, in terms of the ratio between sacrifice and success, nowhere near as costly as other battles in the First World War.

Already, during the night of 12/13 April, the Germans had withdrawn to their well-fortified defence line between Avion, Mericourt and Arleux, near the Scarpe River. Here, their strength was reinforced by 14 April with reserve divisions, and with one man to every 6 ft of ground, their resistance markedly stiffened. The reaction of the British High Command was to attack quickly and prise the Germans out. Three attacks were made to this end, one at Arleux (28–9 April) and two on the Scarpe (23–4 April and 3 May). They failed to dislodge the enemy. Twelve days later, on 15 May, the battles of Arras, of which these were almost the final flickers, petered to an inconclusive close, leaving the Canadian capture of Vimy Ridge very poorly exploited.

However, Arras and Vimy did have uncomfortable consequences for General von Falkenhausen. He was fired for his gross unpreparedness. The French General Nivelle of whom so much, perhaps too much, had been expected was also removed from his post after his Champagne offensive – launched on 16 April in the vilest possible weather – failed to break through the German defence-in-depth. The French lost 100,000 men and on 3 May, the French armies mutinied. On 15 May, Nivelle was replaced as French C-in-C by General Henri Philippe Pétain.

In these circumstances, with the British effort round Arras something of a damp squib and the French campaign an embarrassment and disaster, it was not surprising that so much lustre had attached itself to the Canadians' exploit on Vimy Ridge. This was, in the first place, the first Allied effort in the First World War that could even vaguely be called a success, and the gains made there proved in time to be permanent.

Vimy gave a striking demonstration of just how much could be achieved and just how quickly when warfare was conducted along intelligent, well-coordinated and efficient lines. Marshal Joffre and the other apostles of attrition had shown that sending thousands of men to certain death in the hope of swamping the enemy by force of numbers was neither necessary nor efficacious if battles were to be won.

But in practice the lessons of Vimy Ridge were forgotten as soon as they had been learned. For in the history of the First World War, the Vimy battle makes a fresh filling in a stale and melancholy military sandwich. Six months before it was fought, the battles of the Somme ended. Here, British and French troops were thrown at the enemy in droves – 350,000 of them were mown down like corn. Six months after Vimy Ridge came the battle which cost the British 250,000 men and which serves, even today, as a synonym for nauseating waste and mindless butchery – Passchendaele.

Passchendaele (1917)

Hubert Essame

Much has been written about Passchendaele, or the Third Battle of Ypres, 1917 – a lot of it by writers who were not there. In the process, they have created many myths ranging from the belief that the troops were "lions led by donkeys", and that the generals lived in luxury chateaux whilst the soldiers died in the mud, to the claim that Field Marshal Sir Douglas Haig was a "great master of the field" and justified in his decision not only to stage an offensive on the grand scale east of Ypres on 31 July 1917 but also to continue attacking there for a further 14 weeks. I belong to neither of these schools of thought but prefer to tell what happened to me and what I saw just north of the Menin Road in late July and August.

There was something sinister about the ruins of Ypres in 1917. The painters Hieronimus Bosch, Gustave Doré and Sidney Nolan, had they been living at the time, could, perhaps, have conveyed the eerie horror of the place. A stink of decay from the moat mixed with that of HE defiled the air. In June and July 1917 it was under day and night bombardment. Everybody going to the front had to pass either through the Menin Gate and take the road to Hellfire Corner or the Lille Gate whence a plank road called the Warrington Track ran just north of Zillebeke Lake. Men anxiously waited for the next shell as they marched over the cobble stones of the *Grande Place*. In

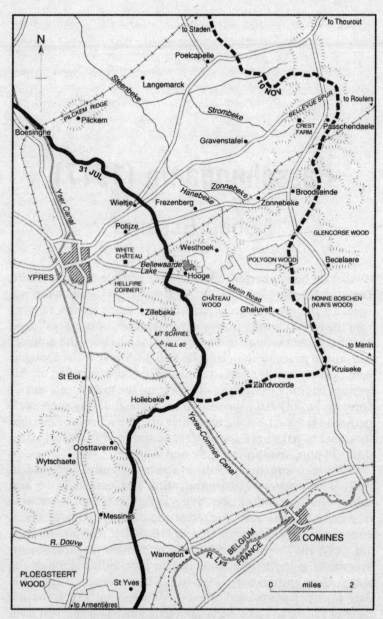

3.5 Passchendaele, July–November 1917

the ramparts there was some cover from the shellfire. By night the Very lights of the front line cast a loop round the city.

Never can the point of attack have been more blatantly advertised. On 7 June we, 2nd Battalion, The Northampton-shire Regiment were in reserve for the Messines battle but not used. A few days later, we, with the rest of our division, the 8th Infantry, were moved into the line to hold the sector about Hooge and to familiarize outselves with the ground over which we were destined to attack. Our guns were so closely packed together for the coming offensive that the northern half had to fire for one part of the night and the southern half for the other. It would have been impossible otherwise for the traffic to get through. Daylight movement east of Ypres was impossible – except for individuals. On our divisional front over 2,000 men worked like moles every night burying cables, digging dugouts at Halfway House and carrying stores to forward dumps under almost continuous shellfire.

Every yard of the Menin Road and the Warrington Track was "taped". Abandoned wagons, corpses, dead horses and mules lined the roads. Limbs and bodies in the twisted distortion of death festooned the shell-holes. Commanding a working party on these roads was a nightmare. It was usual for over 20 per cent of the men to fail to return.

General Sir Hubert Gough, GOC Fifth Army, planned to attack on a front of seven and a half miles from the Zillebeke – Zandvoorde road to Boesinghe with ten infantry divisions. By early July he had concentrated 752 heavy and medium guns, 324 4.5-in howitzers and 1,098 18-pounders to blast his troops forward two miles by a methodical advance in three stages – to the Blue Line about 1,250 yards distant, the Black Line 900 yards farther on and finally a further 1,400 yards to the Green Line. With communications between infantry and artillery as primitive as they were, this may well seem a clumsy plan. But it should be noted that in March and May 1918 the Germans executed successful attacks along these lines on the Somme and the Chemin des Dames.

About 15 miles west of Ypres a full-scale replica of the German positions we were to attack had been marked out with broad tapes in the standing corn. Every day in hot sunshine, under the eyes of the divisional and brigade commanders, we deployed as if for the real attack, advancing behind an imaginary barrage represented by men with red flags moving forward at the rate of 100 yards in four minutes in 25-yard lifts. We had two companies forward and two companies behind them in depth – each company attacking in two waves. They were all intended to go straight through to their objectives leaving one of their four platoons to follow and deal with enemy over-run. Much emphasis was laid on the need to keep as close as possible to the bursting shells of the barrage. All officers also attended an exposition of the divisional plan on a large-scale relief model. This envisaged an advance on a two-brigade front each with four tanks. Two battalions of each brigade would take the Blue Line. Then the other two would pass through to take the Black Line. A pause would then be necessary while the artillery was moved forward. When this was done the third brigade, supported by 12 tanks, would pass through and capture the Green Line.

It had been intended to launch the attack on 25 July. Accordingly we moved back into the line about Hooge on the 23rd. The preliminary day and night bombardment had reached a crescendo. We now found that the French, who were due to attack in the north, were not ready, so the attack had to be put back to the 31st.

As a result of 1916 experience on the Somme each unit going into action left behind within easy reach a so-called "battle surplus" or cadre consisting of understudies at every level of command from lance-corporal upwards. There were about a hundred all told. I was left behind with this party as understudy to the adjutant.

On the afternoon of 26 July a signal from brigade HQ ordered me forward at once. It was a scorching afternoon. The road as far as the outskirts of Ypres was choked with transport, raising huge clouds of dust. Just short of the railway station on the western outskirts all traffic stopped. On reaching the Lille Gate I took the Warrington Track. Not a soul seemed to be moving in the wilderness ahead. It was not a pleasant walk. The observer of a German 77 mm battery apparently thought I presented a worthwhile target and sniped at me all the way to battalion HQ by Zillebeke Lake. Here I found utter confusion. The surface shelter which housed the HQ had sustained a direct hit and the adjutant, the Intelligence officer, the signals officer and the chief clerk had all been blown up and killed or evacuated. Even the leather-faced old RSM looked off colour. But he was still able to call my attention to three jars of rum which had been smashed by the explosion – a contingency Higher Authority was likely to treat with suspicion unless vouched for by unimpeachable evidence.

My CO, 26-year-old Lieutenant-Colonel C. G. Buckle, MC, moved the HQ to a vast dugout by the ruins of Halfway House. This shelter was a triumph of engineering under the marsh, designed to hold about 3,000 men before the attack. The greater part of the battalion were already in residence. There was just room for one man to pass another and the floor was a foot deep in grey mud. Pumping went on continuously. The smell was appalling – a delicate blend of marshes, sewage and human sweat. This vast sewer was spasmodically lit by electric light.

The Germans knew all the exits and kept up a continuous bombardment on them. Every visit to the latrines outside was a dash for life; day and night a never-ending stream of men stepped over us *en route* for the hell outside. We remained in these insanitary quarters for four days – jammed shoulder to shoulder. When the light failed and the supply of candles ran out we sat in darkness.

My main worry concerned not the loss of all the paper about the attack but casualties inflicted on the battalion signallers and runners, amounting to 50 per cent a day. When, on my first night, the signal came through postponing the attack for four days I foresaw that we would probably have to start the battle short-handed. In the event the misty weather on the 27th and 28th and rain on the 30th, ominous though they were in other respects, cut down the casualty rate.

A message on the afternoon of the 30th confirmed that zero hour would be at 0350 the next day. On the previous two nights the German artillery had unleashed exceptionally heavy shelling on our form-up area. There was therefore a feeling of acute tension when we all filed out of the great dugout at about 2100 to assembly trenches just north of the Menin Road at Hooge.

Just in front of the assembly trenches a party had already laid out the tapes marking the start line. It was a dark and cloudy night.

The CO, the Intelligence Officer and I moved to Birr Cross Roads in the middle of the two rear companies with our little party of signallers trailing D3 cable and carrying some unlucky pigeons in baskets. At 0300 all was quiet; half an hour later all companies had reported that they were formed up on the tapes. Suddenly at 0350 the sky behind and on our flanks erupted. The blast was so deafening that we jammed our fingers in our ears; the ground shook. We could see the flashes of the barrage in the murk ahead. There were just a few silvery streaks in the sky to the east. The swish of the 18-pounder shells tempted us to crouch down. In fact, although we could not see them, the two leading companies advancing on compass bearings were clinging to the barrage and moving forward each time it jumped a further 25 yards. The reserve companies and our own headquarters soon started to move forward in the gloom as well.

We reached what had been the German front line. Here, the wire had been blown to bits by our bombardments of the preceding fortnight. Slowly the light strengthened. We could now see about 100 yards and all around us men moved steadily forward. The going was fairly good at first. Five hundred yards farther on we found the two leading companies on their objective rounding up a number of dazed Germans. The two reserve companies now pressed through towards their objective on the Bellwaarde Ridge and soon struck a ravine of sorts full of water and surrounded by the dead stumps of Château Wood. Here were smouldering dugouts which had been treated to a barrage of Thermite (incendiary bombs) fired from mortars. There were also some pillboxes which had been knocked over by heavy artillery fire.

Ploughing through the mud, the two reserve companies could be seen approaching the crest of the ridge which was our final objective. When the CO and I reached a point on the crest they were mopping up some dugouts running along the northern edge of the wood. It was now quite light. We established HQ in a large shell-hole. I could hear a lot of machine-gun fire 100 yards or so away to our left. Evidently the battle here was not yet over. About 100 ft above our heads an RE8 scout plane was sounding its klaxon horn. Looking up I could see the pilot distinctly. The time had come to put out the ground strips indicating our HQ's position and the capture of our objective. The pilot seemed satisfied, for he put the nose of his aircraft up and made off. One of his friends failed to get back to safety. His aircraft had been caught, probably by our own shells, and was burning a few hundred yards away on our left.

I wrote "Objective gained" and our map reference on the flimsy message form which the signals sergeant promptly attached to the leg of a pigeon which was released. I could not have said much else at the time. At that very moment Captain T. R. Colyer-Fergusson was winning his Victoria Cross just 200 yards away. As his "B" Company approached the ridge he found himself in danger of losing the barrage which was already 100 yards ahead. Right in front of him was an enemy trench well wired and occupied by a machine-gun crew which the barrage had missed. Hastily collecting about ten men, amongst whom was Sergeant W. G. Boulding and his own orderly Pte. B. Bell, he rushed forward and gained a footing in the trench which was on the crest of the ridge. Almost at once a German company counter-attacked. Colyer-Fergusson and his little party shot down 20 or 30 of them with rifle fire and the survivors surrendered. The rest of the British company now came up. At the same time a German machine-gun opened fire on them. Leaving his men to hold the trench Colyer-Fergusson and his orderly captured the gun. He then turned the gun on to another group of Germans, killing a large number of them. A few minutes later he was hit in the head by a stray machine-gun bullet and died instantly.

Meanwhile "C" Company on the right had also had a tough struggle for its objective. Here, Second Lieutenant Frost rushed a post which held a machine-gun which was shooting down men of 1st Battalion, The Worcester Regiment, on our right flank. Frost killed a German officer and 14 men. By now Col. Buckle had gone forward and ordered the two companies to consolidate about 150 yards ahead. The liaison officer from the Worcesters reported that they too were on their objective. It was now daylight. I could now see the 1st Battalion, The

Sherwood Foresters, and 2nd Battalion, The East Lancashire Regiment, passing through us and going strong *en route* to the Black Line 1,200 yards ahead on the Westhoek Ridge.

Hours of uncertainty, misunderstanding and confusion descended on the battlefield. It took me a long time to grasp what was actually happening in front and on our flanks. Walking wounded of the Foresters and E. Lancashires said their attack was going well but that they were losing a lot of men from machine-gun fire from their east flank and, surprisingly, from their right rear as well. About 0630 these two battalions were apparently on their objective on the Westhoek Ridge but fighting was still going on. About the same time our own company in Château Wood reported that they were being subjected to very heavy machine-gun fire from their east flank. Looking back I saw our own GOC, Brigadier-General H. W. Cobham, DSO, coming towards us with his brigade major. Suddenly quite close to us the brigade major (Captain A. Holmes Scott, Royal Engineers) was killed by a machine-gun bullet.

On the edge of the tree stumps of Château Wood two tanks were bogged down. They were the only tanks I saw that day. Coming forward from the direction of Hellfire Corner there was a mass of troops from 25th Brigade (Brigadier-General C. Coffin, DSO), destined to carry forward the advance beyond the Westhoek Ridge to the Green Line. About this time my CO, while trying to find out what the situation was on our right flank, was wounded and evacuated. Fortunately Lieutenant-Colonel S. G. Latham, MC, the second-in-command, had found it impossible to restrain himself from coming forward to see if he could be of any help. He never bothered to take cover. We had breakfast – biscuits and cold boiled bacon from our haversacks washed down with cold tea. Latham then went towards the right flank to find out what was really going on there. A lot of machine-gun fire was coming from Nonnebosschen, Glencorse and Polygon Woods. Nobody seemed able to say definitely which group of trees was which. The Worcesters apparently were out of touch with 30th Division which was rumoured to have failed to take Clapham Junction.

The sound of machine-gun fire from this direction continued. About this time our signallers reported that they had line communication with brigade HQ. When I raised the instrument the brigade Intelligence officer's voice seemed far away. I gathered, however, that 30th Division had been checked but were staging another attack on Sanctuary Wood and Stirling Castle. About 1000, the guns on our own front opened up in all-out support for 25th Brigade, now said to be near the final objective for the day – the Green Line on the far side of the Hanebeek stream. Despite the obscure situation on their right flank they seemed to be doing well.

Their progress was a matter of great interest to us as we were due to relieve one of their battalions when it reached its objective. About this time we were heavily shelled. Brigade HQ ordered us to send 60 men at once to Westhoek to act as additional stretcher bearers. A steady stream of walking wounded flowed from the front. They reported that 25th Brigade's three assault battalions were on their objective but had lost a lot of men. Some said they had got their objectives but had been counter-attacked and driven back. Large numbers of Germans had been seen arriving in lorries. By now it was at least clear that they still held Glencorse Wood and Nonnebosschen. The hours dragged by in an atmosphere of continued uncertainty. A wounded officer from 25th Brigade said they were being slowly pushed back to the Westhoek Ridge. Another reported later that Brig.-Gen. Coffin had been forward with his troops all the morning and was now rallying what was left of his brigade on the Westhoek Ridge.

All day the skies had been overcast. At about 1600 it started to rain in torrents. The shell-holes rapidly filled with water. Men were soon sinking knee-deep in the mud. The prolonged preliminary bombardment had shattered the drainage system and the churned-up earth held water like a sponge. The soldiers' ground-sheet capes were poor protection. Very soon we were all soaked to the skin. Only after dark did I fully understand what had happened. The 30th Division on our right, in a maze of shattered tree stumps and wire, had lost the barrage soon after the start. All the tanks supporting them had almost immediately become immobilized in the stinking bog. In the whole day, they had advanced less than 1,000 yards to Stirling Castle after using up all their battalions. For them it had been a nightmare –

almost as bad as the first day of the Somme. It was clear that the Germans still held the high ground of the Gheluvelt Plateau at Clapham Junction and Glencorse Wood. The rest of Fifth Army on our left had had better luck and advanced about 2,000 yards.

It rained all night. Soon after dawn 10th Battalion, The Cheshire Regiment (25th Division) arrived to relieve us and we moved back in small parties towards Ypres. For the moment the guns were silent. Stretcher bearers were still bringing back their heavy loads through the all-pervading swamp of glutinous mud. Compared with 25th Brigade's battalions our casualties of 13 killed and 189 wounded had been light. Altogether the division had lost 160 officers and 3,005 men, mainly due to deadly machine-gun fire from the east flank. This was a fifth of the total British loss on 31 July but we had 600 prisoners to show for it. The divisional artillery exposed in the open for six weeks before the attack had lost more men from mustard gas and HE than they had incurred in the whole preceding period from 1914.

We spent the next ten days in comparative comfort in billets in the little town of Steenvoorde near Poperinghe. The Corps commander, after congratulating us on our efforts, informed us that we would have the privilege of continuing the battle in the same area when the weather improved. I do not recall any unbounded enthusiasm at his announcement, but if anyone disapproved he kept his mouth shut. Meanwhile, the rain continued unabated. On 13 August we returned to the line of shell-holes we had captured two weeks previously with two companies forward just short of Westhoek. Conditions had been bad when we left; they were even worse now. All the holes were full to the brim with water. Everywhere it was hard going through the mud. In some places duckboard tracks sank out of sight almost as soon as they were laid. Aerial photographs showed that the Hanebeek, which had been a mere trickle on 31 July, was now a broad stream. This time the advance to the Green Line which we had captured but failed to hold on the 31st was to be carried out immediately south of the Ypres–Roulers railway on a two-brigade front with Coffin's 25th Brigade on the right. The Northamptonshires were now attached to this brigade as a reserve. On our right Polygon Wood, Glencorse Wood and Nonnebosschen were still in enemy hands. It was abundantly clear that if the 56th Division attacking on our right failed to capture them we would once again be out on a limb and caught under fire as we had been a fortnight earlier.

The battle on 16 August remained imprinted on my mind because it was the only time I ever saw anyone in the act of winning a VC. This time we took into action only 13 officers and 400 men. Zero hour was 0445. The three attacking units of 25th Brigade, 2nd Battalion, The Royal Berkshire Regiment, 1st Battalion, The Royal Irish Rifles and 2nd Battalion, The Lincolnshire Regiment, got off on time despite being shelled when forming up. As the light strengthened, reports passed to us from brigade HQ gave the impression that all was going well and that the Hanebeek had been reached and crossed. Later, however, news came once more that they were being caught in enfilade by machine-guns on right and left flanks. Wounded and stretcher bearers passing by said that Gen. Coffin had gone forward to the hard-pressed front.

In lulls during the bombardment we could once more hear prolonged machine-gun fire from Nonnebosschen and Polygon Wood. Col. Latham therefore ordered Captain C. E. Blake to find out what the situation was there. Working his way to the right, Blake discovered that 56th (1st London) Division had found the tangled mass of dead woods around Inverness Copse and Glencorse Wood concealing considerable numbers of un-located machine-guns which had been too much for it. There could be no doubt that Coffin's brigade was isolated 1,200 yards ahead with open flanks. The expected counter-attack came at about 0930 under a savage bombardment of shells and machine-gun fire. As the morning dragged on there could be no escaping the fact that 25th Brigade were being shot to pieces and slowly pressed back. A little after noon Gen. Coffin ordered Capt. Blake's two forward companies to come forward at once and our other two companies to join him on the Westhoek Ridge with all speed. When we arrived a terrifying situation prevailed. The German shellfire was hellish. Ours must have been just as bad for them. Our forward observation officers had now brought down a dense curtain of fire across our front. Just behind the Westhoek Ridge the massed Vickers guns of the Divisional machine-gun companies had opened up with good observation and deadly effect. In the din you had to shout to make yourself heard.

On the ridge we found Coffin standing upright in the open. He welcomed us with a smile: "Those two companies of yours are a fine lot. They got here just in time." We then discovered that he had led the counter-attack with them and halted the Germans about 150 yards ahead. He and Latham then took the rest of the battalion forward and patched up some sort of line with Royal Berkshire survivors and filled the gap between the right flank and what was left of 167th Brigade (56th Division). Neither Coffin, nor Latham for that matter, showed the slightest inclination to take cover or indeed of being in any way perturbed.

About 1700 quiet descended on the front. It seemed that both sides had had enough for the time being. The sun made a fitful appearance. Three of Coffin's battalions had lost half their strength – the Royal Irish Rifles had only one officer and 60 men left. They were still, however, a disciplined body prepared to fight on. So long as Coffin remained with them they would have gone on to the last man.

Within two weeks my battalion had lost about 330 officers and men. Compared with other 8th Division battalions we escaped lightly. On 16 August our divisional loss came to 81 officers and 2,074 men. When Haig inspected the infantry on 21 August only 3,950 of the 12,000 or so available three weeks previously could be paraded. I do not recollect anything he said. According to the Divisional History, however, he "gave the division many words of encouragement and thanks, inspiring all ranks by his generous appreciation of what they had done."

Junior officers in most battles see only the local picture. Historians therefore tend to treat their accounts with caution. Because I had the luck to act as adjutant in both these battles I probably got a broader impression of what went on than most of my fellow second lieutenants. By some fluke, a copy of the three-page report I wrote on the battle a day or so afterwards has survived. I recollect being very proud of this literary effort at the time and feeling somewhat peeved when my CO signed it after only a cursory glance before dispatch to brigade HQ. I realize that my comments are open to the charge of bias. The loss of so many of my friends may well have embittered me. But, I can at least say that in my limited experience the accusation that divisional and brigade commanders ordered their men to face dangers they were not prepared to share themselves is unfair. Even in minor operations they had little scope for initiative and no option other than to obey orders. The casualty rate in battalion commanders (eight out of our 12 on 31 July), company commanders and lieutenants was proportionately far in excess of that of men in the ranks.

What I failed to understand after these two battles was why Haig chose to attack in an area of reclaimed marshland which two years' experience had already shown would revert to bog when it rained. It should have been obvious that this was no place to employ the 136 primitive tanks committed to battle here. Why did he so blatantly advertise his intention of attacking east of Ypres for six weeks before the actual assault by a vast increase in traffic, a gigantic forward build-up of dumps and a fortnight's preliminary bombardment? This mystified me at the time and still does. Having finally shown his hand and staged a fiasco on the 31 July why did he decide to go on with the battle hoping for fine weather? I was even more astonished when we came back to the muddy horror of Passchendaele in November 1917.

Cambrai (1917)

Bryan Cooper

Accusing as I do without exception all the great Allied offensives of 1915, 1916 and 1917, as needless and wrongly conceived operations of infinite cost, I am bound to reply to the question, what else could be done? And I answer it, pointing to the Battle of Cambrai. *This* could have been done. This in many variants, this in larger and better forms ought to have been done.

Such was Winston Churchill's belief in 1927 and the perspective has only been enlarged since.

At first sight the Battle of Cambrai in November 1917 was no more decisive than most battles fought on the Western Front. Indeed, the initial British advance through the Hindenberg Line that gave such promise of success, and caused church bells in England to ring victory peals for the first time since the Boer War, was repulsed by a German counter-attack that actually took back more ground than had been won. But it was the means of making that original advance, by the first-ever massed attack by tanks with close air-support and an unregistered artillery barrage which established Cambrai as a milestone in the history of warfare. It was a prelude to the tank's decisive role at the Battle of Amiens in August 1918 which signalled the final defeat of Germany.

Although the first, premature and piecemeal use of tanks by the British on the Somme in September 1916 wasted a great chance, it must be remembered that not only tanks were new but also the whole concept of their use. Many Allied commanders continued to disregard their potential but Field-Marshal Sir Douglas Haig, the British C-in-C, made a personal request for 1,000 improved tanks to be built during 1917. It was probably inevitable that the first tanks should be misused in wartime conditions, while those most concerned, crews, designers and commanders, learned from their mistakes. Unfortunately, this was not true of the latter during most of 1917.

The year opened promisingly for the embryo tank force. While a shortage of materials at home reduced Haig's order, there were some 200 tanks available by March, not only improved Mark Is but also a few Mark IVs. These were similar in outline and armament, but had 50 per cent thicker armor in the vital parts, against German armor-piercing ammunition. The Tank Corps, as it was named in June, became better established with at least a rudimentary training procedure. It had also produced its first master of tank tactics and strategy in the person of Lieutenant-Colonel John Frederick Charles Fuller. As Chief General Staff Officer (GSOI) to Brigadier-General Hugh J. Elles, the Tank Corps' first and 36-year-old commander, he devised many of the principles that were to govern the employment of tanks in battle up to and during the Second World War. Fuller saw the tank primarily as a mobile fortress which could escort the infantry into the enemy's defences and emphasized the necessity for surprise. He also saw the need to mass not disperse tanks, and preferably on ground that had not been reduced to a quagmire by constant shelling.

Such concepts were too unorthodox for most of the general staff at Haig's GHQ, especially the artillery commanders who believed that only a long and massive bombardment could soften up the enemy and cut his barbed wire as a prelude to any attack, regardless of the warning this gave. The first 1917 use of tanks was in April during the Battle of Arras, in which some 40 took part. Again strung out along a wide front, diminishing their impact, and despite individual successes, most became bogged down in the mud and unable to avoid

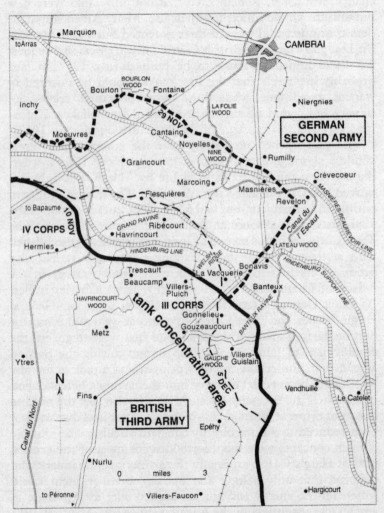

3.6 The Battle of Cambrai, November 1917

German shellfire. At Vimy Ridge, eight tanks were to assist the Canadian Corps, but these foundered before they could even fight.

An even greater tragedy occurred at Bullecourt (NW of Cambrai) where 11 tanks were to help the 4th Australian Division. Due to a heavy snowstorm the attack was postponed for a day; the tanks stood out as easy targets against the white background on a bright clear morning. Nine were knocked out before they reached the Hindenberg Line, and the remaining two were captured, giving the Germans their first chance to examine the new weapon. Australian infantry, following behind the tanks from which they expected protection, suffered appalling losses. They lost their faith in tanks for more than a year.

The worst tank ordeal of all came in Flanders, where the Corps took part in Haig's grand plan to break through the Ypres salient. The start of the offensive, at mine-sprung Messines Ridge on 7 June, was a great success, but 40 new Mark IV tanks were hardly needed, although they gave valuable support to the infantry. It was during the main campaign, begun on 31 July, which resolved itself into the terrible struggle for the village of Passchendaele that tanks, in common with the British Army as a whole, experienced their greatest catastrophe.

The preliminary artillery bombardment reached its highest peak of the war, when in 13 days over four million shells were fired from 3,000 guns, one gun to every six yards of the 11-mile front. This churned the ground into a dreadful condition made even worse by several weeks of non-stop rain and flooding in Flanders. Some 200 tanks were mustered for the Ypres offensive, and when it petered out at the beginning of November, hardly any remained in one piece. Most had sunk deep into the mud and were destroyed by enemy fire, to the point where the Menin Road was known as the "tank graveyard". After three months of bloody fighting, total British casualties were nearly 400,000 men – for the gain of four miles of territory.

GHQ was still unable to see the true value of tanks and held on to an attitude typified by one army commander, who stated after the Ypres campaign: "One, tanks are unable to negotiate bad ground; two, the ground on a battlefield will always be bad; three, therefore, tanks are no good on a battlefield." The War

Office in London had further doubts about whether to build more tanks. But although few realized it at the time, Passchendaele was the last of the senseless battles of attrition, fought in despair of conducting the war in any other way. For on another part of the front the Tank Corps had quietly been planning an attack in conditions of their own choosing, on dry hard ground, and according to their own tactics, that would show that indeed there was another way.

The town of Cambrai lay seven miles behind the Hindenberg Line, opposite General Sir Julian H. G. Byng's Third Army. It was a region of open, rolling countryside and firm ground covered by uncultivated grass that had seen little fighting during the war. The Germans considered their fortifications to be impregnable and were content to hold them while the Allies wore themselves out in reckless assaults elsewhere. As far back as mid-June, in a paper written on the future employment of tanks, Col. Fuller had suggested the idea of a major tank raid, not to win ground but to destroy or capture enemy troops and guns. One area he thought suitable was the country between St Quentin and Cambrai. The idea was originally turned down at GHQ, but early in August, support for it came from Gen. Byng, already thinking of an attack in the Cambrai area.

Further support came from Haig himself. As it became obvious even to him that Passchendaele was a disaster, he wanted to launch a quick operation with a good chance of immediate success in order to raise morale at home and among his own troops. He believed the Tank Corps plan might work. If it failed, he could always blame the tanks for not fulfilling their earlier promise. In such an event, it was not likely that the Tank Corps could have survived. On 13 October, he gave his approval for the attack to take place on 20 November. Conditions were now not nearly so favorable. Flanders had drained the Army's resources, most divisions were battle-weary and under strength, and on top of that the collapse of the Italian Front at Caporetto on 24 October meant rushing five British divisions to Italy to hold the line, leaving Third Army short of reserves.

Byng's intention was to break through the Hindenberg Line along a six-mile front between two canals, the Canal de L'Escaut (St Quentin) on the right and the unfinished and waterless Canal du Nord on the left. This was to be accomplished by three brigades of Mark IV tanks, followed by six infantry divisions with support from another two and three more held in reserve. While the tanks and infantry captured the two main features of the area, the Flesquières and Bourlon ridges, five cavalry divisions (40,000 horsemen) were to pour through the gap and isolate the town of Cambrai. The German forces would be cut off and rounded up, then the way would be clear to drive NE towards Valenciennes. From then onwards the plan was rather vague, but conformed to Haig's doctrine of attacking the German flanks after a breakthrough and "rolling up the front". Supporting the attack would be 1,003 guns, almost a third of 6-in calibre or more, and 14 squadrons (289 aircraft) of the Royal Flying Corps. This novel co-operation between tanks and aircraft was the origin of the German *Blitzkrieg* in the Second World War.

Cambrai itself was an important target, being a major communications center where four railways and a number of main roads and waterways converged, and German defenses were therefore particularly strong. They lay in a wide path, up to five miles deep, between the British front and Cambrai, with three main lines of trenches dug much wider than usual, up to 16 ft and to a depth of 18 ft. Even if tanks were used, the three defending divisions were confident that such vehicles would be unable to cross, and indeed the Mark IV only had a 10 ft trench-crossing capability. Each trench system included concrete dug-outs in which were massed batteries of machine-guns and lay behind acres of dense barbed wire, nowhere less than 50 yards thick. British observers had estimated that it would take five weeks of artillery bombardment to cut down this wire in the normal way.

Col. Fuller reckoned that tanks could crush the barbed wire, although there was always a danger of it becoming entangled in their tracks. The sheer size of the trenches was the biggest obstacle. An answer was finally provided by the Tank Corps Central Workshops. Bundles of brushwood of the kind used for road repairs were bound together by thick chains to make huge 10-ft-long fascines, each weighing 1.75 tons. One would be carried on the roof of each fighting tank, to be dropped into the trenches to form a bridge across.

The fighting tanks were to operate an ingenious leap-frogging system, in sections of three. An advance tank would go forward, flatten the German wire for the oncoming infantry, then reaching the first trench would turn left and drive along the edge, firing down at the enemy to protect the two main-body tanks following 100 yards behind. The first of these would drop its fascine in the trench, cross over, and give covering fire in front of the second trench for the next tank. This in turn would cross the second trench and move forward to attack the third and last line of trenches. Meanwhile, the advance tank would have come up to drop its fascine in the third trench, leading its two companions into the open country beyond. Four platoons of infantry were to follow closely (25–50 yards) behind each tank section to capture and garrison the trenches as they were overcome. Finally, 32 special wire-pulling tanks would roll up the flattened wire with grapnels to make broad pathways for the cavalry advance. In addition to these and 378 fighting tanks, there were 54 supply carriers with nine wireless tanks, a telephone cable laying tank and two bridge layers – making a grand total of 476, the largest tank force ever concentrated.

The week before the attack was due to begin, and after ten days training in the technique described above, the tanks were brought up to the front by rail in great secrecy, arriving by night so that even the British infantry did not know of their presence. Late on the afternoon of 19 November, the tanks began to leave their lying-up positions in woods and fields and made their way to the start-line. Dawn came up very slowly, grey and overcast with a fine ground mist. The shapes of the woods and ridges ahead began to emerge out of the darkness. Coveys of partridges sprang up and larks and crows took to the sky as the British infantry began to cut through their own wire, ready for the assault. There was no sign of the Germans, hidden deep in their trenches and dugouts, confident of the protection given by long, dense belts of barbed wire.

At zero hour, 0620, there was a devastating roar as 1,000 British guns opened up, most firing for the first time, having had their targets mapped and not registered by ranging shots, while from out of the sky swept four RFC squadrons, flying low and spraying the German trenches with machine-gun fire. The Battle of Cambrai had begun. And from the beginning it was different from previous battles. The artillery barrage, instead of continuing for days and even weeks, giving the Germans time to bring up reinforcements, almost immediately began to lift towards targets farther on. At the same time, the tanks moved slowly forwards down tape-marked lanes, the sound of their engines hidden by the noise of the guns and their course set by compass. At last they were to be used in a surprise attack as the pioneers of tank development had always intended.

Right in the center and aboard "Hilda", one of the leading tanks, was Brig.-Gen. Elles, carrying the new Corps flag and insisting on the right to lead his men into the first large-scale tank attack in history. It was one of the very few occasions in the First World War that a general did so. The sight of so many tanks lumbering out of the half-light of dawn, their huge fascines on top making them appear even more like monstrous, prehistoric animals, was too much for many of the German troops, who fled in panic. Those who remained were dismayed to find that their armor-piercing bullets could not penetrate these new Mark IV tanks. And when the tanks opened fire with their 6-pounders and Lewis machine-guns, the demoralization of the enemy was complete. A tank commander called it "almost a cake-walk". And it was recorded that "the infantry had walked behind the tanks smoking and with practically nothing to do except mop up a few dugouts."

By midday, the tanks had broken through the three trench systems as planned and advanced nearly five miles on a six-mile front, a deeper penetration than that achieved after the three months of fighting just over at Passchendaele. The day had yielded captures totalling 8,000 men, 123 guns and 281 machine-guns: two divisions had been annihilated. At HQ German Supreme Command, there was consternation. An immediate counter-attack was ordered, but the necessary reinforcements could not be brought up for at least 48 hours. Now the value of a swift surprise attack became evident.

So serious was the situation that General Erich Ludendorff, commanding the German armies, considered an extensive with-

drawal of the whole Cambrai front, one which might have led to
a general retreat. But the attack's success had also surprised
British GHQ. In fact, many commanders refused to believe it
and valuable time was lost while they awaited confirmation of
reports from the front. The morning objectives, with one
important exception, had been taken with such relative ease
that some advanced infantry units were content to remain in the
captured German trenches, so much more comfortable than
their own. In some instances the infantry failed to keep up with
the tanks, which later had to withdraw for lack of support. But
there still remained the five divisions of cavalry massed behind
the British lines waiting to advance. They had waited for such a
chance in nearly every other battle previously fought. Now it
had come. The great breakthrough had been made.

Unfortunately, Cavalry Corps HQ was five miles behind the
front line, and local commanders were not empowered to make
decisions on the spot. By the time orders came through to
advance, the momentum of the attack had faltered. And in one
vital sector of the center, at Flesquières, the German 54th
Reserve Division was still holding out. The way should have
been clear for 1st Cavalry Division to pass through the village
and move on to the all-important objective of Bourlon Wood on
the ridge covering the approach to Cambrai. But it was here that
the one hold-up of the morning had occurred, largely due to a
lack of co-operation between tanks and the infantry of 51st
Highland Division, for which their commander, Major-General
G. M. Harper, was largely responsible. He did not approve of
tanks, just as earlier he had opposed machine-gun development,
and ignored the instructions laid down by the Tank Corps.
Instead of keeping his men in files close behind the tanks, to
deal with German artillery, he made them follow in extended
order 100 yards or more behind. They had to waste valuable
time looking for the paths that the tanks had cut through the
barbed wire. Meanwhile, as the tanks pressed on alone towards
the crest of Flesquières Ridge, they came under fire from
several German 77 mm field-gun batteries. Sixteen were destroyed (a quarter of the figure lost to gunfire), with no
survivors among the crews. By the time the Highlanders advanced to this point, the Germans had regrouped and the

fighting here lasted until evening. Only then, outflanked on both sides, did the defenders withdraw. But this delay prevented the cavalry advance until next day, and the chance of taking Bourlon without a fight was lost.

By nightfall on the 20th, 179 of the 378 tanks that had moved forward at dawn were out of action. Many of those remaining had fought almost continuously for 16 hours and required maintenance. In spite of the great success achieved, the infantry and cavalry had not taken full advantage of it – perhaps because no one really expected such a breakthrough after the deadlock of earlier battles. Meanwhile, on the German side, five reserve divisions were beginning to arrive around Cambrai. Haig did in fact see the danger. But having provided the British public at home with a victory, the first one for so long, he did not wish to call a halt. The offensive continued.

On the 22nd, the British attack was resumed and very nearly succeeded. With the help of tanks, the infantry managed to fight their way into Bourlon village, while several other tanks almost reached Cambrai itself. But with little by way of reserves to call on, the British offensive lost its impetus. The Germans fought back with grim determination, and for another five days the battle swung first one way, then another. The fighting reached its peak on the 27th in the village of Fontaine, almost within sight of Cambrai. The situation at Bourlon was much the same, with part of the wood and village still in enemy hands. By the end of that day it was apparent to all, even Haig, that the offensive had to be called off. There were just not enough reserves to keep it going.

One week of fighting had achieved little more than the initial success gained in the first few hours, although on the credit side, apart from ground gained, over 11,000 prisoners had been taken, together with 142 guns, 456 machine-guns, 74 trench mortars and large quantities of stores and ammunition. After a hurried conference at GHQ, it was decided to withdraw to a defensive line on Flesquières Ridge, making use of the former German trenches. As far as the British were concerned, the Battle of Cambrai was over. The remaining tanks were pulled back to prepare for entrainment to their winter quarters.

But no one had reckoned with German intentions. On the

morning of 30 November, while the British were carrying out an orderly withdrawal, eight German divisions delivered a massive counter-stroke that took 6,000 prisoners and 158 guns on that day, in many ways just as sudden and surprising as the original British attack. The German plan was nothing less than to cut off and destroy all British troops in the salient formed by their advance on Cambrai. Only 63 tanks remained in the area. These were quickly rounded up and sent into action to help the infantry. They made a vital contribution to preventing what could have been a major disaster. Even so, by the time the German offensive ended in a blinding snowstorm on 7 December they had won back as much ground as they had lost and achieved a more or less even balance in casualties and prisoners, which totalled about 45,000 for both sides.

It was by no means the worst British defeat of the year, but after the promising victory of 20 November, the final result seemed just that much more of a bitter failure. There was a public outcry at home and even a Court of Enquiry which whitewashed the generals and put most of the blame on the junior officers, NCOs, and men. But this time, at least, the tanks could not be blamed. No one could deny their brilliant initial success. They suffered for it as well, particularly during the German counter-attack. Of the 4,000 officers and men of the Tank Corps who had taken part in the whole battle, a total of 1,153 were killed or wounded. Less than a third of the 476 tanks returned to base and all of them required extensive repairs. In fact, few saw action again, for the Mark IV was replaced in 1918 by the more efficient and more heavily armored Mark V. Haig had finished his Cambrai dispatch: "The great value of the tanks in the offensive has been conclusively proved."

Megiddo (1918)

Basil Liddell Hart

On 19 September 1918 began an operation which was both one of the most quickly decisive campaigns and the most completely decisive battles in all history. Within a few days the Turkish armies in Palestine had practically ceased to exist. Whether it should be regarded primarily as a campaign or as a battle completed by a pursuit is a moot question. For it opened with the forces in contact and hence would seem to fall into the category of a battle; but it was achieved mainly by strategic means, with fighting playing a minor part. This fact has tended to its disparagement in the sight of those who are obsessed with the Clausewitzian dogma that blood is the price of victory – and hold, as a corollary, that no victory is worthy of recognition which is not sanctified by a lavish oblation of blood. But Caesar's triumph at Ilerda, Scipio's near Utica, Cromwell's at Preston, and Moltke's, though opportunist rather than sought for, at Sedan, each had the same "pale pink" complexion. In each, strategy was so effective that fighting was but incidental. Yet no one can deny their decisiveness both as victories and on the course of history. A more serious "depreciation" of this final campaign-battle in Palestine lies in the fact that Allenby had a superiority of over two to one in numbers, and more in terms of weapon-values.★ In addition the morale of the Turks had so declined that it is often argued that Allenby had merely to stretch out his hand for the Turkish army, like an overripe plum, to fall into it. There is force in these contentions; but most of the "crowning mercies" of modern history, from Worcester to Sedan, have seen almost as great a disparity of strength and morale between victors and vanquished. And in 1918 Allenby had to outwit such able commanders as Liman von Sanders and Mustapha Kemal, not such men as those who thrust their heads into the sack at Sedan.

When full deduction is made for the advantageous conditions of September, 1918, the conclusion remains that the triumph immortalized by the already immortal name of Megiddo is one of history's masterpieces by reason of the breadth of vision and treatment. If the subject was not a difficult one, the picture is almost unique as a perfect conception perfectly executed.

The question is often asked, whose was the conception? Was it that of the titular commander? Or, did it spring from some gifted subordinate? When the victories of Hindenburg on the Russian front are discussed, even the man in the street speaks of Ludendorff's strategy – and the student of war goes still deeper, or lower, and muses on the unassessable influence of Hoffmann's military genius. But with Megiddo it is possible to dispel doubt, through the unanimous evidence of those most intimately concerned. The broad conception sprang entire from Allenby's mind, whatever the credit due to his assistants for working out its executive details. "Grew", indeed, would be a better word than "sprang", for the original conception was of more modest dimensions – to break through the Turkish front near the coast and, wheeling inwards, turn the flank of their forces in the Judæan Hills. But, returning one day from a ride during which he had been studying the problem, Allenby suddenly unfolded the plan as it was executed, in all its almost

---

★ Allenby's fighting strength was 12,000 sabres, 57,000 rifles and 540 guns. He estimated the Turkish strength at 3,000 sabres, 32,000 rifles and 402 guns. This figure is about double Liman von Sanders's estimate, which, however, seems to be a broad calculation, excluding machine-gun personnel.

breath-taking scope. It abundantly fulfilled Napoleon's maxim that "the whole secret of the art of war lies in making oneself master of the communications". If Allenby had a superiority of strength he was going to use it to make himself master not of one, but of every one, of the Turkish communications. And the success of his attempt to do so owed much to the complementary fact that he had taken thorough measures to be master of his own communications.

The three so-called Turkish "armies", each hardly more than the strength of a division, drew nourishment through a single stem – the Hejaz railway running south from Damascus. At Deraa a branch ran out westwards; crossing the Jordan at Jisr el Mejamie, just north of Beisan, it forked at El Afule in the Plain of Esdraelon, one line going to the sea at Haifa and the other turning south again through the hills of Samaria to Messudieh Junction. This line fed the Seventh (Mustapha Kemal) and Eighth (Jevad) Turkish armies which held the front between the river Jordan and the Mediterranean Sea. The Fourth Army (Jemal) east of the Jordan was fed by the main Hejaz railway.

Now, to cut an army's lines of communication is to dislocate its physical organization. To close its lines of retreat is to dislocate its morale. And to destroy its lines of "inter-communication" – by which orders and reports pass – is to dislocate it mentally, by breaking the essential connection between the brain and the body of an army. Allenby planned to achieve not a single but the triple dislocation, and the third element was not the least important to the success of his plan.

The convergence of both roads and railways made Deraa, El Afule, and, to a less extent, Beisan the vital points in the Turks' rear. To get a grip on El Afule and Beisan would sever the communications of the Seventh and Eighth Armies and also close their lines of retreat, except for the extremely difficult outlet to the desolate region across the Jordan eastwards. To get a grip on Deraa would sever the communications of all three armies and the best line of retreat of the Fourth. But it was considerably further from the British front.

El Afule and Beisan, however, lay within a sixty-mile radius, and hence were within the range of a strategic cavalry "bound", provided that these vital points could be reached without interruption or delay. The problem was, first, to find a line of approach unobstructed by nature, and, second, to ensure that the enemy could not block it by force. How was it solved? The flat coastal Plain of Sharon afforded a corridor to the Plain of Esdraelon and Vale of Jezreel, in which El Afule and Beisan respectively lay. This corridor was interrupted by only a single door, so far back that it was not guarded by the Turks, formed by the narrow mountain belt which separates the coastal Plain of Sharon from the inland Plain of Esdraelon. But the entrance to the corridor was firmly bolted and barred by the trenches of the Turkish front. Allenby planned to use his infantry to force this locked gate and swing it back, as on a hinge, north-east-wards, so leaving a clear path for his cavalry. But having passed through the front gate they would still have to get through the back door. This the Turks could easily close if they had time and warning. Speed on the part of the cavalry was essential. But not sufficient. The attention and reserves of the Turks must be distracted. Even so, there was still a risk. War experience had shown how easily cavalry could be stopped, and a handful of men and machine-guns would suffice to block the two passes through the intermediate mountain belt. To avert this risk the Turkish Command must be made deaf and dumb as well as blind. In this complete paralysis of the Turkish Higher Command lies the main significance and the historical value of the victory of Megiddo.

Let us watch how it was achieved. For it, Allenby had two comparatively novel tools – aircraft and Arabs. Feisal's Arabs, under the guiding brain of Colonel Lawrence, had long been harassing, immobilizing and demoralizing the Turks along the main Hejaz railway. Now they were to contribute more directly to the final stroke by the British forces. On September 16th and 17th, emerging like phantoms from the desert, they blew up the railway north, south, and west of Deraa. This had the physical effect of shutting off the flow of Turkish supplies temporarily – and "temporarily" was all that mattered here. It had the mental effect of persuading the Turkish Command to send part of its scanty reserves towards Deraa.

The Air Force contribution was in two parts. First, by a

sustained campaign it drove the enemy's machines out of the air. This campaign was carried so far that ultimately the fighters "sat" above the Turkish aerodrome at Jenin to prevent their machines even taking off. Thus it closed the enemy's air eye during the period of preparation. Secondly, when the moment came for the execution of Allenby's plan, the Air Force made the enemy's command deaf and dumb – by decisively bombing their main telegraph and telephone exchange at El Afule, a stroke in which Ross-Smith, who later made history by his flight to Australia, helped England to make history. In addition, the enemy's two army headquarters at Nablus and Tul Keram were bombed, and at the second, the more vital, the wires were so effectively destroyed that it was cut off throughout the day both from Nazareth and from its divisions in the coastal sector. Another and earlier form of air activity was, if less military, perhaps of even wider strategic effect. This was the dropping not of bombs but of an equal weight of illustrated pamphlets showing the physical comforts which the Turkish soldier enjoyed as a prisoner of war. Its appeal to half-starved and ragged men was none the less for being imponderable.

While the Arabs and the Air Force were perhaps the two most vital factors in "unhinging" the enemy preparatory to the actual push, the plan had also the wide and purposeful variety of ruses which marks the masterpieces of military history. By these Allenby sought to divert the enemy's attention away from the coast to the Jordan flank. In this aim he was helped by the very failure of two attempted advances east of the Jordan, towards Amman and Es Salt, during the spring. Then, throughout the summer he kept a cavalry force, periodically relieved, in the stifling heat of the Jordan Valley to hold the enemy's attention. When the cavalry were ultimately moved surreptitiously across to the other flank, their camps were not only left standing but new ones added, while 15,000 dummy horses of canvas filled the vacated horse lines. Mule-drawn sleighs created dust clouds; battalions marched by day towards the valley – and returned by night in lorries to repeat this march of a stage army; a hotel was taken over in Jerusalem and elaborately prepared for the mythical reception of General Headquarters; new bridging and wireless activity fostered the illusion; Lawrence sent agents to bargain for vast quantities of forage in the Amman district.

And all the time more and more troops were filtering down by night marches to the other flank near the sea, there to be concealed in orange groves or in camps already standing. By these means Allenby increased his two-to-one superiority, on the front as a whole, to a five-to-one superiority on the vital sector – unsuspected by the enemy. For some time Liman von Sanders had certainly anticipated a big attack, and, indeed, had thought of frustrating it by a voluntary retirement to a rear line near the Sea of Galilee. "I gave up the idea, because we would have had to relinquish the Hejaz railway . . . and because we no longer could have stopped the progress of the Arab insurrection in rear of our army. On account of the limited marching capacity of the Turkish soldiers and of the very low mobility of all draft animals, I considered that the holding of our positions to the last gave us more favourable prospects than a long retirement with Turkish troops of impaired morale."

Although he feared an attack near the coast, he feared still more the effect of one east of the Jordan, and even at the last hour the warning of the first given by an Indian deserter on September 17th was offset by the more positive news of the Arab attacks on the vital railway at Deraa. Deceived by his own preconceived idea, Liman von Sanders was, indeed, too ready to believe that this deserter was a tool of the British Intelligence, and his story a blind to cover Allenby's real purpose. Further, Liman von Sanders rejected the plea of Refet Bey, commanding the coastal sector, who wished to withdraw his troops a mile so that the British bombardment might waste itself on empty trenches. Forbidding Refet to withdraw an inch, he ensured that he should go back a hundred miles, to Tyre, leaving his army behind – dead or prisoners.

On the night of 18 September began what was both the last move of the "distracting" preparation and the first move of the real action. The 53rd Division, which formed Allenby's extreme right, made a spring forward in the hills on the edge of the Jordan Valley. Thereby they would be a step on their way towards closing the only way of retreat – across the Jordan eastwards – left open to the Turks when the main move had fulfilled its encircling purpose.

Far away to the west by the sea all was quiet. But at 4.30 a.m. 385 guns opened fire on the selected frontage. For a quarter of an hour, only, they maintained an intense bombardment, and then the infantry advanced, under cover of a rapid lifting barrage. They swept, almost unchecked, over the stupefied defenders and broke through the two trench systems, shallow and slightly wired – by Western Front standards. Then they wheeled inland, like a huge door swinging on its hinges. Of this door, a French contingent and the 54th Division formed the hinged end; then, with a five-mile interval, the 3rd Indian, 75th and 7th Indian Divisions, formed the middle panel; and the 60th Division, by the sea, the outside panel. The latter reached Tul Keram by nightfall. But what survived of the Turkish Eighth Army had long before been pouring back through the defile to Messudieh in a confused crowd of troops and transport. And upon this hapless mob the British aircraft had swept down with bombs and bullets.

Meantime, through the opened door had ridden the three cavalry divisions of the Desert Mounted Corps (Chauvel). By evening they had reached the Carmel Range, the "intermediate door", sending detachments with their armoured cars to secure the two passes. By morning they were across. One brigade descended on Nazareth where the enemy's General Headquarters lay, ignorant of the events of the past twenty-four hours because cut off from all communication with its fighting body. Liman von Sanders, however, escaped through a failure to block the northern exit of the town, and after a vigorous street fight the cavalry were forced to retire.

The real strategic key, however, was now not at Nazareth but at El Afule and Beisan. These were reached at 8 a.m. and 4.30 p.m. respectively – to Beisan the 4th Cavalry Division had covered seventy miles in thirty-four hours. Passing through the Carmel Range in its wake, the Australian Mounted Division turned south to Jenin to place a closer barrier across the Turks' line of retreat. The enemy's only remaining bolt-hole was east over the Jordan – which flows swiftly, with few fords, through a deep and winding trough, 1300 feet below sea level at the Dead

Sea end. He might have reached this but for the Air Force, as the infantry advance was making slow progress through the hills in face of the stubborn Turkish rearguards. Early in the morning of 21 September, the British aircraft spotted a large column – practically all that survived of the two Turkish armies – winding down the steep gorge from Nablus to the Jordan. Four hours' continuous bombing and machine-gunning reduced this procession to stagnation, an inanimate chaos of guns and transport. Those who survived were merely scattered fugitives. From this moment may be timed the extinction of the Seventh and Eighth Turkish Armies. What followed was but a rounding up of "cattle" by the cavalry.

Only the Fourth Army, east of the Jordan, remained. This, delaying too long, did not begin to retire until 22 September. A broken railway and the Arabs lay across its line of retreat to Damascus. And four days later the 4th Cavalry Division moved east from Beisan to intercept it, while the other two converged directly on Damascus, its goal. Escape was impossible, but its fate was different from that of the other armies, a rapid attrition under constant pinpricks rather than a neat despatch. In this pursuit the Desert Mounted Corps co-operated with, and for the first time met, their real desert allies, hitherto an invisible and intangible factor. Their presence, and identity, was disclosed when a messenger reported – "There's an Arab on the top of the hill over there in a Rolls-Royce; talks English perfectly and in the hell of a rage!" For no pursuit could be fast enough to satisfy Lawrence's ardent spirit as he urged his Arabs on towards the city of desire. To a British cavalry officer with an apt gift of phrase their march looked "like some strange oriental version of an old-time Epsom road on Derby Day", but they outpaced the 4th Cavalry Division.

The fragments of the Turkish Fourth Army were finally headed off and captured near Damascus, which was occupied on 1 October. On the previous day the garrison had been intercepted by the Australian Mounted Division as it was trying to escape through the Barada gorge (the Biblical "Abana"). Sweeping the head of the fugitive stream with machine-guns from the overhanging cliffs the Australian Light Horse rolled it back to Damascus, there to swell the "bag" of prisoners to 20,000.

The next move was a fitting conclusion to this chapter of history. The 5th Cavalry Division was despatched to advance on Aleppo, two hundred miles distant, in conjunction with an Arab force. Its armoured cars led the way and dispersed such slight opposition as was met, reaching the outskirts of Aleppo on 23 October. Two days later the leading cavalry brigade came up. A combined attack was arranged for next morning, but during the night the Arabs slipped into and captured the town on their own. The British force, too weak to press the retreat of the garrison, was awaiting reinforcements from Damascus when the capitulation of Turkey on 31 October wrote "finis" to the campaign. During a brief span of thirty-eight days the British had advanced 350 miles and captured 75,000 prisoners – at a cost of less than 5,000 casualties.

In a war singularly barren of surprise and mobility, those keynotes of the art of war, their value had been signally vindicated at the last, and in one theatre at least. Surprise and mobility had virtually won the victory without a battle. And it is worth noting that the Turks were still capable of holding up the infantry attack until the "strategic barrage" across their rear became known and produced its inevitable, and invariable, moral effect.

Because a preliminary condition of trench warfare existed the infantry and heavy artillery were necessary to break the lock. But, once the normal conditions of warfare were thus restored, the victory was achieved by the mobile elements – cavalry, aircraft, armoured cars and Arabs – which formed but a fraction of Allenby's total force. And it was achieved, not by physical force, but by the demoralizing application of mobility. A new light on Napoleon's dictum that the moral is to the physical as three to one.

4
Asian Incidents

Khalkhin-Gol (1939)

Alan Lothian

Lieutenant General M. Komatsubara's 23rd Infantry Division had been destroyed utterly – scarcely one man in a hundred escaping – on the empty borderlands of the Khalkhin-Gol river between Outer Mongolia and Manchuria. It was late in 1939, while half a world away Poland bled from the new German *Drang nach Osten* (Drive to the East) and the Western democracies indulged themselves in the "Phoney War" along the new Siegfried Line, a lonely and disgraced officer of Imperial Japan brought his life to a private end. Komatsubara might now find redemption in the agonizing rite of *seppuku*: only by ripping out his own entrails with his own short sword might he "prove his sincerity" to the Emperor and his ancestors. But the Khalkhin-Gol disaster was too great to be atoned for by a general's suicide. It was better that it had not happened at all, and the less attention drawn to it the better. Komatsubara, announced Tokyo inscrutably, had died of "an abdominal ailment".

The empty steppe country around the Khalkhin-Gol river had represented the farthest fringe of Japanese expansion. China, invaded in 1937, was still unsubdued but the Imperial grip on Manchuria, annexed in 1931, was firm. Here, in the wilderness of the Mongolian Republic, might Soviet strength be tested. Thirty-five years before, Japan's crushing defeat of the old Tsarist armies had astounded the world; now, perhaps, a border pinprick might develop into a deep thrust at the Trans-Siberian Railway, severing Russia's spinal column and allowing the rich Soviet Far East with its port of Vladivostok to fall into the lap of the Emperor.

For years, Japan's highest military councils had been divided into factions advocating either a "Strike North", at Russia, or "Strike South", at the western colonies. Emperor Hirohito had already decided upon "Strike South", which would in the next few years lead to Pearl Harbor, the fall of Singapore, and ultimately Hiroshima. But in the Army many officers still hankered after an attack on Russia, and the High Command of the Kwantung Army in Manchuria was no exception.

"Border incidents" spanning July–August 1938 at Lake Khasan, near Vladivostok, had shown real Soviet weakness after Stalin's terrifying purges of the Red Army. A Russian general, Lyushkov, had defected to the Kwantung Army with details of dispositions and stories of discontent. Acting first without Hirohito's knowledge, and eventually in direct disobedience, the Kwantung command launched an attack on the Russian forces which met with some success until it ran up against superior Soviet armor and airpower. Enraged, Hirohito refused to allow his air force to fly in support of his own disobedient army, and the situation was eventually settled by a diplomatic return to the status quo. But to save his officers from a catastrophic loss of face, the constant problem of the Japanese Imperial regime, he had to let them try again. After a formal ceasefire had been agreed at Lake Khasan, Hirohito approved a General Staff plan for an organized trial of strength farther west, in Mongolia, during the following summer.

The border area chosen by the Japanese staff was beside the Khalkhin-Gol river, for much of its length a frontier between Japanese-occupied Manchuria or Manchukuo to the east and the Outer Mongolian People's Republic, closely bound to Russia by a mutual-assistance pact in March 1936, to the west. At one point, however, the border bulges east of the river around the village and hill of Nomonhan. On this shallow salient, 46 miles wide, the Japanese planned to test the Soviet pledge to defend Mongolia. The country was steppe, blue-green in the summer with sturdy grass, and populated only by a few tribal herdsmen. East of the river it was more broken, with gullies, dunes, and even a few quicksands.

On 11 May 1939, a few hundred Inner Mongolian horsemen under Japanese control and accompanied by "advisers" from Komatsubara's 23rd Division, crossed the frontier and rode as far as Nomonhan itself before the villagers alerted their border guards, based in a log fort five miles away on the west bank of the river. The following day, the invaders were driven back across the border in an action that resembled an ancient tribal feud rather than a clash between two twentieth-century super powers: whooping Tskirik horsemen riding rings around their Japanese-led Bargut enemies.

But on 14 May the Inner Mongolians reappeared in strength, and this time they had 300 Japanese cavalry as stiffening. Within a few hours the Tsiriks had been driven back to their garrison positions, and that night the local Russian adviser, Major Bykov, was called in. When he reached the picturesque border fort next morning, he found that the twentieth century had arrived at last in the shape of a Japanese air raid which terrified his Mongolian charges and left the place a ruin. Taking no chances, Bykov at once called in 6th Mongolian Cavalry Division and the few Red Army detachments available. But as these troops massed on the Mongolian side of the Khalkhin-Gol, the Japanese on the east bank melted away. On the night of 22 May, Bykov made a cautious reconnaissance in force across the river. In the quiet rough pasture of Nomonhan the Japanese were waiting. Only after fierce hand-to-hand fighting was Bykov able to fall back to the Khalkhin-Gol.

The game of cat-and-mouse continued. On 25 May Bykov cautiously moved his full strength forward and over the next two days cleared the east bank and reoccupied the deserted village of Nomonhan. By now, about 10,000 men had been involved on the Mongolian side, mainly "constabulary" troops with a few specialist Russian companies. The border incident was rapidly escalating, and at dawn on 28 May it went a stage further. Five thousand Japanese regulars, with an accompanying tribal horde, fell on Bykov's troops before daybreak. Only the veteran Russian's canny dispositions enabled him to fall back once more to the river without complete destruction. But the panic button had already been pressed in Moscow and that same evening troops of the Soviet 149th Motorized Infantry Regiment began to arrive, to be sent straight into the fight from their trucks. All that night the battle continued, and the following morning a Soviet–Mongolian counter-attack pushed the Japanese back, once more, to the border with a loss of 400 men.

By now, Moscow was feeling real alarm. Despite accurate intelligence from his master spy Richard Sorge in Tokyo on long-term Japanese planning, Stalin understandably feared the possibility of a disastrous two-front war with Japan and Germany. Accordingly, no effort was to be spared in crushing this Japanese adventure before it threatened all of the Soviet Trans-Baikal. The first step was to release troops from the interior for the mission, and the second was to appoint a commander, someone new, outstanding, trusted, and with a fighting reputation to make. The man Stalin picked was Corps Commander Georgi Konstantinovich Zhukov.

Zhukov in 1939 was a tough, 43-year-old cavalryman turned "tankist" and Deputy Commander of the key Belorussian Military District. Squat, barrel-chested, heavy-browed (his name came from the Russian word *zhuk*, meaning "beetle") he had fought his way up from the ranks of the Red Army in the Civil War to distinction in every peacetime command he had held. He had been in China, perhaps in Spain; he had survived the bloodletting of the 1937 purges unscathed and was already well-known in the Red Army for his short-tempered, no-nonsense thoroughness. As "the general who never lost a battle" Zhukov was to direct forces and fighting of unsurpassed dimensions in the Russo-German war: 1941 would see him halt Hitler's offensive outside Moscow, in 1942 he would mastermind the Stalingrad campaign, and in 1945 he would meet the Western Allies in the wreckage of Berlin as the epitome of the ruthless, crushing might of the Soviet war machine. But in June 1939, as he flew out with a small staff to Mongolia, his future career and quite possibly his life depended on victory at Khal-khin-Gol. And victory alone would not be enough. Only the utter destruction of the Japanese would satisfy Stalin.

On 5 June Zhukov arrived at HQ, Soviet 57th Special Corps, the only major Red Army formation in the area. There he found little cheer. The command was hopelessly out of touch with the front, there was not so much as a kilometer of telegraph wire in the area, co-ordination of troops was poor and reconnaissance, though inadequate, clearly showed a Japanese build-up far greater than any mere border conflict would require. Furthermore the Japanese were making full use of air superiority, both for bombing and reconnaissance. Zhukov, with papers in his pocket appointing him local C-in-C if need be, at once took charge. The Corps commander was relieved and sent home and Zhukov threw all his characteristic energies into organizing a defense.

By early July, the Japanese had about 38,000 men, 135 tanks and 225 aircraft concentrated on the frontier east of the Khalkhin-Gol. Soviet and Mongolian forces together amounted to only 12,500 men, though Zhukov had 186 better tanks and 226 armored cars. He would need them. The Japanese plan involved sending a strong force wide around the Soviet left flank, across the river to seize the dominating high ground of Mount Bain-Tsagan. Then, as the main tank-led force attacked along the general front, this outflanking force would surround and destroy the east bank salient from its rear.

According to the Japanese schedule, offensive operations would be over by mid-July and the campaign wound up before the autumn rains. On 2 July, the first attacks pressed into the weak east bank positions and by the end of the day Japanese tanks and infantry were on the river in the Russian third line at some points. But Zhukov was too shrewd a commander to commit his reserves prematurely. Shortly before dawn on 3 July, the Soviet Colonel I. M. Afonin, Chief Adviser to the Mongolian Army, was inspecting Mongolian 6th Cavalry Division defenses on Bain-Tsagin when he stumbled upon Japanese troops who had made a surprise river-crossing by pontoon bridge. The Mongolians, without the training or equipment of their Red Army mentors, were driven off.

As the sun rose the following morning, Zhukov could not fail to appreciate the danger of the situation. The Japanese only had to roll on to the south for the hard-pressed Soviet forces on the east bank to be completely cut off. At once he ordered his armor – practically his only reserve – into action; 11th Tank Brigade was to attack from the north, 7th Mechanized Brigade from the south, and 24th Motorized Infantry Regiment from the NW through the retreating Mongolians. These forces together deployed over 300 fighting vehicles: the Japanese, on both sides of the river, had less than half that. Zhukov wrote in his 1969 memoirs: "It was impossible to delay a counterblow since the enemy, who saw the advance of our tanks, rapidly began to take defensive measures and started bombing our tank columns. The latter had no shelter whatsoever: for hundreds of kilometres around there was not even a bush in sight."

The speed of the triple-pronged Soviet thrust first startled, then demoralized the Japanese. From 0700 Zhukov's entire bomber force had been pounding them, and for the first time they felt the weight of the brilliantly organized Russian heavy artillery. By 0900 the advance detachments of Russian armor were arriving in the combat area and at 1045 the full attack went in. The Japanese had had little time to dig in thoroughly; their anti-tank training had always been a weak spot and now they paid the penalty. As the battle raged all that day, it was no longer the Russians who were in danger of encirclement.

An attempt at counter-attack on 4 July was broken up by Red Army aviation and artillery; worse, the single pontoon bridge they had laid across the Khalkhin-Gol was destroyed by Russian bombs. Hundreds of soldiers drowned trying to escape, and Komatsubara was lucky to get across with his HQ. Most of the 10,000-strong Bain-Tsagan assault force lay dead and wounded on the slopes of the little mountain, and when the heaviest fighting ended, on the night of 4–5 July, the Japanese had little cause to celebrate, having lost half the tanks available in Manchuria. And though Soviet 3 July tank losses had been over a hundred, the Red Army had successfully exploited glaring Japanese deficiencies in field and anti-tank (AT) artillery.

But the Kwantung Army was by no means willing to abandon its Mongolian campaign. During the remainder of July, it doubled the force committed, stripping divisions elsewhere of AT units to strengthen the Khalkhin-Gol positions. On 10 August, two full Japanese infantry divisions (7th and 23rd), a Manchukuoan brigade, three cavalry regiments, 182 tanks, 300 armored cars and three artillery regiments with over 450 aircraft were combined into the 75,000-strong Sixth Japanese Army under General Ogisu Rippo. A final general offensive along a 43-mile front was planned for 24 August, after an attack on 23 July got nowhere under Soviet bombardment.

On the Russian side of the hill final victory was far from certain. Powerful reinforcements had to be brought over poor communications from the Soviet heartland. But Stalin knew that Soviet international prestige was at stake and his new negotiations with Hitler, no respecter of weakness, had reached a critical juncture. Neither blood nor treasure would be spared. "For Stalin," wrote one former Red officer, "the losses were of no importance whatsoever."

Throughout July and August three infantry and two cavalry divisions with seven independent brigades, including five armored, as well as artillery and air force units, were assembled. This was in itself no mean feat. The Japanese, in the year before their attack, had built a railway to within a few miles of the Mongolian border. The nearest Russian railhead from which the new First Army Group could be supplied was 403 miles away. For Zhukov's coming offensive, 55,000 tons of supplies, including 18,000 tons of artillery ammunition, had to be carried along rudimentary Mongolian roads, the overworked trucks and drivers further tormented by late summer heat and the piercing dust storms of Central Asia. Such was the shortage of trucks that gun-towing tractors from the front had to be pressed into service as supply carriers.

So Zhukov laid his plans. The Japanese had attempted a great envelopment; very well, Zhukov would show them how it was done. He organized his new forces into three groups, North, South and Central, with his armored units, ready to move fast and deep, on the wings. He would be ready by 20 August, four days before the enemy. Until then he kept his plans, his troop movements, and thus his future surprise well masked by painstaking and ingenious deceptions. Fake radio signals ordering large quantities of engineering equipment misled the Japanese into thinking the Russians were digging in for the autumn. Sound effects gave the impression of heavy pile-driving work. The night movements of armored and motorized units were covered by air and artillery bombardments. All day a few tanks stripped of their silencers drove up and down until the Japanese got used to the noise. Zhukov even solemnly issued to his troops the official handbook *What the Soviet Soldier Must Know In the Defence*. By Sunday 20 August, unknown to the Japanese, quietly waiting in the jump-off positions were 35 infantry battalions, 20 cavalry squadrons, 498 tanks, 346 armored cars and 502 guns of all types.

The first the Japanese knew of the coming storm was at 0545 when 150 bombers, escorted by 100 fighters, launched a saturation raid on their forward defenses and artillery positions. Before the stunned Japanese had recovered, Zhukov's 250 heavy guns and mortars were playing on their close reserves and at 0845 his yelling infantry were surging forward behind the tanks. All along the front, the Russian waves broke through the Japanese front. The defenders were "morally and physically suppressed" by the three-hour Red Army artillery bombardment, delivered by twice the number of defending guns which anyhow lacked the wealth of Russian ammunition.

Not that the Japanese crumbled easily. At one point a divisional attack on Japanese fortifications was bloodily repulsed and the division, probably the raw 82nd Infantry sent from the Urals, pinned down under heavy fire. Its commander begged Zhukov for new orders; Zhukov told him to continue his attack. When the divisional commander doubted the possibility, Zhukov said coldly: "I hereby relieve you of command. Give me your Chief of Staff." The Chief of Staff agreed to continue the attack, but the attack failed to materialize. Zhukov picked up the telephone once more: "I hereby relieve you of your command. Wait for the arrival of a new commander." An officer from Zhukov's own staff was sent over, and with reorganized artillery and air support, the attack succeeded despite appalling losses.

Most successful was Zhukov's Southern group. Its powerful armored forces, which included a battalion of SP guns and a company of flamethrower tanks, swept clear around the left and by 21 August were solidly established behind the Japanese operating south of the Khalkhin-Gol's east–west tributary, the Khailastyn-Gol. Two days later the Northern group, assisted by Zhukov's reserve 212th Airborne Brigade (fighting on the ground) cut its way across the Palets Heights round to join them, and the enemy were surrounded. The fighting was bitter and by no means over. Japanese in dugouts had to be burned out by the flame-throwing tanks, and surrenders were rare. But the Red Army too had a determination which took a heavy toll of 600 dead in the savage hand-to-hand fighting in the dugouts and gullies of the Palets Heights as the pincers of encirclement closed.

After a Japanese relief attempt had been beaten off by 6th Tank Brigade on 26 August all hope for the trapped troops was gone. The growing Russian air superiority alone was enough to prevent the movement of fresh Japanese troops into the battle zone. In the first week the Soviet Air Force flew 474 sorties and dropped 190 tons of bombs, modest by later standards but some of the most intense air fighting since 1918. In the dogfights of the first day five Polikarpov I16 fighters shot down two Mitsubishi A5M fighters with 82 mm RS82 rockets – the first likely instance of air-to-air rockets being lethal against aircraft.

But neither Zhukov nor his government were content with a passive containment. With bloody impatience, he set about planning the liquidation of Japanese units trapped on various patches of high ground within the perimeter. For a week the savage business of mopping up went on. In this phase too, Zhukov demonstrated his tactical skill and the technical superiority of his army. Japanese troops on the Remizov Heights had relied on the muddy bottom of the shallow Khailastyn-Gol to protect their southern flank from attack. But by night Zhukov's engineers reinforced the river bed and the tanks with their terrifying flamethrowers drove straight across, as one of the three converging assaults on the last pocket of resistance.

By the morning of 31 August, any Japanese remaining on Mongolian territory were either dead or prisoners. Of 60,000 troops trapped in the cauldron, 50,000 were later listed as killed, wounded and missing. Casualties in the veteran 23rd Division ran as high as 99 per cent. The Russians admitted casualties of 10,000 in killed and wounded throughout the campaign, but it seems likely that this was a considerable underestimate. The outnumbered Japanese Army Air Force claimed to have downed 1,200 Soviet planes (the Russian figure for their "kills" was 660) in the four months of hostilities, but in the days before instant close-support on the battlefield this could not sway the ground-fighting.

Now, on the last day in August, Zhukov's dog-tired, grimy tank crews stared east from the border they had regained, waiting for the order to go on, while the frantic Kwantung Army HQ scraped the depots of Manchuria to find troops to stem what many feared would be a Red flood.

That order never came. In that autumn of 1939, Moscow and the world had other, more urgent problems. On the day Zhukov's pincers met behind the Japanese, Stalin and Hitler had published their Non-Aggression Pact: the Soviet dictator now believed, with unusual trustfulness, that he had bought the time he needed to prepare Russia against war. On 1 September the German *Panzers* rolled into Poland and within a few days the victorious Soviet armor was rattling back across the Trans-Siberian Railway to the new Soviet frontier in Eastern Poland – just in case.

Hirohito had to face up to more than the shock of military disaster. The Non-Aggression Pact surprised no one more than the Japanese, to whom it was a baffling breach of faith. The Prime Minister resigned in shame. Hirohito would have been more than just puzzled and disappointed had he heard Hitler ranting to his generals a few days before. "The Japanese Emperor . . . is weak, cowardly, and irresolute. . . . Let us think of ourselves as masters and consider these people at best as lacquered half-monkeys, who need to feel the knout." To Hitler, the Japanese defeat was no surprise. But thanks to Khalkhin-Gol, the confidence he had in his invasion of Russia was not shared by the Japanese.

Hirohito was on his own. Yet that was not entirely unsatisfactory. The "Strike North" army faction was discredited at last. The Kwantung Army begged to be allowed one more offensive to save its face, but this time the Emperor was firm. In Moscow once more the diplomats took over, and once more the status quo was resumed. A ceasefire was signed on 15

September. In April 1941, a Russo-Japanese Non-Aggression Pact was signed. The Soviet Far East remained safe from Japanese Imperial ambition, and throughout the coming war with Germany, American ships under Soviet flag would sail unhindered from United States arsenals to Vladivostok. Japan would strike south.

5
The Second World War

River Plate (1939)

David Thomas

Commodore Henry H. Harwood, OBE, RN, stabbed a finger on the chart aboard his flagship, the light cruiser HMS *Ajax*: "That's where she'll turn up next," he predicted confidently. But he was quite wrong in thinking his quarry was the German pocket-battleship *Admiral Scheer*, nevertheless the chart position was as accurate as a star sight. He further predicted – though with less skill and some luck – that the enemy ship would arrive astride the rich South American trade routes of the River Plate area on 12 December 1939. He was one day out.

The warship was, in fact, the *Admiral Graf Spee* and at the time she was 2,000 miles away celebrating the sinking of the ninth and last victim of her 12-week cruise as a commerce raider. *Admiral Graf Spee* was one of three brilliantly designed German warships: *Deutschland* (re-named *Lützow* in February 1940) was the first, launched in 1931, followed two years later by *Admiral Scheer*, then on 30 June 1934 the garlanded *Admiral Graf Spee* took to the waters of Wilhelmshaven Naval Dock. They were fine ships, and, curiously, they were the direct product of the 1919 Treaty of Versailles which forbade Germany to construct warships of more than 10,000 tons displacement.

German naval architects had evolved an entirely new type of vessel, nominally of 10,000 tons but in the event *Graf Spee*

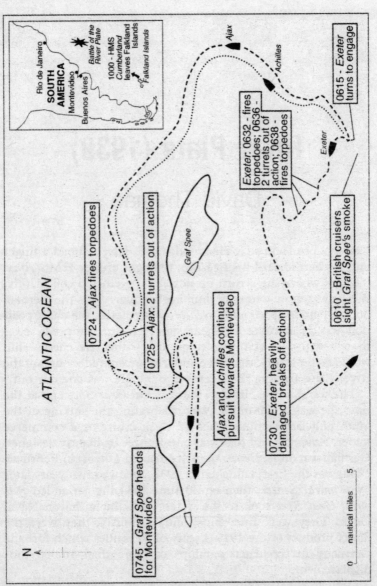

5.1 The Battle of the River Plate, 13 December 1939

displaced 12,100 tons. A design requirement was to mount guns superior to those of a British heavy cruiser and with protective armor thick enough to withstand such a cruiser's (8-in) shells. By employing welded construction and adopting diesel propulsion in place of conventional steam-turbines, by minimizing thick belt and armor protection, sufficient weight was saved to allow a radius of action of 12,500 miles at cruising speed before the need for refuelling. *Graf Spee*'s 54,000 hp engines gave her a trial speed of 27.7 knots.

The three new warships were armed with a main battery of six 11-in (280 mm) guns in two triple turrets and a secondary armament of eight 5.9-in (150 mm) guns. They could outgun every British cruiser. They could outrun every British battleship. Only three ships in the entire Royal Navy had the speed to catch them and the guns to sink them – the First World War vintage battle-cruisers *Renown*, *Repulse* and *Hood*.

Kapitän zur See (Senior Captain) Hans Langsdorff took command of *Admiral Graf Spee* at the age of 44 in 1938, climaxing a naval career of 26 years; the captain and the ship were well matched but when put to the test of battle it was the man who failed, not the ship. *Graf Spee* sailed from Wilhelmshaven on 21 August 1939, ten days before the outbreak of war, destination mid-Atlantic, and then three days later her sister ship, *Deutschland*, sailed for a similar waiting assignment in the North Atlantic. Each was accompanied by a supply ship, the notorious *Altmark*, later captured as a prison ship, being assigned to *Graf Spee*. The pocket-battleships' tasks had been clearly defined as "the disruption and destruction of enemy merchant shipping by all possible means." Action with enemy naval forces was to be avoided at all costs, except to further the primary objective.

Graf Spee entered the sunshine and heat of the South Atlantic and intercepted her first victim, the SS *Clement*, off Brazil on 30 September. But the 5,084-ton ocean-going tramp steamer reported the pocket-battleship as *Admiral Scheer*, a report which confused the eight Raider Hunting Forces formed jointly by the British Admiralty and the French Ministry of Marine. The second victim was the SS *Newton Beech*, one of three ships captured and sunk on the trade routes from the Cape of Good

Hope during 5–10 October. *Graf Spee* then rendezvoused with *Altmark* in mid-South Atlantic from whom she fuelled and to whom she transferred the crews of her victims.

A week later SS *Trevanion* was sunk on 22 October, then *Kapitan* Langsdorff rounded the Cape of Good Hope where the 706-ton tanker *Africa Shell* was sunk on 15 November. *Graf Spee* doubled back, refuelled from *Altmark* on 27 November NE of volcanic Tristan da Cunha island, then a few days later sank the 10,000-ton cargo liner *Doric Star*. Before the end, the liner got away the prescribed distress signal, "R–R–R", signifying Raider.

The day after the *Doric Star* sinking, SS *Tairoa* was sunk. On 7 December *Graf Spee* sank her last victim, the 3,895-ton cargo vessel *Streonshalh*. This sinking brought her total to nine British ships and 50,089 tons. Not a single life had been lost during these sinkings, a source of great pride to Langsdorff. Many of his prisoners subsequently testified to his courteous firmness, his fairness, distinguished bearing, chivalry and professionalism.

The responsibility for the long and anxious search for the elusive *Graf Spee* in the South Atlantic fell upon Forces G, H and K. Their success depended largely upon attacked merchantmen getting off their R–R–R signal and position. In fact, Langsdorff was better informed about British warship movements. He was aware, for example, that the cruisers *Ajax*, *Achilles*, *Exeter* and *Cumberland* were operating off the South American coast, that the two heavy cruisers *Sussex* and *Shropshire* were off Cape Town and that the battle cruiser *Renown* and aircraft carrier *Ark Royal* were off West Africa.

As Commodore Harwood had predicted, Langsdorff determined to quit the mid-ocean patrol and, as if destiny was directing him to destruction, he set course for the River Plate estuary, attracted by the prospect of rich prizes. Also heading for the estuary was Harwood's squadron, one of the British Raider-Hunting Forces engaged in the ever-changing dispositions, wider-ranging even than the later *Bismarck* pursuit from the wastes of the North Atlantic to the southernmost tip of Latin America.

Early in December 1939, 51-year-old Commodore Harwood, as Officer Commanding the South American Division of the American and West Indies Squadron, flew his broad pennant in the 6,985-ton 6-in gun cruiser *Ajax*, commanded by Captain Charles H. L. Woodhouse. His two heavy 8-in gun cruisers, the 8,390-ton *Exeter* (Captain Frederick S. Bell) and the 9,850-ton *Cumberland* were at Port Stanley in case of an enemy attack to revenge the Battle of the Falkland Islands where Count von Spee's squadron was destroyed on 8 December 1914. The 6-in gun cruiser *Achilles* (Captain Edward Parry), to 7,030 tons and partly manned by 327 New Zealanders, was patrolling off Rio de Janeiro. *Ajax* had recently sailed from Port Stanley for the River Plate.

Harwood calculated after the *Doric Star* sinking that the raider could reach Rio by 12 December and be off the River Plate by the following day. Accordingly, he ordered his cruisers to concentrate. *Exeter* was instructed to leave Port Stanley on the 9th and *Achilles* was instructed to head south from Rio to join the flagship on the 10th. *Cumberland* had to remain in the Falklands to complete an imperative self-refit.

By 0600 on 12 December the three cruisers were in company 150 miles off the River Plate. The Commodore had long considered the tactics his squadron should employ on encountering a pocket-battleship. Undaunted by the greatly superior gunpower of such an adversary, he made his intentions clear in a signal to his three captains, timed 1200, 12 December: "My policy with three cruisers in company versus one pocket-battleship: attack at once day or night."

At dawn on 13 December the sea was tropically calm with a light swell. As the light strengthened to promise another beautiful day the three grey British cruisers formed up in line ahead, *Ajax* leading *Achilles* and *Exeter*, 2,000 yards apart, zig-zagging about a mean course of 060° at 14 knots. At 0540 crews stood down from Dawn Action Stations. Visibility rapidly increased with tropical suddenness from a few hundred yards to 20 miles. Twenty minutes before, at 0520, the squadron was in position 34°34′ S, 47°17′ W, 250 nautical miles due east of Punta del Este.

Soon after 0600 Leading Signalman Swanston on *Ajax*'s bridge sighted smoke over the horizon bearing 320°. Harwood ordered *Exeter* to investigate. She swung out of line and at 0616 she signalled by lamp: "I think it is a pocket-battleship," and Capt. Bell ordered Flag N hoisted to the yard-arm – "Enemy in sight".

Graf Spee, heading 155° at 15 knots, logged an almost identical chart position. Langsdorff held the whip hand. He had sighted the British ships 20 minutes before *Ajax* saw the smudge of smoke. At 0552, fine on the starboard bow, there were first two, then four more thin masts. The stereoptic main range-finder measured a distance of 31,000 metres (33,902 yards = 19.26 miles). By 0600 *Graf Spee* was cleared for action and some of the masts had resolved themselves into the unmistakable superstructure of HMS *Exeter* accompanied by what appeared to be two destroyers.

Now, if ever, was the time for Langsdorff to turn about and refuse action. By maintaining course he committed a cardinal error. He went even further and decided to attack contrary to Naval Operations Command instructions. Langsdorff's senior navigator, *Korvettenkapitän* (Lieutenant Commander) J. Wattenberg, reminded him of the order to avoid even inferior enemy forces. "I suspect a convoy." Langsdorff explained. He ordered full speed to close the range. Phase 1 of the Battle of the River Plate had begun even before the British cruisers had sighted the enemy. At 0615 the pocket-battleship eased to port on to a course of 115° for a running action to starboard with a closing range. By now she had identified the "destroyers" as *Ajax* and *Achilles*. Her only safeguard now lay in crushing the opposition by destroying it or putting it to flight. At 0618 the two triple 11-in turrets opened fire with a thunderous crash.

When *Exeter* identified the pocket-battleship, Capt. Bell hauled off to the west while Harwood led *Ajax* round to close the range. *Achilles* conformed to the flagship's movements throughout the action enabling the two light cruisers to concentrate their gunfire with great effect. All three ships increased speed, hoisted battle ensigns and fire was opened: *Exeter*'s 8-in guns opened at 0620, *Achilles*' 6-in at 0621 and *Ajax*'s two minutes later. The range was then about 19,000 yards (10.8 miles). Langsdorff had made no effort to maintain his range advantage and he now found himself, as Harwood intended, confronted with two divisions and the problem of whether to divide his main armament to engage them both – or to leave one unengaged. Initially, *Graf Spee* engaged both but very soon shifted fire of all six 11-in guns to *Exeter*. Her accuracy was formidable and remained so throughout the day.

Exeter's 'A' and 'B' (bow) turrets opened fire at 0620 with "Y" (stern) turret following 2.5 minutes later. She had been steaming on boilers in Boiler Room B only and when the alarm sounded those in Boiler Room A were flashed up and connected. Full speed was ordered at 0620. With his third salvo, the gunnery officer, Lieutenant Commander Richard B. Jennings, straddled *Graf Spee* and prospects looked promising. But *Exeter* herself was under fire and *Graf Spee*'s third main salvo straddled the British ship. A minute or so later – at 0624 – *Exeter* was hit but the 670 lb shell smashed through the deck abaft "B" turret and passed through the ship's side to the sea without exploding.

A minute later *Graf Spee*'s eighth salvo struck an almost decisive blow: within seconds *Exeter* was transformed from an efficient fighting unit into an uncontrollable machine. "B" turret took a direct hit between the two gun barrels, putting it and eight of the crew out of action. Splinters swept the bridge killing or wounding nearly everyone there; the wheelhouse was smashed, vital communications cut. Captain Bell, wounded himself, was compelled to retire to the after-conning position where a human chain of command had to be set up.

While the 11-in salvoes were being directed at *Exeter*, Langsdorff employed his eight 5.9-in guns against the 16 6-in guns of the two light cruisers whose accuracy was such that the pocket-battleship shifted fire from *Exeter* to bring her 11-in guns to bear on *Ajax* and *Achilles*.

During this period – at about 0637 – while still under fire from *Graf Spee*'s secondary armament, *Ajax* managed to catapult into the air one of her two 124 m.p.h. Seafox floatplanes, piloted by Lieutenant Edgar D. G. Lewin; a fine evolution considering that "X" and "Y" turrets only a few feet away were firing at the time. Lewin and his observer, Lieutenant Richard E. N. Kearney, began their spotting reports at 0654. *Exeter*'s two Walrus seaplanes were damaged beyond repair early in the battle and had to be jettisoned. *Graf Spee*'s Arado 196 float-plane was unserviceable because of a cracked engine block and took no part in the battle.

Exeter's shooting astonished the *Graf Spee*'s officers, both for its accuracy and in particular for the rapidity of each following salvo. Her fifth salvo scored a direct hit but the shell passed through the upper part of the bridge without exploding and caused little damage. Another 8-in shell passed a metre above the armored deck, passing through the 5.5-in (140 mm) ar-mored belt and finally exploding amidships. The ease with which this shell penetrated the armor plate contrary to expecta-tion caused great anxiety aboard *Graf Spee*. Pocket-battleships were not, it seemed, inviolable to 8-in cruisers.

At 0632 the damaged *Exeter*, under severe pressure from the accurate German gunnery, fired her three starboard 21-in torpedo tubes. A few minutes later *Graf Spee* made a heavy alteration of course to port and steered NW under cover of smoke. This change of course prevented a "crossing the T" situation by *Ajax* and *Achilles*. From this moment on the battle became a pursuit with the light cruisers maintaining contact with *Graf Spee* while the heavily damaged *Exeter* limped along in company. As a parting shot – at 0638 – she fired her port torpedoes, but they too missed.

During this period *Exeter* took two more 11-in shell hits. "A" turret was damaged and put out of action and a second shell burst in the Chief Petty Officers' flat amidships starting a fierce fire. It was this shell which created the most damage: the 4-in magazine was flooded by burst water mains, all compass re-peaters were out of action and Captain Bell handled the cruiser using a whaler's compass. The ship's upperworks were pierced with splinters, dead and dying littered the decks. Lieutenant Commander Jennings, now stationed on the after searchlight platform kept the single remaining "Y" turret in action under local control. Captain Bell kept adjusting course to keep the turret bearing on the target. *Exeter* took another shell hit under the fo'c'sle, suffered flooding of several compartments and took a 7° list to starboard. Ablaze, she had taken heavy punishment, and was close to being destroyed.

At 0640, when one of *Graf Spee*'s 11-in turrets was being directed against the light cruisers, a shell near-missed *Achilles*, bursting on impact with the sea. Hundreds of splinters penetrated her thin bridge plating and the armor of the Director Control Tower, killing four ratings. Captain Parry and the Chief Yeoman on the bridge were slightly wounded and a splinter severed the halyard for the White Ensign: the battle continued to be fought under the New Zealand flag at the mainmast.

At 0656 Harwood hauled round to the north then west to maintain close range and to keep all guns bearing. He also pursued the tactic of "chasing salvoes" – sailing towards close splashes and away from distant ones to confuse the enemy spotting. *Graf Spee* also made frequent alterations of course to throw out the British gunfire and from 0700 she made much use of smoke. Despite these tactics she continued to be struck by 6-in shells but these 100 lb projectiles inflicted relatively little damage.

By 0724 Harwood had closed the range to 9,000 yards to deliver a torpedo attack. *Ajax* turned to starboard and fired a spread of four 2-in torpedoes. *Kapitanleutnant* (Lieutenant) Rasenack on *Graf Spee*'s bridge later reported, "They came right at us. To avoid them our captain again put them under the direct fire of our heavy guns. One of the torpedoes passed only a few metres from our side." Langsdorff told Captain Patrick G. G. Dove, one of the 62 British Merchant Navy prisoners aboard the pocket-battleship during the battle, "The *Ajax* and *Achilles* came at me like destroyers."

But this daring maneuver took an ugly turn for Harwood when *Ajax* received an 11-in shell hit on the after superstructure at 0725; the shell passed through several cabins, wrecking the machinery below "X" turret and burst in the Commodore's sleeping cabin. Damage was sustained by the "Y" turret barbette, jamming the turret. Thus one shell effectively put both "X" and "Y" turrets out of action, killing and wounding many of the guns' crews. By now *Exeter* was out of the fight, her speed reduced, falling astern of the action, fires raging with 61 officers and ratings killed. *Ajax*, the flagship, had been reduced to only half her main armament. Only *Achilles* remained practically undamaged.

Langsdorff's tactics – British and German naval experts are agreed on this point – are difficult to understand because he should have turned to the southward to finish off *Exeter* before then turning his attention upon the two light cruisers. Yet he deliberately allowed *Exeter* to escape, then pointlessly sought sanctuary in a neutral harbor. Harwood continued to harry *Graf Spee* and by 0728 the range was down to only 8,000 yards (4.54 miles). *Graf Spee* was now being subjected to a deluge of accurate 6-in gunfire and the pocket-battleship even brought into action some of her six 4.1-in (105 mm) AA guns against the cruisers. It was at this stage that the Seafox spotter plane reported torpedo tracks and Harwood altered course to comb them.

Graf Spee, now on a westerly course and clearly heading for the River Plate estuary, was still maintaining accurate fire, one of her last salvoes, at 0738, bringing down *Ajax*'s mainmast with all its radio aerials. Harwood decided to break off the day action, carry out the traditional cruiser duty of shadowing, and close in again after dark. Accordingly, at 0740, 82 minutes since *Graf Spee* had opened fire, the light cruisers turned away to the east under cover of smoke but continued to maintain contact. *Exeter* set course for the Falklands and *Cumberland*, pre-empting a signal from Harwood, sailed at 1000 from the Falklands for the River Plate to take her place.

Langsdorff, who had now recovered from two slight splinter wounds and a bout of unconsciousness from shell blast, made no attempt to pursue Harwood as the cruisers broke off action. He headed for Montevideo in Uruguay at 22 knots and took stock. Senior Surgeon Dr Kartzendorff reported one officer and 35 ratings killed and 61 others wounded. In no way did these casualties reduce the fighting capacity of a ship with a complement of 1,134, but the supply of 11-in shells was only 186–31 per gun.

Damage-control reports revealed a considerable mass of minor damage by 17 6-in shell hits from *Ajax* and *Achilles* and more serious damage by the three 8-in shell hits from *Exeter*. The wireless direction-finding apparatus was damaged and nearly all galleys out of operation. The equipment for purifying lubricating oil was damaged as were the forward ammunition hoists. The armor belt and armored deck had been penetrated: there were 15 holes on the starboard side plating and 12 to port including two in the bows, the largest measuring 6.5 ft wide. Minor items of damage to guns, torpedoes, searchlight and communications was superficial. More important from the point of view of fighting efficiency was slight damage to the main range-finder, foretop, torpedo-ranging device and fire-fighting equipment.

One hit was from a practice shell from *Achilles*, probably loaded in error; it hit aft, killed two ratings, passed through half a dozen cabins and came to rest in the berth of a Petty Officer still identifiable as a drill projectile! It was the large hole in the bows which was serious because *Graf Spee* would ship water in anything for a seaway if she made a dash for Germany. Langsdorff was also worried over the ammunition shortage. He decided, entirely alone and without consultation with his senior officers, to seek shore repair facilities. *Korvettenkapitän* Wattenberg later quoted his captain: 'Our damage cannot be repaired with the means available on board. We must run into port somewhere for repairs.'

Ajax and *Achilles* continued their shadowing for the rest of the day. *Achilles* followed close to the coast. *Ajax* remained to the south to cover a possible doubling back at dusk. At 1915 *Graf Spee* fired two accurate salvoes and at 2048 another three. Sporadic firing finished at 2142 and the pursuit and shadowing phase of the battle ended when *Graf Spee* anchored off Montevideo at 2350.

While the battle and pursuit were in progress the Royal Navy was making dispositions to engage *Graf Spee* whenever she should quit Montevideo. *Cumberland* joined her consorts at 2200 on 14 December after steaming 1,000 miles in 34 hours. The 8-in cruisers *Dorsetshire* and *Shropshire*, carrier *Ark Royal*, battle-cruiser *Renown* and modern cruiser *Neptune* were all directed to the River Plate but this overwhelming strength could not concentrate there before 19 December.

Meanwhile Langsdorff was the center of an unprecedented diplomatic storm in what he later called "the trap
of Montevideo". He had secured a 72-hour extension over
the 24-hour permissible stay of a warship in a neutral port.
British objections were more academic than real for they had
no wish to force *Graf Spee* to sea before the 19th and the
ploy of sailing a British merchant ship each day was
adopted. International Law provided that merchantmen
leaving port had to be given a head start of 24 hours over
an enemy warship.

On 16 December Langsdorff reported to Berlin – erro-
neously – his belief that the British concentration of warships
already lay in wait outside the harbor. *Gross-Admiral* Eric
Raeder, C-in-C of the German Navy, discussed this naval
dilemma with Hitler that same day and they agreed that an
attempted fighting breakout to Buenos Aires was the proper
course of action, failing which scuttling would be preferable
to internment.

At 1815 on 17 December Langsdorff conned *Graf Spee* out of
harbor with a reduced crew aboard: 800 of her company had
been transferred to the German tanker SS *Tacoma* which
followed close astern. Soon after the ship was outside the
three-mile limit she stopped and anchored. Tugs approached.
The ensign was lowered. Six fuses were lit. Boats – the last one
containing Langsdorff – headed away from *Graf Spee* across the
River Plate towards Buenos Aires in Argentina. Six violent
explosions shattered the quiet of evening. The pocket-battleship *Graf Spee* exploded like a volcano and settled in the
shallows of the estuary, deserving of a more dignified end than
a scuttling. She burned like a pyre in position 34°58′ 25″ S, 56°
18′ 01″ W, four miles 117 yards from land.

Langsdorff turned to his senior navigator: "Pilot, enter in the
log book *Graf Spee* put out of service 17 December 1939 at 2000
hours." *Ajax, Achilles* and *Cumberland* steamed by *en route* to
Montevideo with Harwood newly knighted and promoted to
Rear-Admiral on the bridge of his damaged flagship. Two days
later in a suicide letter Langsdorff wrote: "Now I can only
prove by my death that the fighting services of the Third *Reich*
are ready to die for the honor of the flag. I alone bear the

responsibility for scuttling the pocket-battleship *Graf Spee*. I am happy to pay with my life to prevent any possible reflection on the honor of the flag."

Lieutenant H. Dietrich found Langsdorff the following morning. He had shot himself in the right temple. He lay in full uniform stretched out on the flag of the German Imperial Navy.

Dunkirk (1940)

Peter Young

"The Miracle of Dunkirk" has passed into the mythology of the British nation. The successful evacuation of 338,226 men; the valour and efficiency of our seamen; the unsung but nevertheless real contribution of the Royal Air Force, and the calm days in the Channel were all factors which went to make up the feeling of a great Deliverance. And it is certain that without the members of the B.E.F. who came through that ordeal it must have been well-nigh impossible to build up an efficient army to carry on the long struggle that lay ahead. When tribute has been paid to the sailors and airmen who did so much to bring the B.E.F. home, it may be as well to remind oneself that the success of the evacuation was in some measure due to that Army itself.

From the strictly military point of view it could be said that "the Miracle of Dunkirk" was that the B.E.F. went to France without a single horse. We are inclined to forget that both French and German armies depended to an enormous extent, not only on horsed transport, but on horsed cavalry. The present writer has seen the leading scouts of the reconnaissance company of the 7th German Infantry Division dead in a ditch on the Roubaix–Courtrai road, the legs of their horses sticking up in the air. Another unforgettable sight was the first-line transport of a French artillery regiment, six-horsed covered wagons, being dive-bombed between Kemmel and Wytschaete. It was not a pretty scene. But the B.E.F., if it had only one brigade of tanks, at least had no horses. The British Army had thrown off the immobility of 1918 and on German intelligence maps its divisions were marked as motorized. In fact, the infantry were still expected to march from place to place, but in practice the B.E.F. enjoyed a mobility that its allies and its enemy lacked, and which was something completely new in the British Army. That this was so is the more wonderful when one remembers the devotion of successive generations of British soldiers to the cult of the horse. Kitchener's view (14 October 1902) that "hunting and polo are the best and quickest means of developing the qualities and muscles required in the field", was still widely held. Cavalry had had their successes in 1918 – on the Western Front as well as in Palestine – and Haig for one was convinced, as late as 1925, that the horse still had a great future in war, and certainly dash, vigour and the ability to move rapidly are not qualities which any army can afford to despise. Sad to relate, they were little in evidence in the French Army of 1940. Their doctrine, based on the idea of methodical positional warfare, was the heritage of the First World War, as was the Maginot Line. As Frederick the Great had taught his contemporaries, one cannot be strong everywhere, and a linear system, more than any other, demands adequate reserves, a *masse de manoeuvre*. This the French failed to provide. Nor, for reasons of expense, did they complete their famous Maginot Line which, though it stretched from Switzerland to Sedan, did not bar the roads along which the Schlieffen Plan had brought the German right wing in 1914.

The French were very much the senior partners on the Allied side, for the simple reason that they provided 103 of the 146 Allied divisions. It followed that the B.E.F. – as in 1914 – had little strategic control. It was a question of conforming to the French plan, while reserving a right to appeal to the British Government before executing any French order that might – in the opinion of General the Viscount Gort, its commander – imperil the British Field Force.

In 1914 the B.E.F. was plunged into action almost immediately after disembarkation. The B.E.F. of 1939 – rather to its surprise – had six months in which to prepare for the coming onslaught. In the opinion of the Official Historian, "the time was put to good use." In general this is true, but it would be very wrong to suppose that everything was perfect.

The B.E.F. spent most of its time slowly constructing field-works of a very dubious value in places where for the most part it was not going to fight. It did all too little training and – presumably because there were few rifle ranges – hardly any shooting. This was the more deplorable because the great majority of the men were reservists whose military skills badly needed a refresher course. The winter 1939–40 was an abominably cold one and this discouraged activity! On the credit side must be placed the tours which successive formations made to the Saar, where they spent upwards of three weeks each in the various lines of the Maginot system. This was practical training of the best sort, for it accustomed the men to shell-fire, mortar-fire and patrolling, and cost very few casualties.

The "Phoney War" period gave time for a most valuable build-up of forces. The original B.E.F. of four Regular divisions in two corps had grown by May 1940 to ten divisions in three corps and a G.H.Q. reserve. Of these divisions five were Regular and five T.A.

The officers of the B.E.F. right down to lieutenant-colonel had seen service in the First World War, and so had a fair number of the original company commanders, though by the time the fighting began most of these had been promoted. A few of these veterans were for various reasons no longer useful, but in general their experience and example was invaluable in seeing their younger colleagues through their somewhat brusque initiation into the Art of War.

The breakdown of the B.E.F. at the end of April 1940 was:

Main fighting force	237,319
T.A. divisions sent out for labour duties and further training	18,347
Reinforcements held at bases	17,665
Lines of communication duties	78,864
H.Q.s of various services and missions; hospitals and miscellaneous employment	23,545

Drafts *en route*	9,051
Not yet allocated	2,515
Advanced Air Striking Force	6,859
	394,165

Thus the B.E.F. was by this time a very substantial portion of the Allied Army in France. The very large numbers in the rearward areas – 150,000 – were there because it was intended to build up a much larger fighting force as rapidly as possible, and most of them were preparing the bases, depots and installations necessary. Many were skilled tradesmen who wore khaki, but had done little if any training.

When at length the Germans struck they achieved a fair measure of surprise, especially against the Dutch and Belgians, who, of course, had hoped to maintain their neutrality and whose armies were organized purely for defence. The B.E.F., however, was not surprised and carried out the complex move up into Belgium, which had been carefully prepared, with smooth efficiency.

> One unit of the 3rd Division had a frontier barrier closed against them because they could not show the faithful but ill-informed official in charge "a permit to enter Belgium". But they charged the barrier with a 15-cwt truck and the advance of the division proceeded.

From the German Air Force, which was occupied in bombing airfields or acting in place of artillery, in support of their ground forces, there was little interference. Lord Gort's decision to risk moving in daylight was justified, and the B.E.F. established itself beyond Brussels without loss.

The French had two plans for dealing with a possible German invasion of Belgium. One was to advance and hold the line of the River Dyle; the other, less enterprising, but perhaps sounder, was to occupy the line of the River Escaut (Scheldt). It was the former that was now put into operation, and by the afternoon of 14 May the B.E.F. was in contact with the Germans all along the front. On the 15th the British were disposed with three divisions (2nd, 1st and 3rd) in the line, each with two brigades forward and one in reserve; while two divisions, 48th and 4th, were in support. In reserve were 5th and 50th, while 42nd and 44th were back on the Escaut, giving depth to Gort's dispositions.

The German Sixth Army (von Bock) was anxious to break through between Louvain and Namur, so as to prevent the Allies establishing themselves in this position. They lost no time in attacking (14 May), but were beaten off at Wavre and Louvain by the 2nd and 3rd Divisions. But the line of the French First Army on the immediate right of the B.E.F. was broken on a 5,000-yard front and I Corps was compelled to fall back from Wavre to the River Lasne – towards the field of Waterloo.

Meanwhile the Dutch had surrendered and from the French front, where the Germans had forced the passage of the Meuse (14 May), bad tidings began to flow into G.H.Q. On the 16th General Billotte (First Group of Armies) ordered a withdrawal to the line of the Escaut. To the British this was simply incomprehensible. They had advanced sixty miles without any difficulty, had dug in with a skill and keenness unknown the previous autumn, and had beaten off the first German attacks in convincing style. To abandon a great city like Brussels without a struggle seemed unbelievable. But it is part of the strength of the British soldier that he is very far from expecting the Higher Command to behave in a reasonable or understandable way. Without being unduly depressed, the B.E.F. withdrew in reasonably good order to the Escaut.

By this time the campaign was beginning to take on the inconsequential, illogical, dreamlike quality which seems after twenty-seven years to have been its main characteristics. The German Air Force became ever more active; Belgian refugees thronged the roads, always turning up where they were least wanted; such forlorn Belgian soldiers as one saw seemed to have ridden out of the past into a nightmare present. To add to the confusion maps no longer covered the areas where the B.E.F. was operating. But the weather was good, the administration was working, the Escaut was deep and wide, and if a battalion held a front rather longer than Wellington's position at Waterloo, what of it?

It was on 19 May that General Lord Gort, as he puts it, "was unable to verify that the French had enough reserves at their disposal south of the gap to enable them to stage counter-attacks sufficiently strong to warrant the expectation that the gap would be closed". By this time it was clear to General Billotte that nine or, more probably, ten German armoured divisions were operating in the gap, their leading elements already at Peronne and Cambrai. Under these circumstances for the B.E.F. to fall back along its line of communications to the line of the Somme was hardly possible. The only alternative was to withdraw to the sea, which might well mean evacuation.

The B.E.F. was now holding thirty miles of the Escaut with seven divisions in the line, and the German Army Group B was bearing down upon it. The situation on this part of the front was positively comfortable by comparison with the state of affairs on the line of communications, where seven German armoured divisions, advancing through territory for which the French were responsible, were now approaching the *Canal du Nord*. Many of their men had seen action in Poland. To face this horde of tanks Gort had only two of the three T.A. divisions which had been sent out in the spring to complete their training and to carry out labour duties. They had no artillery and only skeleton signals and administrative units; fifteen guns and two howitzers were manned from the R.A. school of instruction, but some were without sights.

A glance at the map reveals the situation facing the scattered brigades of 12th and 23rd Divisions on 20 May. Nobody will be surprised to hear that by that night the Germans were in Albert, Doullens, Amiens, Abbeville and Montreuil, or that the two British divisions had practically ceased to exist. But the Germans had not had everything their own way. At Arras, where the 1st Welsh Guards from G.H.Q. Reserve was the backbone of the defence, Rommel's 7th Armoured Division had been held. Its commander had been surrounded for several hours at Vis-en-Artois by French heavy tanks. It seems his tanks were out of action and that his only escort was his signal staff. These unknown Frenchmen certainly had it in their power to do their Allies a good turn that day! The 8th German Armoured Division was not long delayed by 70th Brigade, which was reduced by that evening to fourteen officers and 219 other ranks.

The War Diary of the 6th German Armoured Division, which now met British troops for the first time, pays tribute to the 5th Buffs

> who fought tenaciously ... The Battle for Doullens claimed the whole attention of the troops. In spite of the use of numerous tanks it was only possible to break down their resistance after about two and a half hours.

At Albert the 7th Royal West Kents fought hard, but were overwhelmed, and in Amiens 7th Royal Sussex fought to a finish and were destroyed. The Territorials had defended themselves stubbornly and at a time when every hour was vital to the rest of the B.E.F. had slowed down the striking force of the Wehrmacht.

> Now that we have reached the coast at Abbeville the first stage of the offensive has been achieved ... The possibility of an encirclement of the Allied armies' northern group is beginning to take shape.

Thus did the War Diary of Army Group A (Colonel-General von Rundstedt) conclude its entry for 20 May. That this possibility was never to be fully realized was due to the moral courage of Lord Gort, who, against all his training and his principles, knew when to disobey the C.I.G.S. and the War Cabinet, and follow the course which he knew to be right. At a time when General Ironside wanted the B.E.F. to move south-west through Béthune and Arras to get back on to its line of communications, Gort determined to withdraw northwards. At the same time he was preparing the operation which is commonly known as the British counter-attack at Arras (21 May).

The object of this operation was to "support the garrison in Arras, thus cutting off the German communications (via Arras) from the east". General Franklyn was "to occupy the line of the Scarpe on the east of Arras" and establish touch "by patrols" with the French. On 20 May Lord Gort said nothing to Franklyn about a counter-attack, nor did he mention the possibility of French co-operation. Not until General Ironside visited General Billotte's H.Q. in Lens did the French agree to make an attack towards Cambrai next day with two divisions. The co-operation of General Prioux (French Cavalry Corps) was arranged for and was in the event forthcoming.

The British "counter-attack" was really a large-scale mopping-up operation. While the major part of 5th and 50th Divisions held Arras, the 1st Army Tank Brigade and two battalions formed into two mobile columns sallied forth under the command of General Martel.

So much that is misleading has been said of this operation that it may be as well to give the breakdown of the force.

Right Column
    7th Royal Tank Regiment
    8th Durham Light Infantry
    365th Battery, 92nd Field Regiment, R.A.
    260th Battery, 65th Anti-Tank Regiment, R.A.
    One platoon 151st Brigade Anti-Tank Company
    One scout platoon 4th Royal Northumberland Fusiliers
      (Motor-cycle)

Left Column
    4th Royal Tank Regiment
    6th Durham Light Infantry
    368th Battery, 92nd Field Regiment, R.A.
    206th Battery, 52nd Anti-Tank Regiment, R.A.
    One platoon, 151st Brigade Anti-Tank Company
    One company and one scout platoon, 4th Royal
      Northumberland Fusiliers (Motor-cycle)

At this period the British Army did not have tank transporters. The 1st Army Tank Brigade had covered long distances without much chance of maintenance and had only fifty-eight Mark I and sixteen Mark II tanks in running order.

The force was to cross the Arras-Doullens road at 2 p.m. The roads north of Arras were crowded with refugees, some of the troops were delayed, and in consequence they crossed the start line without much time to study orders and with none for reconnaissance.

Nevertheless the Right Column, co-operating with the French tanks on their right, cleared Duisans, Warlus and Berneville, taking a number of prisoners. Pushing on to the Doullens road, they met the leading units of the German 7th Infantry Regiment and some of the *S.S. Totenkopf* Division, and were held up by heavy fire from machine-guns and mortars. German aircraft dive-bombed the main body for twenty minutes. The advanced guard, after suffering heavily, fell back to Warlus, and German tanks – presumably from 7th Armoured Division – attacked that village and Duisans, and, though they took neither, got across the road between them.

The Left Column occupied Dainville, Achicourt, Agny and Beaurains, and a small advanced guard pushed on as far as Wancourt. They found that they had run into a far superior enemy force, but managed to hang on to Agny and Beaurains while the 4th Royal Tank Regiment fought off the enemy armour. The fight went on all the afternoon, and both columns suffered heavy casualties in tanks and men before they were ordered to withdraw that evening. Some of the French cavalry hung on near Warlus, where they were surrounded during the night, only a few tanks escaping. Six French tanks and two armoured troop-carriers managed to extricate the infantry from Warlus, bursting through the enemy on the Duisans road. Night fell and, with the help of the carrier platoon of the 9th Durham Light Infantry, the troops from Duisans were able to retire in the dark. Despite heavy bombing of Agny and Beaurains and a further tank attack, the 6th D.L.I. managed to extricate themselves.

Thus ended a day of confused fighting. The 7th German Armoured Division admitted a loss of nine medium and several light tanks, besides 205 killed and wounded and 173 missing. Since the British took nearly 400 prisoners it seems not unlikely that other formations suffered fairly heavy losses as well. Casualties in the outnumbered British force were also heavy, as might be expected, the commanding officers of both tank regiments being among the killed. The British had suffered because the infantry had not been trained to co-operate with tanks, and because the wireless communications of the latter did not work well, owing to lack of time for recharging batteries and for "netting". The German artillery was deployed well forward, and caused heavy casualties to the British infantry and the lighter vehicles, but our heavy tanks were proof against the smaller German guns.

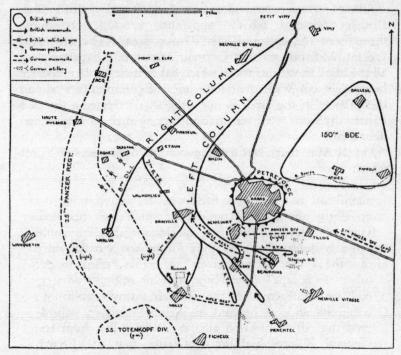

The Counter Stroke, 21 May 1940

To the British soldiers engaged, subjected as they were to heavy air attacks, it must have seemed a doubtful struggle. The most sanguine of them could not have guessed the extent of its strategic success.

The Germans took the British "counter-attack" very seriously. "To Rommel it seemed an attack by 'very strong enemy tank forces', a 'very heavy battle against hundreds of enemy tanks and following infantry'." He admitted that 1st/6th Infantry Regiment, whose defensive front was penetrated, "suffered particularly heavy casualties". Their guns were "destroyed by fire or overrun and their crews mostly annihilated". He complained that the German anti-tank guns "were not effective enough even at close range against the heavy British tanks". It was concentrated artillery fire, he asserted, that finally wrecked the British attack.

Other German commanders were also affected by this sudden British onslaught, which "apparently created nervousness throughout the entire (Kleist) Group area". The orders of the 1st, 2nd, 6th and 8th German Armoured Divisions were all modified in various ways, which led to their further advance being delayed. With their long lines of communications and their flanks in the air it is not altogether surprising that the Panzer divisions were sensitive to thrusts such as Martel had delivered.

On 21 May there was a succession of conferences at Ypres which were

> significant not for what little was decided but for the appalling absence of confidence which was revealed. General Weygand had no confidence that he could order withdrawal to the Yser for he has written since of "the orders I had given, or rather, tried to get others to accept". The King (and his military adviser) had no confidence in the Belgian Army's ability to withdraw and, as he told his Prime Minister, considered the Allied position almost, if not quite, hopeless. General Billotte had no confidence that the French First Army could do more than hold on, for they were "barely capable of defending themselves."

Billotte considered "the British Army alone still consitituted a powerful offensive element". Gort, for his part, was ready to join with the French in a further offensive, if some of his divisions now on the Escaut positions could be relieved by French or Belgian formations.

In the event the B.E.F. held the Escaut position until the night of the 22nd. Although the Germans gained several footholds on the west bank, it was only on the left that they won any considerable advantage. A party that crossed at Escanaffles near

Avelghem on the girders of the partially demolished bridge
were heavily shelled by 30th Field Regiment R.A., who
smashed the roof and scored nineteen direct hits on the front
wall of the factory from which the Germans were supporting
their advanced guard, persuading the Germans to flee into the
field of fire of the 1st K.O.S.B., who took proper advantage of
the target offered. A platoon of the 2nd Bedfordshire and
Hertfordshire Regiment then advanced across a thousand yards
of bare water meadows and dislodged the German bridgehead,
incredibly enough, without loss to themselves. Such is the value
of good artillery support coupled with a sight of the bayonet.
This was on the 21st. On that day the Germans made some
initial progress near Tournai, but both 42nd and 1st Divisions
counter-attacked successfully before nightfall, though the 3rd
Grenadiers were reduced to a strength of two companies.

On the 22nd the Germans were most active on the British left.
The 44th Division had much confused fighting and fairly heavy
losses before they were able to disengage. The 1st/6th Queens
had 400 casualties in two days, and owing partly to the roads
being choked with refugees, and partly to conflicting orders,
thirty-four field guns were lost or destroyed.

Still the line held and once more the British soldiery found
themselves withdrawing much against their will. A platoon
commander of the 2nd Lancashire Fusiliers, finding that his
men looked somewhat unhappy in the cold light of early
morning, had encouraged them with the cheering thought that
it had been "worse than this at Gallipoli". This piece of
regimental folk memory – six V.C.s before breakfast – struck
a chord and when it was time to go back he found the fusiliers
most reluctant.

The line had held, and the long night tramp back to the
Maulde-Halluin line went well enough. Carrier platoons
brought up the rear, picking up such stragglers as fell by the
wayside. The Germans, perhaps almost as tired as their opponents, were slow to follow up and it was late on the afternoon of
the 23rd before the first reconnaissance elements began tapping
at the British outpost line. It is easy to forget that they, too, had
had casualties and, though sustained by success, were beginning
to be wary. Army Group B's situation report for 22 May

credited the B.E.F. with "offering stubborn resistance, supported by strong artillery".

The main body of the British was now back on the French frontier, upon whose fortifications they had spent so many hours the previous winter. After two major withdrawals it was appreciated that everything was not going quite according to plan. Even so the news that the Germans were in Arras, which was evacuated after a splendid resistance on the night of the 23rd, was received with some incredulity. Rations and petrol were still to be had, and the soldiers were for the most part unaware that the enemy had planted himself firmly astride the British lines of communications. An attitude of suspicious alertness was well-developed in the B.E.F., as many a Belgian refugee could testify. Aged peasants with washing hanging in the garden caused the gravest suspicion.

There was something of a lull on 24 May, though the 8th Brigade of Major-General B. L. Montgomery's 3rd Division indulged in a sortie of 1,000 yards towards Wattrelos, which cost it five carriers and 117 casualties. One German unit was identified, but as the Official Historian comments: "It is not clear that any good purpose was served by this somewhat expensive sortie."

But if Bock left the B.E.F. alone his mobile troops could be seen moving across the 4th Division's front toward the Belgian position on the Lys. An attack by four divisions drove our allies back to the line Menin-Moorseele-Winkel St. Eloi.

Meanwhile 2nd, 44th and 48th Divisions, freed from the shortened eastern front, were moving to face the German armour on the Canal Line between La Bassée and the River Yser near Wormhoudt. Thus far improvised forces, such as Macforce, which with great foresight Gort had brought into being as early as the 17th, had held a far from continuous line. The good work done by the units composing these forces and by those sent from England to garrison Boulogne and Calais, was about to pay a great dividend.

The hardest thing in war is to imagine one's enemies' difficulties, and to prevent one's own looming too large. Von Rundstedt, though a first-class soldier, was not unnaturally influenced by his past experience in the more formal campaigning of the First World War. His armoured divisions had performed wonders and had cut the Allied armies in half. It is not too much to say that their Northern Armies now lay within his grasp. He did not quite see it.

The lull on the 24th is partly accounted for by a directive which von Rundstedt issued to the Fourth Army about 6 p.m. on the previous evening. In consequence it was ordered that

> . . . in the main Hoth Group will halt tomorrow; Kleist Group will also halt, thereby clarifying the situation and closing up.

The factors and events which influenced von Rundstedt in his appreciation of the situation were:

(*a*) The possibility of a concerted Allied attack from the north and from across the Somme.
(*b*) The importance of closing up the German mobile formations.
(*c*) British and French attacks about Arras and Cambrai.
(*d*) The need to consolidate his northern front.
(*e*) The failure of XIX Corps to take Boulogne and Calais.
(*f*) The fact that the Somme flank was not yet secure.

When Hitler visited von Rundstedt about 11.30 on the 24th

> He agreed entirely with the view that east of Arras an attack had to be made with *infantry*, while the *mobile forces* could be halted on the line reached – Lens-Béthune-Aire-St. Omer-Gravelines – in order to intercept the enemy under pressure from Army Group B. He emphasized this view by *insisting* that it was in any case necessary to conserve the armoured forces for future operations and that any further compression of the ring encircling the enemy could only have the highly undesirable result of restricting the activities of the *Luftwaffe*.

Thus spake the one-time corporal. When he had departed the Colonel-General, who was not altogether lacking in guile, issued a directive saying:

> By the Führer's orders . . . the general line Lens-Béthune-Aire-St. Omer-Gravelines [Canal Line] will *not* be passed.

It cannot be doubted that this order, which considerably puzzled the thrusters among the German divisional commanders, enshrined one of the most important single decisions of the whole war, for while the Panzers were harmlessly getting on with their maintenance Gort was forming a proper western front to the Allied enclave. Indeed, it was upon this day that G.H.Q. was able to decree the abolition of the improvised forces – Frankforce, Petreforce, Polforce and Macforce – which had so far borne the heat of the day. Even so the B.E.F. and the French First Army were still in an extremely unenviable position, and one is surprised that this was not evident to von Rundstedt, if not Hitler. They were now hemmed in, as the German situation maps must have revealed to a long narrow triangle of territory running inland for seventy miles from the coast. At its widest this enclave was twenty-five miles wide; at its narrowest but thirteen. This area was crowded with troops, most of whom depended on horse-drawn transport for their maintenance and upon their feet for movement. The roads were crowded with frightened, hungry refugees, Belgian and French, who, unable to get away towards the Somme, were wandering round in circles.

It was fortunate for the Allies that von Rundstedt was bent on husbanding his armour, six divisions of which spent the 25th quietly watching the Canal Line, while two (2nd and 10th) were occupied at Boulogne and Calais respectively. The 4th Army (von Kluge), which was part of his Army Group A, found itself held up by tenacious French resistance, though it followed up the withdrawal from Arras. As early as the 23rd the Kleist Group had reported more than fifty per cent casualties to their tanks.

Next day the War Diary of XXXIX Corps (Hoth's Group) noted:

Casualties for each armoured division, approximately 50 officers and 1,500 N.C.O.s and men, killed or wounded; armour, approximately 30 per cent. Owing to frequent encounters with enemy tanks, weapon losses are heavy – particularly machine guns in the infantry regiments. [This is the corps to which Rommel's 7th Armoured Division belonged.]

It is clear that the Germans had not had things entirely their own way.

The 25th was a quiet day on both British fronts, but the Belgians were under increasing pressure. The 12th Lancers (an armoured car regiment) were ordered to watch the left flank of II Corps north of the Lys, and to make contact with the Belgians in the Halluin-Ypres area. The situation was serious and the Belgians appealed for British air cover. But fighters working from England could not keep constant air cover over the Lille-Ypres area, and the Stukas were having things pretty much their own way.

Early in the day a patrol from the 3rd Division made an invaluable capture when it shot up a German staff car. Its passenger was Colonel (later Lieutenant-General) Kinzel, liaison officer between the Commander-in-Chief, Colonel-General von Brauchitsch, and Army Group B. He managed to escape, but he lost two documents of priceless value. One was the German "Order of Battle and Commands" as at 1 May 1940, of which only four copies had been issued to be taken forward. Although a few pages were missing, it gave the German organization down to divisions, including the names of commanders and their chiefs of staff. This windfall "gave the War Office for the first time an authoritative picture of the German Army, a grasp of its composition which was never subsequently lost".

The second document was of more immediate value, for it was the German Sixth Army's operation order for the attack begun that very day.

It revealed that their IX Corps was attacking towards Ypres and VI Corps towards Wytschaete.

At the time Gort "had no reserves beyond a single cavalry

regiment, and the two divisions (5th and 50th) already ear-marked for the attack southwards . . ." He told his Chief of Staff that "he had a 'hunch' that calamity threatened in the north-east and only instant action could avert it". About 6 p.m. he ordered the 5th and 50th Divisions to move at once to the gap that was opening between the British and Belgian armies. This done he informed the Headquarters of the French First Group of Armies of his decision.

Beyond question this timely action saved the B.E.F. The two divisions just managed to reach the gap between Menin and Ypres in time to prevent von Bock achieving the breakthrough which would have cut off the B.E.F. from Dunkirk and brought about its destruction.

While von Bock was closing in from the east, von Rundstedt, as we have seen, was permitting himself to be delayed by a variety of factors. Not least among these was the defence of the Channel Ports, Boulogne and Calais. Gort had no troops to spare to garrison them, but the War Office contrived to produce two brigades for that purpose.

THE DEFENCE OF BOULOGNE

Boulogne is overlooked by high ground and in order to defend it properly the defenders must occupy the surrounding hills, and especially the Mont Lambert feature. This means taking up a front of six miles. When the German armour broke through to Abbeville (20 May) there were a number of troops in the town, but their combat value did not amount to much, for they were either young French and Belgian recruits or men of the British Auxiliary Military Pioneer Corps, who were neither trained nor equipped as infantry. There were in addition groups of men, mostly French, who had fallen back before the German advance, besides details returning from leave or hospital. Add crowds of refugees, and it will be seen that the place was full of "useless mouths". It was Gort's policy to evacuate all personnel in the Channel Ports who were not of military value.

In this emergency the War Office moved with admirable dispatch. On 21 May the 20th Guards Brigade (Brigadier W. A. F. L. Fox-Pitt), which was training at Camberley, was warned "to proceed immediately to Dover for service overseas". It landed at Boulogne within twenty-four hours. Unfortunately it was short of a battalion, being composed of:

2nd Irish Guards
2nd Welsh Guards
Brigade Anti-Tank Company
275th Battery (less one troop) of 68th Anti-Tank Regiment.

To these must be added some fifty men of 7th Royal West Kent, who had survived the destruction of their battalion at Albert, and about 100 of 262 Field Company R.E., both of which bodies were already in the town.

The French 21st Infantry Division was supposed to be coming to hold a line between Samer and Desvres, ten miles south of Boulogne, and General Lanquetot, who had set up his H.Q. in the Citadel, was attempting to organize the defence of the town with the French troops available.

Fortunately it was not until about midday on the 22nd that Kleist Group ordered General Guderian (XIX Corps) to resume his advance. His men had some trouble in overcoming the personnel of a French divisional instruction centre in Samer. In the afternoon they made contact with the Irish Guards on the south-western sector of the defences and were beaten off with the loss of a tank. The Welsh Guards on the north-east of the town beat off two attacks that evening. Meanwhile some of the French 21st Division held up the German 1st Armoured Division until about midday on the 23rd. Unfortunately the rest of the Division was attacked by German tanks while entrained, and dispersed. The R.A.F. was active in its efforts to hamper the enemy advance and shot down twenty-four planes for a loss of four.

At dawn on the 23rd the Germans renewed their attacks, taking Fort de la Crèche from the French and closing in from all sides. By midday the British battalions had been compelled to fall back to the outskirts of the town, and the harbour was under close-range German fire.

Allied destroyers, besides evacuating non-combatants and

wounded, were able to give valuable fire support against German gun sites and machine-gun nests, though not without loss to themselves. The French destroyer *L'Orange* was sunk, while the British destroyers *Keith* and *Vimy* both lost their commanders.

The stout resistance had impressed the Germans, and the War Diary of Guderian's Corps recorded:

> 1445: At about this time Corps Headquarters has the impression that in and around Boulogne the enemy is fighting tenaciously for every inch of ground in order to prevent the important harbour falling into German hands. *Luftwaffe* attacks on warships and transports lying off Boulogne are inadequate: it is not clear whether the latter are engaged in embarkation or disembarkation. 2nd Armoured Division's attack therefore only progresses slowly.

The defenders had succeeded to some extent in confusing the enemy, and won themselves some respite, for there was a lull during the afternoon.

About 4.45 p.m. there was an attack by forty or fifty German planes, which interrupted evacuation for a time, though the R.A.F. intervened and shot down eight enemy aircraft for a loss of three.

At about 6.30 p.m. the 20th Guards Brigade received orders from the War Office to withdraw at once. It was not possible for Brigadier Fox-Pitt to tell General Lanquetot of this order, since the latter was cut off in the Citadel and the Germans were already in the lower town. This was nevertheless unfortunate, for, after all, the French general had himself been charged with the defence of the town, and the two battalions of the 20th Guards Brigade were the backbone of the defence. By this time the whole harbour was under fire at close range, and the British destroyers found themselves firing over open sights at German tanks. Even so they managed to take off some 6,700 men. The *Vimiera* made her second trip at about 1.40 a.m. on 24 May

. . . in an eerie silence. She remained at her berth for over
an hour and took on board 1,400 men. In this dangerously
overloaded state she reached England in safety.

Whitshed, Vimiera, Wild Swan, Venomous, Venetia, Windsor:
these were the ships that achieved the impossible at Boulogne.

Unhappily the *Wessex* had been diverted to Calais and some
300 of the Welsh Guards were left behind. Major (later Brigadier) J. C. Windsor-Lewis, with the remains of his company,
some French infantry and other details hung on to the seaward
end of the mole for another thirty-six hours, despite a heavy fire
from artillery, tanks and mortars, but were finally overwhelmed.

General Lanquetot, despite the withdrawal of the British
brigade, continued to defend the Citadel until the 25th.

It was fortunate for the defenders of Boulogne that the
possibility that the Arras counter-attack might be renewed
had delayed Rundstedt for five hours. Had the 2nd German
Armoured Division appeared before the 20th Guards Brigade
could get themselves organized, the further delay imposed by
the latter formation could scarcely have been so prolonged and
effective.

THE DEFENCE OF CALAIS

Calais was fortified by Vauban, and though overlooked by hills
to the south-west, was still a fairly strong place.

It was not until 22 May when the Germans were already
closing in on Boulogne that the 1st Queen Victoria's Rifles
(T.A.) began to arrive from England. They had been sent
abroad in a hurry and their equipment was incomplete. They
were without transport or 3-inch mortars. They were followed
by the 3rd Royal Tank Regiment with twenty-one light tanks
and twenty-seven cruisers. The 30th Infantry Brigade (Brigadier C. N. Nicholson) sailed from Dover early on the 23rd, with
the object of relieving Boulogne. When the convoy reached
Calais that afternoon the Brigadier found that the 3rd Royal
Tank Regiment had already suffered severe casualties in an
attempt to push south-eastwards to St Omer and Hazebrouck.
The enemy was already closing in on Calais and Nicholson

realized that his first task must be to organize the defence of the town itself – and that without delay. But no sooner had he deployed his men to hold the outer ramparts than he was given the most formal orders to convey 350,000 rations for the B.E.F. to Dunkirk. This proved impossible, despite hard fighting in which the 3rd R.T.R. were reduced to twelve light and twenty-one cruiser tanks.

At dawn on the 24th, German artillery and mortars began a bombardment heralding an attack by tanks and infantry on the western and south-western sectors of the defences. The British outposts withdrew to the ramparts. Only at one point did the Germans penetrate the main defences and here a counter-attack by the King's Royal Rifle Corps supported by tanks cleared up the position.

The Germans mounted further attacks during the afternoon. The French surrendered Fort Nieulay, after heavy shelling, and abandoned Fort Lapin. On the British sector the Germans broke into the town and established themselves in some houses from which they were able to enfilade the ramparts.

Despite these successes, the German 10th Armoured Division War Diary's entry at 4 p.m. reported: "Enemy resistance from scarcely perceptible positions was so strong that it was only possible to achieve quite slight local success", and about 7 p.m. Corps was informed that a third of the German equipment, vehicles and personnel and "a good half of the tanks" were casualties; the troops were "tired out".

After dark Brigadier Nicholson withdrew into the old town "and the quadrangle to the east which is enclosed by the outer ramparts and the Marck and Calais canals". He now received a message telling him that for the sake of Allied solidarity there was to be no evacuation. The Brigade was to fight to the end.

At dawn on the 25th the Germans began to bombard the old town, houses caught fire, rubble blocked the streets, the water mains burst, clouds of dust and smoke filled the air. The last two guns of the 229th Anti-Tank Battery were destroyed; only three British tanks remained in action. The German bombardment grew ever more intense and there was no British artillery to reply, although the Royal Navy gave some gunfire support.

Gradually the defenders were driven back, but, despite heavy losses, the French still held the Citadel, where Brigadier Nicholson had set up a joint H.Q. with their commander. Here in the afternoon a German officer appeared under a flag of truce, demanding surrender. The Brigadier replied: "The answer is no, as it is the British Army's duty to fight as well as it is the Germans".

The Germans returned to the attack, but finding that resistance was not yet crushed broke off, as their Infantry Brigade Commander considered there was not time to finish the operation before nightfall. The ordeal was to last another twenty-four hours.

The fighting flared up again early on the 26th. More guns had been brought up from Boulogne and the Citadel and the western suburbs of Les Baraques between the Citadel and Fort Lapin were heavily bombarded. XIX Corps War Diary recorded: "No visible result is achieved; the fighting continues and the English defend themselves tenaciously."

With the support of heavy dive-bombing, German tanks and infantry, in bitter fighting, gradually drove the stubborn riflemen back into the northern part of the old town, cutting them off from the Citadel.

Though broken up into isolated parties in houses and bastions, the defenders fought on. Late in the afternoon, after repeated attacks, the Germans broke into the Citadel and took the Allied H.Q. Groups still held out in the old town, but by nightfall all was over. The 30th Brigade had fought to the end. Their resolute stand and that of the 20th Guards Brigade at Boulogne gained time for the B.E.F. to reach Dunkirk. Exhorted by Mr Eden, the Secretary of State for War, himself an old rifleman, to "perform an exploit worthy of the British name", they had sacrificed themselves without complaint to symbolize "our continued co-operation with France". In their prison camps the survivors could look back on their fight with satisfaction. One infantryman ended his record of the siege with the comment: "It would not be easy to find any who regret the days of Calais."

*   *   *

With the mass of German armour on the move again the defence of the Channel Ports alone was not enough to occupy von Rundstedt and keep him off the back of the divisions facing von Bock. Further sacrifices were demanded.

The German plan was for a converging attack by both their Army Groups; their aim was to break through to the Poperinghe-Kemmel line and cut off a major part of the Allied armies from the sea. At the same time the Germans intended to make Dunkirk and Ostend unusable and so put an end to all evacuation.

The attack went in at 8 a.m. on 27 May. In heavy fighting Kleist's Group drove back the French 68th Division, which withdrew from Gravelines that night. The Germans were now within four miles of Dunkirk and could shell the port.

The 48th Division held a front of more than twenty miles from Bergues to Hazebrouck. The Germans attacked with four divisions, but though they penetrated the line the key positions, Ledringham, Cassel and Hazebrouck, were held.

The 44th Division held a zigzag line on both sides of the Forêt de Nieppe. The most dangerous attack came from the north, where German armour (6th and 8th Divisions) had pushed through between Cassel and Hazebrouck. The enemy was held up at Eecke, at Caestre – where 5th Royal Sussex (T.A.) knocked out six tanks and took their crews – and at Strazeele. The Germans withdrew in the afternoon with little to show for their losses.

It was upon the 2nd Division that the brunt of the fighting fell. The 27th of May was to be their day of crisis and of sacrifice. If they failed, it might not be possible that night for the main French and British forces to withdraw from the Roubaix-Lille area to north of the River Lys. The Division held a fifteen-mile front from the Lys Canal at St Venant to La Bassée. Lord Gort's dispatch describing this day's work says:

> Second Division, now reduced to less than the strength of an infantry brigade, had fought hard and had sustained a strong enemy tank attack.

One does not expect epic prose in a dispatch, but this bald statement scarcely does justice to the stand made by the 2nd Division. Attacked by three armoured divisions (3rd, 4th and 7th) and one motorized (*S.S. Totenkopf*) they had succeeded in delaying the junction of Army Groups A and B.

A German account from XXXXI Corps (Kleist's Group) describes the fighting:

> At every position heavy fighting had developed – especially at every village and indeed in every house. In consequence the Corps [XXXXI] has not been able to make any notable headway to the east or north-east. Casualties in personnel and equipment are grievous. The enemy are fighting tenaciously, and, to the last man, remain at their posts: if they are shelled out of one position, they shortly reappear in another to carry on the fight. The enemy appear to have very good observation for their artillery fire . . .

It is invidious to single out any particular unit when all, including a pioneer battalion (6th King's Own), fought with great determination. But mention must be made of 1st Queen's Own Cameron Highlanders, whose reserve company, forty-five strong, made an early-morning counter-attack to drive back Germans who had got across the La Bassée Canal. They had artillery support and six French tanks, and they succeeded in ejecting the enemy, but not before they had lost thirty-nine killed and wounded. Later in the day the Battalion was practically surrounded, but they and the 5th Brigade Anti-Tank Company knocked out twenty-one enemy tanks. Eventually ten tanks of the 4th/7th R.T.R. came to the rescue, and though they lost seven tanks extricated the remnant of the Camerons and 7th Worcestershire, now numbering no more than a hundred officers and men.

On this day (27 May) a hundred men of 2nd Royal Norfolk, many of them wounded, were captured, after a stubborn resistance, by men of the *S.S. Totenkopf* Division. They were disarmed and then mowed down by two machine-guns at thirty yards' range. Only two, both badly wounded, managed to escape, hidden by the bodies of their comrades. Captured by another unit, they were well looked after and later repatriated. Although this crime was reported, the German Army authorities did not feel able to do anything about it. The officer who ordered the massacre was himself taken prisoner later in the war, and was sentenced to death by a British court-martial.

Meanwhile on its eastern front the B.E.F. was engaged in a desperate three-day battle (26–28 May) with von Bock's Army Group B. Upon its successful outcome depended the ability of the main body of the B.E.F. to withdraw into the Dunkirk bridgehead, which was already being put into a state of defence.

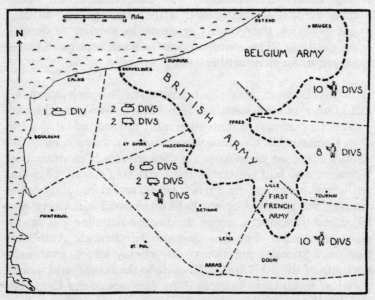

Distribution of German Divisions, 27 May 1940

The situation was aggravated by the imminent collapse of the Belgian Army, which, considering its late mobilization and the early destruction of its air force, had done well to survive so long. The danger was not so much that von Bock's infantry would break the British line, but that they would simply walk through where there was nobody to oppose them. The improvizations which were needed in order to patch up some sort of front were enough to drive a tidy-minded staff officer out of his mind. If the British Army weathered this storm it was due above all to one man: Lieutenant-General A. F. Brooke, the commander of II Corps. He was everywhere and he always seemed able to conjure up some reserve, however small, when there was most need.

At the same time Major-General H. E. Franklyn, who had already distinguished himself at Arras, must have much of the credit, for everything depended on his 5th Division holding out until Brooke's right could be extricated from the Halluin-Roubaix salient.

There was a crisis on the 27th. The 5th Division, spread out in a thin line on the front between Ypres and Comines, was under pressure from three German infantry divisions (18th, 311th and 61st). If the dike should break now, the enemy would come flooding through towards Poperinghe and Kemmel and all would be lost.

Brooke visited 5th Division H.Q. at 10 a.m. on 27 May and after he had studied the situation in silence – according to Franklyn "it was very bad" – the following exchange took place:

> Brooke: *What are you going to do about it?*
> Franklyn: *I'm not worried about my left, but I am uneasy about the 143rd Brigade on my right – they have given and are being pushed back.*

Brooke left without a word. He had already arranged to place 10th Infantry Brigade (4th Division) under Franklyn. He now set out to collect further reinforcements.

> As I had heard that the 1st Division had already started withdrawing three battalions from the line and that these battalions were somewhere west of Ploegsteert Wood, I decided to endeavour to secure their assistance. After some hunting I found I Corps H.Q. in one of the old Lille forts, and I obtained Michael Barker's agree-

ment. I therefore proceeded again to Wambrechies to
see Alexander to request him to issue orders to these
battalions to come under orders of 5th Division and to
move forward at once. Alexander, as I had expected, co-
operated at once, and these three battalions played a
great part in restoring the situation on the right of the
5th Division front.

From 1st Division I motored back again to G.H.Q.
and this time secured seven infantry tanks which were
despatched at once to 5th Division front.

I had now set all that was possible in motion to
reinforce 5th Division, so returned to my headquarters
at Lomme to keep Ritchie, my B.G.S., informed of the
various moves I had carried out, and to discuss orders
for withdrawal with him.

Having seen to these details I again returned to 1st
Division H.Q. to discuss with Alexander his future
moves and to find out at what points I could gain
contact with him during our retirement.

This passage reveals very clearly the methods by which
Brooke ran his battle. Communications had broken down,
and liaison was everything. Frequent visits to his divisions
enabled him to weigh up the situation and to see what he
could do for them.

On this morning his next visit was to the 3rd Division, which
was preparing to pull out of the line and, moving in the dark by
second-class roads, cross the Lys, pass Ploegsteert Wood and
prolong the left flank of the 50th Division.

It was a task that might well have shaken the stoutest of
hearts, but for Monty, it might just have been a glorious
picnic. He told me exactly how he was going to do it, and
was as usual exuberant in confidence. There is no doubt
that one of Monty's strong points is his boundless confidence in himself. He was priceless on this occasion, and I
thanked Heaven to have a commander of his calibre to
undertake this hazardous march.

Montgomery himself thought this "the most difficult operation" his division was called upon to do during the campaign, and comments:

> If this move had been suggested by a student at the Staff College in a scheme, he would have been considered mad. But curious things have to be done in a crisis in war.

Brooke returned to his H.Q. at Lomme, where a revealing incident took place. His Military Assistant, Lieutenant-Colonel Stanyforth, pointed to a body lying in the gutter

> Stanyforth: *They have just shot that chap.*
> Brooke: *Who shot him?*
> Stanyforth: *Oh! Some of these retiring French soldiers; they said he was a spy, but I think the real reason was that he refused to give them cognac!*

Brooke remarks that the episode gave "some idea of the discipline in the French retirement, which at times looked more like a rout", but with scrupulous fairness adds that "some of the formations were living up to the very highest traditions of the French Army . . ." Later in the day he found the main Armentières-Lille road

> . . . practically blocked with four lines of French Army traffic moving against me towards Armentières, two rows of horse-drawn vehicles and two rows of motorized ones. The drivers were unshaven, and with the growth of several days on their faces, their clothes were covered with mud. I saw no officers in charge or any attempt on the part of N.C.O.s to control this mob.

In the evening the Corps Commander managed to visit General Franklyn once more:

> I found him very tired but running an excellent show. He had had a very trying day with continual German attacks, resulting in the loss of ground but had retained his front

intact. The only point that was causing me serious alarm was the junction between the 5th and the 50th Divisions. Franklyn informed me that satisfactory contact had not been established. The 10th Brigade under "Bubbles" Barker had up to the present failed to restore the situation.

The 10th Brigade (4th Division) in fact moved its H.Q. and the major part of two battalions from Roncq to Kemmel, via Wytschaete, during the night 27/28 May. Breaking off from one engagement, it arrived in the dark on the edge of another. A conference was held by the light of a single candle in a house in a side street in Wytschaete, and two of the C.O.s of the Brigade were briefed as to the situation on the front that they were to bolster up if and when their battalions arrived. Someone had a map – an unusual luxury by that time – and described the front that was being held. The 7th Field Company R.E., acting as infantry, was *here*; there were a hundred Inniskillings *here*, and *there* another field company. The line seemed pitifully thin, and the unreassuring recital was punctuated by frequent crashes which one of the senior officers present, with the benefit of 1918 experience, described as coming from a 5.9. The Germans had got a gun up with disconcerting promptitude. Every time a shell landed there was a despairing wail from the house next door, where a number of wounded were lying. The night was already far spent, positions had still to be selected in the dark, and might all too easily prove horribly exposed in the light of dawn. It was one of those times when one just has to remember that "heaviness may endure for a night, but joy cometh in the morning": things are seldom as black as they seem, and the Dunkirk campaign, if it proved nothing else, proved that over and over again.

By midnight on 27 May the Belgian Army had ceased fire. There was now a gap of twenty miles between Noordschote and the coast beyond Nieuport. In it there was nothing except the French 2nd Light Mechanised Division, the 12th Lancers and the 101st Army Field Company, R.E., which was demolishing the bridges between Nieuport and Dixmude.

On General Franklyn's front there was another day of violent fighting. By the end of it the two brigades of the 5th Division numbered no more than 600 men each. Farther north the 50th and 3rd Divisions had a relatively quiet day. During the night the 5th and 42nd Divisions managed to withdraw safely to the River Yser. At nightfall the orderly Germans would usually put up white signal flares all along their front line, marking their progress, and indicating to their administrative services the places to send their rations. Thereafter, they were remarkably peaceful until dawn, which certainly made it easier for their opponents to break contact and withdraw undisturbed.

It may be that the fight against von Bock was more bitter and prolonged than that against von Rundstedt, but at least Brooke was able by brilliant tactics to preserve a more or less continuous front. On the west the British defence was a series of isolated strongholds. The evening of the 28th found the British still in possession of Ledringhem (5th Gloucestershire), Cassel (145th Brigade) and Hazebrouck (Ist Buckinghamshire). The first of these garrisons, what was left of them, got back to the Yser during the night. The second survived a day of heavy shelling. The third, which consisted of the Battalion H.Q. and H.Q. Company, held a "keep" in the middle of the town until the building collapsed at about 6.30 p.m. as the result of continuous shelling. They had previously succeeded in shooting down the men of an enemy battery which was brought up to blast them out over "open sights". Their commanding officer had fallen, their reserve ammunition had blown up, and as a survivor put it they were now "definitely tired".

Farther south the 44th Division suffered heavily before they were withdrawn northwards, but the armoured divisions of Guderian's corps were down to fifty per cent and he considered that the operation was "costing unnecessary sacrifices". Heavy rain during the past twenty-four hours had made the going bad for armour.

It was up to 18th Army (Army Group B) to finish the job. Since Kleist Group now agreed to withdraw Guderian's three armoured divisions, the widely dispersed British garrisons had not sold their lives in vain.

On the east front the Germans reached the outskirts of Nieuport at 11 a.m. on the 28th, only a few hours after the Belgian surrender. The 12th Lancers repulsed the enemy's

leading patrols with loss, but more troops came up, took a
bridge and got a foothold in the town. Since the "infantry" of
the garrison, besides French detachments, consisted of men of
the 2nd and 53rd Medium Regiments, the 1st Heavy A.A.
Regiment R.A. and the 7th Field Company R.E., it is remarkable that the Germans made no better progress. They had now
missed their chance, for General Brooke was moving the 4th
Division back into the bridgehead with all speed. Hastening
back through Furnes it established itself behind the anti-tank
obstacle formed by a series of canals. Against all probability, the
"Race to the Sea" had been won.

Meanwhile the evacuation was getting under way. Already on
the 27th, Kleist Group, who could see the embarkation going on
before their very eyes, had commented that "it is very bitter for
our men to see this". Told that Göring had ordered the
Luftwaffe to attack Dunkirk "in such a manner that further
embarkations are impossible", the Chief of Staff of Fourth
Army painted the picture thus:

> Big ships come alongside the quays, planks are run up, and
> the men hurry aboard. All material is left behind. But we
> do not want to find these men, newly equipped, up against
> us again later.

It is gratifying to record that by this time (28 May) considerable
confusion reigned among the well-trained and formidable Teu-
tons. There was a lack of co-ordination between von Bock's
Army Group and von Rundstedt's. Around Lille the two
became mixed up. Some corps halted to reorganize, while
others pushed on. All were beginning to think in terms of
the coming offensive across the Somme. Beyond question the
B.E.F. had done something to throw the well-oiled machine out
of gear for however short a time.

Actions such as that fought by the 145th Brigade at Cassel
were of vital importance. The garrison was sent orders to retire
on the night of the 28th, but only received them at 6 a.m. on the
29th. They held on until 9.30 p.m. and then tried to fight their

way out. Few indeed got through to Dunkirk, but they had held a key road junction during vital days.

By midday on the 30th nearly all that remained of the B.E.F. was back in the Dunkirk bridgehead. An attack on Furnes was repulsed. The Eighteenth Army (Army Group B), which had been engaged hitherto against the Dutch and the Belgians, was now given the task of destroying the Allied troops in the bridgehead. Von Rundstedt had had his way. He could now preserve his precious armour for the impending thrust across the Somme. This time he was right, for Dunkirk, behind its network of canals, was hardly vulnerable to armour.

By midnight on 30 May a total of 126,606 men had already been evacuated to England. On that day Gort, who, much against his own inclinations, had been ordered home – as had Brooke – held his final conference and gave orders for the withdrawal of II Corps on the night 31 May– 1 June, and told Lieutenant-General M. G. H. Barker (I Corps), who would be in final command, "that as a last resort he would surrender himself and what remained of his corps to the Germans". Montgomery, who was now commanding II Corps, remained behind and had a private word with Gort.

> I then said it was my view that Barker was in an unfit state to be left in final command; what was needed was a calm and clear brain, and that given reasonable luck such a man might well get Ist Corps away, with no need for *anyone* to surrender; he had such a man in Alexander . . . I knew Gort very well; so I spoke very plainly and insisted that this was the right course to take.
>
> Gort acted promptly. Barker was sent off to England and I never saw him again. Alexander took over the Ist Corps. The two corps were now commanded by two major-generals and we met the next day in La Panne to discuss the situation; we were both confident that all would be well in the end. And it was; "Alex" got everyone away in his own calm and confident manner.

If the rest of the story can be told in few words, this is not to say that nothing was happening, but merely that the B.E.F. was no longer under the extreme pressure of the previous days. There was plenty of shelling and even Montgomery remarks that it was "very unpleasant" in La Panne on the evening of the 31st with shells bursting all round the house which was his H.Q.

In the air there was heavy fighting, as the R.A.F. strove to drive off the dive-bombers. While the 4th Division was marching along the beach from La Panne to Dunkirk mole on the morning of 1 June there came a time when not a single ship was to be seen in the offing. The Stukas had disposed of everything in sight. Now and again German planes would streak up the beach, machine-gunning, but they did remarkably little damage.

Evacuation continued until 4 June. During the days that remained the French "fighting for every house and for every foot of ground", were forced back to within two miles of the beaches. Those who could not be embarked finally surrendered at 9 a.m. on the 4th. They numbered some 40,000. Of the troops evacuated 139,097 had been Frenchmen.

And so the B.E.F. lived to fight another day. Looking back to those desperate days, and weighing up the chances of its survival after the German breakthrough, there still seems to be an element of the "miraculous" about it all. Sent overseas shamefully weak in armour and antitank guns, with a R.A.F. component short of aircraft designed for co-operation with ground forces, it had been trapped by a combination of strategic circumstances entirely beyond its control.

Battle of Britain (1940)

Christopher Dowling

On 30 June 1940 Major-General Alfred Jodl, Hitler's closest military adviser, expressed the view that the final German victory over England was "only a matter of time". He had good reason to be confident. Thanks to a run of victories unparalleled since the days of Napoleon, Germany was master of Western Europe from the Arctic to the Bay of Biscay. The much-vaunted French army had been destroyed in a campaign lasting barely six weeks. The British, who had sent a token force to France and Belgium, had been bundled off the Continent. Although the greater part of the British Expeditionary Force had managed to escape, it had been compelled to abandon almost all its heavy equipment and, for the time being, was incapable of offensive action. With the fall of France Britain lost her only ally in Europe. Despite Churchill's defiant speeches, many, including President Roosevelt and his advisers, doubted whether Britain would be able to resist the expected German onslaught.

Paradoxically, the very magnitude of their triumph over France had created intractable strategic problems for the German High Command. No plans had been made for a direct attack on England because the possibility that the Wehrmacht would inflict a decisive defeat on the French army had scarcely been contemplated. At most, Hitler had hoped to occupy bases in the Low Countries and northern France from which a naval and air blockade could be mounted against the British Isles. On 21 May, after the German armour had reached the Channel coast, Hitler briefly discussed the idea of invading England with the commander-in-chief of the navy, Admiral Raeder, but he was too preoccupied with the Battle of France (which was far from over) and then with the armistice negotiations to give much thought to the matter. In any case he was convinced that the British, for whom he had a grudging respect, would recognize the hopelessness of their position and sue for peace. He was anxious to bring the war to a speedy conclusion so that he could fulfil the mission which had always been the ultimate aim of his policy: the carving out of a great land empire in the East.

Hitler's hopes of a settlement with Britain were not finally dispelled until the third week of July, when Churchill contemptuously rejected his ill-conceived "peace offer". In the meantime he and his advisers had begun, in a somewhat leisurely manner, to consider possible courses of action should the British refuse to see reason. Britain, with her insular position, her powerful navy and her rapidly expanding air force, was an awkward opponent for the Wehrmacht, which, as the relative size and strength of the three armed services demonstrated, had been designed for Continental warfare. Germany's naval weakness and her lack of long-range aircraft ruled out a strategy of blockade – even if the necessary forces had been available this was bound to be a lengthy process. An invasion seemed the quickest and surest method of bringing Britain to her knees. However, in view of the Royal Navy's overwhelming superiority in surface ships, it was clear that troops could only be landed after air supremacy had been achieved and that even then the operation would be fraught with risk. Unlike some of his generals, Hitler did not regard the voyage across the Channel as merely "an extended river crossing". As Raeder was at pains to point out, the navy, which had been decimated in the Norwegian campaign, could provide little or no protection for the invasion fleet. Hitler lent a sympathetic ear to Raeder's arguments and it was agreed that invasion should be a "last resort", to be launched only when the British had been softened up by air bombardment. If, as its commander-in-chief

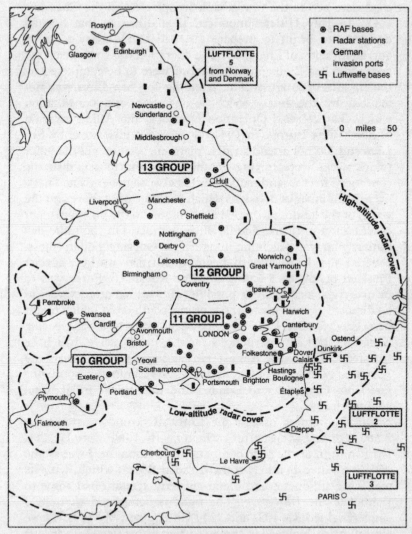

5.2 The Battle of Britain, July–September 1940

Hermann Goering boasted, the Luftwaffe was capable of knocking Britain out single-handed, the government might capitulate before the first assault troops crossed the Channel.

On 16 July Hitler announced in a directive that he had decided "to begin to prepare for, and if necessary to carry out, an invasion of England". The operation was to be given the codename Sea Lion and preparations were to be completed by the middle of August. The planning for Sea Lion was not marked by the inter-service co-operation and consultation which characterized Operation Overlord, the Allied invasion of north-west Europe in 1944. Goering set little store by Sea Lion and did not attend a single planning session, yet the other two services were relying on the Luftwaffe to establish the conditions for the landing. Disputes between the army and navy over the number of divisions which could be put ashore and the width of the landing front led on 1 August to the postponement of Sea Lion until the middle of September. On the same day Hitler, who was becoming impatient at Goering's dilatoriness, ordered the Luftwaffe to begin intensified warfare against England on or after 5 August. The Royal Air Force was to be overcome as quickly as possible, after which attacks were to be directed against ports; those on the south coast which might be needed for Sea Lion were, however, to be spared. Goering issued his tactical instructions for the air offensive, which he christened Eagle, on 2 August. He had so poor an opinion of the RAF that he allowed only four days for its elimination south of a line from Gloucester to London and four weeks for its total annihilation.

For the coming assault the Luftwaffe could muster some 2,500 serviceable aircraft, of which nearly 1,000 were He 111, Do 17 and Ju 88 medium bombers. In addition there were some 260 Ju 87 dive-bombers – the dreaded Stuka, which, with its menacing silhouette and blood-curdling scream, had come to symbolize the *Blitzkrieg*. The fighters comprised about 800 single-engined Me 109s and 220 twin-engined Me 110s. These aircraft were deployed in three *Luftflotten* (air fleets). *Luftflotte* 2, which was based in Holland, Belgium and northern France, was under the command of Field-Marshal Albert Kesselring, a former artillery officer who had transferred to the Luftwaffe in

1933. His genial manner had earned him the nickname "Smiling Albert". Further west lay *Luftflotte* 3 under Field-Marshal Hugo Sperrle, who had commanded the Condor Legion during the Spanish Civil War. It was intended that the 150 or so bombers of *Luftflotte* 5, under General Hans-Juergen Stumpff, should create a diversion by attacking targets in north-east England from their bases in Norway and Denmark. Of the three *Luftflotten* commanders, Sperrle was the only one who had flown in the First World War.

Although the Luftwaffe had officially been in existence for little more than five years it had already acquired a legendary reputation. It had played a spectacular and decisive part in the Polish, Norwegian and French campaigns; in the euphoria of victory the check it had suffered at the hands of the RAF over Dunkirk in May 1940 was soon forgotten and its significance was overlooked. Yet, formidable though it was, the Luftwaffe was in many respects ill equipped for the task which it had been given and which its leaders had embraced so readily. It had been designed not for independent strategic bombing but rather for the tactical support of the army in the field, a role which it had performed with brilliant success. Its organization, the training of its crews and the weapons with which they were provided reflected this purpose. The Luftwaffe lacked the essential instrument for an effective air offensive, a long-range heavy bomber. The medium and dive-bombers which formed its striking force did not have the necessary range, armament or bomb-carrying capacity for strategic operations and were vulnerable to the latest fighters, the dive-bombers particularly so. Had the ambitions of the first chief of the Luftwaffe General Staff, the gifted and far-sighted General Walther Wever, been realized, Germany might by the summer of 1940 have possessed a fleet of heavy bombers capable of reaching every target in the United Kingdom. As early as 1936 – the year in which the British Air Staff first issued the specification for a four-engined bomber – prototypes of the Do 19 and Ju 89 were ready for testing. However, after Wever's death in an air crash both models were scrapped and the heavy bomber programme was given a low priority.

The Luftwaffe was also severely handicapped by the limited endurance (about 80 minutes) of its standard fighter, the Me 109, which in other respects was an outstanding aircraft. The return journey across the Channel took approximately an hour; this left only 20 minutes for combat over England. The longer-ranged Me 110, on which extravagant hopes had been placed, proved incapable of holding its own against the RAF's Hurricanes and Spitfires and had itself to be protected by the faster and more nimble Me 109. As the German bombers were too vulnerable to fly without escort in daylight, their operational zone was necessarily restricted to the Me 109's radius of action – that is, to London and the south-east corner of England, where the British defences were concentrated. Moreover, owing to the comparative neglect of the fighter arm before the war, there were not enough Me 109s to provide adequate cover for the bombers, each of which needed an escort of at least two fighters. This, in effect, reduced the number of bombers that could be launched against Britain at any one time to a mere three or four hundred.

The Luftwaffe High Command was only vaguely aware of these deficiencies. Goering, who was more of a politician than an airman, greatly overestimated the strength of what he fondly regarded as "his" Luftwaffe. He had been a dashing fighter pilot during the First World War, but he had resigned his commission in 1922 and since then had lost touch with the development of military aviation. Hitler took little interest in air warfare and was content to leave the management of the Luftwaffe entirely to his faithful party henchman. Though he was not without ability, Goering had neither the technical knowledge nor the professional experience to command a modern air force. He lacked the capacity for sustained work and concerned himself only spasmodically with Luftwaffe affairs, preferring to lead a life of self-indulgent ease on his country estate at Karinhall. His chief of staff, the youthful Hans Jeschonnek, was an ardent Nazi and was not disposed to challenge his overbearing superior. In any case, he, like the two field commanders Kesselring and Sperrle, shared many of Goering's illusions about the Luftwaffe's potential.

While the Battle of Britain was, from the Luftwaffe's point of view, an improvised operation hastily mounted with the resources to hand, the RAF had been preparing for it over a period of more than four years. By the summer of 1940 a sophisticated system of air defence had been evolved under the direction of the commander-in-chief of Fighter Command, Air Chief Marshal Sir Hugh Dowding. The cornerstone of this system was the chain of 52 radar (originally called RDF or radio direction-finding) stations which lined the coast from Pembrokeshire to the Shetlands. In the early 1930s the problem of intercepting enemy bombers before they reached their targets had seemed insoluble, since the defending fighters had to be alerted when the raiders were still well out to sea. In 1935, however, Robert Watson Watt demonstrated that radio waves might be used to detect and locate approaching aircraft. His ideas were taken up by another distinguished scientist, Sir Henry Tizard, who harnessed the new device of radar to operational requirements. Although the radar screen was not quite complete when the Battle of Britain began, it was able to provide accurate information on the distance and bearing of hostile aircraft at ranges of 70 miles or more and to give a rough indication of their height and numbers. Once the aircraft had crossed the coast their movements were tracked by the keen-eyed volunteers of the Observer Corps, whose methods Churchill rather tactlessly described as 'early Stone Age'. The Germans were aware of the existence of the radar stations – their towering masts made them an obvious landmark – but they underestimated their efficiency and did not realize how closely they had been integrated into the British defence system. Radar enabled the British fighters to be in the right place at the right time and obviated the need for standing patrols. Without its magic eye Fighter Command would have been at a hopeless disadvantage.

Information from the radar stations and Observer Corps posts was passed by means of an elaborate network of communications to the four groups into which Fighter Command was divided. The most important of these was No. 11 Group, which was responsible for the key area of London and the south-east of England. Its commander was Air Vice-Marshal Keith Park, a New Zealander, who, though very different in personality from Dowding, saw eye to eye with him on the handling of the fighter force. No. 12 Group, under Air Vice-Marshal Trafford Leigh-Mallory (brother of the famous mountaineer George Mallory), covered the Midlands; No. 13 Group, under Air Vice-Marshal R. E. Saul, Scotland and the north of England; and No. 10 Group, under Air Vice-Marshal Sir Quinton Brand, the south-west. Each group comprised a number of sectors. There were seven sector stations in No. 11 Group: Tangmere, Northolt, North Weald, Debden, Hornchurch, Biggin Hill and Kenley. The sector commander ordered aircraft into the air in accordance with the orders he received from group headquarters and directed their movements from the ground by the then advanced method of radio telephone. Although Fighter Command Headquarters at Bentley Priory near Stanmore had a general view of the situation as it developed from minute to minute, the actual conduct of the battle was left to the various groups and sectors. In addition to the radar stations, Observer Corps centres and fighter squadrons, Dowding had at his disposal the 1,500 barrage balloons of Balloon Command, and the 1,300 heavy and 700 light guns of Anti-Aircraft Command.

At the beginning of August the RAF had a front-line strength of 1,200 aircraft, nearly 700 of which were fighters. (The 500 or so bombers were not directly involved in the battle.) All but a handful of the 55 fighter squadrons were equipped with Hurricanes or Spitfires, whose eight wing-mounted Browning machine-guns were capable of destroying a bomber in a two-second burst of fire. The Hurricane has been overshadowed in the popular imagination by the more glamorous Spitfire, and it is not always recognized that it formed the backbone of the fighter defences. It was a steady, robust and highly manoeuvrable aircraft but it was inferior in performance to the Me 109. There was little to choose between the Me 109 and the Spitfire, though the system of direct fuel injection which enabled the German machine to go into a steep dive without any loss of power perhaps tipped the scales in its favour. In terms of the number and quality of their single-engined fighters and the skill and courage of the men who flew them the two sides were evenly matched. The British, however, had the greater reserves and, thanks to the forceful methods of Lord Beaverbrook, the Minister of Aircraft Production, were producing more than twice as many aircraft as the Germans. Between June and September 1940 deliveries of Me 109s averaged only 190 a month, compared with 470 Hurricanes and Spitfires.

The position as far as pilots were concerned was less encouraging. Nearly 300 fighter pilots had been lost during the Battle of France (a third of the total complement), and at the beginning of August Fighter Command was still 154 pilots below establishment, despite the welcome addition to its ranks of trained recruits from France, Belgium, Czechoslovakia, Poland, the United States and the Dominions. On the other hand the British enjoyed the advantage of fighting over their own territory: RAF pilots who baled out or crash-landed could be in action again within a few hours, whereas their opponents were marched off to prisoner-of-war camps. Similarly, many of the British aircraft that were shot down could be salvaged.

Fighter Command was fortunate in being led by men of unrivalled professional ability and experience. Dowding, who but for the outbreak of the war would have been retired in 1939, was a career officer with a keen interest in the application of science to modern warfare. Just as the Grand Fleet of the First World War was moulded by Lord Fisher, so Fighter Command was largely Dowding's creation. Austere, reserved and dedicated, he presented a complete contrast to the flamboyant and vainglorious Goering. By his tenacious opposition to the War Cabinet's proposal to send additional fighter squadrons to France after the German breakthrough in May 1940, Dowding ensured that he had sufficient forces with which to fight the Battle of Britain. Unlike their German counterparts, many of whom had army backgrounds, Dowding and his senior officers had behind them a quarter of a century of continuous service in military aviation.

The Battle of Britain, like the Battle of the Atlantic and the Battle of France, was, strictly speaking, a campaign rather than a battle. In fact it was a campaign within a campaign, for it formed part of a major German air offensive against Britain which lasted from June 1940, when the first bombs fell on British soil, to May 1941, when the bulk of the Luftwaffe was transferred to the Eastern Front in preparation for the attack on Russia. Although there is no agreement about its exact time span, the Battle of Britain consisted in essence of a series of daylight engagements fought in the skies above south-east England between 12 August and 30 September 1940. During these critical weeks the Luftwaffe sought to destroy Fighter Command in order to pave the way for a landing or for the unopposed occupation of a country paralysed by bombing. As Fighter Command could only be engaged in daylight the night raids by unescorted bombers, which began to assume a regular pattern after 24 August, cannot properly be regarded as part of the Battle of Britain, except perhaps for those that supplemented the daylight attacks on London during the last three weeks of September. After September the daylight fighting gradually died down and the Battle of Britain merged imperceptibly into the Blitz.

The prelude to the battle was an attempt by Goering early in July to wear down Fighter Command by attacking ports and shipping in the Channel. Neither side was at full strength, for the Luftwaffe had not yet completed its redeployment after the French campaign, and Dowding prudently refused to commit more than a small number of squadrons in conditions which usually favoured the enemy. The *Kanalkampf*, as the Germans called it, continued with mounting intensity until well into August. The results of these preliminary skirmishes were inconclusive. The Germans sank 30,000 tons of shipping and succeeded in establishing air superiority over the Straits of Dover in daylight, but their losses in aircraft were twice those of the British.

The Battle of Britain proper can be said to have begun on 12 August, when the Luftwaffe struck its first real blows at the RAF's fighter airfields and radar stations. Of the six radar stations attacked, one, Ventnor on the Isle of Wight, was so badly damaged that it was out of action for ten days, though this was skilfully concealed from the Germans. The Luftwaffe, however, failed to follow up the limited success it had achieved. Owing to faulty planning and slipshod staff work the long awaited Eagle Day on 13 August, which was to herald the opening of the main air assault, proved to be a flop. No attempt was made to repeat the attacks on the radar stations, and the aerodromes at Eastchurch, Detling and Andover were heavily bombed in the mistaken belief that they were fighter stations.

On 15 August the Luftwaffe made its greatest effort of the battle, flying no fewer than 1,786 sorties. Every available fighter was thrown in and for the first and last time all three *Luftflotten* were committed. The outcome was a notable victory for Fighter Command, which shot down 75 German aircraft at a cost of 34 of its own. The weakly escorted bombers of *Luftflotte* 5 came in over the North Sea expecting to encounter little or no opposition. They were set upon by fighters from Nos 12 and 13 Groups when they were still some distance from land and suffered such crippling losses that they took no further part in the battle. There was heavy fighting on 16 and 18 August before a spell of cloudy weather brought the first phase of the struggle to an end.

Although Fighter Command was putting up stiff resistance, Goering, whose wishful thinking was reinforced by wildly inaccurate intelligence estimates, believed that Dowding had only about 300 fighters left – this was less than half the true figure. By concentrating his attacks on Fighter Command's vital airfields in south-east England he hoped to draw the British into an all-out fighter action in which Dowding's remaining squadrons would be wiped out. Hitherto, on Park's instructions, the British fighter pilots had engaged the bombers and avoided combat with the Me 109s. This had driven the Germans to employ their fighters in a close escort role rather than in the offensive sweeps for which they were best suited. In order to provide the strong escorts which Goering demanded for the bombers, almost all the Me 109s in Sperrle's area were transferred to Kesselring. The Ju 87s, which had been severely mauled, were withdrawn. Further attacks on the radar stations were discouraged by Goering, who considered them a poor investment, and after 18 August they were left unmolested.

The second and most crucial phase of the battle opened on 24 August with a devastating raid by *Luftflotte* 2 on No. 11 Group's forward aerodrome at Manston, which was so badly knocked about that it had to be evacuated. During the next fortnight the Luftwaffe began for the first time to gain the upper hand. The new German tactics of maintaining continuous patrols over the Straits of Dover and of delivering feint attacks across the Channel confused the British defences. Park's fighters found it difficult to get to grips with the German bombers, which were now protected by swarms of Me 109s. The disparity in losses narrowed sharply. From 31 August to 6 September the Luftwaffe lost 225 bombers and fighters, the British 185 fighters. As bombers accounted for about half of the German figure the British losses in fighters were considerably higher. Of even greater concern than the dwindling reserves of aircraft was the wastage of trained pilots: weekly casualties were running at more than 10 per cent of Fighter Command's total combat strength and the strain of almost daily action was beginning to tell. The Luftwaffe was also causing serious damage on the ground. At Biggin Hill, which was raided six times in three days, the operations room was wrecked, hangars, workshops and barracks destroyed and nearly 70 station staff killed or wounded. Early in September the Luftwaffe was close to winning some measure of air superiority over Kent and Sussex. This would have forced Park to withdraw his squadrons to airfields north of the Thames, from which an effective defence of south-east England would have been impossible.

But on 7 September Goering relaxed the pressure on Fighter Command's ground organization by switching the main weight of the offensive to London. Shortly after 5 p.m. over 300 bombers escorted by some 600 fighters converged on the capital and dropped a hail of bombs and incendiaries on the East End and the London docks, kindling numerous fires. Fighter Command was taken by surprise and the German bomber losses were comparatively light. The blazing warehouses and oil refineries acted as a beacon for a further 250 bombers, which continued the work of destruction during the night. When dawn rose over the smoke-laden city 306 civilians were dead and 1,337 seriously injured.

There were two reasons for what, in the event, proved a disastrous change of strategy: one military, the other political. The time of decision for Sea Lion was fast approaching. Already, in the first week of September, hundreds of barges and tugs had begun to creep round the North Sea coast to the ports of embarkation in the Channel, yet the Luftwaffe had still not achieved the necessary degree of air superiority to justify launching the invasion. Goering and Kesselring, though not the more realistic Sperrle, were convinced that Fighter Command was on its last legs and that mass daylight raids on a target as important as London would hasten their victory by forcing Dowding to expend his few remaining fighters. The possibility that ruthless bombing of the civilian population might break the British will to resist was an added inducement. The political reason for the assault on London was Hitler's demand that reprisals should be carried out for British raids on Berlin, which had themselves been ordered as reprisals for the accidental bombing of London by the Luftwaffe on the night of 24 August.

Because of unsettled weather and the growing fatigue of its aircrews the Luftwaffe was unable to sustain its daylight offensive against London. In the week that followed the big attack of 7 September there were only three days – 9, 11 and 14 September – when sizeable forces were sent over London, though it was heavily bombed every night. The raid on 9 September was a failure, but two days later the Luftwaffe inflicted greater losses than it incurred, while in the fighting on 14 September honours were even. The opposition was patchy and it seemed to the Germans that the British fighter defences were at last on the point of collapse. Encouraged by Goering's jubilant account of the Luftwaffe's recent achievements, Hitler determined to wait until 17 September before making a final decision about Sea Lion. In the meantime the raids on London were to continue.

The weather on the morning of 15 September was clear and sunny. Sensing that the day would not be devoid of incident, Winston Churchill paid one of his periodic visits to No. 11 Group's headquarters at Uxbridge. As Park accompanied the Prime Minister and his wife down to the operations room, 50 feet below the ground, he remarked: "I don't know whether anything will happen today. At present all is quiet." Shortly after 10.30 a.m. radar plots revealed that enemy aircraft were massing over the Pas de Calais, and it soon became apparent that a major attack was imminent. The Germans neglected to carry out their usual feints and Park was able to deploy his forces to the best advantage. When the German bombers crossed the English coast at about 11.30 a.m. they were engaged by successive squadrons of British fighters and harried all the way to London. Although a considerable amount of damage was done few of the bombers succeeded in reaching their targets. After a two-hour interval, which gave the British fighters an opportunity to rearm and refuel, a second and heavier attack was launched. It too was repulsed. One of the features of the day's fighting was the timely intervention of a wing of five squadrons from No. 12 Group, aggressively led by Squadron Leader Douglas Bader. Park, who believed in using his squadrons singly or in pairs rather than in the large formations advocated by Leigh-Mallory and Bader, had, on previous occasions, complained bitterly about the lack of support from No. 12 Group.

As the German bombers straggled back to their bases, many with their wings and fuselages riddled with bullets and with dead or wounded men on board, it became clear that the Luftwaffe had taken a severe beating. The British thought that they had shot down 185 German aircraft, and on the strength of this grossly inflated estimate 15 September has come to be celebrated as Battle of Britain Day. The actual German losses were about 50 – fewer than on 15 and 18 August. Even so, the two actions on 15 September, if not particularly significant from a tactical point of view, were strategically decisive. The German fighters had once again held their own but they had been unable to protect the bombers. There was no disguising the fact that Fighter Command, which had lost only 26 aircraft, was still very much in being and that air supremacy was as far away as ever. Furthermore, since 4 September Bomber Command had been mounting nightly attacks on the Channel ports and had sunk or damaged more than a hundred barges and transports. On 17 September Hitler postponed Sea Lion indefinitely. Two days later, after Bomber Command had struck further damaging blows, he ordered the invasion fleet to be dispersed.

The abandonment of Sea Lion (formally cancelled on 12 October) did not, as might have been expected, bring the Battle of Britain to an end, for Hitler was anxious to keep up the threat of a landing and Goering, who was not one to admit defeat, still nourished the hope that his stubborn adversary might yet be vanquished. After 15 September the Luftwaffe turned increasingly to night bombing – a tacit acknowledgement that it had failed to win the daylight battle – but daylight attacks on London and other targets by mass formations of bombers continued for another fortnight. The fighting did not go in the Luftwaffe's favour and at the beginning of October, in order to avoid further bomber losses, Goering resorted to the use of fighter-bombers, which relied on speed and altitude to evade the British defences. These raids were mere pinpricks compared with what had gone before and they served no real strategic purpose. Nevertheless the battle dragged on, its finale being the belated intervention of the Italian air force, which made two gallant but ineffectual raids on 29 October and 11 November. The crew of one of the antiquated Fiat BR20 bombers which was shot down over East Anglia presented an incongruous spectacle: they wore steel helmets and were armed with bayonets.

There were many reasons for the Luftwaffe's defeat in the Battle of Britain: Goering's muddled strategy and his boundless capacity for self-delusion; the failure of the Germans to destroy or neutralize the British radar screen; the shortage of Me 109s and their unsuitability as bomber escorts; the high courage and superb morale of Fighter Command's pilots and ground crews, whose belief in ultimate victory never wavered; and, not least, the resolute strategy and skilful tactics pursued by Dowding and Park. Ironically, their conduct of the battle, in particular their reluctance to employ their fighters in big wings, earned official disapproval, and both were removed from their commands before the year was out. Few battles of comparable importance in world history have been won at such a small cost in human life: between 10 July and 31 October 1940 (the official British dates for the Battle of Britain) Fighter Command's casualties were only 449, though these were nonetheless grievous losses. In the course of the battle Fighter Command lost 915 aircraft, the Luftwaffe 1,733. Tactically the fighting was inconclusive, since neither air force was able to do irreparable harm to the other. At the end of the battle Fighter Command's strength in aircraft was greater than it had been at the beginning. The Luftwaffe took longer to recover, largely because of Germany's low rate of aircraft production, but it had made good its losses both in aircraft and in personnel by the spring of 1941, and its operational efficiency was not noticeably impaired. Its leaders, however, failed to take action to remedy the shortcomings which the Battle of Britain had exposed. Little attempt was made, for example, to step up aircraft production, or to expand the woefully inadequate training programme, or to accelerate the development of a four-engined bomber. It is a remarkable fact that the only major new aircraft type introduced into service in Germany between 1939 and 1944 was the Focke-Wulf 190. In so far as the Luftwaffe never again enjoyed the prestige or the relative striking power that it had possessed in June 1940, the Battle of Britain marked the beginning of its decline.

Dowding's victory in the Battle of Britain was no less significant than Nelson's at Trafalgar, with which, indeed, it has sometimes been compared. Yet in many ways Lord Howard of Effingham's victory over the Spanish Armada in 1588 affords a closer parallel. The defeat of the Spanish Armada was the first great naval battle of modern times, the Battle of Britain the first (and almost certainly the last) great air battle. Like the Battle of Britain, the duel between the English fleet and the Armada was not a setpiece encounter but a string of engagements of varying size and intensity. Both were successful defensive battles, though neither decided the issue of the war. Nor was the disparity in strength between the respective fleets and air forces nearly as wide as was thought at the time: the two battles were more akin to the combat between Hector and Achilles than to that between David and Goliath. Like some of the German generals, notably Field-Marshal von Rundstedt, the Duke of Parma, whose troops were to carry out the landings, was indifferent to the invasion project. The antipathy which existed between Drake and Frobisher finds some echo in the clash between Park and Leigh-Mallory over tactics. Just as Howard was criticized for failing to annihilate the Spanish fleet, so it was argued in some quarters that Dowding and Park could have inflicted greater losses on the Luftwaffe by adopting a more aggressive policy. There, however, the parallel ends, for whereas the defeat of the Armada led to a revival of Spanish naval power, the defeat of the Luftwaffe, as we have seen, was one of the signposts on the road to its ultimate demise.

The failure of the Luftwaffe to destroy Fighter Command in the summer of 1940 had far-reaching strategic consequences. It was the first setback suffered by the Wehrmacht in the Second World War and it dented the myth of German invincibility in much the same way as Napoleon's repulse at Aspern-Essling in 1809 had shown a demoralized Europe that the all-conquering Grand Army could be mastered. Furthermore, it shattered Hitler's hopes of a swift victory and ensured that the struggle would be a protracted one; Germany, whose economy and armed forces were geared to a *Blitzkrieg* strategy, was ill-equipped to fight this kind of war. Hitler realized that in view of Britain's rapidly growing military strength an invasion in 1941 would not be feasible. Germany was thus forced to seek alternative avenues to victory, which involved her in costly campaigns in the Mediterranean. Although the frustration of the German attempt to conquer Britain had nothing to do with the attack on Russia, planning for which had started several weeks before Eagle Day, operations in the East seemed to offer a solution to the stalemate in the West. Hitler was obliged to embark on the invasion of Russia with an unsubdued enemy in his rear. The threat of British intervention on the Continent pinned down more than 35 divisions, thereby reducing the forces available for Operation Barbarossa. Perhaps the last word should be given to von Rundstedt. Shortly after the war he told a group of Russian officers that had the Luftwaffe won the Battle of Britain Germany would have defeated Russia in 1941. The Russians had come to ask him which he considered to be the decisive battle of the war, expecting him to name Stalingrad. When he replied, "The Battle of Britain", they closed their notebooks and went away.

Kiev (1941)

John Strawson

Hitler hailed it as "the greatest battle in the history of the world". For on 16 September 1941 the German *Panzergruppen* of Colonel-Generals Heinz Guderian and Ewald von Kleist had joined hands in the Ukraine at Lokhvitsa, 125 miles east of Kiev. The Soviet commander in the Ukraine, Marshal Semyon Mikhailovich Budenny, had just been sacked by Stalin, but his army group was encircled. Within ten days the Germans captured 655,000 prisoners, 884 tanks, 3,718 guns and 3,500 motor vehicles. Colonel General Franz Halder, Chief of the German General Staff, called Kiev the principal strategic blunder of the Russian campaign. His view seems irreconcilable with Hitler's. How had it all come about?

The answer lies in the planning and aims of Hitler's invasion of Russia. As early as 1924, Hitler's book *Mein Kampf* was explicit: "We stop the endless German movement to the south and west, and turn our gaze towards the land of the East. If we speak of new territory in Europe today, we can primarily have in mind only Russia and her vassal border states . . . This colossal empire in the East is ripe for dissolution." Hitler's foreign policy was not just to abolish the Treaty of Versailles and extend the *Reich*'s frontiers to include all Germans. These aims were virtually achieved by 1939 without recourse to war. But *Lebensraum* (living space) demanded far more than what was "rightly" Germany's. It needed Russia for ideological as well as strategic reasons.

Despite all the campaigns in the west and the south, it can be argued that Hitler concentrated three-quarters of his forces with his prime object clearly in view – the defeat of Russia. Only then could he settle 100 million Germans of pure Aryan stock on lands east of Germany to ensure that the New Order would last for a thousand years.

Hitler knew that the establishment of a German empire in the East, would, sooner or later, mean war with Russia. Even in 1934 he was telling Hermann Rauschning: "We cannot in any way evade the final battle between German race ideals and pan-Slav mass ideals. Here yawns the eternal abyss which no political interest can bridge . . . We alone can conquer the great continental space, and it will be done by us singly and alone."

It might be necessary to make arrangements with the Soviet Union along the way, but only the more quickly to erase Russia completely for "it will open to us the mastery of the world." In July 1940, with France crushed but England defiant, Hitler turned his arguments inside out when trying to persuade his Commanders-in-Chief about how to defeat England. England's hope lay in Russia and the United States. If Russia dropped out of the picture, America would too, for Russia's elimination would make America think only of Japan's threat to themselves. "Decision: Russia's destruction must therefore be made part of this struggle. The sooner Russia is crushed the better. The attack will achieve its purpose only if the Russian state can be shattered to its roots with one blow . . . if we start in May 1941, we will have five months in which to finish the job."

In December 1940 Hitler's War Directive No 21, *Case Barbarossa*, sent a shiver down the spines of those first privileged to read it. "The German Armed Forces must be prepared, even before the conclusion of the war against England, to crush Soviet Russia in a rapid campaign." The bulk of the Red Army stationed in Western Russia would be encircled and destroyed by deeply penetrating armored forces. Above all, any Soviet forces still able to fight would be prevented from withdrawing into the depths of Russia. Herein lay the reason for the battle of

Kiev. Hitler's directive gave a broad outline of the conduct of operations and the final objective – the creation of a barrier against Asiatic Russia on the general line of the Caspian Sea at Astrakhan to Archangel in the Arctic. It did not say how and where the Soviet armies were to be destroyed. This failure to draw up an absolutely clear and realizable master plan for the Red Army's annihilation ensured that the astonishingly successful Kiev battles made no difference to the final outcome of the war.

Hitler had always maintained that "we have only to kick the door in and the whole rotten structure will come crashing down." In order to foment this instant collapse three Army Groups were assembled. Army Group North would strike for Leningrad. Army Group Centre with the two main *Panzergruppen* (1,770 tanks) was aimed at Smolensk. Field Marshal Karl Gerd von Rundstedt's Army Group South was to deal with the enemy west of the Dnieper river in the Ukraine. Throughout planning, Hitler constantly reiterated the need to wipe out, not just put to flight, the main enemy forces. But he consistently failed to lay down any absolute strategic plan or objective to which all operations would contribute and be subordinate.

As *Barbarossa* developed, the Führer constantly chopped and changed, or worse still, vacillated. In spite of rapid advances and huge bags of prisoners, there was little sign of the whole Soviet structure crashing down. Army Group North got to Leningrad, but was repulsed before the city itself and had to be content with investing it. Field Marshal Fedor von Bock's Army Group Centre executed a great pincer movement converging on Minsk and by 10 July, 20 days after the start of the campaign, claimed 300,000 prisoners. The battles around Smolensk started a week later and lasted for three more. They produced a comparable number of prisoners, but took such a toll of von Bock's armies that the advance towards Moscow from Smolensk was not resumed until 2 October. It was this lack of a conclusive decision in the north and center, combined with Hitler's constant change of heart over what constituted decisive objectives, which led to glittering but illusory success in the Ukraine.

On 19 July Hitler issued his War Directive No 33. This directive (and its supplement on the 23rd) caused furious controversy between the Führer and his generals. In the first place Army Group Centre was instructed to keep advancing on Moscow, while its vital *Panzer* formations were hived off. *Panzergruppe 3* was to join in the battle for Leningrad. Guderian's *Panzergruppe 2* would attack the Ukraine in conjunction with von Kleist's *Panzergruppe 1* from Army Group South. Hitler made it clear that the priorities were the capture of Leningrad whose fall, he believed, would lead to the collapse of the regime it politically symbolized, and the Ukraine, an economic objective to be denied to Russia and used by Germany.

Col. Gen. Halder, Chief of the General Staff, argued that the whole campaign was endangered by the lack of a clear aim. Were the Führer's aims military conquest or economic exploitation? Hitler replied that both were equally important. But when Halder supported by von Bock, von Rundstedt, Field Marshal Walther von Brauchitsch (C-in-C of the Army) and Guderian insisted that a final autumn thrust must be made on Moscow, Hitler simply lectured his Commanders on the economic aspects of conducting war. Hitler only conceded Army Group Centre a defensive role after losing its *Panzergruppen*. It would not have to push on to Moscow with infantry alone. A 12 August supplement to Directive No 34 made it plain that the new offensives would be directed north on Leningrad and southwards to the Crimea, Kharkov, the Donets river basin and the Caucasus mountains. Large enemy forces on the flanks of Army Group Centre, especially the Soviet Fifth Army in the Pripet Marshes north of Kiev, were to be destroyed. This was the foundation of the great Kiev battles.

Among those who attempted to dissuade Hitler was the very man who did most to make the Kiev battles a stupendous triumph. In a last-ditch attempt to overturn the decision, Guderian obtained an interview with Hitler in the *Wolfsschanze* ("Wolf's lair" HQ at Rastenburg in E. Prussia) on 23 August. He pointed out that Moscow was the objective which ordinary soldiers understood. It was also a vital communication center, the political solar plexus of the Soviet Union, industrially important and psychologically perhaps conclusively so. He maintained that to capture Moscow first and destroy the Russian forces defending it (half a million men had escaped from the Smolensk encirclement) would make the subsequent over-running of the Ukraine easy. To go for the Ukraine first would rob the *Wehrmacht* of the chance to take Moscow before winter came.

Guderian heard what was planned for his own *Panzergruppe* – movement to the Ukraine and back involving more than 600 miles – he commented, "I doubt if the machines will stand it, even if we are unopposed." But having been told by Hitler that Moscow must wait and the Ukraine offensive go ahead, Guderian assured the Führer that he would do his best. Hitler used Guderian's acquiescence to parry the continued doubts of Halder. He was always dividing and ruling his servants. But whatever the decision-making process, the outcome was that the main striking power of the German Army went north and south, not east to Moscow.

If there was discord among German military leadership about where to continue the offensive, there was just as much discord in STAVKA, the Soviet High Command, about how to stem its seemingly invincible advance. Colonel General M. P. Kirponos's SW Front had been pushed back into the Ukraine, while Hitler's Rumanian satellite armies from the Balkans begun to move into Bessarabia and towards Odessa. The Soviet problem here was the unenviable one of trying to defend a broadening front with disintegrating forces. STAVKA decided to amalgamate Southern and SW Fronts into one SW Theater. Stalin appointed as its Commander his old crony, Marshal Budenny. The Commissar with a main job of evacuating industry was none other than the 47-year-old Lieutenant General Nikita S. Khruschev. The 58-year-old Budenny, having held no real field command for 20 years, had little to recommend him save political "reliability" against the German professionals, von Rundstedt and von Kleist.

As if choosing so questionable a commander was not enough, Russian strategy itself was soon a matter of violent disagreement. At a meeting in Moscow on 29 July, General Georgi K. Zhukov, Chief of the General Staff, urged that Kirponos's SW

Front be withdrawn from the Dnieper river-line, even though this meant giving up Kiev. Stalin angrily rejected such a course, and instantly accepted Zhukov's offer to resign. Zhukov therefore went off to command the Reserve Front. The ailing Marshal Boris M. Shaposhnikov became Chief of the General Staff again. In any event, Stalin's decision to fight on the line of the Dnieper prevailed. Kiev, capital of the second most important Socialist Republic, was to be held at all costs.

Marshal Budenny's army group was positioned in an enormous salient about 150 miles wide, stretching from Trubchevsk in the north to Kremenchug in the south with Kiev as the apex of the salient sticking out to the west. The opportunity for encirclement and annihilation was therefore present from the outset. Budenny had the best part of 1.5 million soldiers in his area, about eight armies, mainly at Uman and Kiev itself.

The German recipe for annihilation was *double* encirclement. The first and *inner* ring would be drawn by three infantry armies; the Second moving SE from Gomel, the Seventeenth striking north from Kremenchug and the Sixth keeping Russian attention riveted on Kiev itself. Meanwhile the *outer* ring would be closed by Guderian's *Panzergruppe* driving south with some 500 tanks from Trubchevsk to meet von Kleist's 600 tanks striking north from Kremenchug, at a point some 125 miles east of Kiev. It was the strategist's dream, a re-creation of the unique victory won by Hannibal over Rome at Cannae in 216 BC. The Carthaginian military genius had destroyed 70,000 out of 86,000 Romans for a cost of only 5,700. His infantry had lured 16 legions into the heart of their concave formation while the cavalry smashed the Roman wings and enveloped the infantry – to charge into their rear.

While the German plan unfolded, the Russians seemed to be paralysed and incapable of decisive action. Had Budenny had any inkling of the scope of German plans, he might have reversed his troop concentrations to withdraw behind the Dnieper. But having no notion of the kind of battle about to be fought, he reinforced those very areas, like Uman, which were to be engulfed even before the main battle was launched. While Uman was being reinforced, von Kleist's three *Panzer* Corps were dashing eastwards roughly between the two main

Soviet concentrations at Uman and Kiev. By the end of July the *Panzers* were more than 100 miles SE of Budenny's main forces. The noose east of Uman was looped by Eleventh Army infantry crossing the river Bug and pushing on to Novo Ukraine where they joined up with 14 *Panzer* Corps from the north. Uman was a foretaste of greater things to come – by 8 August 103,000 prisoners had been taken from 21 divisions of three encircled Russian armies. The week's reduction of the pocket yielded booty totalling 850 field guns, 317 tanks, and 242 AT and AA guns. One German artillery battery pounding these targets fired more ammunition in four days than it had in the entire six-week 1940 campaign in France.

At this point in the Russian campaign – it was still only August – seven weeks after the start, the morale of the *Wehrmacht* was at its peak despite checks at Leningrad. In the south they were advancing fast without too much opposition. When the Russians did counter-attack, they usually signalled their coming by a lot of radio conversation *en clair* and then stuck to their normal pattern of a short artillery bombardment followed by wave after wave of infantry. Sometimes they were supported by tanks or trucks crammed with soldiers which simply drove straight at the German positions until inevitably knocked out. These were halcyon days and it was as well that the Germans enjoyed them for there would not be much more to enjoy after the autumn. This gallop across the Ukraine was recalled by C. Malaparte:

> During the night-time all fighting ceases. Men, animals, weapons rest. Not a rifle shot breaks the damp nocturnal silence. Even the voice of the cannon is hushed. As soon as the sun has set, and the first shadows of evening creep across the corn field, the German columns prepare for their night's halt. Night falls, cold and heavy, on the men curled up in the ditches, in the small slit trenches which they have hastily dug amid the corn, alongside the light and medium assault batteries, the anti-tank cannon, the heavy anti-aircraft machine-guns, the mortars . . . Shielded from sudden attack by the sentries and patrols the men abandon themselves in sleep. There in front of us,

concealed amid the corn and with the solid dense mass of the woods – over there beyond the deep, smooth, bleak fold of the valley, the enemy sleeps. We can hear his hoarse breathing. We can discern his smell – a smell of oil, petrol and sweat.

By 7 September German operations were crystallizing. During a visit to von Rundstedt's Army Group South HQ, Halder agreed final details of the plan involving both this army group and Army Group Centre by which all enemy in the Kiev–Dnieper–Desna bend would be destroyed and Kiev itself taken. From Army Group Centre, Guderian would continue his 12-day-old thrust southwards from Starodub to Romny and Priluki with Second Army covering the right flank of the *Panzer* advance. From Army Group South, Seventeenth Army would pin the Soviet forces on the Lower Dnieper below Cherkassy and get a bridgehead over the river at Kremenchug. Then von Kleist could drive northwards from it to link up with Guderian in the general area Romny–Lokhvitsa thus cutting off some six Soviet armies. Field Marshal Walther von Reichenau's Sixth Army would cross the 700-yard wide Dnieper opposite Kiev and attack the encircled Soviet forces there.

Within a few days the German armies had made great strides. Seventeenth Army crossed the Dnieper on 11 September and von Kleist was packing his tanks into the bridgehead. To counter these moves, Budenny's only recourse was a desperate appeal to Stalin on 11 September for permission to withdraw.

It is possible, when we remember that he had given Budenny over a million men, to sympathize even with Stalin's exasperation and his refusal to authorize retreat to the east. Instead the Party slogan was "Stand fast, hold out, and if need be die." But by this time it was virtually too late. From the outset Russian leaders just could not believe that Hitler would abandon Moscow as his prior target when it looked as if he could reach it even earlier in the year than Napoleon (14 September 1812) – so while Guderian was seen to be heading south, it was thought that he was only trying to dodge round the strong Soviet forces barring the direct route to Moscow. Russian mobility, despite mechanization tied essentially to the foot soldier, could never hope to match that of the German *Panzer* troops who roamed more or less at will, at least six times as fast.

What is more, after von Kleist's breakthrough, there was nothing to stop them. Indeed with his *Panzers* ranging as far east and south as Dnepropetrovsk, Krivoi Rog and Nikolayev, von Rundstedt's difficulty was not so much that he could not gain his objectives, but to know what these objectives were. All southern European Russia, including the whole of the Donets basin, was his for the taking. There was nothing to stop him swarming on into Asiatic Russia except possibly a shortage of petrol. What should he aim for, what objective was there that would actually finish off the Russians? Their scorched-earth policy, emphasized by the blowing up of the Zaporozhe Dam which supplied power for the Dnieper bend industries, was hardly encouraging or likely to lead to realization of Hitler's prediction that the whole rotten structure would come crashing down. Von Rundstedt, therefore, in keeping with the broad directive of the whole campaign to prevent large bodies of Russian troops from retiring into the hinterland, had switched his *Panzers* back north in order to meet Guderian's drive south and so close the door on the huge prize of Kiev and nearly 750,000 Red Army troops.

Guderian's 24 *Panzer* Corps was being led by two *Panzer* divisional commanders, both wounded in the battle, who subsequently achieved fame. Lieutenant General (later Field Marshal) Walther Model of 3rd *Panzer* Division became known as the Führer's "Fireman" of 1944 because of a knack for putting out fires, that is, of restoring collapsing fronts both east and west. But now the future "Lion of the Defence" was displaying the dash and elan of a Rommel. General Ritter von Thoma, the Spanish Civil War tank expert who commanded 17th *Panzer* Division, was later to take over the *Afrika Korps* and be captured by the British at El Alamein. Once Model took the Desna bridges at Novgorod-Severskii, there would be no proper terrain obstacle between Guderian and Kleist. On 26 August Model's division punched into the town on the north bank of the marshy river. The Russians blew the small pedestrian bridge, but a headlong scramble by a special engineer assault detachment secured intact the vital 750-yard wooden road bridge. Lieutenant Störck calmly dealt with the final obstacle – an adapted aerial bomb planted right in the middle of the bridge – by unscrewing the detonator.

Model poured men and equipment along the vital artery to carve out a bridgehead that was to be proof against eight days of Soviet counter-attacks. Thoma's division made a crossing higher up the Desna and led a flank cordon that stretched and stretched to a N–S length of 155 miles but always just held against piecemeal Russian assault. On 9 September, despite late summer torrential rainstorms that churned roads into quagmires and dwindling fuel supplies, 3rd *Panzer* Division captured Romny, the last town before the pincers' rendezvous.

Meanwhile Kleist was about to join up with Guderian. His pincer had been held back so long lest the Russians recognize the threat of double envelopment too soon. On 12 September, the day snow first fell on the Eastern front, 16th *Panzer* division sliced 43 miles north after breaking out of the bridgehead at Kremenchug. The division's infantry needed a day and a half to master Lubny, fiercely defended by workers' militia and NKVD secret police. The closing pincer spearheads were still 60 miles apart. By the 15th, 3rd *Panzer* Division was down to ten battle-ready tanks but under Guderian's stimulus had struggled on beyond Lokhivitsa while the bulk of its units were still mudbound along the road back to Romny. Reconnaissance parties from *Panzergruppen* made contact and on the 16th the greatest encirclement of the entire Russo-German conflict was achieved. Twenty-two days after the opening of the battle 50 Soviet divisions had been trapped. Three days earlier Budenny, specially flown out, had finally been relieved of his command and Marshal Semyon K. Timoshenko, Stalin's indispensable "rescue" general, appointed in his place.

From 16–19 September the Second and Seventeenth German infantry armies closed in on Yagotin, target of the inner ring of encirclement, while Sixth Army took Kiev on 20 September. For the next week what became known as the Kiev cauldron – originally about 130 miles wide and deep – which for all its efforts outside the Red Army was not able to burst into and meet the belated breakout efforts begun during the night of the 17th–18th, was broken up by the Germans. Some six Soviet armies (5th, 21st, 26th, 27th, 38th and 40th) were either wholly or partially destroyed. One army commander extracted just 500 survivors. Besides having no proper direction, the Russian soldiers simply had not enough ammunition or fuel – two indispensable commodities of modern war – to conduct a co-ordinated battle of any sort. Courage they did have and in a series of fanatical and desperate counter-attacks made by men down to five bullets apiece were simply annihilated.

> During the fighting the words of Stalin, magnified to gigantic proportions by the loudspeakers, rain down upon the men kneeling in holes behind the tripods of their machine-guns, din in the ears of the soldiers lying amid the shrubs, of the wounded writhing in agony upon the ground. The loudspeaker imbues that voice with a harsh, brutal, metallic quality. There is something diabolical, and at the same time terribly naive about these soldiers who fight to the death, spurred on by Stalin's speech on the Soviet Constitution. By the slow deliberate recital of the moral, social, political and military precepts of the Commissars, about these soldiers who never surrender; about these dead, scattered all around me; about the final gestures, the stubborn, violent gestures of those men who died so terribly lonely a death on this battlefield, amid the deafening roar of the cannon and the ceaseless blaring of the loudspeaker.

The killing went on for the best part of a week, and then the surrenders began. Once they started they went on and on until over 600,000 Russian soldiers were prisoners. A colossal part of the Red Army, perhaps a third of its June 1941 strength, had been removed from the battle. It was not enough. No matter how many times Hitler might trumpet that "The Russian is finished," he obviously was not. The Russian Bear refused to lie down and expire. He insisted on fighting on. And within three months of their fantastic Kiev victory, something like despair was to grip leading German formations as they stumbled to a halt before Moscow and then began to withdraw.

For irony of all ironies, having condemned his generals' notions of capturing Moscow in no moderate terms – "Only

completely ossified brains, absorbed in the ideas of past centuries could see any worthwhile objective in taking the capital"
– Hitler insisted Moscow be captured. But he still made the fatal
mistake of trying to go for Leningrad and the Caucasus as well.
Soon after resuming his advance in the center, *two months* since
halting after the Smolensk battle, von Bock had taken another
600,000 prisoners and by 15 October his spearhead was at
Mozhaisk, a mere 65 miles from the capital. If even at that
point Hitler had gambled all, concentrating the dwindling tank
strength of all four *Panzergruppen* on the drive for Moscow,
while merely defending the northern and southern fronts, then
surely victory – if by that we mean destruction of the Soviet
armies defending Moscow and capture of the city itself – would
have been within his grasp. Instead he failed to observe the
never-to-be-forgotten principles of singleness of purpose and
concentration of resources to that end. By the time he had
realized it, the chill breath of winter and defeat was breathing
down the necks of ordinary soldier and High Command alike.

From the Russian point of view the greatest numerical
military catastrophe of their history was caused by Stalin's
refusal to give up his regime's tenuous ideological grip on
the Ukraine without a fight. Surely in this he may be judged
right for to have chucked his hand in there would simply have
given the Germans more time and resources to finish off the job
in the center. Moscow's loss might well have brought about a
total collapse of the Red Army's will to continue as opposed to
the willingness of hundreds of thousands of its soldiers to
surrender. The same sort of ideological and military question
mark had also been half-posed in 1919 during the Russian Civil
War when anti-Bolshevik forces were converging on Moscow
from all points of the compass. But given that the Ukraine was
to be defended in 1941, Budenny's defense ensured that had the
Germans been allowed to choose their enemy's response they
could not have done better. For the Germans indeed the battle
was a brilliantly executed operation of war – the technical and
tactical highpoint of the *Blitzkrieg* era.

Yet strategically it was a flop. All the slaughter, all the
advances, all the planning and controversy and triumph went
for nothing. The magnitude of Russia's resources proved equal

to the enormity of the loss. Four million out of her 10 million military casualties occurred in the first six months of almost four years' fighting, but in 1941 alone four million reserves were mobilized. Kiev was a second Cannae – but, as after the first, the losing side would fight on to eventual and total victory.

Leningrad (1941)

Alan Clark

What brought the *Wehrmacht* to a halt at the very gates of Leningrad in 1941? Was it the indomitable spirit of a beleaguered citizen army? Could it have been a breaking from within the German impetus in its thrust forward into Russia's vitals? Or was it the desperation of a population caught frighteningly between a German hammer and the anvil of Communist political oppression?

The three primary objectives for the Germans in their invasion of Russia on 22 June 1941 were the coal and iron fields of the Donet basin in the south, the capital, Moscow, in the centre, and the city of Leningrad at the extreme northern point of the front. And to each of these objectives the Germans had assigned a separate army group concentrating their tanks in *Panzer* groups. These were to clear the way and weld the chains of encirclement around the more cumbersome Soviet forces, whose surrender would be forced by the slower moving infantry divisions that followed in the *Panzers'* wake. In their advance, the Luga River was the last major obstacle facing the German army before the city of Leningrad. But on 8 August 1941 the Russian armies collapsed and the 41st *Panzer* Corps, commanded by General Georg-Hans Reinhardt, broke into open country. The German tanks had already travelled nearly 500 miles on their own tracks and the motorized equipment was overdue for servicing after six weeks of continuous use in the dust and summer heat of Northern Russia. The soldiers themselves were exhausted. They had had only four to six hours sleep a night: but morale was at its height. Now, they felt certain, there would be nothing to stop them capturing Leningrad, the ancient Tsarist capital.

The situation was severe enough for the Russian Chief of Staff, Major General D. N. Nikishev, to report two days later to Marshal Boris M. Shaposhnikov, the Red Army Chief of Staff: "The difficulty of restoring the situation lies in the fact that neither divisional commanders, army commanders, nor front [army group] commanders have any reserves at all. Every breach down to the tiniest has to be stopped up with scratch sections or units assembled any old how."

In the city itself, citizens were being conscripted ruthlessly into the *Opolchenye* (militia). But this was little more than an enthusiastic rabble, indifferently armed, without signals or communications equipment, and whose training had been confined to weekends in local Party camps. A contemporary Russian account says that "in addition to some rifles and machine-guns . . . the workers were armed mainly with Molotov cocktails and hand-grenades; they also had 10,000 shotguns and about 12,000 small calibre and training rifles donated by the city's population."

Gloomily, and with the threat of a firing squad hanging over him, Lieutenant General M. M. Popov, the Russian Commander in Chief of the Northern Front, reported to his superiors in Moscow: "To suppose that opposition to the German advance can be resisted by militia units just forming up, or badly organized units taken from the North-Western Front command after they have been pulled out of Lithuania and Latvia . . . is completely unjustified." And yet even at this moment a plan to storm Leningrad was not part of the German strategy. As early as 8 July Colonel General Franz Halder, the German army's Chief of Staff, had noted that: "It is the Führer's firm decision to level Moscow and Leningrad and make them uninhabitable, so as to relieve us of the necessity of feeding the population during the winter. The city will be razed by the Air Force. Tanks must not be used for the purpose." And on 15 July the

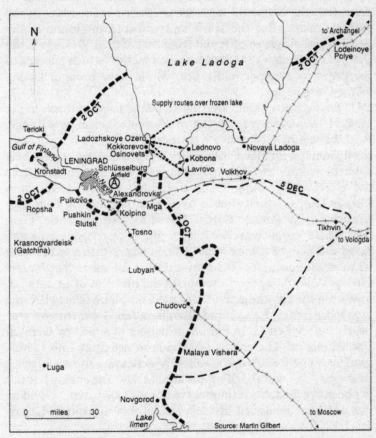

5.3 The Siege of Leningrad October 1941–January 1944

German Commander of Army Group North, Field Marshal Ritter von Leeb, was given express instructions that "the immediate mission is not to capture Leningrad but to encircle it."

It is possible that Gen. Reinhardt's corps could have driven without a halt to the Nevsky Prospect in those early August days; that the SS could have set up their headquarters in the Winter Palace. But the spirit and enforced discipline of the Soviet citizens was so different from that of their Western Allies that it is unlikely the German army's tactics (which succeeded the previous summer in France) would have brought lasting victory in Russia.

Then, between 14 and 18 August, all the Russian forces in the area, at the urgent prompting of Moscow, began to advance. And this counter-offensive – uncoordinated, extravagant, tactically inept, with masses of cavalry and unarmored lorries, with soldiers making costly frontal charges – did, nonetheless, have the effect of diverting General Erich von Manstein's 56th *Panzer* Corps, which should have been reinforcing Gen. Reinhardt's 41st *Panzer* Corps. For three critical weeks Gen. Manstein's corps marched and counter-marched across the dried-out marshes of the upper Illmen river, further exhausting its men and machines. It was not until September that *Panzer* Group IV could again contemplate the problem of Leningrad.

Within the city the activities of the Communist Party became ever more frenzied: "Comrade Leningraders! Dear friends! Our dearly beloved city is in imminent danger of attack by German Fascist troops. The enemy is striving to penetrate into Leningrad . . . The Red Army is valiantly defending the approaches to the city . . . and repelling his attacks. But the enemy has not yet been crushed, his resources are not yet exhausted . . . and he has not yet abandoned his despicable plan to capture Leningrad."

Marshal K. E. Voroshilov and Lt. Gen. A. A. Zhdanov organized a "Military Soviet for the defense of Leningrad" – an independent move which even at this time of acute danger was bitterly resented by Marshal Josef Stalin who expressed his "extreme dissatisfaction". Voroshilov's answer was that "it corresponded to the actual requirements of the situation." But Stalin brushed this aside and demanded "an immediate review of the personnel", and both Voroshilov and Zhdanov were dismissed.

In order to assert the Party supremacy over the Army, Foreign Ministers Vyacheslav M. Molotov and Georgi M. Malenkov were sent from the Committee for the Defense of State to replace them. A special order was issued to the troops:

> Individual soldiers, commanders, and political workers are forgetting . . . their pledge and are revealing in battle a criminal absent-mindedness, faint-heartedness, and cowardice. Not only are there commanders and political leaders who do not set an example of courage and audacity and do not carry along their soldiers by their example, but there are also loathsome self-seekers who hide in fox-holes and do not lead the fight. Such disgraceful individuals cannot be tolerated in the Red Army. Those who fail to perform their duties have no place in our ranks.

The rattle of firing-squads could stiffen discipline, but Party theorists were of small value in handling men in battle. And at the end of the month Stalin sent General Georgi K. Zhukov, who was given absolute power. In his day, Zhukov was to visit and stabilize in turn every dangerous sector of the Eastern Front. Few commanders, with the possible exception of Montgomery before Alam Halfa in North Africa, can have arrived at their headquarters with so little time to spare.

On the German side, Wilhelm Ritter von Leeb was clear about his personal ambition – to seize Leningrad, the most prestigious prize of the campaign, by force, thus confirming entitlement to his field-marshal's baton. But Hitler had different ideas. His imprecise instructions were: "to level the town, make it uninhabitable and relieve us of the necessity of having to feed the population through the winter." The German High Command were against getting involved with the civilian population at all. One of them, Lieutenant General Walther Warlimont, prepared a memorandum. "Normal" occupation was rejected. It might be acceptable to evacuate the children and the old people "and let the remainder starve," but this could lead to "new problems". Perhaps the best solution, said

Lt. Gen. Warlimont, would be to seal off the whole town, and surround it with an electrically charged wire fence, guarded by machine-guns. But there remained the danger of epidemics spreading to the German front.

In case Warlimont's proposals should be adopted, corps commanders were alerted to the need for using artillery against civilians trying to break out of the city. It was thought "doubtful whether the infantry will shoot at women and children trying to break out."

There was also the possibility of the Germans making propaganda capital out of the affair. It was suggested that an approach be made to: "the philanthropist Roosevelt to send either food supplies to the inhabitants not going into captivity, or to send neutral ships under the supervision of the Red Cross, or to ship them off to his continent." Naturally, any response to this which threatened to assume real shape would not have been accepted.

The proper solution was to: "Seal off Leningrad hermetically, then weaken it by terror [air raids and artillery bombardment] and growing starvation. In the spring we shall occupy the town . . . remove the survivors into captivity in the interior of Russia, and level Leningrad to the ground with high explosives."

But first the Russian defenders had to be put to rout. Unfortunately for von Leeb's plans, Führer-Directive No 35, issued on 6 September, ordered the diversion of the whole of General Erich Hoepner's *Panzer* Group IV to Army Group Center, where it was to participate in the attack on Moscow. The 8th Air Corps, of close-support dive-bombers, was to co-operate. But Leeb ignored this signal. His plans for a final assault were already complete. By taking advantage of a provision in the Directive that the redeployment be subject to "first achieving a close encirclement" he staged what was, in effect, a full-scale assault on the city's defenses, with the 1st *Panzer* Division following the left bank of the Neva and 6th *Panzer* straddling the main railway to Leningrad from the south.

Both divisions were soon enmeshed in a net of anti-tank ditches and straggling earthworks which had been thrown up by the construction battalions and *Opolchenye* during the previous weeks. These defenses were often poorly sited and crudely finished, but they were extensive. The Russians were seriously deficient in artillery, and indeed in all arms not produced on the spot at Leningrad and its environs. But they had a large number of medium and heavy mortars whose weight of fire, at the ranges of the first day's battle, was nearly as effective as regular field artillery.

On the coastal sector, between the sea and Krasnoye Seloe, the 12-in guns of the Baltic fleet pounded away at the German rear. Over the battlefield, massive KV tanks roamed singly and in pairs, manned sometimes by civilian testers and mechanics from the Kirov factory where they were still being produced at the rate of about four a day. This was the kind of close in-fighting where Russian courage, obstinacy, cunning in camouflage and ambush more than counterbalanced the deficiencies in command and technique which had crippled them in the open battlefields on the frontier and on the Luga.

The *Panzers*, in contrast, were suffering as armored troops always do when they encounter close defenses after weeks of mobile fighting. Like the British 8th Army when it hit the Tunisian mountains after months in Libya, the tank commanders took fearful punishment as they sought to adapt their tactics in an unfamiliar element. In the first day of the assault four successive commanders of 6th *Panzer* were casualties.

By the evening of 10 September the Germans had penetrated as far as the last line of Russian defenses, which ran along the crest of some shallow eminences known as the Dudergof heights – about six miles to the south-east of Leningrad. During the night many of the tanks of the leading division, 1st *Panzer*, lay out on the battlefield, forward of the main German positions, and fought throughout the hours of darkness to beat off the succession of counter-attacks which the Russians always put in during the night.

By the glare of blazing petrol bottles and sodium flares the Germans broke up one Russian formation after another as they assembled to charge the positions captured during the day. At first light, the *Stuka* dive bombers returned to the battlefield and 41st *Panzer* Corps braced itself for "one last heave". The 1st *Panzer* had lost so many tanks that there was only one battalion left with over 50 per cent effective strength, yet they gradually inched their way forward during the day and by 1600 had scaled "Height 167", a hill 450 ft high, the topmost point in the Dudergof ridge to the south-east of the city.

"In front of the victorious troops stood the city of Leningrad in the sunlight, only 12 kilometres away, with its golden cupolas and towers and its port with warships that tried with their heaviest guns to deny us possession of the heights."

On the left flank of the *Panzer* corps the infantry were slowly edging their way across the valley, and once the Russian guns and observers had been cleared off Height 167 the Germans were able to make better progress, entering the suburban districts of Slutsk and Pushkin, and, on the evening of 11 September, Krasnoye Seloe.

By 12 September, the fourth day of the assault, it was painfully obvious to the *OKH* that a full-blooded engagement was raging in an area from which they were trying to draw reinforcement. Col. Gen. Halder ordered F. M. Leeb that the city "was not to be taken, but merely encircled. The attack should not go beyond the Peterfog– Pushkin road." For another five days close fighting continued although at a diminishing tempo. The German resources were not enough to cope with the dilution of their technical superiority which street fighting imposed.

The only alternative to closing down the operation was massive reinforcement on a scale which, one year later, was to be granted to Field-Marshal Friedrich Paulus at Stalingrad. Halder wrote the epitaph of the battle in the *OKH* diary: "The ring around Leningrad has not yet been drawn as tightly as might be desired, and further progress after the departure of 1st *Panzer* and 26th Motorized from that front is doubtful. Considering the drain on our forces on the Leningrad front, where the enemy has concentrated large forces and great quantities of material, the situation will remain critical until hunger takes effect as our ally."

The weight now shifted from the Red Army's soldiers in Leningrad's defenses to the civilian population, although the Communist Party continued for some months to direct its energies at "stiffening" the army in case a further assault should develop. A "letter campaign" from schoolchildren mailed every infantryman with a stilted request that "you at the front must strike harder at the enemy who had the gall to attack our great cities and villages", and resolutions were constantly sent out from the factory workers to the soldiers in the field:

> With great pain and bitterness we hear that among you there are sometimes cowards and deserters . . . The coward and deserter thinks that he will succeed in hiding from the people's censure and anger. He is mistaken. He will be cursed by his own mother, his wife will turn from him, his name will be spoken with loathing by his own children. With hatred and contempt – that is how his friends and comrades will greet him. A bullet in the head is what such a scoundrel and self-seeker will get.

September passed, and October, and with the leaves stripped from the trees along the Neva came the first frosts, followed by snowfalls. Food was already short, for supplies had not been stockpiled in the town. The German advance to Schlusselburg had occurred so suddenly and the demand for purely military items such as ammunition had been so acute that very little had been brought into the town before the ring of encirclement was sealed.

In two months, and before the ice on Lake Ladoga began to harden, everything that was edible in the city was consumed. Rats were considered a great delicacy. So too was the earth that came from near the Badaev warehouses where the sugar and chocolate had been stored and which had been burned down in one of the *Luftwaffe* raids. As winter tightened its grip, fuel became as scarce as food.

One Leningrader remembered:

> First, the feeling of being cold. One gets up with it, one walks with it, one goes to bed with it. It seems to wander around somewhere under the skin; it penetrates the bones and sometimes it seems as if it even enters the brain. One can't escape from it. It penetrates under all shirts, sweaters, and jackets, no matter how many one puts on. The second is the feeling of hunger. This feeling has many

shadings – from a dull, painful, sharp, unbearable one, which appears as soon as one has eaten one's ration of 125 grammes, to being tortured by fantasies.

Soviet records show that of the 26,600 persons who took the basic civilian military training course (the *Vzevobuch* programme) in the month of November over 6,000 were too ill or weak to finish the course. Of these 800 died of starvation while under training. Another 10,000 were so frail that they could only be given a short course. Trainees were very reluctant to fail as an allocation to the front-line units meant a different and improved ration scale. As fuel ran out so was electricity power confined to military use from emergency generators. In the short days of November and December, Leningrad must have seemed a city of the dead, shrouded in snow and freezing mists from the Baltic, without light or movement. In the factories, starving and frozen workers toiled for 14 hours a day making armaments, many dropping dead at their lathes.

Medical attention for civilians was virtually nil. In hospitals

the absence of electricity, heat, and water made work extremely difficult. The temperature in the wards usually stood between 30° and 35° Fahrenheit. The patients lay fully clothed, with coats and blankets, and sometimes even mattresses, piled on top of them. The walls were covered with frost. During the night water froze in pitchers. The hunger had the effect of causing diarrhea among the patients, many of whom from weakness were unable to use the bedpans. Sheets on the beds were filthy – no water for laundering. The only medicine available was sodium bromide, which the doctors prescribed under various names.

The only hope for Leningrad was to bring supplies across the ice on Lake Ladoga from the harbors of Lednevo and Kabana to Osinovets. The lake was not smooth ice. October gales had made the ice pile up in irregular heaps and there were always some crevasses that never froze. On 18 November, when the ice was only 5 in thick, a small reconnaissance party made the crossing on foot followed by a man on horseback, and for a few days supplies were brought in by ponies drawing sleds with light loads. The first truck column on 24 November lost nine of its vehicles crashing through gaps in the ice into the water. Only two of the drivers survived. But by the end of November there were 500 trucks in use, battling against arctic blizzards, mechanical breakdowns and constant strafing by the *Luftwaffe*.

It was not until January that the ice was thick enough to allow trucks to carry full loads. Few survived more than three journeys on the ice and over 1,000 trucks were lost before the middle of January when the ice was 3 ft thick and could bear almost any load. Yet, in spite of the efforts on the "ice road", Leningrad never had more than one or two days of food in hand. Even during the previous October the bread ration had been reduced to 400 grammes a day for workers and 200 grammes for other categories and on 20 November these were reduced to 250 and 125 grammes. Under these conditions it was simply a matter of waiting for death by starvation. A schoolgirl, Tania Savich, kept a diary:

Jenia died on 28 December, 1941, at 12.30 a.m.
Grandmother died on 25 January, 1942.
Lena died on 17 March, 1942.
Uncle Lesha died on 10 May, at 4.00 p.m.
13 May, at 7.30 a.m. darling Mama died.

Then Tania herself died.
A Leningrad doctor describes his experiences:

I entered without knocking. My eyes beheld a horrible sight. A dark room, the wall covered with frost, puddles of water on the floor. Lying across some chairs was the corpse of a 14-year-old boy. In a baby carriage was a second corpse, that of a tiny infant. On the bed lay the owner of the room, K. K. Vandel – dead. At her side, rubbing her chest with a towel, stood her eldest daughter, Mikkau. . . . In one day Mikkau lost her mother, a son, and a brother who perished from hunger and cold. At the entrance, barely standing on her feet from weakness, was a neighbor, Kizunova, her horrified gaze fixed on the dead. She, too, died the next day.

Had the Germans been as skilled at offensive warfare under winter conditions as the Soviet Army it is possible that a surprise assault in that first bitter winter of 1941–2 might have overcome its emaciated garrison and populace.

The awful winter passed, and during the spring and early summer of 1942 the reinforcement of Leningrad by the sea route across Lake Ladoga gathered momentum. Freight steadily increased from 1,500 tons in May to 3,500 tons in June, and the ships took out wounded and non-combatants instead of returning empty. It gradually became apparent to the Germans that Leningrad was threatening their extreme northern flank, and plans were laid for a full-scale assault.

For this, Manstein's 11th Army, which had by now fought a successful Crimean campaign culminating in the capture of Sevastopol, was given the support, once again, of the 8th Air Corps. In addition, a special siege train of 800 heavy artillery pieces was concentrated round the city. But the German plans were foiled by a series of spoiling attacks which the Russians launched at the end of August. Before Manstein had completed the deployment of his forces most of the German resources were used up in preventing the rupture of their corridor to Lake Ladoga.

At the beginning of 1943 the siege was lifted when the Red Army succeeded in forcing a narrow passage about five miles wide along the southern shore of Lake Ladoga and a rail link was established. From then – although the siege of Leningrad was effectively over – the city's fate was ultimately dependent on the outcome of the great battles that raged in southern Russia.

With hindsight we can see that the Germans might have rushed the city in August of 1941. Had the Germans been able to fight aggressively in the depths of winter their best chance would have been at Christmas 1941 when the citizens and the soldiers' spirits were at their lowest. But the intractable problem remained: highly trained and disciplined troops lose their advantage when dispersed over acres of rubble. Street fighting places a premium on numbers and tenacity. It is unlikely that the Germans could ever have succeeded in storming Leningrad any more than (with much greater resources) they could have been successful at Stalingrad the following year.

But they did come very near to starving the city out. Was it the iron discipline and terror of the Communist Party system that kept it alive?

Pearl Harbor (1941)

Paul Hutchinson

"All hands, general quarters! Air raid! This is no drill!" The alarm sounded for an attack that was to kill 2,403 American citizens as well as cripple her Pacific Fleet. But the Japanese attack on Pearl Harbor on 7 December 1941 was the key that released the unrivalled military might of the US. The eventual fate of the fascist powers – both east and west – was sealed.

Japan's strike at Pearl Harbor is often presented as a surprise attack on the US Navy, yet relations between the two countries were so strained because of Japan's colonizing policies it was practically inevitable that, for Japan to get her expansionist way in Asia, she would have to use force against the US.

In May 1940 the US Pacific Fleet was moved from San Diego to Pearl Harbor. The Fleet had been taking part in maneuvers off Hawaii the previous month and was ordered to stay in Pearl Harbor by Roosevelt when the exercises were finished. This decision did much to spur Japan into signing the Tripartite Pact with Italy and Germany the following September.

By mid-1940 it seemed that the fascist powers were everywhere triumphant. Nazi Germany controlled the better part of Europe and looked menacingly towards Britain from the coast of France. Meanwhile, Imperial Japan was locked in her expansionist war with China – a conflict of almost unsurpassed brutality. America was deeply involved in the fight against the aggressors in both theaters and short of military intervention was giving all possible help.

Public opinion in the US was deeply split over whether or not to go to war, with the majority firmly in the isolationist camp. But President Franklin D. Roosevelt saw clearly enough that unless the dictatorships were defeated the US's own independence would eventually be threatened.

On 27 September 1940 Japan joined the Axis when she entered into a tripartite pact with Germany and Italy. Under the terms of this agreement "the leadership of Japan in the establishment of a New Order in Greater East Asia" was acknowledged. By this time Britain had been pressured into closing an important life-line to China – the Burma Road. America imposed a partial embargo on exports to Japan. This embargo was later intensified and anything regarded as a strategic war material was included in the restrictions.

It soon became painfully clear in Tokyo that Japan's empire-building conquests in Asia could not possibly continue for much longer without the raw materials of war – especially oil.

Relations between America and Japan continued to deteriorate into 1941 and an armed clash appeared increasingly likely. But US naval strategists did not think an attack on Pearl Harbor at all likely. According to them, such an action would be an impressive but rather pointless piece of sabre rattling – yielding Japan no great benefits. It was for the same reason that the Japanese rejected the idea when it was proposed by Admiral Isoruku Yamamoto in September 1941. Its lack of any military value apart, an attack on Pearl Harbor would snap the already strained relations between the two countries and all-out war would result.

Yamamoto – himself opposed to war with America – kept his faith in the viability of his plan. He had put the finishing touches to this as early as the spring of 1941. But for the attack to succeed, Yamamoto realized that absolute security was essential. There was in existence a cryptographic code which enabled Japanese naval officers to communicate with no risk of American interception reading their messages. Another risk to security in a venture of such importance was the inevitable prolonged argument and counter-argument within the Japanese

High Command. The chances of a "leak" were enormous, so Yamamoto bypassed the High Command altogether and approached Emperor Hirohito's brother Prince Takamatsu, then a navy staff officer based in Tokyo. He was intrigued and told his brother, who gave the go-ahead for the idea to be studied in secret.

As relations between Japan and the US went from bad to worse, Yamamoto trained his men. The harbor at Kagoshima was chosen for dummy dive-bombing and torpedo dropping because the lie of the land was similar to that of Pearl Harbor.

In late July the French were pressured into handing over Southern Indochina to the Japanese. America retaliated promptly. Japanese assets in the US were immediately frozen and the partial embargo already imposed on strategic material was made total. Britain and Holland joined in the economic boycott. The stark choice facing Japan was certain economic collapse or an armed clash. War with the US was no longer a question of "if" – only "when". Unless the flow of oil was swiftly resumed Japan would have to abandon the Chinese mainland – an intolerable loss of face for the military. The absolute deadline for a solution was October.

Talks were held throughout the summer and autumn of 1941. Cordell Hull, American Secretary of State, made his country's position clear – all sanctions would be lifted only if Japan took her forces out of China and Indochina. But the negotiations were nothing but a device for buying time. Hull knew perfectly well that Japan would never accede to such a demand. Despite the pleadings of the Japanese Prime Minister, Prince Fumimaro Konoye, the Emperor and War Minister General Hideki Tojo refused to countenance any compromise. They were convinced of Japanese invincibility against all comers. "The day after war begins we will have to issue an Imperial Declaration of War. Please see to it," Emperor Hirohito told his Lord Privy Seal, Koichi Kido, on 13 October.

Also in October, the US was warned of a planned strike on Pearl Harbor by an unusual source. Richard Sorge, Moscow's master spy in Tokyo, had passed the information to Josef V. Stalin, who in turn had informed Washington. But American naval strategists still considered an attack on Pearl Harbor unlikely.

Anxious for a peaceful settlement with the US, but outnumbered in the cabinet and overruled by his emperor, Prince Konoye resigned as Prime Minister on 16 October 1941. The extreme hawk Gen. Tojo took his place. At this point the Japanese Ambassador in Washington, Kichisaburu Nomura, asked Tokyo to recall him. His request was refused and the expert diplomat Saburo Kurusu was dispatched to buy time by supervising yet another round of "negotiations".

At this point it is worth speculating whether President Roosevelt was really ignorant of Japan's aggressive intentions. Apart from Richard Sorge's warning, the President also had access to *Magic* information – the decoded transcriptions of Japanese secret messages. It has also been suggested that Churchill thought that a Japanese attack on Pearl Harbor would demolish the case of the isolationists and bring America into the war and that Roosevelt agreed.

On 5 November Japan decided to make one more diplomatic approach to Washington before unleashing the now fully rehearsed attack on Pearl Harbor. This approach was sure to fail and was not intended to succeed – merely to give Japan the international veneer of "peacemaker". Presuming the breakdown of the talks, the Japanese Supreme Command's operational orders ended with: "War with the Netherlands, America, England inevitable; general operational preparations to be completed by early December."

Also on 5 November, the US Chiefs of Staff (Army and Navy) met Roosevelt to discuss the Far East. A month before, Generalissimo Chiang Kai-Shek, the Chinese Nationalist leader, had pleaded with America and Britain for help. US Secretary of State Cordell Hull feared that any further aid to China would provoke Japanese retaliation and General George Crook and Admiral Harold R. Stark urged the President to tread carefully. But it was resolved that if Japan undertook any military action against British, Dutch or US territory, America would intervene militarily.

After this decision the November talks between the two sides had no meaning whatever. Japan demanded a totally unacceptable retreat from America's stated position and tied her diplomats to a deadline of 29 November. This came and went with nothing resolved.

The force destined to attack Pearl Harbor had left Japan almost a fortnight before the 29th and congregated at Tankan Bay in the Kurile Islands. It was a powerful force – six aircraft carriers and nine destroyers, with tankers and supply ships, two cruisers and two battleships in support. Twenty ocean-going submarines acted as an advanced guard. Five of these were equipped with two-man midget subs. This force, commanded by the brilliant Vice Admiral Chuichi Nagumo, was the cream of the Imperial Japanese Navy.

On 26 November, the strong armada left the Kuriles and set course for Pearl Harbor – adopting a route that would bring them towards the US Pacific Fleet from the north. Japanese met forecasters had told the task force that the weather was expected to be bad in the regions it would pass through. This would make the necessary refuelling tricky, but if they approached from the north there was less chance of being spotted by the Americans.

By 6 December, American naval strategists were still saying an attack on Pearl Harbor was most unlikely. Their grounds for such confidence were the unequivocal reports from US and British reconnaissance planes that Japan was launching a full-scale amphibious operation in the south, and Japanese ships laden with soldiers were reportedly entering the Gulf of Siam. American opinion could not accept the idea that Japan was capable of mounting two naval operations at the same time.

As dawn broke on 7 December, the Japanese carrier force had reached a position 275 miles north of Pearl Harbor. Fifty-one Aichi "Val" dive-bombers, 43 Mitsubishi Zero-Sens "Zeke" fighters, 40 Nakajima B5N2 "Kate" bombers with shallow-running torpedoes and 50 high-level "Kates" left the decks at 0600. Eighty Vals, 54 Kates and 36 Zeros followed up.

The ships lying at anchor at Pearl Harbor were charged to keep a "Condition 3" state of preparedness. Every fourth gun was supposed to be manned. But as America still regarded herself precariously at peace, none of the main guns was manned and the ammunition for the machine-guns was in locked boxes. The keys were in the charge of officers – some of whom were not even on duty.

A boatswain's mate saw between 20 and 25 aircraft approaching at 0730 but he could not see who they belonged to. All doubt was dispelled when the first bomb dropped just before 0800. Pearl Harbor's naval commander, Admiral Husband E. Kimmel, got the news of the attack three minutes later. Naval air commander, Rear-Admiral Bellinger, broadcast the words that were to smash the isolationist grip on America: "Air Raid, Pearl Harbor, this is no drill!"

Even the ambitious Yamamoto could scarcely have hoped for a more total surprise attack. The US Pacific Fleet was caught with its pants well and truly down. Blunders and bad luck brought about this American debacle. One certain blunder was when two NCOs, manning a radar station, saw Japanese planes closing in and watched them for 40 minutes. They tried to raise the alarm by telephone, but failed to contact anybody who believed their report. USS *Ward* gave another warning at 0645 when she sank a midget submarine at the mouth of Pearl Harbor. This too was ignored.

"Tora–Tora–Tora!" (Attack, attack, attack!) Commander Mitsuo Fuchida, in charge of the first wave, signalled to his airmen at 0749. Six minutes later the bombs began to fall. Their target was Battleship Row – eight battleships at the SE of Ford Island. Low-flying torpedo Kates roared in on the hapless ships. Four of them were holed or damaged in five minutes. While the Kates punished the vessels below the waterline, Vals were busy smashing decks, bridges and gun turrets. Other Kates were finishing off the job with high-level bombing.

The initial attack inflicted shattering losses on the Pacific Fleet. USS *Arizona* (32,600 tons) blew up and snapped in two. More than 1,000 men were drowned. The carnage continued when three torpedoes smashed into *Oklahoma* (29,000 tons). She turned over – imprisoning what was left of her crew below decks. When holes were later cut in her bottom only 32 survivors crawled out. A total of five hits – four torpedo, one bomb – put paid to the 31,800-ton *West Virginia*, while the *California* (32,600 tons) blazed for three days after fires reached her fuel tanks. Then she sank.

USS *Nevada* (29,000 tons) tried to steam out of the harbor, but Japanese bombers caught her and she finally beached on a mudflat at the entrance to the harbor. *Maryland* and *Tennessee* escaped relatively lightly. They were shielded from torpedoes by *Oklahoma* and *West Virginia*, which were moored on the seaward side. The 33,100-ton flagship of the US Pacific Fleet, *Pennsylvania*, was in drydock and was more or less unscathed at the end of the attack.

The old battleship *Utah* had been in use as a target ship for some time before the Japanese attack. Denuded of her superstructure, from the air she looked like an aircraft carrier. Japanese pilots expended valuable torpedoes on this worthless relic.

At the NW shore of the harbor Japanese aircraft damaged the light cruiser *Helena* and the seaplane tender *Curtiss*, while the light cruiser *Raleigh* was crippled. The minelayer *Oglala* was sunk. The destroyers *Shaw*, *Cassin* and *Downes*, the light cruiser *Honolulu* and the repair ship *Vestal* all suffered damage.

While the Pacific Fleet in the harbor was being pulverized, the airfields on the mainland were also taking a hammering. At the US Marine Corps' Ewa Field were 49 airworthy planes. By the time the Japanese were through with them only 16 remained intact. Kaneohe was a flying-boat base equipped with 36 Catalinas. After the attack an incredible 27 were complete write-offs while six others were severely damaged. This was one of the most punishing attacks on air bases in the Second World War. Of 148 first-line naval aircraft, at least 112 were destroyed, as were 52 out of the 129 Army planes. Thirty-eight American planes did take off. Ten of them were shot down.

The first Japanese wave then departed. Its attack had lasted 25 minutes. In that time thousands of American lives had been lost and millions of dollars worth of strategic weaponry destroyed. But there was more to come.

At 0845, 36 Zekes, 54 torpedo Kates and 80 high-level Kates provided Japan's second wave. But now the Americans had woken up and were a little more prepared. Shore batteries opened up as did still-serviceable ships' guns. Japan lost only nine planes in the first wave. In the second the score rose to 20 in return for little effect – its value being confined to finishing off already crippled installations. The submarine base escaped unscathed as did the fuel depot. Here was stockpiled almost as much oil as Japan had in her entire reserves.

President Roosevelt spoke of the "day that shall live in infamy." If it was, it was also a day of appalling military cost to the United States. The Japanese had lost 29 aircraft and 55 men. For this meager expenditure 2,403 soldiers, sailors, airmen and civilians had been killed, 164 planes destroyed and six battleships and three destroyers sunk, while a number of others had been badly damaged. Apart from the dead, the Japanese left 1,178 wounded Americans in Pearl Harbor. The only section of the US Pacific Fleet to escape damage was its carrier force. It was not at Pearl Harbor at the time of the attack.

If the Japanese had sent in a third wave – as Cdr Fuchida wanted – there is little doubt that they could have totally devastated Pearl Harbor. But Fuchida did not have his way. Vice-Adm. Nagumo, the task force commander, believed that he and his men had done more than a good day's work and the effectiveness of the strike had certainly surpassed all expectation. His force turned tail and settled down to a quiet journey home to Japan.

At 1347 Washington time, news of the attack reached Cordell Hull. Abruptly breaking off the now pointless diplomatic wrangle he unceremoniously dismissed Nomura from his presence.

The isolationist grip on America was at last smashed and she was now at war with Japan. The attack on Pearl Harbor, while brilliantly successful in itself, unleashed the might of the US military machine against Japan, as well as her German and Italian partners. For Japan the end would not come until she was utterly demoralized and Hiroshima and Nagasaki had been flattened by the atom-bomb. The entry of America into the war ensured the eventual defeat of fascism in both theaters.

Singapore (1942)

C. C. M. Macleod-Carey

It was Friday, 13 February 1942 and I was watching the sun rise from my Command Post on top of Mount Faber, Singapore. The rays from the red orb of the sun radiated in ever widening shafts of red; just like the old "Rising Sun" flag of Japan used to be.

I remember that I was feeling pretty gloomy at the time but this evil omen gave me an uncomfortable sense of impending doom. Singapore at that time was obviously in its death throes and there seemed to be very little future in it. The Japanese Army had driven right down the length of Malaya and the city was closely besieged by a ruthless and efficient enemy.

About midnight the following night, a signal came from HQ at Fort Canning saying an unidentified ship had been located just outside the minefield covering the entrances to Keppel Harbour and that no British ship was in the area. I was at that time second-in-command of the 7th Coast Artillery Regiment covering Keppel Harbour with its powerful armament of 15-in, 9.2-in, 6-in and a host of other smaller weapons. There was another similarly equipped regiment defending the Naval Base at Changi. I rang up the Port War Signal Station, our line with the Navy, which was manned by sailors. There was no reply and we discovered later that it had been evacuated but for some reason no one had informed us. I then ordered the 6-in batteries

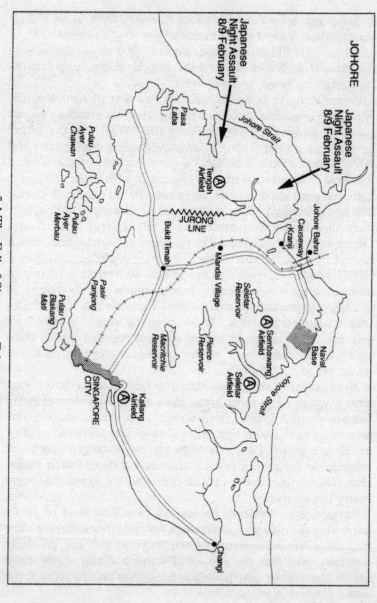

5.4 The Fall of Singapore, February 1942

JOHORE

Japanese
Night Assault
8/9 February

Japanese
Night Assault
8/9 February

Johore Strait

Pasa Laba

Pulau Ayer Chawan

Pulau Ayer Merbau

Tengah Airfield

JURONG LINE

Bukit Timah

Mandai Village

Seletar Reservoir

Johore Bahru

Causeway

Kranji

Naval Base

Pasir Panjong

Macritchie Reservoir

Pierce Reservoir

Sembawang Airfield

Seletar Airfield

Pulau Blakang Mati

SINGAPORE CITY

Kallang Airfield

Johore Strait

Changi

at Serapong, Siloso and Labrador to sweep the area with their searchlights. Almost immediately a ship which seemed to be of 8,000 tons was illuminated at a range of 7,000 yards, just outside the minefield. We challenged the ship by Aldis lamp but the reply, also by lamp, was incorrect.

Fortunately, in order to assist in this sort of situation, the Navy had posted an excellent rating who was standing by my side. We had a copy of *Jane's Fighting Ships* and the rating pointed to a photograph of a Japanese landing craft carrier and said, "I reckon that's it, sir." I gave the order "Shoot" and within seconds all six 6-in guns opened up with a roar. The guns had been permanently sited, and even without radar, which had not been installed, their instruments and range-finding gear were so accurate that preliminary ranging was unnecessary. Direct hits were scored at once. Flames, sparks and debris started flying in all directions. The crew could be seen frantically trying to lower boats but it was all over in a matter of minutes, after which the ship just disappeared into the sea.

This action was reported to Fort Canning but it is strange that it has never, so far as I know, been mentioned in an official account. Most likely the record was lost together with a good many other documents in the subsequent events after the surrender of Singapore.

Next morning we were ordered to fire the guns at the very large number of oil tanks situated on the islands around Pulau Bukum about 3.5 miles from Keppel. Something like 200,000 tons of oil were set on fire. After that we were ordered to blow up all the guns. This was achieved by placing a charge of gelignite in the breech of each gun and another in their magazines. Time fuses were lit and the resulting explosions were pretty impressive.

Singapore in its death throes has been described in all its harrowing details by a good many writers. It is not a pretty story but the overriding factor of which everyone was painfully conscious was that the supply of water had just about dried up. In fact, troops were having to break into houses to get at the water remaining in the cisterns.

On the evening of 15 February, the gunners manning the Command Post on Mount Faber had been joined by a small

Indian Commando unit and were holding a line across the main road near Keppel Golf Course below Mount Faber. At about sunset we distinctly heard Japanese troops farther up the road shouting "Banzai!" "Banzai!" "Banzai!" Shortly afterwards orders were received from Fort Canning that we were to cease fire and we were informed that the great fortress of Singapore had surrendered. The Coast Artillery had done its best and the fact is that the power and efficiency of its armament had the effect which it was designed for. It was exceedingly unlikely that the Japanese naval forces would be so rash as to make a frontal attack on Singapore because it is doubtful if they would have survived the encounter.

The plans for countering the expected invasion of Malaya by the Japanese were based on this factor and they were well conceived. The 11th Indian Division was poised on the frontier of Malaya and Thailand in December 1941, and Operation Matador was to send 11th Indian Division into Thailand and occupy the beaches at Singora and Sungei Patanie before the Japanese landed. British officers dressed in plain clothes and riding bicycles had been sent into Thailand to reconnoiter the area, where they met Japanese officers doing precisely the same thing. Air reconnaissance had reported large numbers of Japanese transports heavily escorted by warships and yet Operation Matador was called off for political reasons. So we got off to a bad start and our troops were caught on the "wrong foot". It soon became apparent that Japanese methods of warfare were totally different from ours and we had an awful lot to learn.

Part of my job was to direct the fire of the coast guns on to landward targets. It was mostly harassing fire, sometimes at the request of the Army and sometimes at targets picked at random, such as likely landing places on the north and west side of Singapore Island. There was no possible means of observing and correcting the fall of shot at 27,000 yards (15.3 miles) or more, so what the results were, goodness only knows. The only live Japanese I saw was a little perisher perched on top of a telescopic mast where he was probably spotting for his own guns. He was about three miles from where I was watching with my binoculars and just behind the grandstand of the racecourse near Burkit Timah. I turned the Connaught 9.2-in battery on to him and fired about thirty rounds. The little man disappeared in a cloud of smoke, dust and debris most of which came from the grandstand. Coast Artillery was not designed for this job but it certainly made a lot of noise, particularly the 15-in guns, whose flashes at night were quite spectacular. It was all a matter of firing at map references and hoping for the best.

I am anxious to dispel the myth that the Coast Artillery did not turn round and shoot at the enemy, so I propose to deal with each of the main batteries in turn.

The searchlights were manned by locally enlisted Malays who deserted overnight the day before the surrender. They just vanished – with one exception. He was a half-caste whom we promoted to Bombardier because he spoke English and Malay fluently and was very useful. He stayed and the curious thing is that he reported to me a month later in Colombo (Ceylon) and asked me if he could be sent back to Malaya. Intelligence grabbed him, gave him a course of training and, eventually landed him with a wireless set on the coast of Malaya. I hope he survived.

The following is an account of the actions of the Coast Artillery batteries.

Faber Fire Command

Pasir Laba Bty.   Fired at the Japanese crossing Johore Strait in boats but the battery was a sitting duck for the Japanese who brought up mortars and lobbed bombs from concealed positions until the battery was put out of action. The guns were blown up and the detachments withdrew.

Buona Vista Bty.   When Vickers installed the two 15-in guns in 1938 they fitted Magslip cables that were too short for all-round traverse. These cables carried an electric impulse from the Plotting Room to actuate the dials on the guns. The result was that stops were put on the traversing arcs of the guns which prevented them from pointing inland. The Japanese broke into the battery area but were driven out by the gunners and Australian infantry. The guns were then blown up and the personnel marched to Mount Faber and next day were attached to an infantry battalion with their battery CO Major Phillip Jackson.

Siloso and Labrador Btys. Both batteries fired a good deal of HE at Japanese troops advancing along the coast road through Pasir Panjang. It was reported to me by an infantry sergeant that the guns had caused a lot of Japanese casualties.

Serapong and Silingsing Btys. Owing to hills and buildings, they were not well sited to fire inland and I do not know whether they actually fired or not. It is possible that they fired counter-battery programs.

Connaught Bty. The three 9.2-in guns fired a considerable amount of ammunition including all their 90 HE rounds. Targets which I know were engaged included Johore Bahru, right across Singapore Island, where the Japanese had their HQ, possible landing places on the south bank of Johore Strait, a tank attack on the Bukit Timah road, Tengah Airfield, Jurong road and the Japanese artillery spotter already mentioned. Also counter-battery programs.

Changi Fire Command

Most of the action took place on the western side of the island. It is difficult to obtain accurate information on this Fire Command but it is obvious that the guns could only in many cases have been fired at extreme range.

Johore Bty. I do know that the three 15-in guns fired a great deal of their AP ammunition, notably at Johore Bahru and the reservoir area. They had all-round traverse but they had to knock down some of the concrete emplacements in order to get the shields round. Colonel Masanobu Tsuji, Chief of Staff Japanese Twenty-Fifth Army (Lieutenant General Tomoyuki Yamashita), records coming under their fire on the newly captured Tengah Airfield (11 February). Abandoning his car, he was blown into a ditch and watched the 50-ft-wide shell-holes appear around the drainage pipe he crawled into.

Tekong Bty. The three 9.2-in guns fired at several targets including the 400 Japanese landing on Pulau Ubin island.

Counter Battery An organization was hastily set up with OPs (observation posts) on the tops of high buildings such as the Kathay Building and other places. Bearings of enemy gun flashes were fed into an operation room, probably in Fort Canning.

There must have been plenty of enemy batteries to neutralize. The Japanese did not make great use of their artillery in their advance through Malaya, relying mostly on their infantry guns and mortars which they were very expert at handling. For the final assault on Singapore Island they deployed a very large concentration of artillery which they managed somehow to transport all the way down the peninsula. Japanese Army engineers excelled in repairing broken bridges. They brought up a considerable amount of heavy artillery which, judging by the effect of their shells, must have been up to 6-in caliber. Their preparatory bombardment (from 440 guns) before crossing Johore Strait was almost of First World War proportions.

One was constantly aware that once the small supply of HE was used up the guns could only fire armor-piercing (AP) projectiles. These are made with very thick, hard steel walls and nose, designed to penetrate the thick armor-plate of a warship without collapsing. They have a delay-action fuse fitted to the base of the shell. The effect is that the shell detonates inside the ship and, as the quantity of ammatol or lyddite explosive is comparatively small, due to the thickness of the walls, the shell casing breaks up into very large chunks of steel. These smash up boilers, steam pipes, electric cables and machinery and generally create havoc inside the ship. As a man-killing instrument of warfare AP ammunition is not very effective. I expect the shells with a high angle of descent drilled a hole about 20 ft deep and there was none of the fragmentation which is essential for antipersonnel requirements.

It is interesting to indulge in that well-known pastime of hindsight and wisdom after the event. The lessons of Singapore were learnt and applied with considerable urgency in Ceylon. Colombo and Trincomalee were the last remaining bases for the Royal Navy in the Far East and were vitally important. The following measures were taken and, had they been applied in Singapore, it is reasonable to suppose that the Coast Artillery could have been more effective.

1 The post of C-in-C and Governor-General was created and ably carried out by Admiral Sir Geoffrey Layton. This ensured there was little likelihood of politics rearing its ugly head and cramping the style of the Service Chiefs in the way that it did in Malaya. The atmosphere in Ceylon was electric – "There is not going to be another Singapore here."

2 Both Colombo and Trincomalee had quite powerful Coast Artillery of modern 9.2-in and 6-in guns. All guns were given all-round traverse and overhead cover against air attack.

3 Each Fire Command was given an armored, tracked vehicle which was fitted with a No. 19 wireless set, to act as a mobile OP for co-operation with the field army.

4 Permanent OPs were established round the perimeter of each port. These OPs had a permanent telephone line to an operation room.

5 Each coast bty had its own 40 mm Bofors AA gun manned by coast gunners.

6 Each Fire Command had on its establishment a fully equipped eight-gun 25-pounder field battery. This had the good psychological effect of identifying the coast gunners with the field army instead of being out on a limb as they were in Singapore.

7 An expert in counter-battery work was sent down from India who organized a workable counter-battery organization. He also instructed the officers in that important aspect of artillery work.

8 The proportion of HE ammunition was augmented.

In conclusion it can be stated that the coast artillery did its job just by being there. Singapore was one of the most heavily defended ports anywhere and the existence of its enormously powerful artillery dictated the strategy of the war in those parts. The Japanese were fully aware of this and we knew that they knew, so the campaign started more or less exactly as it was expected it would. The Coast Artillery locked the front door and it was up to the field army to bolt the back door.

Santa Cruz (1942)

Michael Orr

In 1942, the seemingly unstoppable expansion of Japanese imperialism threatened to engulf the whole of SE Asia and even Australia. American forces in the Pacific fought desperately to stem the tide. The Battle of the Santa Cruz Islands was of vital importance. There was no clear victor at the time but it was to significantly affect the war in the Pacific. Why?

Between May and October 1942 a series of four naval/air battles in the western Pacific established that the aircraft carrier had replaced the battleship's supremacy in the world's fleets. The battleship era was by no means completely finished and a number of vital battleship actions were still to be fought, but the aircraft carrier had become the linchpin of the fleet. The battleship and every other type of warship were now its subordinates. This change vastly increased the potential of seapower. The ability of the battleship to influence a war directly was limited to a score of miles – the range of its guns. But the carrier was a far more flexible weapon – able to strike over hundreds of miles and influence events over huge areas.

The strategic problems which the two sides faced were very similar. Guadalcanal lay at the end of a long and difficult line of communication and competed with other areas for scarce resources. The Japanese were very slow to realize the island's importance, giving more priority to the war in China and the threat of a war with Russia. The Imperial Navy therefore was forced to make do with the troops already in the SW Pacific. On the American side, Guadalcanal had to compete with the Battle of the Atlantic and the need to supply Russia. And preparations were reaching a climax for the Operation Torch landings in North Africa. It was not surprising that the Marines on Guadalcanal were soon thinking of themselves as a forgotten army.

After several months of fierce fighting neither side wanted to risk their depleted fleets without the certainty of decisive victory. The Japanese chose to wear their enemy down until they could re-establish an effective superiority. The waters between the American base at Espiritu Santo, in the New Hebrides islands, and the Solomons were so heavily patrolled by Japanese submarines that the area was dubbed "Torpedo Junction". Henderson Field, near Lunga Point, was in the possession of the Americans. They took advantage of this to control the waters around Guadalcanal during daylight.

A pattern of operations was soon established. American convoys delivered supplies from Espiritu Santo to their garrison while day lasted, but withdrew at nightfall. Under the cover of darkness the "Tokyo Express" of Japanese troop-carrying destroyers and cruisers would rush down "the Slot" to land stores and reinforcements or bombard the American positions. But they would have to leave in a hurry in order to be out of range of avenging aircraft from Henderson Field before daybreak. Thus neither side was able to achieve a superiority in ground forces on the island. The Japanese were particularly short of supplies, rather than men. They had few landing craft and had to rely on fast destroyers and small boats. The Americans found fuel for Henderson's aircraft their greatest problem.

A series of skirmishes and minor battles established the Japanese superiority in night fighting and turned the water north of Guadalcanal into a wreck-strewn "Ironbottom Sound". An attempt by the Japanese to force through a larger convoy than usual resulted in another carrier battle on 24 August.

The honors of the Battle of the Eastern Solomons were fairly evenly shared. A Japanese light carrier, the *Ryujo*, was lost. The American carrier *Enterprise* was damaged and had to return to Pearl Harbor. The next weeks saw several successes for the

Japanese policy of attrition. The carrier *Wasp* was sunk, and the carrier *Saratoga* and the battleship *North Carolina* damaged. At one time the Americans had only one carrier in the Guadalcanal area. Better news for the Americans came with the Battle of Cape Esperance on 11 October when a Japanese cruiser force was severely damaged in a night action.

By this time the Japanese had decided to break the stalemate on Guadalcanal, which was also delaying the progress of the New Guinea campaign. In mid-September Imperial Army and Navy Staffs agreed that: "After reinforcement of Army forces has been completed, Army and Navy forces will combine and in one action attack and retake Guadalcanal Island airfield. During this operation the Navy will take all necessary action to halt the efforts of the enemy to augment his forces in the Solomons area.' The capture of the airfield was left to the Army. After its experience at Midway, the Navy was apparently chary of risking a major battle while the enemy had the use of an "unsinkable aircraft carrier" – Henderson Field. During October the "Tokyo Express" increased its work, with heavy bombardments of Henderson Field and other American positions. It brought the Japanese strength on the island up to 20,000 men.

The Americans were fully aware of their own danger. On 15 October Admiral Chester W. Nimitz, C-in-C in the Pacific, considered that his forces could not control the sea. Supplying American positions could be done, but only at great military cost. By 18 October Vice Admiral William F. Halsey had been appointed to succeed Vice Admiral Robert L. Ghormley as Comsopac (Commander, South Pacific Area). Halsey's reputation in the Pacific was second to none. He had commanded the carrier task forces which had first struck back at the all-conquering Japanese and in particular had commanded the group from which the Doolittle Raid on Tokyo was launched. His strategy was "Kill Japs! Kill more Japs!" At last, with the Torch convoy on its way, Washington was prepared to increase its support of the South Pacific operations.

The Japanese had planned to capture Henderson Field on 21 October, but the unexpected strength of the American garrison (which rose to over 23,000 Marines and GIs) caused them to postpone the attack until 23 October. The delay did not do them much good. They lost over 2,000 men and all their tanks. However, on the 24th Admiral Isokuru Yamamoto, the Japanese naval C-in-C, warned his military colleagues that the fleet, which had been at sea since 11 October, was running dangerously short of fuel and would soon have to withdraw. The attacks on Henderson Field therefore continued and a false report of victory in the early hours of 25 October brought the Japanese fleet hurrying south, only to reverse their course as soon as the report was denied. At 1200, two Japanese carriers were spotted by a Catalina flying boat but they immediately turned away and so avoided the search aircraft of the American carriers.

Another night of doubt and indecision followed for both fleets. On land the Japanese mounted another attack, but were eventually forced to admit defeat. The first part of the Japanese plan had failed. The outcome of the land attack was so uncertain that the units of their fleet had been drawn much farther south than intended. On the night of 25/26 October elements of the Japanese navy were twice sighted and attacked by Catalinas. In his headquarters at Noumea, in New Caledonia, Admiral Halsey was in no doubt what his orders to his commanders at sea should be: "Attack – Repeat – Attack!"

Task Force 64, led by Rear Admiral Willis A. Lee, in *Washington*, was responsible for protecting Guadalcanal from night bombardments and operated independently throughout the battle. During the night of 25/26 October, the battleship *Washington* was patrolling west of Savo Island. Task Force 16, under Rear Admiral Thomas C. Kinkaid, was based on the carrier *Enterprise*. Rear Admiral George D. Murray commanded Task Force 17 from the carrier *Hornet*.

Enterprise and *Hornet* were sister-ships, completed in 1938 and 1941 respectively. In October 1942 they were the last word in carrier design and represented the fruits of the USN's interwar experience of aircraft carriers. With a displacement of 19,000 tons (*Enterprise*) and 20,000 tons (*Hornet*) they were capable of speeds up to 34 knots and could operate between 80 and 100 planes. Both ships were veterans of the Pacific war, having worked together on the Doolittle Raid to Tokyo and at Midway.

The battleship *South Dakota* of Task Force 16 was one of a new generation of fast ships. With a displacement of 35,000 tons, she was capable of 28 knots and had a main armament of nine 16-in guns. She was fresh from Pearl Harbor where her AA guns had been increased to include 68 of the new 40 mms in quadruple mounts and 78 20 mm guns. Captain Thomas L. Gatch, her commander, neglecting the conventional "bull", had concentrated on gunnery practice. The battle that followed proved that he had made a trained and efficient fighting team of his inexperienced ship's company.

The Japanese divided their fleet into a number of smaller units as well, but on principles which differed significantly from those of the Americans. The two main elements were the Advance Force, under Vice Admiral Nobutake Kondo, in *Atago*, and the Striking Force under Vice Admiral Chuichi Nagumo. The Advance Force was intended for the close support of the troops on Guadalcanal and had been responsible for most of the night bombardments of the American positions during October. On 26 October it consisted of two battleships, four heavy cruisers and a destroyer screen. Originally two carriers had provided air cover, but *Hiyo* had developed engine trouble and had been forced to return to Truk on 22 October. This left only her sister ship *Junyo*, completed as recently as May. Both ships were converted passenger liner hulls. For their size, 24,000 tons, they carried a small complement of aircraft, just over 50, and were underpowered, being capable of only 25.5 knots.

The Striking Force to deal with any major interference by the American fleet, was sub-divided into a Carrier Group, under Nagumo, of three aircraft carriers and their screen, and a Vanguard Force, under Rear Admiral Hiroaki Abe, of two battleships, three heavy cruisers and a destroyer screen. The carriers *Shokaku* and *Zuikaku* were sister-ships, designed as fleet carriers to work with the *Yamato*-class super-battleships. They displaced 25,000 tons, but with engines capable of 160,000 SHP they had a speed of 34 knots. Able to handle air groups of over 80 planes, they had operated together at Pearl Harbor and the Coral Sea. Damage in the latter battle ensured that they missed Midway. *Zuiho* was a light carrier, originally designed as a submarine tender. Displacing 11,000 tons, she could reach 28 knots with up to 30 aircraft.

The Japanese practice of dividing their fleets into sections has been criticized. The fault lay not so much in the division itself but the way in which it was done. By separating the individual parts too much and dividing their carriers between the parts they generally ensured that only a fraction of their available carrier strength would be able to intervene in any battle. This happened at Midway and, to a lesser extent, at Santa Cruz. Within the main divisions of the fleet, the carriers operated as a unit, but without the support of other types of ship, save destroyers. Although this made it easier to co-ordinate aircraft operations, it meant that the carriers were exposed to air attack.

Once their carriers were sighted, all the Japanese eggs were in one basket. And they lacked the fearsome AA fire of the Americans. At Midway four Japanese carriers were caught together and three were sunk. The fourth escaped temporarily because of a fortuitous rainstorm. On the other hand the Japanese, although they sighted one American carrier group at Midway, remained ignorant for a long time of the presence of another, stronger, group. A further Japanese disadvantage was that their carriers had restricted bridges and limited radio facilities. This made them unsuitable as flagships, yet they had to be used as such.

First light on 26 October came shortly after 0500, revealing a fine day, with just enough cloud in the sky to conceal a dive-bomber attack. The American carriers were by then north of the Santa Cruz Islands. They chose to approach Guadalcanal from that direction rather than risk encountering Japanese submarine patrols in Torpedo Junction. Their course was north-westerly and less than 200 miles ahead of them were the Japanese forces in a triangular formation. The Vanguard Group of the Japanese Striking Force was leading the carriers by 60 miles. One hundred miles to the west was the Advanced Force, with the carrier *Junyo* maneuvering independently even farther west. The Japanese forces were all steering northwards. Both sides were aware that the enemy's carriers were at sea, but neither knew the other's exact location. Delays in transmission meant that Kinkaid had not received the report of the Catalina which had attacked *Zuikaku* during the night. This was unfortunate because the overwhelming advantage in carrier battles went to the side which struck first. Kinkaid ordered an aircraft search from *Enterprise*. Sixteen Dauntless dive-bombers took off. Each was armed with a 500-lb bomb. They fanned in pairs to the north and west. One group saw a "Kate" torpedo bomber on a similar mission and at 0617 the Vanguard Group, led by Admiral Abe, was sighted. There was no sign of the carriers until 0650. The first pair of scouts could not break through the fighter patrols. Then at 0740 another pair, having heard the sighting report and altered course, made an unobserved approach. They attacked the light carrier *Zuiho* and both scored a hit. A 50 ft hole in the flight deck made the carrier useless. But it was too late to prevent a strike taking off.

The "Kate" spotted by *Enterprise*'s aircraft had identified a carrier task force at 0658. At 0700 a 65-strong force of "Zekes", "Kates" and "Vals" flew off and another group was soon being ranged. The American carriers did nothing about their sighting reports until 0720. Even then, the attack was not co-ordinated. At 0730, 15 Dauntless, six Avenger torpedo bombers and eight Wildcat fighters left *Hornet*. *Enterprise*'s first strike consisted of eight Avengers and eight Wildcats and only three Dauntlesses. The carrier was by now critically short of dive-bombers. Six had not returned from the previous evening's attempt to find the Japanese carriers, six more were on anti-submarine patrol, and the 16 scouts had not yet come back. The *Enterprise*'s strike flew off at 0800 and was followed at 0815 by *Hornet*'s second strike – nine Dauntlesses, nine Avengers and seven Wildcats. With their targets nearly 200 miles away there was neither time nor fuel for the aircraft to circle the carriers until a concentrated strike could be built up. Squadrons flew in a long-drawn-out gaggle. As they flew they passed the incoming Japanese strike. Some Japanese fighters left their convoy to attack the *Enterprise* group. Four Wildcats and four Avengers were either shot down or severely damaged and forced back to the carrier. The size of the *Enterprise*'s strike had been halved at a cost of only three "Zekes".

The American fleet was expecting the Japanese strike. Every possible step was taken to avoid a disastrous carrier fire, such as that which had destroyed the *Lexington* at the Coral Sea. Aircraft were secured in the hangar deck, aviation fuel lines were filled with carbon dioxide, and damage control parties were on constant alert. Speed was maintained at 28 knots and around the carriers their escorts were poised to provide massive AA fire.

The first line of defense was the 38 Wildcats of the combat air patrol (CAP). This was directed from the *Enterprise*. But the officer in charge was new to his job, having recently replaced a Midway veteran whom Halsey had taken to Noumea. For some time the fighter-direction team could not distinguish between the American and Japanese air groups on their cluttered radar screens. It was 0857 before a clear picture emerged. The CAP was too near the fleet, and too late – only 10 miles out at 0906. Although the Wildcats claimed some victims, neither they nor the American gunners could break the co-ordination of the Japanese attack.

At about 0900 *Enterprise*'s group was hidden by a rain squall. This left *Hornet* – lacking the close support of a battleship like *South Dakota* – to face the full might of the Japanese attack alone. "Val" dive-bombers began the assault, scoring one hit and two near-misses. The squadron commander, his plane having been hit, made no attempt to drop his bombs but kept on diving. The "Val" bounced off the carrier's funnel and burnt through the flight deck. The dive-bombers suffered heavily, but their attack covered the approach of a squadron of "Kate" torpedo bombers from astern. Two torpedoes crashed into *Hornet*'s engine-rooms and she slowed to a halt under a pall of black smoke. A sitting target, *Hornet* was hit by three more bombs and then a burning "Kate" made a suicide run into the ship's port side. It was all over in ten minutes. The Japanese had lost 25 planes, but the once-formidable *Hornet* was a listing, blazing wreck.

Meanwhile the American air groups were approaching the Japanese fleet. But their straggling formation had been disturbed by the fighters. They were unable to deliver a united attack, or even find the same target. Fifteen Dauntlesses from *Hornet* led the attack. The first wave of defending fighters was kept at bay by their escorting Wildcats but the Dauntlesses were then left without protection. At 0930 *Shokaku* and *Zuiho* appeared below and the main Japanese CAP above. Even so, 11 bombers got through and scored between three and six hits on *Shokaku*. The 1,000 lb bombs tore her flight deck apart and started a tremendous blaze in the hangar. But there were no torpedo bombers to finish the job. *Hornet*'s Avengers had lost touch with the rest of the strike and so *Shokaku* and *Zuiho* went unmolested as they limped towards Truk. The Avengers made contact with Abe's Vanguard Group, but they were so short of fuel that they could not continue to search for the carriers. At 0930 they made an unsuccessful attack on the cruiser *Suzuya*. The rest of the American aircraft also missed the carriers and attacked Abe's group. *Hornet*'s second wave damaged the cruiser *Chikuma* but *Enterprise*'s aircraft had no luck at all.

As the American aircraft turned for home the result of the battle was still very much in the balance. Two Japanese carriers were out of action, but the second strike from *Shokaku* and *Zuikaku* had not yet attacked. *Zuikaku* was ready to gather up the survivors of all three carriers and prepare another strike. *Junyo* was hurrying westwards and, as Nagumo's flagship *Shokaku* was out of action, he transferred command of flying operations to Rear Admiral Kakuji Kakuta on board *Junyo*. She was still more than 300 miles from the American task forces. Even so, Kakuta ordered a strike to commence. Her aircraft were to land on *Zuikaku* or *Shokaku* after the attack.

On the American side, *Hornet*'s fires had been brought under control, although at one stage the order to abandon ship had been given. By 1005 the 9,050-ton cruiser *Northampton* was ready to begin towing the carrier when an unsuccessful attack by a stray "Val" disrupted operations.

Although Task Force 16 had not yet been attacked, it was the scene of increasing confusion. Overhead were stacked the surviving aircraft from both carriers. They were by now nearing the end of their fuel. At 1002 the destroyer *Porter* was torpedoed by a Japanese submarine while picking up the crew of a crashed aircraft. The *Porter* was so badly damaged that she had to be sunk by gunfire, her crew transferring to another destroyer, *Shaw*. A submarine was the last thing which any carrier wanted to encounter while forced to keep a straight course for aircraft to land.

Then (almost as soon as the landings started) the second Japanese strike was detected on the *South Dakota*'s radar. *Enterprise* suspended operations and prepared to defend herself. Fortunately this attack was not so well co-ordinated as that on *Hornet*. The dive-bombers arrived 20 minutes before the torpedo-bombers and were met by the heaviest AA fire yet seen in the Pacific War. *South Dakota*, only 1,000 yards from *Enterprise*, showed to perfection her crew's gunnery skills. She shot down 26 "Vals", *Enterprise* claimed another seven. But two bombs found their mark, damaging the flight deck and starting fresh fires in the hangar. But the torpedo-bombers were too far behind to deliver the final blow.

When they finally arrived they were attacked by the combat air patrol. One Wildcat pilot, Lieutenant Vejtasa, shot down six before he ran out of ammunition. About 14 "Kates" got through to the Task Force. Five of these were destroyed by AA fire. Then the surviving Japanese moved in on the luckless *Enterprise*, attacking on both sides. Full-speed maneuvering by her captain once more saved the carrier. One "Kate" did not even try to launch its torpedo, but dived straight onto the forecastle of the destroyer *Smith*. The blazing ship used *South Dakota*'s wake to douse her fires and so survived the battle.

On board *Enterprise*, the ship's company worked with disciplined but feverish haste to clear the flight deck and complete the recovery of the circling aircraft before they ran out of fuel. The appearance of a submarine periscope made things more difficult. Then at 1101 *Junyo*'s aircraft appeared on *South Dakota*'s radar screen. Alerted by this, her gunners opened fire on six unidentified aircraft at 1110. These proved to be returning Dauntlesses. By the time that this mistake had been sorted out *Junyo*'s aircraft were hidden in the cloud over the Task Force. Twenty attacked in a two-minute flurry, but achieved only one near-miss on *Enterprise* and lost eight planes. At 1127 two isolated "Vals" dived on *South Dakota* and the AA cruiser *San Juan*. One bomb exploded on *South Dakota*'s foremost turret, without penetrating the armor. But Captain Gatch was wounded by splinters and for a moment the battleship was not under command.

As *South Dakota* headed towards *Enterprise*, *San Juan* was hit astern and her rudder jammed. The tight formation of Task Force 16 was shattered as the ships maneuvered out of the way of their careering consorts. Both ships were soon under control and *Enterprise* was able to land aircraft again. But with her forward elevator out of action the carrier was slow in getting aircraft below and several planes were forced to ditch before their turn came. *Enterprise* launched a CAP, but did not attempt to renew the battle. All morning the carrier had been steering south-eastwards into the wind, but at 1400 she turned east. Admiral Kinkaid had decided that with only *Enterprise*'s limited capacity to operate aircraft he could not risk an offensive against an unknown number of Japanese carriers.

The Japanese still had two carriers left in the battle, but had lost over 100 aircraft. *Zuikaku* and *Junyo* collected the mixed assortment of aircraft and sent them off in penny packets. Kondo and Abe also increased the speed of their battleship squadrons, hoping to finish off the crippled American ships after nightfall.

The cruiser *Northampton* was inching *Hornet* to safety when they were spotted at 1515 by Japanese aircraft. *Northampton* cut her tow, leaving the stationary carrier an easy target for the approaching torpedo planes. One hit was enough to seal her fate. The order to abandon ship was given, but three more Japanese formations attacked before all the survivors had been taken off. Then *Hornet* showed the same endurance as her sister-ship *Yorktown* at Midway. Destroyers fired nine torpedoes into her and over 400 5-in shells. But *Hornet*, burning from stern to stern, was still afloat when she was sighted by Abe's ships at 2120. The Japanese at least had the satisfaction of avenging the Doolittle Raid by giving the *coup de grâce* to the ship which launched it.

During the night, the Japanese carriers were once again attacked by Catalinas. It was not until the afternoon of the 27th that the Combined Fleet began its withdrawal to Truk.

At the end of the battle neither side had suffered decisive losses. The Americans had lost *Hornet* and a destroyer. *Enterprise*, *South Dakota*, *San Juan* and a destroyer had been damaged. No major Japanese unit had been sunk, but two carriers and a destroyer had been damaged. *Shokaku* was out of action for nine months. The Japanese also lost 100 aircraft, against American casualties of 20 planes destroyed in action and another 54 missing or damaged.

What was the final result of the battle? Admiral Samuel E. Morison claims in the Official History of the battle, "The Struggle for Guadalcanal", that "Measured in combat tonnage sunk, the Japanese had won a tactical victory; but other losses forced them back to the Truk hideout." This is less than fair to the Japanese. Truk was no more a "hideout" than Noumea, and the American fleet turned for home first. The real reason for the retirement of the Japanese fleet was the failure of their army to capture Henderson Field. The struggle for Guadalcanal reverted to its former pattern: supply runs by day and night and a long, hard fight on land. Eventually the Americans won the reinforcement battle and in February 1943 Japan evacuated the survivors of her garrison.

With the advantage of hindsight it would be easy to argue that the Battle of Santa Cruz made little difference to the final result. But this is to ignore the question of what might have been. After Santa Cruz the Japanese had four undamaged carriers and the Americans had only the damaged *Enterprise* and the escort carrier *Long Island* in the Pacific. Japan had the opportunity to exploit her carrier superiority and win the decisive victory which had escaped both sides. She failed to do so because, although she had the carriers, both aircraft and pilots were lacking.

The Japanese fleet, lacking both air cover and the striking power of the carrier, could not check the American daylight convoys. By the time the Japanese carrier fleet had been repaired and re-equipped it was too late to save Guadalcanal. When the two fleets next met, in the Philippine Sea in June 1944, Japan could send only nine carriers and 430 aircraft against 15 carriers and 891 aircraft. Whether or not Santa Cruz was a setback for the Americans it bought them enough time to ensure final victory.

Kokoda Trail (1942)

John Laffin

One of the least known of all the campaigns of the Second World War is that of the Kokoda Trail over the Owen Stanley Mountains in Papua New Guinea. But among land battles it ranks with Stalingrad and the Burma Campaigns for sheer toughness, and with Stalingrad, Alamein and the Normandy landings in importance.

A no-holds-barred fight between the Australians and Japanese, the Kokoda Trail campaign – sometimes called the Battle of the Ranges – lasted seven months and put an end to the myth of Japanese infantry invincibility. It also saved Australia from invasion – with the naval battle of the Coral Sea – and gave Australian military history a name to place alongside Gallipoli and Tobruk.

After their attack on Pearl Harbor in December 1941 and their steam-roller successes in the Pacific and SE Asia, the Japanese turned their eyes to Australia. No matter how successful a landing on the Australian mainland might be, they first had to capture the islands to Australia's north. Lightly defended, New Britain and New Ireland quickly fell. Next on the list was New Guinea, whose northern part was Australian mandated territory, while the southern part, Papua, was Australian soil.

The capital, Port Moresby, was the Japanese target. On the southern coast of the island, it was the most vital supply link with Australia. A second force would take Milne Bay at the eastern end of New Guinea and a third would menace the Bulolo Valley and another key settlement, Wau, in the north.

The first people to know of the Japanese arrival off the north coast, 63 air-miles from Moresby, were a lieutenant and a sergeant at Buna Government Station, who, on 21 July 1942, watched an enemy cruiser shell shore targets. The sergeant ran to the radio hut and on emergency frequency sent off his report:

A JAPANESE WARSHIP IS SHELLING OFF BUNA, APPARENTLY TO COVER A LANDING AT GONA OR SANANANDA. ACKNOWLEDGE, MORESBY. OVER. . .

Over and over again, the message was repeated, but Moresby did not acknowledge.

Soon it was too late to matter. The Japanese had landed their vanguard of 2,000 troops to begin a thrust across the forbidding mountains. There was little that generals in Port Moresby or their leaders in Australia could do.

The elite divisions of the volunteer Australian Imperial Force were not available at the time. The 6th and 7th were either on their way back from fighting German, Italian and Vichy French troops in the Middle East or regrouping in Australia, the 8th had been lost in the lightning Japanese conquest of Malaya and the 9th was Eighth Army's trump card in the first Battle of Alamein. Until the 6th and 7th Divisions could be brought in, the defense of Papua depended on militia battalions. The militiamen had not volunteered for service outside Australia, most were city conscripts and many considered they had been "shanghaied" to Port Moresby without being told where they were going.

The men of the Australian Imperial Force (AIF) – volunteers to a man – despised the militiamen as "chokos", chocolate soldiers. With some outstanding exceptions, morale was low in the militia units. In Moresby many were unloading stores from ships, digging slit trenches for air-raid defense and guarding airfields. Virtually untrained in jungle warfare, the most arduous of fighting, they rotted in tropical heat.

Meanwhile a formation known as "Maroubra Force" (after a famous Sydney beach) commanded by Lieutenant-Colonel W. T. Owen was trying to stem the Japanese advance. The striking unit of this "force" consisted of one grossly understrength battalion – the 39th – formed of a few hundred militiamen and stiffened by AIF reinforcements. Their average age was 18. If the Japanese could defeat them and take Kokoda airfield – the only way the defenders could receive adequate reinforcements and supplies – they might well be in Port Moresby before the AIF veterans could arrive.

The battle developing was to be fought in a terrible climate in jungles, swamps and mountains. The Owen Stanley range, which reaches a height of 13,000 ft, is a maze of ridges, spurs, valleys and rivers. Each big river is laced like a shoe with numerous small ones. The northern coast has flat and perpetually swampy ground, blanketed with dense and smelly rain forest which the sun never penetrates. The mountain jungles drip water continuously. Such tracks as exist are steep, muddy and treacherous. In places the jungle is thick with vines and creepers armed with spikes the size of fingers. Paths had to be hacked with machetes.

Vast areas are infested with malarial mosquitoes, leeches and other insects which burrow into the flesh and cause painful, itchy swellings. Here and there the jungle is broken by clearings of *kunai* – elephant grass. But because these were ideal for ambush, troops learned to avoid them.

Much fighting took place on a one-man front – the width of the track. Many Australians were killed or wounded by Japanese snipers, tied into position high up in the trees. They would allow perhaps a hundred troops to pass while they waited to pick off an officer or NCO. As a precaution the Australians abandoned badges of status and nobody was addressed by rank. Even senior officers were known by a makeshift codename. A CO might be "Dick" or "Curly" to his troops. The Japanese sniper who waited so patiently for a target was nearly always killed – as he knew he would be – by the troops he had allowed to pass.

The Japanese who landed at Gona and Buna trapped many Europeans at the plantations, missions and hospitals. Only a few escaped and crossed the mountains to safety. Most of those captured were murdered. In front of terrified natives, an Anglican mission party – two ministers, two women, two half-caste mission workers, a six-year-old boy and an army officer – were beheaded one by one with a sword – the boy last of all.

After several aggressive rearguard actions Col. Owen's battered battalion was forced back. When the forward Japanese troops met opposition they deployed and engaged while support moved in with machine-guns and mortars. With probing attacks the Japanese found out the width and depth of the defenses by drawing Australian fire. Stronger support units would then move around the Australian flanks to force a withdrawal or to wipe out the enemy by a rear attack. The Japanese often shouted, fired furiously, blew whistles and pulled noisily at the jungle in attempts to frighten the Australians into withdrawal. They sometimes shouted orders or requests in English to lure them into ambush, but without mastery of the Australian accent or slang this rarely worked.

The administration post of Kokoda – 1,200 ft above sea level and 45 miles from Port Moresby – possessed the only airfield between Port Moresby and the northern coast. To defend this vital place Col. Owen had about 80 men in all – 60 young soldiers and a handful of Papuans from the Papuan Infantry Battalion under Major Watson. This small exhausted force cheered mightily when they saw aircraft approaching with reinforcements. Then the planes sheered off, climbed steeply and vanished. Word had been flashed to them from Army HQ in Melbourne, 2,000 miles away on the mainland, that Kokoda had fallen. Had those planes landed the epic of the Kokoda Trail might never have happened.

That night 500 Japanese attacked Kokoda. In this first pitched battle on Papuan soil, attackers and defenders became mingled in the confused fighting. Col. Owen was mortally wounded. Maj. Watson, assuming command, extricated the survivors and withdrew to the native village of Deniki.

For several days the 39th, under Major Alan Cameron, fought a savage rearguard action. With malaria and dysentery adding to their casualties, the battalion was in poor shape by the

time it reached Isurava. Here on 16 August, what was left of
Maroubra Force was taken over by an AIF veteran officer,
Lieutenant-Colonel Ralph Honner, who had been ordered
hurriedly to the crumbling front.

Honner, with service in Libya, Greece and Crete, looked at
his thin, gaunt and tattered men. They had been unable to
change their clothing for weeks. Their boots were rotting on
their feet. Despite great care, their Bren light machine-guns and
Lee-Enfield rifles were rusting. When it got through, their food
was bully beef and biscuits. They lived in continual rain without shelters or groundsheets. At night they shivered, blanket-
less, in the cold. Supplies were dropped from aircraft but much
was lost in the jungle. Yet these men could still fight and
Honner decided on a stand at Isurava. He had a few hundred
men and his largest weapons were 3-in mortars firing a 10 lb
shell. Against this puny force were three battalions of the
Japanese 144th Regiment, with another full regiment, the
41st, coming up fast. Supporting them were a mountain artillery battalion and two engineer units – about 4,000 men in all.

Despite these odds, the Australians fought the Japanese
hand-to-hand in a series of ambushes and raids for two weeks.
One group of 39th sick and wounded were on their way down
the trail to Moresby. Upon hearing that their battalion was
fighting for its life they disobeyed orders, turned round and
hurried back into action.

Another battalion placed under Honner's command, the
53rd, was not so valiant. Slow to move forward and reluctant
to fight, it was removed from an offensive role after its CO was
killed. Its men were made carriers and porters on the Kokoda
Trail.

On 25 and 26 August, Major General Horii, the Japanese
commander, launched a full-scale offensive. On the 28th the
Japanese, shouting "Banzai!" made frontal attacks on Australian positions. Violent hand-to-hand fighting followed. Horii
did not know it then but he was too late to win the campaign.

The AIF had arrived at Isurava.

The 150 survivors of the 39th had left Isurava the day before
the battle, fighting their way out down the trail. They were
young, tired veterans who had held on for as long as they had

been asked. The Japanese now faced men of the first AIF battalion to reach the battle – the 2/14th, soon joined by part of the 2/16th, both part of the 21st Brigade. On 29 August, Gen. Horii concentrated five battalions in a narrow valley for a decisive blow against the still heavily outnumbered Australians. Along the entire 350-yard Australian front he unleashed a storm of artillery shells, mortar bombs and continuous machine-gun fire; then wave after wave of infantry went in. The Australian veterans fought off every attack. One platoon repulsed 11 attacks of 100 or more men. It lost its commander and every NCO. A private soldier took command, with other privates acting as NCOs.

During the fighting on this day Sergeant R. N. Thompson led a fighting patrol of seven men to push the enemy back along the track. One of his men was 24-year-old Private Bruce S. Kingsbury, armed with a Bren and grenades. Seeing that the Japanese were getting ready for a fresh assault, Kingsbury charged them. Japanese machine-gunners opened fire on him from farther back but Kingsbury ran on, sweeping the enemy positions. The patrol finished what Kingsbury had begun and regained 100 yards of track – considerable in jungle warfare. While Thompson was preparing a holding position a Japanese sniper killed Kingsbury. He was awarded a posthumous VC. At another point Acting Corporal Charles McCallum – wounded three times – killed 40 Japanese in a brief, furious action while extricating the survivors of a forward platoon from a dangerous position. He won the Distinguished Conduct Medal.

The Australians held Isurava for four days before Japanese pressure became too great. The Australian commander, Brigadier A. W. Potts, could not challenge Horii's control of the upper spurs and ridges without weakening the defense of the main track, the Australians' lifeline route to Moresby. The 2/14 and 2/16th Battalions made a slow, deliberate withdrawal. A bloody bayonet charge checked the Japanese but their out-flanking movements isolated parties of Australians. Those captured were killed on the spot.

Others finally reached safety after such privations that only a tropical, mountainous jungle can inflict. One badly wounded soldier crawled for three weeks on his hands and knees. Most

wounded men were luckier, being carried to medical help by
native porters – lauded by the Australian public as "the Fuzzy-
Wuzzy Angels".

At Iora Creek an ever-thinning line of Australians killed 170
Japanese and kept their line intact before withdrawing to Imita
Ridge, the last defensible point of the Owen Stanleys. Here they
held while the Japanese dug in on the facing ridge – Iorabaiwa.
Horii had a chance to smash through but again he was too late.
The three battalions of a fresh AIF Brigade, the 25th under
Brigadier K. W. Eather, relieved the exhausted 21st Brigade.

While the Japanese were striking for Port Moresby over the
mountains a linked action was developing at Milne Bay, 200
miles to the east. The Royal Australian Air Force (RAAF) had
established Kittyhawk fighter-squadrons there in July 1942 and
the 7th Infantry Brigade (militia) and 18th Infantry Brigade,
AIF – both under Major-General C. A. Clowes – were moved in
to defend them. A few hundred Americans had also arrived. On
24 August a Japanese invasion got under way and troops and
tanks landed from barges the following day.

On 4 September the first VC of the New Guinea campaigns
was earned at Milne Bay by Corporal John Alexander French.
When Japanese machine-guns held up the advance, Corporal
French ordered his section to take cover and with grenades
rushed the first of a group of three machine-guns. He silenced
the first, returned for more grenades and put paid to a second.
Firing a Thompson sub-machine-gun he rushed the third gun
and killed its crew. He died from wounds on the edge of the
gunpit.

By 7 September, after much patrol fighting, Japanese naval
attacks and RAAF strikes on enemy troop barges, the Japanese
had lost the battle and at least 1,000 dead – mostly elite marine
assault troops. Fighting was invariably savage. One Australian
was found dead with 30 Japanese corpses around him. The
heads of two had been smashed in with the butt of the Australian's sub-machine-gun.

Crackers with a slow-burning wick led a few Australians to
their deaths. A Japanese would creep through the long grass,
place a lighted cracker and then steal away and position himself.
When the cracker exploded, an Australian would turn towards

the sound and perhaps advance towards it. The Japanese sniper would see the sudden movement and have time to aim and fire. Here, as elsewhere in New Guinea, men often died without ever seeing the enemy in the impenetrable jungle darkness.

Milne Bay was the first clear-cut land victory over the Japanese anywhere in the war. Strategically it confined the main Japanese operations in Papua to the Buna–Kokoda area and spelt failure for the Japanese plans to capture Port Moresby.

This was not clear at the time and in the Owen Stanleys the Australian 25th Brigade was preparing for the counter-attack which would push the enemy out of the mountains. These men had already beaten the Foreign Legion in Vichy French Syria.

Using the Australian-made Owen gun, a 9 mm light sub-machine-gun for close quarter fighting, the Australian infantry soon dominated the valley between the Imita and Iorabaiwa ridges. For the first time the Australians had artillery – two 25-pounders painfully dragged up the tracks. Australian aircraft, for the first time able to help their infantry, destroyed the bridge over the wide, treacherous Kumusi River – cutting Horii's supply lines. On 26 September Horii, obeying an order from his HQ at Rabaul, began a withdrawal. Men too sick or weak to keep pace were simply left to die.

The Australian pursuit was governed by the ability of the RAAF to drop supplies. Ground troops rarely recovered more than 30 per cent of a drop. The track was so bad that, even without enemy opposition, a battalion would sometimes cover only a mile a day. Every day at noon, rain fell in solid sheets over the mountains, turning the tracks into narrow streams of black and yellow mud. Hidden in this mud were countless tree roots to catch the boots of tired soldiers. Steps cut into the track deteriorated into mudpools.

On one spur of Imita Ridge engineers cut and blocked with logs 2,000 steps – ironically nick-named the Golden Stairway. This was not the record number; Maguli Ridge had 3,400 steps.

The track was disheartening. For every 1,000 ft of altitude the troops climbed they dropped 600 ft to the start of the next ascent. Between Uberi and the crest of the Owen Stanley range the track climbed more than 20,000 ft in this switchback fashion. It crossed many rivers by log or vine bridges. At times it climbed or skirted precipices.

The temperature lurched from humid, oppressive heat to bitter cold. When not rain-drenched the soldiers were sweat-soaked. In these conditions a man was too old for jungle warfare at 30. The Japanese were so hungry that they frequently ate flesh cut from Australian or their own dead. But they often turned and fought back – on one occasion holding the Australians for eight days. Beheading or bayoneting captives, the Japanese remained a disciplined and formidable foe. Cleverly concealing their weapon pits which they made proof against mortar fire, they had to be prised out of every position.

Their food supply improved as they fell back to their bases. They could also use artillery, which the Australians were denied. The guns could not be taken across the ranges. But the Australian advance was irresistible and, on 3 November, they re-entered Kokoda.

To commemorate the recapture the Australian commander, Major-General G. A. Vasey, raised the Australian flag and presented medals to five natives for loyal and meritorious service. A great crowd of carriers assembled for the ceremony – the first of its kind in the campaign. "Without your help", Vasey told the natives through an interpreter, "we would not have been able to cross the Owen Stanleys." All the carriers received gifts of knives and rami – the native kilt-skirt.

Vasey might have added that without Dr G. H. Vernon and Captain Herbert Kienzle the natives would not have been an effective force. Vernon had fought in the First World War as Regimental Medical Officer to the 11th Light Horse Regiment and had returned to Australia with the Military Cross. Stone deaf – from a bursting shell at Gallipoli in 1915 – he was working in Papua as a government medical officer when the war with Japan broke out. The Australian Government evacuated the women, children and older men. Although Vernon was 60, he refused to leave, even when threatened with arrest. Instead, he took upon himself the medical care and much of the organization of the native carriers between Owen's Corner – at the end of the motor road from Port Moresby – and on to Kokoda. His first dramatic act was to post himself to the 39th

Battalion when he heard that the unit was temporarily without its medical officer. In this way he served through the first battle of Kokoda, patching up many wounded and treating the dying Col. Owen. He was one of the last four men out of Kokoda.

Resuming his work with the natives, Vernon – himself a strong mountain walker – kept the carrier line working. Everything that went up to the troops was carried on the backs of these natives. Unavoidably loaded and worked to the limit they came to love Dr Vernon. He saw to it that they had proper rest periods and treatment. Having taken supplies up, the natives became stretcher bearers and brought out many badly wounded men. On those tortuous tracks and crossing rushing rockstrewn rivers, eight men were needed for each human load. Carrying a stretcher in these conditions was an appalling task. Sometimes it had to be held at arm's length above the head. Yet the bearers always managed to be gentle and careful.

Herbert Kienzle – a rubber planter when war came – was also responsible for organizing and maintaining much of the native line of communication across the Owen Stanleys.

Strangely, Vernon got no official recognition for his extraordinary labors, which contributed in no small measure to his death in 1946, aged 64. Kienzle received an MBE, the lowest class of the Order of the British Empire.

From Kokoda, the Australian infantry pushed on steadily. At Gorari on 11 November two battalions of the 25th Brigade – 2/25th and 2/31 st – made fierce bayonet charges, killing 580 Japanese in fighting that lasted five days.

This action – by jungle warfare standards a major battle with serious casualties – demonstrated Gen. Vasey's tactical skill. By clever maneuvering he had caught the rarely surprised Japanese off guard. The victory precipitated the collapse of organized resistance outside the Buna–Gona beach-head. The able, determined Gen. Horii, in an effort to evade capture, tried to cross the white-water Kumusi River on a raft and was drowned when it overturned.

The last bitter phase of the fighting was fought at Buna, Sanananda and Gona in a vast morass of swamp, mud and battle-torn jungle. Many Australians, exhausted by combat, fever, lack of sleep and poor food went out on patrols with high temperatures. In November 1942 alone the evacuations numbered 1,500, but by now American troops were reinforcing the Australians. Their numbers and weight of firepower were decisive. In other parts of northern New Guinea fighting would go on until 1944 but the Battle of the Ranges was over.

The 39th Battalion, which had begun the Battle of the Kokoda Trail, was in at the end. Colonel Honner led it back over the mountains to victory in action at Gona.

On 23 January 1943, the Kokoda Trail campaign completed, the battalion held a roll call. Its strength amounted to seven officers and 25 men – out of a normal 800.

Stalingrad (1942)

E. D. Smith

Nearly 300 miles beyond the German frontline that existed in the spring of 1942 lay the city of Stalingrad. Even farther away, over 350 miles distant, was the Caucasus with its rich oil fields. Adolf Hitler decided that these two objectives would be captured during his summer offensive against the Red Army.

At first glance, Hitler's intentions seemed to be sound, designed to destroy the Russians before another cruel winter came to their aid. If the German Army could cross the Volga in the Stalingrad area, then Russia's main north-south line of communications would be cut. And, if simultaneously the production of the rich oil fields in and near the Caucasus could be harnessed to the German war effort, then the whole situation in the East would be changed and the prospects of an outright victory considerably enhanced.

It was a gamble, however, because Hitler's objectives, being some 350 miles apart, meant that two separate, divergent operations had to be mounted. To capture two such remote and distant objectives meant bringing fresh divisions to the Eastern front and these had to come from Germany's allies – Rumania, Hungary and Italy. Prior to 1942 only élite units from these satellite nations had fought alongside their German masters. Now complete corps or even armies of one nationality were to fight at ever-increasing distances from their homelands. Such a vast increase in battalions gave some substance to Hitler's dreams. He was intoxicated by their numbers but the seeds of disaster had already been sown when he launched his offensive at the end of June. The soldiers of Germany's allies followed the spearhead of the attack with a reluctance that increased as they moved deeper into Russia.

The campaign, under the operation Code word "Blau", began with a series of victories. In July Krasnodar on the Kuban River and Voroshilovsk close by the foothills of the Caucasus mountains were captured. Thousands of prisoners were taken. By the end of August the German flag had been hoisted on the peak of the Elbrus, the highest point in the Caucasus. At this stage, 4th Army's panzers suddenly stopped on Hitler's orders and turned north east to help 6th Army in its drive to the Volga. No further progress was to be made in the Caucasus. The attention of both sides was drawn inexorably to the Stalingrad front.

In the early days of August the Germans struck across the steppes from the south west, advancing along the Salsk-Stalingrad railway. The rail centre of Kotelnikovo, 73 miles from Stalingrad, was captured on 2 August. Thereafter the forces used in these efforts swelled in mid-August from a total of 17 divisions to 23 but there was to be no dramatic breakthrough by General Friedrich von Paulus and his experienced 6th Army. By now Stalin had issued his stirring cry: "Ni shagun nazad" (Not a step backwards). Stalingrad, in 1941 a sprawling industrial giant of half a million people was going to be defended street by street, block by block, house by house. The German 6th and 4th Panzer Armies were being sucked into all-out attacks on the city – with their long open flank on the River Don guarded by apprehensive satellite divisions.

A midnight on 23 August the 16th Panzer Division had outrun the support of the other divisions and reached the outskirts of Stalingrad. Earlier in the same day the Luftwaffe began a series of terrible air raids, levelling the city until it looked as if a giant hurricane had lifted it into the air and smashed it down into a million pieces. Thousands of frightened civilians, whose presence in the smoking ruins was no longer necessary, were evacuated, crossing the Volga in a fleet of

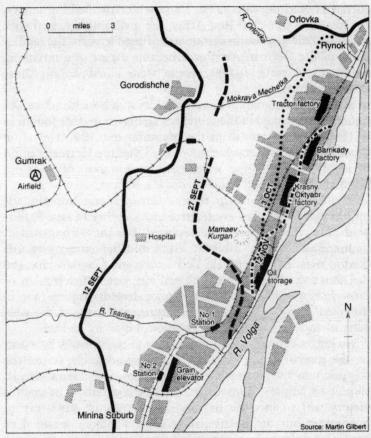

5.5 The Battle for Stalingrad, September 1942–February 1943

battered tugs, ferries and steamers. The Stukas tried to stampede the civilian population by bombing the jammed embankment beside the main ferry landing. Clusters of bombs found them and the footpaths near the Volga were slippery with blood, while many of the boats of the rescue fleet sank with few survivors reaching safety. For those who remained in the city, the troops of the 62nd Red Army, the civil militia armed with rifles, and the workers in certain important factories, the regular visits of the German Air Force became a part of a terrifying nightmare. Nearly 40,000 people were killed during those brutal air raids.

Stalin's determination to save the city that bore his name was not always reflected in the morale of all his troops that fought in the Stalingrad sector during the late summer of 1942. Defection was rife, few Russian soldiers believed that the Germans could be stopped short of the Volga, and the numbers of prisoners pouring into German hands became a torrent.

The Commander of the 62nd Army, General Lopatin, admitted that he had lost confidence in his ability to save Stalingrad. He was sacked and replaced by the strong-willed, pugnacious General Chuikov. From mid-September onwards the partnership of Generals Yeremenko and Chuikov changed the situation. Anyone who showed any signs of defeatism or pessimism was thrown out; they demonstrated complete faith in the 62nd Army by bringing reinforcements across to the west bank of the Volga when the situation was at its blackest.

No longer could the Germans expect to take the city by storm on the march. Gone were the lightning advances across the steppes; now the panzers were bogged down in narrow streets, shot at by snipers, doused by Molotov cocktails. The cost of victory was to increase day by day as August gave way to September but the possibility of such a victory lessened as winter approached, as the Russians made plans to break through the German "corridor" that thrust its way to Stalingrad. The Russian High Command was well aware that the left flank of the German Army Group "B" was manned by non-German troops, with the Rumanians closest to Stalingrad, the Italians farther to the west, and the Hungarians farther west still. Indeed, the German General Staff had already begun warning Adolf Hitler about this vulnerable flank but his answer was unchanged. "Where the German soldier sets foot, there he remains. You may rest assured that nobody will ever drive us away from Stalingrad" (Speech to the German people in October 1942). Instead of a strategical withdrawal before winter came, General Paulus was told to battle his way through Stalingrad to the Volga – regardless of cost to men and machines.

On 13 September two German assault groups, infantry and tanks, smashed into the positions held by Chuikov's 62nd Army. After a day of bitter fighting the German troops made some gains. Next day the Soviets tried to counter-attack but with the whole weight of many hundreds of guns supported by Stukas, tanks and truck-loads of infantry fought their way towards the Volga and threatened the central landing stage, the very lifeline of the besieged army. By now, the Germans were only 800 yards from Chuikov's HQ. Never faltering, he made the important and fateful decision to summon the 13th Guards Division to his aid even though more than a thousand of its members had no weapons to fire. After a hazardous crossing of the Volga in small boats and barges, strafed by Stukas during daylight hours and targets for observed artillery and small arms fire, the Guards riflemen joined the other defenders who were fighting for survival: men who had nowhere to retreat, who were lacking food and water, who were constantly under attack from air as well as being embroiled in a deadly struggle that went on by day and night. At a very high cost, the German onslaught against the centre of the city was blocked and the 62nd Army won a few more precious hours.

Contrary to German expectations, the city did not fall into their hands rapidly nor did the Red Army pull back entirely onto the eastern bank of the Volga. Each building in Stalingrad became its own battleground. Factories, railway stations, streets, squares, even single ruined walls, were all defended with a stubborn tenacity by soldiers, militia and the workers themselves. The Central Railway Station changed hands many times. The struggle for the hillock, Mamaev Kurgan, was equally intense. On the southern boundary of 62nd Army stood a giant grain-elevator in which German and Soviet soldiers fought for several days and nights for parts of the building. Elsewhere there were dozens of strongpoints which took a heavy toll of lives, German and Russian.

The commanders on both sides were shaken by the terrible casualties, wondering whether they would run out of men before their opponents did, but by 22 September, the Germans appeared to be on the verge of victory. General Friedrich von Paulus was telling journalists from his own country that the city would fall "anytime now, anytime". In his heart, however, he had lost most of his hopes for a quick victory. Moreover, Paulus envisaged no solution other than butting his way through the factory districts, using his tired army as a human battering ram.

The 52-year-old Army Commander was a typical German General Staff officer; tall and handsome, impeccably groomed at all times, the ambitious Paulus had solid grounds for thinking that the capture of Stalingrad would lead to further promotion. Nevertheless, he was worried by the long open left flank in his rear, guarded by the puppet forces of Germany's Allies. Stubbornly sticking to his earlier tactics Paulus continued to hurl his army against Russian defences. Weakened by nagging dysentry, he sent a series of complaints back to his superiors, asking for more of everything; instead he received a sapper battalion specially flown out from Germany to help in the house-to-house fighting which was decimating his infantry units. The build-up meant that by the first week in October General Chuikov considered that he was facing nine German divisions, with the Volga less than 4,000 yards behind the front line.

There could be no retreat. There was none. By the middle of October nearly 100,000 Russian reinforcements had been ferried across the river into Stalingrad. They were killed so quickly that in less than a month the 62nd Army had lost more than 80,000 men, killed, wounded or missing. The German 6th Army was in no better plight. In a period of six weeks they had lost over 40,000 casualties. The struggle for the key to the city, the factory area, continued throughout October with the northern sector under constant siege. The Germans narrowed their attacks down to sectors, two to four hundred yards wide, concentrating on taking the shortest way to the Volga. Such tactics were to bring some success. In four places they broke through the narrow-waisted city to the river. General von Paulus set up his HQ in a basement store on Heroes of the Revolution Square, in the centre of Stalingrad. Like his army he was committed to stay in Stalingrad. For a few days both sides stood limp and exhausted from their murderous struggle in the smoking ruins, the graveyard of a city.

The 6th Army had all but taken Stalingrad; they had a death-grip on the ruins along the Volga. An order of the day from Paulus to his exhausted army claimed an outright victory adding, "the actions of the leadership and the troops during the offensive will enter into history as an especially glorious page. Winter is upon us . . . the Russians will take advantage of it. It is unlikely the Russians will fight with the same strength as last winter".

Brave but ill-considered words. The Germans held most of Stalingrad but all around them was gathering a storm, a storm that was due to break on 19 November. For while the 6th Army had been hurling itself against Stalingrad, only limited German operations had been continuing in the Caucasus, and elsewhere along the front the German High Command had left the other Red Armies alone, free to reorganise, able to regroup. Under Stalin's supervision, Marshals Zhukov and Vasilevsky were drawing up their final plans for Operation "Uranus", designed to encircle and trap their enemy within the gates of Stalingrad. Such a counter-offensive, which involved three fronts, Stalingrad, Don and South-Western, meant that thousands of Russian troops were on the move days before the date Stalin had selected far the attack to begin – and the Germans were fully aware that an onslaught was about to be launched to coincide with the Russian winter.

On many occasions, Hitler had been told that the left flank of Army Group "B" was exposed, the Achilles heel of Paulus and his army. General Zeitzler, Chief of the Army General Staff advocated a withdrawal westward from Stalingrad, which would shorten the front and would do away with the long corridor with its vulnerable flanks.

Such a solution proved totally unacceptable to Hitler. To even suggest the abandonment of Stalingrad, the hard-won prize of his summer and fall offensives, was enough to cause the Führer to rant and rave. For him the retention of Stalingrad had become a question of personal prestige. Nobody, and nothing, could make him change his mind.

In desperation his General Staff devised other expedients. A small reserve was created behind the threatened flank. It consisted of a single weak Panzer corps, comprising two armoured divisions, one German and the other Rumanian. In addition, small German units, such as anti-tank battalions, were interspersed amongst the satellite divisions. These units were intended to bolster the threatened front. In the event of the non-German units being overrun, the "bolster units" were to stand fast, to limit the enemy's gains, and in holding out in such a manner, to create more favorable conditions for a German counter-attack. In theory there was some merit in the plan but should the allied troops collapse too quickly, or too completely, then it was obvious that the German units would find themselves hopelessly swamped by sheer weight of numbers. Other measures included posting liaison groups, containing German General Staff officers and signal units, to the senior headquarters of the non-German formations.

Radio deception was practised on a large scale, with the purpose of concealing from the Russians the fact that there were no German troops along the threatened flank and also of giving them a false picture of the German strength in that sector.

These were but some of the precautions taken but, efficiently though they were put into operation, the Russian High Command was not deceived. During the first half of November the picture of the future Russian offensive became increasingly clear. That they were going to attack north-west of Stalingrad became obvious. German Intelligence felt that the sector held by the Rumanians would be the one selected but what they could not gauge was the date on which such an attack would be launched. Even the puppet allies had begun sounding the alarm. The Commander of the Rumanian 3rd Army, in position on 6th Army's left flank at the Don, sent a cry for help that was forwarded to East Prussia for Adolf Hitler's consideration. What was the German Army going to do about the build-up opposite his Army? Hitler gave his reply in a political speech during which he said: "I wished to reach the Volga at a certain point, near a certain city. That city happens to bear the name of Stalin himself . . . I wished to take that city; we do not make exaggerated claims and I can now tell you that we have captured it . . . Now people may ask: Why does not the Army advance faster? But I do not wish to see a second Verdun. I prefer it to reach my objectives by means of limited assaults. Time is of no importance . . ."

In Moscow, the Russian General Staff was overjoyed when the Germans continued to rivet their attentions to the ruined city near the banks of the Volga. The German Luftwaffe did what it could to harass the Soviet build-up. Planes were sent to the Kletskaya and Serafimovich bridgehead areas to strike against rail lines and troop concentrations. Long-range artillery bombardment was used to maximum effect but the most that this could hope to achieve was a postponement of the date fixed for the attack. The Germans did not possess total, overwhelming air supremacy nor did they have an air force of the requisite size on the Eastern Front.

General Richthofen, the aggressive, flamboyant Air Fleet IV commander, wrote in his diary on 12 November, "The Russians are resolutely carrying on with their preparations for an offensive against the Rumanians . . . When, I wonder, will be attack come? The guns are beginning to make their appearance in artillery emplacements. I can only hope that the Russians won't tear too many big holes in the line!".

Such was the situation when the Russian winter broke upon the Germans with all its fury. Now they knew that the counter-offensive would not long be delayed. Three days later the outspoken Richthofen, in a telephone conversation with General Zeitzler, gave vent to his anger and frustration: "Both the command and the troops are listless . . . we shall get nowhere. Let us either fight or abandon the attack altogether. If we can't clear up the situation now, when the Volga is blocked and the Russians in real difficulty, we shall never be able to".

Zeitzler agreed – but there was nothing that he could do. The final authority lay with Adolf Hitler.

Early on the morning of 19 November 1942, the Russian

offensive opened. The liaison staff with the Rumanians reported, "Very heavy artillery bombardment of the whole Rumanian front north-west of Stalingrad". The single reserve corps under command Army Group "B", Panzer Corps "H", the 48th Corps, was made ready for action immediately – but application had to be made to Hitler for its release from reserve. It required, as usual, a tremendous effort to convince the Führer that the reserve had to be used at once. Meanwhile the Russian shelling of the Rumanian positions had redoubled in intensity; then, under cover of a heavy snowstorm and with the thermometer showing 20 degrees below zero, the Red Army attacked. For Chuikov and his Army, it meant that the 68 days of fighting in Stalingrad were about to be rewarded. Their stubborn defence had bought time and enabled the gigantic counter-offensive to be prepared and launched. Now he and his men would wreak their vengeance on the German 6th Army.

Three Red Army Groups launched the carefully planned offensive from north-west and south-west of Stalingrad. The Russian 5th and 21st Tank Armies burst through the Rumanian Army in the wake of the heavy artillery bombardment. The bewildered, frightened Rumanians offered little resistance, with only a few staying to fight the Russian tanks. The German 48th Panzer Corps was sent to challenge the Russian 21st Army rampaging south of the Don. Its efforts were hampered by the fleeing Rumanians who were scattering in terror across the snowfields. The foul weather grounded both air forces so that General Richthofen was unable to help the stricken Rumanians, whose officers had defected, leaving thousands of soldiers to wander aimlessly around the steppes, nor was he able to assist 48th Panzer Corps in seeking out the Russians. The prospects of a successful counter-attack soon diminished. The Panzer Corps was incapable of stabilizing the situation and became hopelessly embroiled in the general confusion, fighting desperately for its own survival.

South of Stalingrad more Russian forces massed along a 125-mile front. The 64th, 57th and 51st Armies were facing the vastly over-extended 4th Rumanian Army. Its task was to protect the German 6th Army's right flank. At 1000 hours, on 20 November, General Yeremenko began his attack. The soldiers of the Rumanian 4th Army fled in all directions and within a matter of hours, 10,000 prisoners had been taken by the Russians. North and south of the "Corridor", the Russians swept forward, trapping units as they retreated into defensive pockets where they were isolated without communications with each other or Higher Command. Only in the fading afternoon light of 21 November did the Germans gain a victory. The 29th Motorized Division thrust at the right flank of the Russian mechanized column. A sudden counter-attack caught the Russians off guard and many of their tanks were lost in the ambush. Before the Divisional Commander could annihilate the burning enemy force he was ordered to pull back to guard 6th Army's rear at the Don. Such a victory brought a brief respite only; its significance was soon forgotten as disaster followed disaster elsewhere. The Stalingrad Army was thus threatened with encirclement from both flanks and it was only a question of hours before the two Russian pincers closed behind 6th Army's rear. When General Paulus suggested that his Army should withdraw to the south-west, a sharp command was received to hold fast, to stand firm.

"To HQ 6 Army, Führer Order. 6 Army will hold position despite threat of temporary encirclement. . . . Keep railroad line open as long as possible. Special orders regarding air supplies will follow."

The order implied that the 6th Army would be supplied from the air after forming a hedgehog defence. General Richthofen is reported to have phoned Göring's deputy and said: "In the filthy weather we have here, there's not a hope of supplying an army of 250,000 men from the air. It is stark staring madness." Such considerations were brushed aside by Hitler and on 23 November the Russian pincers met at Kalach. The encirclement movement was complete. The Rumanian divisions had been defeated, most of them caught and slaughtered by the surprise Red Army crossing of the unfrozen river Don. Inside the Red Army ring were twenty-two divisions, twenty German and two Rumanian. There were also troops from the engineers, artillery, assault gun battalions, pioneers, in addition to the headquarter staffs of five corps and General Paulus's own Army Headquarters. The Luftwaffe was represented by parts of an anti-aircraft artillery corps and by the ground staff personnel. It is impossible to establish the exact number of troops encircled, the figure given ranging from 215,000 to something approaching 300,000. Small elements of 6th Army were not caught in the encirclement when first it was formed while units belonging to other armies were. The only means of communication between the entrapped Army and the outer world was by airplane and radio. Initially, there were three or four airfields within the pocket and an efficient radio-telephone link was established between General Paulus and the Commander, Army Group "B".

One of the first orders which Hitler issued after the Russian pincers had met, ran as follows: "The forces of the 6th Army encircled at Stalingrad will be known as the troops of Fortress Stalingrad". However, Stalingrad was a fortress in name only, even if the German civilian population were hoodwinked into thinking that the defenceless trapped army could withstand a long siege. There were no fortifications, the bombastic and meaningless title bestowed upon the 6th Army did nothing for the morale of the soldiers. Sixth Army was to hold a pocket of some 25 miles from east to west and about 12 miles, north to south. Outside the ruined city, the country was steppe, with scarcely a tree or bush to be seen. Sections of Stalingrad were still in Russian hands with its eastern boundary on the right bank of the Volga. And now the stricken army, in conditions of extreme cold, in blizzards, with the thermometer far below freezing point, had to build fortifications where none had existed before. Although General Paulus was convinced his Army should begin its retreat towards the west, he continued to wait for Hitler's approval, putting all units on the alert to move quickly in case permission was granted. The authorization was never to be forthcoming – although Zeitzler and his colleagues tried to persuade Hitler that Paulus must be given freedom to act on his own and be allowed to break out. Occasionally, Hitler lost all self-control, crashing his fist down on the table, shouting: "I won't leave the Volga! I won't go back from the Volga!". He put his faith in the efforts of Army Group "D" and the arrival, on the Russian front for the first time, of the new heavy tank, the Tiger. Efficient though the prototype Tigers, were, it was stretching fantasy to extremes by expecting a single battalion of tanks not only to succeed in breaking through the Russian lines but to keep the "Corridor" open thereafter.

If relief was to come, then it had to be in the shape of a force commanded by Field Marshal Erich von Manstein, the newly appointed Commander-in-Chief of Army Group Don. Before Manstein's attack was to begin, however, an even more crucial problem had to be resolved. Could Reich-Marshal Göring and his Luftwaffe keep 6th Army supplied by air?

The Reich-Marshal had assured Hitler that this was possible but the beleaguered army in Stalingrad required some 500 tons of resupply each and every day. Early figures were not encouraging; 110 tons, 120, sometimes 140 tons. On many days no supplies arrived at all. This was not the fault of the German air crews nor of their immediate commanders who did their utmost, but Göring had undertaken a task which was far beyond the capacity of the Luftwaffe. The winter weather meant that there were many days when planes could not fly. The pilots had to run the gauntlet across a belt of enemy-held territory which became wider and wider as the Russians pushed the German forces further to the west. As more and more German planes were shot down so the capacity to lift in the required tonnage decrease. In the "Fortress" the situation deteriorated as shortages became more and more acute. The soldiers of the 6th Army called the Fortress "Der Kessel" (the Cauldron). It was a tragedy for 6th Army that General Paulus was not able to act against the wishes of the Führer, especially when he knew in his heart that to stay in Stalingrad meant disaster. The only hope for Paulus and his men lay in Field Marshal Erich von Manstein, conqueror of Sevastopol, hero of the French campaign whose plan to out-flank the Maginot Line had led to the downfall of France within six weeks. If anyone was to save Paulus and his army, it was Manstein – but he needed more troops and armour than circumstances allowed him in the middle of December 1942. In addition, 6th Army would have to abandon Stalingrad and fight their way west to meet him.

Meanwhile, the Russians had been surprised by the success of their Operation "Uranus". In their wildest dreams they never expected to trap nearly 300,000 men within their giant encirclement. But now seven Soviet Armies were hugging 6th Army in a hostile embrace. There remained the problem of exterminating such a big force. There is a Russian tale about a hunter who bet a friend that he could catch a bear single-handed. He went out, grappled with the bear, and called back to his friend: "See, I've got him. The only thing is, now, he won't let me go". The question was whether the 6th Army would let its encirclers go or would they try to break out without help from a relief force? Zhukov predicted that they would stand fast, that a relief force would attempt to evacuate the trapped army and, in his opinion, the 6th Army pocket should be cut in half. But before this could be put into effect, Operation "Winter Storm", the attempt to break through to 6th Army had begun.

From the suburbs of Kotelnikovo, tanks and trucks of the 6th Panzer Division fanned out and raced for Stalingrad. To begin with, General Hoth and his Fourth Panzer Army advanced steadily and six days later they were little more than 40 miles from the southern perimeter of Stalingrad. Three days later the city was only 30 miles away. For the first twelve days, as Manstein and Hoth pushed forward, the Russian resistance was negligible, then the opposition hardened with Soviet T-34 tanks and anti-tank guns being thrown against the Germans. The attack slowed to a snail's pace.

On 17 December the Russians struck another blow, this time against two Italian divisions, fifty miles west of Serafimovich. The attack was aimed at seizing the city of Rostov, thereby entrapping the entire German Army in Southern Russia. The Italian army failed to hold and it was clear that Manstein would have to go to their rescue. He urged Hitler to issue an order for Operation "Thunderclap", an order that would mean that 6th Army, weakened though it was, would begin to move back westwards across the steppe, fighting the Russians on all sides in a bid for salvation and safety. But the Führer forbade Paulus to withdraw from Stalingrad. His reasoning was arrogant and typically blind, adding that "too much blood has been spilled there by Germans". Manstein sent his intelligence officer into Stalingrad by air so that he could discuss the situation with Paulus. By now it was clear that 4th Panzer Army could only continue to drive forward for a very limited period; that some divisions might have to move away and go to the assistance of the Italians. It was doubtful whether General Hoth's tanks could advance many more miles towards Stalingrad. Could Paulus extend his own drive a further 25 kilometers to the south? In Paulus's opinion this was not feasible as 6th Army was desperately short of fuel for its tanks and all arms needed urgent supplies of food and ammunition. General Paulus was not prepared to accept the risk of making the link-up until more supplies had been received or unless his Führer so ordered a complete evacuation of Stalingrad.

Before his attack ground to a halt some 30 miles from Stalingrad, Field Marshal von Manstein made one more attempt to persuade Hitler to change his mind. Zeitzler spent many hours with the Führer, arguing and pleading. Eventually Hitler said that a message could be drafted addressed to Paulus, asking him how far he could get if he was ordered to break out. Zeitzler immediately drafted the signal in Hitler's presence and gave it to him to sign. The Führer read it, picked up a pencil and inserted the words: "the condition being that you continue to hold the line of the Volga". Such a condition missed the whole purpose and nature of the proposed operation. Instead of a full-scale evacuation, Hitler intended a link-up which was intended to bring further supplies into the Stalingrad garrison. Paulus's reply came, "about 25 miles", a shorter distance than that which separated him from the vanguard of Field Marshal von Manstein's force. Once again, salvation had been denied Paulus and his besieged army by Adolf Hitler. That was the very last moment at which the 6th Army might still have been saved. All it could do was to defend Stalingrad against increasing pressure from all sides – without any hopes beyond death or captivity.

On 24 December the Red Army under General Malinovsky struck against Manstein. In three days he pushed the relieving forces back to their starting point and on 29 December captured Kotelnikovo. The distance between 4th Panzer Army's foremost troops and the outposts of the 6th Army was increased, once again, to over 60 miles. Another successful attack of the Russian winter offensive, west and south of Stalingrad, was beginning to threaten the German Army Group "A" in the

Caucasus. If the Russians captured Rostov the whole of that Army Group would be in imminent danger of encirclement. At first it appeared as if the Führer would not withdraw from the Caucasus but eventually he relented, thus saving his armies from the fate that had befallen their fellow countrymen in Stalingrad.

At the end of December the situation within the fortress had badly deteriorated, although, as yet, the Russians had not undertaken any major direct assaults. The airlift was totally inadequate and shortages became more and more acute. The troops' rations were cut and cut again; these were now insufficient to keep the men alive for any length of time. It was obvious that a further reduction would soon be inevitable. The failure of the attack by 4th Panzer Army had demoralized both the commanders and the troops – all the more so since they had been encouraged to hope and believe that salvation was on its way. The defenders dug deep in the basements of the city and hacked holes in the frozen earth. They received 25 to 30 cartridges daily, with orders to use them only in self-defence. Four ounces of bread and a ration of horse meat, with the temperature well below zero, with a burning cold wind from the east which whipped across the barren earth: such was their lot. To describe such conditions is virtually impossible, and those who have survived invariably maintain that the last days in Stalingrad were akin to hell – but that the weeks and months spent as prisoners of the Russians were far worse – quite beyond description and outside the comprehension of those who were not there to share their sufferings.

The 8 January 1943 was the date which marked the beginning of the end for General Paulus' Army. This was the day on which the Russians sent two officers, accompanied by a bugler and carrying a white flag, towards the German lines. As their bugler sounded a call, the Germans answered them with a hail of fire, which sent the Red Army men scampering for cover; but they came back, waved their flag, sounded their bugle again, and on this occasion the German lines were silent. The Germans blindfolded them and took them to Paulus in his headquarters.

The emissaries carried an ultimatum, a demand for surrender, addressed to General Paulus and signed by the Russian General commanding the Don Front, Lieutenant-General Rokossovsky. In it the Russian Commander-in-Chief described the hopeless position of the encircled 6th Army and promised that if the soldiers surrendered they would be guaranteed life, security and their return to Germany, or whatever other country they came from, as soon as the war was over. The document ended with the threat that if the Army did not now capitulate, then it would be annihilated. The time limit fixed for the reply was 1000 hours, 9 January 1943.

There was no need to send a delegation to seek a reply from the Germans next day, and the Russians never came. The ultimatum had been turned down. Paulus had contacted Hitler at once and asked for freedom of action. The General's request was immediately and curtly refused. Hitler ordered his army to fight to the death and that they would do. Again, Soviet loudspeakers called on the Germans to surrender, but to no avail. Firing was resumed and two days later, on 10 January the Red Army launched an offensive against the starving, desperate Germans.

Why did Hitler condemn a whole army to death and destruction? He was a man of such varying moods. It is impossible to say whether he really understood the significance of his "last round, last man" edict. In his New Year message to the Stalingrad army he promised them they would be relieved and delivered from the hands of the Russians. To the German people he repeated over and over again that the sacrifice and fortitude of Paulus and his men had been vital and had enabled other fronts to be preserved intact. Their defence would yet be crowned with victory – said the Führer. There is no direct evidence as to Hitler's true feelings except that General Jodl, his most intimate military crony, said at his trial at Nuremberg:

"I feel great compassion for General Paulus. He could not know that Hitler considered his army lost from the moment when the first winter storms began to blow about Stalingrad."

We can only assume that Hitler was a prisoner of his own obstinate conviction that where the German soldier once set his foot, there he remained.

Early on the morning of 10 January, the Russian artillery laid down a heavy barrage which heralded a major attack against the "Fortress". Their infantry began an assault against its northern, western and southern flanks. The defenders, weak with hunger and short of ammunition, fought with desperation and heroism. Casualties on both sides were severe. But the 6th Army could not stop the Russians breaking through on all flanks and large sections of the defensive front had to be abandoned: the pocket was being steadily constricted and this continued throughout the next few days.

By 16 January, the pocket was barely 15 miles long and about 9 miles deep at its widest. The most serious loss was that of the Pitommik airfield through which the defenders had been supplied. Now even Hitler's blind optimism could not continue. For the first time the German people were told about the serious situation which was developing in Stalingrad. Nevertheless, the Führer still refused to give Paulus the freedom of action which the Army commander had repeatedly requested. In Stalingrad, Paulus found that several of his subordinate generals were plotting mutiny, convinced that further resistance was futile. He seemed dazed by the calamity that had overtaken him. An observer wrote, "Sorrow and grief lined his face. His complexion was the colour of ashes. His posture, so upright otherwise, was now slightly stooped". Indeed, his Chief of Staff, Lieutenant General Artur Schmidt, had begun to assume control of the defeated army. Schmidt was a bulwark of strength, shining in adversity, bullying defeatist officers and threatening would-be deserters with the firing squad.

Like a Greek play, the tragedy was drawing to its close. By 26 January, the Russians had broken the German force into two small, isolated groups, one west and the other north of Stalingrad. For the ordinary soldier fighting there, each day simply brought a renewed dose of hunger, privation, bitter cold, hardship of every sort, fear of freezing or starving to death, fear of being wounded when little could be done to tend the wounds. For supplies had ceased almost completely. If something was lost, then it was gone for ever and could never be replaced. There was no shelter for the wounded, no bedding, no medicine. Surgeons and doctors alike were powerless because they had nothing to work with to alleviate pain or suffering.

The once proud 6th Army began to disintegrate. Senior commanders who could no longer endure the strain either committed suicide or went out in the open, firing at the Russians until at last a bullet put an end to their agony. Some junior officers and men set off to try and reach the main German front. In March one solitary sergeant managed to reach the German lines after weeks of incredible hardship. He died a few days later, worn out by the privations he had suffered.

The Führer's reply to General Paulus, when he asked, once again, for freedom of action, was to promote him to Field Marshal as well as issuing dozens of decorations and promotions to the starving, dying survivors in Stalingrad. Within Germany, Dr Goebbels' propaganda machine began to extol the exploits of Paulus and his men. Reich-Marshal Göring spoke of the greatest and most heroic fight in all the annals of the German race and compared the 6th Army to the Greek heroes that fought to the last man at Thermopylae.

On 31 January the western group was smashed and Paulus, the general who had subordinated himself completely to Hitler's whims, and in so doing had lost control of his destiny, was captured. Unshaven, but immaculate in his full dress uniform, Friedrich von Paulus went into captivity after being reassured that his men would be given proper rations and medical care.

Unfortunately neither of these conditions was to come to pass. Hundreds of defenceless and wounded German troops were killed where they lay. When the final attack was made early in the morning of 2 February, Germans who had fired their last ammunition at the attackers were beaten to death by the enraged Russians.

The battle for Stalingrad was over. In five months, 99 per cent of the city had been reduced to ruins and rubble. Of the half-million inhabitants of the previous summer, only some 1,500 civilians remained. Of the 500,000 Germans, Italians, Hungarians, Rumanians, who were captured in the Stalingrad sector or in the city itself, it is estimated that in three months, between February and April of 1943, more than 400,000 of them were to perish somewhere in Russia. The Russian High

Command had never expected to take such numbers into captivity. They left most of them to their own devices and to the cruel mercy of a harsh Russian winter. Those that survived did so, in many cases, by accepting Communist indoctrination because co-operation meant at least some food – and life.

For Paulus, too, there was to be no happy ending. Hitler raged against his newly appointed Field Marshal, one who preferred captivity to death. Hitler said that he had not expected this; had he done so, he would never have promoted Paulus. In captivity, Paulus eventually let it be known that he believed that Communism was the only hope for post-war Europe and lent his name to the Anti-Fascist Officers group which flourished in Soviet prisons. Paulus was to spend the rest of his life behind the Iron Curtain, living in Russia until 1952, when he moved to East Germany. His final years were bitter ones. Stung by memoirs that accused him of subservience to Hitler and of apathy in adversity, he wrote copiously to rebuff these charges.

The disaster at Stalingrad profoundly shocked the German people and armed forces alike; indeed, it truly horrified them. Never before in Germany's history had so large a body of troops come to so dreadful an end. It is true that the Eastern Front was stabilized during 1943 and there were to be some notable German successes. But the gap torn in the ranks of the German Eastern Army, when the twenty divisions of the 6th Army, almost all formations of the highest class, were annihilated, could never be made good. The Battle of Stalingrad was the turning point of the entire war. Adolf Hitler not only condemned an army to death; he ensured that the German nation could not win the struggle against the Allies.

Midway (1942)

Donald Macintyre

Pearl Harbor was a scene of intense activity during the last week of May 1942: a feeling of great impending events pervaded the atmosphere. On the 26th the aircraft-carriers *Enterprise* and *Hornet* of Task Force (TF) 16 had steamed in and moored, to set about in haste the various operations of refuelling and replenishing after a vain race across the Pacific to try to go to the aid of Rear-Admiral Frank Fletcher's Task Force 17 in the Battle of the Coral Sea. On the next day the surviving carriers of TF 17, the *Yorktown*'s blackened sides and twisted decks providing visible signs of the damage sustained in the battle, berthed in the dry dock of the naval base where an army of workmen swarmed aboard to begin repairs.

Under normal circumstances, weeks of work lay ahead of them, but now word had reached the dockyard that emergency repairs in the utmost haste were required. Work was to go on, night and day, without ceasing, until the ship was at least temporarily battle-worthy. For at the headquarters of the C-in-C Pacific, Admiral Chester Nimitz, it was known from patient analysis and deciphering of enemy signals that the Japanese fleet was moving out to throw down a challenge which, in spite of local American inferiority, had to be accepted.

So, on May 28, Task Force 16 sailed again, the *Enterprise* flying the flag of Rear-Admiral Raymond Spruance, and vanished into the wide wastes of the Pacific. Six cruisers and nine destroyers formed its screen; two replenishment tankers accompanied it. The following day the dockyard gave Nimitz the scarcely credible news that the *Yorktown* was once again battleworthy. Early on the 30th she, too, left harbour and, having gathered in her air groups, headed north-westward to rendezvous with Task Force 16 at "Point Luck", 350 miles northeast of the island of Midway. Forming the remainder of Task Force 17 were two cruisers and five destroyers.

The main objective of the Japanese was the assault and occupation of the little atoll of Midway, 1,100 miles west-north-west of Oahu, and forming the western extremity of the Hawaiian island chain. Together with the occupation of the Aleutian Islands, the capture of Midway would extend Japan's eastern sea frontier so that sufficient warning might be obtained of any threatened naval air attack on the homeland – Pearl Harbor in reverse. The plan had been given added impetus on 18 April by the raid on Tokyo mounted by Colonel Doolittle's army bombers taking off from the *Hornet*.

Doubts on the wisdom of the Japanese plan had been voiced in various quarters; but Yamamoto, the dynamic C-in-C of the Combined Fleet, had fiercely advocated it for reasons of his own. He had always been certain that only by destroying the American fleet could Japan gain the breathing space required to consolidate her conquests and negotiate satisfactory peace terms – a belief which had inspired the attack on Pearl Harbor. Yamamoto rightly believed that an attack on Midway was a challenge that Nimitz could not ignore. It would bring the US Pacific Fleet out where Yamamoto, in overwhelming strength, would be waiting to bring it to action.

The Japanese plan was an intricate one, as their naval strategic plans customarily were, calling for exact timing for a junction at the crucial moment of several disparate forces; and it involved – also typically – the offering of a decoy or diversion to lure the enemy into dividing his force or expending his strength on a minor objective.

Between 25/27 May, Northern Force would sail from Ominato, at the northern tip of Honshu, for the attack on the Aleutians. The II Carrier Striking Force, under Rear-Admiral

Kakuta – comprising the small aircraft-carriers *Ryujo* and *Junyo*, two cruisers, and three destroyers – would be the first to sail, its task being to deliver a surprise air attack on Dutch Harbor on 3 June. This, it was expected, might induce Nimitz to send at least part of his fleet racing north, in which case it would find waiting to intercept it a Guard Force, of four battleships, two cruisers, and twelve destroyers.

Kakuta's force would be followed two days later by the remainder of the Aleutians force – two small transport units with cruiser and destroyer escorts for the invasion of Attu and Kiska on 5 June. Meanwhile, from Hashirajima Anchorage in the Inland Sea, the four big aircraft-carriers of Vice-Admiral Nagumo's I Carrier Striking Force – *Akagi, Kaga, Hiryu*, and *Soryu* – would sail for the vicinity of Midway. There, at dawn on the 4th, their bombers and fighters would take off for the softening-up bombardment of the island prior to the assault landing two days later by troops carried in the Transport Group.

The original plan had called for the inclusion of the *Zuikaku* and *Shokaku* in Nagumo's force. But, like the *Yorktown*, the *Shokaku* had suffered damage in the Coral Sea battle and could not be repaired in time to take part in the Midway operation, while both carriers had lost so many experienced aircrews that replacements could not be trained in time.

In support of the Transport Group, four heavy cruisers under Vice-Admiral Kurita would also sail from Guam. Finally, three powerful forces would sail in company from the Inland Sea during 28 May:

- The Main Body, comprising Yamamoto's splendid new flagship *Yamato*, the biggest battleship in the world mounting nine 18-inch guns, the 16-inch battleships *Nagato* and *Mutsu*, with attendant destroyers;
- The Main Support Force for the Midway invasion force – two battleships, four heavy cruisers, and attendant destroyers – under Vice-Admiral Kondo;
- The Guard Force (mentioned above).

Parting company with Yamamoto's force after getting to sea, Kondo was to head for a supporting position to the south-west of Midway, while the Guard Force would proceed to station itself near the route from Pearl Harbor to the Aleutians. Yamamoto himself, with the Main Body, was to take up a central position from which he could proceed to annihilate whatever enemy force Nimitz sent out. To ensure that the dispatch of any such American force should not go undetected, Pearl Harbor was to be reconnoitred between 31 May and 3 June by two Japanese flying-boats via French Frigate Shoal (500 miles north-west of Hawaii), where a submarine was to deliver them petrol. As a further precaution, two cordons of submarines were to be stationed to the north-west and west of Hawaii by 2 June, with a third cordon farther north towards the Aleutians.

Yamamoto's plan was ingenious, if overintricate: but it had two fatal defects. For all his enthusiasm for naval aviation, he had not yet appreciated that the day of the monstrous capital ship as the queen of battles had passed in favour of the aircraft-carrier which could deliver its blows at a range thirty times greater than that of the biggest guns. The role of the battleship was now as close escort to the vulnerable aircraft-carriers, supplying the defensive anti-aircraft gunpower the latter lacked. Nagumo's force was supported only by two battleships and three cruisers. Had Yamamoto's Main Body kept company with it, the events that were to follow might have been different.

Far more fatal to Yamamoto's plan, however, was his assumption that it was shrouded from the enemy, and that only when news reached Nimitz that Midway was being assaulted would the Pacific Fleet leave Pearl Harbor. Thus long before the scheduled flying-boat reconnaissance – which in the event failed to take place because French Frigate Shoal was found to be in American hands – and before the scouting submarines had reached their stations, Spruance and Fletcher, all unknown to the Japanese, were beyond the patrol lines and poised waiting for the enemy's approach. Details of this approach as well as the broad lines of Yamamoto's plan were known to Nimitz. Beyond sending a small force of five cruisers and ten destroyers to the Aleutians to harass the invasion force, he concentrated all his available force – TF 16 and 17 – in the area.

He had also a squadron of battleships under his command, to be sure: but he had no illusions that, with their insufficient speed to keep up with the aircraft-carriers, their great guns could play any useful part in the events to follow. They were therefore relegated to defensive duties on the American west coast.

For the next few days the Japanese Combined Fleet advanced eastwards according to schedule in its wide-spread, multi-pronged formation. Everywhere a buoyant feeling of confidence showed itself, generated by the memories of the unbroken succession of Japanese victories since the beginning of the war. In the I Carrier Striking Force, so recently returned home after its meteoric career of destruction – from Pearl Harbor, through the East Indies, and on to Ceylon without the loss of a ship – the "Victory Disease" as it was subsequently to be called by the Japanese themselves, was particularly prevalent. Only the admiral – or so Nagumo was subsequently to say – felt doubts of the quality of the many replacements who had come to make up the wastage in experienced aircrews inevitable even in victorious operations.

Spruance and Fletcher had meanwhile made rendezvous during 2 June, and Fletcher had assumed command of the two task forces, though they continued to manoeuvre as separate units. The sea was calm under a blue sky split up by towering cumulus clouds. The scouting aircraft, flown off during the following day in perfect visibility, sighted nothing, and Fletcher was able to feel confident that the approaching enemy was all unaware of his presence to the north-east of Midway. Indeed, neither Yamamoto nor Nagumo, pressing forward blindly through rain and fog, gave serious thought to such an apparently remote possibility.

Far to the north on 3 June, dawn broke grey and misty over Kikuta's two aircraft-carriers from which, soon after 0300 hours, the first of two strike waves took off to wreak destruction among the installations and fuel tanks of Dutch Harbor. A further attack was delivered the following day, and during the next few days American and Japanese forces sought each other vainly among the swirling fogs, while the virtually unprotected Kiska and Attu were occupied by the Japanese. But as Nimitz refused to let any of his forces be drawn into the skirmish, this part of Yamamoto's plan failed to have much impact on the great drama being enacted farther south.

The opening scenes of this drama were enacted early on 3 June when a scouting Catalina flying boat some 700 miles west of Midway sighted a large body of ships, steaming in two long lines with a numerous screen in arrowhead formation, which was taken to be the Japanese main fleet. The sighting report brought nine army B-17 bombers from Midway, which delivered three high-level bombing attacks and claimed to have hit two battleships or heavy cruisers and two transports. But the enemy was in reality the Midway Occupation Force of transports and tankers, and no hits were scored on them until four amphibious Catalinas from Midway discovered them again in bright moonlight in the early hours of 4 June and succeeded in torpedoing a tanker. Damage was slight, however, and the tanker remained in formation.

More than 800 miles away to the east, Fletcher intercepted the reports of these encounters but from his detailed knowledge of the enemy's plan was able to identify the Occupation Force. Nagumo's carriers, he knew, were much closer, some 400 miles to the west of him, approaching their flying-off position from the north-west. During the night, therefore. Task Forces 16 and 17 steamed south-west for a position 200 miles north of Midway which would place them at dawn within scouting range of the unsuspecting enemy. The scene was now set for what was to be one of the great decisive battles of history.

The last hour of darkness before sunrise on 4 June saw the familiar activity in both the carrier forces of ranging-up aircraft on the flight-deck for dawn operations. Aboard the *Yorktown*, whose turn it was to mount the first scouting flight of the day, there were Dauntless scout dive-bombers, ten of which were launched at 0430 hours for a search to a depth of 100 miles between west and east through north, a precaution against being taken by surprise while waiting for news from the scouting flying boats from Midway.

Reconnaissance aircraft were dispatched at the same moment from Nagumo's force. One each from the *Akagi* and *Kaga*, and two seaplanes each from the cruisers *Tone* and *Chikuma* were to search to a depth of 300 miles to the east and south. The seaplane carried in the battleship *Haruna*, being of an older type, was restricted to 150 miles. The main activity in Nagumo's carriers, however, was the preparation of the striking force to attack Midway – 36 "Kate" torpedo-bombers each carrying a 1,770-pound bomb, 36 "Val" dive-bombers each with a single 550-pound bomb, and 36 Zero fighters as escort. Led by Lieutenant Joichi Tomonaga, this formidable force also took off at 0430.

By 0445 all these aircraft were on their way – with one notable exception. In the cruiser *Tone*, one of the catapults had given trouble, and it was not until 0500 that her second seaplane got away. This apparently minor dislocation of the schedule was to have vital consequences. Meanwhile, the carrier lifts were already hoisting up on deck an equally powerful second wave: but under the bellies of the "Kates" were slung torpedoes, for these aircraft were to be ready to attack any enemy naval force which might be discovered by the scouts.

The lull in proceedings which followed the dawn fly-off from both carrier forces was broken with dramatic suddenness. At 0520, aboard Nagumo's flagship *Akagi*, the alarm was sounded. An enemy flying boat on reconnaissance had been sighted. Zeros roared off the deck in pursuit. A deadly game of hide-and-seek among the clouds developed, but the American naval fliers evaded their hunters. At 0534 Fletcher's radio office received the message "Enemy carriers in sight", followed by another reporting many enemy aircraft heading for Midway; finally, at 0603, details were received of the position and composition of Nagumo's force, 200 miles west-south-west of the *Yorktown*. The time for action had arrived.

The *Yorktown*'s scouting aircraft were at once recalled and while she waited to gather them in. Fletcher ordered Spruance to proceed with his Task Force 16 "south-westerly and attack enemy carriers when definitely located". *Enterprise* and *Hornet* with their screening cruisers and destroyers turned away, increasing to 25 knots, while hooters blared for "General Quarters" and aircrews manned their planes to warm-up ready for take-off. Meanwhile, 240 miles to the south, Midway was preparing to meet the impending attack.

Radar had picked up the approaching aerial swarm at 0553 and seven minutes later every available aircraft on the island had taken off. Bombers and flying-boats were ordered to keep clear, but Marine Corps fighters in two groups clawed their way upwards, and at 0616 swooped in to the attack. But of the 26 planes, all but six were obsolescent Brewster Buffaloes, hopelessly outclassed by the highly manoeuvrable Zeros. Though they took their toll of Japanese bombers, they were in turn overwhelmed, seventeen being shot down and seven others damaged beyond repair. The survivors of the Japanese squadrons pressed on to drop their bombs on power-plants, seaplane hangars, and oil tanks.

At the same time as the Marine fighters, ten torpedo-bombers had also taken off from Midway – six of the new Grumman Avengers (which were soon to supersede the unsatisfactory Devastator torpedo-bombers in American aircraft-carriers) and four Army Marauders. At 0710 they located and attacked the Japanese carriers; but with no fighter protection against the many Zeros sent up against them, half of them were shot down before they could reach a launching position. Those which broke through, armed with the slow and unreliable torpedoes which had earned Japanese contempt in the Coral Sea battle, failed to score any hits; greeted with a storm of gunfire, only one Avenger and two Marauders escaped to crash-land on Midway.

Unsuccessful as these attacks were, they had important consequences. From over Midway, Lieutenant Tomonaga, surveying the results of his attack, at 0700 signalled that a further strike was necessary to knock out the island's defences. The torpedo attacks seemed to Nagumo to bear this out, and, as no inkling of any enemy surface forces in the vicinity had yet come to him, he made the first of a train of fatal decisions. At 0715 he ordered the second wave of aircraft to stand by to attack Midway. The "Kate" bombers, concentrated in the *Akagi* and *Kaga*, had to be struck down into the hangars to have their torpedoes replaced by bombs. Ground crews swarmed round to move them one by one to the lifts which took them below where mechanics set feverishly to work to make the exchange. It could not be a quick operation, however, and it had not been half-completed when, at 0728, came a message which threw Nagumo into an agony of indecision.

The reconnaissance seaplane from the *Tone* – the one which had been launched thirty minutes behind schedule – was fated to be the one in whose search sector the American fleet was to be found; and now it sent back the signal – "Have sighted ten ships, apparently enemy, bearing 010 degrees, 240 miles away from Midway: Course 150 degrees, speed more than 20 knots." For the next quarter of an hour Nagumo waited with mounting impatience for a further signal giving the composition of the enemy force.

Only if it included carriers was it any immediate menace at its range of 200 miles – but in that case it was vital to get a strike launched against it at once. At 0745 Nagumo ordered the re-arming of the "Kates" to be suspended and all aircraft to prepare for an attack on ships, and two minutes later he signalled to the search plane: "Ascertain ship types and maintain contact." The response was a signal of 0758 reporting only a change of the enemy's course: but twelve minutes later came the report: "Enemy ships are five cruisers and five destroyers."

This message was received with heartfelt relief by Nagumo and his staff; for at this moment his force came under attack first by sixteen Marine Corps dive-bombers from Midway, followed by fifteen Flying Fortresses, bombing from 20,000 feet, and finally eleven Marine Corps Vindicator scout-bombers. Every available Zero was sent aloft to deal with them, and not a single hit was scored by the bombers. But now, should Nagumo decide to launch an air strike, it would lack escort fighters until the Zeros had been recovered, refuelled, and re-armed. While the air attacks were in progress, further alarms occupied the attention of the battleship and cruiser screen when the US submarine *Nautilus* – one of twelve covering Midway – fired a torpedo at a battleship at 0825. But neither this nor the massive depth-charge attacks in retaliation were effective; and in the midst of the noise and confusion of the air attacks – at 0820 – Nagumo received the message he dreaded to hear: "Enemy force accompanied by what appears to be a carrier."

The luckless Japanese admiral's dilemma, however, had been disastrously resolved for him by the return of the survivors of

Tomonaga's Midway strike at 0830. With some damaged and all short of fuel, their recovery was urgent; and rejecting the advice of his subordinate carrier squadron commander – Rear-Admiral Yamaguchi, in the *Hiryu* – to launch his strike force, Nagumo issued the order to strike below all aircraft on deck and land the returning aircraft. By the time this was completed, it was 0918.

Refuelling, re-arming, and ranging-up a striking-force in all four carriers began at once, the force consisting of 36 "Val" dive-bombers and 54 "Kates", now again armed with torpedoes, with an escort of as many Zeros as could be spared from defensive patrol over the carriers. Thus it was at a carrier force's most vulnerable moment that – from his screening ships to the south – Nagumo received the report of an approaching swarm of aircraft. The earlier catapult defect in the *Tone*; the inefficient scouting of its aircraft's crew; Nagumo's own vacillation (perhaps induced by the confusion caused by the otherwise ineffective air attacks from Midway); but above all the fatal assumption that the Midway attack would be over long before any enemy aircraft-carriers could arrive in the area – all had combined to plunge Nagumo into a catastrophic situation. The pride and vainglory of the victorious carrier force had just one more hour to run.

When Task Force 16 had turned to the south-west, leaving the *Yorktown* to recover her reconnaissance aircraft, Nagumo's carriers were still too far away for Spruance's aircraft to reach him and return; and if the Japanese continued to steer towards Midway, it would be nearly 0900 before Spruance could launch his strike. When calculations showed that Nagumo would probably be occupied recovering his aircraft at about that time, however, Spruance had decided to accept the consequences of an earlier launching in order to catch him off-balance. Every serviceable aircraft in his two carriers, with the exception of the fighters required for defensive patrol, was to be included, involving a double launching, taking a full hour to complete, during which the first aircraft off would have to orbit and wait, eating up precious fuel.

It was just 0702 when the first of the sixty-seven Dauntless dive-bombers, twenty-nine Devastator torpedo-bombers, and twenty Wildcat fighters, which formed Task Force 16's striking force, flew off. The torpedo squadrons had not yet taken the air when the sight of the *Tone*'s float plane, circling warily on the horizon, told Spruance that he could not afford to wait for his striking force to form up before dispatching them. The *Enterprise*'s dive-bombers led by Lieutenant-Commander McClusky, which had been the first to take off, were ordered to lead on without waiting for the torpedo-bombers or for the fighter escort whose primary task must be to protect the slow, lumbering Devastators. At 0752, McClusky took departure, steering to intercept Nagumo's force which was assumed to be steering south-east towards Midway. The remainder of the air groups followed at intervals, the dive-bombers and fighters up at 19,000 feet, the torpedo-bombers skimming low over the sea.

This distance between them, in which layers of broken cloud made maintenance of contact difficult, had calamitous consequences. The fighters from the *Enterprise*, led by Lieutenant Gray, took station above but did not make contact with Lieutenant-Commander Waldron's torpedo squadron from the *Hornet*, leaving the *Enterprise*'s torpedo squadron, led by Lieutenant-Commander Lindsey, unescorted. *Hornet*'s fighters never achieved contact with Waldron, and flew instead in company with their dive-bombers. Thus Task Force 16's air strike advanced in four separate, independent groups – McClusky's dive-bombers, the *Hornet*'s dive-bombers and fighters, and the two torpedo squadrons.

All steered initially for the estimated position of Nagumo, assuming he had maintained his south-easterly course for Midway. In fact, at 0918, having recovered Tomonaga's Midway striking force, he had altered course to north-east to close the distance between him and the enemy while his projected strike was being ranged up on deck. When the four air groups from TF 16 found nothing at the expected point of interception, therefore, they had various courses of action to choose between. The *Hornet*'s dive-bombers decided to search south-easterly where, of course, they found nothing. As fuel ran low, some of the bombers returned to the carrier, others made for Midway to refuel. The fighters were not so lucky: one by one they were forced to ditch as their engines spluttered and died.

The two torpedo squadrons, on the other hand, low down over the water, sighted smoke on the northern horizon and, turning towards it, were rewarded with the sight of the Japanese carriers shortly after 0930. Though bereft of fighter protection, both promptly headed in to the attack. Neither Waldron nor Lindsey had any doubts of the suicidal nature of the task ahead of them. The former, in his last message to his squadron, had written: "My greatest hope is that we encounter a favourable tactical situation, but if we don't, and the worst comes to the worst, I want each of us to do his utmost to destroy our enemies. If there is only one plane left to make a final run in, I want that man to go in and get a hit. May God be with us all."

His hopes for a favourable tactical situation were doomed. Fifty or more Zeros concentrated on his formation long before they reached a launching position. High overhead, Lieutenant Gray leading the *Enterprise*'s fighter squadron waited for a call for help as arranged with Lindsey, thinking that Waldron's planes were the torpedo squadron from his own ship – a call which never came. From the cruisers and destroyers of the screen came a withering fire. One by one the torpedo-bombers were shot down. A few managed to get their torpedoes away before crashing, but none hit the enemy. Only one of the pilots, Ensign George H. Gay, survived the massacre, clinging to a rubber seat cushion which floated away from his smashed aircraft, until dusk when he could inflate his life-raft without attracting strafing Zeros.

Five minutes later it was the turn of Lindsey's fourteen Devastators from the *Enterprise*. Purely by chance, as he was making his attack on the starboard side of the *Kaga*, the torpedo squadron from the *Yorktown* came sweeping in from the other side, aiming to attack the *Soryu*, and drawing off some of the fighter opposition.

The *Yorktown*'s strike group of seventeen dive-bombers led by Lieutenant-Commander Maxwell F. Leslie, with twelve torpedo-bombers of Lieutenant-Commander Lance E. Massey's squadron and an escort of six Wildcats, had taken departure from their carrier an hour and a quarter after the strike groups of Task Force 16. A more accurate assessment of probabilities by Leslie, however, had brought the whole of this force simultaneously over the enemy to deliver the co-ordinated, massed attack which alone could hope to swamp and break through the defences. In addition, at this same moment, McClusky's dive-bombers also arrived overhead. McClusky, after reaching the expected point of interception, had continued for a time on his south-westerly course and had then made a cast to the north-west. There he had sighted a destroyer steering north-east at high speed. This was the *Arashi*, which had been left behind to depth-charge the *Nautilus*. Turning to follow her, McClusky was led straight to his objective.

The simultaneous attack by the two torpedo squadrons brought no result of itself. Scores of Zeros swarmed about them, brushing aside the puny force of six Wildcats. The massacre of the clumsy Devastators was reenacted. Lindsey and ten others of his force were shot down. Of Massey's squadron, only two survived. The few torpedoes launched were easily evaded.

The sacrifice of the torpedo-bombers had not been in vain, nevertheless. For, while every Japanese fighter plane was milling about low over the water, enjoying the easy prey offered to them there, high overhead there were gathering, all unseen and unmolested, the dive-bombers – McClusky's eighteen and Leslie's seventeen. And now, like hawks swooping to their prey, they came plummeting down out of the sky.

In the four Japanese carriers the refuelling and re-arming of the strike force had been almost completed. The decks were crowded with aircraft ranged for take-off. Nagumo had given the order to launch and ships were turning into wind. Aboard the *Akagi*, all eyes were directed downwards at the flight-deck.

Suddenly, over the rumbling roar of engines, the high-pitched rising scream of dive-bombers was heard. Even as faces swivelled upwards at the sound, the black dots which were 1,000-pound bombs were seen leaving three "Hell-Divers" as they pulled out from their near-vertical dive. Fascinated eyes watched the bombs grow in size as they fell inexorably towards that most vulnerable of targets, a full deck load of armed and fuelled aircraft. One bomb struck the *Akagi* squarely amidships, opposite the bridge and just behind the aircraft lift, plunged down into the hangar and there exploded, detonating stored torpedoes, tearing up the flight deck, and destroying the lift. A second exploded in the midst of the "Kates" on the after part of the deck, starting a tremendous conflagration to add to that in the hangar. In a matter of seconds Nagumo's proud flagship had been reduced to a blazing shambles. From time to time she was further shaken by internal explosions as the flames touched off petrol tanks, bombs, and torpedoes. Within a few minutes Captain Aoki knew that the damage and fires were beyond control. He persuaded the reluctant Nagumo that it was necessary to transfer his flag to a ship with radio communication intact Admiral and staff picked their way through the flames to reach the forecastle whence they lowered themselves down ropes to a boat which took them to the light cruiser *Nagara* of the screen.

Only three dive-bombers from the *Enterprise* had attacked the flagship. The remainder of the air group, thirty-four dive-bombers, all concentrated on the *Kaga*. Of four bombs which scored direct hits, the first burst just forward of the super-structure, blowing up a petrol truck which stood there, and the sheet of flame which swept the bridge killed everyone on it, including the captain. The other three bombs falling among the massed aircraft on the flight deck set the ship ablaze and started the same fatal train of fires and explosions as in the *Akagi*. Within a few minutes, the situation was so beyond control that the senior surviving officer ordered the transfer of the Emperor's portrait to an attendant destroyer – the custom obligatory when a ship was known to be doomed, and conducted with strict naval ceremony. The *Kaga* was to survive for several hours, nevertheless.

Simultaneously, with the *Akagi* and *Kaga*, the *Soryu* had also been reeling under a devastating attack. Leslie of the *Yorktown* was leading veterans of the Coral Sea battle, probably the most battle-experienced aviators in the American navy at that time. With deadly efficiency they dived in three waves in quick succession from the starboard bow, the starboard quarter, and the port quarter, released their bombs and climbed away without a single casualty. Out of the shower of 1,000-pound bombs, three hit. The first penetrated to the hangar deck and the explosion lifted the steel platform of the lift, folding it back against the bridge. The others landed among the massed aircraft, causing the whole ship to be engulfed in flames. It took Captain Ryusaku Yanaginoto only twenty minutes to decide to order "Abandon Ship" to save his crew from being burnt alive, though the *Soryu*, like her sisters, was to survive for some hours yet.

Thus, in five brief, searing minutes, half of Japan's entire fleet carrier force, her naval *corps d'élite*, had been shattered. For the time being the *Hiryu*, some miles away, remained untouched. She was to avenge her sisters in some measure before the day was over; but before going on to tell of her part in the battle let us follow the remainder to their deaths in the blue Pacific waters.

On board the *Akagi*, though the bomb damage was confined at first to her flight and hangar decks and her machinery spaces remained intact, the fires fed by aviation petrol from aircraft and from fuel lines were beyond the capacity of the Japanese crew to master. They fought them for seven hours but by 1715 Captain Aoki had decided there was no hope of saving his ship. The Emperor's portrait was transferred to a destroyer and the ship was abandoned. Permission was asked of the C-in-C to hasten her end but it was not until nearly dawn on the following day – when Yamamoto at last fully understood the fullness of the Japanese defeat – that he gave his approval and the *Akagi* was sent to the bottom by torpedoes from a destroyer.

Petrol-fed fires similarly swept the *Kaga* and defeated all efforts to save her. Lying stopped and burning she became the target for three torpedoes from the *Nautilus* which, after her earlier adventure, had surfaced and chased after the Japanese carriers. Even the stationary target, however, was too much for the unreliable torpedoes with which the Americans were at that time equipped. Of three fired, two missed, and the third struck but failed to explode. At 1640 orders were given to abandon the *Kaga*, and at 1925 two great explosions tore her asunder and sent her to the bottom.

The *Soryu*'s story was a similar one, of intermittent internal explosions from within the great mass of flame and smoke which she had become. When Captain Yanaginoto gave the order "Abandon Ship", he determined to immolate himself, dying in the flames or going down with her. A party of his men returning on board with the intention of persuading him or, if necessary, of forcing him to save himself, fell back abashed at the heroic, determined figure of their captain, standing sword in hand, facing forward, awaiting his end. They left him to his chosen fate. As they did so they heard him singing the Japanese national anthem. Yanaginoto's resolution held fast till 1913 hours when at last the *Soryu* and the bodies of 718 of her crew slid beneath the surface.

Much had taken place in the meantime before Nagumo's three aircraft-carriers suffered their death throes. The first survivors of the American strike groups to land back on their ships made it clear that one Japanese carrier had not yet been located. This was the *Hiryu* which, at the time of the attack, had become separated from the remainder. Admiral Fletcher therefore launched a ten-plane search from the *Yorktown*, and sent up a defensive patrol of a dozen Wildcats. It was none too soon. At a few minutes before noon, the *Yorktown*'s radar gave the warning of enemy planes coming in from the west.

These were the *Hiryu*'s attack group of eighteen dive-bombers and six fighters, led by Lieutenant Michio Kobayashi, a veteran leader who had taken part in every operation of the Nagumo force. As soon as they had flown off, a further strike of ten torpedo-bombers and six Zeros, to be led by the redoubtable Tomonago, was ranged up. Kobayashi's force had followed some of the *Yorktown*'s attack planes back and now concentrated on Fletcher's flagship. Wildcats – for once outnumbering the escorting Zeros – broke through to get at the "Vals", shooting down ten of them, including the leader. Of the eight which remained, two were knocked down by anti-aircraft fire from the cruiser screen.

The six survivors, however, showed that they had lost none of their skill as they screamed down on the carrier. One "Val" broke up under anti-aircraft fire, but its bomb sped on to burst on the flight-deck, killing many men, and starting a hangar fire below. A second bomb plunged through the side of the funnel and burst inside, starting more fires. With three boiler uptakes smashed and the furnaces of five or six boilers extinguished, the carrier's speed fell away until, twenty minutes later, she came to a stop. A third bomb penetrated to the fourth deck where for a time a fire threatened the forward petrol tanks and magazines.

His flagship immobilized, her radio and radar knocked out, Admiral Fletcher transferred his flag to the cruiser *Astoria*, and ordered the *Portland* to take the aircraft-carrier in tow. The damage-control organization worked wonders, however. Before the towline had been passed, the *Yorktown* was under way again and working up to 20 knots, and the refuelling of the fighters was in progress. Prospects seemed bright. Then a cruiser's radar picked up Tomonaga's air group, 40 miles away and coming in fast. There was just time to launch eight of the refuelling Wildcats to join the four already in the air, but they were unable to get through the screen of fighters to get at the "Kates" – though they shot down three of the "Zeros". A tremendous screen of bursting shells spread itself in front of the attackers, while the cruisers raised a barrage of splashes with their main armament, a wall of water columns through which it seemed impossible that the skimming "Kates" could fly.

Five "Kates" were shot down, but the remainder, coming in from four different angles, displayed all their deadly skill, boring doggedly in to drop their torpedoes at the point-blank range of 500 yards. It was impossible for the carrier to avoid them all. Two hit on her port side, tearing open the double-bottom fuel tanks and causing flooding which soon had her listing at 26 degrees. All power was lost, so that counter-flooding was impossible. It seemed that the *Yorktown* was about to capsize. At 1500, Captain Buckmaster ordered "Abandon Ship".

Meanwhile, however, the dive-bombers from Spruance's Task Force 16, operating some 60 miles to the north-east of the *Yorktown*, had wreaked vengeance on the *Hiryu*. Twenty-four Dauntlesses, of which ten had been transferred from the *Yorktown*, arrived overhead undetected soon after the few survivors of *Hiryu*'s attack had been recovered. The aircraft-carrier circled and swerved to avoid the bombs from the plummeting dive-bombers, but in vain. Four of them hit, one of which blew the forward lift bodily on to the bridge. The others started the inevitable fires and explosions, and the same prolonged death agonies as the *Hiryu*'s sisters were still suffering. By 2123 she had come to a stop. Desperate efforts to subdue the flames went on through the night; but at 0230 the following morning she was abandoned to be torpedoed by her attendant destroyers.

When the night of 4 June closed over the four smoking Japanese carriers and over the crippled *Yorktown*, the Battle of Midway was, in the main, over. Neither of the opposing commanders yet knew it, however, and manoeuvres and skirmishes were to continue for two more days. The Japanese commanders, except Nagumo, were slow to realise that the shattering of their four fleet carriers signified defeat and the end of the Midway operation. Admiral Kondo, with his two fast battleships, four heavy cruisers, and the light carrier *Zuiho* had set off to the help of Nagumo at midday on 4 June, and soon afterwards Yamamoto was signalling to all his scattered forces to concentrate and attack the enemy. He himself, with the main body of his fleet, was coming up fast from the west bringing the 18-inch guns of the giant *Yamato* and the 16-inch ones of the *Nagato* and *Mutsu* to throw in their weight. Still underestimating his opponent, he was dreaming of a night encounter in which his immensely powerful fleet would overwhelm the American task force and avenge the losses of the previous day. The great "fleet action" with battleships in stately line hurling huge shells at each other was still his hope and aim.

Such a concept had been forcibly removed from American naval strategy by the shambles of Pearl Harbor. Raymond Spruance, one of the greatest admirals to come to the fore during the war, was not to be lured within range of Yamamoto's battleships, above all at night, when his carriers, at this time untrained for night-flying, would be at a tremendous disadvantage. At sunset he turned away eastwards, aiming to take up a position on the following day from which he could either "follow up retreating enemy forces or break up a landing attack on Midway".

The Japanese C-in-C refused to credit the completeness of the disaster that had overtaken his fleet and the Midway plan until early on 5 June when, at 0255, he ordered a general retirement. Thus, when Spruance, after prudently steering eastwards to keep his distance from the still overwhelmingly superior Japanese surface fleet, and reversing course at midnight so as to be within supporting distance of Midway at daylight, sent a strike of 58 dive-bombers from his two ships during the afternoon of the 5th to seek out Yamamoto's Main Body, his airmen encountered nothing but a lone destroyer sent to search for the *Hiryu*.

Two final incidents remain to be briefly recounted. When Yamamoto ordered his general retirement, the squadron of four heavy cruisers of Admiral Kurita's Support Force, the *Kumano, Suzuya, Mikuma*, and *Mogami*, was to the westward of Midway, steering through the night to deliver a bombardment at dawn. They now swung round to reverse course full in view of the American submarine *Tambor*. As they steadied on their retirement course, from the flagship the *Tambor* was sighted in the moonlight ahead. The signal for an emergency turn to port was flashed down the line but was not taken in by the rear ship, *Mogami*. Failing to turn with the remainder she collided with the *Mikuma*, suffering serious damage which reduced her speed to 12 knots. Leaving the *Mikuma* and two destroyers to escort the cripple, Kurita hurried on with the remainder.

News of this attractive target soon reached Midway. Twelve army Flying Fortresses took off but were unable to locate it; but twelve Marine Corps dive-bombers sighted the long oil slick being trailed by the *Mikuma*, followed it up – and at 0805 dived to the attack. Their bombs failed to achieve direct hits, but the plane of Captain Richard E. Fleming crashed on the after turret of the *Mikuma*. Petrol fumes were sucked down into the cruiser's starboard engine-room and exploded, killing the whole engine-room crew.

The two cruisers nevertheless continued to limp slowly away, until the following day when Spruance, having abandoned hope of delivering another blow on Yamamoto's Main Fleet, was able to direct his dive-bombers on to them. The *Mikuma* was smothered and sunk, but the *Mogami* miraculously survived, heavily damaged, to reach the Japanese base at Truk.

While these events were taking place, far to the east the abandoned *Yorktown* had drifted crewless through the night of 4/5 June. She was still afloat at noon the next day and it became clear she had been prematurely abandoned. A salvage party boarded her and she was taken in tow. Hopes of getting her to port were high until the Japanese submarine *I-168*, sent by Yamamoto for the purpose, found her, penetrated her anti-submarine screen, and put two torpedoes into her. At 0600 on 7 June the *Yorktown* sank at last.

At sundown on the previous day Spruance had turned his force back eastwards to meet his supply tankers. That the Battle of Midway was over was finally clear to all.

El Alamein (1942)

J. F. C. Fuller

The first three weeks of July 1942, on the El Alamein line [in North Africa] were devoted to attack and counter-attack. Rommel's one aim was that the front should not become static, and Auchinleck's aim was to make it so. The latter won the tussle and the outcome of the campaign became a question of reinforcements and supplies.

Faced with this situation, Rommel calculated that up to mid-September the advantage would be his; but in this he was badly deceived, because from the end of July on Auchinleck switched the main weight of his air offensive from the forward positions to the ports of Mersa Matruh, Bardia, and Tobruk, which left Rommel with Benghazi – 680 miles away – as his nearest secure base of supply. The results were that by the middle of August he was still short on establishments of 16,000 men, 210 tanks, 175 troop carriers and armoured cars and 1,500 vehicles; his army consumed double the amount of supplies that crossed the Mediterranean, and had it not been for the vast enemy dumps captured in Marmarica and western Egypt, "it would", as he says, "never have been able to exist at all."

Rommel was severely criticized for not halting on the Egyptian frontier after he had taken Tobruk. True enough, had he done so he would have curtailed considerably his communications, but this in itself would not have solved his supply

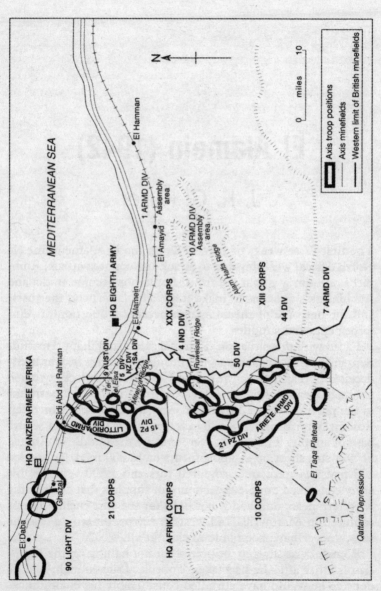

5.6 The Battle of El Alamein, 23 October 1942

problem, because, as long as Malta remained in British hands in the long run it was impossible for him to out-stockpile his enemy. Further, once his attempt to rush the Alamein position failed, he could not fall back on a rear position because he had not sufficient transport simultaneously to supply his forward position and build up a position in rear. Since to remain where he was could not solve the problem of driving his enemy out of Egypt, he realized that he would have to attack, not when he was fully ready – that he could never hope for – but before his enemy's deficiencies had been made good.

It should be remembered that because Rommel was nominally subordinated to Marshal Bastico, Marshal Cavallero, the Italian Chief of Staff, whom Ciano calls "that crook" and "this charlatan," was responsible for the supply of Rommel's army. In order to clarify the supply situation, Rommel asked Cavallero and Field-Marshal Kesselring to meet him in Egypt. This they did on 27 August, and when they guaranteed to supply him with 6,000 tons of petrol, one-sixth of which Kesselring promised to deliver by air, Rommel decided to attack. But to be doubly assured, he turned to Cavallero and said that the outcome of the battle would entirely depend on its receipt, to which the latter replied: "You can go on with the battle, it is on its way." Unfortunately for Rommel, Kesselring failed to mention the recent arrival in Malta of Spitfire aircraft, which profoundly altered the situation.

When Rommel was thus engaged, General Alexander arrived at Cairo on 8 August, and four days later he was joined by General Montgomery, who at once assumed command of the Eighth Army.

Montgomery was a man of dynamic personality and of supreme self-confidence. Known to his officers and men as "Monty", he was a past-master in showmanship and publicity; audacious in his utterances and cautious in his actions. Though at times smiled at by his officers, his neo-Napoleonic personal messages – "I am proud to be with you" . . . "YOU have made this Army what it is. YOU have made its name a household word" . . . "*YOU* and I together will see this thing through," etc., etc., interlarded with "The Lord Mighty in Battle" and "hitting the enemy for six", electrified his men. He was the right man in the right place at the right moment; for after its severe defeat the Eighth Army needed a new dynamo and Montgomery supplied it.

As soon as he arrived at his headquarters he summoned a meeting of his staff and said that his mandate was to destroy the Axis forces in North Africa, and if anyone doubted this he had better clear out. He added that he had ordered all withdrawal plans to be burnt; that the defence of the Delta meant nothing to him; and that in a fortnight he would welcome attack, but he did not intend to assume the offensive until he was ready to do so. In order to carry it out, it was essential to have a *corps d'élite*, like the Afrika Korps; therefore he would at once create one out of two armoured and one motorized divisions. Further, it was also essential that Army and RAF headquarters should live in close proximity, so that the planning of the great offensive he had in mind might be a joint effort from the start.

Except for the Wadi Akarit position north of Gabes, the El Alamein Line was the only one in North Africa that offered no flank that could be turned from the south. Rommel's tactical problem was how to penetrate this position, and because of his enemy's minefields and the tactical features in rear of them, it was by no means easy to solve. The former ran from Tel el Eisa, close by the Mediterranean, to Hunter's Plateau, which fringed the Qattara Depression, the northern border of which was girt with precipitous cliffs; and the latter comprised two ridges, the Ruweisat, about 200 ft above sea level, which ran from the centre of the front eastward, and the Alam el Halfa, to its south-east, which at its highest point was a little over twice the height of the former, and which extended in a north-easterly direction towards El Hamman on the Alexandria–Mersa Matruh railway.

Auchinleck's plan, which Alexander and Montgomery accepted as the basis of their own, was to hold as strongly as possible the area between the coast and the Ruweisat Ridge; lightly to hold but heavily to mine the area south of it to Hunter's Plateau; and to hold in strength the Alam el Halfa Ridge so that, should the enemy's mobile forces penetrate the front either north or south of the Ruweisat Ridge, they could be counter-attacked in flank, and should they break through along the ridge itself, then they could be met frontally.

When Montgomery assumed command of the Eighth Army he found the front held by the XXXth and XIIIth Corps, the former north of the Ruweisat Ridge and the latter south of it. The former consisted of the 9th Australian, 1st South African and 5th Indian Divisions and the 23rd Armoured Brigade; the latter of the 2nd New Zealand and 7th Armoured Divisions. Alexander had in reserve the 8th and 10th Armoured and the 44th and 51st Infantry Divisions, also the 1st Armoured and 50th Infantry Divisions, both refitting. At once Montgomery asked for the 44th and 10th Armoured Divisions, the one to hold the Alam el Halfa Ridge and the other to occupy its western extremity as a mobile striking force.

Rommel's army was disposed as follows: In the north the German 164th Infantry Division, then the Italian XXIst Corps, which consisted of the Trento and Bologna Divisions and Ramcke's German Parachute Brigade, and lastly the Brescia Division of the Italian Xth Corps; all these formations were in front line. As his striking force Rommel had the Afrika Korps, which consisted of the 15th and 21st Panzer Divisions; the German 90th Light Division (motorized infantry); and the Italian XXth Mobile Corps, which comprised the Ariete and Littorio Armoured Divisions and the Trieste Division. In rear, at Mersa Matruh and Bardia, were the Italian Pavia, Folgore, and Pistola Divisions in reserve.

Rommel's plan was to make a feint attack in the north, a holding attack in the centre, and the main attack in the south. On the night of 30–31 August, lanes through the southernmost sector of his enemy's minefields – which he believed to be weak, but which were strong – were to be cleared by German and Italian infantry. Next, at dawn on the 31st, the Afrika Korps was to follow through, take the Alam el Halfa Ridge and make for the area south-west of El Hamman. In the meantime the 90th Light Division and the Ariete and Littorio Armoured Divisions were to break through to the north of the Afrika Korps and cover the left flank of its advance. His idea was to cut off his enemy from his supply depots, while the 90th Light Division and XXth Mobile Corps held the enemy, and then annihilate him. He sought a decisive battle, and for its success it was imperative that the Alam el Halfa Ridge should be overrun early on the 31st.

According to General Alexander, the opposing forces were evenly matched on the southern half of the front. Both had about 300 field and medium guns and 400 anti-tank guns; Rommel had 500 medium and light tanks, and the XIIIth Corps 300 medium and 80 light tanks and 230 armoured cars. Besides these, 100 tanks with the 23rd Armoured Brigade constituted a reserve. Though numerically evenly matched, Rommel was badly outclassed, because half his tanks were Italian and they were very indifferent machines.

For Rommel, the battle of Alam el Halfa was a desperate gamble because the plan on which it was based was the only one feasible with the means at his disposal, and precisely because of this Montgomery expected Rommel to adopt it. For Montgomery, whose intention it was to maintain a firm defensive until he was fully prepared to attack, it was a heaven-sent opportunity; not only did it enable him to rebuild the morale of his army, but at the same time it enabled him to weaken that of his opponent and thereby doubly assure the success of his eventual offensive. In order to impede an attack on the southern sector of his front Montgomery considerably added to its minefields that on the night of 30–31 August when the Germans and Italians began to clear lanes through them, they were greatly delayed. To add to this difficulty, General von Bismarck, commander of the 21st Panzer Division, was killed by a mine, and the commander of the Afrika Korps, General Nehring, was severely wounded. Further, Rommel was so sick that he was unable to leave his truck. This, Desmond Young considers, was "perhaps the greatest handicap of all", because Rommel – like Charles XII – "relied much more on his personal observation and judgement during the progress of a battle than on a preconceived plan."

The results of these misfortunes were that there was no surprise; the advance of the Afrika Korps was delayed; that of the 90th Light Division still more so; and the Ariete and Littorio Divisions could not penetrate the minefields. Rommel, bereft of half his striking force, was compelled to abandon his sweep to the north-east and restrict the attack of the Afrika Korps to the western end of the Alam el Halfa Ridge. But its advance was so impeded by soft sand and by air attacks that at 4 p.m. it had to be called off.

During the night of 31 August–1 September the Italo-German forces were so pounded by the RAF that, on 1 September, Rommel was compelled to abandon any attempt to carry out a major operation, and only desultory fighting on the Alam el Halfa Ridge followed. In the meantime Montgomery, when he saw that the battle was in his hands, switched the 10th Armoured Division from the south to the west of the ridge preparatory to carrying out a counter-attack southward with the 2nd New Zealand Division directly he had exhausted his enemy's offensive.

On 2 September, still under constant air attack and desperately short of petrol, Rommel renewed his offensive, but with so little success that he ordered a withdrawal for the morning of the 3rd. Montgomery then launched his counter-attack, and at the same time ordered his 7th Armoured Division to harass the enemy's southern flank. After stiff fighting he drove him back to the minefields, and at 7 a.m. on 7 September called off the battle. Rommel's losses were nearly 3,000 men killed, wounded and missing, 50 tanks, 15 guns, 35 anti-tank guns and 400 lorries lost; and Montgomery's losses were 1,640 killed, wounded and missing, and 68 tanks and 18 anti-tank guns put out of action.

Kesselring's opinion is that if Rommel had not been sick he would never have pulled out of the battle because he had "completely encircled his enemy". This is a fantastic statement, and more especially as it is made by a highly experienced soldier. There was no encirclement, and once the battle had opened Rommel was under no illusion that his enemy's command of the air predoomed his defeat. He has much to say on this question, and among other things that,

Whoever enjoys command of the air is in a position to inflict such heavy damage on the opponent's supply columns that serious shortages must soon make themselves felt. By maintaining a constant watch on the roads leading to the front he can put a complete stop to daylight supply traffic and force his enemy to drive only by night, thus causing him to lose irreplaceable time. But an assured flow of supplies is essential; without it an army becomes immobilized and incapable of action.

This should be remembered when we come to the part played by Rommel in the Normandy campaign of 1944.

"With the failure of this offensive," writes Rommel, "our last chance of gaining the Suez Canal had gone." He knew that the battle for supplies was irretrievably lost, if only because the large convoy of "well over 100,000 tons, laden with the very latest weapons and war material for the Eighth Army", which he expected "would arrive at Suez at the beginning of September," arrived there on 3 September with Roosevelt's gift of 300 Sherman tanks. He knew that his enemy would attack, and in all probability under a full moon. Kesselring remarks: "Was it right under these circumstances to wait for the British offensive?" and adds that neither OKW nor the Comando Supremo would have objected to a withdrawal. Although this assumption is highly improbable, possibly the reason why Rommel stayed where he did was that either a voluntary withdrawal was repugnant to him, or that he had not the petrol and vehicles to carry it out. This latter reason is supported by Ciano, who, on 2 September, entered in his diary: "Three of our tankers have been sunk in two days," and on the 3rd, "Rommel's pause continues, and, what is worse, the sinking of our ships continues." But had Rommel fallen back shortly before the next full moon, he would have disrupted his enemy's plans.

Whatever his reasons, he decided to stand and accept battle. His plan was to hold with outposts only his forward belt of minefields, in which some 500,000 mines and vast numbers of captured British bombs and shells had been sunk, and to fight his defensive battle in a mined zone 1,000 to 2,000 yards behind. On his northern flank he posted the German 164th and 90th Light Divisions in depth; allotted to the Italians the defence of the front south of them; and divided his armoured divisions into two groups, the 15th Panzer and Littorio Divisions in the north, and the 21st Panzer and Ariete Divisions in the south. Tactically this was a faulty distribution and unlike any Rommel had hitherto adopted; possibly it was forced upon him through lack of petrol. In all he had 300 Italian tanks of little fighting value and barely fit for action, and 210 German tanks, of which 30 were Panzer IVs armed with 75 mm guns, and the remainder Panzer IIIs with 50 mm guns.

As he was then a very sick man he decided to return to Germany, and on 22 September he handed his command over to General Stumme, an experienced tank officer, and informed him that should the enemy attack he would at once return. This was not a very satisfactory arrangement. Back in Germany, on 10 October he was presented with his Field-Marshal's baton, which had been awarded to him immediately after the fall of Tobruk.

While Rommel was engaged on his unenviable task, his opponent, General Alexander, prepared for an all-out offensive. On 10 August Mr Churchill had handed to him a directive to annihilate the German–Italian Army "at the earliest opportunity", but the date was governed by certain factors. First, Operation Torch had been scheduled for 8 November; and it was considered of vital political importance, in order to win over the French in Morocco and Algeria, that the Axis forces in Egypt should be decisively defeated before the invasion was launched. Secondly, because the 300 Sherman tanks would not arrive until early in September, and when they did several weeks' training with them was imperative, as well as a full moon under which to attack, the date fixed upon was the night of 23–24 October.

The next problem was one of grand tactics: where should the decisive blow be struck on the 40-mile front? Although in the front's southern sector the minefields were less extensive than in the northern, because a successful penetration in the south would drive the enemy northward towards his communications – the coastal road – it was decided to deliver the main blow in the north, to gain an outlet on to the coastal road, and to cut off the bulk of the enemy forces south of it. This settled, the next problem was one of minor tactics.

Because minefields can no more be rushed by tanks than wire entanglements can be rushed by infantry – and in the northern sector they were from 5,000 to 9,000 yards in depth – it was agreed that the initial advance would assume the form of an old-fashioned infantry attack accompanied by mine clearing parties and covered by artillery and bomber aircraft, with tanks in rear.

On 6 October, Montgomery issued his plan. The main attack was allotted to the XXXth Corps (Lieutenant-General Sir Oliver Leese) on a four divisional front of six to seven miles in width. Its task was to cut two corridors through the minefields; the northern south of Tel El Eisa, and the southern across the northern end of the Miteiriya Ridge. Once this had been done, the Xth Corps (Lieutenant-General Sir Herbert Lumsden) which comprised the 1st and 10th Armoured Divisions, was to pass through and engage the enemy's armour. In the meantime, to mislead the enemy and pin down the 21st Panzer Division in the extreme south, the XIIIth Corps (Lieutenant-General Sir B. C. Horrocks) and the 7th Armoured Division were to carry out two subsidiary attacks against the enemy's right flank. In all Montgomery had seven infantry divisions, a formation of Free French, a Greek brigade, three armoured divisions and seven armoured brigades; a total of 150,000 men and 1,114 tanks, of which 128 were Grants and 267 Shermans, both armed with 75 mm guns, and 2,182 pieces of artillery, of which 1,274 were anti-tank guns of various types. The battle was to be opened by a short intense counter-battery bombardment, to be followed, once the infantry advanced, by a bombardment of the enemy's defences. From 6 October to the night of the 23rd the RAF (500 fighters and 200 bombers) was to intensify its attack on the enemy's communications and transport, next, to support the artillery bombardments, and finally to concentrate on the areas in which the enemy's armour was located.

In addition, there was an elaborate cover plan, the aim of which was to make good lack of strategical surprise by deceiving the enemy. The first task was to conceal the various concentrations as much as possible, and the second, by means of dummy hutments, dumps, tanks, vehicles, gun emplacements, water installations and a pipeline, to mislead the enemy about the probable date, and direction, of the attack. Until the invasion of Normandy, it was the most elaborate fake undertaken, and its principle was – hide what you have and reveal what you haven't.

At 9.40 p.m. on 23 October, under a brilliant moon, the whole of the artillery of the Eighth Army, nearly 1,000 guns, simultaneously opened fire on the enemy battery positions. Twenty minutes later the infantry advanced, and on the XXXth Corps front by 1 a.m. on the 24th the enemy forward defences were captured without serious loss. Half an hour's halt was then made in order to reorganize, after which the advance was resumed and met with stern opposition. Nevertheless, by 5.30 a.m. the Australians had secured most of their final objective, and the New Zealanders the whole of theirs; but in the centre the 51st Division was held up by strongpoints in the middle of the northern corridor some 1,500 yards from its final objective, and in the south the 1st South African Division was held up for several hours.

The Xth Corps crossed its starting line at 2 a.m., but the engineers, who worked behind the infantry, were so greatly delayed in lifting the mines that it was not until 6.30 a.m. that the southern corridor was sufficiently cleared to permit the 9th Armoured Brigade, followed by the 10th Armoured Division, to move forward. When the latter did go ahead it gained a footing on the eastern slope of the Miteiriya Ridge, but came under such heavy fire that it could proceed no farther. In the meantime, the 2nd Armoured Brigade and the 1st Armoured Division had been seriously delayed by mines and artillery fire in the northern corridor, and it was not until 3 p.m., after an intense artillery bombardment and a combined attack by the 51st Division and the 1st Armoured Division, that the corridor was finally established. These delays put back the timetable and prohibited a break-out on the 24th.

In the south the operations of the XIIIth Corps met with so limited a success that Montgomery instructed Horrocks to press the attack no farther, but to resort to "crumbling" action – local attacks of attrition – without the 7th Armoured Division being involved.

On the Axis front the situation rapidly deteriorated, for although the outposts had fought staunchly, the terrific enemy bombardment so smashed the network of communications that command was paralysed. General Stumme went forward at dawn on the 24th to find out what was happening, and shortly after had a heart attack and died. When this became known hours later, General von Thoma, Commander of the Afrika Korps, assumed the chief command.

When the battle opened, Rommel was in hospital at Semmering, and on the afternoon of the 24th he was telephoned by Field-Marshal Keitel, who inquired whether he would be well enough to return to Africa. He replied that he was, and at 7 a.m. on the 25th took off for Rome. When he arrived there at 11 a.m. he was met by General von Rintelen, the German military attaché, who informed him that only "three issues of petrol remained in the African theatre", which was equivalent to "300 kilometres worth of petrol per vehicle between Tripoli and the front". As experience had shown that one issue of petrol was required for each day of battle, it was obvious to Rommel that the battle was as good as lost, for without petrol the army could no longer react to the enemy's movements.

That evening Rommel learnt from von Thoma that ammunition was so short that Stumme had forbidden the bombardment of the enemy's assembly positions on the night of 23–24 October, and that on the 24th and 25th the petrol situation had so deteriorated that major movements were no longer possible, and that only groups of the 15th Panzer Division had been able to attack; that they had suffered frightful casualties; and that the division was now reduced to 31 effective tanks.

In spite of this crippling shortage of means, the Axis forces put up so determined a defence that Montgomery realized that his 'crumbling' attacks were too costly. He decided to switch the axis of the offensive more to the north, and instructed the XXXth Corps to order the 9th Australian Division to direct its offensive toward the coast, to cut off the enemy in the salient which had been created north of the Tel el Eisa Ridge. At the same time the 1st Armoured Division was ordered to fight its way westward toward what the British called Kidney Ridge and the Germans Hill 28. These attacks resulted in the most savage fighting of the battle. The Australian advance was successful, but the 1st Armoured Division made no appreciable progress until nightfall, because Rommel brought forward the 90th Light Division, elements of the 15th Panzer and Littorio Divisions, and a battalion of Bersaglieri. He writes: "Rivers of blood were poured out over miserable strips of land", and after it had grown dark: "Never before in Africa had we seen such a density of anti-aircraft fire. Hundreds of British tracer shells criss-crossed the sky and the air became an absolute inferno of fire." At length, during the night, the 1st South African and 2nd New Zealand Divisions gained 1,000 yards more depth on the Miteiriya Ridge, and the 7th Motor Brigade of the 1st Armoured Division established itself on Kidney Ridge.

On 26 October it became apparent to Montgomery that the momentum of his attack was on the wane, and that his break-in area was still hedged in by a strong anti-tank screen. He decided to assume a temporary defensive, and to regroup his forces and build up fresh reserves for a renewal of the offensive in the north. He ordered the 2nd New Zealand Division to be relieved by the 1st South African Division and brought into reserve, and the front of the latter to be taken over by the 4th Indian Division, which was placed under the command of the XIIIth Corps. Further, he instructed the XIIIth Corps to send north the 7th Armoured Division and three brigades of infantry.

While these moves were under way, on the night of 26–27 October Rommel moved the 21st Panzer Division north, and on the 27th violently attacked Kidney Ridge, but was repulsed at such heavy cost that Montgomery was able to withdraw the 1st Armoured Division and the 24th Armoured Brigade into reserve. At the same time he ordered the 9th Australian Division to attack the enemy in the coastal sector on the night of the 28th–29th. Apparently Rommel expected this attack, and in order to reinforce his left he was compelled to denude his southern front of practically all heavy weapons and German units and to replace them by part of the Ariete Division which had been engaged in the north.

The Australian attack was launched under cover of an intense bombardment at 10 p.m. on the 29th in the direction of the coastal road between Sidi Abd el Rahman and Tel el Eisa. For six hours the battle raged furiously, and "again and again", writes Rommel, "British bomber formations flew up and tipped their death-dealing loads on my troops, or bathed the country in the brilliant light of parachute flares." So intense was the fighting that, on the morning of the 30th, Rommel began to

consider a withdrawal to the Fuka position, which ran from the
coast 50 miles west of El Alamein southward to the Qattara
Depression. This is the first intimation of a contemplated
retreat which, irrespective of the severity of the fighting, was
being pressed to the fore by petrol shortage. On 27 October only
70 tons had been delivered by the *Luftwaffe*, and on the 29th
Ciano entered in his diary: "Another oil tanker was sunk this
evening . . . Bismarck has learned from Rintelen that Rommel
is optimistic about the military quality of the troops, but that he
is literally terrified by the supply situation. Just now not only is
fuel lacking but also munitions and food."

During the morning of 29 October Montgomery became
aware that the 90th Light Division had been moved into the
Sidi Abd el Rahman area, and as this indicated that Rommel
had reacted to his intent to break out along the coastal road, he
decided to shift the axis of his break-through attack southward
so that it would fall mainly on the Italians. In order to cover this
operation and pin down the 90th Light Division, he ordered the
9th Australian Division to resume its attack on the night of the
30th–31st. In the meantime the 2nd New Zealand Division was
to be brought up in readiness to force a gap through the enemy's
front a little to the north of the existing northern corridor, and
once it had been made the Xth Corps with the 1st, 7th, and 10th
Armoured Divisions was to pass through it into the open desert.
This operation was code-named "Supercharge". Montgomery
writes: The operation

> was to get us out into the open country and to lead to the
> disintegration of Rommel's forces in Egypt. We had got to
> bring the enemy's armour to battle and get astride his lines
> of communication. Second New Zealand Division's tasks
> involved a penetration of some 6,000 yards on a 4,000
> yards front. I made it clear that should 30 Corps fail to
> reach its final objectives, *the armoured divisions of the 10th
> Corps were to fight their way through.*

On 30 October, Rommel had the Fuka position reconnoitred,
and although he realized that because the Italian infantry had
practically no transport they would be no more than a dead

weight in the open desert, he nevertheless planned to load as many of them as he could on his transport columns and withdraw them under cover of night, after which his remaining motorized forces were, on a wide front, to beat a fighting retreat to the west. "But first," he writes, "we had to wait for the British move, to ensure that they would be engaged in battle and could not suddenly throw their strength into a gap in our front and then force a break-through."

It came that night, when the Australians resumed their attack toward the coast and, after they had reached it, they turned eastward and cut off the Panzer Grenadiers of the 164th Division in the northern salient. But most of the grenadiers, helped by counter-attacks delivered by elements of the 21st Panzer Division and the 90th Light Division, effected their escape.

Montgomery's original intention had been to launch 'Supercharge' on the night following this attack, but the situation compelled him to postpone it for 24 hours, and it was not made until 1 a.m. on 2 November, after an intense artillery bombardment, reinforced by relays of bombers. Under cover of a creeping barrage two brigades of the 2nd New Zealand Division, supported by the 23rd Armoured Brigade, moved forward on a 4,000-yard front; their task was to drive a lane 4,000 yards in length through the enemy's position, clear it of mines and open a path for the 9th Armoured Brigade, which before dawn was to push forward another 2,000 yards to the track which ran south from Sidi Abd el Rahman, and establish a bridgehead from which the 1st, 7th, and 10th Armoured Divisions could debouch into the open desert and bring on a decisive armoured battle.

The lane was successfully cleared, but when a little before daylight the 9th Armoured Brigade reached the track, it ran into a formidable anti-tank gun screen and suffered a loss of 87 tanks – over 75 per cent of its strength. In the meantime the 1st Armoured Division debouched and was at once engaged by the Afrika Korps. A fierce tank battle followed around Tel el Aqqaqir. Although Rommel's tanks were outclassed by his enemy's, and their 50 mm and 49 mm (Italian) guns could make little impression on the British Grant and Sherman machines, the attackers were brought to a halt and the penetration sealed off. Nevertheless, Rommel was under no illusions; he realized that the battle was lost. Not only were there signs of disintegration – units of the Littorio and Trieste Divisions streamed to the rear – but the supply situation, he writes, was "absolutely desperate". During the day his army had expended 450 tons of ammunition, and only 190 tons had been brought to Tobruk by three destroyers. He also states: "The Afrika Korps had only 35 serviceable tanks left."

"This then", writes Rommel, "was the moment to get back to the Fuka line," and especially as "the British had so far been following up hesitantly and that their operations had always been marked by an extreme, often incomprehensible caution." He then made what he acknowledges was a crucial blunder. Early on the morning of 3 November he sent his ADC, Lieutenant Berndt, to report direct to Hitler and to ask him for full freedom of action. He did not doubt that it would be given and ordered part of the Italian formations to retreat. At 1.30 p.m. he received Hitler's answer: stand fast and yield not a yard of ground. "As to your troops," it read, "you can show them no other road than that to victory or death." Rommel then halted the withdrawal, and in the evening sent Berndt back to Hitler with a message to inform him that to stand fast meant annihilation.

Early on 4 November Kesselring arrived at Rommel's headquarters and, according to Rommel, said to him, "that the Führer had learnt from his experiences in the East that, in circumstances like these, the front must be held at all costs." In his *Memoirs* Kesselring contradicts this, and writes that he told Rommel, "there could be no question of any such folly, that Hitler's order must be ignored," and that he would accept full responsibility for ignoring it.

When on the morning of 3 November Montgomery learnt of his enemy's withdrawal westward, he asked the Desert Air Force to switch the whole of its weight to the retreating Axis columns. But it was not until nightfall that he ordered the 51st Division and a brigade of the 4th Indian Division to move forward on a four-mile front and to break through the southern sector of the enemy's anti-tank screen and win a gap through which he could pass his three armoured divisions. This was successfully done by the morning of the 4th.

Of this, the final action of the battle, Rommel supplies the following dramatic description:

> Enormous dust-clouds could be seen south and south-east of headquarters, where the desperate struggle of the small and inefficient Italian tanks of XX Corps was being played out against the hundred or so British heavy tanks which had come round their open right flank. I was later told by Major von Luck, whose battalion I had sent to close the gap between the Italians and the Afrika Korps, that the Italians, who at that time represented our strongest motorized force, fought with exemplary courage. Von Luck gave what assistance he could with his guns, but was unable to avert the fate of the Italian Armoured Corps. Tank after tank split asunder or burned out, while all the time a tremendous British barrage lay over the Italian infantry and artillery positions. The last signal came from the Ariete at about 15.30 hours: "Enemy tanks penetrated south of Ariete. Ariete now encircled."

By nightfall the XXth Italian Corps had been destroyed; the Afrika Korps on its left had been broken through and its commander, General von Thoma, captured; a 12-mile gap had been driven through the Axis front; and Rommel had no reserves and no petrol. In spite of Hitler's insane order, retreat became compulsory, and Rommel tried to save what he could of his army. Next morning a message arrived from Hitler's headquarters to authorize the withdrawal.

That Rommel was ever able to withdraw even his motorized units was firstly because of Montgomery's instinctive cautiousness, and secondly because of the reluctance of the RAF to engage in low flying attack, as it had done so successfully after the battle of Vittorio-Veneto. According to General Alexander, the Eighth Army could still muster "very nearly six hundred tanks against eighty German"; it needed only a modicum of audacity by Montgomery to turn his enemy's retreat into a rout. On the second point, de Guingand writes:

With the virtual air superiority we possessed, and the state
of disorganization of the enemy, it looked to us in the
Army that here was the "dream target" for the RAF. In
the event, the results appeared very disappointing. When
setting out along the road between Alamein battlefield and
Daba, I had expected to see a trail of devastation, but the
visible signs of destroyed vehicles were few and far between. After Daba much better results had been obtained
but even here a lot of the vehicles we found had stopped
through shortage of petrol.

This he rightly attributes to the RAF's trust in high-level
bombing instead of low-level machine-gunning, with the consequence that training in low flying attack had been neglected.
Had it not been for this, his opinion is that Rommel's withdrawal would have been paralysed.

The crux of Rommel's retreat was the pull-out on the night of
4–5 November, when chaos reigned, but fortunately for him his
methodical opponent, fearful of the difficulties of a night pursuit, halted his forces. "On 5 November", Montgomery in-
forms us, "I regrouped for the pursuit." Thus he lost some 18
invaluable hours. When he had regrouped he decided that the
Xth Corps (1st, 7th Armoured and 2nd New Zealand Divisions)
were to lead the chase; the XXXth Corps was to come into
reserve between El Alamein and Mersa Matruh; and the XIIIth
was to clear up the battlefield. In spite of this delay, by an
outflanking movement through the desert he nearly cut off his
enemy at Mersa Matruh. But on 6 November the van of the 1st
Armoured Division was brought to a halt through lack of petrol
and Rommel succeeded, as he says, "in forming a fairly firm
front and beat off all enemy attacks." He adds that his enemy
"still continued to operate with great caution."

It is also stated that "conditions on the road were indescrib-
able. Columns in complete disorder – partly of German, partly
of Italian vehicles – choked the road between the minefields
[south of Mersa Matruh]. Rarely was there any movement
forward and then everything soon jammed up again. Many
vehicles were on tow and there was an acute shortage of petrol,
for the retreat had considerably increased consumption."

To add to the difficulties of both sides, and more particularly to the pursuers, on the 6th torrential rain made the desert tracks impassable. For 24 hours the pursuit was bogged down. According to Montgomery the rain saved Rommel "from complete annihilation."

Kursk (1943)

Alan Wykes

The German armies in Russia were prepared for a massive offensive to reverse the disaster of Stalingrad. The finest divisions of both the *Wehrmacht* and the *Waffen SS* were gathered in an enormous concentration of men and armor. Armed with the latest tanks, their morale high, they expected to be unstoppable, even if the Russians were ready. But "Whenever I think of this attack", said Hitler, "my stomach turns over" – and his queasiness was understandable. For now, in the spring of 1943, both he and his generals knew that only a decisive victory over the Red Army could ease the relentless, threatening pressure on the Eastern Front.

The cracks in the wall of Axis domination were becoming ever more numerous and more apparent. The Allies were beginning to overcome the efforts of the U-boats. Italy was in a more parlous state than ever before. Japan's advances in Burma and the south-west Pacific had been stopped, and were going into reverse. The bombing of German industrial centers was disrupting essential war supplies. The hit-and-miss methods of the Red Air Force were being offset by increasing numbers of planes and the increasing skill of the Russian air crews. And the threat of a Second Front kept many German divisions tied up in Europe, reducing the possibility of any major effort on the Russian front.

Then, in March, came Field Marshal von Manstein's great victory at Kharkov for Army Group South and it seemed for a moment as if the tide was turning. But it was a short-lived hope. The victory, so far as the restoration of the German initiative was concerned, was incomplete. A great Russian-held salient remained – a bulge roughly semi-circular in shape, driven some 75 miles westward into the German lines at Kursk, with its base measuring more than 100 miles from north to south. Within the salient were said to be a million men, and armaments in proportion. Clearly, a pincer movement thrown across the base of the salient would cut off and destroy the forces contained in it and considerably weaken the total power of the Soviet army, and von Manstein planned such a movement to clinch his victory.

As so often before, however, the weather took a hand. The spring thaw turned vast tracts of frozen ground to mud, rivers rose, swamps appeared, ruined villages were mirrored in the desolation of floods. There was nothing von Manstein could do but withdraw his armor to save it from getting bogged down, and leave the infantry in possession while a plan was worked out. But there was a catch: the longer the Germans remained purely on the defensive, the sooner there would be an attempt by the Russians to widen the salient and breach the German front completely.

At a time when speed and decisiveness of action could have produced results, the Germans vacillated. Hitler changed his mind. His generals feuded among themselves. And there were conflicting interpretations of the demands of the situation in Europe. Even the promise of a new assault on the Don and an advance towards Moscow after the salient had been pinched out could not bring the Führer to decide. Tanks and other heavy assault weapons – particularly the Tigers and Panthers – were not reaching the army in the expected numbers. It was 11 April before the semblance of a design was arrived at, and it was in essence the same design that von Manstein had been unable to fulfill after Kharkov. It was indeed the obvious plan – and its obviousness was now appreciated equally by the Russians, who made haste to improve their defenses round Kursk. Any chance of surprise had been lost. Now, the only possibility lay in an assault so tremendous that no defenders could resist it.

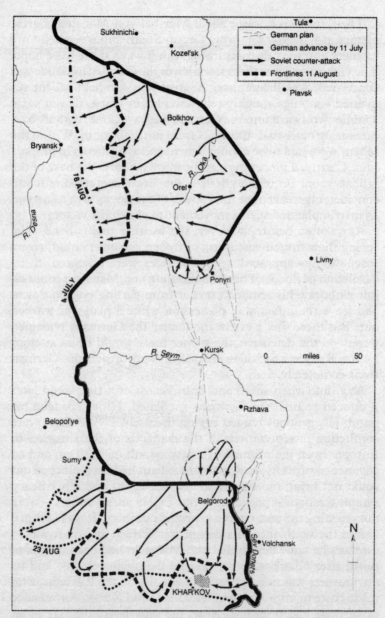

5.7 The Battle for the Kursk Salient, July–August 1943

Such an attack meant risking far more armor than the Germans could afford to lose, and if infantry support was to be forthcoming for the tanks it also meant imprudently weakening the front both north and south of the salient.

Hitler was himself caught in a pincer movement of commitment. On the one hand he had the conflicting views of his advisers as to the possibility of success. Field Marshal von Kluge, the Army Group Center commander, and Generals Keitel and Zeitzler of the Army General Staff were in favor; Colonel-General Guderian, the Inspector-General of Armored Troops and, by this time, von Manstein himself were equally strongly against. On the other hand, there was the assurance of Speer, Minister of Production, that the necessary tanks would be available, and the certainty that without a German offensive the whole weight of the Soviet forces would come crashing against the over-stretched *Wehrmacht*.

While Hitler hesitated, General Vatutin and the Red Army went ahead – not merely with defenses as impenetrable as they could be made, but also with the preparation of a large-scale counter-attack. The news filtered back to Hitler intelligence reports and alarming air photographs that indicated the withdrawal of the Russian mobile forces from the area west of Kursk in obvious preparation for a counter-attack. But at last, on 10 May, Hitler gave his consent to the plan – it was to be called Operation Zitadelle – emphasizing his underlying reluctance with the words "It must not fail."

The forces were decided. Colonel-General Model's Ninth Army, with seven *Panzer*, two *Panzergrenadier*, and nine infantry divisions was to attack from the north. Colonel-General Hoth's Fourth *Panzer* Army, with ten *Panzer*, one *Panzergrenadier* and seven infantry divisions would sweep up from the south. The two arms of the pincer would meet east of Kursk, thus enclosing the salient and cutting off huge Russian forces. But, although the plan and deployment were decided, Hitler continued to hesitate.

Knowing that the Russians were building up their defenses, he postponed the first mooted date for the start of Zitadelle from 13 June until the beginning of July so that an extra couple of battalions of Panthers could be sped off the production line and allotted to Model's northern pincer. The opening of what was to become known – justifiably – as the greatest tank battle in history was finally fixed for 1500 on 4 July, despite continued proposals for abandonment from von Kluge, von Manstein and Guderian.

Opposing the 36 German divisions was a force of 11 Russian Armies, including the crack Sixth and Seventh Guards Armies that had fought so well at Stalingrad and the First Tank Army. Each Russian "army" corresponded approximately with a German corps in size. In terms of manpower there was little to choose between the conflicting forces, but the Russians had reinforced the north corner of the salient, which would bear the brunt of Model's attack, with thickly sown minefields – so dense that, according to Marshal Rokossovski, who was the joint commander on the Kursk front with Vatutin, "you could not have put one of Goering's medals between them." There were 2,200 anti-tank and 2,500 anti-personnel mines per mile of the defensive front, four times the density at Stalingrad. In addition there were no fewer than 20,000 guns of various kinds, including 6,000 76.2 mm anti-tank guns and more than 900 *Katyusha* rocket guns. For attack they had the famous T34 tank – one of the best armored vehicles to be produced during the war – with its long-range 76 mm gun and great reliability.

The German attacking force was largely based on the new Panther D, a fine tank in many ways but with numerous technical faults caused by hasty production. But the Germans still had considerable superiority in the air, as was to be proved by the squadrons of Stuka dive-bombers.

But if the opposing forces were fairly matched there were other factors that would determine the course of the battle – not least the lost element of surprise, which had been frittered away in argument and indecision.

The ground over which the battle was to be fought was reasonably good for tank warfare. Kursk lies in the basins of the Don and Dneiper and the countryside which surrounds it and formed the salient is characterized by low hills and wide-ranging plains of fertile arable land. The ground is watered by numerous brooks and tributary rivers – one of them, the Pena, being a swift stream running between steep banks. Cornfields stretch for unbroken miles across the landscape. Such roads as there are are for the most part sandy cart-tracks that become unusable by wheeled traffic during heavy rain. Numerous scattered villages lie in the shallow valleys and small thickets bristle on the low hills. To the north of the village of Beresowka there is a thickly wooded area, roughly circular in shape and some four miles in diameter.

Along the southern front of the salient, Hoth's Fourth *Panzer* Army was lined up along a slight curve extending some 30 miles from west to east. First the 3rd and 11th *Panzer* divisions and the *Gross Deutschland* division (a *Panzergrenadier* unit with a high complement of tanks under 48 *Panzer* Corps); then the three SS divisions, *Leibstandarte Adolf Hitler*, *Totenkopf* (Death's Head) and *Das Reich* in the SS *Panzer* Corps; and on the right wing the 6th, 19th and 7th *Panzer* divisions of 3 *Panzer* Corps. There had been the closest co-operation between ground and air forces and the utmost care had been taken to get the huge force of tanks into position under cover of darkness. "Morale", according to Model, "was high" – and was raised even higher by a message from the Führer:

> Soldiers of the Reich! This day you are to take part in an offensive of such importance that the whole future of the war may depend on its outcome. More than anything else, your victory will show the whole world that resistance to the power of the German army is hopeless.

Unfortunately the message arrived during a four-hour intense artillery bombardment from the Russians which confirmed that the defenders were well aware that the attack was about to be launched. The intensity of the bombardment inevitably had its effect on the striking power of the attackers, but the attack began as planned at 1500 after a return bombardment by German artillery and some devastating strikes on the forward Russian lines by dive-bombing Stukas.

By 1900 advance infantry and grenadiers of the three divisions on the German left flank of the southern pincer had thrust into the Russian forward line at Luchanino, Alexejewka and Sawidowka – three villages only lightly held by the defenders.

The ease with which they were taken was characteristic of the tactic, much used by the Russians throughout the battle of Kursk, of luring the attackers into a position that subsequently proved to be untenable.

Model's northern pincer managed to break into the salient on a 15-mile front and 47 *Panzer* Corps pushed forward about five miles during the next 30 hours, but at great cost in huge Porsche Ferdinand (or *Elefant*) assault tanks. These lacked machine-guns and, as Guderian had warned long before, quickly proved vulnerable. As their escorting light tanks were knocked out, they found themselves at the mercy of infantry who dashed out from slit trenches and directed flame-throwers into the engine louvres, thus setting the fuel systems alight and forcing the crews to either be roasted alive or to bale out into captivity. The Model thrust was to gain only five more miles to south and west during the next week. Engineers who tried, under covering fire, to clear lanes through the minefields found that this only aided the Russians, who deftly scored many hits with rockets and 76 mm guns as the tanks passed through.

"For all our bitter struggling in the north", one young officer wrote subsequently, "we moved virtually nowhere – we stood still. It was like Verdun in 1916. There was a little village called Teploye. We saw it first on the second day and we never saw it more clearly than then. Thick black smoke from brewed-up tanks blew about and each time the smoke cleared away we saw Teploye again, but it was like a mirage. We never got any nearer."

In the south, Hoth's forces gained ground by advance detachments of infantry and grenadiers, but only at great cost. During the night the defenders withdrew and the front line was shelled throughout its length. Paul Hausser, commander of the three SS divisions *Leibstandarte*, *Totenkopf* and *Das Reich*, wrote afterwards: "Again and again we showed this weakness of tactics that made us insist on holding ground that had been too easily gained. Having chased Ivan out, we should have withdrawn ourselves and let him bombard the place out of existence. Then we could have moved the armor forward relatively safely."

This lack of imagination, which was characteristic of German planning, in this particular case won an undeserved reward.

During the night a cloudburst caused an immediate overflowing of the Pena and its tributary streams and turned the ground into an impassable morass. But for this, all the tanks would have been moved up into the line of bombardment. Even as it was, the losses were considerable because of the difficulty of taking up camouflaged positions, so that when daylight illuminated the swamped valleys the Red Air Force easily picked out the stranded tanks and attacked.

Luftwaffe Stukas attacked too and had considerable success in demolishing Russian artillery batteries, but as one pilot, Hans Rudel, has recorded, "The Russian guns were almost as numerous as their mines, and the camouflage was masterly . . . you had to assume that every copse was a gun battery and dive down to treetop level . . . four times out of five you found you scored a hit on a 76 . . . if it didn't get you first."

This success, however, did little to neutralize the trouble that faced the tanks on the morning of 5 July. The whole of 48 *Panzer* Corps – 3rd and 11th *Panzer* divisions and *Gross Deutschland* – were ordered to move up from the bombarded villages to the next Russian line of defense and capture Ssyrzew and Ssyrzewo, which lay beyond the Pena river, and wheel round to the north-west to capture the wood at Beresowka and the three small hills that lay beyond it. The floods from the cloudburst, however, made this impossible without the aid of engineers to bridge the river and the flooded cornfields on either side of it, and the engineers were continually harassed by snipers and Soviet planes. As the grey day advanced, the dense formation of tanks along 48 Corps' entire front was seen to be extremely vulnerable – many of them bogged down because they had approached too near the swamped ground round the Pena, and all of them on open ground that made them easy prey for aerial attack.

The three SS divisions on 48 Corps' right were more fortunate. The ground over which they attacked was slightly higher and much of it was outside the cloudburst area, so that the hazard of swampy ground was considerably reduced. Sepp Dietrich of SS *Leibstandarte*, a commander of great skill and daring, forced his tanks forwards some seven miles during the day, knocking out 27 T34s in his advance. By late afternoon his patrols reported the village of Gremutshy clear of enemy, but Dietrich was not to be caught in the lure of a deserted objective. He halted his tanks, got them hull down in folds in the ground and saw that they were well camouflaged. His cunning was rewarded. At sunset the bombardment of Gremutshy began and continued till midnight. Then the whole of the *Leibstandarte* moved forward – without having lost a single tank in the baited trap. Gremutshy had been reduced to a smoking ruin by shelling. Its thatched cottages still blazed fiercely and dust rose in clouds from the rubble as, in the moonlight, Dietrich's tanks skirted the razed village and got into position for a dawn attack.

Dietrich supposed, rightly, that the Russians believed their bombardments had disabled or destroyed many German tanks and that they were therefore unprepared for the attack. But, since surprise was of the essence, there was no time for such refinements as the clearing of minefields, and there were a good many casualties as SS *Leibstandarte* pressed on. But by midday the huge Panthers, which were impervious to 76 mm fire except at point-blank range, had penetrated the Russian defensive positions south of Werchopenje and were making for Hill 260 a mile south of Nowosselowka – one of the objectives that had been unattained by 48 Corps. Their losses had been heavy, however – as much from breakdowns as from Russian attacks. The day ended with stalemate on that middle section of Fourth *Panzer* Army's front.

It was in fact only on the third day, 7 July, that any real success was achieved by the southern pincer. By that time the sun had dried out the swampy ground and the battle-field presented a different, though equally desolate, appearance: miles of devastated cornfields, hundreds of burnt-out tanks of both sides, and the bodies of the dead already swelling obscenely in the heat. A soldier's diary records, "One man had been caught by bomb blast while squatting in a ditch with his trousers down. It seemed the ultimate in humiliation."

The minefields had created great devastation and the black-ened flesh and bones of those who had been blown up were strewn grotesquely over the battlefield:

Coming stealthily upon a small copse I looked warily up to meet the face of a sniper poised in a tree. Panic-stricken I fired my pistol up at him before he could get me; but it was just a head, a blown-off bodiless head, still – it seemed to me – smiling craftily, that had lodged in the branches there. When I climbed up I dislodged it and it fell to the ground with a thud, the crafty smile undisturbed.

By this time, the Russians had moved back into the ruins of Gremutshy in preparation for a counter-attack. While they were forming up for this, 48 *Panzer* Corps launched their delayed attempt to make their two-pronged wheel to the north-west. They caught the enemy by surprise, broke through on both sides of Ssyrzew in great force and caused havoc among the assembling Seventh Guards Army, which fled in disorder to shelter behind Hill 243 beyond Werchopenje, losing 70 tanks and artillery pieces in the carefully timed and aimed German barrage.

With the ground clear before them, *Gross Deutschland* now gained momentum and wheeled round to Ssyrzewo with only the most minor casualties. The Russians seemed for the moment nonplussed. But by afternoon they had recovered and launched their counter-attack on Ssyrzewo. It resulted in a head-on collision in which 500 tanks simply faced each other and went on firing until, after several hours, the reverberation of guns along the steep banks of the Pena diminished and night fell on the still-blazing hulks.

No ground had been gained by either side, and it became clearer than ever that the chief characteristic of the Battle of Kursk – which town, though less than 40 miles to the north, remained to the Germans as remote as the moon – was the huge wastage of men and arms in a fight that lacked any subtlety of direction. Mass was posed against mass in a conflict that, in theory, should have been brief and sharply decisive, but in five days showed no sign of reaching a climax.

Dietrich, one of Hitler's oldest friends, said in one of his rare criticisms of the Führer:

Perhaps the feeling of failure had permeated the troops on the Russian front since Kharkov. Not to be able to clinch the victory then was a bad thing. Then Hitler's uncertainty was a sign. The conflict between the top commanders was another. There were personal feuds. Kluge and Guderian hated each other; they nearly came to blows once. Hitler's intuition was always right, and he should have allowed it to overcome the pressure of the generals who wanted Zitadelle to go on for their share of the glory. Also, the way the Russians poured men and machines into the fray was absolutely unlimited. They simply had a disregard for numbers. It didn't matter to them that they were losing a million. Another million were packed behind them ready to be fed into the battle machine.

It was true, although it could hardly be said that Hitler was sparing in his expenditure of men and machines either. But his was the expenditure of desperation, and the Russian High Command knew this very well. Viewing the battle in retrospect Stalin declared to the Supreme Soviet: "We were an immovable mass against which the Fascists tried to pitch an irresistible force. A scientific impossibility in any case. But they were outmaneuvered by our generals also. They never had a chance."

That was untrue. There were a number of occasions when Russian tactics were as unimaginative as the Germans', and many more when the jaws of the pincer seemed to be closing. But it was always a piecemeal closure by isolated units, never a concerted forward movement. The shoulder-to-shoulder positioning of Hoth's entire Fourth *Panzer* Army within a 30-mile front had packed a punch that could hardly have failed. Yet it was a punch that was weakened by circumstances that should have been anticipated. Such simple devices as the lure of the abandoned village were overlooked, and the enemy's ability to contain Model's northern force in, so to speak, a salient within a salient was not appreciated. This last factor dealt the death blow to the whole operation. With every abortive attempt Model made to press southward it became increasingly difficult for Hoth to link up with him. "The Russians have learnt a lot since 1941," he told Manstein, "They are no longer peasants with simple minds. They have learnt the art of warfare from us."

Wherever they had learnt it, their knowledge was nowhere more apparent than in the intense fighting that took place around the railway junction of Orel, north of the salient. The Russian Third Army had forced its way forward with the object of encircling Model's Ninth Army in a sweep to the south-west. In that objective it failed, but it did keep most of Model's infantry and artillery engaged in defense instead of attack. The German infantry were thus unable to lend support to the southward armored thrusts that were meant to link up with the Fourth *Panzer* Army on the heights east of Kursk. For three continuous days and nights from 9 to 11 July, Orel in the north and Belgorod in the south – where the Seventh Guards Army was attempting a similar tactic to split the SS divisions from their supporting battle group in 48 *Panzer* Corps – were subjected to bombardment after bombardment. "It was a continual earthquake," one eye-witness put it, "The ground just split asunder and any tank on the move would tip into the fissure."

Yet another blow was delivered by the Red Air Force, which succeeded in bombing the German supply base at Poltava and destroying the railway line to Kharkov, making lengthy and delaying engineering work necessary. There was no doubt that, whether newly learnt or not, the art of warfare was much in evidence in the Russian designs.

By the time both German pincers had been fighting unáinterruptedly for a week, they were showing signs of exhaustion. A shortage of supplies and ammunition, abetted by the cutting off of the railhead, was also making itself felt. But on the left flank of the southern pincer they managed to drive the enemy off the main road from Rakowo to Kruglik and head for the Beresowka forest. Once that objective was attained there was a good chance of capturing Hill 247 with the help of the northwest sweep of the SS division on the right flank, which was intended to wheel round from Hill 260 south of Nowosselowka and make a synchronized attack on Hill 247 from the east.

During the night of 9 July the 3rd *Panzer* Division entered the village of Beresowka from the west, much reduced in numbers – at least a third of its heavy tanks lay burnt out on the battlefield – but tenaciously holding on to every inch of ground it had fought for up the Kruglik road. Help was on its way in the form of one regiment of SS *Leibstandarte* that was making its way unopposed across open country from Werchopenje. Rudolf von Ribbentrop, son of the German Minister, was in command and reported later that he had got to within half a mile of the woods north of the village when a strong Russian counter-attack met them. "Russian tanks of all sizes came streaming out of the forest and fanned out to meet us," he said, "Visibility was bad because of the cornfields, but there was a battle royal and we shot up two of their big mobile guns before the *Luftwaffe* came in to help."

As one of the pilots described it: "In the first attack four tanks explode under the hammer blows of my cannon; by evening, after four more sorties, the total rises to 12. The evil spell is broken, and in the Stuka we possess a weapon which can speedily be employed everywhere and is capable of dealing successfully with the formidable numbers of Soviet tanks."

This was wishful thinking on his part, however. Nothing could deal wholly successfully with the huge number of Soviet tanks. On every section of the battlefield those that were destroyed or immobilized were replaced with seeming magical rapidity. Supplies were endless "and appeared from nowhere," as Manstein told Hitler at a conference at the Führer's headquarters on 12 July. By that time the railhead at Poltava was operating again, but there were no endless supplies coming from Germany. The enormous force of fighting vehicles with which Manstein and Kluge had opened the battle to close the Kursk salient had been depleted by more than half. There was continual activity at the repair shops to get into some sort of fighting order those tanks – especially Panthers and Tigers – that had been retrieved from the battlefield. An equally continual effort was made to overcome the successes of the Soviet aircraft in attacking the ammunition trains for which every German tank still left in the field was desperately waiting.

It was now being proved only too clearly that Hitler had indeed put in hazard far more armor than he could afford to lose. Although no resolution of the Kursk conflict could yet be seen, developments in Europe were calling for a speedy conclusion of the offensive and the transfer of forces to the western theater. For, by 12 July, the Allies had landed in Sicily.

The climax to the battle of Kursk was reached during the two days 12 to 14 July, although it amounted to only the fadeaway ending of a battle of attrition. For nine days the two contestants had been slugging at one another like heavyweights swinging giant blows that consistently failed to achieve the knockout.

Early on the morning of 12 July, Hoth summoned his corps commanders and planned for a breakthrough before the Russians could intensify their defenses between Kruglik and Nowosselowka and build up their forces for a big push southward. He had received intelligence reports indicating that the extreme southern tip of Army Group South's fortified line along the Donetz and Mius rivers, between Taganrog and Stalino, was under the threat of a Russian attack. "We shall be needed there," he told Hausser, commander of the SS Corps. "Let us finish the issue of Kursk once and for all."

Brave words. His armored strength consisted now of only 600 operative tanks to spearhead the attack. Every man in Fourth Army was suffering from battle exhaustion, and ammunition was at a premium. In contrast, Vatutin had new machines, including the new 85 mm SU85 self-propelled gun, and men fresh to the front. He also had the entire Fifth Armored Army in reserve and ready for action. It was not difficult to see where the advantage lay. This climactic action came to be known as "The Death Ride of Fourth Panzer Army."

"It's a fine day for a joyride," Sepp Dietrich said laconically to the driver of his command tank. "It won't rain."

Nor did it. It was a day of intense dry heat. The interiors of the tanks were like ovens despite the air induction systems and fan coolers. The high speed traffic of heavy vehicles over the sandy roads threw up clouds of dust that made it virtually impossible for the *Luftwaffe* to pick out their targets. On one occasion, according to Dietrich, a T34 and a Panther collided head on as they rolled through the dust. "Ivan had broken through our anti-tank screen and his progeny were streaming like rats all over the battlefield."

The "all over" certainly suited the situation. The Fifth Armored Army had come charging into action with all the zest of experienced troops who had waited too long in reserve positions. As the spearhead of the SS *Panzer* Corps rolled towards Prokhorovka it met the full force of this fresh and eager force. Slightly outnumbered, but with more heavy tanks, Hausser's exhausted tank crews met their match. The thick dust prevented the Tigers from making full use of their superior range, and many fell prey to the T34s. The battlefield was littered with burning wrecks – more than 300 tanks were lost by each side. But it was the Germans who could least afford such heavy losses. The onslaught of the *Panzers* was over. By evening the Russians had recaptured Berezowka and cut off 3rd *Panzer* Division and a large wedge of *Gross Deutschland* that had forced its way through the woods to the rescue.

For the Germans, the battle was clearly lost. All the open country between Belgorod, where Seventh Guards Army had broken through as far as the rear echelons of the SS corps, and Orel to the north was possessed by the Russians. Only isolated pockets of Germans were evident in the villages.

From the three hills so fiercely fought for and now relinquished by the Germans, the Russians had a straight line of fire down on to the irrepressible attackers, whose commanders were continually reminding themselves of the Führer's words: "It must not fail."

Nevertheless it did fail. The immediate cause of failure, or anyway of termination, was the Führer's own order, relayed through Manstein and radio link to Army Group South's headquarters: "Operation Zitadelle is cancelled forthwith."

It is of course impossible to stop a raging battle instantaneously unless both sides are given the same order. A withdrawal meant fighting a rearguard action, and it was two weeks before Hoth's forces got themselves back to their original positions on the starting line – with further considerable losses. In the north, Model's Ninth Army, having advanced so little, had correspondingly little to cover in retreat. The situation at Orel was still critical, however, and Manstein had to order two *Panzer* divisions north to help deal with this threat. He sent two more to the south, where the Taganrog–Stalino sector was also being increasingly threatened.

During the whole of the operation, from H-hour to cancellation, the advances made by the two jaws of the pincer, collectively or by individual units, had never reduced the breach across the base of the salient to less than 60 miles. Twenty *Panzer* divisions, the pride and joy of the *Wehrmacht*, had been bled white, and although on the credit side could be counted the huge number of Russian prisoners and the vast booty and destruction of the battlefield it was only too clear that with Allied assistance the Russians could afford losses on this colossal scale far more easily than the Germans could.

The Death Ride of the Fourth *Panzer* Army signaled the approaching end of the German struggle for Russia. By December, the reconstituted Ninth and Fourth *Panzer* Armies had been pushed back to, and beyond, the Dneiper. The whole of the Eastern Front from Nevel in the north to Kirovograd in the south reflected the turning of the tide, for it had been subjected to unremitting Soviet attacks against the weakening power of Hitler's armies. Now, not even a stalemate could be achieved. The Kursk gambit had been played and had failed.

The Battle of the Atlantic (1943)

Herbert A. Werner

The cruel waters of the Atlantic were always destined to be a major battlefield of the Second World War. An overpopulated island, Britain was peculiarly needy of imports; in 1939 over half its food was imported. So was all of its oil, and much of its non-ferrous metal. All were conveyed to the island by the largest merchant fleet in the world. Cognizant of lessons learned in the First World War, when hostilities commenced in 1939 the Royal Navy organized merchantmen into trans-Atlantic convoys under the protection of its 220 escort vessels (mostly destroyers).

Cognizant, meanwhile, of Britain's dependence on its waterly supply line it became German strategy to disrupt, better still destroy, this self-same supply line. There were occasional raids on sea lanes by the battleships of the Kriegsmarine *(although Hitler was almost paranoically scared of squandering his big sea guns) and E-boats were a constant menace in British coastal waters. Much the most effective, however, of Germany's weapons was the* Unterseeboot: *the U-boat. Admiral Karl Donitz began the war with just 57 U-boats; by July 1942 the U-boat fleet had reached 300 strong and was sinking 7 million tons annually. Small wonder that*

*Churchill, after victory, declared that "the only thing that
really frightened me during the war was the U-boat peril".
Disaster for Britain was only averted by the entry of the US
into the war (Uncle Sam was soon building three "Liberty"
merchant ships a day for the Atlantic supply route), the
breaking of German U-boat wireless "traffic" by the crypto-
graphers at Bletchley Park (henceforth U-boats could more
easily be obviated or hunted) and advances in avionics which
allowed the RAF to patrol greater and greater distances into
the Atlantic. Depite reactive improvements in U-boat tactics
and technology, notably the invention of the* schnorkel *which
allowed U-boats to cruise submerged whilst using their diesel
engines, the tide of the Atlantic war turned ineluctably
against the* Kriegsmarine. *In 1943 twice as many U-boats
were sunk as were built. The chance to starve Britain into
submission had gone.*

*Herbert Werner was an officer in the German U-boat
force, the most dangerous branch of any service, Allied or
Axis, in the Second World War. Of the 39,000 men who
served aboard U-boats between 1939 and 1945 28,000 perished.*

2 May [1943]. The weather was serene, the sea calm and
irridescent. At 1408 Riedel spotted a fast-moving target behind the southern horizon, a loner. We raced at highest speed
on a track that would intersect the vessel's mean course. After
three hours of running, during which we left the cargo ship
cautiously behind the horizon, we dived leisurely, having
plenty of time before the vessel would become visible. One
hour later, our hopes of shooting the first torpedo vanished.
The ship was identified as a Swedish freighter travelling the
"Philadelphia Route", which we had guaranteed as a safe path
for neutrals.

After we had allowed the Swede to pass, we intercepted a
signal from one of our boats: CONVOY IN AJ 87 COURSE
NORTH-EAST. SUNK TWO TOTAL 13,000 TONS.
KEEP CONTACT. U-192. Grid square AJ 87 lay between

Newfoundland and Greenland – far beyond our reach. We had to leave the convoy to wolves patrolling that area.

5 May. *U-230* charged towards her allotted square. During the morning, we intercepted a signal that confirmed our worst fears. Riedel handed me the deciphered message in silence: DESTROYER. ATTACKED. SINKING. U-638. This report was the last act of *U-638*. Nothing was heard of her again.

Two hours later, a fresh distress signal was hastily decoded: ATTACKED BY DESTROYERS. DEPTH CHARGES. LEAVE BOAT. U-531. This second alarming call alerted us to the fact that the battle at that convoy had produced unusually fierce countermeasures by its defence.

6 May. It was still dark when another signal from the battle-field flashed across the Atlantic: ATTACKED BY CORV-ETTE. SINKING. U-438. This third death message angered and puzzled us. What caused this sudden stream of messages which told us of nothing but dying?

Now another was intercepted: AIRCRAFT. BOMBS. RAMMED BY DESTROYER. SINKING. U-125.

A fourth casualty! Our anger changed to shock.

7 May. *U-230*, cruising with extreme caution under a star-strewn sky, intercepted still another last report: AIR AT-TACK. SINKING 47N 05W. U-663. I checked the victim's position on our mildewy chart and marked the spot of her destruction, in the centre of the Bay of Biscay, with a black cross. She was the fifth boat to go to the bottom within three days. But seven hours later I had to revise the total when, after repeated requests by Headquarters to report their positions, *U-192* and *U-531* had not answered. They had met their fate while attacking that convoy southeast of Greenland.

10 May. It was a sunny day. We arrived in the designated square, a small area almost in the centre of the Atlantic. Here we were supposed to intercept the convoy reported earlier. With us in ambush lurked six boats, and many more sailed between our patrol and the British Isles. *U-456* our companion since our departure from Brest, hid somewhere behind the horizon. The trap was set.

11 May. Another obituary, again originating in the Bay of Biscay: ATTACKED BY AIRCRAFT. SINKING. U-528.

We were outraged and determined to pay back the loss of our friends a hundredfold.

One hour later we received, as a consolation, attack orders from Headquarters: ALL U-BOATS IN GRID SQUARE BD INTERCEPT EASTBOUND CONVOY IN BD 91. ATTACK WITHOUT FURTHER ORDERS. At once we set *U-230* on a new course at high speed; her bow split the water ahead into two sparkling fountains. Preparing for action, I ordered a complete overhaul of all torpedoes.

12 May. At 0400, the tension was apparent throughout the boat as I mounted my watch. At 0540, as the new day dawned. Prager shot several stars and established our position. At 0620, he reported from below that we had arrived on the convoy's calculated mean track. I reduced our speed and turned *U-230* onto a westward course, toward the convoy, cautiously probing ahead. The eastern sky turned bloodred as the sun prepared to rise over the horizon; only a thin line in the west remained dark.

0615: The sun shot like a fireball out of the ocean. At that spectacular moment, I spotted a smear over the southwesterly horizon – the convoy! I called Siegmann to the bridge and said as he arrived, "I have a present for you, Sir."

"Thanks, Exec, encouraging news at last."

We watched the smudge grow bigger and wider. Soon the Captain turned the stern of the boat toward the gray and black fumes. Three mastheads crept over the sharp horizon in the west and mounted higher. Emerging fully, the three ships were seen to be escorts, the sweepers in front of the convoy. They zigzagged closer, moving jerkily like puppets on an empty stage. We proceeded slowly eastward, maintaining safe distance, to determine the convoy's exact course.

0638: Mastheads appeared over a wide section of the horizon. Then the funnels followed. These were the cargo ships, the targets we were after. A mighty display of masts and funnels rose ever higher out of the sea. We were almost dead ahead of the parade, in excellent position. Within one hour, I calculated, we would have plenty of targets at our disposal.

0655: Siegmann acted. "Clear the bridge! On diving stations."

I was in the conning tower as the alarm bell sounded the call to action. Five minutes later the boat was properly trimmed and floated just below the surface. The Captain, seated at the scope, informed the crew over our intercom system. "We have sighted an extremely large convoy, probably over one hundred vessels. We shall attack submerged. I need not remind you that this is no holiday cruise. I expect your utmost effort to make this attack a success." Then he activated the motor of the scope.

0705: No visible contact yet. Siegmann ordered all tubes prepared for firing.

0710: I reported *U-230* combat-ready as the convoy's thumping roar spread through the depths.

0716: The soundman conveyed news that ruined our plan for a submerged assault: "Convoy apparently has changed course. Sound band changed to three-one-oh."

The Captain, visibly annoyed over the unexpected change, raised the scope further into the air to catch a view of the parading fleet. The high-pitched spinning of escorts' propellers echoed through the water, and the grinding noise of the huge armada hit our hull like the beating of countless jungle drums.

"Damn dirty trick," muttered Siegmann. "The convoy zigzags to the northeast. There are at least a dozen corvettes spread over its starboard side."

The convoy steamed away at 11 knots while *U-230* floated undetected by the outer defence, unwilling to attack till she had passed through the cordon of destroyers. The rhythmical thrashing of a hundred propellers penetrated the heavy steel of our hull and bounced forth and back inside the boat. The Captain relinquished his seat at the scope, snarling, "Come over here, Exec, take a look. If I only had a faster boat I could roll up the convoy like a carpet."

I swung into the seat. Seven miles on port I saw an amazing panorama. The entire horizon, as far and wide as I could see, was covered with vessels, their funnels and masts as thick as a forest. At least a dozen fast destroyers cut the choppy green sea with elegance. As many as two dozen corvettes flitted around the edges of the convoy. I said in awe, "Quite a display of power, sir. It's probably the largest convoy ever."

"You might be right. Once we are close to that wall of ships our torpedoes can't miss."

Before we could risk surfacing to race into a new attack position, we had to put distance between us and the convoy. The swishing of propellers, the pounding of piston engines, the singing of turbines, and the chirping of Asdic pings accompanied us on our clandestine run. For almost two hours we travelled diagonally away from the giants of steel.

0915: *U-230* surfaced. Mounting the bridge while the deck was still awash, I took a hurried look in a circle. Far to the northeast, mastheads and funnels moved along the sharp line which divided the ocean from the sky. *U-230* forged through the sea, parallel to the convoy's track, in an attempt to reach a forward position before dusk. Riedel flashed the message of our contact to Headquarters and the other wolves in ambush: CONVOY BD 92 COURSE NORTHEAST ELEVEN KNOTS. STRONG DEFENCE. REMAIN SURFACED FOR ATTACK. U-230.

0955: A startled cry at my back, "*Flugzeug!*"

I saw a twin-engined plane dropping out of the sun. The moment of surprise was total.

"Alarrrmmm!" We plunged head over heels into the conning tower. The boat reacted at once and shot below surface. At this moment of our maximum danger and minimum ability to act, our lives depended upon a miracle, an accident, or the good luck that had so far saved us from extinction.

Four short, ferocious explosions shattered the water above and around us. The boat trembled and fell at a 60-degree angle. Water splashed, steel shrieked, ribs moaned, valves blew, deck-plates jumped, and the boat was thrown into darkness. As the lights flickered on, I saw astonishment in the round eyes of the men. They had every right to be astounded: the attack out of the sun was a complete mystery. Where had the small plane come from? It did not have the range to fly a round-trip between the nearest point of land and the middle of the Atlantic. The conclusion was inescapable that the convoy launched its own airplanes. It seemed highly likely, though we did not want to believe it, that the planes returned to convoy and landed on an aircraft carrier. The idea of a convoy with its own air defence smashed our basic concept of U-boat warfare. No longer could we mount a surprise attack or escape without meeting savage counterattacks.

1035: *U-230* came up to periscope depth. A careful check with our "sky scope", an instrument similar to the periscope, revealed no aircraft. We surfaced at high speed.

The hunt went on. We pressed forward obstinately, with that terrible constriction in the stomach. The diesels hammered hard and pushed the boat swiftly ahead. I glanced only occasionally at the dense picket fence along the horizon and concentrated on the sky. Thickening white clouds scudded along at medium height under a stiff breeze from the west. The wind pitched the water up on deck and once in a while blew a sheet of spray across the bridge.

1110: I detected a glint of metal between the clouds. It was a small aircraft, and it was diving into the attack.

"Alarrrmmm!"

Fifty seconds later, four explosions nearby taught us that the pilot was a well-trained bombardier. Shockwaves rocked boat and crew. Friedrich, struggling to prevent the boat from sinking, caught her at 180 metres, balanced her out, and brought her up to periscope depth.

1125: *U-230* surfaced. We drove forward and clung to the fringes of the convoy with grim determination. Instinct forced us ahead, kept us moving despite the constant threat from above, made us numb to the repetitious detonations. We raced in defiance of fear and sudden destruction – always forward, toward the head of the convoy.

1142: "Aircraft – alarrrmmm!"

U-230 plunged into the depths. Four booms twisted the hull, but the boat survived the savage blows. We waited for the plane to disappear with our hearts beating under our tongues.

1204: We surfaced in an increasingly choppy sea and surged ahead, the boat jolting and shaking. The convoy had slipped into a north-westerly position, and despite our constant harassment we had gained considerable headway on it. I spotted the escorts on the horizon but the real danger lurked above. The clouds had lowered and thickened, covering the last patches of blue sky.

1208: A call from below reached us on the bridge: "Message for Captain, signal just received: ATTACKED BY AIR-CRAFT. SINKING. U-89." Again we were stunned. With a shudder. I pictured what would happen to us, once our own hull was cracked.

1217: "Aircraft dead astern, alarrrmmm!"

U-230 dived once more and descended rapidly. I bit my lip and waited for the final blast. At 45 seconds, four booms whipped the boat with violent force. Every second we were able to snatch from the pursuing aircraft brought us closer to the convoy and success. But if we dived a second too late, bombs would end our hunt with sudden death.

1230: We surfaced again. This time only three men went to the bridge, the Captain, the first seaman's mate, and I. We raced ahead stubbornly, plagued by the thoughts of being annihilated within the hour.

1315: A twin-engined plane dropped suddenly out of a low cloud, only 800 metres astern. It was too late to dive. After freezing for a horrifying instant, Siegmann yelled, "Right full rudder!" I jumped to the rear of the bridge to shoot while the mate manned the second gun. The small aircraft grew enor-mous fast. It dived upon us, machine-gunning the open rear of the bridge as the boat turned to starboard. Neither the mate nor I were able to fire a single bullet; our guns were jammed. The aircraft dropped four bombs which I saw falling toward me, then roared over the bridge so close that I could feel its engines'. hot exhaust brush my face. Four bombs in a row erupted alongside our starboard saddle tanks. Four high fountains collapsed over the two of us at the guns. *U-230* was still afloat, still racing through the rising green sea. The aircraft, having used up its bombs, turned and disappeared into the direction of the convoy.

1323: Our radio mate delivered an urgent message to the Captain: ATTACKED BY AIRCRAFT. UNABLE TO DIVE. SINKING. 45 NORTH 25 WEST. HELP. U-456.

"Have Prager check position," Siegmann shouted back. "Maybe we can save the crew."

The Captain's impulse to rescue our comrades might well result in suicide. We were closer to death than to life ourselves.

But help was imperative – we would have expected the same. Moments later, Prager reported that *U-456* was only 12 miles ahead, 15 degrees to starboard. Immediately, the Captain changed course.

1350: We spotted a plane circling four miles ahead. Then my glasses picked up the bow of *U-456* poking out of the rough sea. The men clung to the slippery deck and to the steel cable strung from bow to bridge. Most of them stood in the water up to their chests. The aircraft kept circling above the sinking boat, making it foolhardy for us to approach. Another danger prevented rescue: astern, a corvette crept over the horizon, evidently summoned by the plane. Now our own lives were in jeopardy. We turned away from the aircraft, the escort, and *U-456*, and fled in the direction of the convoy.

1422: "Aircraft astern!"

Again it was too late to dive. The single-engined plane came in low in a straight line exactly over our wake. I fingered the trigger of my gun. Again the gun was jammed. I kicked its magazine, clearing the jam. Then I emptied the gun at the menace. The mate's automatic bellowed. Our boat veered to starboard, spoiling the plane's bomb run. The pilot revved up his engine, circled, then roared toward us from dead ahead. As the plane dived very low, its engine sputtered, then stopped. Wing first, the plane crashed into the surging ocean, smashing its other wing on our superstructure as we raced by. The pilot, thrown out of his cockpit, lifted his arm and waved for help, but then I saw him disintegrate in the explosion of the four bombs which were meant to destroy us. Four violent shocks kicked into our starboard side astern, but we left the horrible scene unharmed.

The downing of the aircraft must have upset the enemy's flight schedule. Minute after minute passed without a repetition of the attacks. Running at highest speed, *U-230* gained bearing ahead of the convoy. In about an hour, we approached the calculated intersection with the convoy's track.

1545: A report from the radio room put our small victory into proper perspective: DEPTH CHARGES BY THREE DE-STROYERS. SINKING. U-186. This new loss was the 11th we had heard of since our patrol began. A naval disaster seemed to be in making. But we could not afford a moment of sorrow for all the men who died that one death that every submariner pictures a thousand times.

1600: *U-230* cut into the projected path of the convoy. I saw four columns of ships creep over the sharp horizon in the southwest, headed in our direction. We had to halt them, had to spread fire in their midst and blow gaps in the mass of steel and iron.

1603: "Aircraft, bearing three-two-oh."

We plummeted into depth. Four detonations, sounding like one, drove the boat deeper and caused rudders and hydroplanes to block in extreme positions. Minutes later, more explosions occurred in the vicinity, but in defiance of our attackers, Siegmann ordered his boat to periscope depth. He raised the scope but downed it instantly, cursing angrily, "*Verdammt!* The fellow has dropped a smoke bomb and has dyed the water yellow."

Despite the dye marking the spot of our submergence, the Captain ordered an attack on the convoy before the escorts could attack us. Chirping Asdic pings, bellowing detonations, and the grinding roar of a hundred engines provided grim background music for our assault.

1638: Up periscope. Then: "Tubes one to five stand ready."

"Tubes one to five are ready," I answered quickly, then held my breath.

Siegmann swiveled around to check the opposite side. Suddenly he cried, "Down with the boat, Chief, take her down for God's sake, destroyer in ramming position! Down to two hundred meters!"

I fully expected the bow of a destroyer to cut into the conning tower momentarily. As the boat swiftly descended, the harrowing sound of the destroyer's engines and propellers hit the steel of our hull. It grew so fast, and echoed so deafeningly, that we were all unable to move. Only our boat was moving, and she went downward much too slowly to escape the blow.

An earshattering boom ruptured the sea. A spread of six depth charges lifted the boat, tossed her out of the water, and left her on the surface at the mercy of four British destroyers. The screws of *U-230* rotated in highest revolutions, driving us ahead. For seconds there was silence. For seconds the British were baffled and stunned. After a whole eternity, our bow dipped and the boat sank – and sank.

A new series of exploding charges lifted our stern with a mighty force. Our boat, entirely out of control, was catapulted toward the bottom five miles below. Tilted at an angle of 60 degrees, *U-230* tumbled to 250 metres before Friedrich was able to reverse her fall. Floating level at a depth of 230 metres, we thought we were well below the range of the enemy's depth charges. *U-230* was speedily rigged to withstand pursuit. Once again we were condemned to sit it out in crushing depths.

1657: Distinct splashes on surface heralded the next spread. A series of twenty-four charges detonated in quick succession. The bellowing roar slammed against our boat. The explosions again pushed her into a sharp down tilt while the echo of the detonations rolled endlessly through depths.

1716: A new spread deafened us and took our breath away. The boat listed sharply under the shattering blow. The steel knocked and shrieked and valves were thrown into open position. The shaft packings leaked, and a constant stream of water soon filled the aft bilge. Pumps spouted, the periscope packings loosened, and water trickled into the cylinders. Water everywhere. Its weight forced the boat deeper into the depths. In the meantime, the convoy crawled in a thunderous procession over our boat.

1740: The uproar was at its peak. A sudden splash told us that we had ten or fifteen seconds to brace against another barrage. The charges went off just beyond lethal range. While the ocean reverberated under the blasts, the bulk of the convoy slowly passed the spot of our slow execution. I pictured the freighters making a detour around the escorts massed above to end our existence. Perhaps we should risk going deeper. I did not know where our limit was, where the hull would finally crack. No one knew. Those who had found out took their knowledge into the depths. For hours we suffered the punishment and sank gradually deeper. In a constant pattern, spreads of twenty-four charges battered our boat every twenty minutes. At one time we thought we had won. That was when the escorts departed and rushed to take their positions in the convoy. But our hope was short-lived. The hunters had only left the *coup de grâce* to the killer group following in the wake of the armada.

20:00: The new group launched its first attack, then another, and another. We sat helpless 265 metres below. Our nerves trembled. Our bodies were stiff from cold, stress, and fear. The mind-searing agony of waiting made us lose any sense of time and any desire for food. The bilges were flooded with water, oil, and urine. Our washrooms were under lock and key; to use them then could have meant instant death, for the tremendous outside pressure would have acted in reverse of the expected flow. Cans were circulated for the men to use to relieve themselves. Added to the stench of waste, sweat, and oil was the stink of the battery gases. The increasing humidity condensed on the cold steel, dropped into the bilges, dripped from pipes, and soaked our clothes. By midnight, the Captain realized that the British would not let up in their bombardment, and he ordered the distribution of potash cartridges to supplement breathing. Soon every man was equipped with a large metal box attached to his chest, a rubber hose leading to his mouth, and a clamp on his nose. And still we waited.

13 May. Over 200 canisters had detonated above and around us by 0100. Several times we had used a ruse in an effort to escape. Through an outboard valve, we repeatedly expelled a great mass of air bubbles. These screens of air floated away on the current, reflecting the Asdic impulses like a large solid body. But our attackers were fooled into chasing the decoys only twice, and both times they left at least one vessel behind, directly over our heads. Unable to sneak away, we gave up the game and concentrated on conserving our power, our compressed air, and our dwindling supply of oxygen.

0400: The boat had fallen to 275 metres. We had been under assault for twelve hours and there was no sign of relief. This day was my birthday and I wondered whether it would be my last. How many chances could one ask for?

0800: No lessening of the attacks. The water in the bilges rose above the deck plates and splashed around my feet. The bilge pumps were useless at this depth. Whenever a charge erupted, the Chief released some compressed air into the tanks to assure the boat's buoyancy.

1200: The boat's down angle had sharply increased. Our compressed-air supply was dangerously low, and the boat slipped ever farther away.

2000: The air was thick, and even more so as we breathed it through the hot cartridges. The devil seemed to be knocking on our steel hull as it creaked and contracted under the enormous pressure.

2200: The barrage increased in violence as dusk closed in on surface. Wild attacks at shorter intervals indicated that the enemy had lost his patience.

14 May. By midnight, we had approached the limit for boat and crew. We had reached a depth of 280 metres and the boat was still sinking. I dragged myself through the aisle, pushing and tossing men around, forcing them to stay awake. Whoever fell asleep might never be awakened.

0310: A thunderous spread rattled down, but without effect. We were closer to being crushed by the mounting pressure than by the exploding canisters. As the echo of the last blast slowly subsided, something else attracted our attention. It was the thrashing of retreating propellers. For a long time we listened to the fading sound, unable to believe that the Tommies had given up the hunt.

0430: For over an hour there was silence. We spent all that time doubting our luck. We had to make sure, so we turned on our fresh-water producer, went high with the motors. No reaction from above. Using the last of our compressed air and battery power, the Chief managed to lift the overloaded boat, metre by metre. Then, unable to slow her upward movement, Friedrich let her rise freely and yelled, "Boat rises fast . . . fifty metres . . . boat has surfaced!"

U-230 broke through to air and life. We pushed ourselves up to the bridge. Around us spread the infinite beauty of night, sky, and ocean. Stars glittered brilliantly and the sea breathed gently. The moment of rebirth was overwhelming. A minute ago, we could not believe that we were alive; now we could not believe that death had kept his finger on us for thirty-five gruesome hours.

Abruptly I felt the impact of the oxygen-rich air upon my system. Almost losing consciousness, I sagged to my knees and slumped over the rim of the bridge. There I stayed until I regained my faculties. The Captain recovered quickly, and we congratulated each other on another miraculous survival.

Then the Captain called out, "Both diesels half ahead. Steer one-eighty. Ventilate boat. Secure from action stations." Siegmann had thrown the dice again.

The diesels coughed to life. Since the convoy had disappeared long ago, we travelled south, towards our last position. The engines muttered reassuringly, topping off our drained batteries and pushing the boat toward a new sunrise. The bilges were emptied, the foul air expelled, and the accumulated refuse thrown overboard. When the darkness dissolved and a new day dawned, *U-230* was again ready for combat.

Still numb from the murderous assault and stiff from the cold depth, we added up our account. Three U-boats in our group had been sunk. Well over 100 Allied ships had ploughed past us, and we had not been able to sink a single one. We might now expect that some 700,000 tons of war material would safely reach the British Isles. It was not a pretty picture.

Sicily (1943)

Hubert Essame

The invasion of Axis-occupied Sicily, Operation Husky, in July 1943 was the greatest seaborne assault of the Second World War. Almost eight divisions – 181,000 troops – were simultaneously put ashore along a hundred mile stretch of the island's coastline. Backing the men was an array of technological expertise and military might that from then on was the hallmark of the Western Allies at war: 14,000 vehicles; 600 tanks; 1,800 guns; 750 warships (including six battleships, 15 cruisers and 128 destroyers) and 5,000 aircraft. For Sicily, the United States contributed her latest inventions – the "walkie-talkie" radio, and the versatile DUKW six-wheeled amphibious truck. By contrast, in the invasion of Normandy a year later, only 133,000 men were landed over the 45-mile stretch of D-day beaches. Husky marked not only the return of the Allies to the mainland of Europe, but also signalled their determination to knock Mussolini's Italy out of the war.

By January 1943 it was apparent that the Axis forces in Tunis were trapped in the vice being closed by the Allied armies from west and east, and that their destruction was only to be a matter of time. Field Marshal Albert Kesselring, Axis Supreme Commander in the Mediterranean, predicted that the Allies would soon be "in possession of a jumping-off base for an assault on Europe from the south". There was an urgent need, therefore, for President Franklin D. Roosevelt and Prime Minister Winston Churchill to meet with their Chiefs of Staff to decide the next move. They met on 14–23 January 1943 in French Morocco for the Casablanca Conference, with Major General George S. Patton, commanding the United States forces in Morocco, as host.

After discussing – and discarding – the possibilities of a second European front to take the strain off the hard-pressed Soviet Armies, the conference decided that when the North African campaign was over, the Allied forces, under General Dwight D. Eisenhower, should stage Operation Husky – the invasion of Sicily by two armies, one American, under Patton, and one British, led by General Sir Bernard Montgomery, both under command of General Sir Harold Alexander. It was hoped to placate Stalin by drawing German forces away from the Russian front; to open up the Mediterranean to Allied shipping; and to give the war-weary Italians an excuse for overthrowing Benito Mussolini and getting out of the war.

Sicily is about the size of the state of Vermont, and a little larger than Wales. The terrain generally favors the defense. Inland, the ground is rugged and mountainous, with Mount Etna, in the north-east corner, rising to 10,000 ft. Good roads ran along the east and northern coasts; elsewhere they were few, badly surfaced and with many sharp corners and steep gradients. Deployment off the roads would inevitably be difficult. Only in the Plain of Catania could armor move with any degree of freedom. The Allied plan made the capture of the 30 Sicilian airfields a priority, for it was these bases that posed such a threat to Allied shipping in the Mediterranean. They had also sustained the Axis defense in Tunisia. The airfields fell into three groups: the Gerbini group in the Plain of Catania; the Castelvetrano group south-west of Palermo; and the Conte Olivio Comiso group near the south coast ports.

Combined operations were still in their infancy. No one knew to what extent it would be possible to maintain the invading forces over the beaches with the DUKWs, LSTs, LCMs and LCIs. It was therefore considered vital to gain possession of the major ports as soon as possible. Messina, the largest of these, was out of fighter range and known to be strongly defended.

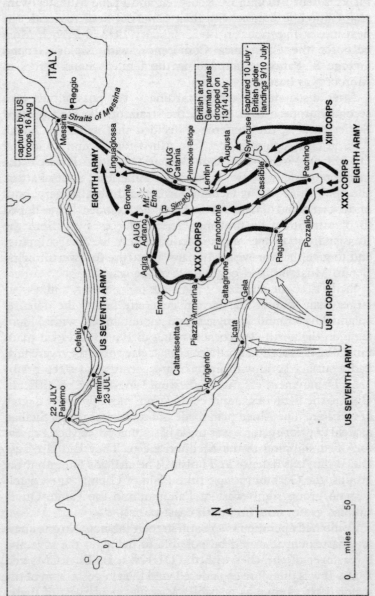

5.8 The Invasion and Conquest of Sicily, July–August 1943

Palermo, Trapani and Marsala, also out of fighter range, could maintain about half the invading force; Catania, Augusta and Syracuse, within range, would supply the other half. Operation Husky was proving as formidable to prepare as Operation Torch, the previous (and first) Anglo-American amphibious landing of the war.

For the assault the admirals stressed the advantages of dispersed landings from the naval point of view. The airmen, their case forcibly put by Air Chief Marshal Sir Arthur Tedder, demanded the neutralization of the airfields on the island as a first priority: both British and American logistic staffs insisted that they must have the use of Palermo and the southern and south-eastern ports at a very early stage. After seven invasion plans had been discussed, Eisenhower gave the final decision: the two armies would land side by side, the Seventh US Army about Gela and the Eighth British Army in the south-east corner of the island. July would be the deadline for the landings.

Most post-war comment gives the impression that the Americans and British in the Mediterranean were continually at loggerheads. But the reverse was the case, due largely to the magnanimity and vision of Eisenhower, the Supreme Commander. Seldom did the Allies work together so cheerfully and unselfishly. Eisenhower had in Alexander the most experienced and tactful commander in the British Army to handle his two brilliant but brittle Army commanders – Patton and Montgomery. Finally in Vice Admiral Sir Bertram H. Ramsay, his Deputy Commander, he had the admiral who had organized the largest evacuation in history – Dunkirk – to help him execute the largest combined operation in history.

The air strength of Tedder and Lieutenant General Carl Spaatz (USAAF) was formidable – 267 squadrons, 146 of which were American and the rest British, totalling over 5,000 aircraft and thus outnumbering the 520 Axis planes by ten to one. Immediately after the fall of Tunis, the Allies turned to the task of securing the air dominance over Sicily which must be gained before a single ship could safely approach it or one soldier step ashore. First, the Allied aircraft ranged far and wide against strategic targets in Italy. Then they began an intense bombardment of the enemy airfields and radar stations within striking distance of Sicily and the proposed routes of the convoys. Tedder interrupted the first stage of his air plan to seize Pantellaria; the island fortress Mussolini had constructed as rival to Malta.

Starting in May, the bombardment of this island gradually increased in intensity till 7 June. Thereafter for four days it rose to a crescendo: over 5,000 tons of bombs were dropped. On 10 June, the third anniversary of Italy's entry into the war, a force from 1st British Division approached the island covered by a precision attack by American flying Fortress B17 bombers. The garrison of 4,600 surrendered without a struggle. For the first time victory had been gained by air power alone.

At the end of June, Alexander's plans for the assault were complete. Montgomery and Eighth Army, embarking at ports between Syria and Sfax were to land on a 30-mile front with two corps, 13th Corps (Lieutenant General Sir Miles C. Dempsey) just south of Syracuse and 30th Corps (Lieutenant General Sir Oliver Leese) astride the Pachino peninsula to capture the airfield there. Patton planned to land his Seventh Army on a 70-mile front in three simultaneous seaborne assaults; two on the east flank by Major General Omar N. Bradley's 2nd Corps with 45th Division at Scoglitti and the 1st at Gela, and 3rd Division (Major General Lucian K. Truscott), directly under his own command, at Licata. As a floating reserve he had 2nd Armored Division and part of 9th Division. All were battle-hardened with the exception of 45th Division.

Initially Alexander prescribed the establishment of beach-heads and the early seizure of Syracuse, the Pachino and Ponte Olivo airfields and the port of Licata. Thereafter Montgomery was to seize Augusta, Catania and the Gerbini group of air-fields. Patton planned to advance about 15 to 20 miles inland on the first day. Both armies were to link up on a common boundary – the Yellow Line. But what was to be done thereafter was, unfortunately, not clear. Patton suspected (with good reason) that the major role of exploitation would be given to Montgomery. He protested to Alexander but when overruled, like a good soldier for the moment raised no further objection. Both British and American landings were to be preceded by airborne assaults: the British 1st Airborne Division in gliders and the 82nd American Airborne Division parachuting.

Meanwhile, in early June, Generale d'Armata Alfredo Guzzoni had assumed command of the Italian forces on the island with his Sixth Army headquarters at Enna. He found, even by Italian standards at this stage of the war, an appalling situation. There was a total Italian garrison of 30,000 men and 1,500 guns but only four divisions out of 12 were relatively mobile. The rest were scattered in low-grade coast defense units on the scale of 41 men to the mile. Many of them were of local origin and virtually untrained; the standard of their officers was exceptionally low. Most of their arms and equipment were obsolete and the coast defenses, except near the ports, were either perfunctory or non-existent. One Corps headquarters presided over the destinies of these depressing troops at the east end of the island and another at the west. Only German assistance gave cause for any hope.

Guzzoni had attached as adviser Major General Fridolin von Senger und Etterlin, a Bavarian who had distinguished himself at the head of a *Panzer* Corps in Russia. Detached from 14 *Panzer* Corps on the mainland were 15th *Panzer Grenadier* Division under Major General Eberhard Rodt and *Hermann Goering Panzer* Division under Lieutenant General Paul Conrath, a former Nazi police chief, making a total of about 30,000 troops and including a Tiger tank company of 17 Mark VI tanks and approximately 90 Mark IIIs and IVs.

Anticipating landings at opposite ends of the island, as the Allies had originally planned, Guzzoni and von Senger deployed 15th *Panzer Grenadier* Division in the west and the *Hermann Goering* Division in two battle groups; one near Caltagirone about 20 miles north of Gela and the other under Colonel Schmalz in the Catania Plain. With these troops and the *Livorno* Division, south of Caltanisetta near the Ponte Olivo airfield, the Axis counted on holding the ring by rapid counterattack until reinforced by the rest of 14 *Panzer* Corps from the mainland.

The day before the invasion, 9 July, started hot with scarcely a ripple on the sea. Rear Admiral Louis Mountbatten, the British Director of Combined Operations, with Adm. Ramsay on board the command ship *Antwerp*, watched the six invasion convoys as they passed on their way to the rendezvous south of Malta. Seven and a half divisions, totalling 160,000 men, were afloat in 2,760 ships and landing craft. They came from the Clyde, from Norfolk, Virginia; and ports along the African coast from Beirut to Algiers. Incredibly there was not a single enemy aircraft in the sky.

At noon, a light breeze sprang up from the west; by mid-afternoon it was blowing Force 7. Almost all the troops in the smaller craft were sick. As the British came under the lee of the land, conditions for them improved but for the Canadians and Americans there would be no respite. They would have to land sick to death and soaked to the skin. But the rough weather was not an unmitigated disaster. Most of the defenders of the Sicilian coast retired to bed, deciding that no man in his senses would attempt to land in such conditions.

First to land in the blackest hours of the night were the British 1st Air Landing Brigade in Waco and Horsa gliders. Their target was the Ponte Grande area near Syracuse. But it was disastrous. Partly owing to the lack of experience of the pilots of their towing aircrafts and due also in part to the high winds their landing was widely scattered. Seventy of the 134 gliders were released too soon and lost in the sea. Only eight officers and 65 men out of a total 2,075 emplaned in Africa, reached their objective. But they managed to hang on until relieved by the 5th British Division. The 82nd Airborne Division (for the same reason) had an equally difficult landing. About 200 paratroopers of 505th Parachute Regiment managed to seize the vital high ground near Piano Lupo to set up and defend road blocks. They were to prove of great value when the expected counter-attack came later that day. Others roamed far and wide, cutting communications and generally spreading despondency and alarm amongst the Italians, rudely wakened from their slumbers.

On the Eighth Army front the guns of the four supporting battleships quickly silenced any coastal batteries and field guns that dared open fire and the landing proceeded smoothly, partly owing to the thorough training the troops had received and partly to the absence of Italian resistance. At one stage, Montgomery received a report that the Royal Marines had been charged by cavalry! In fact they had inadvertently stampeded the horses of the Italian 206th Coastal Division. These they rounded up, mounted and themselves charged inland. By nightfall the British had taken Syracuse and all their objectives for the day.

On the American front, 45th Division at Scoglitti, although delayed for an hour by the gale, had similar good fortune. At Licata, 3rd Division, in the new beaching craft (LSTs, LCIs and LSTs), landed on time and almost without a hitch. Mountbatten was impressed by the coolness, discipline and efficiency of the US Navy crews and the rapid organization of movement inland. By 0830, guns and tanks were freely coming ashore. Only at Gela was there serious opposition.

As Force X, a special force of Rangers attached to 1st Division, approached the shore, the enemy blew up the pier. Simultaneously the coast defense guns opened up. But they were quickly silenced by devastatingly accurate fire from the 5-in and 6-in guns of the destroyer *Shubrick* and the cruiser *Savannah*. As the Rangers touched down they dashed forward into Gela with the leading troops of 1st Division close on their heels. By 1000 Patton, in the headquarters ship *Monrovia* with Vice-Adm. Hewitt, had 3rd Division holding eight miles of coastline and forces moving rapidly inland. At Gela 1st Division held the road junction of Piano Lupo, the town itself and the airfield. The 45th Division reported that its leading troops were five miles inland.

Now that the Allies had shown their hand, Gen. Guzzoni's reaction was prompt but ill-starred. Clearly there was no risk of a landing at the Palermo end of the island. *Kampf Gruppe Schmaltz* could be relied upon for the moment to guard the Gerbini group of airfields. The major threat was posed by the Americans at Gela. Guzzoni therefore set the 15th *Panzer Grenadier* Division in motion towards Enna, thus creating a reserve under his own hand, and ordered the *Livorno* Division, plus two mobile groups and the *Hermann Goering* Division, to make a co-ordinated attack on Gela and drive the Americans into the sea. The orders for the *Hermann Goering* Division went astray: in consequence the Italians attacked on their own at 0830 with infantry and about 20 light tanks. They struck the 16th Regimental Combat Team supported by the guns of the Navy who were in no mood to be pushed aside. Their attack was a costly fiasco.

The German counter-attack during the early afternoon came with greater vigor, accompanied by heavy shelling of the beaches and determined low-flying attacks by the *Luftwaffe* on the mass of shipping now lying offshore. Despite the courage of the Germans it was a muddled affair and came to nothing. About an hour later they renewed the attack, this time supported by Tiger tanks. This too petered out in confused fighting which continued till nightfall, leaving the Americans in possession of all their first day's objectives except the Ponte Olivo airfield.

To Patton it was evident that 11 July would be the crucial day and that his army would have to bear the brunt of a full-dress counterstroke by the bulk of the German armor. To the consternation of the staffs, he therefore scrapped the pre-arranged landing schedules and ordered 2nd Armored Division and the 18th RCT ashore with all speed. Disembarkation proceeded at a frantic rate throughout the night. He was thus ready to meet the thrust on Gela soon after dawn by the *Hermann Goering* Division who attacked in three columns from the east and by the *Livorno* Division from the west. When he disembarked from Adm. Hewitt's barge at 0900, German 88 mm guns were pounding the beach. When his scout car had been de-waterproofed he set off into Gela for the headquarters of the 1st Division. On the way he decided to look in on the HQ of Colonel Darby, one of the Rangers.

It was a lucky decision. In fact, the *Hermann Goering* Division had cut off the 1st Division from the Rangers and a confused battle was raging along the eastern outskirts of the town. From an observation post close to the front, Patton was able to watch a battle between the Rangers, using a captured battery of Italian 77 mm guns and *Livorno* Division. Every gun the enemy could bring to bear was used. They turned Gela into a shambles. In the nick of time, ten Shermans joined in the fray, having driven all the way from Licata. Deadly and accurate fire from the 6-in guns of the *Savannah* was brought to bear on the

Livorno Division. By mid-morning they had had enough and retired badly mauled.

Patton now moved on to the 1st Division's front which only had two tanks ashore. Outside the town Conrath had flung in all his 60 tanks with orders to hurl the Americans into the sea. Burning tanks soon littered the Gela Plain. The 32nd Field Artillery Battalion, disembarking their guns from DUKWs, went straight into action and engaged the German tanks over open sights. The infantry of the 1st Division stood like a rock. Three miles inland, the Germans reeled back before the 16th Infantry at Piano Lupo. Meanwhile, the tanks of 2nd Armored Division, struggling through the sand of the beaches, roared into action. Deadly and accurate fire from the Navy added to the inferno. The German tanks faltered and then turned back leaving over half their number behind in flames. Patton then got through to Major General Terry de la Mesa Allen, commander of the 1st Division, to congratulate him and at the same time remind him that he still had to take his D-day objective, Ponte Olivo airfield, four miles inland. Meanwhile, farther to the east, the paratroops had put up a magnificent resistance on Biazzo Ridge and disembarkation had continued. By nightfall the bridgehead at Gela was secure. As Patton had foreseen, this was the bloodiest day of the campaign.

An unfortunate incident that night marred a story of outstanding success. Patton had arranged for 504th Parachute Regiment, consisting of two battalions of parachutists, to be dropped on the Gela airfield and had taken every precaution to warn his own troops of the operation. He and his staff were assured that all the anti-aircraft gunners of the huge supporting fleet had also been told. Regrettably, and perhaps due to the 550 Axis air sorties in two days, enemy AA guns in the fleet opened up against the aircraft carrying the parachutists. As a result, the men were dropped far and wide. When daylight came, out of 2,000 men and equipment, all that could be mustered at the landing zone were a scratch company and a few light howitzers.

With both Eighth and Seventh Armies firmly ashore, the first phase of Operation Husky was nearing its end. By the evening of 12 July Montgomery had captured Augusta and was on the point of advancing on a front of four divisions into the Catania

Plain. Patton had linked up with him and was nearing the Yellow Line 20 miles inland which was his first objective. Meanwhile, Guzzoni had been moving his armored forces into the Catania Plain and reinforcements from 14 *Panzer* Corps were arriving opposite the British front. The time had clearly come for Alexander to decide which line of advance the Allied armies should take. It seemed obvious to the Americans and others that Patton rather than Montgomery was better sited to strike due north on Enna and the north coast.

On 14 July, Montgomery, in his drive towards Catania, found himself held up by 29th *Panzer Grenadier* Division and two regiments of parachutists flown in from Avignon as well as Battlegroup Schmalz. General Hans Valentine Hube, of 14 *Panzer* Corps, a one-armed veteran of the Eastern Front, had taken charge. Montgomery, without even mentioning the fact to Patton (but apparently with Alexander's acquiescence), now set in motion a left-hook round the foot of Mount Etna on Route 124, which was within the American area of operations. Of the three good roads running north he now had two. That evening, to the consternation of Patton and Bradley, a directive arrived from Alexander allotting to Montgomery the main effort against Messina, on both sides of Mount Etna.

The Americans, cramped for space and resentful of the fact that they had not even been consulted, found themselves relegated to the invidious task of guarding the British left flank. Later, they were to have the consolation prize of a ride to Palermo, when Messina was in Montgomery's grasp. Stung, Patton took off for Tunis to see Alexander and to express his disappointment. Only now did Alexander realize how deeply Patton felt the affront. But it was too late to halt Montgomery. Alexander therefore gave Patton a free hand in advancing towards Palermo and the north coast.

Released from his strait-jacket Patton launched his spectacular all-out drive on Palermo. To this end he created a provisional Corps under Major General Geoffrey T. Keyes, his Chief of Staff. The 82nd and 3rd Divisions were to make for Palermo from the south and south-east, with 2nd Armored Division in their wake for the final advance on the city. Meanwhile Bradley's Corps was to strike due north and cut the coast road. During a six-day lightning campaign in torrid heat Keyes' Corps, with the infantry riding on the tanks, thrust forward 100 miles and took 53,000 prisoners. On 22 July Patton, with 2nd Armored Division, entered Palermo in triumph to the plaudits of the inhabitants and took up his quarters in the Royal Palace. Next day Bradley's Corps reached the north coast at Termini Imerese.

After the war attempts were made to detract from Patton's achievement. It was claimed that, before the campaign started, contact had been made by Intelligence officers through 'Lucky' Luciano, head of the Mafia in the United States (and serving a 30-year prison sentence), with his opposite number in Sicily, Don Calogero Vizzini, to ensure that the Italian troops put up no resistance to the invaders. In particular, it was alleged that Mafia agents persuaded Colonel Salemi's battle group (consisting of a battalion, some field guns and several Tiger tanks) holding a very strong position in the mountainous Cammarata area which dominated the two roads to Palermo, to let Patton's columns through on 20 July. That there were contacts with the Mafia in Sicily is probably true – they would have been almost impossible to avoid – but to suggest that their influence was in any way decisive is ludicrous.

With every justification the Press were jubilant. The Americans now had a deep-water port capable of handling ships coming direct from the United States and were no longer dependent on supply over beaches; the 9th US Division landed at Palermo. Magnanimously Patton restored his Sicilian prisoners to their families, which reduced the demand on Allied food supplies. Alexander now directed Patton to swing along the north coast towards Messina. Montgomery was to make a short hook with the Canadians about Regalbuto to give Bradley room to maneuver. Thus the so-called inter-Allied race for Messina.

Although the Allies had not secured a military decision in Sicily their progress now finally precipitated the fall of Mussolini and his government. Hitler was still sane and the time had not yet come when a policy of "No withdrawal" would be his strategic panacea. The disasters at Stalingrad and in Tunisia, and now his appalling losses in his Russian summer offensive, Operation Zitadelle, at last brought home to him that his manpower resources were running down. On 26 July, the day Marshal Pietro Badoglio arrested Mussolini, Hitler gave Kesselring permission to abandon Sicily, before the Allies made their invasion of Italy.

Next day Kesselring, ignoring Guzzoni, told Hube to prepare for evacuation. The chances of success must have seemed slim, for he gave orders that men rather than equipment were to have priority. Hube accordingly planned a slow withdrawal to a series of five defensive positions across the Messina peninsula. The rugged country was in his favor: it gave him magnificent artillery observation; the roads were narrow and winding, often passing through defiles which were easy to block. The anti-aircraft defenses at Messina under Colonel Ernest Guenther Baade were very strong and Captain von Liebenstein of the German Navy had an excellent ferry service across the three-mile-wide straits.

When Patton and Montgomery resumed operations at the end of July they found themselves condemned to attack side by side against a series of excellent defensive positions held by first-class troops, whose morale remained unshaken. For neither the British nor the Americans was there great scope for maneuver: German mines and demolitions harassed their every move. Montgomery had 13th Corps on the right and 30th Corps on his left. In Seventh Army, 45th and 1st US Divisions led first, later giving way to 3rd and 9th Divisions. The weather was hot and the dust appalling. There were many casualties from malaria. Patton, determined at all costs to reach Messina before Montgomery ordered "a sustained relentless drive until the enemy is decisively defeated". Inevitably the terrain channelled the advance along narrow lanes or on to ridges and up valleys devoid of cover and in full view of the enemy's artillery observers. Air co-operation on the fronts of both armies left much to be desired. There were far too many incidents of friendly aircraft bombing their own troops.

At Troina, the 1st Division, slogging along rugged hillsides to outflank immensely strong German positions, fought for four days the bitterest battle of the campaign. Allen and his deputy commander were at loggerheads; their men were tired and beginning to feel that they were being called upon to shoulder more than their fair share of the fighting, having been through the whole Tunisian campaign. When Troina finally fell, on 6 August, Patton had to take the decision to relieve both the divisional commander and his deputy.

Exasperated by the delay and worried by the increase in the numbers of men evacuated with battle neurosis, Patton staged three amphibious hooks. But incredibly only enough landing craft could be provided to lift a battalion group. The first run was abortive. The second landed at Brolo on 11 August just behind 29th *Panzer Grenadier* Division's position on the north coast road. It was not strong enough to cut off the battlegroup opposing 45th Division but, helped by the fire of American warships, accelerated the German withdrawal by 24 hours. Regrettably the *Panzer Grenadiers* made up lost time by hanging on to the next position for an extra day. For the night of 15 to 16 August Patton staged a further end run, this time of regimental size. It was a blow in thin air. The Germans had fallen back to the next position and the amphibious force waded ashore not behind the Germans but to meet the leading infantry of 3rd Division.

A similar landing by No. 40 British Royal Marine Commando, just south of Scaletta on the same night, found nothing to stop it except demolitions. But so impeded was their advance into Messina that when they entered the town on the morning of 17 August they found that the 7th Infantry Regiment of 3rd US Division had arrived ahead of them, and Patton had won the race to Messina. He had already accepted the surrender of the city at 1015. There was an element of anti-climax in these last days of the campaign. Despite the overwhelming strength of the Allies in the air and on the sea, Hube had succeeded in evacuating nearly 40,000 German troops with 9,605 vehicles, 47 tanks, 94 guns and 17,000 tons of ammunition. It was a miniature German version of Dunkirk in which typically they had saved a much greater proportion of their heavy equipment than the British. In addition some 62,000 Italians had escaped across the straits.

Baades' 350 dual-purpose anti-aircraft guns had maintained a barrage described as "heavier than the Ruhr", over the four evacuation routes starting on 11 August, along which 140 small

craft plied. From 13 August, von Liebenstein decided to risk
working by daylight as well as by night. Losses were remarkably
light. Surprisingly, the Allies did not realize until 14 August
that the Germans were pulling out. Judged objectively by
professional standards, Hube and von Liebenstein were the
winners of the race to Messina.

Kesselring was astonished that the Allies should have failed
to secure an overwhelming victory, in the last week of the
campaign, by landing another amphibious force on the toe of
Italy, seize the ferry terminals at Reggio and hamstring the
withdrawal across the Straits of Messina. The Allies had ample
reserves of troops in North Africa. Their navies could have
provided the landing craft if they had been asked and would not
have hesitated to bring their big ships within range of the
coastal batteries if ordered. They had unchallenged superiority
in the air which they failed to concentrate over the straits.

Finally, Adm. Cunningham was not prepared to risk his
warships in the straits at night; the only other foolproof method
of disrupting the frantic Axis ferry service. There was no
capitulation in Sicily because, before the landing, no agreement
had been reached as to whether or not Husky should be
followed by the invasion of Italy. It was therefore left to
Eisenhower to exploit his victorious landing as he thought
fit. As operations progressed, Alexander failed to use his initiative, awaiting orders which never came.

Nevertheless, the campaign had achieved its major objects. It
had unseated Mussolini. It had set in motion the negotiations,
through the British embassies in Lisbon and Madrid, which
would soon result in the Italians abandoning their German
Allies and surrendering their fleet. The Mediterranean was at
last freed for Allied shipping and in particular for tankers from
the Persian Gulf.

Much battle experience had been gained and many good
commanders, notably Bradley, had come to the fore. Casualties,
at 9,000 British and 8,735 American, were remarkably light.
The Germans had lost 32,000 and the Italians 132,000, mostly
prisoners of war. And the threat the Allies now offered to "the
soft underbelly of Europe", although it did not swing Turkey
over to the Allied side, undoubtedly induced Hitler to call off

the ghastly battle of Kursk (Zitadelle) on 14 July and to divert reserves from the Russian front in order to retain his grip on the Italian mainland. The experience gained in the invasion of Sicily, especially in amphibious operations, ensured the success of Overlord, the invasion of North West Europe, less than a year later.

Admin Box (1944)

Patrick Turnbull

In the latter half of 1943, Lieutenant General Renya Mutaguchi, Japanese Fifteenth Army commander, and his divisional commanders, were summoned to a series of conferences at Lieutenant General M. Kawabe's Burma Area Army HQ in Rangoon. They were there to discuss operations for the coming year. The outcome of these meetings – held under considerable strain, since Tokyo had impressed on Kawabe the necessity for speedy victory in Burma to boost flagging morale at home – was the plan for an offensive – Operation *U-Go* – on the central Assam/Manipur front by Fifteenth Army. Its objective was the destruction of 4th Indian Corps, and an advance to the Bengal frontier. It was somewhat optimistically reckoned that success – and it was stressed that failure could not even be contemplated – would spark off a general uprising in India against the British Raj, and what Japanese propaganda was to refer to as "The March on Delhi".

But it was not until the general outline of *U-Go* had been approved by Southern Area Commander, Field Marshal Count Hisarchi Terauchi, that a rider for a preliminary, diversionary, operation in Arakan – code name *Ha-Go* – was added. To be carried out by 55th and elements of 54th Divisions under the recently arrived Lieutenant General Tadashi Hanaya, the object of this limited offensive was to pin down, and draw off, British-Indian reserves from the main central front.

Japanese hopes of a resounding victory in Burma seemed justified. Early in 1943, an attempt by 14th Indian Division to recapture the Arakan port of Akyab ended in ignominious failure. Though eventually expanded to six brigades, 14th Division had failed to break through the Japanese defenses on the Donbaik Chaung. This was at no time manned by more than two battalions and by as little as two companies to begin with. Finally, in early April, the recently arrived Japanese 55th Division staged a brilliant counter-attack, driving 14th Division and its replacement 26th Indian Division back well beyond their starting point.

At his Ranchi HQ, Lieutenant-General Sir William J. Slim, commanding 15th Indian Corps, who had been called to take charge of the Arakan battle too late to do other than convert a threatened rout into an orderly withdrawal, was one of the very few not afflicted by the wave of pessimism following this disaster. The jungle, he insisted, was the reverse of the desert – infantry, not tanks and fighter-bombers dominated the battlefield. Therefore until the British copied the Japanese, and made the infantry the *corps d'élite*, there could be little or no hope of victory. Acting on his own theory, Slim devoted the Monsoon period to the intensive battle training of his reconstituted Corps, 5th and 7th Indian Divisions, commanded by Major-Generals Harold R. Briggs and Frank W. Messervy, both veterans of East Africa and the Western Desert, and Major-General C. G. Woolner's 81st West African Division. The Bihar jungle was the scene of tough exercises under active service conditions. Non-combatants – clerks, storemen, wireless operators, cooks – had to join in, warned by Slim that "in the jungle every man, whatever his job, is likely to find himself engaged in hand-to-hand fighting with the enemy".

When the 1943/44 dry season operational plans were made known, 15th Corps was gratified to learn that it was to be given the opportunity for a "return match". While in Manipur, 4th Corps' activities were to be confined to "a limited offensive up to the Chindwin", 15th Corps was entrusted with the job of clearing the enemy forces from Arakan, and (possibly) to follow up with the capture of Akyab.

As the Monsoon abated, 15th Corps left Ranchi *en route* for Arakan, but within a few days of setting up his HQ at Bawli Bazar, Slim was called upon to command the newly created Fourteenth Army. His place was taken by Lieutenant-General Philip Christison from 33rd Corps in Southern India.

Arakan's terrain, as 14th Division had found to its cost, heavily favored the defense. A narrow strip oriented north–south, it is bounded on the east by almost trackless jungle-covered hills, the Arakan Yomas and Arakan Hill Tracts, on the west by the Bay of Bengal. What flat ground there is consists of *padi* fields and swamps, furrowed by wide, swift-flowing rivers, and tidal creeks. The Mayu Peninsula, ending at Foul Point opposite Akyab Island, is bisected by a dragon-crested spine of hills, the Mayu Range. Its precipitous jungle slopes rise to 2,500 ft in places, crossed east–west by only three passes. The Goppe and Ngakyedauk Passes were barely fit for mules. But the Tunnels Road was suitable for mechanical transport. This was formerly the track of a narrow-gauge railway connecting the little port of Maungdaw on the west, at the mouth of the Naf river, with Buthidaung on the east, at the point where the tidal Mayu River became the Kalapanzin, and cutting through the range by two short tunnels. This road – 16 miles in length – was the line on which Lt. Gen. Hanaya had chosen to base his main defenses, giving the whole area the picturesque name of "The Golden Fortress".

Since the destruction of the Japanese, rather than territorial gain, was Christison's objective, this concentration of enemy forces suited him. Advance was on a two-divisional front, 5th Division to the west, 7th Division to the east of the Mayu Range. After making a wide sweep to the east the West Africans were moving on a pack basis down the Kaladan Valley, acting as a flank guard. Christison had met with only token resistance. By the New Year of 1944, he was poised for the first phase of his main attack; an assault on the Golden Fortress's western bastion, Razabil, just south of Maungdaw. The choice of Razabil as the first objective was dictated by the urgency of securing Maungdaw with its harbor facilities, since, till the port became operational, 15th Corps had to rely on a single supply line. This was a road on the west, coastal, side of the Mayu Range – built the year before by 14th Division's engineers.

In the first week of January, 161st Brigade (5th Division) began to probe the outer edges of the Razabil defensive network. They met such determined opposition that what was hoped would be the decisive blow could not be delivered until 26 January. Though preceded by heavy aerial and artillery bombardments, and supported by the Corps' armored unit – the 25th Dragoons in Lee-Grant medium tanks – hardly any progress was made. After three days of abortive assaults, heavy losses – the Sikh company of 1st Battalion, 1st Punjabi Regiment was reduced to 21 men, while the 4/7th Rajputs lost 27 killed and 129 wounded – Christison had to call a halt.

He planned to switch the main weight of his renewed offensive to 7th Division's front. With this in mind he ordered 25th Dragoons to move to the eastern side of the Mayu Range via the Ngakyedauk Pass, by then capable of taking heavy vehicles, thanks to superhuman efforts on the part of the engineers, since the track included a rise and fall of 1,000 ft in three miles. It was renamed, and since immortalized, as the "Okey-doke" Pass.

At the same time the eastern exit in the neighborhood of Sinzweya was converted into an administrative area, with petrol and ammunition dumps, vast stores of rations, spare parts, and medical supplies, manned by Ordnance, Service Corps, Transport and Medical units. Its defense against possible tip-and-run raids was entrusted to the 24th Light Anti-Aircraft/Anti-Tank Regiment, commanded by a peace-time solicitor, Lieutenant-Colonel R. B. "King" Cole.

By 3 February the redeployment was almost complete. The offensive was fixed for 7 February. But unimpressed by the fact that he was outnumbered, and anxious to repeat his division's earlier triumph, Hanaya struck first.

For the tactical execution of *Ha-Go* he detailed a force of roughly 8,000 men under the command of Major-General T. Sakurai (commander of 55th Divisional Infantry Group; an appointment without equivalent in the British Army) which was split into three columns. Though the main striking force of these three was designated *Sakurai* Column, it was in fact led by Colonel S. Tanahashi. He was a dynamic officer who had played a major role in 14th Division's discomfiture. At the head of his own 112th Infantry Regiment, supported by an artillery and an engineer group, his task was to pass through the advanced posts of 114th Brigade (7th Division) strung out on the eastern bank of the Kalapanzin, capture Taung Bazar, then, crossing to the west bank, swing left and "destroy the enemy forces between the Kalapanzin river and the Mayu Range" – the bulk of 7th Division.

While this was in progress, a smaller column of only one battalion under Colonel Tai Koba, marching rapidly north, was to make a left-wheel near the Goppe Pass, cross the Mayu Range, and establish a road block across 5th Division's lifeline – the Bawli Bazar–Maungdaw road. To pin down forward troops while these outflanking movements were being performed, two battalions, under Colonel Doi, were to mount a series of holding attacks along the entire front from the Kalapanzin to the sea.

Relying on the element of surprise, *Sakurai* Column took almost suicidal risks when it set out from Kindaung at 2300 on 3 February. In a solid phalanx, 16 men abreast, together with their mules, 112th Regiment marched down a narrow valley, barely 400 yards wide, knowing that units of 114th Brigade were in positions on the ridges on either side. The gamble paid off, helped by the fact that the night was moonless and by a thick mist blanketing the valley. Brigade HQ reported hearing the sound of movement, of muffled voices and the clanking of mule accoutrements, but assumed that the sounds came from Royal Indian Army Service Corps supply columns taking advantage of the cover of darkness. As a result, the few troops installed in Taung Bazar were taken completely by surprise at first light, and wiped out.

By evening most of 112th Regiment had crossed to the west bank. There were indecisive skirmishes with elements of 89th Brigade, divisional reserve, the next day, but by 7 February Col. Tanahashi had reached the Ngakydeauk Pass. Meanwhile Col. Koba had descended on the coastal road near Briasco bridge, spanning the widest of the tidal *chaungs* (Burmese name for watercourses), and overrun a Field Park and a Workshops Company. With only a weak battalion, Koba could not hold his ground. A morning counter-attack beat him back to the foot-hills after he had set fire to most of the vehicles and damaged the bridge. The vital road was soon reopened, even though convoys were often under fire. Tanahashi on the other hand was soon firmly astride the Ngakyedauk, successfully separating 5th and 7th Divisions.

Christison appreciated from the start the primary importance of retaining the Sinzweya administrative area – from then on referred to as the "Admin Box". Having first directed 26th Indian Division, then in reserve at Chittagong, to move forward with all haste, he telephoned Maj.-Gen. Briggs of 5th Division instructing him to order 9th Brigade commander, Brigadier Geoffrey C. Evans, to move immediately with all his spare troops to the Box, and hold it to the last.

Even with the reinforcements Evans could count on in the next hour or so, the chances of holding out against attacks by crack Japanese troops, with a garrison composed mostly of non-combatants, seemed slender. Furthermore all advantages of the terrain lay with the attacker. Never foreseeing that it would become the scene of a major battle, it had been chosen for its flatness and absence of scrub and jungle. Even so, the clearing measured a bare 1,200 yards in diameter. This meant that not a square inch would be out of range of small arms fire. It was a tactical trap; a bowl, the bottom naked, the sides and encircling rim densely covered in jungle. Ammunition dumps piled up at the foot of the western face of a central 150 ft hillock – "Ammunition Hill" – were particularly vulnerable.

Evans realized that the defenders would be under direct observation, while the enemy could approach unseen to the edge of the perimeter from any direction. Again, although every man from storeman to cook and muleteer would have to take his place in the defenses, there would still not be enough to provide an unbroken line. Concentrating, therefore, on the most likely lines of enemy attack, Evans was obliged to leave the eastern and north eastern sectors dangerously open, counting on his mobile reserve – the veteran 2nd Battalion, The West Yorkshire Regiment, commanded by the experienced Lieutenant-Colonel "Munshi" Cree, and two squadrons of the 25th Dragoons under their second-in-command, Major Hugh Ley.

Frantic digging was in progress when at 1430 on 6 February, a ragged group appeared from the jungle to the east. It was Maj.-Gen. Messervy, with a number of his staff. His 7th

Division HQ had been overrun that morning. Throughout the afternoon more stragglers arrived, giving hair-raising accounts of their escape. By evening Messervy, in touch with his brigades, had resumed command, but had also made it clear that the defense of the Box was to remain in Evans's capable hands. At 1700 the latter called a conference of his commanders, to issue his orders. His instructions were brief – "Stay put and keep the Japanese out."

By evening the garrison had been strengthened by the arrival of two companies of the 4/8th Gurkhas – the other two temporarily lost in the jungle – a mortar battery of 139th Field Regiment RA, and a battery of 6th Medium Regiment. A troop of the 8th (Belfast) Heavy Anti-Aircraft Regiment, and two batteries of the 24th Mountain Regiment were ordered to abandon their positions to go to the Box immediately.

During the afternoon there was a low-level attack by Zero fighters, causing a number of casualties, but it was not until midnight that a first assault was delivered at a sector held by an Indian mule company. The muleteers – many of them Pathans – showed exemplary fighting discipline, holding their fire, unflustered by streams of tracer, until the yelling Japanese were almost on top of them. No determined attempt was made to press home the attack – possibly because no serious opposition had been expected.

The next day, the 7th, started badly. A patrol up the Ngakyedauk Pass was ambushed – making clear the fact that the Japanese had severed communications with 5th Division. Then, the two companies of the 4/8th Gurkhas, ordered to occupy a low jungle-covered hillock dominating the "eastern gate" of the Box (Point 315), were violently attacked before reaching their objective. Forced to give ground, their retreat was followed up by the Japanese who smashed through the perimeter – only to be halted by fire of the 25th Dragoons' 37 mm and 75 mm tank guns, then hurled back in confusion by "D" Company of the West Yorkshires. The Gurkhas were later able to seize and dig in on part, but not all, of Point 315.

The afternoon and evening were quiet, but in the early hours, Evans heard "rifle and automatic fire . . . accompanied by screams and cries for help." A Japanese raiding party had infiltrated the forward positions and entered the Box hospital. This had been set up in three widened and deepened dried-up *chaung* (watercourse) beds, at the foot of a hillock known as MDS Hill. The raiders' first act was to bayonet a number of the badly wounded as they lay helpless on their stretchers. Six doctors were then lined up and shot. An Indian doctor, Lieutenant Basu, escaped by smearing himself with blood and feigning death. When, at dawn, a counter-attack was organized, the survivors, wounded and medical staff alike were used as human shields to protect the retreating Japanese, only to be later murdered in cold blood.

Another crisis developed at first light on 9 February. During the night before, the Japanese manhandled their 70 mm infantry howitzers to the crest overlooking Ammunition Hill, and opened up on the ammunition dumps. Fires were soon raging and crates of .303-in and 25-pounder shells exploding with much the same effect as if the enemy had reached the center of the Box. Having recovered from the surprise, the Dragoons and the Belfast Heavy AA troop engaged the Japanese guns in an extraordinary artillery duel over open sights. As the Lee-Grant's 65 mm (2.56-in) armor was proof against 70 mm shells, it was not long before the enemy batteries were silenced and the surviving crews killed by the West Yorkshires' bayonets. But the burning dumps continued to explode. It was not until late afternoon that the last fires were extinguished.

Early the next morning a partial revenge for the hospital murders was exacted. Regimental Sergeant-Major J. Maloney, "B" Echelon, 9th Brigade, with a handful of HQ clerks, normally considered too old for combat, held a trench overlooking a dried-up *chaung*. At around 0200 the sound of approaching footsteps and voices was heard. Seconds later, about 50 Japanese headed by an officer came into view. Maloney held his fire until the enemy was level with his trench. Then, at his word of command, a volley of grenades and Sten submachine-gun bursts at point blank range wiped out the entire party. It was a minor victory all the more appreciated when it was found that the dead men's packs were stuffed with hospital rations.

The first phase of the battle was over by 11 February. The Japanese had failed to destroy 5th and 7th Divisions. They had not even thrown them into confusion. On the other hand, rather than mopping up the Golden Fortress, 15th Corps was grimly battling for survival. Yet Christison had sound reason for optimism. Convoys, though sometimes under fire, flowed down the vital coastal road. The isolated *Koba* Force, driven back to the foothills, faced starvation. The Box, despite furious onslaughts, showed no sign of being swamped or running short of supplies. From the 10th the defenders were receiving all they needed, not only in the way of vital rations and munitions, but also such comparative luxuries as toothpaste, mail, rum and spare clothing, by air. Allied Troop Carrier Command's Dakota transports flew a total of 714 sorties, dropping 2,300 tons of supplies without which, starving, their guns silent, Evans's men might well have suffered the fate of Dien Bien Phu.

Over the rest of 7th Division area, the three brigades – 114th, 33rd, and 89th – had dug themselves into subsidiary boxes, and though individually cut off were holding fast and hitting back hard. The advanced elements of 26th Indian Division were in contact with detachments of *Sakurai* Column north of Taung Bazar, while the army reserve, 36th Indian Division was at sea, *en route* from Calcutta to Chittagong.

At this stage, common sense dictated that Hanaya withdraw what was left of Sakurai's original force to the still intact Golden Fortress. His offensive had been halted. Soon his badly mauled regiments would be faced by no fewer than four divisions, two of them fresh to the battle. He had no armor, and the enemy was master of the skies. But he suffered from the besetting Japanese military sin – inflexibility. Once having issued an order, he could not tolerate the thought of modifying it. Furthermore his overconfident dispatches had encouraged Tokyo to broadcast – "It's all over in Burma". Sakurai was ordered to press home his attacks with even greater vigor, an order with which he endeavored, loyally, to comply. From 10–18 February the fate of the Box often hung in the balance.

A major onslaught was directed at "Artillery Hill", held by 24th LAA/AT Regiment, a bare 200 yards from Evans's HQ. Hidden by the jungle, the Japanese advanced to within yards of the gunners' trenches. Their first charge swamped the position, and a hastily organized counter-attack was thrown back.

By then Evans and his commanders had devised a plan for tank/infantry co-operation. It was to prove brilliantly successful. As the infantry left their starting position, the tanks saturated their objective with high explosive, until when, within assaulting distance, the infantry commander fired a Very light. This was the signal for the tanks to switch from HE to solid shot. The Japanese were still forced to keep their heads down, but as they pushed forward the attacking infantry were not exposed to fragmentation. The tanks were, therefore, able to keep up their fire until the leading sections, as close as 15 yards to the enemy, could make the final charge with grenade and bayonet, before the stunned Japanese had time to react. Employing these tactics, "A" Company of the West Yorkshires, supported by a squadron of the Dragoons, retook "Artillery Hill" by evening. Only 24 hours later this maneuver was repeated with equal success, after the Japanese had overrun "C" Company Hill, overlooking the eastern exit of the Pass.

After ten days of ceaseless harassment, Evans could congratulate himself that not one of the Box's main positions had fallen. But casualties were mounting alarmingly. Continuous night attacks, though not on a major scale, were achieving the dual purpose of stopping the exhausted defenders gaining any proper rest and necessitating a frightening expenditure of ammunition.

Efforts were also made to knock out the tanks which at night moved into laager – their machine-guns dismounted and laid on fixed lines. The most determined attack was launched at daybreak from Point 315. Caught in the open by the combined fire of tank guns and machine-guns, the Japanese were all slaughtered before covering half the distance.

Outside the Box, there were setbacks. On the 13th, the 2/1st Punjabis and 4/7th Rajputs (123rd Brigade of 5th Division) overran the key to the Ngakyedauk Pass – the fortified hill feature Point 1070. It seemed the relief of the Box could be only a matter of hours. But during the night, the company of the 1/18th Royal Garwhal Rifles, ordered to hold the position, was subjected to continual *kamikaze* attacks. At dawn the survivors were hurled back down the slopes, leaving the feature firmly in enemy hands. On 10 February a gallant attempt by three companies of the 1st Lincolnshire Regiment (26th Division) failed to clear Point 315 overlooking the "eastern gate". One of the company commanders, Major Ferguson Hoey, earned for himself a posthumous VC in this clash.

By the 19th, though the garrison had been strengthened by the 4/8th Gurkhas and the 2nd King's Own Scottish Borderers, general conditions in the Box were deteriorating. The hospital was a shambles as the wounded piled up. Flies by the million infested the primitive wards where the two surgeons labored without rest in the most unhygienic surroundings imaginable. Ammunition proved a constant source of anxiety. Dumps were repeatedly hit. In trying to put out a fire threatening to destroy the entire stocks, "King" Cole was badly wounded. He refused to leave his post till the siege ended.

On 21 February, however, Point 1070 fell at last to the 2/1st Punjabis, led by Major Sarbjit Singh, holder of the DSO and Bar. This successful assault opened the way to the Box, and 123rd Brigade moved steadily down the Pass, mopping up isolated posts. At last forced to admit failure, Hanaya was obliged to cancel *Ha-Go* while 7th Division's brigades, breaking out of their individual boxes, fanned out into the jungle in an attempt to cut off Sakurai's withdrawal.

But the ordeal of the Admin Box was not over. Night attacks redoubled in their ferocity. On the night of 21/22 February the Japanese broke through to within 20 yards of 9th Brigade HQ. The morning revealed 30 enemy dead ringing the officers' mess. That same morning, a suicidal charge came near to swamping Cole's HQ. But for the murderous volume of fire the Box could then command, it might well have succeeded.

At dawn on 24 February Maj.-Gen. Briggs, who had spent the night at 123rd Brigade HQ, climbed into a Lee-Grant. The last Japanese had been driven from the immediate neighborhood of the Pass, and the tank "grumbling out of the eastern entry", crossed the shell-cratered ground until it came to a shattered tree marking Messervy's HQ. Clambering from the turret, Briggs held out a bottle of whisky. "Messervy grinned and took it, and the two shook hands, and the siege was officially at an end."

For Hanaya, the failure of *Ha-Go* was a disaster. Out of Sakurai's picked 8,000, less than 3,000, starving, exhausted men fought their way back to the Golden Fortress. He had not only failed to destroy 15th Corps (3,506 casualties), but had not entirely pinned down Fourteenth Army's reserves. When *U-Go* got under way in mid-March, 5th and 7th Divisions were airlifted to the central front where both played a major role in the defeat of Mutaguchi's ultimate offensive.

Compared with the scale of that subsequent battle of Imphal-Kohima, the Box was a minor skirmish. Nevertheless the defeat of *Ha-Go*, like Stalingrad and Alamein, was one of the moral turning points of the Second World War. For the first time in their history as a modern power, the Japanese had suffered a major defeat on land at British-Indian hands.

Anzio (1944)

John Keegan

The little Italian port of Anzio was the scene, in early 1944, of one of the great "might have been" battles of the Second World War. Like Arnhem which might have ended the war in the west in September 1944, or Army Group Center's offensive in August 1941 which might have defeated Russia in the first four months of Operation Barbarossa, Anzio might have broken the costly stalemate of the Italian front before midsummer of Invasion year, captured Rome, 33 miles to the north, and driven the Germans deep into northern Italy.

This single stroke would have released vitally needed shipping for the D-day operation, brought the Allied bombers closer to their targets in southern Germany and outflanked German positions in the Balkans, one of her major sources of oil and mineral supplies. It would have also dealt a considerable blow to Hitler's prestige and almost certainly cost him a major part of the very large force he maintained in southern Italy to keep the Allied Mediterranean Expeditionary Force at bay. Anzio, in fact, achieved none of these things. Why was the operation, so rich in promise, so empty of fulfillment?

In the early winter of 1943, the Allied armies, landed near Naples in September, were brought to a frustrating halt in the mountains south of Rome. They had run into exceptionally difficult terrain and an unexpectedly severe winter of rain and snow. The Germans also presented problems – there were more of them than the Allied High Command had anticipated and they had built a belt of fortifications, the Gustav Line, which, with the advantages of climate and geography, gave a coherency to their defensive line.

The only progress made by the Allies' two armies, the American Fifth on the Mediterranean coast and the British Eighth on the Adriatic, was by set-piece assaults on strongly defended river lines. These were time-consuming to prepare and costly to execute. Since they had run up against the heavily fortified and well-manned Gustav Line, in early November, they had made virtually no progress at all.

It was against this background that plans for a seaborne invasion behind enemy lines were formulated. The Allied High Command realized that their earlier belief that the Germans would withdraw into northern Italy if heavily pressed was mistaken. General Dwight D. Eisenhower and General Sir Harold Alexander concluded that the enemy's current strategy of making the Allies win Italy inch by inch could be countered only by a seaborne landing in their rear. Alexander, in a directive dated 8 November 1943, laid down a timetable for such an operation: it entailed a triple offensive, first by the Eighth Army to attract German reserves onto the Adriatic coast, then by the Fifth to set the campaign again in motion towards Rome and finally by an amphibious force, landing near Rome, and linking up with the Fifth across the river lines of the Mediterranean coastal plain.

The plan was orthodox – but the means to execute it were not immediately available. The plan demanded ships – but shipping was needed for the coming Normandy invasion and had been directed to leave the Mediterranean forthwith. Troops were needed – but the necessary divisions were also wanted for Normandy. They had begun to leave and had not yet been replaced by the Free French Army which was training in Africa. The plan, code-named Operation Shingle, was, after a feasibility study, therefore shelved. But it was not forgotten. As the winter fighting increased in severity, and apparent futility, the idea of a seaborne descent near Rome came to appear more and more attractive to the protagonists of the original plan, notably Alexander and the British Prime Minister, Winston Churchill.

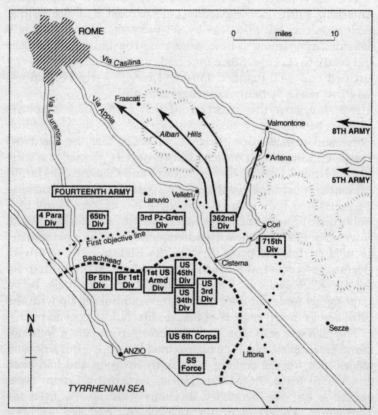

5.9 The Battle for Anzio, May 1944

On 22 December, Shingle was officially canceled; but on the following day Churchill insisted that it be reconsidered. As the author of the heart-breaking Gallipoli failure of the First World War, Churchill's credentials to oversee a revived Shingle did not bear close examination. But he could well argue, if anyone had drawn the parallel, that the Allied position in the Mediterranean was far more favorable in 1944 than in 1915, and that while the objectives Shingle proposed were more limited than those intended at Gallipoli, the investment required was proportionately more limited.

He could and did argue that Shingle made excellent military sense – if only by contrast with the fighting along the narrow mountain roads and hidden defiles to which their current strategy condemned the Allies. There they were unable to disguise either the timing or the direction of their strokes and could gain little advantage from their air superiority. A seaborne movement offered the chance to surprise the enemy both in space and time, and to force him into battle on the naked plain, while supplying themselves plentifully along the broad highway of the Mediterranean. If the enterprise were successful, moreover, it would give them Rome, put the Balkans under threat and perhaps – and here the argument became speculation – even make Operation Overlord, the invasion of Normandy, unnecessary.

It was vital, if Shingle was to work at all, to delay the transfer out of the Mediterranean of the necessary shipping. By direct intervention with President Roosevelt, Churchill secured the retention, first until 15 January, then until 5 February, of 68 Landing Ship Tanks (LSTs), the basic requirement of a seaborne landing. As planning proceeded, Churchill made further requests for logistic supplies and secured them. At the same time he ensured that there was no wavering in the enthusiasm of Gen. Alexander, Army Group Commander, and of Lieutenant General Mark Clark, the American Fifth Army Commander, two of the three men who had chosen Anzio for the invasion point.

In fact, this was unlikely for both had strong, if different, personal motives for wishing the operation well. Alexander, disappointed that Eisenhower, rather than himself, had been appointed Supreme Commander, was resolved that the struggle for Italy should not become a stalemated sideshow – and, without Shingle, it threatened to become just that.

Gen. Clark, who felt that his Fifth Army had not been given the credit its achievements deserved, ached for the glory of capturing Rome. His American and British divisions, now pinned to the river valley floors by fire from the heights of the Monte Cassino range, were 100 miles short of the capital. He counted on Shingle to release them from the stalemate of the plains below Monte Cassino. Seventy miles separate Anzio from Cassino, and Clark thought that, given determination, the launching of concentrated offensives from the two spots should break the German defense on the west coast and lead him into Rome.

This was Churchill's hope and, having secured the necessary equipment for his commanders, he left them to put the plan into action. But the translation of military decisions into effect always reveals unanticipated difficulties. The preparation of Shingle was no exception. Further staff study suggested that the Germans would probably react strongly to the initial landing, and that a two-division landing, for which Churchill had had to commit his personal prestige to find the shipping, might not survive the onslaught. Further shipping, and more men, had to be found to land with three divisions.

The final order of battle, therefore, included, besides the British 1st and American 3rd Divisions, the American 45th Infantry and 1st Armored Divisions, as well as members of American Parachute and Ranger and British Commando battalions. The whole was to be subordinate to a Corps headquarters – the US 6th Corps. This was debatably too small to handle the operations of a force though it had grown from the initial planning figure of 24,000 to a final 110,000. Doubts also emerged about the efficiency of the force itself. At a dress-rehearsal in Naples Bay, both the 1st and 3rd Divisions mishandled their equipment, losing 40 DUKWs (the amphibious lorry on which cross-beach mobility depended) and two batteries of 105 mm howitzers; while the naval parties operating the landing craft made a series of unnerving mistakes. It was not a happy augury.

These events badly worried the already anxious commander of 6th Corps, Major General John R. Lucas. An experienced and respected soldier, Lucas was not happy with the Anzio idea and expressed his doubts strongly and continuously in the pages of his diary. He described himself as unusually tender-hearted for a general in an army which traditionally took a blood-and-guts attitude to the prospect of casualties and he feared he was leading, or worse, sending, his men to their deaths.

Hence his growing obsession, which the weeks of preparation made more and more apparent, with reinforcement and re-supply considerations. It was vital, in his view, that the men in the beach-head should have ashore with them the largest possible quantity of armored vehicles and artillery pieces as well as ammunition and petrol. Given these, and air support, the beach-head troops would be able to repel a counter-attack, which Lucas expected to come swiftly and in strength, despite the different story from Allied Intelligence.

His superior, Mark Clark, an abler man than his posturing suggested, was sensitive to Lucas's anxieties, which to some extent he shared. Consequently, he refrained from giving Lucas the additional responsibility for a decisive breakout from the bridgehead. The orders Clark issued to 6th Corps were for "an advance on" the Alban Hills – the feature which commands the land between Anzio and Rome – not for an advance "onto". This ambiguity gave Lucas the option of halting his troops short of the objective if he felt that the strength of enemy reaction threatened his beach-head.

The Germans were also making their plans. The *Luftwaffe* Field Marshal Albert Kesselring had been preferred to Field Marshal Erwin Rommel for the post of Commander-in-Chief in Italy because of his optimistic and generally correct forecasts of the way events would go in the peninsula. Kesselring was aware that, over a distance of several hundred miles, both his flanks were vulnerable to amphibious assault. He suspected, however, that the coast near Rome was the most likely spot for the Allies to choose, and he accordingly kept two divisions in reserve nearby. They were divisions he could hardly spare, for his armies were at full stretch on the Gustav Line, the cross-peninsula German defense line from which, Hitler had ordered, there was to be no retreat. He was aware, moreover, that even this reserve might not be sufficient to contain a landing, for the Allies might outnumber it before reinforcements, which could only come from southern France, the Balkans and the far north of Italy, had arrived.

On 18 January, and only after receiving the firmest assurances of the unlikelihood of an Allied landing in the near future, from his own and higher Intelligence sources, he agreed to send his two reserve divisions from Rome to Cassino, where Clark's Fifth Army had just succeeded in forcing the line of the Garigliano. General Heinrich von Vietinghoff, commanding the Tenth Army, had represented this breach of his sector of the Gustav Line as potentially catastrophic, for it threatened to outflank the Monte Cassino position on which the whole line hinged. Kesselring was persuaded by his entreaties. What neither appreciated was that Clark, though delighted by this local success, had planned it precisely as a means of clearing the Anzio area of anti-invasion forces. Once Lucas was ashore Clark then intended to launch a major offensive from the Garigliano bridgehead, directed towards Anzio, the Alban Hills – and Rome. The Germans in between, if the strategy proved right, would flee, or surrender to the pincer attack.

Thus Lucas, thanks to an excellent stroke of strategic deception by his own commander, and to the enemy's faulty Intelligence, was to enjoy the most precious advantage an amphibious force leader can obtain – total surprise. His fleet of 240 landing craft and 120 warships made an undetected overnight passage northwards from Naples. In the early morning of 22 January 1944, they began to unload the two assault divisions – 1st British, 3rd US – on beaches left and right of Anzio without interruption from the enemy, apart from some light, uncoordinated cannonading by a few, soon-silenced, batteries. By midnight nine-tenths of the assault force (36,000 men and 3,000 vehicles) had come ashore for a loss of 13 dead, and had established a perimeter between two and three miles inland. The Allied air forces had flown 1,200 sorties, but had not been opposed. The port had been captured intact and was now ready to receive supplies from the fleet which swung untroubled at anchor offshore.

Lucas felt, and rightly felt, that he had done well. Indeed as landings go, the first day at Anzio must be regarded as an impeccable exercise in that particular tactical form. But success did not dispel Lucas's anxieties, for he now feared a major enemy counter-blow. Rather than cripple the expected counter-attack by seizing commanding terrain features and communication centers inland, he redoubled his concentration on building up his base and perimeter defenses. For the next few days the American 3rd Division pushed cautiously inland, the British 1st Division, on its left, rather more boldly. But both failed to reach their obvious objectives, Campoleone and Cisterna, from which an advance on the Alban Hills must start; and neither was urged onward with any fervency by Lucas. He was now directly under the eye of Clark, who had come to see the bridgehead for himself. But even the presence of his superior could not stir him to action, though his diary reveals that it rattled him. When he was ready, he wrote, he would move. He thought he would be ready by 30 January.

Unfortunately for the Allies, the Germans were ready also. If there was one thing at which their staffs had always excelled, it was the rapid improvisation of defense and counter-attack, and this war had given them all the practice they needed at perfecting their procedures. The landing had badly frightened them – Vietinghoff was so alarmed that he had begged Kesselring for permission to withdraw from the commanding Cassino position. But *Oberbefehlshaber* (CinC) Kesselring was not prepared to fall for Clark's ploy and had kept his nerve. He called up his *Alarmeinheiten* and settled down to win the build-up. *Alarmeinheiten* were "paper" units, formed from clerks, drivers and men returning from leave and all German headquarters had plans to form such units in an emergency. German headquarters in Rome sent several of these units to the beach-head in the first day.

Meanwhile Kesselring called for better units to replace them. From the north of Rome came the 4th Parachute and Hermann Goering *Panzer* Divisions, from southern France the 715th Division, from the Balkans the 114th, from northern Italy the 92nd, 65th and 362nd Divisions and the 16th SS *Panzer* Grenadier Division. From the Gustav Line, which Kesselring insisted should be thinned out, came the 3rd *Panzer*, the 1st Parachute and the 71st Divisions. Not all of these were destined for Anzio. Kesselring had two crises on his hands, the Anzio beach-head and Cassino, and needed a surplus of units with which to juggle his way to stability. By 30 January, he had extracted sufficient force from these newly liberated reserves to have sealed off the Allied bridgehead and to be contemplating his own counter-offensive, which he had scheduled for 2 February.

Lucas's methodical preparation of his offensive had thus ensured the conditions which would bring about its failure. For his postponement of the capture of Cisterna and Campoleone had not only allowed the Germans to build up opposition on the commanding ground of the region; it had also betrayed to them what would be the thrust of his eventual attack. If he had taken these two places, his forces could have moved north-west, north or north-east. Cramped within his original bridgehead, with the coast on his left and the impassable inundations of the Pontine Marshes on his right, he could only attack straight ahead, due north. There the Germans sat and waited for him.

Lucas planned his H-hour, the attack time, for 0200 on 30 January. This timing gave his infantrymen some advantage for darkness covered the movements of the Ranger force he sent along the dry bottom of the Pantano ditch towards Cisterna. But it also concealed the Germans assembling stealthily to ambush them. Of the 767 Rangers who set out on this commando penetration only six returned to the Allied lines. Their comrades of the 1st and 3rd Armored Divisions, following up in a conventional assault, suffered fewer casualties but nevertheless met desperate resistance and, after an advance of three miles in three days, which brought them near to the vital Highway 7, were forced to a halt. Only in the British sector was there promising progress. Here the veteran 1st Division had launched its attack from the positions it had won a week before near Aprilia. (These were "The Factory", as the Allies termed the Fascist model farm at Aprilia, and "The Flyover", a road bridge which carried a minor road over the Anzio–Campoleone road.) But it was made at a dreadful price.

The countryside beyond the roads was a maze of gullies or "wadis", and these denied protection to the flanks of 3rd Brigade, attacking up the Anzio–Campoleone highway. Its three battalions suffered crippling casualties as a result; one, the 2nd Sherwood Foresters, was almost completely destroyed in the final assault on Campoleone. "There were dead bodies everywhere," wrote an American visitor to the scene, "I have never seen so many dead men in one place. They lay so close I had to step with care."

Though the offensive of 30 January to 3 February was a failure, in that it cost much for little, fell short of a break-out and further depressed Lucas at a time when buoyant leadership was becoming vital to the beleaguered invaders, it did achieve some positive gains for the Allies. It had inflicted heavy losses on the Germans, who had no way of suppressing the fire of the Allied fleet or of chasing off the Allied air force, and had no real answer to the enormous weight of artillery the Allies could always deliver. Both the British 1st and American 3rd Divisions had penetrated Kesselring's main line of resistance; and the upset they had inflicted forced him to postpone the planned 2 February offensive.

The Allied assault had averted a German offensive designed to obliterate the Anzio beach-head and sweep the Allies into the sea. But if it had avoided another Dunkirk, Colonel General Eberhard von Mackensen, whose Fourteenth Army Headquarters Kesselring had brought down to oversee German operations at Anzio, was determined not to let the Allies consolidate. He inaugurated the first of a series of minor attacks, beginning on 3 February, and chiefly aimed at the British Campoleone salient. All of these were designed to win the ground necessary for a major counterblow. He was unable to shift the British on 3 February but kept them subjected to fierce pressure which, the next day, drove them out of most of their salient. On 7 February, Mackensen attacked towards "The Factory" and nearly took it. On 9 February he got possession of Aprilia village but failed to take "The Factory". It fell next day, was retaken by the British in a counter-attack, and only passed finally from their hands on 11 February.

The British 1st Division had now lost half its strength, which, as always in a stricken infantry formation, meant much more than half its infantrymen. A fresh British division, the 56th, had landed but it was needed elsewhere in the line and could not relieve the 1st and much of its front was, on Lucas's orders, taken over by the American 45th Division with the aim of fighting the Germans out of Aprilia. Lucas seemed to have little fight left in him. Badgered by his superiors, Mark Clark and Alexander, who were frequent visitors to the beach-head; menaced by the appointment of a deputy commander, Major General Lucian K. Truscott, whom he suspected of being kept ready to supplant him, and more distressed than ever by the losses his men were suffering, Lucas busied himself in supervising the preparation of a "final beach-head line" of strongpoints, roughly following the perimeter of 24 January.

In the coming days the men at the front, who were also frantically strengthening their tactical positions, were to feel grateful for the sense of refuge the final beach-head line offered, for on 16 February Mackensen unleashed his long-prepared offensive. There were two thrusts to the assault. The first, against the British 56th Division on the west bridge-head, was by 4th Parachute and 65th Divisions. The other, and main attack, by 3rd *Panzer* Grenadier, 114th and 715th Divisions, with 29th *Panzer* Grenadier and 26th *Panzer* Divisions in support, was down the now dreadfully familiar axis of the Campoleone–Anzio road. It was spearheaded by a unit chosen specially for the task by Hitler – the *Infanterie Lehr* Regiment. Successor to the *Lehr* Regiment of the Kaiser's Guard, and brother to the mighty *Panzer Lehr* Division, the regiment looked, and thought itself, invincible. In fact, the only activity it was accustomed to were military displays and demonstrations in Germany. It was inexperienced and overconfident. Exposed to the defiant resistance of the American 45th Division, astride the main road, the Nazi regiment suffered heavy casualties and its discipline broke.

Equally disappointing – for those like Hitler, who believed in fancy solutions to old-fashioned military problems – was the performance of the "Goliath", a remote-control miniature tank. Each of the 13 such tanks used in the attack carried 200 lb of explosive at 6 m.p.h. for a maximum distance of 2,000 ft. It was supposed to open a cheap way into an enemy position. All bogged down on the approach; Allied fire destroyed three, the rest were dragged ignominiously back to base.

But these two reverses were compensated by substantial German successes on 16 February. Although unable to deploy their tanks off the road, just as the Allies had been unable to do during their offensive, Mackensen's divisions had inflicted substantial loss on the British 56th and American 45th Divisions and driven both back. Behind one of their rare air bombardments they continued their attacks during the night, and attacked again early next morning down the main road. A further air raid in mid-morning aided their advance, and by noon they had secured a salient two miles deep and one mile wide in the 45th's front. They were now only a mile from Lucas's "final beach-head line". But the Germans could get no farther. Lucas found reinforcements, which included the battered British 1st Division, and with the help of these troops the 45th held out.

The Germans, by the end of the day, had suffered such heavy losses in their engaged infantry battalions, which were down to a rifle strength of 150 to 200 men, that Mackensen persuaded Kesselring that he could only continue if allowed to commit his *panzer* reserve – 26th and 29th Divisions. Kesselring, though not optimistic, agreed. They attacked next day, 18 February, and managed to enlarge the breach considerably. Then they ran into a carefully prepared fire-trap laid on by a "grand battery" of 200 Allied guns. Five times the Germans tried to break through the barrage that the battery laid around the Flyover on the Anzio road but each time their formations were broken up and driven back. Still they rallied to attack again in the afternoon and only the committal of final Allied reserves from Anzio, and more self-sacrifice by the 45th and 56th Divisions, turned back the assault.

The Germans had very nearly broken through on the afternoon of 18 February and Mackenson continued to attack, at a lower intensity, for the rest of the month. But after 18 February both he and Kesselring accepted that their offensive must end. With the cessation of the great Allied attack on Cassino on 13 February, the reason for the German offensive had gone. They had also, with 5,000 casualties in five days, run out of troops and supplies were low.

The Allies too had suffered heavy losses in men. But their supply line, though occasionally interrupted by the new German radio-controlled glider bomb – most spectacularly when the ammunition-ship *Elihu Yale* was blown up – was never broken and continued to provide ammunition in a quantity the enemy could not hope to match. Profusion of ammunition, after stark bravery, was the principal reason for the Allies' survival in the beach-head. After 20 February the German commanders tacitly accepted that the continued existence of the beach-head was a situation they would have to live with.

For the Allies, however, mere survival fell rather short of a victory. It was enough to satisfy Lucas, but not his superiors who, in the aftermath of the German winter-offensive, promoted him out of his command and into obscurity. With his departure, and the Germans' exhaustion, the beach-head relapsed into a lethal slumber. Maj.-Gen. Truscott, who could have won the ground Lucas dared not grasp for, was ironically compelled to oversee a prolonged period of siege-warfare – something for which his predecessor was perfectly fitted.

Yet perhaps it was still not Lucas's sort of battle. For despite the lack of movement on either side, Anzio remained a place of death, the death of young soldiers whom Lucas had cherished more deeply with each day of battle. And the deaths they were to suffer, in this gentle Italian landscape, warming to the spring, were those of a different war in another country – the deaths of soldiers of the First World War in the trenches of Flanders. For at Anzio, as at Ypres, the lines ran within grenade-throwing distance of each other, and men spent their days, throughout the "lull" of March, April and May, pressed against the earth walls of their bunkers, listening for the distinctive discharge noises of short-range weapons and bracing themselves to withstand the shock of the explosion. Rest, when it came, took tired units no more than three or four miles from the line where shelling, which at least they were spared "up front" by their proximity to the enemy, was a constant harassment and killer.

There was also the German propaganda barrage. Its message meant nothing to many soldiers; to others it was demoralizing and provocative. Radio broadcasts from Rome warned of the danger and horror of further fighting and encouraged desertion. Leaflets fired over in shells alleged unfaithfulness on the part of wives and girlfriends at home – leaflets for the British troops spoke of English girls enjoying themselves with the Americans encamped in "Merry Old England" while, for the American soldiers, the villain was the archetypal Jew. One of the most effective leaflets carried the chilling legend, "The Beachhead has become a Death's Head" and showed a map of Anzio over which a skull was superimposed.

All who survived the "lull" at Anzio testify to the tension, caused by constant alarms and persistent sense of claustrophobia, they experienced within the perimeter. When orders came, on 23 May, to break out and meet the spearhead probing north from Monte Cassino, they were greeted with the sort of genuine enthusiasm soldiers rarely accord the prospect of risk. The Allies had been too long at Anzio. It had proved no short-cut from the path to Rome.

Ought Anzio to have worked? Mark Clark thought so; Alexander thought so; Churchill continued to think so, long after the war's western focus of effort had moved out of the Mediterranean. Were they all wrong? It depends whether one wants a tactical or strategic answer to the question. Tactically, there seems little doubt that Lucas might have seized the high ground between the beach-head and Rome – the Alban Hills – had he pressed on hard from his perimeter in the first three or four days after the landing. But equally there seems little doubt that to have pressed on farther, to Rome itself, would, even though the city lay temporarily undefended, have resulted in the destruction of his Corps.

Hitler's snap judgement about Anzio was that it betrayed an Allied reluctance to risk a cross-channel invasion and he was willing in consequence to release reserves from much farther afield than usual to crush the landing. Given this reaction, Lucas's caution looks justified. But, his critics argue, bolder action would have frightened the Germans into thinning out the Cassino front which, in turn, would have heightened the chance of the Allies breaking the Gustav Line and dashing to his rescue.

That argument shifts the debate from the tactical to the strategic level. Its validity is dubious also – Cassino and Anzio are so far apart (about 70 miles) that the two Allied forces, given their strength relative to each other and to the enemy's, could not mutually assist each other. A much stronger punch at Cassino, a much bigger landing at Anzio, a weaker Tenth Army, a slower, smaller reinforcement by Hitler – any of these would have turned the trick for Mark Clark, Alexander, Churchill, perhaps even for the depressive Lucas. But these alterations in the strategic equation presuppose a major revision of priorities in the Allied plans for the conduct of the war in 1944. Not only was there no such revision but American opinion, at the highest level, was rockfast against it.

Roosevelt and Marshall were determined to transfer the focus of Allied war-making out of the Mediterranean and into Normandy, agreed to Anzio with bad grace and resolved to concede it with no more than would pacify Churchill. Given their attitude, the 70 miles between Cassino and Anzio were unbridgeable by any Allied effort. Hitler's hopes and fears – fears that he might be about to lose both the Balkans and Italy; hopes that a brutal extinction of the Anzio beach-head might deter the Allies from risking a landing elsewhere – determined that the Germans would give Lucas and Mark Clark no help either. It was this combination of enemy determination and Allied lack of enthusiasm which robbed the Anzio operation of its chance of success and made the subsequent battle so terrible.

Monte Cassino (1944)

E. D. Smith

When I first saw the monastery it was intact, an ancient and magnificent building set on the top of the steep slopes of Monte Cassino. It dominated the surrounding countryside. As we drove towards the battlefield, at every turning, at the top of every crest, there was the monastery getting bigger and clearer. On a cold February morning in 1944 it presented a noble sight with the pale winter sun shining on the glass of its windows and the great towers and dome outlined against the grey sky.

During the next two weeks, at a comparatively safe distance from the monastery and the town of Cassino, I acted as a supernumary liaison officer, and was a spectator, removed from the fierce struggle that was taking place on the hills across the Rapido valley. Some two or three miles away from our vantage point we could see and hear the battle being waged in the ruined town, among the rocks and scrub on the ridges under the shadow of the monastery, against the background of Monte Cassino, and, to the north, the towering snow-capped peak of Monte Caira where the French wrestled with the elements as well as stubborn German defenders.

Under a clear sky on the morning of 15 February and with token opposition only from the Germans, an armada of bombers made their appearance over the monastery and for four hours wave after wave of bombs pulverized the building; the planes dropped their bombs from heights between 18,000 ft and 10,000 ft. It was an impressive and awe-inspiring spectacle. Even from our remote vantage point we found it difficult to envisage anyone surviving the punishment being meted out. Then, to add to the destruction, the Allied artillery began to batter away as soon as the bombers had returned to their bases. By now the monastery looked like a gigantic decayed tooth and in our innocence most of us thought it would never dominate the valley again. We were wrong. Without scruple, the Germans were now able to use the ruins for defense.

German paratroopers constructed loopholes in the ruined walls from where they could fire in several directions. Artillery and mortar observers kept a ceaseless watch from posts that gave them a perfect view over the terrain below, the ground over which Americans, British, Indians and Poles hurled themselves against defenses until the monastery was abandoned on 17 May 1944.

On 7 March the call came for me to join my battalion, 2/7th Gurkha Rifles, which was holding a position on the hills north of Monte Cassino. The journey forward was on foot and it is etched clearly in my memory. The track up the hills, little used by day, was the life-line of the battalions from 4th Indian Division that were holding the sector around Snakeshead Ridge. Up and down this crude path worn out of the mountainside, went everyone and everything. New, clean soldiers going up, prematurely old bedraggled men returning; some wounded, others acting as escorts to mules. The mules were moving in both directions, being urged on by Italians, Indian and the occasional British voice. How we depended on those mules in Cassino! There was no other way of getting rations, ammunition and other stores up the mountains to the forward positions. It was a dangerous, uncomfortable walk.

The noise of gunfire never stopped. Far behind Mount Trochhio, on the south side of the valley, we could see the flashes of the Allied guns. Ahead we could hear the thump of the German artillery replying, and the sound of tearing silk as the shells flew above our heads in both directions. Occasionally

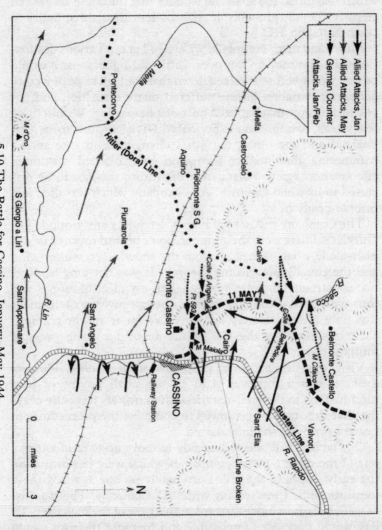

5.10 The Battle for Cassino, January–May 1944

a shell or mortar exploded on the rocks nearby or in a ravine which magnified the noise: no wonder that the climb seemed an eternity though probably it took us less than three hours to reach battalion HQ.

Mules and men, eventually we arrived at our various destinations. The journey up was over. Little did I guess that it would be five weeks before I walked down that trail, all hope of victory gone, our battalion having suffered many casualties, and not one inch nearer that battered hulk of a monastery. Within those five weeks, two fine and experienced Divisions, one from New Zealand and the other, the 4th Indian, were to take such a hammering that neither formation ever reached maximum effectiveness again. Fortunately the future was not to be disclosed to us when I joined "A" Company which was then in a reserve position.

The Company was not holding or defending any ground. The Gurkha soldiers were sheltering in holes behind rocks or beside man-made stone "sangars" from the snow, sleet, winter wind and the equally unwelcome shelling. It was not long before I had constructed my own stone shelter, my place of refuge, and thus we stayed seemingly forever, though my diary tells me it was only a week. Rarely did we move far from our cramped shelters unless for the call of nature or for some pressing military chore.

Visits to toilets had to be postponed until evening. Then, at dusk, it was a common sight to see small groups of bare hindquarters in the semi-darkness, their owners fervently praying that they might be allowed to complete the proceedings in peace before the shelling started.

Our tactical role was to be ready to move up to reinforce any one of the three forward companies which were in position on the early slopes of the hill. Fortunately no one attacked those localities while I was serving with "A" Company. This was just as well, because a move forward in full view of the monastery by day would have been impossible and by night the path would have been difficult.

We had been told that a third attempt to capture Monte Cassino was to be launched under the code name "Bradman", but winter struck with all the violence of a fresh enemy so that the attack was postponed from day to day because there was no chance of aircraft even flying, let alone carrying out pinpoint bombing against Cassino town. Friend and foe, German, British and Indian, clung to exposed positions on those mountains during the worst storm in an Italian winter which held us all in its icy grasp. Long-drawn-out days, followed by nights of activity meant that the morale and physique of our Gurkhas was severely tested. I wrote in my diary:

Each night we pray that the following morning will bring a change in the weather, a respite from the rain and snow and the endless vigil that is never a quiet one because the whine and crump of the guns and mortars continue by day and night. As day succeeds day, anxiety about the next attack has changed into a desperate longing to do anything rather than sit for ever undergoing an ordeal that tests minds and bodies alike.

Such a winter could not go on for ever, even at Cassino, and on 13 March the sky began to clear and the prospects looked brighter. We were told that the long-postponed attack was due to begin on the 15th morning: it was to be preceded by a bombardment of Cassino town by over 500 bombers. Next day dawned clear and at 0830 wave upon wave of bombers arrived, to begin pounding the town which was soon shrouded in billows of smoke and dust. It was a terrifying exhibition, even to us cowering down in our foxholes below Point 569. After a few minutes I felt like shouting – "That's enough!" but it went on and on until our ear drums were bursting and our senses befuddled. Several bombs fell astride the company position and I found myself shouting curses at the planes.

It's no fun being bombed by anyone, but the feeling of bitterness at being bombed or shelled by your own side is beyond description; the sight of friends killed or mangled by the mistakes of friendly supporting arms arouses the deepest of emotions in the hearts of front-line soldiers. That evening I wrote in my diary: "What an inferno is Cassino now! Dear God – take pity on those men, if there are any survivors in the town, which I doubt."

In spite of that terrible ordeal, many German paratroopers survived amongst the collapsed walls and the deep craters caused by the bombs. The German High Command decided to stand firm and, although casualties were heavy, they had been less than expected in proportion to the damage caused by the aerial bombardment. The battle went on. Next day, Maj. Beckett would not let us carry out the mission which had been given us by brigade HQ. Already he had seen too many costly attacks, all of which had ended in failure. Moreover, he was deeply concerned about the safety of Castle Hill itself: an active fighting company of Gurkhas near at hand and ready to help his defenders would be of far more use than another broken band of men who, he knew, would eventually trickle back like their unfortunate predecessors. He refused to let us commit suicide and told brigade HQ accordingly. As a consequence, I lived to write this story.

Later that afternoon a direct hit by a heavy German shell caused one of the castle walls to collapse, engulfing and burying several Essex soldiers under the rubble. Without hesitation their comrades, British, Indian and Gurkha, began tearing at the stones in an attempt to save their lives. After a few minutes came German paratroopers from foxholes, some only 75 yards away, to join in the rescue operations side by side with our soldiers. In the middle of the Cassino battle there began an unofficial and very local "ceasefire". Friend and foe worked together, talked and exchanged cigarettes. My company commander spoke German fluently and he learnt that the enemy's view of Cassino was very similar to ours – it was Hell, the weather bloody, and the end impossible to predict.

It is not surprising that this incident remains clearly in my mind, truly an extraordinary commentary on the senselessness of war. My Gurkha orderly summed it up by saying that the "Dushman" (enemy) were so like "our Sahibs" that he wondered if there had not been a mistake somewhere! Why were we not all fighting the Japanese instead? However, his comments and the rescue operations were brought to an abrupt end by the Allied artillery which, for some inexplicable reason, opened up: the German snipers scuttled back and almost as if someone had said "Let battle commence," we were shooting away at one another once more. A few men were never released from the rubble.

I was ordered to return and brief "A" Company who were still waiting at the foot of Castle Hill. Not wishing to retrace my steps along the slippery path at the top of the deep ravine, I sought another route. I met four Indian soldiers, Sikhs, who were hiding behind some rocks on the stony hillside. Their faces reflected fatigue and cold. I greeted them cheerfully, even jauntily, but their hearts were heavy. I asked them the quickest way down to the bottom of the hill. One huge Sikh replied that there was a short cut along the ridge but on this they had lost several men from accurate sniper fire. The alternative path that would take longer, was the slippery precipitous mountain track that I had used before. "One way you get shot, Sahib, the other you slip to your death." And he grinned without humor.

Being impetuous and wishing to carry out my mission as soon as possible, I decided to take a chance and dash down the track that snaked its way along the ridge to the base of the hill. I waited and waited. All was quiet. Nothing moved on the path below. Nothing appeared to be moving in the town – indeed there had been a lull in the fighting for some time although, behind me, the sound of battle around the castle continued as fiercely as ever. I rose to my feet at the top of the hill and charged down the track: nothing mattered but to get to "A" Company. It seemed as if I was going to be lucky when something flicked off my black side-cap as I threw myself behind a rock. I lifted my head and saw the bullet mark. The bullet had only just missed my head. Something had prompted me into diving for cover. It was a cold day, but in a second I was covered in sweat. Cold sweat. Everything seemed to stop: the noise of battle, the guns. Probably less than a minute or two passed. It seemed like an age. I crawled forward and willed myself to make another dash. I prayed with great sincerity, prayed for speed. I prayed that the sniper would think I had already been hit. Into the open, zigzagging down the track at the fastest speed I had ever attempted. Once again the crack, crack, a blow on my haversack and then the safety of another rock. Breathless, I lay as dead until a glance at my watch spurred me on, this time to safety. The Gurkhas welcomed me, surprised to find that I was alive because they had seen me drop twice on the track above.

It had been an exciting day, but it was not yet over. While the company remained at the foot of Castle Hill in close support of the besieged garrison, I was told to make my way through the town and report to brigade HQ to act as liaison officer and, possibly, return with fresh orders. After dark my Gurkha orderly, Rifleman Rambahadur Limbu, accompanied me as we scrambled a way down to the battered Cassino below us. It was not long before I realized that the landmarks that had appeared to be so prominent in fading daylight, from an observation point on the hill, were not nearly so easy to find in pitch darkness among rubble and ruins. After about ten minutes I was convinced that we were lost. Unfortunately, Rambahadur and I could not agree on the direction we should be taking. We appeared to have gone round in a complete circle but Rambahadur had no doubts whatever: he was sure he knew the way and so, against my better judgement, I agreed to let the Rifleman lead. The town, or the remains of it, was strangely quiet after a day of close-quarter fighting when the noises of machine-guns and grenades had continued to pay testimony to the bitter struggle that was being waged in Cassino.

The two of us shuffled and groped an uncertain way around walls, skirting bomb craters, and scrambling over piles of stones. Occasionally we heard voices or smelt cooking which wafted out of the darkness from improvised cellars and hiding places. It was quite impossible to tell who was friend and who foe: occasionally we saw movement at a distance. Suddenly a dark form appeared in front of Rambahadur and challenged him – in German. As Gurkha and German stood frozen in mutual surprise, I fired at the enemy sentry with my tommy-gun, saw him drop, hit by the burst of fire. We dashed down the remains of an alleyway to throw ourselves behind a wall. Within seconds, several Germans, who had been cooking or eating their evening meal below ground, were shouting furiously at each other and shooting at random. Fortunately no one came to look for us and after about five minutes all was quiet.

This time I took the lead and soon we recognized one of the lost landmarks and, without any further incidents, located brigade HQ. Here we were told to rest but although I was near the end of my tether, the clamor of battle and the nervous strain was too much for me: I could not sleep so back I went to the improvised Operations room where the brigadier informed me that "A" Company would be returning before dawn. I was to guide them to a quarry nearby which was to be our temporary position until further orders. Rambahadur and I spent some considerable time searching for the best route before meeting them at the outskirts of the town. There was no sleep for any of us that night.

"A" Company had been withdrawn into reserve because a German force had infiltrated its way down the large ravine behind Castle Hill in an attempt to isolate the British defenders by cutting off supplies of food and ammunition. The quarry afforded us some protection from intermittent shelling and mortaring which increased in intensity during the afternoon. As darkness fell, the Germans rushed up to hold a sector and, for the rest of the night, both sides fired indiscriminately at one another without any apparent gains in territorial possession. The next day, 21 March, proved to be just as dangerous – the pressure never relenting for one moment. Throughout the morning the Germans kept up their shelling of our position while we tried to construct stronger defences and to cover any gaps with mines. By now we were so exhausted that even sleep became impossible. I have never been a good sleeper and I was so wound up that I thought madness was close at hand even if I managed to survive German fire and bullets. Nature eventually saved me when I was going round the company's positions after three sleepless days and nights. My legs buckled under, I hit my head and passed out. At the Regimental Aid Post, the Indian doctor who had already supplied sleeping pills without success, soon diagnosed my comatose state. Events did not let me sleep for more than six hours, but I was restored to sanity again.

So it went on, the merciless shelling and mortaring that claimed many victims. "A" Company was near the end of its tether. Our Gurkhas' normal resilient cheerfulness, their toughness, their fatalistic attitude towards life generally, all these admirable qualities that make them such magnificent soldiers had evaporated. This was not their kind of soldiering. It provided no opportunities for them to get to close grips with the enemy: for hour upon hour they were targets for mortars, shells and the banshee screams of the *nebelwerfers*. In retrospect, I wonder if we could have held on for another 24 hours, but fortunately our ordeal was nearly over.

During the morning of 22 March, the shelling of our positions became more intense and accurate. It was an inferno all day but early in the evening came the news that saved the lives of the survivors – and our sanity. Later that night we were to move back to rejoin our own battalion which had been resting while we were being hammered.

For five hectic days and nights we had been on detachment away from the 7th Gurkhas. My chief recollection was the noise that never stopped. It was to be two days before we recovered our spirits. Fortunately our colonel decided to send us back to act as reserve company again, while the other three rifle companies held the front line near the Snakeshead Ridge.

Unbeknown to us, however, the generals above had realized that 4th Indian Division was exhausted and would have to be withdrawn. We had shot our bolt and had little to show for our efforts. Our friends of the 1/9th Gurkha Rifles, still clinging to the isolated position on Hangman's Hill, were ordered to begin their withdrawal after dark on 25 March. By a miracle they made their way down the hillside and through German outposts without any major incident. Eight officers and 170 Gurkha ranks abandoned Hangman's Hill without relief: later the Germans claimed to have counted 185 dead Gurkhas in and around their old position, the price that battalion paid for the nine days spent under the walls of the monastery.

And our turn was soon to come. In the early evening of 25 March, an advance party from the Lancashire Fusiliers arrived to begin the take-over of our positions. For me the relief could not have been delayed because by that time I was suffering from a nasty bout of diarrhea. In my diary I wrote: "Now very weak – how long can I continue?" Next morning brought confirmation that we were to be relieved by 78th British Division during that night, a complicated and dangerous operation of war because the German outposts were, in some places, less than 100 yards from ours. And then we faced a long march back across the valley of the Rapido to our waiting transport.

The distance was probably less than five miles, but during the time in the front line many men had hardly walked at all for six weeks. We had been cramped in foxholes, we were unfit, mentally exhausted, and many of our soldiers had lost their willpower. Even though the ordeal was nearly over, the fact did not seem to be understood. The Germans did little to hamper or harass us – indeed I believe they were relieving their own units but this was not known at the time. All we knew was that our group of dejected, tired soldiers, had to be across the valley before the sun rose the next morning. No one looked back. They just stared ahead with eyes that seemed to see nothing and kept on following the man in front, trying to force one foot past the other.

Never will I forget that nightmare of a march. Officers, British and Gurkha, shouted at, scolded, cajoled and assisted men as they collapsed. At times we had no alternative but to strike soldiers who just gave up; all interest lost in everything, including any desire to live. By dint of all the measures we could think of, most of our battalion reached the waiting transport and survived to fight another day, elsewhere, in Italy.

Cassino for us was over – a few weeks later it was to be over for the Germans as well. The third battle had been a grim struggle with few prisoners being taken, by either side, with every yard contested and no quarter given. Like many others who fought at Cassino, I remember how the decencies of war were observed to an astonishing degree. There were many examples of feelings, akin to comradeship, recounted by soldiers who fought at Cassino. Many wounded men survived because stretcher bearers were allowed to carry out their missions of mercy under the Red Cross flag in the forward areas: the contestants had a mutual respect and understanding of each other's problems. The German High Command's cautious claim to a victory was a true assessment because their defenders had won the battle: it was a victory, however, dearly bought because their losses were as distressingly high as ours.

When we left Cassino, the monastery still glowered down at us, an impregnable fortress. The ruins did not fall to any direct assault or succumb to the heaviest weapons available to the Allies. Monte Cassino continued to dominate the lives of the soldiers that fought under its shadow.

Omaha Beach (1944)

Nigel Bagnall

"You guys going to stay here until you're all dead? Like to see me attack alone?" The American lieutenant rushed towards the barbed-wire entanglement and blew a hole in it with an assault charge. "Come on, let's go!" Three hundred exhausted men of the 1st US Division, 5th Corps, death staring at them on their bitterly contested toehold of Nazi Europe, flung themselves after the lieutenant. At last the Americans began to move forward from the slaughter of "bloody Omaha" beach on D-day 6 June 1944, the first day of the Allied invasion of Europe.

At 2130 on Sunday 4 June Group Captain Stagg, senior meteorologist, reported to General Dwight D. Eisenhower, Supreme Commander Allied Forces, and his senior commanders that the bad weather, which had already forced one postponement of the Allied invasion, was improving.

A rain front over the planned assault area was expected to move in two or three hours and the clearing would last until Tuesday morning. Stagg expected the high winds to moderate and cloud conditions to permit bombing during Monday night and Tuesday. But a heavy sea would still be running and the cloud base might not be high enough to permit spotting for naval gunfire.

Eisenhower faced a critical decision. Such weather conditions would be barely tolerable but to decide on another postpone-

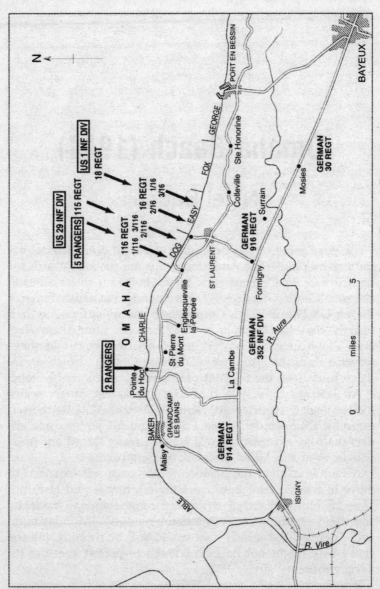

5.11 The Invasion of Normandy–Omaha Beach, 6 June 1944

ment meant that the invasion would have to wait until 19 June before the right conditions of moon, tide and daylight returned. The choice was between a risky disembarkation of troops or postponement – and the longer the delay, the shorter the likely duration of good campaigning weather on the Continent. Admiral Sir Bertram Ramsay, Commander-in-Chief Allied Naval Forces, reminded the Supreme Commander that he had to make a decision within half an hour for by then, if the invasion were to go ahead, orders must be given to the first convoys to sail. Turning to General Sir Bernard Montgomery, Ground Force Commander, Eisenhower asked, "Do you see any reason for not going on Tuesday?" "I would say Go," replied Montgomery. At 2145 Eisenhower announced his decision. "I am quite positive we must give the order . . . I don't like it, but there it is . . . I don't see how we can do anything else."

With the decision taken, the detailed plans that had been prepared over the years began to unfold. The invasion would take place along the 40 miles of coastline between the Vire Estuary and the River Orne in western Normandy. This area offered several advantages – it was near the ports in southern and south-western England, the beach-heads would be within Allied fighter range, it was near the major port of Cherbourg which, hopefully, would be captured early, and Allied air attacks on railways and bridges might be able to isolate the assault area and slow up the arrival of German reinforcements and supplies.

The initial assault landings were to be carried out by 21st Army Group, under Montgomery's command, consisting of six reinforced infantry divisions landing from the sea, and three airborne divisions. On the east was the British 2nd Army and on the west the United States 1st Army. Five beach-heads had been selected – "Utah" and "Omaha" for the United States 1st Army; "Gold", "Juno" and "Sword" for the British 2nd Army.

A number of factors governed the selection of D-day. A long period of daylight would enable maximum advantage to be gained by Allied air power. The moon should be nearly full to aid the airborne troops and the tide should be strong. Beach obstacles would thus be fully exposed at low water and vehicle landing craft could ground, unload and withdraw on a rising tide. The requirements of the actual timing of the landing, H-hour, also entered into the calculation.

The Allies had learnt several lessons from previous amphibious operations and these had to be considered in selecting H-hour. At Tarawa, the Americans learnt that naval fire support could not be relied on to neutralize beach defenses, unlocated gun positions, or to provide close fire support for the assaulting troops. Admiral Ramsay studied the full report and observed that "the heaviest casualties were caused by the failure to neutralize enemy positions during the period immediately before and after the touch down of the assault."

The final period selected for D-day was between 5 and 7 June and H-hour was to be staggered, varying by about an hour from the easternmost British and westernmost American landings, because of the different tidal and beach conditions.

On the German side, an invasion in the west had been expected since 1942. To protect the 3,000 miles of coastline Germany controlled, an "Atlantic Wall" was planned. This fortification existed largely in Hitler's mind and though it was good propaganda it was never completed. Their manpower situation was also discouraging. On paper there were between 50 and 60 German divisions in the west but they rarely had more than 25 efficient, full-strength field divisions available at any one time.

The 5th Corps assault at Omaha was planned to extend over 7,000 yards of beach which curved landward in a slight crescent, flanked at both extremities by 100-ft-high cliffs rising almost directly out of the sea. Above high-water mark there was a sloping bank of shingle, in places 15 yards wide, which extended into sand dunes on the eastern two-thirds of the beach. On the remaining western third of the beach, the shingle butted against a sea wall, between 4 ft and 12 ft high.

Behind the dunes, which formed an impassable barrier to vehicles, was a shelf of sand some 200 yards wide in the center but narrowing sharply at either end. Beyond this sand shelf, the grass-covered ground rose sharply to between 100 ft and 180 ft before opening on to a plateau of rolling farm land. Four small wooded valleys extended inland from the beach area to provide natural corridors onto the plateau. Near the eastern end, there was a fifth, less distinct, exit.

Below the high-water mark the beach sloped very gently but with an 18 ft tidal range, some 300 yards of firm sand would be exposed at low tide. Here the Germans had built three bands of obstacles which would be concealed at high tide. None of the bands was unbroken but together the three formed one continuous obstacle over 100 yards wide and 250 yards out from the high-water mark at its seaward edge. The first two belts consisted of waterproofed Teller mines fixed to iron frames and upright logs and the third comprised a series of metal "hedgehogs" designed to hole assault craft that had avoided the mines.

The German shore defenses at Omaha were based around 12 strongpoints though not all of them had been completed by June. Each of these strongpoints was a small complex of pill boxes, gun casements and firing trenches, surrounded by mine-fields and wire. Only two of the complexes were bomb-proof. Deep trenches or tunnels connected the various components and there were underground living quarters and ammunition stores. The strongpoints were mainly sited to block the valley exits from the beach though they could also cover the tidal flat and the whole beach with both flanking and direct fire. Machine-gun emplacements, weapon pits, barbed wire and minefields fortified the areas between the strongpoints. In all there were 35 pill boxes with artillery pieces of various sizes and/or automatic weapons, four artillery batteries, 18 anti-tank guns, six mortar pits, 35 rocket-launching sites, each equipped with four 38 mm rocket tubes, and 85 machine-gun nests.

There was no heavy coastal artillery in the Omaha sector and only two batteries of mobile field guns in the immediate vicinity, but there were about 60 light artillery pieces within the strongpoints. The Allies had been informed that the defensive positions were held only by a reinforced infantry battalion, 800 to 1,000 strong, belonging to the 716th Infantry Division. Fifty per cent of these were supposed to be non-Germans. But this intelligence assessment was wrong.

Field Marshal Erwin Rommel, Army Group B Commander-in-Chief, and responsible for coastal defenses between Denmark and the Pyrenees, knew from his experience in North Africa that it was folly to use massed armor against an enemy who had air superiority. If the German army could not fight the Allies on something like equal terms, then its only chance of offering a successful defense was to fight from the strongest natural positions. The battle for the West, Rommel considered, would be decided at the water's edge, and the decision would come within the first 48 hours of the Allied landing. He therefore wanted to move the German armored divisions forward into the coastal areas, so that at least elements of them could intervene.

But Rommel was overruled by von Rundstedt. He was only permitted to make a few moves forward nearer to the coastline. This proved to be very fortunate for the Allied troops at the Omaha beach-head. Allied intelligence estimated that the nearest German reserves to the Omaha sector were two more battalions of the 716th Division, but they judged that it would take them two to three hours to arrive, and then they would be able to do little more than help contain the Allied landings. A full scale counter-attack would have to await the arrival of the 352nd Infantry Division, thought to be in the St Lo–Caumont area some 20 miles farther inland, and the Allies believed that it was not capable of delivering such an attack until the afternoon of D-day.

The objectives of 5th Corps were then laid down with the aim of gaining an adequate foothold or lodgement area as quickly as possible. The assault echelons (an echelon is a formation of troops in parallel divisions, each with its front clear of the one ahead) were to break through the beach defenses within two hours of landing, and then clear the exits leading out through the valley by H + 3 hours. This achieved, 5th Corps' D-day objective was to advance four miles inland and secure the plateau up to the river Aure, where the Corps was to be prepared to repel German counter-attacks. Later 5th Corps was to push southwards towards Caumont and St Lo, conforming with the British 2nd Army on its left flank.

Fifth Corps consisted of three infantry divisions; the 1st Division, which had seen action in the Mediterranean, and the 2nd and 29th Divisions. Since the Corps' subsequent operations were to develop on a two-divisional frontage, it was necessary to land elements of both divisions in the assault echelons, so as to avoid having to pass one formation through another within the restricted bridgehead. There was neither sufficient shipping nor room on the beach to allow both formations to assault at once.

The Corps would then conduct its landing in four basic echelons, the two assault ones each consisting of some 15 waves of landing craft. The first echelon (Force O) and the second echelon (Force B) were commanded by the headquarters of the 1st and the 29th Divisions respectively but were made up from elements of both formations. The 2nd Division formed the third echelon, and a miscellany of units the fourth and last.

Embarkation of Forces "O" and "B" began on 31 May and 1 June and both were completed by 3 June. The numbers of men and vehicles involved was enormous – for Force "O", the first assault echelon, 34,000 men and 3,300 vehicles were loaded into 300 landing craft. Two battleships, three cruisers, 12 destroyers, 33 minesweepers and 105 other ships supplied the escort, minesweeping and fire-support requirement. In addition, 600 vessels of different types were ready for a variety of support and service work. The main convoy of Force "O" left Portland harbor in Dorset on the afternoon of 5 June and made an uneventful crossing of the English Channel under continuous Allied air cover.

At 0300 the armada arrived at a point 12 miles off Omada. The wind gusted between 10 and 18 knots and waves were 3 ft to 4 ft high. Into this swell the assault craft were unloaded from larger ships. Some were winched down fully loaded, but to get into others soldiers had to scale the scramble nets over the sides of the parent ships. This was a hazardous operation as the craft were tossing and bucking in the heavy sea. The men were heavily laden – each soldier was equipped with weapons, a rubber life-preserver, a gas mask, a first-aid kit, entrenching tools, a canteen, knives and rations and extra ammunition and explosives.

Ten small craft sank almost at once, throwing 300 heavily laden men into the sea. The assault craft circled the transport area, getting into formation. As dawn lightened the sky, the craft edged towards the beaches. Discomfort followed the soldiers as waves sloshed over the blunt bows of the landing craft and they had to bail out with their helmets. Seasickness added to the misery.

The sea also took a toll of the guns and armor that were to follow the assault craft. Thirty-two amphibious tanks were launched too early into the swell and sank within minutes. Some crews escaped, others drowned in their vehicles. Ninety-six tanks were planned to follow the soldiers onto the beaches – a third of that number had now been lost without ever coming under fire. The DUKWs that were to ferry support artillery ashore also ran into difficulties. The small, heavily laden craft foundered – the 111th Field Artillery Battalion lost all but one of its 105 mm howitzers and the 16th Infantry Cannon Company and the 7th Field Artillery fared little better.

With 40 minutes to go to H-hour, when the troops would reach the beaches, the Allied aerial and naval bombardment of the enemy defenses reached a climax. The Allies had a massive air superiority on D-day. A total of 3,467 heavy bombers, 1,645 medium, light and torpedo bombers, 5,409 fighters and 2,316 transport aircraft were stationed in England on 6 June. Against this the Germans could muster only 319 aircraft, of which 100 were fighters. Field Marshal Hugo Sperrle, Commander of *Luftwaffe* Air Fleet III, had requested more aircraft before D-day – the *Luftwaffe* simply could not spare any from the defense of Germany's industrial centers. German naval patrols had been canceled on 5–6 June because of bad weather and the ships stayed in port. In fact the German navy did not consider the weather suitable for an invasion and, because they had no weather stations in the west, they were unable to detect the improvement in the weather noted by the Allies. German E-boats did approach the Allied fleet by accident but the mighty steel shield of warships that protected the invasion force was impenetrable. One German rating, on seeing the Allied force, said in astonishment that "It's impossible. There can't be that many ships in the world!"

At Omaha, 500 heavy bombers of the US 8th Air Force mounted a concentrated attack on the German defenses. The US battleships *Texas* and *Arkansas* poured 3,500 shells into the enemy positions from their total of ten 14-in, 12 12-in and 12 5-in guns. A variety of fire-support craft softened up the landing areas. But even this did not convince German High Command that the invasion point was between Cherbourg and the Seine and not the Pas de Calais area which, to strengthen the illusion, the Allies had bombed extensively in the days leading up to 6 June.

In the assault craft the cold and miserable vanguard of the invasion, bailing frantically to remain afloat, paused to look up and cheer the flying shells that were to destroy the German coastal defenses. The landing craft moved closer and closer to the shore of occupied Normandy and still no response came from the enemy defenses.

It was a silent prelude to disaster. The naval bombardment had overshot many of the front-line enemy positions. Some had been neutralized but only temporarily. The final aerial bombardment did not deliver a single bomb on the beaches – for fear of hitting their own men the aircraft crews had delayed a few seconds in dropping their bombs. They fell three miles inland. The landing craft, in a strong lateral current, had tended to drift eastward: the landmarks, seen so often in aerial photographs and in training exercises, were shrouded in smoke and dust and early morning mist. And so the troops, trained for specific tasks in their planned landing areas, found themselves in a confused and unexpected situation.

But this was the least of their immediate problems. The German shore batteries opened up, crashing into the bobbing, awkward landing craft. Artillery, mortars and machine-guns thundered all along the four-mile stretch of Omaha beach. Those units whose job it was to ensure that the successive waves of assault craft could beach safely and disembark their men and equipment on the rising tide suffered badly. The special Engineer Task Force was responsible for clearing gaps through the belts of obstacles during the first half-hour of the landing. Only five of the 16 assault ferries carrying the Engineers landed in the correct sectors and of these, three of the teams had no infantry or tank support. Sixteen bulldozers were to have come ashore with the task force – only six reached the beach and three of these were quickly disabled by artillery fire. Much of the equipment needed to mark lanes through the obstacle belts was lost or destroyed.

To add to the Engineers' problems they came in behind schedule and became mixed up with infantry, some of whom sought shelter behind the obstacles the Engineers were intended to blow. The Germans singled them out for special attention, with sniper fire detonating the mines fixed to the obstacles while the Engineers were working on them and mortar fire detonating rows of mines. At the end of the day there were 50 per cent casualties among this special unit.

Despite the difficulties, the Engineers managed to clear six lanes through the belts of obstacles before the incoming tide submerged them. Four of these lanes were in the 16th Regiment's sector and two in that of the 116th Regiment. But only one of these lanes could be marked and this created casualties and confusion as waves of assault craft, unaware of the situation, approached the areas. One craft struck a mine and disintegrated, showering the Engineers with debris and spreading blazing fuel over the water.

On 5th Corps' right flank, the invasion plan was for the 116th Infantry Regiment to land four companies in the first assault wave on each of their four beaches – code-named Dog Green, Dog White, Dog Red and Easy Green. A Ranger Company was to land slightly farther to the right on Charlie beach and from there it was to assault a strongpoint just to the west of Vierville. The 16th Infantry Regiment should also have landed four companies in the first assault wave in Easy Red, Fox Green and Fox Red.

Because of the general eastward drift of the landing craft few touched down in the correct sectors and sub-units became hopelessly mixed. Few landing craft made dry landings, most of them grounded on sandbanks up to 100 yards from the beach and in some places troops were disembarked into water that was neck deep.

F and G Companies came ashore on Dog Red and Easy Green. Although under heavy fire and disorganized by landing in the wrong place, many of them crossed the 200 yards of tidal flat to shelter behind the sea wall and shingle. Those who stopped at the water's edge were under direct German observation and suffered casualties. The right wing of 5th Corps' assault wave had practically disintegrated and the four companies of the 116th Infantry Regiment were no longer a fighting force. A Company had been cut to pieces on the shore line, F Company was disorganized by heavy casualties, scattered sections of G Company were trying to find their correct sector and E Company had veered widely off course, landing on the eastern extreme of the 116th Regiment, on the left flank.

To the west of the 116th Regiment, on the extreme right flank of Charlie beach, the 2nd Ranger Battalion had suffered severely. Their objective was an enemy strongpoint to the west of Vierville. One of their two landing craft was sunk by artillery fire and the other came under direct machine-gun fire as soon as the ramp was lowered. By the time the soldiers had reached the base of the cliff, 200 yards from the water's edge, only half the 65-strong unit was still alive. By nightfall, only 12 remained.

There were heavy casualties on the left flank, in the 116th Regiment's sector, but the majority of the supporting tanks had got ashore. Four tanks landed on Easy Red, a mile-long beach marking the junction point of the 116th and 16th Infantry Regiments, but only about 100 men landed with them – unfortunate for the Allies, for here enemy resistance was light. E and F Companies were scheduled to land on Easy Red but the bulk of both companies drifted too far to the east. The result was that only elements of these companies, together with part of E Company of the 116th Regiment, came ashore in the right sector in the first assault wave and these were bunched on the extreme eastern part of the beach.

Some of the troops were disembarked in waist-high water but then had to cross a deep channel to get to the beach. This pulled them even farther to the east and though casualties were light, with only two men killed, most of their heavy equipment such as flame throwers and mortars and some personal weapons were lost. Others landing slightly farther to the east were less fortunate – not only were they disembarked in deep water but they came under heavy fire. Only 14 men reached the shingle.

Stiff enemy resistance, faulty navigation and delays contributed to the critical situation that was now developing on Fox Green. Two companies from the 116th Infantry were scheduled to land in the first assault wave but the bulk of four companies, including elements of E Company of the same regiment, landed hopelessly intermixed in a comparatively restricted sector. Few casualties had been incurred in the final approach to the beach but as soon as the leading landing craft lowered their ramps and disembarkation got under way interlocking enemy machine-gun fire swept the water and inflicted heavy casualties. The survivors struggled to the water line and here, with most of their officers dead or wounded, they stopped.

I and N Companies of the 16th Infantry Regiment, which should have formed the first assault wave on Fox Green, were delayed – and they missed the disaster. I Company drifted widely off course and were an hour behind schedule. N Company was 30 minutes late and landed beyond the eastern limit of Fox Green. The company lost a number of men at sea and during the landing but it disembarked at a point where the tidal sand reached almost to a steep escarpment. This was the only company, of the nine that formed the first assault wave, that was ready to act as a unit.

At 0700, 30 minutes after the first assault wave had landed, a second group of five follow-up waves approached the beaches. These included the support battalions of the two leading regiments and was timed to go ashore at 0740. None of the follow-up assault waves arrived under the conditions that were expected. The tide had risen nearly 8 ft and now covered most of the beach obstacles. Only six lanes through the obstacles had been cleared and these were still not properly marked. The initial assault waves had not advanced beyond the sea wall or shingle and neither the surviving tanks nor the infantry from the first wave were in a condition to provide more than spasmodic covering fire. Nowhere had the enemy defenses been neutralized.

The troops in the second wave were organized, briefed and equipped to do no more than mop up any enemy positions that had been by-passed by the first wave. They were then to move inland, by boat loads, to their respective battalion assembly areas. Only a few sections of the second waves had special assault equipment – flame throwers, demolition charges and bangalore torpedoes for clearing lanes through minefields once ashore.

The troops in the second waves, as they approached the shore, could see the carnage wrought among the first wave. Debris from sunken assault craft bobbed among half submerged bodies and struggling survivors. Broken or discarded stores, weapons, lifejackets, equipment of every kind littered the shore line. Silent, wounded soldiers were grouped among the desolation, many in severe shock. One sergeant recalled a "terrible politeness among the more seriously injured" and a soldier of the 741st Tank Battalion saw a man sitting at the water's edge, oblivious to the machine-gun bullets that spattered about him, "throwing stones into the water and softly crying as if his heart would break." Medical orderlies, there to treat the wounded, did not know "where to start or with whom".

On the right wing, in the 116th Infantry Regiment's sector, the 1st Infantry Battalion had landed only A Company in the initial assault wave; the other three companies in this wave belonged to the 2nd Infantry Battalion. The 1st Battalion's three remaining companies were to come ashore in the second wave on Dog Green in echelon formation at ten-minute intervals. They assumed that A Company's assault wave had cleared most of the enemy positions.

At 0700, B Company started to come ashore but it was badly scattered over an area extending to nearly a mile on either side of its intended sector. A few assault craft beached in the correct area but were subjected to the same heavy fire that had decimated A Company 30 minutes earlier. The survivors of B Company struggled ashore to mingle with those of A Company along the shore line. Only three widely dispersed groups on the flanks played any effective part in the subsequent battle.

C Company was scheduled to land directly behind B Company at 0710. A major navigational error prevented it from doing so – and it was saved the disastrous fate of B Company. The company came ashore 1,000 yards to the east on Dog White beach. One of its six assault craft became entangled on the mined obstacle belt and it took 20 minutes of gentle maneuvering before it got free. The remaining five assault craft approached the shore in reasonably good order but the vessel carrying the special assault equipment capsized in the surf when its ramp jammed and the entire load was tipped into 4 ft of water. The unit recovered from this set-back and suffered only six casualties in disembarking and crossing the sand, largely because smoke from grass fires in the escarpment obscured enemy observation. C Company moved up to the sea wall and started to reorganize.

At 0720 D Company began to disembark having lost two assault craft, one swamped and the other hitting a mine. The remainder of the company got no farther than the shore line, having come under fire as soon as they disembarked. Most of the heavy support weapons were lost. To add to the disruption, the three assault craft carrying the battalion command group, the Headquarters Company and the Beachmasters party for Dog Green were widely scattered several hundred yards to the west. They came in directly under the cliffs and suffered heavy casualties in doing so. They stayed in the same position for most of the day and played no part in co-ordinating the scattered remnants of the battalion.

The 2nd Infantry Battalion had landed three of its companies in the initial assault wave – now only G Company survived as a fighting unit. Machine-gun fire ripped into the ranks of the supporting H Company and of the battalion headquarters as the ramps were lowered. Men scrambled for shelter behind disabled tanks near the water's edge. The battalion commander, together with his command post and elements of H Company, braved the fire, running up the open beach to the shingle bank where they joined the leaderless survivors of H Company. Because of the faulty radio communications it was over an hour before further progress could be organized. Eventually an attack by about 50 men was mounted against the enemy positions in and around Les Moulins, but it was beaten back to the crest of the shingle bank.

While this was in progress, the four sections of G Company, trying to move along the beach to get near their objectives on Dog White, gradually lost cohesion. One by one individuals or small groups stopped to take cover, only to become mixed and separated as they progressed westwards along the shingle bank crowded with survivors of other companies. By the time the remnants of G Company had reached their correct sector at about 0830, the main action was already over.

The 3rd Battalion of the 116th Infantry Regiment was scheduled to arrive directly behind the 2nd Battalion on Dog White, Dog Red, and Easy Green between 0720 and 0730. But the battalion was ten minutes late and came in well to the east on Easy Green and Easy Red along a thousand-yard frontage. Only a few scattered elements of the first assault wave had landed in this sector. K and I Companies came in behind them in close formation on Easy Green, and suffered only a handful of casualties in crossing the tidal flat to the shingle, but having arrived there safely they appear to have become immobilized.

L Company disembarked on either side of the junction between Easy Green and Easy Red, where they met only light enemy fire, which many men seem not to have noticed. M Company landed farther to the east on Easy Red and, encountering enemy fire on first disembarking, they stopped at the water's edge. Eventually, when the rising tide began to push them forward, the whole Company moved to the embankment as a body and, as one of them later remarked, "the Company learned with surprise how much fire a man can run through without getting hit."

Although the enemy defenses had not been breached, the second assault group suffered much less severe casualties than the initial one. Altogether five of the eight companies of 116th Infantry Regiment were capable of developing and holding a precarious toe-hold which they had established. Troops who were demoralized and lacked inspired leadership found this supplied when, at 0730, the Command Group of the Regiment, which included the assistant divisional Commander Brigadier General Cota and Colonel Canham began to land on Dog White. Both men were fearless soldiers and could not have arrived at a more opportune moment nor at a better place to influence events. To their left troops were crowded along the embankment of a few hundred yards, while the main Ranger contingent was about to land in the same area. Ahead of them, behind the embankment, smoke from burning grass obscured the enemy's view and rendered his fire largely ineffective.

The experience of the 16th Infantry Regiment was similar to that of the 116th. Although the initial assault wave all landed on Fox Green, leaving the large 2,000-strong force on Easy Red beach with only a handful of infantry operative, the second group started to land, and casualties were high. The main problem was the dislocation of command posts, faulty landings, casualties, the loss of radio sets and the physical difficulty commanders experienced in imposing control. Except for those immediately around them, they could exert little influence over the many men lying against the sea wall – a shelter they were all too reluctant to leave. Behind them the troops could see successive waves battling through the same fierce defense they had been through and the bodies of dead and dying comrades, and in front of them lay the enemy and a beach flat littered with minefields and wire obstacles.

The situation looked critical and further vehicles and support weapons could not come ashore until the exits had been cleared. But slowly, desperately slowly, inspired leadership and individual heroism began to turn the tide. General Cota and Colonel Canham, the latter already wounded, walked up and down the beach oblivious to enemy fire and bluntly directed officers and NCOs to get their men moving. Slowly groups of men, often from different units, and in other places units of company size, started to move forward supported by the few remaining tanks. Behind Easy Red beach an engineer lieutenant and a wounded sergeant walked forward under fire to clear a lane through the wire obstacles. Their task done they returned and looking down in disgust at the men huddled behind the shingle, exhorted them to get forward before they were killed where they lay. Advances were made in a world of smoke and confusion, each group isolated from its neighbors. An impetus developed, however, as successive penetrations brought a slackening of enemy fire.

The most significant advance in the 116th Regiment's sector came from Dog White beach. Here C Company and the 5th Ranger Battalion were spurred forward by General Cota at about 0750.

German defenses in this area consisted of lightly manned weapon pits connected by deep trenches sited just on the crest of the escarpment. The machine-guns were mainly sited to provide flanking fire down other sectors of the beach, rather than to deal with a direct assault. On the opposite side of the sea wall there was a double apron wire obstacle which had to be breached before the infantry could get through. After an initial setback, a gap was eventually blown by a bangalore torpedo and the infantry started to filter through under cover of heavy smoke from the grass fire drifting eastward along the face of the escarpment.

The leading infantrymen were joined by others who had cut their way through the wire and together they moved forward to the high ground giving access to the plateau. Progress was slow here through fear of mines, and the company advanced in column following an indistinct track. On gaining the top of the escarpment the enemy positions were found to be unoccupied and, after suffering only six casualties since leaving the shelter of the sea wall, the advance was resumed for a farther 200 yards when, still moving in column, the company encountered machine-gun fire from a flank and went to ground.

At 0810 the 5th Ranger Battalion, without knowing exactly what C Company was doing ahead of them, crossed the beach flat after blowing four lanes through the wire and started to climb the escarpment. Heavy smoke forced some of the men to put on their respirators and contact was lost between the various sub-units. However, for the loss of only eight men, the few enemy positions still holding out on the edge of the escarpment were overrun, and, after pausing to reorganize, the Rangers resumed their advance.

By 0830 a penetration 300 yards wide had been made and the last groups of infantrymen were leaving the sea wall. It was not in itself an advance of great significance but similar actions, frequently on an even more reduced scale, were being conducted all along the beaches. These isolated penetrations were then gradually linked together, expanding the bridgehead laterally and, what was of equal importance, giving it some depth so that further reinforcements of both men and equipment could be brought ashore as the beach exits were first cleared and then developed.

On the 16th Regiment's front, a gap opened up by G Company became an exit for movement off the beach during the remainder of the morning. The Regiment's command group landed in two sections at 0720 and 0815. The second section included Colonel Taylor who got his disorganized and leaderless men moving with terse instructions: "Two kinds of people are staying on this beach, the dead and those who are going to die – now let's get the hell out of here!" As soon as the engineers had cleared gaps through the wire obstacles and scattered minefields, the infantry were organized into haphazard groups and sent forward under the command of the nearest available officer or NCO. As they moved forward through the gap, there was intermittent enemy fire from both flanks and the already congested route became a scene of even greater confusion as leaderless groups stopped to shelter below the crest.

Strenuous efforts by the officers who had landed with the various command groups in the later waves encouraged the troops forward onto the plateau and gradually the bridgehead was extended. Progress inland was aided by a few isolated but determined groups of Rangers who had landed to the flanks of the main assault, and then fought their way forward unaware of what was happening elsewhere. As the penetrations which had been made between 0800 and 0900 started to link up, a new but still fragmented phase of the battle began. German defenses along the immediate coastline had begun to crumble and there were no significant reserves available to the enemy in the Omaha sector. A more immediate threat to the Germans came on the flank of 5th Corps attack. Here the British 2nd Army had broken through the German defenses in a number of places, and to the west, the American 7th Corps was firmly ashore with men and vehicles pouring across the beaches almost unhindered.

The inland battle behind Omaha developed into three generally unconnected and largely uncoordinated actions around Vierville, St Laurent and Colleville. Although there was only scattered resistance from small but determined enemy groups, seldom as much as company strength, progress was slow for a variety of reasons. Little fire support was available since most of the tanks and heavy support weapons had been lost during the landings, vital communication links were missing, units were frequently still hopelessly mixed, and control amongst the thick hedgerows was extremely difficult.

By 1100, however, Vierville had been cleared after a frontal attack by two battalions of the 116th Regiment, who then tried to extend the bridgehead laterally to link up with the Rangers who had landed farther to the west. By late afternoon this advance had been halted and Colonel Canham decided to withdraw and concentrate on the defense of Vierville, where the scattered Engineers, with only a quarter of their equipment, struggled to open up the beach exit giving access to Vierville. East of the Les Moulins valley, the 3rd Battalion of the 116th Regiment fought their way forward in small groups until they were stopped just short of St Laurent. Farther to the east, two battalions of the 16th Regiment fought a series of confused and fragmented actions in an advance towards Colleville, which was halted short of the town by a local German counter-attack.

At sea, the 115th Infantry Regiment had been held as a floating reserve only to be committed if the situation became critical. The desperate situation which had developed during the 116th Regiment's landings on the right wing of 5th Corps assault demanded their committment so the 115th Regiment was ordered to land at H + 4 (1030) to give immediate support. The same eastward drift which had disrupted the earlier assault waves dislocated the landings of the 115th Regiment. Pulled eastward by the incoming tide sweeping up the English Channel, the Regiment landed on top of the 18th Infantry Regiment in the process of disembarking east of St Laurent. It was not until early afternoon that the confusion on the congested beaches could be sorted out and the 115th Regiment headed for its assembly area south-west of St Laurent. After an unsuccessful attempt to take the town, the regiment halted short of the St Laurent–Colleville road.

The 18th Infantry Regiment, whose disembarkation had been disrupted by the unscheduled arrival of the 115th Regiment in their rear, was tasked with taking over the 16th Regiment's D-day objectives. However, because of delays and enemy resistance, their orders were changed and it was directed onto the high ground beyond the St Laurent–Colleville

road to fill a gap between the 16th Infantry on the right, but at
dusk it had not managed to reach the road.

At the end of the day 5th Corps had established two footholds, the first in a narrow sector between St Laurent and
Colleville, nowhere more than a mile and a half deep; the
second, slightly farther to the west, around Vierville. The cost
of these modest gains had mounted to 2,000 killed, wounded
and missing, together with the loss of a large amount of
equipment which included about 50 tanks and 26 artillery
pieces. The whole of the landing area was still under enemy
artillery fire and of the 2,400 tons of supplies planned to be
onloaded during D-day, only about 100 tons had actually
arrived. Beach obstacles were only about a third cleared, even
after a low tide during the afternoon had enabled the Engineers
to resume work on them; beach exits had not been developed,
nor had the essential beach organization, necessary to ensure
the orderly handling of successive landings, been properly
established.

The principal cause of 5th Corps' setback was the unexpected degree of enemy resistance. Not only were prisoners
taken from the 726th Regiment which was known to be in the
area, but also from the fully combatant 352nd Division whose
presence on the coast came as a complete surprise. How much
of the 352nd Division was actually in the Omaha area is not
known – certainly not the whole formation, since elements of
it were encountered as far east as Bayeux in the British 2nd
Army sector. The division appears to have been moved into
the area between Grandchamp and Arromaches – in order to
stiffen the second-line coastal formations deployed within the
immediate beach defenses. In this manner, all the prepared
strongpoints and their various interconnecting weapon pits
were fully manned and the artillery of the 352nd Division,
consisting of three field and one medium battalion, was at least
in part able to support the German troops confronting the
Omaha landings.

Had it not been for the massive assistance of the Allied navies
and air forces during this critical period of 5th Corps' landing, it
is doubtful whether the shaken and depleted troops of the
assault waves would have been able to recover, reorganize

and then develop an offensive which was to deepen and widen their bridgehead in the succeeding days.

Omaha is a story of near disaster but no shame. Largely unseasoned troops, subjected to all the hazards of a vast and complex amphibious operation, further compounded by unfavorable weather conditions and stubborn opposition, were initially near paralysed by shock but, under the shield of fire provided by the allied navies and air forces, rallied and resumed a dogged offensive.

Aachen (1944)

Hubert Essame

The greatest US involvement in ground fighting during the Second World War was not in the battle of the "Bulge" nor the recapture of the Philippines, but in the little-known battles of Aachen in the autumn of 1944. They were in some respects akin to the Meuse–Argonne offensive of 1918 which holds a similar place in the First World War, but the Aachen battles were not ultimately successful. After three months two US armies only penetrated 22 miles into Hitler's Reich at a cost of 140,000 casualties, then they were subjected to a totally unexpected German winter counter-offensive in the Ardennes. Allied hopes of victory in 1944 died with the protracted and frustrating campaign on the Siegfried Line.

Back in the heady days of the Normandy breakout, comparatively little stress had been laid on the spectacular success of Lieutenant General Courtney H. Hodges' First US Army in their helter-skelter advance from the Seine, in accordance with General Dwight D. Eisenhower's "Broad Front" policy, towards the Aachen Gap and Cologne. Hodges, in the last days of August, advancing on a three-Corps front with Major General "Lightning Joe" Lawton Collins' 7th Corps on the right flank suddenly swung it NE towards Mons. Approaching this area were disjointed elements of 20 routed German divisions flushed out of Normandy by the British. Neither had been forewarned of the other's approach and both stumbled into an impromptu battle which ended in more than 2,000 Germans being killed and another 30,000 POWs being rounded up. First Army in fact had destroyed the last reserves of both Seventh and Fifteenth Armies leaving the way ahead to Liege and Aachen virtually open. It was this little-advertised victory which enabled US patrols to be first across the Belgian border into Germany west of Aachen on 11 September. The First Army closed up on the west bank of the river Wurm.

Thereafter Eisenhower gave priority for supply to Field-Marshal Sir Bernard Montgomery's airborne carpet thrust towards Arnhem. Hodges closed down offensive operations on 22 September to shorten his front and bring forward another Corps to fill the gap in the Ardennes between his army and Patton's. Ahead on either side of Aachen from Geilenkirchen to the Huertgen Forest stretched one of the strongest parts of the West Wall. Hodges also knew that whatever its military value Hitler would not lightly let Aachen go. The days when cities could be carried at a run in the confusion of the pursuit were over. First Army would once more have to face new problems demanding novel techniques. In Normandy it had been hedge-rows, now it would be concrete pillboxes, minefields and all the bedevilments of fighting in a densely populated industrial area. Inevitably success would depend more on the courage and skill of the individual infantryman than on air support or armored strength.

On purely military grounds retention of Aachen had little to recommend it, surrounded as it was by hills and lying within two defensive belts of the West Wall. The city's roads were relatively unimportant as First Army had already found adequate ones leading towards the Rhine both north and south of the city. Over a millennium before, however, in the days of the Emperor Charlemagne, Aachen (Aix-la-Chapelle) had been capital of the Holy Roman Empire and thus had become identified with the mythology of National Socialism. To strike at Aachen was to strike at a symbol of Nazi faith. Hodges therefore decided to encircle it using 30th Division and 2nd Armored Division of 19th Corps to strike south to link up with 7th Corps NE of Aachen near Wuerselen and thereafter reduce the city at leisure. West and north of Aachen lay a densely built-up urban area. Major General Leland S. Hobbs, commander of 30th Division, therefore chose to make the first penetration of the West Wall on a narrow front along the Wurm nine miles north of Aachen where the country was more open.

On 26 September over 300 guns began a systematic attempt to knock out all the pillboxes on the divisional front; results were disappointing. Heavy bomber support was arranged with the proviso by 30th Division that the USAF should avoid bombing them instead of the enemy as they had done with disastrous results at St Lo in Normandy – 75 men killed and 505 wounded by American bombs. Bad weather resulted in the attack's postponement until 2 October. When the air strike went in, many of the medium bombers missed their targets – one group bombed a town in Belgium 28 miles away! The fighter-bombers, although they found their target area, failed to knock out a single pillbox. The 117th Infantry Regiment had to fight its way forward supported only by its own artillery, mortars, heavy machine-guns and tanks. There followed a day of small battles amongst the houses of Marienberg and Palenberg.

A volunteer flame-thrower operator of Lieutenant Robert P. Cushman's platoon, Private Brent Youenes, advanced within 10 yards of the first of two pillboxes and squirted two bursts into the embrasure. Private Willis Jenkins then shoved a pole charge into it. Out came five badly shaken Germans, lucky to be still alive. The platoon next shot up a machine-gun crew in a trench outside the pillbox and, creeping round the back of another, tossed hand-grenades through the embrasure. Pte Youenes squirted it with flame and the garrison surrendered. The platoon then dealt with three more pillboxes in like manner. An observer's comment, "These infantrymen have guts" erred on the side of understatement. Meanwhile the Engineers worked on treadways across the quagmires of the Wurm to enable the tanks to cross; none, however, could get into action before nightfall.

On the next day house-to-house fighting in Palenberg often lapsed into hand-grenade duels. One rifleman, Private Harold G. Kiner, spotted a hand-grenade that landed between him and his fellow riflemen, threw himself upon it and saved his companions at the cost of his own life. He was posthumously awarded the Medal of Honor. On the right flank of 117th Infantry, the 119th Infantry Regiment established a shallow bridgehead along the Wurm in the face of intense artillery fire.

Close infighting like this characterized the struggle among concrete and wire for the next three days. On 4 October the Germans staged a full-dress counter-attack with tanks and assault guns supported by well-directed artillery fire: even the *Luftwaffe* made an appearance. They got nowhere despite goading by Field Marshal Walther Model. By the 6th, superior American morale and armament swung the issue in their favor. On the left, 2nd Armored Division attacking SE carried all before it; on their right. 30th Division, despite fatigue, burst into the ghost town of Arlsdorf and the squalid streets of Merkstein. It was here that Private Salvatore Pepe refused to take cover but, rushing forward alone firing his rifle and tossing hand-grenades, wounded four Germans and caused 50 more to surrender. The 30th Division was now only three miles from Wuerselen, the planned point of junction with 7th Corps attacking from the south. Inch by inch the advance continued. By the evening of the 7th, Hobbs, justifiably exuberant, could report to his Corps Commander, "We have a hole in this thing big enough to drive two divisions through . . . this line is cracked wide open." His division and 2nd Armored had literally ruptured the West Wall in the face of a surprisingly large concentration of heavy and medium artillery and over 50 assault guns. Both divisions had taken in their stride the shock of the abrupt change from exhilarating pursuit to a grim battle in fortified zones.

It was now the turn of 7th Corps to strike north with 1st Division and complete the encirclement of Aachen by advancing to Wuerselen. Major General Clarence R. Huebner of 1st Division planned to do this with the 18th Infantry Regiment. Only a two-and-a-half-mile advance was involved, but it would take them through a dense maze of pillboxes and over exposed hill crests. To take these hills was no easy task; holding them thereafter under heavy artillery bombardment would be even more difficult. In Aachen itself there were about 12,000 Germans. Furthermore, unknown to the Americans, Field Marshal

Gerd von Rundstedt had promised to provide 3rd *Panzer-grenadier* Division and 116th *Panzer* Division under 1 SS Corps for counter-attack when the situation was ripe. Huebner's preparations included the provision of special pillbox assault teams equipped with flame-throwers, Bangalore torpedoes and pole and satchel charges. A battery of 155 mm guns and a company of tank destroyers were also provided to hurl point-blank fire against the pillboxes.

Attacking at night on 8 October and again on the 9th, the 18th Infantry fought their way forward to Verlautenheide, halfway to Wuerselen. Here they had to endure the most intense artillery fire yet encountered in the campaign. Despite fatigue, the 18th Infantry faced the prospect of a counter-attack with determination. It came in full force during 15–16 October. German losses were heavy; over 250 dead were counted in front of 16th Infantry Regiment. Altogether a third of the attackers were killed to no avail.

Meanwhile, from the north, 30th Division had turned southwards to meet 1st Division, in the process attracting particularly vicious attacks by 1 SS *Panzer* Corps. Amidst the slag heaps and pit heads around Bardenberg the reserve battalion of the 120th Infantry Regiment knocked out six tanks and 16 half-tracks, the CO, Major Howard Greer, personally accounting for two with his bazooka. Almost hourly fresh German units were fed into the struggle. But divisional morale remained unshaken, despite 2,020 casualties sustained in the past ten days. All efforts on their part to get forward still continued to meet vicious and obstinate resistance. The pressure on Hobbs from his superiors to close the now mile-wide gap and get on to Wuerselen became almost unendurable. On 16 October he struck again with 119th Infantry as his spearhead against the dug-in tanks and pillboxes blocking the way forward. In the mid-afternoon, 18th Infantry in the south spotted American troops on the ridge SW of Wuerselen. They were the two survivors of a patrol of 119th Infantry, Privates Edward Krauss and Evan Whitis. At 1615 these two, quickly reinforced, had the honor of closing the ring around Aachen.

Aachen itself, already a wilderness of rubble as a result of RAF attention earlier in the year, now found itself the target of

7th Corps artillery and fighter-bombers of 9th Tactical Air Force. An ultimatum to surrender delivered under a flag of truce, broadcasts on Radio Luxembourg and leaflets shot into the ruins by artillery on 10 October were all scornfully rejected by the garrison commander, Colonel Gerhard Wilck. Huebner had to commit 25th Infantry to a tedious battle within the ruins "from attic to attic and sewer to sewer". German resistance, reinforced by SS Battalion *Rink*, continued obstinate to a degree. Methodically, 26th Infantry inched their way forward. Outside the perimeter all attempts by 1 SS *Panzer* Corps to re-establish contact with the encircled garrison came to nought. Finally on the 19th Model abandoned the city to its fate.

But Col. Wilck issued an order of the day, "The defenders of Aachen will prepare for their last battle. Constricted to the smallest possible space we shall fight to the last man, the last shell, in accordance with the Führer's order." Over the air he continued to affirm his "unshakeable faith in our right and our victory". By the night of 20 October, 26th Infantry, reinforced by two battalions of tanks, had corralled his few remaining soldiers into the western and SW suburbs. Next morning, Lieutenant Colonel John T. Corley's battalion, supported by a 155 mm gun, approached a big air raid bunker at the northern end of the city. Faced by the threat of being blasted into eternity, Colonel Wilck surrendered. He had fought to a finish. The battle for Aachen was over; the once proud city, the first city of the Reich to be captured, lay in utter ruin. Burst sewers, broken gas mains and dead animals raised an overpowering stench.

It had been a costly battle. The 30th Division lost over 3,000 men, the two battalions of 26th Infantry 498. Throughout the armor had been forced to fight in penny packets cheek by jowl with the infantry. It had been a soldiers' battle in which Allied air power and material superiority counted for less than the fighting spirit of the infantry and the tank crews. Between them 1st and 30th Divisions had taken some 12,000 prisoners. What was surprising was the skill with which the German commanders had handled the many miscellaneous elements thrown piecemeal into the fighting as the days went by. Even more surprising was the tenacity with which their troops continued to fight.

Long before the battle it had become evident that Model, commander of Army Group B, whose frontage coincided almost with that of General Omar N. Bradley's 12th Army Group, had succeeded in establishing a well-organized defense of the West Wall astride the Aachen Gap. The morale of his troops was high, and even his second-class troops, established in fixed defenses, built-up areas and woods, could be formidable. Stolberg's 4,000 defenders put up a week's street fighting. Much bitter fighting in ever-shortening hours of daylight and deteriorating weather would have to be faced before the line of the river Roer, 12 miles ahead, let alone the Rhine, could be reached.

It is an indisputable fact that on the whole the German Army still outclassed the Allies in the flexibility and simplicity of its organization and in the professional skill of its battle-experienced corps and divisional commanders and their staffs. In the debacle at the end of August and the first week of September, although the Seventh and Fifteenth Armies had been reduced to skeletons, most of their staffs had survived and still continued to function. With the aid of Military Police and *Waffen* SS detachments they succeeded in regaining a measure of control. Hitler rushed forward First Parachute Army to fill the gap between what remained of Seventh and Fifteenth Armies.

Heinrich Himmler, commanding the Home Army in addition to his duties as Minister of the Interior, Chief of Police and Head of the SS, had put all his weight behind the drive to fill the ranks of 43 *Volksgrenadier* (the People's Grenadiers) Divisions now being formed. To supplement the artillery Hitler ordered 12 motorized brigades (about 1,000 guns), 10 *Werfer* Brigades, 10 assault-gun battalions and 12 machine-gun battalions to be raised. Himmler diverted the best of the manpower and equipment into the *Waffen* SS which now composed one third of the *Panzer* and one fourth of the *Panzergrenadier* divisions. The great strength of these divisions lay in their young officers – Nazi to a man, coarse, arrogant and cruel, but well trained and ruthless in battle. From them Hitler planned to produce a new generation to replace the regular officers of the *Wehrmacht*.

"Unconditional surrender" and the announcement of the Morgenthau Plan on 24 September, which revealed the Allied intention of turning Germany into a third-class agricultural state, reinforced Joseph Goebbels' propaganda appeals to the German people. Now that the enemy stood on the sacred soil of the Fatherland a deeply felt, instinctive love of country prompted all, soldiers and civilians alike, to fight on in the belief that the Führer in some mysterious way would emerge finally triumphant like Frederick the Great when all seemed lost in the Black Year of 1759. Behind the ramparts of the West Wall and depths of the Huertgen Forest they would fight on as the nights grew longer and the autumn rains slowed down the Allied armies and diminished the threat from the air.

As a matter of strict nomenclature, defined by the US Army Military History Department, the battle of Aachen ends with the fall of the city. Popularly, in the Allied Armies of the time and in European eyes, especially German, it also embodies all the operations of First and Ninth Armies east and west of Aachen in November and the first half of December.

At Brussels on 18 October Eisenhower revealed to the Army Group commanders his intention of continuing the battle on the Aachen front with First and Ninth Armies as a first step towards enveloping the Ruhr. He made it clear that serious logistic difficulties must first be overcome. Until the mouth of the Scheldt was cleared, enabling the port of Antwerp to be opened, no large-scale offensive could be sustained. Two other serious supply problems were causing him great anxiety. Surprisingly, US factories had failed to keep up with the Army's needs and an acute shortage had developed, which would take some time to make up. Eisenhower broadcast a personal appeal to the United States. Casualties, especially infantry riflemen and tank crews, had been much heavier than anticipated. Drastic steps had to be taken to comb out and retrain as infantry men from other arms. For these reasons and the vagaries of the weather affecting air support a resumption of the battle was deferred for nearly a month. If there was no fog over the airfields in Great Britain there was always fog over the target area and vice versa. As a result, autumn, with overcast skies, damp depressing fogs, persistent rain and ever shortening hours of daylight, was already far advanced when on 16 November Bradley renewed his offensive towards the Rhine.

Immediately south of Aachen, First Army, now numbering 12 divisions, was to make the main effort. In particular it was to take the seven Roer dams at Schmidt, so that Eisenhower's future plans for the Second British and Ninth Armies could be implemented. North of Aachen the Supreme Commander brought in the Ninth Army, fresh from America, to advance simultaneously and protect First Army's northern flank. Some seven miles ahead and almost parallel to the front lay the river Roer, initial objective of both Armies. To reach it First Army would have to fight its way through the dense Huertgen Forest, three miles deep, flanked by extensive built-up areas. On Ninth Army's front the country was more open for tanks and for controlling the large forces now to be engaged.

By this time, although the Allies had not an inkling of his intentions, Model's plans for an Ardennes counter-offensive in December with Fifth and Sixth *Panzer* Armies and Seventh Army were already far advanced. Facing First and Ninth Armies he had Fifth *Panzer* Army and Seventh Army; in their immediate rear Sixth *Panzer* Army had already started to assemble. Altogether some 30 divisions would be concentrated here and large stocks of fuel and ammunition built up. Model had over 1,000 guns centrally controlled and plenty of ammunition. His losses of the early autumn had been replaced and his intentions were crystal clear – to fight the Americans in the Devil's Garden of the West Wall and Huertgen Forest; under no circumstances would he allow the Americans to cross the Roer. Furthermore, the Sixth *Panzer* Army, destined to execute the main effort in the Ardennes, must be kept out of the battle on the Aachen front but look like joining it.

Bradley imagined that an overpowering aerial bombardment would shatter German morale and then he intended to blast his way through with massed artillery. Over 1,200 heavy bombers of 8th USAAF and RAF Bomber Command were to "take out" the towns of Duren, Julich and Heinsberg on the Roer. The forward troops would have 750 fighter-bombers on call. Late on the morning of 16 November vast fleets of aircraft passing over First and Ninth Armies signalled the start of Bradley's offensive. Results were disappointing – the 9,400 tons of bombs, for safety reasons, were dropped so far behind the German forward troops that they almost completely missed them. The attacking troops, four divisions on a 25-mile front, although supported by 1,000 guns, found themselves greeted by deadly small arms, artillery and mortar fire. It was small consolation and no help to them that six miles ahead three towns on the Roer had been destroyed in the heaviest tactical air bombardment yet launched.

Thus inauspiciously began the month-long battle of attrition which occupies a place and significance in the history of the American Army similar to that of Verdun for the French and Passchendaele for the British. In the end it absorbed some 17 divisions, resulted in severe casualties both from enemy action and sickness and severely tested the morale of the troops. It was fought in vile weather – damp grey mist alternating with heavy downpours reduced the battlefield to a ghastly quagmire and precluded effective air support. Everything favored the enemy. In the Huertgen Forest, First Army plumbed the depths of misery. Here, hidden from view amongst the closely planted trees, protected by barbed wire, anti-personnel mines, log bunkers, log-covered foxholes and machine-gun emplacements, a few men could hold up whole battalions. There were so many mines that the attackers were reduced to using pitch forks to uproot the new wooden and glass types. Charles B. Macdonald, American Official Army Historian, vividly recorded the fighting in *The Siefried Line Campaign*:

It was attrition unrelieved. Overcoats soaked with moisture and caked with freezing mud became too heavy for men to wear. Seeping rain turned radios into useless impedimenta. So choked with debris was the floor of the forest that men broke under the sheer physical strain of moving supplies forward and evacuating the wounded. The fighting was at such close quarters that hand grenades were often the decisive weapon. The minefields seemed endless. A platoon would spend hours probing, searching, determining the pattern, only to discover after breaching one minefield that another just as extensive lay 25 yards ahead. Unwary men who sought cover from fire in ditches or abandoned foxholes might trip over lethal

booby traps and turn the promised sanctuary into an
open grave.

The swollen bodies of the dead in grotesque positions added to
the general horror. So bitter was the fighting that the village of
Huertgen changed hands 14 times and the village of Vossenack
eight times. Inevitably there were unfortunate incidents in
which both officers and men cracked under the strain. More
than 24,000 killed, missing, captured and wounded fell a prey to
the fighting here; a further 9,000 succumbed to the misery of
the forest itself, the wet and the cold, trench foot, respiratory
diseases and combat fatigue. To some extent, too, the torpor
which comes from prolonged exposure without relief to shellfire
and bad weather was reflected at command level.

In the more open country on the northern part of the front
Ninth Army had better fortune and reached the Roer from
Julich to Linnich on 28 November. Thanks to realistic training
in the United States and the support of more lavishly supplied
British artillery, the army stepped off on the right foot in this its
first battle. It would be another two weeks, however, before
First Army was able to close up with the river opposite Duren.
The testimony of British officers who saw the American troops
at this time should also be recorded. During the battle many
officers and men of Guards Armoured Division were exchanged
with the Americans. Their impression was that "their methods
might be somewhat curious and unorthodox, but there could be
no doubt about the excellent results when put into practice.
Divisions such as the 29th and 30th Infantry who fought in this
battle could have challenged comparison with the finest of our
own." Lieutenant-General Sir Brian Horrocks, commanding
the British 30th Corps on the extreme left flank of the offensive,
and with the 84th US Infantry Division under his command,
was most impressed by their performance in their first battle,
their bravery, initiative and ability to learn from experience.

The first snow fell on 9 December; thereafter the days were
chill and the sky overcast. By 15 December First and Ninth
Armies, having advanced eight miles in a month, had reached
the high ground overlooking the river Roer. But three miles to
the south the Germans still held Schmidt and the vital dams

despite persistent attack. Attempts by the RAF to burst them with their heaviest bombs had failed. On their right, on a 100-mile front in the Ardennes, Bradley only had some four divisions, two new to battle and two badly mauled in the Huertgen Forest. The Germans, fighting what was an essentially defensive action, had reinforced the front with 11 divisions including two *Panzer*. Of these, however, only one, 10th SS *Panzer*, was scheduled to take part in the now imminent Ardennes offensive. American losses, mostly in front-line units, in killed, wounded or missing in the Aachen battles since September now totalled 68,000, plus over 70,000 sick as a result of fatigue, exposure, accidents and disease.

Fifty years later it is fair comment to say that First Army fought in the wrong place. They would almost certainly have had greater success if they had advanced in September, as originally planned, south of the Ardennes in conjunction with Patton's Third Army. Better still, they could have been sent through the Ardennes, which, as the Germans had proved in 1940 and would soon confirm, were not the barrier to large-scale military movement they had traditionally been assumed to be.

At 0530 on 16 December in darkness and fog from south of Monschau came the rumble of 2,000 German guns, their heaviest artillery barrage of the whole campaign. Model launched 13 infantry and seven armored divisions, followed by a further ten, a thousand tanks and 250,000 men into the Forest of the Eifel. The battles of Aachen were over. Another had begun.

Ardennes (1944)

Peter Young

Not since Pearl Harbor had the Americans received so rude a shock as when the dawn of 16 December 1944 was broken by the thunder of a thousand guns: German guns, heralding a most determined onslaught.

Ever since July, Hitler, with a strategic sense which one is compelled to admire, had been building up a reserve, a *masse de manoeuvre*, of 250,000 men. It was little enough for a two-front war, nor were they the soldiers of 1940, but it was still a force capable of delivering a heavy blow. And it was commanded by von Rundstedt, a man of whom miracles could still be expected. He had already performed one when he stabilized the German line on the Western Front after the débâcle in Normandy. Now he performed another by concentrating Hitler's last army (Model's Army Group B) in the Eifel area without attracting the attention of the American High Command. How did the Allied intelligence fail to see a quarter of a million men, their vehicles and 1,100 tanks? They saw what they wanted to see. The Germans, they thought, were licked – and anyway who would think of mounting an offensive in the Ardennes in the middle of winter? A certain number of suspicious troop movements were reported by prisoners, civilians, and by airmen, but their significance was discounted. As the Germans hoped, these were thought to be reinforcements for the fighting round Aachen.

Although von Rundstedt was to command the offensive, he did not favour it. It was Hitler's own brain-child. Physically the Führer was not the man he had been before the bomb attempt of 20 July. Lt-General Hasso von Manteuffel saw him as "a stooped figure with a pale and puffy face, hunched in his chair, his hands trembling, his left arm subject to a violent twitching which he did his best to conceal, a sick man apparently borne down by the burden of his responsibility. When he walked he dragged one leg behind him." But this miserable, shambling creature could still make himself obeyed. Whatever his physical condition his willpower was unimpaired. Temperamentally unstable, he was incapable of playing a waiting game. He deliberately sought a decision. Moreover, that acute if unbalanced mind could detect certain factors in favour of his plan.

In 1940 the Ardennes had been the weak link in the French chain. Now the Monschau–Echternach sector was the weakest part of Eisenhower's front. Lt-General Courtney H. Hodges (First Army) was holding 85 miles with only five divisions and three of them (2, 4, and 28) had suffered heavily in the recent fighting round Aachen. Only about 100 miles to the NW was Antwerp, the great Allied supply base, which had recently been opened to seaborne traffic. The German commanders knew the narrow roads of the Ardennes with their hairpin bends and steep hillsides very well. They had come that way in 1940. Bad weather could be expected to nullify the Allied air superiority. Otto Skorzeny's Panzer Brigade 150, disguised in American uniforms, would cause confusion behind the lines.

Von Manteuffel had a conversation with Hitler on 2 December, when the latter admitted that there was

a certain disparity between the distant objective of Antwerp and the forces which were to capture it. However, he said, this was the time to put everything on one throw of the dice, "for Germany needs a pause to draw breath." Even a partial success, he believed, would retard the plans of the Allies by eight to ten weeks . . . Temporary stabilization on the Western Front would enable the Supreme Command to move forces from there to the threatened central sector of the Eastern Front.

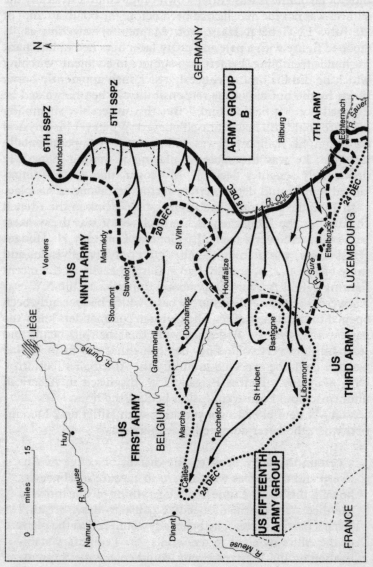

5.12 The Battle of the Bulge, December 1944

The German generals were not unnaturally concerned about the question of air cover. After the Berlin conference Manteuffel told Hitler that "in our sector of the front we never saw or heard a German aeroplane these days." He received this curious reply: "The *Luftwaffe* is being deliberately held back. Göring has reported that he has three thousand fighters available for the operation. You know Göring's reports. Discount one thousand, and that still leaves a thousand to work with you and a thousand for Sepp Dietrich."

When the attack came the SS General Sepp Dietrich with the Sixth SS Panzer Army fell upon the US V Corps (Major-General Leonard T. Gerow) and thrust towards Liège. The Americans were driven back to the Eisenborn Ridge, but in three days' desperate fighting they denied the enemy the direct road to Liège, the main communications centre of Bradley's Twelfth Army Group. A German armoured column did succeed in thrusting forward through Malmédy, Stavelot, and Stonmont, but as luck would have it narrowly missed not only the Allies' main fuel dump but Hodges' HQ at Spa. By 19 December it had been brought to a halt.

Fifth Panzer Army, though weaker than Sixth, made much more progress. Von Manteuffel achieved tactical surprise by attacking without a preliminary bombardment, relying on close co-operation between his armour and his infantry. His onslaught shattered the US VIII Corps (Major-General Troy H. Middleton), which was strung out upon a long front. On Manteuffel's right a corps cut off two regiments of the inexperienced US 106th Division in the Schnee Eifel. On his left two panzer corps broke through the US 28th Division, and reached the outskirts of Houffalize and Bastogne.

Seventh Army (General Erich Brandenberger) was supposed to cover Manteuffel's left flank by thrusting forward towards the Meuse. It made some progress at first especially on the right, but after a few days was held up by the US 4th Infantry Division and elements of the 9th Armoured Division.

Dietrich's failure meant that the Germans were not going to retake Antwerp. Hitler determined nonetheless to exploit Manteuffel's narrow breakthrough.

In 1940 Gamelin had had no theatre reserve, no *masse de manoeuvre*. Eisenhower had the XVIII Airborne Corps; this he now sent to General Hodges.

Eisenhower ordered General Omar N. Bradley (12th Army Group) to attack each flank of the German breakthrough with an armoured division. But he saw that if Model succeeded in widening the shoulders of the breakthrough Bradley's army group might be split right down the middle. Practical as ever, he placed all the US forces north of the breakthrough (First and Ninth Armies) under Montgomery (21st Army Group), leaving Bradley in command of the forces to the south.

Like Joffre in 1914, Eisenhower was willing to give up ground rather than let his line break. Patton (Third Army) was to disengage, make a tremendous left wheel, and drive northwards. The 6th Army Group in Alsace would have to take over Patton's sector in the Saar even if this meant giving ground in Alsace and perhaps abandoning Strasbourg. General de Gaulle was *not* pleased. But in fact the Germans were in no position to mount another offensive, and although the northern corner of Alsace was evacuated, Strasbourg itself was saved.

While Eisenhower was taking a grip on the situation, his front-line troops, though hard-pressed, were putting up a fight which compared more than favourably with the resistance of the French IXth Army in 1940. The unfortunate Corap had had few if any tanks. It was the American armour that won time for Eisenhower's measures to take effect. The 7th Armoured Division denied St Vith to the enemy until 21 December. Part of the 10th Armoured Division delayed von Manteuffel just long enough to allow 101st Airborne Division to establish itself in Bastogne.

Bastogne stood like a rock. Fifth Panzer Army, unable to drive through, had to go round, shedding considerable forces to contain the improvised fortress. Summoned to surrender 22 December Brigadier-General Anthony McAuliffe, a modern Cambronne, curtly answered "Nuts".

The Germans had not quite shot their bolt. Sixth Panzer Army got going again and Manteuffel's two panzer corps drove on westward and on Christmas Eve his 2nd Panzer Division was in sight of the Meuse, near Celles, three miles east of Dinant. But the attack had lost its momentum.

Meanwhile, the Allied counter-attack was getting under way. The weather had cleared and 5,000 Allied planes were strafing the transport strung out nose to tail all the way to the German frontier. In the words of General Arnold "We prepared to isolate the battlefield." Moreover it was air supply that saved Bastogne, while Patton pushed up from the south to its relief.

In the line north of the gap Montgomery had three American corps under Hodges (V, XVIII Airborne, and VII) with the British XXX Corps in reserve on the Meuse. Hodges' centre was still vulnerable and to shorten it Montgomery evacuated a salient round Vielsalm – *reculer pour mieux sauter* is no bad tactical axiom.

The US 2nd Armoured Division (VII Corps) cut off and destroyed Manteuffel's spearhead at Celles on Christmas Day. Next day the US 4th Armoured Division broke through to Bastogne. Thus ended the first phase of the battle.

By Christmas Day von Rundstedt realized that the battle had been lost, but Hitler was not the man to admit defeat or to cut his losses. Instead he thought up a new double offensive. He would begin by taking Bastogne and then, wheeling north, would take the First Army in flank while a secondary attack engaged it from the direction of Roermond. In the New Year he would mount yet another offensive in Alsace.

At the same time Eisenhower was planning a counter-offensive which had rather more substance. Bradley and Montgomery were to strike simultaneously.

Bastogne was still the storm centre. The corridor to the town was only a mile wide in places. Patton was determined to drive off the two German corps that were squeezing its lifeline. At the same time Manteuffel was concentrating for the attack which would rid him once and for all of this thorn in his flesh. On 30 December they met head on, and locked in a deadly winter battle which ranged blindly and fiercely through the snow-clad woods and ravines of the Ardennes.

By the time the battle died down the Germans were spent. On 8 January 1945 Hitler reluctantly agreed to limited withdrawals, and next day Patton broke out of Bastogne. Model, helped by a break in the weather, began to disengage his forces. On the 13th, owing to the Russian winter offensive, the German Supreme Command withdrew Sixth SS Panzer Army from the Ardennes battle, and permitted a general retreat. Patton and Hodges joined hands at Houffalize on the 16th and Bradley was able to resume command of his army and restore his original line. By 28 January it was all over.

The battle cost the Allies 76,980 casualties, but it ruined Hitler's last reserve army both morally and physically. The Germans lost 70,000 casualties and 50,000 prisoners, besides 500–600 tanks and 1,600 planes. The Russians had launched their great winter offensive on 12 January, and Hitler no longer had his *masse de manoeuvre* to meet it: a terrible price to pay for the six weeks delay it imposed on the Western Allies.

It was a great victory. Even so the Germans, though less well trained than three years earlier, had hacked a wound 50 miles deep in the American line. They had fought with all their old devotion. The more credit to the Americans who beat such men.

The part of the air forces must not be underrated. The *Luftwaffe* was still able to send over 700 aircraft on New Year's Day, 1945, to attack Allied airfields and to destroy nearly 200 planes on the ground. On 22 January the Anglo-American air forces claimed to have destroyed 4,200 pieces of heavy equipment; railway engines and trucks, tanks, motor and horse-drawn vehicles.

There are those who regard General Eisenhower as a very indifferent general, little more than a sort of Grand Liaison Officer. It is true that in the battle of the Ardennes his original lay-out was faulty. Major-General Fuller even goes so far as to say: "The enormity of Eisenhower's distribution can be measured by supposing that it had been made in May, 1940. Had it been, then there can be little doubt that his armies would have suffered a similar fate to Gamelin's." But this is going altogether too far, and ignores the fact that up to mid-December 1944 Eisenhower had had the initiative on the Western front, and was not simply sitting waiting to be attacked. Once the battle began he made the right decisions and he made them in time. In the event his 33 divisions mauled 26 German divisions.

One can only judge a general by his works, good or ill, and it seems to the present writer that Eisenhower's stature is greatly enhanced by this macabre winter battle.

> *Few, few shall part where many meet*
> *The snow shall be their winding sheet*
> *And every turf beneath their feet*
> *Shall be a soldier's sepulchre.*

    (Thomas Campbell, *Hohenlinden*)

Berlin (1945)

John Strawson

In all the talk that went on in the last months of the Second
World War about strategy and objectives and partitioning
Europe, one vital point was overlooked by everyone. It was
that the only military objective whose capture or elimination
could actually bring the war to an end lay in the person of
one man – Adolf Hitler. It was Hitler's will alone which
kept the German people on their dreadful path to destruction. He had made his intention clear to his generals on the
eve of the Ardennes offensive in December 1944: "We must
allow no moment to pass without showing the enemy that,
whatever he does, he can never reckon on a capitulation.
Never! Never!" Indeed he had already said it countless
times – in *Mein Kampf* and in his endless table talk years
before. "We shall not capitulate – no, never. We may be
destroyed, but if we are, we shall drag a world with us – a
world in flames."

The battle for Berlin turned this reckless prophecy into the
reality of *Götterdämmerung*. Albert Speer, technocrat, and
Minister of Armaments and War Production, described the
helplessness to which Hitler's miscalculations had reduced the
once mighty Reich: "Howling and exploding bombs, clouds
illuminated in red and yellow hues, droning motors and no
defence anywhere – I was stunned."

Before 1945, when it was hard to see how it could be done, both the Russians and the Western Allies had repeatedly named Berlin as their goal. But such definitions made little sense unless it was possible to make a proper plan to capture the city. This was not feasible until the beginning of 1945. Once the *Wehrmacht* had at last recognized that there was nothing left but a strategy of defense, in the East on the Vistula and in the West on the Rhine, once Germany itself was on the point of being invaded, that is in January 1945, the battle for Berlin – then only a few hundred miles away from each main enemy army – was on.

Planning the final battle of the war began in the Soviet High Command in October 1944. It was intended to advance from the Vistula to Berlin and beyond in six weeks. The offensive was to start on 20 January 1945. Later the date was brought forward to 12 January. Three army groups or "fronts" were to attack – 1st and 2nd Belorussian commanded respectively by Marshals Georgi K. Zhukov and Konstantin Rokossovski, and 1st Ukrainian under Marshal Ivan S. Koniev – 2.5 million men against fewer than a million Germans. The Russians' material superiority was even greater. When the attack started it had immediate and startling success. The Eastern Front collapsed, as Colonel General Heinz Guderian, Chief of the German General Staff, had forecast, like a house of cards. By early February the Red Army had reached the River Oder opposite Berlin. They were only 40 miles from the city. Here they paused.

Why did Stalin not push on after his first brilliant success? Was it simply that with Berlin virtually in the bag he wanted to get his hands on as much of SE Europe as he could? Still more interesting is the question he put to his generals: "Who is to capture Berlin, we or the Allies?" – and this at a time when it had already been agreed with the Americans that they would halt their armies well to the west of the city.

Zhukov maintained that because of so many casualties to men and equipment suffered during the January battles, difficulties of supply and air support, as well as the German counter-attack capability, further advance was impossible. Colonel General Vasili I. Chuikov, on the other hand, commanding 8th Guards Army under Zhukov, claimed that the war could have been

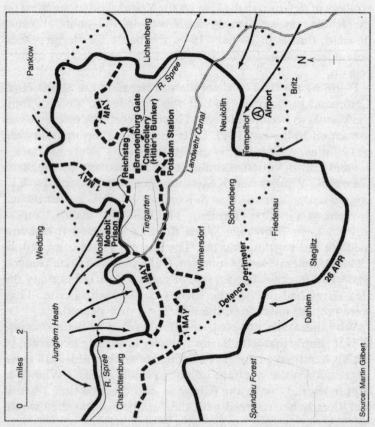

5.13 The Fall of Berlin, April–May 1945

Source: Martin Gilbert

ended in February. He also recorded that when on 4 February the advance on Berlin was being discussed, Stalin telephoned Zhukov and told him to halt the advance on the city and attack the German forces in Pomerania instead.

The result was that the final thrust on Berlin did not start until 16 April. Broadly, Zhukov was to take the city while Koniev would cut off the German Army Group Vistula from Berlin and secure Zhukov's southern flank. Zhukov had no illusions about the problems facing him:

> The unusual and highly complex offensive against Berlin required the most careful preparation at all front and army levels. Troops of the 1st Belorussian front were expected to break through a deeply echeloned defense zone extending from the Oder River all the way to heavily fortified Berlin. Never before in the experience of warfare had we been called upon to capture the city as large and as heavily fortified as Berlin. Its total area was almost 350 square miles. Its subway and other widespread underground engineering networks provided ample possibilities for troop movements. The city itself and its suburbs had been carefully prepared for defense. Every street, every square, every alley, building, canal and bridge represented an element in the city's defense system.

Yet four days after the attack started, his artillery opened up on Berlin and on 21 April the leading troops of three armies, 3rd Shock, 2nd Guards Tank and 47th broke into the outskirts of the city. The last phase of the battle had begun. Eleven days later on 2 May, General Helmuth Weidling, Berlin Commandant, surrendered. It was all over. The battle between 16 April and the German capitulation had cost the Red Army a terrible 300,000 casualties.

"How pitiful is their Berlin!" announced Marshal Zhukov after his troops had captured it. It was the Red Army and Allied bombing which had made it so. Yet the courage and perseverance of the Berliners themselves should not be forgotten. The long road to Berlin had cost the Russians 20 million men since that day almost four years earlier when the two great armies had clashed head on. And all of it had been brought about by the man who at the height of the fighting for Berlin conducted, or thought he conducted, the battle which he claimed would cause the Russians to suffer their bloodiest defeat.

That it was the Russians and not the Americans who reached Berlin first was because of decisions and actions taken during the first two weeks of April 1945. Lieutenant General William H. Simpson's US Ninth Army crossed the Elbe astride Magdeburg on 12 April, and reached Tangemunde – only 50 miles from Berlin. The Russians' next offensive was not planned to start for another four days, 16 April, and they were at this time 40 miles from Berlin on the Oder. The day before, Simpson asked General Omar N. Bradley to let his troops expand the Elbe bridgehead and push on in force for Berlin. That he would have got there seems more or less certain for he had suffered very few casualties and opposite him were only scattered, ill-equipped and untrained formations of General Walther Wenck's Twelfth Army which had no air support at all. Wenck commented: "If the Americans launch a major attack they'll crack our positions with ease. After all what's to stop them? There's nothing between here and Berlin." But Eisenhower vetoed the idea.

On the same day Stalin sent a message to the American Ambassador in Moscow to the effect that the Red Army was about to renew the offensive. The main thrust would be on Dresden with a subsidiary one on Berlin. This information was hardly accurate. The main Russian forces were directed at and astride the German capital. Could the *Wehrmacht* withstand the forthcoming Russian steamroller? Colonel General Gotthard Heinrici in command of Army Group Vistula (still called this although it had long since left the Vistula far away) had two armies – General Theodor Busse's Ninth Army, directly in the path between the Red Army and Berlin, and General Hasso von Manteuffel's Third *Panzer* Army which was on the Oder 30 miles NE of the city and was deployed as far north as Stettin. He would be attacked by three Russian Fronts – Rokossovski's aimed at Stettin, Zhukov's at Berlin and Koniev's at Dresden.

It took the Red Army only ten days from 16 April to surround Berlin. But it was by no means a walkover for them. The battle for the Seelow Heights, a critical position, was hard and costly. Despite all their superiority in artillery, the Russian troops came under heavy AT and machine-gun fire which took such a toll of the advancing troops that they were stopped. This caused Stalin to order Koniev to direct his armored forces on Berlin so that on 17 April two Soviet fronts were making for the city. This was too much for Busse's Ninth Army, and by 20 April the Germans defending the approaches to Berlin were overrun. One Russian witness, Konstantin Simonov, saw the remnants of a German battle group:

> In front of us lay Berlin, and to our right a forest clearing, now a chaos of jumbled tanks, cars, armored cars, trucks, special vehicles and ambulances. They had uprooted hundreds of trees, probably in an attempt to turn round and escape. In this black, charred confusion of steel, timber, guns, cases and papers, a bloody mess of mutilated corpses lay strewn along the clearing as far as the eye could see . . . Then I noticed a host of wounded men lying on greatcoats and blankets or leaning against tree trunks; some of them bandaged and others covered in blood, with no one to tend to them.

Before the Russian attack on the Oder position started, Heinrici had explained to Speer that there would be no proper battle for Berlin because the two wings of Army Group Vistula would simply withdraw respectively north and south of the city. But when it was clear to him that Zhukov had broken through, Heinrici did make an attempt to organize the *Volkssturm* (home guard) battalions to establish some defenses to the east of the city. But *Volkssturm* battalions without transport and with inadequate supplies of ammunition could never stop the Red Army.

On 20 April Soviet artillery began to shell Berlin. Next day 2nd Guards Tank, 3rd Shock and 47th Armies – all Zhukov's formations – reached the outskirts of the city. At the same time Koniev was moving forward with 3rd Guards Tank Army. Then with two huge pincer movements, the Russians encircled the German Ninth Army to the SE of Berlin and Berlin itself, while their spearheads pushed on to the Elbe. By 25 April the Russians had surrounded Berlin and contacted US forces at Torgau. Now there was only one thing left to do – take Berlin and finish the war in Europe.

Col. Gen. Chuikov has left his recollections of it all:

A battery of heavy howitzers was stationed on an open grassy space beside a wood. Dark, ragged clouds were sailing across the sky. The earth seemed to doze, shivering a little from time to time from shellfire in the distance. The gun crews had already run out the howitzers, and were awaiting the command to fire. The muzzles were trained on Berlin . . . on the fortifications of Fascist Berlin – "Fire!" The heavy shells flew up, cleaving the air with a whistling sound. The path had been opened. In the morning I went up to my observation post. It was in a large five-storeyed building near the Johannisthal aerodrome. From a corner room here, where there was a jagged hole in the wall, one got a view of the southern and southeastern parts of Berlin. Roofs, roofs without end, with here and there a break in them – the work of landmines. In the distance factory chimneys and church spires stood out. The parks and squares, in which the young leaves were already out seemed like little outbreaks of green flame. Mist lay along the streets, mingled with dust raised by the previous night's artillery fire. In places the mist was overlaid by fat trails of black smoke, like mourning streamers. And somewhere in the center of the city ragged yellow plumes rose skywards as bombs exploded. The heavy bombers had already started their preliminary "working-over" of the targets for the forthcoming attack . . . Suddenly the earth shuddered and rocked under my feet. Thousands of guns announced the beginning of the storming operation.

The "Fascist beast" himself had made much of making *Festung Berlin* an impregnable fortress. It was a myth. In March 1945 a "Basic Order for the Preparations to Defend the Capital" had been signed and issued, but little had been done to turn

Berlin into a proper defensive position. The city was defended more by words than deeds. The battle for Berlin would decide the war, Hitler claimed. So it did, but not in the way he meant. The Basic Order envisaged an outer perimeter about 20 miles out, another one 10 miles out, a third following the S-Bahn (the railway serving the suburbs), and a final citadel around the government buildings.

A plan was all it was without troops and weapons, ammunition and supplies or a proper command system to control everything. The battle for the city itself never really developed. It was simply a gigantic mopping-up operation. The Red Army isolated Berlin with overwhelming numbers. Then it slowly crushed the city's life. It was impossible to fight a full-scale battle there with nearly two million inhabitants, mostly old men or women and children living in shelters. Allied bombing had forced them below ground. In any event the military organization defending the city was a lame skeleton. So-called *Panzer* divisions had a mere dozen or so tanks and armored vehicles. After engaging the advancing Russians, they inevitably retreated, leaving the dead and wounded lying in the streets. The fighting itself was done in the midst of civilians who had themselves either been killed by rockets and shells, were cowering in cellars or desperately trying to find further cellars behind the retreating soldiers in order not to fall into Soviet hands. The streets were littered with bodies. Yet in some extraordinary way the spirit of the Berliners survived. They scrawled defiant messages on walls, proclaiming ultimate victory in spite of retreat. It was not the *Götterdämmerung* that Hitler had foreseen. But it had its moments of glory.

Up to 22 April Hitler was still nominally in charge of operations. One day earlier he directed his last battle. How did he conduct himself? First, he gave exact instructions to General Karl Koller, a *Luftwaffe* officer and Goering's Chief of Staff. When Goering had left the Bunker, Koller stayed. Like so many others he was unable to stand up to Hitler. Earnest and fussy, he would accept the Führer's raving invective and threats with misgiving but without dissent. Instead he would wring his hands and examine his conscience. On this occasion, as so often before, Hitler's orders were given in the greatest detail. He selected precisely which troops were to be brought back into reserve from the northern part of the city in order to launch a counter-attack on the Russians in the southern suburbs. He laid down exactly which ground units of the *Luftwaffe* were to be employed and in what way. The attack would be an all-out and final attempt to turn the tide. Every man, every gun and every tank would be committed, the *Luftwaffe* would put every available plane into the skies. All would be staked on a final desperate blow. An SS general, *Obergruppenfuehrer* (Lieutenant General) Felix Steiner, would command the operation.

The tactical plan for Steiner's attack was that it would be launched from the Eberswalde into the gap between von Manteuffel's Third *Panzer* Army and Busse's Ninth Army, so smashing the spearhead of Zhukov's drive on the city. But Army Group Steiner was a figment of Hitler's imagination. It had nothing like the strength required to mount an attack of the sort envisaged. Nonetheless Hitler told Steiner on the telephone to withdraw every man available between Berlin and the Baltic up to Stettin and Hamburg. The order was absurd. Steiner had no communication with any of these troops. Even had he the means of giving orders, there was no transport to move them. Yet when Steiner protested, Hitler broke in with an assurance that the Russians would suffer their bloodiest defeat before the gates of Berlin.

The shortage of troops was made up for by an abundance of threats. Commanding officers who did not thrust home would not live to tell the tale. Steiner's written instructions contained a specific promise that he was answerable with his life for the execution of his orders. "The fate of the Reich capital depends on the success of your mission." Koller too was assured that his own head would guarantee both the vigilance of the effort to be made and the success that would result. All was in vain. Hitler's granite willpower was powerless now. Skeleton German battalions could never hold back the fully manned and equipped Russian divisions. The attack never came off. It did not even cross the start-line. German withdrawal in the north simply allowed Russian tanks to stampede through to the center of Berlin. The Steiner attack had made a desperate military position still more hopeless.

Weidling, on the other hand, who became Commandant of Berlin on 25 April, knew the city was almost surrounded. That evening on reporting in the Bunker to the Führer and his entourage, he showed them from a sketch map that the ring around the city would soon be finally closed. In fact the ring was already closed. After explaining the dispositions of enemy and German forces, Weidling gave his view that despite the defenders' efforts, the Russians were slowly and surely advancing to the center of Berlin. The encirclement involved eight Soviet armies. On the same day, 25 April, Hitler ordered the *Wehrmacht* to re-establish contact with Berlin by attacking from the NW, SE and south – so bringing the battle of Berlin to "a victorious conclusion". The only troops Weidling had, would ever have, were some *Volkssturm* battalions, *Luftwaffe* ground personnel and Hitler Youth units, and the remainder of his own 56 *Panzer* Corps. These he organized into defense sectors.

Despite all these difficulties Weidling made a plan which he put to the Führer on 26 April for effecting Hitler's escape from the city. Hitler rejected it. He was not prepared to be caught wandering about somewhere in the woods: "I stay here to die at the head of my men. But you must continue to defend the city." While inspecting defenses that day Weidling saw little to comfort him:

The Potsdamer Platz and the Leipziger Strasse were under strong artillery fire. The dust from the rubble hung in the air like a thick fog . . . shells burst all round us. We were covered with bits of broken stones . . . The roads were riddled with shell craters and piles of brick rubble. Streets and squares lay deserted. Dodging Russian mortars we made our way to the underground station by jumps. The roomy underground station was crowded with terrified civilians. It was a shattering sight . . . Colonel Barenfanger, who commanded in this sector, pressed me for more men and more ammunition. I could promise him neither. Most of his men were *Volkssturm* troopers who had been sent into the exceptionally severe fighting with captured arms . . . No ammunition for these guns could be found in the whole of Berlin.

Exactly how Berlin would finally fall remained to be seen. Lieutenant Colonel Pavel Troyanovski, a "Red Star" correspondent, was there on the same day as Steiner's abortive attack:

It seemed as though we were confronted not by a town, but by a nightmare of fire and steel. Every house appeared to have been converted into a fortress. There were no squares or gardens, but only gun positions for artillery and mine throwers . . . Our guns sometimes fired a thousand shells on to one small square, a group of houses or even a tiny garden. Then the German firing points would be silenced, and the infantry would go into the attack . . . From house to house and street to street, from one district to another, mowing their way through gunfire and hot steel, went our infantrymen, artillery, sappers and tanks . . . On 25 April the German capital was completely encircled and cut off from the rest of the country. At the height of the street fighting Berlin was without water, without light, without landing fields, without radio stations. The city ceased to resemble Berlin.

On 23 April Stalin laid down the boundary between Zhukov and Koniev. The *Reichstag* (Parliament Building), where the Soviet flag was to be raised, was given to Zhukov. His soldiers captured the *Reichstag* and ran up the Red flag at about 1430 on 30 April – an hour before Hitler committed suicide. But German resistance, recalled one German soldier, continued in the hands of an SS officer:

The close combat boys went into action. Their leader was SS-*Obersturmführer* [First Lieutenant] Babick, battle commandant of the *Reichstag*. Babick now waged the kind of war he had always dreamed of. Our two battery commanders, Radloff and Richter, were reduced to taking orders from him. Babick's command post was not in the *Reichstag* itself but in the cellar of the house on the corner of Dorotheenstrasse and the Hermann Goring Strasse, on the side nearer the Spree. There he ruled from an air-raid shelter measuring some 250 sq ft. Against the wall stood an old sofa and in front of it a dining table on which a map of the center of Berlin was spread out. Sitting on the sofa was an elderly marine commander and next to him two petty officers. There were also a few SS men and, of course, SS-*Obersturmführer* Babick bending over his map. He played the great general and treated everyone present in the dim candle-lit room to great pearls of military wisdom. He kept talking of final victory, cursed all cowards and traitors and left no one in any doubt that he would summarily shoot anyone who abandoned the Führer.

Babick was tremendously proud of his successes. He was hoping for reinforcements. From somewhere or another, marines had come to Berlin on the night of 28 April, led by the very Lieutenant-Commander who was now hanging about the cellar with nothing to say for himself. Babick never moved from his map, plotting the areas from which he expected reinforcements and even the arrival of "Royal Tigers" [heavy tanks]. Babick was still bubbling over with confidence. For one thing, he thought himself perfectly safe in his shelter. SS sentries were posted outside, others barred the corridor to the *Reichstag*, and Royal Tigers, our finest weapons, were apparently just around the corner. He had divided his men into groups of five to ten. One group was commanded by SS-*Untersturmführer* [Second Lieutenant] Undermann; he was posted south of the Moltke Bridge in the Ministry of the Interior (the building the Russians called "Himmler's House") and the bridge itself lay in his line of fire.

Then an SS ensign, aged about 19, came to Babick with the report that Undermann and his men had come across some alcohol and that they had got roaring drunk. As a precaution he had brought Undermann along; he was waiting outside. Babick roared out the order: "Have him shot on the spot!" The ensign clicked his heels and ran out. Seconds later we heard a burst of fire from a submachine-gun. The boy reappeared and reported: "Orders carried out." Babick put him in charge of Undermann's unit. Our ranks in the *Reichstag* got thinner and thinner. Part of our battery gradually dispersed, and by the night of 30 April, no more than 40 to 50 people, soldiers and civilians, were left in the cellar. This remnant was now busy looking for the safest possible hiding-places. There we intended to sit tight until the Russians came. But they kept us waiting for another 24 hours. At dawn on 1 May, we heard over our portable radio that the Führer had "fallen in the battle for the *Reich* Capital," his wife at his side. Goebbels and his family had gone the same way. We were our own masters, at long last.

The only thing still to be done was to negotiate with the Russians in order to surrender what was left of the city. By this time all that was left in German hands were the Government buildings, part of the adjoining *Tiergarten* and the area between the Zoo and the Havel river. Hitler had forbidden Weidling to capitulate but he had authorized a break-out. After Hitler's death Martin Bormann, the Deputy Führer, had sent a telegram to Admiral Karl Dönitz in Plön, appointing him as Hitler's successor. Dönitz, not realizing that Hitler was dead, replied: "My Führer! My loyalty to you will be unconditional. I shall do everything possible to relieve you in Berlin. If fate nevertheless compels me to rule the Reich as your appointed successor, I shall continue this war to an end, worthy of the unique, heroic struggle of the German people." But Goebbels and Bormann were trying above all to put an end to the pointless bloodshed. They therefore made contact with the Russians who agreed to receive a German representative.

This was Lieutenant General Hans Krebs, Chief of the General Staff since Guderian's dismissal on 28 March, who spoke Russian and had been in Moscow as Military Attache. He met Gen. Chuikov, Commander of the 8th Guards Tank Army, at Schulenburgring near Tempelhof Airport, at 0400 on the morning of 1 May. He had been authorized to negotiate only a truce or armistice, but the Russians, despite suspicions that the Western Allies were contemplating a separate peace with the German armies in the West, refused to consider anything except unconditional surrender. When Krebs referred to 1 May as a day which their two nations shared as a holiday,

Chuikov drily observed that it might be a fine day in Moscow, but he could not say the same for Berlin. Thus Krebs failed and he committed suicide after returning to the Bunker. Next Weidling tried to negotiate. On the following morning he crossed the line dividing the two armies and surrendered the Berlin garrison with its 70,000 troops. The battle for Berlin was over. The question now was how would the Russians behave?

Rape, looting, burning and murder became commonplace. Hitler's very last War Directive of 15 April had made it clear what fate threatened a defeated Germany: "While the old men and children will be murdered, the women and girls will be reduced to barrack-room whores." Even at the end Hitler's reliance on propaganda and foresight did not desert him. But better things were on the way for Berlin. The Red Army positioned more disciplined regiments there: American troops reached the city on 1 July; the British arrived next day.

Iwo Jima (1945)

Paul M. Kennedy

Iwo Jima made an unremarked appearance on the island-littered map of the Pacific when, over 70 years ago, an underwater volcano spewed out ash and mud. The eight square miles of barren ash and soft, freshly formed rock might have remained in obscurity but for the strategic significance of this speck of land in the battle for the Pacific in the Second World War. Vital to the American campaign of rolling back the newly acquired Pacific empire of the Japanese to attack the enemy homeland, the grim battle for the tiny island lasted over a month and at the end 5,800 Americans and nearly 22,000 Japanese lay dead. Seizure of the island would deny the Japanese an excellent strategic base and give the Americans a bomber base only 660 nautical miles from Tokyo. Previous bombing missions had flown from the Marianas, 2,800 miles from Japan – a range which precluded fighter escort and led to heavy B29 Super-fortress casualties. Iwo Jima was also a necessary link in the air defenses of the Marianas and it had to be captured, not merely isolated. There was a final consideration – the island was traditionally Japanese territory, administered from Tokyo, and its fall would be a severe psychological blow to the enemy.

Such blows were important. The Japanese had expanded their empire at a phenomenal rate. In the first five months of 1942 they had captured territory stretching from Burma in the west, through the Malay archipelago, to the central Pacific island groups of the Gilberts and the Marshalls. Control of these islands, small in size, gave them air command of the surrounding area, and command of the skies was vital to control of the seas.

The Americans responded in two ways. They built up fast carrier-based forces which could gain command of the air in disputed areas, from which land and sea control could follow. To gain land control they devised sophisticated amphibious assault techniques to capture island bases. The land targets were so small that such invasions were, in reality, direct attacks on fortified positions and the landing was not an orthodox preliminary move, it was the battle itself.

Naval victories at the Coral Sea on 7 May 1942 and a month later at Midway, on 4–5 June, started the American comeback. On 7 August, 19,000 Marines under Major General Alexander A. Vandegrift landed on the island of Guadalcanal in the southern Solomons. The move took the local Japanese commanders by surprise and there was no need for an amphibious assault. On the nearby island of Tulagi, however, the Marines had a grim struggle with the local garrison and learned their first lesson – that the Japanese soldier, even if his position was hopeless, would fight to the death rather than surrender.

The next step in the Pacific re-conquest was a two-pronged assault. General Douglas MacArthur thrust into the south-west Pacific, taking the Solomons, isolating Rabaul on the island of New Britain, and "hopping" along the northern coast of New Guinea. Admiral Chester W. Nimitz's central Pacific forces captured the Gilbert, Marshall and Mariana groups, and isolated the Carolines. So swift was the American drive that on 20 October 1944 the re-conquest of the Philippines began, against which the Japanese could offer only sporadic resistance after their naval defeat at Leyte Gulf.

The US Marines played a decisive part in the drive across the Pacific, particularly in the central Pacific advance. In their first attack, against the Gilbert Islands in November 1943, the Corps suffered heavy losses in the confused and bloody assault on Tarawa. Yet they learned a lot from the assault and in later and larger operations in the Marshalls and Marianas the benefits of

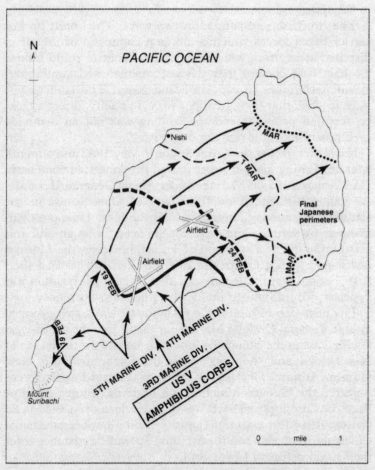

Inside the map, the following labels appear:

N

PACIFIC OCEAN

• Nishi

11 MAR

7 MAR

Final
Japanese
perimeters

Airfield

24 FEB

11 MAR

Airfield

19 FEB

19 FEB

Mount
Suribachi

5TH MARINE DIV.   4TH MARINE DIV.

3RD MARINE DIV.

US V
AMPHIBIOUS CORPS

0   mile   1

5.14 The Campaigns in the Pacific, 1943–5

earlier experience were clearly revealed. Now, at the beginning of 1945, with Japan pushed almost back to her national boundaries, the Marines were preparing for their toughest assignment yet – the assault on Iwo Jima.

The Japanese were also aware of Iwo Jima's importance and began speedy reinforcement towards the end of 1944. A garrison of 23,000 men under Lieutenant General Tadamichi Kuribayashi was sent to the island with orders to hold out as long as possible – American air and naval superiority ruled out further reinforcement. Kuribayashi was a courageous and dedicated soldier, described by Tokyo Radio as one whose "partly protruding belly is packed full of strong fighting spirit."

The Japanese took with them 120 big guns of over 75 mm caliber, 300 anti-aircraft guns of over 25 mm, 20,000 small guns, including machine-guns, 130 8 cm and 12 cm howitzers, 20 20 cm mortars, 70 20 cm rocket-guns, 40 47 mm and 20 37 mm anti-tank guns, and 27 tanks. The building of pillboxes began in October 1944 and five months later 360 were complete. A superb network of deep, interconnected caves, which were almost impervious to naval bombardment, was built. All this on an island of eight square miles.

Adm. Nimitz entrusted overall control of the Iwo Jima operation to Admiral Raymond Spruance's Fifth Fleet which, with its fast carrier and battleship units supported by a mobile fleet train, was the most powerful naval body in the world. Its role was to give distant cover against enemy air or naval attack and to participate in the bombardment of the island. Rear Admiral Richmond Kelly Turner, probably the most experienced leader of amphibious operations during the Second World War, was given command of the landings. The US troops, 84,000 in all, were to come from 4th and 5th Marine Divisions, with 3rd Marine Division in floating reserve, along with Major General Harry Schmidt's 5th Marine Amphibious Corps.

Major General Groves B. Erskine's 3rd Division had fought at Guam and Bougainville and the 4th Division, under General Clifton B. Cates, had seen action at Saipan and Tinian. Major General Keller E. Roche's 5th Division did not have combat experience but they were trained and strengthened by many veterans. Lieutenant General "Howlin' Mad" Smith, the vigorous leader of the Marine Division at Guadalcanal and now commander of the Fleet Marine Force, Pacific, was the commanding general of the Expeditionary troops. With such a tried team of commanders and good calibre soldiers, there was little doubt about the eventual outcome of the invasion. The question was, how easy – or difficult – would the Marines find the assault?

From late 1944 the most intensive softening up yet of the Pacific War began. Army bombers flew raids by day, Marine ones by night with ever-increasing intensity in the weeks leading up to the invasion, which was scheduled for 19 February 1945. Three days before the landings, Admiral William Blandy's Amphibious Support Force, which included five battleships, began an intensive bombardment of the island. At the same time, Spruance supervised carrier forces in their aerial attacks on Honshu to prevent any possible Japanese air strikes against the invasion fleet.

The shelling of Iwo Jima proved completely inadequate, as Schmidt had forecast in repeated requests for a longer, ten-day bombardment. The Americans received a shock on 17 February when 11 of 12 gunboats supporting beach demolition teams were sunk by enemy fire. Blandy realized from this that the island's defenses were far heavier than had been expected and accepted Schmidt's advice to concentrate bombardment on the beaches and nearby areas. Iwo Jima, like Tarawa, was so small that it was virtually all beach – unless enemy fire could be neutralized before the assault the Marines would be completely exposed.

The "gunboat incident" benefited the Americans in two ways. It forced a reassessment of the enemy defenses and also exposed many Japanese gun positions. It seems unlikely that the orders to open fire came from high-ranking commanders – the first of Kuribayashi's "Essential Battle Instructions" demanded that "while the enemy bombardment is going on, we must take cover in the dugouts and we must keep our casualties to a minimum." Kuribayashi was swift to order redeployment of the guns that had opened fire.

With a broad rocky plateau in the north and the extinct volcano of Mount Suribachi at the southern tip of the porkchop shaped island of Iwo Jima, the only place a full-scale invasion could be mounted was on the black cinder beaches along the south-east coast. From this point it was only a short distance to airfield No. 1; but a landing here also meant that the open beaches would be subjected to an intense fire from higher ground to the north and the south.

At 0640 on 19 February, just before sunrise, Blandy's ships, now reinforced by two battleships and 13 cruisers from Spruance's fleet, opened up with a stupendous close-range bombardment of the island. The astonishing number of 450 ships ringed the island. Blasted by shells ranging from five-inch to 16-in in diameter, the beaches seemed to be torn apart. Shortly afterwards, rocket-firing gunboats attacked the Motoyama plateau while other gunboats lobbed mortar rounds at Mount Suribachi. Then, as the firing was temporarily checked and the various ships moved into their final positions, carrier aircraft and heavy bombers from the Marianas showered the areas surrounding the beaches with rockets, napalm and bombs. After a further ten minutes the naval shelling recommenced, joined by ten destroyers and over 50 gunboats which steamed as close inshore as possible in an effort to screen the approaching invasion armada. The whole co-ordinated action was immensely impressive – one history of the battle describes the bombardment as "a power-laden deployment packing the utmost momentum yet devised by the mind and engineering of man. This was the acme of amphibious assault."

As the naval bombardment, now a creeping barrage, reached its crescendo, the landing-ships lowered their ramps and the first of the five assault waves emerged, 5,500 yards from the shore. Each wave consisted of 69 amphtracs, armored amphibian tractors which could take 20 troops each right onto the beach and scramble over coral reefs if necessary. The first wave, the 4th Marine Division on the right, the 5th on the left, moved virtually undisturbed towards the shore. At 0902, after 30 minutes' steaming, the amphtracs hit the beach, spewing out their men and the armored mortar and rocket-firing vehicles.

They were immediately up against two unexpected physical obstacles – black volcanic ash into which men sank up to a foot or more, and a steep terrace 15 ft high in some places, which only a few amphtracs managed to climb. Most stayed on the beach, getting in the way of oncoming waves, while the troops jumped out and struggled through the ash. One Marine described how he "tried to sprint up the terrace wall but my feet only bogged in the sand and instead of running I crawled, trying to keep my rifle clean but failing." Fresh waves of assault troops arrived every five minutes and soon 10,000 men and 400 vehicles were on the beach. Despite inevitable confusion the first combat patrols pushed 150 yards inland, then 300. And then the enemy opened up.

From rabbit-holes, bunkers and pillboxes, small arms and machine-gun fire crashed into the Marines. Heavy artillery and mortars, from deep emplacements and caves on Suribachi and the Motoyama plateau, and trained exactly on the beaches well in advance, thundered out, destroying men and machines. The Japanese garrison, true to their orders, had withheld fire during the landings – only five amphtracs were lost from the early waves. As the momentum of the assault slowed at the terrace and the creeping barrage out-distanced the Marines, the defenders nearest the beach were able to recover and man their weapons. The ash on the beach cushioned all but direct blasts from the mortars and artillery – but one war correspondent stated that "nowhere . . . have I seen such badly mangled bodies." It soon became clear that to stay on the beach was near-suicide – but to move off it meant moving into fire from the well-developed defense system.

At this point – and probably only here – the outcome of the battle was in doubt. If the Japanese had mounted a counter-attack, they might have routed the disorganized Marines. But the lessons of Tarawa, Roi-Namur, Saipan and Guam were that furious counter-assaults upon the invaders simply exposed the defenders to the overwhelming American firepower. Kuribayashi's task was to deny Iwo Jima to the enemy for as long as possible and his troops were ordered to stay strictly on the defensive. Many of the guns were firing only sporadically to conserve their ammunition, although no one at the beach-head would have believed this. The initiative still lay with the Marines – they and their equipment were successfully ashore. Now they could, they *must*, go forward.

Slowly, desperately slowly, the Marines pushed inland, a confused collection of small groups rather than a united force. Each bunker, each rabbit-hole meant a fight to the death. Each enemy position was supported by many others – the Japanese would disappear down one hole and pop up at another, often behind rather than in front of the advancing Marines. The Marines struggled on, pouring bullets, grenades and flame into enemy positions. Flail tanks rumbled forward with the Marines, detonating land mines, tank-dozers carved channels through the terrace and ordinary tanks relieved the pressure on the Marines by knocking out machine-gun nests and pillboxes. But it was no pushover, even with the armor. Facing 4th Division's lines, for example, were ten reinforced concrete blockhouses, seven covered artillery positions and 80 pillboxes. A battalion commander asserted that "whenever a man showed himself in the lines it was almost certain death." By mid-afternoon the reserve battalions of four regimental combat teams and two tank battalions had been committed to the battle to relieve the pressure on the leading units.

As dusk fell on this first, bloody day of the campaign, the numbers of Marines had risen to 30,000, with the committal ashore of the reserve regiments for both divisions. On the left flank Colonel Harry B. Liversedge's 28th Regiment had pushed across to the ridge which overlooked the beaches on the south-west; but fierce enemy opposition had halted its progress towards its main target, Mount Suribachi. Next in line was Colonel Thomas A. Wornham's 27th Regiment, which had similarly been brought to a halt in its efforts to overrun airfield No. 1. Farther to the right were the two regiments of the 4th Division, Colonel Walter W. Wensinger's 23rd Marines and Colonel John R. Lanigan's 25th Marines; both had come under extremely heavy fire from the entire Motoyama plateau area, and the 25th Regiment, being farthest on the right, suffered many casualties – one battalion had only 150 men left in the front line.

Although the Marines had failed to reach their first day's objectives, they had secured a foothold and, aided by the inflow of reserves, were digging in to await the expected counter-attack. It didn't come. Instead, the Japanese kept up a deadly accurate mortar and artillery fire against the beaches, causing great damage and loss of life. Most feared of all were the 60 kg and 250 kg bombs which the Japanese had converted into rockets, which came screaming out of the blue to burst upon impact. "A nightmare in hell" was one description of the scene.

On the second morning, after a 50-minute naval bombardment, the Marines moved on again. But progress was, if anything, even slower than on the previous day. Liversedge's 28th Regiment, making repeated attacks upon the approaches to Mount Suribachi with the aid of artillery, half-tracks and destroyers positioned nearby, advanced only 200 yards that day. To the north the 4th Division reached their objectives on No. 1 airfield and then swung right to face the rising ground that constituted Kuribayashi's first major defense line. Here, too, early progress soon petered out. On the next day this line remained virtually static but the 28th Regiment, again assisted by naval and aerial bombardment, penetrated almost to the foot of Suribachi.

The rugged volcanic mountain, rising steeply out of the sea to a height of 556 ft, was not of central importance to the defense of Iwo Jima. Yet it offered fine observation and artillery siting positions and, because of its imposing appearance, control of it tended to symbolize mastery of the island. Recognizing that it would soon be cut off, Kuribayashi had allocated only 1,860 men to its defense; but to its natural advantages had been added several hundred blockhouses, pillboxes and covered guns around its base together with an intricate system of caves in the slopes. As always, each position had to be taken separately, using a variety of weapons: mortars, tanks, rockets, flame-throwers and dynamite. When the Marines reached the caves, they went in with knives to kill the Japanese in close combat. Some of the defenders, out of ammunition, were reduced to rolling stones down the slopes, but still they fought on. By the morning of 23 February, the Marines were approaching the summit and 40 men under Lieutenant Harold Schrier carried an American flag to signify their victory. At 1020 it was raised amid cheers while fighting was still going on in the vicinity; and at noon it was replaced by a much larger flag. The planting of the second flag was photographed by Joe Rosenthal of Associated Press and the picture became probably the most famous of the entire war.

The end of the campaign was far from in sight – the worst had yet to come. Anticipating a fierce struggle, the Americans had committed the 3rd Marine Division on the same day to the middle of the front line, with the 4th on the right and the 5th on the left, and General Schmidt had come ashore to take direct control of what was the largest group of Marines yet to fight under a single command. Only 2,630 yards of island were left but it was obvious that every one was to be paid for dearly.

Kuribayashi had systematically turned the plateau region into an armed camp. Rockets, artillery and mortars, one a 320 mm weapon that lobbed 700 lb shells, were in good supply and blockhouses and pillboxes were numerous. Caves were elaborate and well fortified – one could hold 2,000 troops and had 12 exits – and the defenders were well trained and in high morale. They were prepared to hold a position to the death, infiltrate Marine lines, or throw themselves under an enemy tank with a bomb strapped to their backs. It was all deadly, frighteningly inhuman. Admiral Turner called it "as well defended as any fixed position that exists in the world today."

Fortunately this kind of operation was exactly what the Marines were trained for. During the Pacific War, as they fought from one atoll to the next, the Marines endured a much more personal and individual form of combat than that seen in actions in Western Europe or North Africa, and against a fanatical enemy who would not surrender.

To reduce the casualties of the attacking force, weapons of modern military technology were brought to their aid. The Japanese positions were bombarded by the guns of warships, they were battered by heavy bombers, the rockets and machine-guns of fighters, as well as dive-bombers. Tanks, artillery, mortar and rockets hammered the positions, flame-throwers scorched them, and dynamite blasted them. But the Marines knew, as they looked ahead over the next ridge, along the next gully, that the capture of virtually every position also involved close-in fighting – with machine-gun, pistol, grenade, knife, digging-tool, even hands – before the defenders were fully overcome. This was how the hell on earth of Iwo Jima had to be taken.

The battle for the second airfield, sited almost in the dead center of the island, was typical of this form of fighting. There the Japanese had constructed hundreds of pillboxes, rabbit-holes and concealed emplacements, which defied the concentrated American firepower for two days. On 24 February, the two battalions of the 21st Marine Regiment rushed forward to take the enemy lines with bayonet and grenade, the terrain being too difficult for tanks. Not only did the Japanese fire upon them from all their entrenched positions, but many rushed into the open and engaged in a struggle reminiscent of some medieval carnage, with the bayonet as the key weapon. Casualties rose steeply on both sides. The Marines, thrown back by this fierce counter-attack, re-formed and charged again. By nightfall of the next day, they had captured the airfield and were pressing towards Motoyama village, with only the prospect of another bitter struggle ahead: to the right of them lay the formidable Hill 382, a position which became so difficult to secure that the Marines referred to it ominously as "the Meat Grinder".

The fighting in the days following was the same. The Americans had to take the higher, central part of the enemy's lines first, for whenever the 4th and 5th Divisions pushed ahead on their respective flanks they were heavily punished by the Japanese who overlooked them. The problem was that it was this middle zone where it was hardest to deploy tanks and artillery, or to direct the naval support fire with accuracy. Although the elements on the flanks helped, the Marines had the main job, the slow and deadly job, of clearing the area. By the tenth day of the fighting, though, the supporting fire for the 3rd Division had been substantially increased and the forward battalions found a weak spot in the Japanese line, and poured through. By evening Motoyama, now a heap of stones and rubble, was taken and the Marines could look down upon the third airfield. Once again, though, further momentum was broken by Kuribayashi's second major defense line, and there remained many areas to wipe up. Hill 382 was fiercely held by its defenders for two more days, and Hill 362 in the west was equally difficult. The whole operation was taking much longer than the ten days Schmidt had estimated for it, and the Marines were tired and depleted in their ranks: some units were down to 30 per cent of their original strength.

On Sunday 5 March, the three divisions regrouped and rested as best they could in the face of Japanese shellings and occasional infiltration. On that day, too, the Marines had the satisfaction of seeing a B29 with a faulty fuel valve returning to Tinian from a raid on Tokyo make an emergency landing on airstrip No. 1. Iwo Jima was already fulfilling its function.

For the Japanese, the situation was serious. Most of Kuribayashi's tanks and guns and over two-thirds of his officers had been lost. His troops were in a serious position, reduced to such desperate measures as strapping explosives to their backs and throwing themselves under American tanks. The Marines were moving relentlessly forward, however slowly, and this forced a gradual breakdown in Kuribayashi's communications system. This meant that, left to their own devices, individual Japanese officers tended to revert to the offensive. This may have been more appealing to the Samurai but it exposed the greatly depleted Japanese forces to the weight of American firepower. One attack, by 1,000 naval troops on the night of 8–9 March, was easily repulsed by 4th Marine Division with Japanese losses of over 800 men. The pressure on the defending forces was starting to tell; they were losing their cohesion.

On the afternoon of 9 March, a patrol from the 3rd Marine Division reached the north-eastern coast of Iwo Jima and sent back a sample of salt water to prove that the enemy's line had been cut in two. There was no stopping the American advance but even now there was no sign of Japanese surrender – the only indication of their desperate condition was the increasing number of "banzai" charges. Kuribayashi's reports, however, describe the deteriorating situation: 10 March. American bombardment "so fierce I cannot express nor write of it here"; 11 March. "Surviving strength of northern districts (army and navy) is 1,500 men"; 14 March. "Attack on northern district this morning. Much more severe than before. Around noon one part of the enemy with about ten tanks broke through our left front line and approached to 220 yards of divisional HQ"; 15

March. "Situation very serious. Present strength of northern district about 900 men."

On 14 March the Americans, believing all organized resistance to be at an end, declared Iwo Jima occupied and raised the Stars and Stripes. Yet underground, in their warren of caves and tunnels, the Japanese lived on. Kuribayashi told the survivors on 17 March: "Battle situation come to last moment. I want surviving officers and men to go out and attack enemy until the last. You have devoted yourself to the Emperor. Do not think of yourselves. I am always at the head of you all."

Clearing out pockets of organized resistance with tanks, demolition teams, rifle fire and flame-throwers took until 26 March. On this day the Japanese staged their last desperate fling when 350 troops rushed an Air Force and Seabee (Civil Engineers of the US Navy) construction camp. They were destroyed by a Marine pioneer battalion after a day of wild fighting. Kuribayashi committed suicide in the northern corner of Iwo Jima in the last few days of the battle. He promised that to help revive the Japanese army after his death, "I will turn into a spirit." One US Marine hoped that "the Japs don't have any more like him."

Only 216 Japanese had surrendered by 26 March; 20,000 were dead. In the following two months 1,600 Japanese were killed and another 370 captured as sporadic resistance was crushed. The American casualties, considering their air and sea control and their superior firepower, were equally daunting. A total of 275 officers and 5,610 men of the Marine Corps were killed and 826 officers and 16,446 men were wounded. Thirty per cent of the entire landing force and a staggering 75 per cent of the infantry regiments of the 4th and 5th Divisions were battle casualties. So depleted were some units during the action that one battalion commander commented that "the appearance of a war dog and its handlers seemed like heavy reinforcements." Twenty-four Medals of Honor were awarded and there were 2,648 "combat fatigue casualties" – both facts telling evidence of the gruelling nature of the battle for Iwo Jima.

Iwo Jima soon justified the strategic value which the Joint Chiefs of Staff and, in particular, the Air Force had attached to it. Before the end of the war against Japan, more than 20,000 crewmen in crippled planes had landed upon the island's airstrips; and from 7 April onwards, thanks to the efforts of the Seabee construction units, Mustang fighters were able to escort the daylight raids of the Superfortresses against Tokyo and other Japanese cities.

General Smith called the battle "the toughest we've run across in 168 years" but also insisted that "When the capture of an enemy position is necessary to winning a war it is not within our province to evaluate the cost in money, time, equipment, or most of all, in human life. We are told what our objective is to be and we prepare to do the job." Admiral Nimitz summed up the achievement of the assault troops: "Among the Americans who served on Iwo Island, uncommon valor was a common virtue."

6
The Korean War

Inchon (1950)

Sydney L. Mayer

The Inchon landings of September 1950 were to prove the turning point of the war in Korea. General Douglas MacArthur conceived of the landings as a way of breaking the Communist stranglehold on the South. When UN forces had succeeded in taking Inchon they were to push on to the main prize – the South Korean capital, Seoul. The struggle for the control of this city was to prove the most savage of the whole war.

On Saturday 24 June 1950 United States President Harry S. Truman heard some grim news. Secretary of State Dean Acheson telephoned – the North Koreans had invaded South Korea. He advised the President to call on the United Nations Security Council to declare that an act of aggression had taken place. The following day Acheson called again. There was no doubt that a full-scale invasion had taken place but the United Nations was unlikely to do more than call for a ceasefire – and the call would probably be ignored. The United States therefore had to decide what degree of support, if any, it would give to South Korea.

The Japanese surrender in August 1945 left the US and Russia in Korea and they decided on the 38th Parallel as a purely military demarcation line between their two forces. In September 1947 the US turned the Korean problem over to the UN. By this time Korea had become a pawn in the rivalry

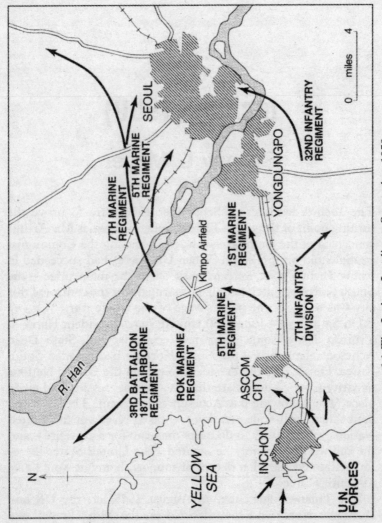

6.1 The Inchon Landings, September 1950

between the two major world power blocs. A UN call for all-Korean elections was ignored by the Russians and elections were held in the South only. In August 1948 the Republic of Korea (ROK) was established in the south under the veteran nationalist Dr Syngman Rhee. In September the Democratic People's Republic of Korea was created in the north, with former guerilla leader Kim Il Sung as premier. There were now two mutually antagonistic Korean regimes, each claiming rights to the whole country and each backed by one of the two world power blocs. Sporadic fighting took place along the 38th Parallel and though the US believed an invasion of the south was possible, Acheson admitted that "its launching in the summer of 1950 did not appear imminent."

Despite appearances, it had happened. President Truman, like most Americans, was acutely aware of the dangers of appeasement. The dictators had not been stopped in 1931 when Japan invaded Manchuria; in 1935 when Mussolini invaded Abyssinia or in 1938 when Hitler marched into Austria. The result was a massive and bloody war. If the US did not react to the agression, so the reasoning went, the Communists would seek to extend their conquests and this would inevitably lead to a third world war. There were pressing domestic considerations too – failure to act would encourage the arch witch-hunter of Communists, Senator Joseph McCarthy, to charge the government with appeasement, possibly fostered by subversives within the President's own staff.

In Washington, the State and Defense Departments presented joint recommendations. General Douglas MacArthur, then stationed in Japan, was ordered to evacuate all Americans from Korea but to attempt to keep the key airports open. The US air force was to remain south of the 38th Parallel and ammunition and supplies for the South Korean army were to be delivered by air drop and other means. The Seventh Fleet was to sail to the Formosa Strait to prevent any possible conflict between the nationalist Chinese on Formosa and the Chinese Communist mainland. American policy had altered – Korea and Formosa now fell within the US defense perimeter.

To MacArthur, news of the invasion was like a nightmare, a repetition of Pearl Harbor. As soon as he received orders from

Washington he sent aircraft to evacuate Americans from Korea but did nothing else. But soon, orders came to commit US troops to the field and MacArthur took immediate action.

Events had given MacArthur a new role. After a successful military career in the Second World War and a smoothly run administration of post-war Japan, MacArthur had little more to look forward to than an honored retirement. Now, as commander of US, and later UN, forces in Korea he had another chance of glory and fame in the field. Thrilled by the challenge, MacArthur prepared his staff for his last great military campaign.

In the meantime, the UN voted to support American operations in Korea. MacArthur was now leader of a nominal UN force – nominal because, especially at the start, the only active participants were the retreating South Koreans and whatever American forces could be shipped or flown from Japan.

By the start of July, North Korean forces had crossed the Han river, pushing streams of dispirited ROK forces before them. At the same time, the first US combat troops arrived in Korea. MacArthur's arrogant hope that the North Koreans might "turn round and go back when they found out who was fighting" came to nothing and on 19 July North Korean tanks smashed through American defenses at Taejon and rolled towards the Naktong river, the last major natural obstacle guarding the Pusan perimeter.

The Pusan perimeter was a 140-mile line running west and north of Pusan, from the Korea Strait to the Sea of Japan. Organized by Lieutenant General William Walker, commander of the US 8th Army in Korea, the Pusan perimeter held out against intensive North Korean pressure while US tanks, artillery and troops arrived through the port to reinforce the bridgehead. UN aircraft flew sorties against North Korean supply lines and the enemy's failure to mass forces for a decisive penetration at one point along the perimeter also contributed to the Americans' ability to hold the line.

By September 1950, the situation was deadlocked along the Pusan perimeter. Although North Korean forces seemed unable or unwilling to launch a major attack against the perimeter line,

ROK and American forces were not of sufficient strength for a land assault on the enemy lines.

MacArthur considered that the only way out of the impasse was to attempt an amphibious landing behind enemy lines. The risks involved in such an action were enormous. Failure would result in irreparable damage to UN credibility in Korea and devalue the stature of the organization. Its ability to effectively intervene in any crisis situation would be greatly impaired.

The idea of landing at Inchon dated back to MacArthur's first visit to Korea following the start of open war between North and South. North Korean supply lines were stretched to the limit. A landing at Inchon would force the enemy to fight on two fronts. The result of this, MacArthur calculated, would be the total breakdown of enemy supply lines. As a result, they would be forced to withdraw from the Pusan perimeter within weeks.

If a landing at Inchon was successful the UN would enjoy a considerable propaganda boost. It would also make possible the recapture of Seoul, the South Korean capital, 18 miles to the east.

Codenamed Operation Chromite, plans for the Inchon landings went ahead. Meanwhile, thousands of reservists were sent from the West Coast of the United States to Japan. The first objective was to capture the island of Wolmi-do, at the entrance to the port of Inchon. Once taken, large numbers of troops could be brought forward, and the island would act as a springboard for the invasion proper.

The next step was to capture the city of Inchon itself. The prime objective – the recapture of Seoul – would now be in the UN forces' grasp. To make this possible, Kimpo – Seoul's major airport – had to be taken. At the same time as preventing the North Koreans from bringing in reinforcements, control of the airport would allow the UN to do just that.

MacArthur fervently believed that the North Koreans would be forced to retreat. He thought that, while fleeing, they would be trapped between the UN troops controlling Seoul and the forces heading north – freed from their "prison" behind the Pusan perimeter.

Once the plan for the Inchon landings had been constructed, it was necessary to select the right personnel to head the operation. It was decided that the 10th Corps, commanded by General Almond, would be landed at Inchon by Rear Admiral James H. Doyle. Doyle was Amphibious Group Commander of the Pacific Fleet. His flagship, *Mt McKinley*, was anchored at Tokio. The landing force was to be in two groups – a marine division to push south and the 7th Division to cover their flank. Both these divisions would then form a defensive buffer against the North Koreans as the 8th Army moved north from the Pusan perimeter.

From the moment the idea of an amphibious landing had been mentioned, the Joint Chiefs supported it. But they were not so keen about the choice of Inchon as a landing place. Their reasoning was that because Inchon was far to the north and so near Seoul, the North Koreans would almost certainly put up a savage defense. Also, Inchon's unusually high tides would make a quick and easy landing very difficult. UN casualties could be enormous before they even reached dry land. There was little room for failure. In contrast to the attitude of the Joint Chiefs, MacArthur had supreme confidence in his own judgement.

After much pressure, the Joint Chiefs finally gave MacArthur the go-ahead on 28 August, and the plan was finally ready for operation on 4 September. The assault on Inchon was set for 15 September. This date was chosen because the tide would be at its highest. Some doubts were voiced by navy and marine personnel – and rightly so. On that day the morning tide was at 0659 and the evening tide at 1919. A tide of at least 23 ft was necessary to enable the LSTs to navigate their way to the narrow peninsula of Wolmi-do, from where the landings were to be staged.

It was planned that a Battalion Landing Team (BLT3) of the 5th Marines would land at Green beach. This was to take place at 0630 with the morning tide. The sea front of Inchon itself, *Red beach*, was to be taken by BLT-1 and 2 at 1730. Back-up forces bringing tanks, bulldozers and engineers in eight LSTs would be brought forward. The 25 ft of tide would be just enough. Three heavily armed battalions would be landed at Blue beach simultaneously. Their task was to be the most demanding of all – to move forward and seize the main road and rail links between Inchon and the capital Seoul. Precise timing was vital for this operation. No margin of error could be afforded. Because of the tide, landing craft had to arrive and depart within a strictly laid-down timetable. Otherwise they ran the risk of being stranded on a sand bar.

MacArthur suspected that the Marines would have to use ladders to go into Inchon. This suspicion was confirmed when Lt. Eugene Clark was sent to inspect the beaches in the landing zone. He discovered that the mud was waist-deep at the harbor wall.

To complicate matters still further, the North Koreans launched an offensive against the Pusan perimeter in early September. General Walton Walker, in the perimeter, feared that if the Marines left for Inchon the North Koreans would have taken over Pusan by the time the landings took place.

MacArthur insisted that his plan to land at Inchon was the only way to avoid a protracted conflict, as well as a likely UN defeat in Korea. So, after further argument and appeal to President Truman for confirmation, MacArthur had his way.

About 70,000 men had to be transported from Japan and Pusan to Inchon. An armada of 260 ships from the United States, France, Britain, Canada, New Zealand and Holland was formed. They were to link with support units at a prearranged series of points.

Things seemed to be going smoothly when a typhoon blew in from the Pacific with wind speeds of up to 125 m.p.h. The ships held their course. Any delay would have wrecked the whole plan. Remarkably, the typhoon passed – causing little harm.

The flagship *Mt McKinley*, with MacArthur aboard, arrived off Inchon on 14 September. By this time the coast had been under almost continuous bombardment for five days. Wolmi-do was singled out for the heaviest of the fire in order to clear the way for one of the three planned landings.

A thin causeway linked Wolmi-do with the mainland. If one of the mainland landings failed, UN troops could defend the island for some time while awaiting reinforcements. But for this to be feasible, Wolmi-do had to be captured swiftly.

The 5th Marines started to land on Green beach, on Wolmi-do, at 0633 on the 15th. It was held lightly and they encountered only scattered resistance. The total enemy presence on the island was around 350 men. By 0655 the "battle" was virtually over and UN forces raised the flag on Radio Hill – the highest point on the island. This first step in the Inchon plan which had caused the Chiefs of Staff so many sleepless nights, was completed by 0800. Wolmi-do had been captured without a single fatality.

UN forces bombarded Red beach from sea and air for the rest of that day. But the landing had to wait for the evening tide, 1730, and as the tide flowed in the landing operation began. This time, things did not go so easily for the UN forces.

There was a fierce battle for the control of Cemetery Hill in the city of Inchon itself. A North Korean bunker held down the Marines below a sea wall. But by midnight the Marines had established a firm line across Observatory Hill – and had complete control of Red beach. Within six hours, UN forces had entered the very heart of Inchon.

So far, things seemed to be running smoothly and to plan. A number of landing craft became stuck in mud some 300 ft out from Blue beach, forcing Marines to wade ashore, and some vehicles stalled when a road collapsed. After a sea wall was dynamited, however, the landings at Blue beach were made easier. The Marines reached their objective by midnight and by the following day the North Koreans had fled Inchon.

Inchon had been taken at the cost of 196 casualties, including about 20 dead. The Joint Chiefs' fears had been proved unfounded and MacArthur's stock had never been higher. But it still remained to capture Kimpo airfield and Seoul itself. This had to be done quickly, but it was not going to be so easy.

The North Koreans had decided to abandon Inchon to avoid unacceptably high losses. However, they intended to dig in their heels at Seoul. The capital was turned into a virtual fortress.

Once Inchon was theirs, MacArthur, Almond and Admiral Struble visited the battlefields. MacArthur believed that he could take Seoul within five days. Almond thought it would take almost a fortnight. Almond was right.

The first target – Kimpo airfield – was captured on 18 September. As it happened, Kimpo was hardly used at all by the North Koreans, but within days it became one of the world's busiest airports as the Americans airlifted in reinforcements. It seemed inevitable to the Americans that Seoul must fall very soon. But they had reckoned without the ferocity of the North Korean defense of the city. The Americans had to bombard the city with all the firepower they possessed. Many civilians were trapped and burnt to death in an inferno from which there was no escape.

MacArthur was a great respecter of the virtues of technology. He believed that tanks, artillery and aircraft should be used to the full in order to save lives. The North Koreans, however, were not equipped with so much sophisticated hardware and, consequently, thought quite differently. Almost all they had was men. They were to fight to the last.

To the Americans, Seoul was a political symbol of the first importance. If this had not been the case, it would have been possible – and certainly wiser – to by-pass the city and join up with the northward bound 8th Army. MacArthur, however, was determined to capture the city and had to pour in more and more forces in the attempt to do so. In Seoul itself there were 20,000 North Koreans who were determined to fight it out until every one was dead.

This was unfortunate for the citizens. Living in Seoul soon became a nightmare. Prior to the Marines moving into the city, aerial bombardment had devastated whole districts. The badly built wooden dwellings of most of the people were burnt to the ground. Often, their owners went with them. North Korean suicide squads threw themselves at the advancing tanks but failed to slow them in any way.

When the Americans finally entered the city, most of the defenders were dead. Thousands of civilians – men, women and children – had been slaughtered and many more were horribly maimed by fire. Panic-stricken homeless refugees were everywhere.

The situation was made still worse as the surviving North Koreans fought a last-ditch, street-by-street battle with the Americans. This fighting was desperate and vicious. Intense heat from the burning buildings added to the horror. The fighting continued until 27 September when the Marines reached the "Capitol of the Republic of Korea" and raised the American flag above it. By the time the North Korean defenders were finally overcome, more than 130,000 prisoners had been taken.

On 29 September MacArthur entered the shattered city and in the South Korean National Assembly pronounced that Seoul was restored as the seat of government. On that same afternoon he returned to Tokio. As a city, Seoul suffered one of the greatest hammerings to be perpetrated in modern warfare. Thousands of its people were dead or homeless. Its buildings were mostly rubble. MacArthur had confounded his critics and scored the greatest triumph of his military career.

Imjin River (1951)

A. H. Farrar-Hockley
and E. L. Capel

The Stalinist regime of North Korea launched a major offensive in the Korean War on 22 April 1951, breaking through the line held by the United Nations west of Chung-pyong Reservoir. The situation was only saved by the stand of the Gloucestershire Regiment at Imjin River against a much larger enemy force, composed mostly of Chinese communists. The Glosters' action was later termed "the most outstanding example of unit bravery in modern warfare" by the UN Commander in Korea, General James Van Fleet. A. H. Farrar-Hockley, the co-author of this account of the Glosters' stand was the Adjutant of the regiment during the Imjin River battle.

The battalion moved back towards the battle line on 21 March 1951, a monumental date for the past and, did they but know it, for the future. But the first step towards the Imjin river was neither very demanding nor challenging: Colonel Carne was ordered to site and dig a battalion position covering Uijongbu. The sector belonged to the 3rd United States Division and its Commander was anxious to have a long stop on the road leading

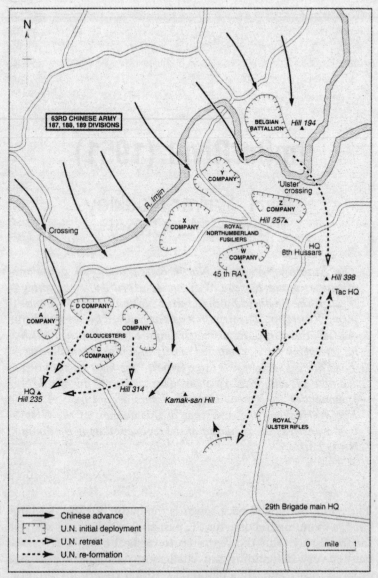

N

63RD CHINESE ARMY
187, 188, 189 DIVISIONS

BELGIAN BATTALLION ▲ Hill 194

R. Imjin

Y COMPANY

'Ulster' crossing

Z COMPANY

Hill 257 ▲

X COMPANY

ROYAL NORTHUMBERLAND FUSILIERS

Crossing

W COMPANY

45 th RA

HQ 8th Hussars

▲ Hill 398

Tac HQ

A COMPANY

D COMPANY

GLOUCESTERS

B COMPANY

C COMPANY

HQ Hill 235

Hill 314

Kamak-san Hill ▲

ROYAL ULSTER RIFLES

29th Brigade main HQ

	Chinese advance
	U.N. initial deployment
	U.N. retreat
	U.N. re-formation

0   mile   1

6.2 The Battle of Imjin River, April 1951

south from the river through the hills at this point. Though little more than a rough track it had been used successfully by the Chinese less than three months previously as a main thrust line to Seoul. It was, indeed, an ancient invasion route by the armies of Imperial China. So the Glosters dug and wired, grumbling cheerfully as British soldiers do when they are obliged to prepare defences without an enemy in sight.

Even when, at the beginning of April, they moved north through the hills along this route to the Imjin itself, there was no sign of the enemy, and this was in many ways a comfort; for though the river formed the front edge of the UN defensive line "Kansas", there were so few troops to man it that the gap between the Glosters' left and the nearest ROK unit was three miles. On the right, the nearest friendly element was a company of the Fifth Fusiliers, almost two miles distant. Thus isolated, the battalion was required to deny to the Communist Forces the use of the road running south.

The Glosters relieved the PEFTOK (Phillipines Expeditionary Force, Task Organization Korea) and these small, brown, friendly men withdrew to the south. They had been in the position only a few days and had very little intelligence about enemy locations or strengths. It seemed to Colonel Carne that he had better do something to remedy this lack of knowledge as soon as his companions had settled. "A" Company, under Major Pat Angier, was left forward on the old Castle Site, a high point (148) west of the village of Choksong. "D" under Major "Lakri" Wood, were on the hill feature south-east of the village. "B" Company, commanded by Major Denis Harding, somewhat to the east guarded the right flank approaches. "C" (Major Paul Mitchell) lay in reserve on the high ground directly above battalion headquarters. The headquarters site was at a point where the road running south entered the hills and swung across a shallow stream. The open valley mouth towards the river was held by the Drums. Troubled by a triangular-shaped height immediately to the west overlooking this site, the colonel put out on it his only uncommitted force, the assault pioneers under Captain "Spike" Pike.

It was a carefully considered deployment which made the best of a frontage of seven miles and depth of five. Any enemy approach would lie through the small arms fire of at least two companies, and two sections of the Vickers machine-guns. The guns of 45 Field Artillery Regiment, backed potentially by the United States 3rd Divisional artillery, the mortars of "C" Troop, 170 Mortar Battery and the Glosters' own 3-inch mortar platoon were able between them to cover both companies and approaches with shell or bomb. The difficulty was to detect enemy movement by night. A change in darkness to a tight defensive position was not practicable because of the shortage of defence stores. It took eight days to get the first truckload of barbed wire and the second did not reach the battalion until it had been in position for 17 days. Much had happened in that time.

An active patrol programme confirmed that the ford across the Imjin river, carrying the road from Seoul northwards, was intact and the enemy defences covering it on the far bank empty. But there had been movement in the high ground immediately to the north amongst a series of bunkers. "A" and "D" Companies combined in a night operation to close on these and sweep them at dawn. Apart from a radio mishap at the outset, this was most successful, though when the troops searched the bunkers these were also found to be abandoned. Where had the enemy gone?

A major sortie followed in daylight: two company groups and Major George Butler's squadron of the 8th Hussars moved north across the Imjin to a distance of seven miles in an operation named "Cygnet" – young swan. At last a few half-starved and very miserable Chinese soldiers were captured. Was this the rearguard of the mighty Chinese Peoples' Volunteers?

As a matter of fact it was. Weakened by the severity of the winter and defeated by the advancing United Nations forces, the mass of Chinese divisions had broken away from their pursuers during March. There had thus been no pursuit into the heart of North Korea as in 1950. General Ridgway had now replaced General MacArthur as Supreme Commander, Allied Powers, and his orders were to hold on or about the line of the 38th Parallel of latitude – the old demarcation line between north and south – which, in this sector, was roughly along the course of the Imjin. A few exhausted Chinese and North Korean units had been left to hold an outpost line while, 20 miles to the north over a period of six weeks, the Chinese commander-in-chief, Peng Teh-Huai, refreshed, replenished, and reinforced his armies. Then, with the winter finally past, he gave orders on 13 April for a fresh offensive. Small reconnaissance parties were sent south to discover and infiltrate between the UN positions, travelling only by night, resting and watching by day. On the night of the 21st, the mass of the attacking armies began to march south after them, amongst them the 63rd Army of three divisions* – the 187, 188, 189 – with orders to force open the ancient route to Seoul.

Various sources of intelligence had disclosed to the United Nations commander in Korea, General James van Fleet, that an offensive was impending. All units were ordered to be ready and thus all were watchful. A little after midday on 22 April, the Glosters' artillery observation posts saw 20 enemy moving south in file . . . dressed in dark uniforms. A larger body moved round behind hill . . . immediately north of the Imjin ford known as Gloster Crossing. Air recce began to search as Colonel Carne accompanied a patrol to a vantage point close to the river from which to observe. The adjutant joined the colonel and the intelligence officer, Lieutenant Henry Cabral, on the bank. Five more enemy parties between 10 and 20 strong were observed occupying the old positions on the high ground immediately to the north, in which they were severely shelled. But otherwise the colonel's orders, sent back to the adjutant, were clear: the companies were to take pains to lie low and conceal themselves from what were obviously enemy scouting parties. A fighting patrol was to be prepared in "C" Company – one platoon – to lay an ambush on the south side of the ford as soon as it was dark. Meantime, "A" Company's observation post was to watch this sensitive point until dusk and to shell and mortar any attempt to seize it in daylight.

The afternoon passed in an atmosphere of excitement. Everyone in the battalion sensed that a major clash was imminent. Men rested in all positions. At 5 p.m. the hot evening meal was eaten and before dusk a comprehensive check of weapons and

* A Chinese Communist Forces (CCF) Division was about 9,000 strong, mostly infantry with six to eight batteries of light artillery and about twice this number of medium and heavy mortars.

ammunition had been completed. Half the reserve ammunition was brought forward from "A" Echelon to the headquarters site. As the light waned, the ambush party from "C" Company, Lieutenant Guy Temple's platoon, came down from their hilltop and made their way to the river and ford.

The task of the "C" Company platoon was to surprise and destroy the enemy attempting to cross to the south of the Imjin. It was only partially successful for two reasons. First, because the weight of the enemy seeking to cross were far greater than had been expected from air reconnaissance and ground observation reports during the afternoon and evening. At dusk on the 22 April, the main body of the enemy were not within 12 miles of the river. They closed on the Imjin in a forced march of three hours carrying all their battle gear. Lieutenant Temple's platoon destroyed the enemy's advanced party attempting to seize the crossing by *coup de main* early in the night but were then pressed by a battalion backed by two more. Seventy Field Battery, "C" Troop of 170 Mortar Battery, the mortar platoon and the small arms of the ambush fired continuously for some hours but they could not stem indefinitely the flood of Chinese soldiers.

Meantime, unknown to the Glosters, a second enemy brigade was crossing the Imjin at another ford, of which they were unaware, one-and-a-half miles downstream. This was the second reason for the limited success of the ambush and a consequence of the excessive frontage held by the battalion. Even while the ambush held the enemy to its front in check, a strong assault was being launched against "A" Company on the Castle Site by about two battalions while a third crossed the road to the east to attack "D" Company.

Upstream, the left flank company of the Fifth Fusiliers holding a ridge overlooking the river and lateral road had been attacked and forced to withdraw. A battalion from this area moved south to attack "B" Company of the Glosters. Not long after midnight, therefore, the three forward rifle companies of the Glosters were in action, "A" Company being critically pressed by an enemy outnumbering them by six to one.

At battalion headquarters, Captain Reeve-Tucker, the signals officers, entered the command vehicle with a message from the ambush party.

"They're still trying to cross in hordes, sir," he said to the colonel. "In another five minutes, he [Temple] reckons they'll be out of ammunition."

The colonel looked across at Major Guy Ward, the battery comander, and the adjutant.

"Tell him to start withdrawing in three minutes," he said to the adjutant. "Guy, I'm going to ask you for one last concentration, and then start dropping them short of Gloster Crossing as soon as the patrol is back at the first cutting south of the river."

The advantage of the United Nations' Forces as their line was, almost everywhere, assailed that night was in the power of their weapons, particularly artillery, to drop destructive fire accurately into the enemy masses. Their weakness lay in the length of front which resulted in numbers of fragmented battles, each of which needed to be won by the defence if Line Kansas was to be held. The artillery could not engage so many targets adequately. The morning light would permit the UN air forces to add their weight of firepower. The question was, would it be enough?

At a number of points, air strikes forced the enemy to withraw temporarily by 9 a.m. on the morning of the 23rd but there were none available to the Glosters.

Before dawn on the 23rd the battalion Command Post had moved up to the ridge held by "C" Company. From there, in a bunker constructed under RSM Jack Hobbs' supervision some days before, the colonel could overlook the battle on the two hill positions to the north. The desperate nature of the struggle was manifest before the morning sun rose. By night, the calls for fire support, each fresh report from "A", "B" or "D" Company headquarters and the artillery radio links had made it all too clear that the attack was in strength. Just after dawn, in the command post, Corporal Walters told the adjutant that Major Angier, commanding "A" Company, wished to speak to him.

"I'm afraid we've lost the Castle Site. I'm mounting a counter-attack now but I want to know whether to expect to stay here indefinitely or not. If I am to stay on, I must be reinforced as my numbers are getting very low."

When the message was passed to the colonel he was already

considering what his options were now that daylight had come. Two questions were in his mind: would the Chinese continue to press their attack in daylight with the threat of intervention by UN aircraft; and, secondly, how long would it be before the Chinese discovered that both battalion flanks were completely open and encircle his battalion?

He questioned Major Angier briefly and then gave his orders: "You will stay there at all costs until further notice."

At all costs and until further notice . . . The need for "A" Company to hold its position was this: notwithstanding the loss of the highest point of their position, they had still observation over the approaches to "D" Company as well as forward to the two river crossing points. If the company was precipitately withdrawn, the Chinese would reinforce freely the force on the south bank, overwhelm "D" Company, and in turn, "B".

The adjutant sent forward a supply of ammunition in a pair of Oxford carriers under Lieutenant Cabral.

"Don't worry about us," said Major Angier on the radio; "we'll be all right." He returned to the fight. The counter-attack was in progress to regain the Castle Site on which, in one of the company's bunkers, the Chinese had installed a medium machine-gun. Lieutenant Philip Curtis led his platoon forward as the guns of 70 Field Battery fired in support. But the overhead cover in the bunker protected the enemy machine-gun crew and they fired freely into the attacking platoon, driving them back within half a minute. Amongst the wounded dragged into cover was Lieutenant Curtis. Corporal Papworth of the Royal Army Medical Corps began to attend to the injuries. Curtis did not wait for his attention.

"We must take the Castle Site," he said.

"Just wait until Papworth has seen you, sir," said a soldier at his side. But he would not wait. Alone he ran forward painfully, a pistol in one hand, a grenade in the other. Possibly waiting until this single figure advancing reached point-blank range the Chinese machine-gunners held their fire. Curtis pulled the pin from his grenade and threw it. As it flew through the air, the Chinese opened fire and killed him; but were themselves killed a few seconds later as the grenade landed directly in the bunker opening and blew away the muzzle of their gun. Then, as Major

Angier was directing a platoon to close upon this key point, he was killed and command of the company passed to the only surviving officer, Lieutenant Terry Waters. By the time he came up to take over, the opportunity to recover the Castle Site had passed.*

To the east, "D" Company was under command of Captain M. G. Harvey.† By about 0830 on that morning, 23 April, it was apparent that neither "A" nor "D" Companies could hold against the weight of successive attacks unless air support was available. At 0730, the brigade commander had given permission to Colonel Carne to withdraw his forward positions. When it became clear about 50 minutes later that the Glosters' request for air strikes would not be satisfied, the colonel gave the order to withdraw. "A" and "D" Companies were brought into positions immediately north-west and west of battalion headquarters and "B" Company to a hill feature below the great height of Kamak-San to the east of the road.

In breaking away from the enemy, the whole fire potential of the battalion, Captain Frank Wisbey's heavy mortar troop and the three batteries of 45 Field Regiment was used against the enemy of the 187 CCF Division. Their dead and wounded lay in heaps on the hill slopes they had occupied and in the gulleys along which they had sought to infiltrate past the main position. With "A" and "D" Company positions in their hands, they had had enough and by noon the battlefield fell quiet.

The adjutant recalled a series of incidents of that day, "clear in themselves but joined by a very hazy thread of continuity."

Colour Sergeant Buxcey organizing his Korean porters with mighty loads for the first of many ascents to the new "A" company positions . . . When Buxcey's anxious face has left my mind, I can still see Captain Bob Hickey, the doctor, working at the Regimental Aid Post, one hand still wet with blood as he turns round, pausing for a moment to clean himself before he begins to minister to yet another

---

* Lieutenant Curtis was to receive a posthumous Victoria Cross for his gallantry.
† Major W. A. Wood was away with a leave party in Japan.

wounded man. The ambulance cars are filled; the jeep that
Bounden drives has been out time and again with the
stretchers on its racks. Sergeants Baxter and Brisland,
Corporal Mills, the whole staff of the RAP is hard at
work with dressings, drugs, and instruments . . . I remember watching the slow, wind-tossed descent of a
helicopter that came down for casualties to whom the
winding, bumpy road back south would have meant certain death . . . Shaw, my driver, and Mr Evans, the Chief
Clerk, went off to Seoul . . . Captain Carl Dain, the
counter-mortar radar officer came in to say, "I'm sending
my vehicles back, except for my jeep. I've decided to stay
with you to make up your numbers of Forward Observation Officers" . . . Lieutenant Donald Allman, the assistant adjutant, was sent to reinforce "A" company, now
under its second-in-command, Captain Anthony Wilson
. . . That morning the Padre, Sam Davies, said a funeral
service for Pat Angier, whose body had been brought back
on one of the Oxford carriers by Lieutenant Cabral. Pat's
body was the only one to which we could pay our last
respects – but we did not forget the others. Three of us
stood by while the solemn words were said: then we
saluted and walked away, each busy with his own
thoughts. Pat lay at rest beside the soft-voiced stream,
quiet in the morning sunlight.

Later that morning, the battalion second-in-command, Major Digby Grist, came forward to see what was to be done by
way of support for the battle which must surely come to life
again as soon as darkness fell. While discussing the prospect,
news came that rear battalion headquarters ("A" Echelon)
five miles back, had been attacked and forced to withdraw:
the enemy had infiltrated strong patrols this far south. The
colonel said, "I think you'd better go back at once, Digby, to
see what is happening." Well aware that he was almost
certainly about to run a gauntlet of fire, the second-in-
command set off calmly with his driver, Bainbridge. Thirty
minutes later, they were driving for their lives through an
enemy ambush.

On the right flank, Major Harding had managed to withdraw from his former position secretly and his new site was unknown to the enemy. He was determined not to reveal it until compelled to do so. When observers reported the approach of enemy patrols, Sergeant Pethrick was sent out to lay an ambush on the most likely approach. Not long after he had settled, expecting to catch a patrol, about 200 Chinese obligingly entered his position and a fire fight began. The Chinese, part of 188 CCF Division, reinforced and began to work round the flanks of the ambush. Sgt Pethrick was ordered back while other detachments from his company went forward, greatly assisted by medium and heavy mortar fire, to hold the enemy off the main position. Backwards and forward, all among the little knolls that lay below the peak of Kamak-San, engagements flared up and died, only to be renewed elsewhere.

Notwithstanding the capture of the forward company positions of the Glosters, the commander of 63 CCF Army was dissatisfied, as we are now aware, with the progress of his force after 24 hours of attack. The 187 Division had failed to destroy the battalion holding the old road running south through Solma-ri. On the night of 23/24 April, it had been planned that 188 Division should march down this road to cut in behind the bulk of the British 29th Brigade and the 3rd United States Division. Due to the casualties inflicted on the 187 Division, the 188 had now to complete the elimination of the Glosters though, as the battle line stood, the tactical opportunity seemed still to be open to the 63rd Army. The 29th Brigade and 3rd Division were fighting in positions east-north-east of the Glosters: if the latter could be disposed of during the first hours of darkness of that night, it should prove possible to march rapidly down the road to Uijongbu. For this reason, Chinese patrolling and probing attacks began early in the evening, particularly against "B" Company, with the aim of finding a route into the heart of the battalion's position and a bypass along which part of the division might slip to the south.

Under the arrangements of Sergeant Smythe, the signal sergeant, telephone cables had been run to all new company positions. At ten minutes to midnight on 23 April, Major Denis Harding telephoned the battalion command post.

"Well, we've started. They're attacking Beverly's [Lieutenant Gael's] platoon now – about 150 I should think."

This explained the noise from this direction. Captain 'Recce' Newcome, the artillery FOO, was directing defensive fire from the guns. From "C" Company came similar news. The 188 Division was attempting to force the right flank of the battalion while simultaneously making for the highest ground in the area, the peak of Kamak-San. In character, the assaults on the rifle companies followed the pattern of the previous night: wave after wave of men armed with grenades and sub-machine-guns stormed the positions under cover of medium machine-guns and mortar fire, were halted by the fire of the defence – small arms, mortars, guns – and driven back with heavy loss.

At the outset of the engagement on the night of 23/24 April, the Chinese were at a disadvantage. The information gained by their patrols was faulty largely due to Major Harding's deceptive tactics: they attacked late and obliquely the battalion right flank, so that the assaults, pressed blindly for the first few hours, were struck by enfilade fire. Some time after two o'clock in the morning of the 24th there was a lull during which it seems probable that a fresh regiment came forward, with a truer idea of the Glosters' positions.

About a quarter to three, intense enemy mortar and machine-gun fire fell among "B" and "C" Companies. The soldiers waiting – regulars, national servicemen, recalled reservists; west countrymen predominantly, with a scattering from London and almost every other county of the British isles; but long since moulded in comradeship by the fortunes of war – stood to their weapons to face another onslaught. Despite the slaughter inflicted on the enemy by their courage and skill, the Glosters' numbers were dwindling. There seemed to be no limit to the casualties the Chinese commanders were prepared to sacrifice to their aim. There was a limit to the casualties that the British battalion could accept if it was to sustain an effective defence.

At three o'clock the telephone from "C" Company rang in the command post. Major Paul Mitchell spoke to the adjutant. "I'm afraid they've overrun my top position and they're reinforcing hard. They're simply pouring chaps in above us. Let me know what the colonel wants me to do, will you?"

The colonel had no doubt as to what had to be done. With the enemy in strength on the commanding ground of "C" Company's ridge, the right half of the battalion had been cracked open. Below this lay the headquarters site with the radios connecting the battalion to brigade headquarters and the guns, the regimental aid post with the wounded sent down during the night, the battalion 3-inch mortars and the artillery heavy mortars.

"Pack the headquarters up," the colonel said to the adjutant, "and get everyone out of the valley up between 2 Company and the anti-tank platoon position. I'm going to withdraw 2 Company in ten minutes; and I shall move 2 over to join us after first light." The withdrawal of "C" Company was an extremely difficult operation in darkness, and as a result only one-third of the Company eventually joined the battalion on Hill 235 – the final position.

By dawn, all but "B" Company were on the high ground overlooking the valley from the west. The next problem was to disengage "B" Company and bring them into the main position; a taxing problem because they were still under attack. By fortunate chance, the local Chinese commander decided to concentrate his force against one platoon, Lieutenant Geoffrey Costello's, and no less fortunately Costello's platoon held firm, the wounded standing with the unwounded. Across the valley in the main position, Captain Dain was able to bring shellfire down amongst the Chinese infantry scrambling up the hillside and Sergeant Syke's section of Vickers opened fire effectively into this target at 2,000 yards range. At first slowly and painfully, Major Harding managed to draw away what remained of his company. With the rearguard of Lieutenant Arthur Peal's platoon, Harding himself broke away at last. A group of the enemy followed them, closing as they approached the foot of the Glosters' hill but were driven back as Private "Lofty" Walker of "C" Company, entirely of his own initiative, ran down to meet them, firing a Bren light machine-gun from the hip into the approaching foe. Twenty of "B" Company survived the journey. Colonel Carne combined them with the remnant of "C" Company under Major Harding's command.

During and after the movement of "B" Company, three important matters had to be attended to: the detailed knitting together of the defences in the new position on Hill 235* against renewed attack; the clarification of the battalion's position in relation to the remainder of the battle in the sector; and a check of physical resources in weapons, ammunition, radio batteries, water, medical supplies and food. The colonel was engaged in the first between seven o'clock on the morning of the 24th, when the sun broke through a haze of grey clouds, and 0845. His round of the battalion was not without incident. Prior to "B" Company's move he came across a group of Chinese infiltrating forward and, supported by two of the regimental police and his driver, he drove them back with the loss of two dead.

'What was all that about, sir?' asked his adjutant as he came back over the ridge.

'Oh, just shooing away some Chinese.' He continued on his way. A few minutes later, the brigade major† came on to the radio to answer the adjutant's request for information about tactical intentions. He had cheering news. PEFTOK – the Filipinos – were on their way forward to reinforce the battalion and on 25 April armour and infantry in brigade strength would come up in relief. The battalion should be back in reserve by the evening of the 25th.

Meantime, it had to maintain its powers of defence. An expedition was arranged to descend the steep path to the headquarters site to collect ammunition and all the other supplies which were needed. RSM Jack Hobbs and CSMI "Muscles" Strong of the Army Physical Training Corps assembled men and porters. Major Guy Ward got together a parallel party of gunners to pick up batteries for their radios. Captain Dain screened the sortie with smoke shells and discouraged Chinese intervention by an occasional salvo of shrapnel. By nine o'clock all had safely scrambled back, heavily laden.

Through the morning and afternoon came several reports about the progress of the relief column. They were not encouraging: Chinese forces were said to be blocking the southern entrance to the hill road. Tanks of the 8th Hussars were sent to

---

* Later to be called Gloster Hill.
† Major Jim Dunning, who was acting in place of Major K. R. S. Trevor, on leave.

help them but in the afternoon the news was that the latter had lost its leading troops in an ambush. The tank carcases were blocking the road in a gorge. But this was not all. The brigadier came on the radio to say that the unrestricted passage of the Chinese past the Glosters would lead to the remainder of the 3rd Division, including the 29th Brigade, fighting to the east, being cut off from their withdrawal route. Though unlikely now to be reinforced on 25 April, it was essential for the Glosters to remain in position.

The colonel had been studying his map as he listened to this statement. When Brigadier Brodie had finished he put his map on top of the radio and replied.

"I understand the position quite clearly," he said. "What I must make clear to you is that my command is no longer an effective fighting force. If it is required that we shall stay here, in spite of this, we shall continue to hold. But I wish to make known the nature of my position."

It was a plain statement of fact. The numbers in the position capable of fighting were about 350, many of whom were wounded. A lot of weapons had been smashed. There had been no resupply of ammunition since the 22nd. Radio batteries might last a further 12 to 15 hours. Once darkness fell, the battalion had no means of stopping the enemy from using the road below.

The brigadier recognized this but stressed that by remaining in position the battalion must pose a threat to the Chinese. They would be obliged to keep attacking and thus retain forces close to the Imjin which would otherwise be used to the south against division and corps.

Seen from the view of the commander of the 1st United States Corps, Lieutenant-General Frank W. Milburn, it was essential for the battalion to remain. This did not ease Colonel Carne's difficulties of holding fast against a third night of attacks. Yet with a calm face he set off up the hillside to the topmost ridge to consider night positions while the adjutant settled arrangements for emergency resupply by Auster aircraft and a full supply by Fairchild Packets the next day. There would be no helicopter for the wounded that night, but perhaps that also might manage to reach the Glosters' hill next morning.

For the moment, a night battle had to be reckoned with: dawn on the 25th was 12 hours distant.

The remainder of the afternoon passed. Colonel Carne arranged to draw in his force tightly round spot height 235, the centre of the feature: on the north-west, "A" Company; to the east, "D" Company; south, "B" and "C"; south-west, Support Company, now grouped together under their commander, Major Sam Weller. Battalion headquarters was to be sited between "A" and Support Companies. At dusk, when the Chinese could no longer see their movement, the Glosters moved together, carrying their wounded among them.

The ridge was generally bare apart from patches of sere dwarf oak and a copse of scrubby trees. The ground was rocky; tools were few. But none doubted the need to dig and, where this was impracticable, rock sangars were raised. By 2000 hours all was quiet.

It was a time for contemplation among the defence. Some of those awaiting the enemy attack were fearful and all were apprehensive of a series of desperate battles ahead. Yet there were no signs of panic or recrimination; none of despair. A sense of determination to fight the battle out successfully was manifest. It was a mood which owed a good deal to individual valour but stemmed, too, from the immense confidence all felt in their commanding officer. He had been amongst them a good deal that day, making the occasional, quiet remark as he was apt to do, neither purveying false confidence nor betraying fears. He gave the impression of being unshakeable and they believed that he was.

By the night of the 24th/25th, according to Chinese prisoners-of-war, the 188 Division had lost over 4,000 killed and wounded since it had cross the Imjin. 189 Division began to cross the river at dusk with orders to clear away the Glosters once and for all. Commanders of the leading regiment had crossed earlier in the day to study the ground and plan the night attack. It was to begin quite silently, the assault companies creeping forward to a range at which they might effectively throw grenades – say, 25 yards. So six companies marched from their assembly area behind the Castle Site to the foot of Hill 235 as soon as it was dark and began stealthily its ascent.

The Glosters had put out trip wires with tins to rattle. These warnings revealed the enemy's approach at 2045 and within a few minutes the faithful guns of 45 Field Regiment were firing into the densely packed enemy. Even so, several hundred Chinese got right up to the Glosters' defences, blowing trumpets and whistles, calling commands shrilly as they sought to overwhelm their dogged foes. Gradually, they were driven back until 2300 hours when all became quiet once more. The Glosters set aside their dead in hollows and sent back the wounded to Captain Bob Hickey in his makeshift RAP.

Three hours later, the Chinese returned. Again the guns, the rifles and machine-guns fired, grenades were exchanged, the battle swayed to and fro. Towards dawn fresh numbers began an ascent across the little valley to the east with many trumpets directing them.

"It will be a long time before I want to hear a cavalry trumpet playing after this," said the colonel to the adjutant.

"It would serve them right, sir," said the adjutant, "if we confused them by playing our own bugles. I wonder which direction they'd go if they heard Defaulters played!"

"Have we got a bugle up here?" asked the colonel. The adjutant called down the question to Drum-Major Buss on the eastern slope.

"Got one in my haversack," came the reply.

"Well, play it, Drum-Major," said the adjutant.

"What shall it be, sir?"

"It's getting towards daylight; play Reveille – the Long and the Short. And play Fire call – in fact, play all the calls of the day as far as Retreat, but don't play that!"

There were a few preliminary peeps from the Drum-Major as he tried out his lips and then his calls rang in the morning air: Reveille, Defaulters, Cookhouse, Officers Dress for Dinner, Orderly NCOs and many more. When the last sweet note died away there was silence. Certainly surprised, perhaps confused and apprehensive of a counter-attack, the Chinese stopped their movement for a while.

The attacks began again after dawn, principally from the north, assault after assault. "A" Company were driven back from their position, being reduced to one officer, CSM

Gallagher and 27 soldiers. The adjutant took them back in a counter-attack and remained to command. He asked the guns of 54 Field to fire deliberately on the restored company position when a Chinese assault flowed into it. This ejected them but they massed again. The forward observation officer with the company, Captain Ronnie Washbrook, brought in with great skill a series of air strikes using napalm against those on the northern slopes. It was a joy to the defenders to see six more pairs of F 80s attack concentrations of troops from Hill 235 to the Imjin. Daunted at last, the Chinese drew back. It was 0610 on the morning of 25 April.

The morning news came from brigade headquarters. Pressure on the route to the east had become so great that all forces were falling back towards Uijongbu. There were no troops available to fight a way forward to the Glosters. The battalion was to fight its own way back, given maximum support from the guns. Orders were passed to Major Weller, the adjutant, Captain Harvey, Lieutenant Temple representing Major Harding, Henry Cabral, Major Ward of 70 Battery and Captain Wisbey of the heavy mortar troop. Captain Hickey was present from the RAP. After pointing out the route to be taken and giving orders for tactical movement, the colonel paused and looked at the doctor.

"Bob, I'm afraid we shall have to leave the wounded behind."

"Very well, sir. I understand our position."

Ten o'clock was to be the hour of disengagement from Hill 235. In each defensive location beforehand, everything of value was destroyed, to prevent it falling to the Chinese. At 1000, the colonel met the adjutant.

"Let Sam Weller know that I have just been told by the brigadier that the guns are unable to support us – the gun lines are under attack themselves. Our orders are quite simple; every man to make his own way back."

Word was hastily passed: soon officers and men were hurrying down the hillside in the warm sunlight. The adjutant passed the RAP. "Come on, Bob," he called to the doctor. 'The colonel will be off in a moment and that will be the lot."

"I can't go," he said. "I must stay with the wounded."

Soon none of the battalion was left on Hill 235 but the dead, the wounded and the gallant RAP staff, Padre Sam Davies amongst them.

The long ridge two miles to the south of Gloster Hill was held in strength by the Chinese and thus blocked the attempts of the Glosters to break out. Some of those running and marching away were shot down and some were captured by the enemy sallying down from the hilltops or advancing to occupy the abandoned hill.

A group under Captain Harvey took fortuitously a route first north and then west and some of this number survived a hail of fire to reach friendly lines (a total of 46 all ranks).

By the evening of the 25th, about 350 of the battalion and its supporting Arms were being marched north across the Imjin River as prisoners of war. So too were the 63 CCF Army which had been so mauled that its remnants were withdrawn over the river to recover.

At brigade headquarters, Brigadier Brodie had written in the operations log his own documentary: "No one but the Glosters could have done it."

So passed Lieutenant-Colonel Carne's battalion of the 28th/61st Foot from view – at least for a time. But almost at once a new battalion came into being. The remaining fragment of the Glosters was ordered to the rear until a decision could be taken as to the future. This disposal reckoned without the character of Major D. B. A. Grist who had assumed command. He gathered in every officer and soldier, including those who had just escaped from the line, returned from leave or arrived from the reinforcement camp and formed them into a fighting body. Replying to a special message of encouragement from the Colonel-in-Chief, he signalled, "we are already operational again." Thus continuity was maintained. As it happened, the main battle was fast waning: the Chinese strength was insufficient to carry the battle across the Han and CCF units north of Seoul began to draw back on 30 April.

From 26 April to 23 May, the Glosters with the remainder of the 29th Brigade were deployed on the Kimpo Peninsula, watching the right flank of the UN line. It was a quiet sector and here all units were reinforced and equipped anew. Major Grist was promoted to lieutenant-colonel and confirmed in command of the battalion. Officers, warrant officers and NCOs of the regiment came from far and wide to fill out the companies; many had hastened to return of their own volition as soon as they heard the news of the battalion's loss. Comrades old and new shared a unique occasion when, on 8 May, General James van Fleet, presented a Distinguished Unit Citation to the battalion and "C" troop, 170 Heavy Mortar Battery, by command of the President of the United States.

In the last week of May, once more at full strength, the British brigade returned to the Imjin, the Glosters holding the reserve position but taking an active part in patrolling north of the river. Those who had been there before were happy to see tons of defence stores arrive. The front was covered with wire; trenches were properly revetted and covered. In August, the battalion moved forward from reserve into many of their old positions and, finally, in September, to a sector north of the river where a new line, "Wyoming", was dug and wired. From its place in this sector, the battalion was relieved by 1st Battalion, The Welsh Regiment, in November 1951.

A year and a month after leaving, the 28th/61st returned to England. Despite the pleasure of being safely at home once more, the thoughts of many of its members were often with those left behind in the prison camps.

Two main columns of British prisoners had been formed up at the end of April from those captured out of the British 29th Brigade. Amongst them were a few members of the United States Air Force shot down in the same battle area. As they marched, certain individuals and small groups escaped but the majority were secured effectively by the Chinese guards as the columns marched nightly in stages of 12–15 miles until a point was reached beyond the range of day-fighter/ground attack aircraft of the United Nations. Thereafter the marches were made by day. Some of the prisoners were passed over to the North Koreans for intelligence interrogation at the notorious "Pak's Palace" at Pyongyang, in which conditions were so bad that hundreds of UN prisoners died. The majority were marched to Chiangsong on the Yalu river where a dull life was not enlivened by daily political lectures aimed at subverting the loyalties of United Nations prisoners.

In the officers' camp, Colonel Carne was singled out for prolonged isolation and beatings due to his immense prestige. Many of his officers and soldiers were also confined and beaten, and some were tortured for escape or defiance of Chinese demands for information. Less than one per cent of the British prisoners co-operated with their captors against their own country or fellow prisoners.

With the failure of their offensive in the spring of 1951, the Chinese had abandoned the hope of driving the United Nations Forces from Korea. Their problem was how to end a war which they saw they could not win, and which was unduly expensive in war material, without sacrificing all political prospect for the communist camp. Armistice negotiations dragged on from May 1951 until August 1953. Only then, at last, were the prisoners-of-war able to move south to be exchanged at Panmunjon, close to the 38th Parallel. Amongst the whole body of prisoners originally taken, many had died of neglect or starvation. Among the 33 dead of the Glosters' group none had died more honourably than Lieutenant Terry Waters, attached to the 28th/61st from the West Yorkshire Regiment, who had chosen to die of his wounds rather than make propaganda broadcasts against his own nation.*

In the autumn of 1953, what remained of Colonel Carne's battalion sailed back into Southampton water. Sirens and hooters sounded as they came ashore to be reunited with wives and families. They were astonished and a little embarrassed to find themselves famous as men who had made history. Such is the way of the British soldier: may it always be so.

---

* Lieutenant Waters was posthumously awarded the George Cross.

7
Vietnam

Dien Bien Phu (1953)

Charles Mey

Dawn is about to break over the North Vietnamese airfields of Gia-Lam and Bach-Mai, just outside Hanoi in the north-east corner of Vietnam. Over 1,800 French and South Vietnamese are ready in full fighting kit, tense and waiting to go into battle. With them are their three commanders, Major Marcel Bigeard, Major Jean Brechignac and Major Jean Souquet, all seasoned veterans of the Indo-China war. On the runway, 67 C47 Dakotas sit, their crews ready to take off. It is 20 November 1953.

Another Dakota, 190 miles away, is circling over a valley shrouded in mist and drizzle. Three French officers, Lieutenant General Pierre Bodet, Brigadier General Jean Decheaux and Brigadier General Jean Gilles, are aboard. They will soon give the go-ahead for the dropping of three parachute battalions who are waiting to attack a small village held by the Viet Minh. It is the village of Dien Bien Phu.

Suddenly, at 0700, the sky clears. An order goes to the parachute battalions outside Hanoi. It is the beginning of Operation Castor. Over Dien Bien Phu, the swarming Dakotas fill the air with their roar and thousands of Thai peasants stare up in surprise. The planes discharge their cargoes of men, and hundreds of white parachutes blossom against the blue sky. Viet Minh soldiers rush to their battle stations. On the dropping

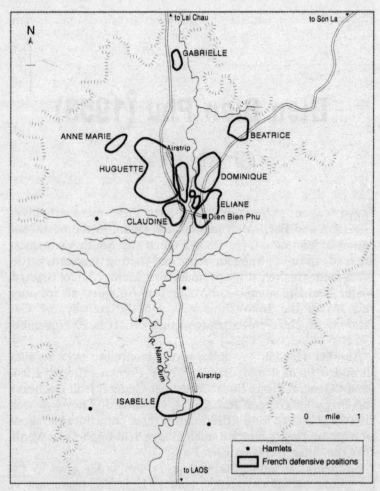

7.1 The Siege of Dien Bien Phu, March–May 1954

zone (DZ) Natasha, a Viet Minh company on exercise has already skirmished with Maj. Bigeard's paratroopers of the 6th Colonial Parachute Battalion. The DZ covers a large area and already the recovery of the tons of equipment parachuted into it is becoming difficult. Machine-guns, 81 mm mortars and radio sets litter the ground. But many of the radios have not survived the drop. Worse, some of the mortars cannot be found.

Farther to the south, on DZ Simone, Maj. Brechignac's paratroopers, from the 2nd Battalion of the Parachute Chasseurs Regiment, have been dropped in difficult conditions and it is proving difficult to rally the soldiers and get them into action as a concerted force. Without waiting for support, Bigeard has left the DZ to attack the village of Dien Bien Phu with three of his four companies. But the Viet Minh regular soldiers defend doggedly. At 1500, Souquet's 1st Colonial Parachute Battalion, who have jumped in support of Bigeard, arrive to take part in the mopping-up action. The 148th Regiment of the People's Army withdraws in good order and the villagers flee into the mountains. French losses are only 13 dead and 40 wounded. It is confirmation of the value of surprise blows struck by well-trained parachute units.

On the second day, 21 November, a second force of paratroopers jumps into the valley of Dien Bien Phu. These are the legionnaires of the 1st Foreign Legion Parachute Battalion and the soldiers of the 8th Vietnamese Parachute Battalion, with their commanding officers, Lieutenant Colonel Pierre Charles Langlais – who breaks a leg on landing – and Gen. Gilles, commander of the whole Dien Bien Phu operation. Heavy supplies are now dropped on DZ Octavie, but one of two bulldozers parachuted in buried itself in the ground after its chute had failed to open fully. The French forces on 22 November are 4,560 men, after a fresh battalion of Vietnamese had arrived. It was time to begin the construction of defensive positions.

After the airborne landing of 20 November, Dien Bien Phu is soon to be a fortified zone, capable of holding 12,000 soldiers. Why is it sited in such an area? Because the French High Command's patience is wearing thin. Embroiled in a war with Ho Chi Minh's revolutionary army since 19 December 1946, a spectacular victory is badly needed. And with Gallic daring, they have chosen to occupy Dien Bien Phu, a base 200 miles inside the enemy's territory.

The French High Command at Saigon is not sure about the role which Dien Bien Phu is being called upon to play. Is it a rallying point for the Lai Chau garrison? A "hedge-hog" in an essential strategic position? Or a start point for an offensive, as Major General Renee Cogny declares? Perhaps it is a trap sprung for the army of General Vo Nguyen Giap, of the Vietnamese People's Army. Or could it be a diversion in anticipation of an attack on the Red River Delta?

Before being replaced by General Henri Navarre, General Salan, Chief of Staff of the French Expeditionary Force in Indo-China, said that Laos could only be defended by holding Dien Bien Phu, as well as Na-San and Lai-Chau. Navarre will come under severe criticism for his action here in establishing Dien Bien Phu as a fortress, sited as it was in the bottom of the valley. But he saw the ten-mile-long and six-mile-wide valley floor as an ideal base. From it he could make sorties to attack the Viet Minh. He felt that the enemy could not surround his fortification, nor could they effectively use artillery against the airstrip from the hills ten miles away.

For some time, Dien Bien Phu is almost a tourist venue for many high-ranking French officers and politicians, together with their Government's military visitors. The fortress is praised from all sides, although one man, General Blanc, has his criticisms about the area in times of monsoon. His warning is not heeded. Among the visitors are General Spears, British Military Attache and High Commissioner Malcolm McDonald, many American Generals including John ("Iron Mike") O'Da-niel, US Army Commander in the Pacific. But none of these highly expert people question the ability of Dien Bien Phu to withstand attack.

There is a collective blindness on the part of senior French officers. And this notwithstanding the fact that the archives hold details of defense preparation, backed by information from the Deuxième Bureau on the movement and capability of the enemy forces.

But from December 1953, events will show that if Navarre has set the scene, it is Giap who will script it. The situation created by the French airborne landings at Dien Bien Phu on 20 November is analyzed by the Viet Minh Council of War. Orders are given to the 316th Division to attack Lai-Chau so that it will be compelled to fall back to Dien Bien Phu. But in December 1953 the French forestall the Viet Minh plans. The Lai-Chau garrison is evacuated in 183 sorties by air transport four days before the arrival of the North Vietnamese troops. Over 2,000 men who had to be left behind have to try to make the 60-mile jungle journey to Dien Bien Phu on foot. But only 175 T'ai soldiers make it. The rest die in ambush. Many desert.

With the Viet Minh fallen back from Dien Bien Phu, the offensive and reconnaissance missions ordered by Gen. Cogny immediately begin to be costly. Two missions, Operations Ardèche and Régate, are undertaken by a paratrooper task force commanded by Lt. Col. Langlais. They leave the base to link up with the Laotian light infantry and Moroccan *Tabors* from Laos. The rendezvous is to be in the Sop Nao region, a mountainous area with thick jungle, providing perfect ambush sites. The task force is harried by a mobile enemy and the losses make it necessary to abandon these long-range penetrations and to concentrate efforts on the mountains that surround Dien Bien Phu itself.

In the fortress, information from French intelligence is that the 351st, 308th and 312th Divisions are moving towards Dien Bien Phu. Soon Giap is mobilizing his forces and the French are preparing for a siege. Their engineers calculate that enormous quantities of equipment will be needed – 36,000 tons. This would take an impossible 12,000 Dakota trips from Hanoi. All the engineers get is 4,000 tons – and 75 per cent of that is barbed wire.

There is another battle between the French and the Viet Minh. It is one of logistics. And the French will lose this one too. All their fortification work is accurately mapped. It can be seen clearly from the surrounding high ground. The smallest trench stands out clearly in the bare earth. As for the French, they see nothing of the enemy's movements in the dense jungle. They do not know that 55,000 regular and locally raised troops surround them. Giap's forces open five routes through the jungle towards Dien Bien Phu. They are used by 600 Russian-built 2.5-ton lorries which travel by night with all lights extinguished. The French air attacks on the passes of Lung Lo and Phadin cause sections of these precarious roads to slide into ravines, and torrential rains make fords impassable and turn valleys into marshes.

But traffic is never interrupted for more than a few days. Thousands of coolies work day and night maintaining the Viet Minh supply routes. In addition, on the narrow tracks packhorses, mules and convoys of bicycles, each one laden with 220 lb, head towards the battlefield. Nothing can stop this conveyor belt of human ants. But the fortress can count only on transport aircraft. Everything has to come from Hanoi.

Ten M24 Chaffee tanks stripped down (each requiring five C47s and two Bristols to lift them), 105 mm and 155 mm guns, rations for 11,000 men, generators, water-purifiers. But French airpower, even with the help of a squadron of C119s supplied by the Americans, could not meet the demands of Dien Bien Phu.

Even before the real trial of strength begins the French have lost the logistics battle. When the airstrip is destroyed and the parachute is the only means of supply, the consequences will be disastrous for the French.

Gen. Giap's artillery strength around Dien Bien Phu is impressive. On the day before the attack the besiegers have 144 field-howitzers (American 75s and 105s), 48 120 mm heavy mortars, 30 75 mm recoilless guns and 36 37 mm AA guns. And during the course of the battle 12 six-barrel Katyusha rocket-launchers will come into action. The physical effort of dragging these guns into place over wet and slippery slopes by human muscle power must have been enormous.

On D-Day, Giap has at his disposal stocks of shells far greater than the French thought possible. From 13 March to 8 May 1954 his guns will fire about 150,000 shells, about 30,000 of them from the 105s. And the French artillery will need an airlift of incredible proportions to keep the guns firing. A total of 95,000 rounds of 105 mm and 8,500 rounds of 155 mm ammunition are parachuted into the base. But a quantity falls beyond the ever-shrinking perimeter into Viet Minh territory.

The besieged French have six batteries (24 guns) of 105 mm, one battery of four 155 mm howitzers and 32 120 mm heavy mortars. Colonel Piroth, who commands the base artillery, considers they can stop any enemy infantry attack, and are good enough for effective counter-battery work. He said: 'No Viet Minh gun will fire three rounds without being destroyed.' The French have underestimated the enemy's artillery strength, the supply of ammunition, the skill of his gunners and the effectiveness of his camouflage.

Bur Dien Bien Phu's firepower inferiority is also the result of other factors. Contrary to expectations the Viet Minh guns are served by excellent crews, trained in camps in south China. Their fire is directed and controlled by observers with uninterrupted views of the airfield and the unprotected French batteries. From the first day of the attack their power and their precision will come as a bitter shock. The French counter-battery work is random and will have no effect.

The Viet Minh 105s, in fact, are undetectable and practically invulnerable, because they are well dug-in, though this is at the expense of wide fields of fire and large handling crews. Dummy guns are used by the Viet Minh to deceive the French spotters in the base. And so the battle of Dien Bien Phu was going to start under unfavorable conditions for the defenders. Their officers either know or sense it and it seems that Navarre and Cogny have their doubts. But by this time the die has been cast.

"Gentlemen, it is at 1700 tomorrow." Colonel Christian de la Croix de Castries had just completed his briefing on the evening of 12 March 1954. The unit commanders have been waiting this moment for several weeks. Less than six miles away, Giap issues his final orders for the attack. He knows the importance of the battle and its cost: "We will have to sustain losses in the course of the battle. Victory is bought at the price of blood and paid for, like all revolutionary conquests, with sacrifices."

At D-day the attackers have a superiority of eight to one: there are only 6,500 French front-line troops against the 50,000 seasoned combat troops of the elite 308th, 312th, 316th, 304th, the 351st (engineers and artillery) divisions and the 148th local regiment. The French have five Foreign Legion battalions, but eight others are composed of Algerian and Moroccan riflemen,

Thais, Vietnamese, Montaguards and mobile police. On 13 March Viet Minh movements are spotted around Beatrice and Gabrielle strongpoints, as two regiments of the 312th Division move up to their start-lines less than 100 yards from the French defenses. Two C47s and a fighter are destroyed by artillery fire on the airstrip.

At 1715 the first 105 mm shells land on Beatrice which is held by 3rd Battalion, 13th Demi-Brigade of the Foreign Legion. Two 105 mm guns in the position are destroyed and Colonel Gaucher, the commander, killed. The Viet Minh infantry attack in the failing light after sappers have blown paths through the wire. Regardless of casualties the enemy move forward, overrunning bunkers and dug-outs. Hand-to-hand fighting with grenades occurs in the trenches and amongst the ruins. At 2100 only one strongpoint is still holding out. Shortly after midnight a heavy silence settles over Beatrice. The garrison of legionnaires has lost 75 per cent of its numbers and fewer than 200 men regain the main French lines.

In the entrenched camp the French are dumbfounded. A strongpoint, defended by the Legion, overrun in six hours! Thousands of men look towards the lost position and try to understand. Col. de Castries, who has sat up all night by his telephones and has lived out the agony of Beatrice, alerts his HQ in Hanoi. He is promised reinforcements and air support. The airfield is all but closed and enemy shelling forces those fighter-bombers still intact to escape to Laos. In addition a quarter of the French 105 mm ammunition has been exhausted in one night.

On the next day, 14 March, the 5th Vietnamese Parachute Battalion is dropped in reinforcement and de Castries contemplates a counter-attack on Beatrice. But low cloud and a violent storm make close air support impossible, besides which it is known that Giap's next objective will be Gabrielle. At 1800 the Viet Minh batteries begin their shelling of the strongpoint, which is held by a battalion of Algerian riflemen and eight Foreign Legion 120 mm mortars. The Viet Minh send in 88th and 165th Regiments of the 308th Division to the attack. It is eight battalions against one. Benefiting from their in-depth defense the Algerians resist the first onslaught. But by dawn on 15 March only one redoubt is still in French hands and awaiting a promised counter-attack by the main part of the garrison.

The counter-attack consists of two companies from the Legion and one battalion of Vietnamese paratroopers supported by six M24 tanks. It fights its way to within 1,000 yards of the position and enables 150 men to regain the French lines before the thrust is called off. The second outlying strongpoint has gone. Within two days of the start of Giap's offensive the French illusions have been shattered. Dien Bien Phu is a trap. Gen. Navarre is directing the battle from his office in Saigon, more than 1,000 miles from the fighting. Gen. Cogny, installed in Hanoi, has the immediate responsibility for the battle. Knowing of the setbacks of 13 and 14 March and realizing what they portend, another battle is to be fought in secret between these two officers.

Navarre finally arrives at Hanoi where a message signed by Cogny awaits him: "One has to envisage the possibility of a defeat at Dien Bien Phu with the attendant loss of our personnel who are at present located there." Cogny, having recognized inevitable defeat, wishes to make certain that responsibility for it does not fall on him. Henceforth, relations between the two generals conducting the same battle will be restricted to exchanges of written notes. But this does not stop them trying to find scapegoats – the engineer officers who designed the fortifications, the photographic interpreters, the transport and ground-attack crews, and – of course – the French civilian government.

At this point both Navarre's and Cogny's responsibilities are crushing and it is made worse by the fact that knowing the enemy's capabilities, they themselves chose the ground on which the battle is being fought. In 1953–4 the Vietnamese People's Army is a well-balanced force of divisions, regiments, battalions and companies, all well-equipped with up-to-date weapons and well led and disciplined. In addition it is fighting for its own country and for a cause in which it passionately believed. To present this modern army as a collection of rebel bands was perhaps necessary for propaganda's sake but to believe it was absurd.

By 15 March morale in the Dien Bien Phu garrison is at its lowest ebb. During the night Col. Piroth, unable to face the defeat of his artillery, takes a hand-grenade and kills himself in his dug-out. In the command post, several officers have cracked. And de Castries hesitates, overwhelmed and overtaken by events. He lacks neither courage nor panache but rather the qualities needed to direct a battle of this magnitude. Later he will be taken to task for his passivity. But it must be remembered that he was ordered to defend Dien Bien Phu after several generals and colonels had "declined the honor".

A soldier of much sterner stuff is the hatchet-faced Langlais, commander of the airborne troops. On 24 March de Castries effectively hands over command of the entrenched camp to him with the exception of Isabelle which is put under the control of Colonel André Lalande. It is an unofficial transfer of authority and a tacit recognition of the plight of the garrison. Langlais is also aided by Bigeard, sent back to the valley some eight days earlier with his battalion. Bigeard is to be Langlais' adjutant. Ultimately the paratroop "Mafia" will take over the defense of the base.

Taking advantage of several days rest from shelling, all those capable of wielding pick and shovel have been put to work reinforcing the dug-outs and bunkers. But on 16 March the 3rd Thai Battalion on Anne Marie sense that things are going against them. They decide to leave the field and return to their villages. And several hundred North African and Vietnamese desert and go to ground in the dug-outs on the banks of the Nam Yum.

Giap and the Front Military Committee have considered the lessons of the first phase of the offensive. Losses have been very heavy and it is decided to pursue the policy of strangling the base. In ten days his front-line troops will dig more than seven miles of trenches and approach routes. A 50-yard tunnel will be dug to place an enormous explosive charge under the position known as Eliane. On the night of 30 March, after a violent preliminary artillery bombardment, the 312th and 316th Divisions launch their attack on the five hills that make up Dominique and Eliane. The battle rages for four days with hand-to-hand fighting for positions that are lost, recaptured and lost again. On one day, the defenders fire 13,000 rounds of 105 mm ammunition. This is largely responsible for the enemy's terrible losses and their failure to take their objectives. But they have made some progress and continue to erode the defended area.

The situation becomes critical on 2 April after units from the 308th Division are thrown against Huguette. At this point Bigeard scrapes together forces for a counter-attack and Viet Minh units break off the action, leaving 800 dead on the wire. The morale of the besieged forces soars and is maintained when Bigeard and his paratroopers recapture one of Eliane's lost strongpoints. Into a harrowing battle, Giap throws four battalions but in vain. Overall, the French position has not improved. Several thousand men are still isolated and trapped. There is little they can do but delay defeat. The Viet Minh divisions have been exhausted by their efforts. Giap is forced to launch a campaign for the "mobilization of morale and rectification of right-wing tendencies."

But on 1 May he orders a general offensive to begin at 2200. On that day there remains for the garrison three days' rations, 275 rounds of 155 mm, 14,000 rounds of 105 mm and 5,000 rounds of 120 mm mortar ammunition. Two strongpoints fall in the first assault, but Langlais and Bigeard hope to be able to hold on with reinforcements of men, supplies and ammunition parachuted into the base.

But the advantage of the attackers is overwhelming. Towards midday on 6 May Giap orders his Katyusha rocket-launchers, the "Stalin Organs", into action to blow up the dumps and spread terror in North African and Vietnamese ranks. By dawn on 7 May the base has been reduced to a rectangle of half a square mile. Incredibly Bigeard mounts another counter-attack with two companies supported by the last Chaffee tank. By 1800 all firing had ceased. The base does not surrender, it is simply overwhelmed.

The price paid in the 56-day defense of Dien Bien Phu is more than 2,000 French dead, 7,000 wounded and missing, and 7,000 prisoners *en route* for the death camps. And it has cost Giap 8,000 lives and 15,000 wounded to secure his "revolutionary conquest".

The French High Command was relying heavily upon the firepower of its medium and fighter-bombers to destroy the supply lines of Giap's divisions and to smash those artillery batteries which had escaped the fire of the base's 155 mm guns. It was mistaken reliance. In fact, the French Expeditionary Corps' air support is ridiculously weak, no more than a hundred strike aircraft, of which three-quarters are committed to the battle at Dien Bien Phu. More pitifully still, there are only 80 transport planes and too few pilots.

Dive-bombing attacks on the supply lines, just as those on the edges of the entrenched camp, have only a limited effect because of the meticulous camouflage of the Viet Minh. Napalm, which had been used with devastating effect two years earlier at Vinh Yen, on the edge of the Red River defenses, is rendered less effective by the different thicknesses of vegetation in the dense forest. On the other hand, the Viet Minh anti-aircraft weapons (36 37 mm cannon and 50 12.7 mm machine-guns) are very formidable. It is soon obvious that French airpower cannot change the course of the battle.

In December 1953 Navarre had studied the operation which, coming from Laos, would crush the Viet Minh army brought to Dien Bien Phu. He had given this the name Condor. By April this was to be the last hope of relief for the defenders of Dien Bien Phu. Three thousand men, two-thirds of them Laotian Light Infantry, would march on the base to attack the Viet Minh's rear areas. At the same time the guerillas of Colonel Trinquier's Mixed Airportable Commando Group would be mobilized, together with Mollat's commandos and all those groups of irregulars fighting in the Viet Minh areas. And an airborne task force would be sent as reinforcement in good time.

But on 22 April Navarre cancels the promised reinforcements and leaves the units already engaged freedom of action to continue or break off. These troops will get close to the perimeter and recover the 78 men to escape from the valley but on 7 May they will receive the order to pull back.

A breakout and withdrawal of the Dien Bien Phu garrison towards Laos would have been, without any doubt, fraught with danger. But it was the only chance to escape annihilation. Capture of all the garrison, if it remained where it was, appeared inevitable. There was a possibility of trying to break out on 3 May under the code name Albatross. But the breakout, covered by all the guns and combat aircraft, would only have been towards the south-east by those still capable of carrying four days' rations and their personal weapons. In the effort to save some of the 6,000 men still able to fight, the wounded would have to be abandoned. But HQ in Hanoi vetoed the plan as being dishonorable. The forces inside the entrenched camp were left to their fate, to fight on heroically without hope until overwhelmed.

The debacle of Dien Bien Phu was due to a number of grave errors in the siting, supply and quality of the French defensive positions. Its ultimate destruction was due to the inability of the French to sustain an adequate supply of men, ammunition and provisions for the besieged garrison. To this must be added the brilliance of General Giap's powers of leadership and the unexpectedly high quality of his battalions.

The loss of Dien Bien Phu was not only the end of a battle, it was the first time an Asian subject people had beaten their European masters in battle. And it was the finish of France as a colonial power in Indo-China.

Hamburger Hill (1969)

John Pimlott

In the aftermath of the Tet Offensive in early 1968, the Americans and their allies in South Vietnam enjoyed a distinct military advantage. Despite the failure of the Communists to trigger a countrywide revolt, by the end of February the Communists had suffered grievous manpower losses and had been forced back to their border bases. With half a million troops in-country, the Americans could contemplate offensive operations into such bases, inflicting yet more casualties while impressing upon the North – about to engage in peace negotiations in Paris – that the costs of continued aggression would be crippling.

General Westmoreland, in his last weeks as MACV commander, looked particularly toward the A Shau valley on the far western edge of Thua Thien province in ICTZ. About 28 miles long and up to 2 miles wide, this "slash in the mountains", close to the Laotian border, had long been a natural route for NVA troops and supplies entering South Vietnam. Surrounded by towering, jungle-covered mountains, the valley was isolated and exceptionally difficult to penetrate, especially during the monsoon with its torrential rain and thick fog.

US and South Vietnamese Special Forces had established camps at A Loui, Ta Bat, and A Shau village, but the first two were abandoned in December, 1965, and the third was overrun by the NVA in a bruising battle the following March. Since then, the A Shau valley had been abandoned to the Communists, something that Westmoreland found deeply frustrating. In April, 1968, he ordered the 1st Cavalry Division to mount an offensive – codenamed Delaware – to reassert Allied control.

US aero-rifle teams entered the valley on 14 April, intending to seize the former Special Forces camp at A Loui in the northern sector. They encountered a wall of anti-aircraft fire which 200 B-52 and 300 fighter-bomber sorties failed to quell; and, although battalions of the 7th Cavalry did take A Loui, conditions were appalling. Low cloud and rain effectively negated the advantages of airmobility; Delaware was called off on 11 May.

This pattern was repeated in August, when the 101st Airborne Division entered the valley in Operation Somerset Plain. The only answer seemed to be the construction of a road from the coast into the A Shau, reducing the dependence on helicopter resupply. By the end of 1968, this had been pushed to the eastern edge of the valley, but if it was to go further, operations would have to be carried out to clear the way.

These began in January, 1969, with Operation Dewey Canyon – a Marine assault south through the Da Krong valley into NVA Base Area 611 astride the Laotian border. It enjoyed a degree of success, persuading the new MACV commander, General Creighton Abrams, to order a follow-up offensive.

In March, the 2nd Brigade, 101st Airborne, air assaulted the central sector of the valley in Operation Massachusetts Striker. It culminated in a three-day battle at Dong A Tay ("Bloody Ridge"), in which the 1/502nd Infantry lost 35 men killed and over 100 wounded. The NVA were clearly prepared to fight.

Massachusetts Striker forced the NVA back toward the north-western sector of the valley, around a mountain (Dong) known as Ap Bia, but marked on US maps as Hill 937. Situated close to the Laotian border, 937 and its neighboring ridges – Hills 900 and 800 to the south and Hill 916 to the south-west – were covered in thick jungle, tangled vines, and impenetrable bamboo. In residence since 1964, the NVA had fortified the area, building log-covered bunkers and camouflaged spider-holes to protect all avenues of approach. By May, 1969, when the A Shau valley was chosen as an objective of the 101st in

Operation Apache Snow, Ap Bia was being held by over 1,200 men of the crack NVA 29th Regiment.

Apache Snow began on 10 May with helicopter assaults by five Allied battalions (three from the 101st Airborne Division and two from the 1st ARVN) into the northern A Shau. At LZ2, about 2,000 yards north-west of Hill 937, Lieutenant Colonel Weldon Honeycutt's 3/187th Infantry landed without incident and began to conduct RIF (reconnaissance-in-force) operations toward the mountain and Laotian border. A more permanent LZ and battalion command post was set up closer to 937 and, with no reaction from the NVA, Company B was ordered to seize the summit.

Starting out at 1640 hours, the paratroopers followed a trail to the south-east of the new LZ which took them into thick jungle, enclosed by tall trees, matted vines, and bamboo. Moving forward over fallen trees, the lead scouts trod warily while their comrades, sweating in the dank, humid air, plodded behind. As they crossed a low saddle, the NVA struck, firing RPGs (rocket-propelled grenades) and AK-47s into the American column. Airstrikes were called in, and, as dusk was gathering, the company pulled back into an NDP (night defensive position).

With only three men wounded, the skirmish was hardly significant, but when another ambush was sprung in the same area the following morning, killing three Americans, it was obvious that the enemy had been found. This suited Honeycutt, who immediately revised his plan. Recalling Company C from its RIF along the Trung Pham River, he ordered it to attack, parallel to Company B, along a ridge that ended between Hills 900 and 937, while Company D worked around the northern edge of the mountain. The aim was to have all three companies in position to assault the summit by first light on 13 May. It did not work.

The companies moved out at 0830 hours on 12 May, after intense air and artillery "prepping" fire. They entered a nightmare of close-quarter fighting that was to continue with little respite for eight days. During that time, the 3/187th was to be shattered, both mentally and physically, as enemy resistance hardened and conditions deteriorated. On Company B's line of advance, the NVA drew the Americans closer to the mountain, into a clearing that sheltered line after line of bunkers, each of which seemed impervious to airstrikes or artillery strikes.

Day after day, the company moved up, attacking the bunkers with grenades, recoilless rifles and machine-guns, only to be forced to pull back, dragging their wounded to safety. By 15 May, Company B was exhausted and had to be replaced by Company D, itself less than strong after terrible experiences farther north. On 12 May, the company had found its way blocked by a steep-sided ravine. On reaching the bottom 24 hours later, they had been ambushed and forced to reverse their journey, in the dark and under torrential rain, manhandling seven of their wounded (including the pilot of a downed medevac helicopter) up a virtually sheer slope. They had then returned to recover seven dead, killed in the initial ambush.

Horrific as all this was, it did not match the experiences of Company C as it pushed along its designated ridge. Once again, the NVA drew the Americans closer to the mountain before springing a carefully prepared ambush on 13 May. The company lost two dead and 35 wounded in a matter of minutes: Honeycutt had no choice but to withdraw the survivors to his command post, sending Company A to take their place. It fared no better, stalling in front of a line of bunkers which defied all efforts at destruction. Meanwhile, the 1/506th, ordered to move from the south toward Hills 916 and 900, made little progress amid a maelstrom of enemy fire and violent thunderstorms.

By 16 May, all attacks had ground to a halt, and soldiers were beginning to react to the appalling strain of the situation. Honeycutt, with his repeated demands for action, became the focus of the men's discontent: "If that sonofabitch wants to take this . . . mountain so bad, why don't he do it himself?"

But the fighting did not end. On 17 May, the 1/506th edged closer to Hill 900 and, 24 hours later, the weary assault companies of the 3/187th made enough progress to suggest that one final effort would take the summit of 937. They were blocked, not by the enemy, but by one of the most spectacular thunderstorms yet experienced. As visibility declined to zero, the rain turned the slopes of 937 – by now devoid of vegetation – into a sea of sticky mud. The attack was called off.

During the night of 18/19 May, Major General Melvin Zais, commanding the 101st, ordered three fresh battalions – the

2/501st, 2/506th, and 2/3rd ARVN – to join the battle. They landed without incident on the 19th, taking up blocking positions to the south-east and north-east of Ap Bia. On 20 May, all five battalions attacked, surrounding the NVA and cutting them off from their bases in Laos.

As the 2/501st and 2/3rd ARVN climbed the precipitous north-eastern and eastern faces of 937, respectively, the 1/506th put in a three-company assault across Hill 900 and into a deep draw – the major NVA escape route – to the south-west. At the same time, Honeycutt's men continued their attacks over familiar ground, gradually clearing the bunker lines and reaching desperately for the summit.

Enemy fire did not slacken, even when small groups of Company C scrambled onto the western edge to set up a defensive perimeter. But once they were joined by squads from Company A, the paratroopers were able slowly to clear the mountaintop. By 1655 hours, the fighting was dying down.

In any other war, the Battle of Dong Ap Bia – soon to be dubbed Hamburger Hill by the 3/187th, "because they say this mountain turns men into hamburgers" – would have been hailed as a great victory. Despite heavy casualties – the Americans lost 70 killed and 372 wounded in the ten days of fighting – over 630 enemy bodies were found, and a well-defended base had been taken. But Vietnam was different, and, as news of the battle filtered out, controversy began.

Publicly condemned by Senator Edward Kennedy as "senseless and irresponsible", the action fueled the anti-war lobby, particularly when, on 5 June, the 101st abandoned Ap Bia and allowed the enemy to return. Military arguments that the strategy was to impose casualties, not occupy real estate, cut little ice, especially when, on 27 June, *Life* magazine ran a misleading feature on "The Faces of the Dead in Vietnam. One Week's Total."

Many readers imagined that the 241 photographs shown were all of men killed at Ap Bia. Under considerable political and public pressure, President Nixon ordered Abrams to cease offensive operations in NVA-controlled territory, accelerating the process of Vietnamization to allow US troops to be withdrawn. US involvement in Vietnam was drawing to a close.

8
The Six-Day War

Jerusalem (1967)

Ashley Brown

Shortly after 0930 hours on the morning of Tuesday, 6 June 1967, Colonel Mordechai Gur, commander of the Israeli 55th Parachute Brigade, spoke on the radio net to his waiting paratroopers. "We stand on a ridge overlooking the Holy City. Soon we will enter the city, the Old City of Jerusalem about which countless generations of Jews have dreamed, to which all living Jews aspire. To our brigade has been granted the privilege of being the first to enter it."

The capture of Jerusalem was the most potent symbol of Jewish victory in the Six-Day War of 1967, for the control of the Holy Places, such as the Temple Mount and the Wailing Wall, was enormously important to the young state of Israel. The honour of being the troops who would physically take possession of this great prize had been earned by Gur's men, who had shown great courage and skill over the past two days. In particular, they had wrested control of northern Jerusalem from the experienced and well dug-in forces of the Jordanian Army in the early morning of 6 June.

Tension had been building between Israel and her Arab neighbours for some time when, on the morning of 5 June, the Israeli Air Force launched a sudden strike against the Egyptians. This was totally successful, but in the confusion of that morning's events, King Hussein of Jordan was led to

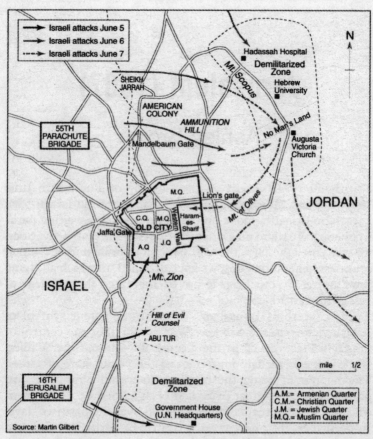

Legend:
- → Israeli attacks June 5
- → Israeli attacks June 6
- ⤏ Israeli attacks June 7

N

Hadassah Hospital
Mt. Scopus
Demilitarized Zone
Hebrew University
SHEIKH JARRAH
AMERICAN COLONY
AMMUNITION HILL
No Man's Land
Augusta Victoria Church

55TH PARACHUTE BRIGADE
Mandelbaum Gate

M.Q.
Lion's gate
Mt. of Olives
JORDAN

C.Q. M.Q.
OLD CITY
Western Wall
Haram-es-Sharif
Jaffa Gate
A.Q. J.Q.

Mt. Zion

ISRAEL

Hill of Evil Counsel
ABU TUR

0   mile   1/2

16TH JERUSALEM BRIGADE

Demilitarized Zone

Government House (U.N. Headquarters)

A.M.= Armenian Quarter
C.M.= Christian Quarter
J.M.= Jewish Quarter
M.Q.= Muslim Quarter

Source: Martin Gilbert

8.1 The Capture of Jerusalem, 5–7 June 1967

believe that the Israelis had themselves been hard hit, and agreed to send his forces in to attack Israel. At 1100 hours a bombardment began from the Jordanian side of the heavily fortified border, and the Jordanian Air Force flew sorties into Israeli air space. This was a foolhardy move that Hussein was to regret bitterly. Within hours, the rampant Israelis had put his entire air force out of action, and Major-General Uzi Narkiss, in charge of Central Command, was putting into operation his contingency plans for an offensive against Jordanian territory.

The Israelis had to cope with an unpromising strategic situation. Their main problem was that a long, narrow finger of land, inviting attack or artillery barrage from the Jordanian territory on either side, was the only link with the Israeli-held areas of Jerusalem. This corridor had to be made secure, and so Narkiss used the tanks of Colonel Ben Ari's 10th Mechanized Brigade to push north of the corridor and seize the ridge linking Jerusalem with the important centre of Ramallah; at the same time, Latrun was attacked and overrun. Meanwhile, to the south of the corridor, the 16th Jerusalem Brigade launched a series of attacks that cut the main Jordanian communications with their forces in Hebron. The success of these two sets of operations, greatly helped by the command of the air that the Israeli Air Force was now exerting, gave the situation a new complexion. Far from being the side with the strategic initiative, the Jordanians were now vulnerable, and their position in Jerusalem under threat.

Within Jerusalem, the possibilities and prospects for either side were complicated by two factors. First, there was a substantial Israeli enclave within Jordanian territory on Mount Scopus, comprising the Hadassah Hospital and the Hebrew University. A prime Israeli goal was to relieve this enclave (which had been maintained, under United Nations auspices, since 1948) while the Jordanians in turn wished to overrun the position. The second factor affecting operations in the city was that in the two decades since the establishment of the existing frontier, both sides had built up complex sets of fortifications. These networks of deep concrete bunkers, carefully sited linking trenches, mines and barbed wire promised to make a frontal offensive a difficult, if not impossible, task.

The main Jordanian force in the city was the 27th Infantry Brigade, under Brigadier Ata Ali. Further brigades were in support to both north and south, while a tank battalion was stationed behind the main built-up areas in the Kidron valley. The Israeli Air Force made every effort to cut the communication lines of these forces with the Jordanian concentrations further to the north and east, but Ali was a competent officer and he had been reinforced. His men, basically the former Arab Legion under a different name, were well trained and confident of the strength of their defensive positions. Against them, the Israelis decided to throw in one of their crack formations – the 55th Parachute Brigade.

The 55th Parachute Brigade was a body of men trained to expect shock action and to be in the forefront of any Israeli offensive. Under its experienced commander, Colonel Mordechai Gur, were many veterans of raids on Arab territory, although some of the most senior officers had not yet seen action. Raised to a fever pitch by the days of waiting before the air strike that marked the beginning of the Six-Day War, the paras had expected to be used against the Egyptians in the Sinai, and at noon on the 5th were told to prepare for a jump against El Arish, to give impetus to the northern axis of advance. However, such was the pace of the Israeli success that by 1600 hours the decision was taken to use the whole brigade against the Jordanians in Jerusalem.

The basic plan was for the 66th and 71st Battalions of the 55th Brigade to attack along a front running from the Mandelbaum Gate to a point opposite the Jordanian-held Police School building. When a breakthrough had been made, the 28th Battalion would push through to exploit southwards, towards the walls of the Old City. Some support would come from the tanks attached to the Jerusalem Brigade, but the paras would have to fight their way through an awesome set of obstacles with only minimum support before the attack could gather momentum.

The staff of the 55th Brigade urgently prepared for the assault. It was due to go in as soon as possible, but in the event, the battalions would not be ready before 0215 hours on the 6th. The crews manning the 81 mm mortars were especially concerned, because the shells they needed were very slow in arriving. They were anxious to start rangefinding, but could not risk running short of ammunition. Units were getting lost as they struggled to find their place in the line and Jordanian shells, falling at random, were causing casualties. In addition, the deputy commander of B Company, 71st Battalion, had mistakenly attached his men to the convoy of buses carrying mortars forward, and with him was all the communications equipment for the battalion. But eventually all was just about in position and, at 0215 on 6 June, the barrage began.

With buildings on the Jordanian side bursting into flame and lines of tracer flicking through the darkness, the first Israeli platoons approached the Jordanian positions. They thrust bangalore torpedoes below the coils of barbed wire, and then hastily pulled back and hit the deck. The 71st Battalion in particular had trouble in their sector: bangalore torpedoes were not exploding, and then further wire obstacles were looming up after the first breach had been made. The delays meant that men moving forward to exploit the expected breach caused over-crowding, and the milling soldiers could have been very vulnerable to Jordanian shells. Eventually the way through was cleared. Waving green torches (usually the recognition signal for assembly after a night jump) to indicate that the path was open, officers led the platoons through into the next phase of the assault.

Once through the wire, the 66th Battalion was to exploit northwards, through the Police School, taking the important position of Ammunition Hill, while the 71st Battalion was to move through the Sheikh Jarrah area and the American Colony towards the Wadi El-Joz. The men of the 66th knew that they would face enormous difficulties. Ammunition Hill was a vital point, and the Police School itself was well fortified. The paras were heavily laden, carrying extra magazines for their Uzi sub-machine-guns and knapsacks stuffed with grenades. In some cases, men were unable to get up when they fell over, and in one narrow trench Israeli troops got stuck because they were too bulky to pass along.

Giant searchlights illuminated the white walls of the Police School; Jordanian flares suddenly lit up the whole scene.

Blazing houses made the darkness around them seem even darker, and the constant explosions of tank, mortar and Jordanian 25-pounder shells provided a deadly backdrop as the paras pushed ahead. It was impossible to see exactly where the enemy small arms fire was coming from. If a trench or emplacement was seen, then it could be attacked and wiped out, but the main priority was to push on to the important objectives. In spite of their loads, and in spite of the fire, the men of the 66th Battalion kept going.

First into the Police School was A Company, cutting a way through a cattle-fence outside. The long passages inside were completely dark, a darkness rendered even more impenetrable by the sudden shell flashes outside. Groups of four men cleared the rooms, two throwing in a grenade and then spraying a room with fire, while the other two moved on to the room next door. But the paras kept tripping and falling in the pitch blackness; in the end, the officers had no option but the dangerous one of using torches. When they had taken the school, A Company moved on towards the Ambassador Hotel, together with D Company; B and C Companies moved towards Ammunition Hill.

As dawn broke (at about 0340 hours) the paras were engaged in a deadly, exhausting fight for the hill. In the trenches and bunkers it was often very difficult to tell friend from foe, and the fighting was further confused by Jordanian sniping from hills to the north. Tanks came up in support, but close-quarters fighting against prepared positions is a tanker's nightmare, and they needed infantry protection against bazookas and recoilless rifles. Soon, the paras had emptied the spare loaded magazines they had brought with them, and had to refill magazines by hand from ammunition boxes – a tiring, fiddly task when under fire. But gradually, the hill was cleared, and the final, so-called "great bunker" was taken at 0515.

Meanwhile, the 71st Battalion was also meeting stiff resistance in its attack. Having had the most problems in assembling for the assault, this battalion also had difficulty in finding its way once it was into the Jordanian lines. The difficulty of finding the right road in the darkness with only photographs to guide them was magnified by the need to clear hidden

Jordanian positions. Dropping grenades into emplacements, and carefully moving along the sheltered sides of streets, the Israelis began clearing the area between the frontier and the Nablus Road, and had a stroke of luck when the Jordanian defenders of the street leading to Wadi El-Joz were taken by surprise. A company of paras moved rapidly down the street to set up positions at this important intersection.

Although the advance was generally going well, the Jordanian support weapons soon picked out the assembly area of the Israelis, and the brigade's mortar crews and recoilless rifle operators suffered casualties as artillery fire began to zero in on them. The breaches in the front-line defences were soon being crossed by the wounded returning from the fight up ahead, some stoical but others screaming with pain. The medical resources of the brigade were becoming dangerously stretched by the mounting casualties in the attacking battalions and among the support units that were under artillery and machine-gun fire.

One heavy machine-gun in particular had caused great concern as it swept the breaches with fire before it was knocked out by a bazooka; and in spite of many efforts, a light machine-gun proved endlessly troublesome. It would stop as soon as a shell burst near it, then open up again. A group of staff officers from the 28th Battalion volunteered to finish it off; but when they tried to approach it they were caught in a trap, and the commander of the support company, leading the attempt, was seriously wounded.

With bullets flying and shells bursting around them, the men of the 28th Battalion moved off to begin their part of the assault soon after the 71st Battalion had gone through the breach in the wire. One shell chanced to injure the deputy commander of D Company, while there were serious officer casualties when a Jordanian 25-pounder struck lucky and hit battalion headquarters. After a seemingly interminable wait, it was dawn before the first members of the 28th Battalion had got to the Jordanian side of the wire, and then they had to fight their way south.

Fighting in the daylight proved, in some ways, worse than the night fighting. Now, snipers could fire without the flash of their muzzles giving away their position, and Jordanian artillery observers had a better view of events. Some of the districts through which the men of the 28th were moving were supposed to have been cleared, but the Israelis soon found that enemy troops could easily infiltrate back into good positions. The building of the Moslem Council had to be cleared three times to make certain that a single shot, or a carefully lobbed grenade, would not take its toll of the advancing Israelis.

The task of moving down Saladin Street was given to C Company but, unable to identify the area properly, it went down Nablus Road. Here the paras had to flush out the YMCA building, from which there was considerable fire. Entering it cautiously, they found most of it empty, finding only the base of a machine-gun mounting. Suddenly the squad that was investigating the situation was fired upon, and men went down wounded. Time was too short to waste it on just one obstacle, and a hand-to-hand combat would have resulted in further casualties. The squad pulled out, and a supporting tank put two shells into the upper stories; the advance went on.

About 0500, there was a lull and the men of the 28th Battalion were ordered to halt. This was a nerve-racking moment, because the risk of a sniper's bullet, or of a well-aimed salvo of artillery shells was as great as ever. Then the advance began again with more tank support. The main task now was to get to the Rockefeller Museum, an imposing new building that dominated the approaches to the north-east corner of the Old City. The roar of the tank guns when they fired almost deafened the paratroopers as the sound echoed between the high buildings. The paras also found it difficult to communicate with the tank crews because the cables for the external telephones had been cut by shrapnel, or were turned off so that the tankers could listen to the stream of orders they were getting on their radio net. But in spite of these problems, the tanks were a real boon, for they drew fire away from the men on foot and they certainly gave the Jordanian defenders second thoughts about opening up at short range.

By 0800, the 55th Brigade had performed brilliantly. All its objectives were secured, and it had set the scene for further advance. From Ammunition Hill in the north through Sheikh Jarrah, the Ambassador Hotel, and down to Wadi El-Joz, a line had been established that gave contact with the slopes of Mount Scopus and promised imminent relief for the besieged garrison; while in the south, the capture of the Rockefeller Museum made an assault against the Old City a practical possibility. Indeed, paras of the 28th Battalion had set themselves up in the Rivoli Hotel opposite Herod's Gate, and when they were not engaging the defenders of the walls of the Old City they were able to sample the delights of the hotel's kitchens, and have a bath.

The casualties sustained by the brigade in reaching these objectives had been horrific – but the achievement had been immense. Gur visited the troops at the Rockefeller Museum. Although many had no previous experience of real action, he noted that already they were comporting themselves like veterans; they knew exactly where enemy fire might come from, and where to find precisely the safest places to sit and relax.

The ranks of the three battalions were thinned by the pounding they had taken during the assault, but there was no shortage of volunteers to replace the dead and wounded. The mortar crews and anti-tank personnel were now anxious to get into the front line – especially as the Old City was beckoning. Morale was sky-high, and Gur prepared to move the 66th Battalion further south for another day's fighting.

Narkiss, desperate to finish things off and to get into the Holy City, ordered Gur to concentrate on taking the last Jordanian strongpoint in the region, the Augusta Victoria Hospital on a ridge to the south of Mount Scopus, and then to prepare an encirclement of the Old City. The plans for the assault were swiftly drawn up, and it was decided to wait until after 1930 hours, when darkness fell, before attacking.

The assault on Augusta Victoria Hospital got off to a bad start, when some troops strayed too close to the walls of the Old City and were fired on from there; and then, at 2140, Gur was informed that 40 Patton tanks of the Jordanian Army had been seen on the reverse side of the slope his men were to attack. With only four Shermans as support, Gur could not risk the assault. He decided to wait until the next day, when aerial support could be called in. Anti-tank dispositions were made and then the soldiers tried to sleep.

Gur's new plan was to attack at about 1130 hours on 7 June, by which time the Israeli Air Force should have dispersed the Pattons. The Israeli high command decided, however, that the attack should go in much earlier in the morning, at 0830. Again, there was frantic haste to reschedule operations, for the new attack was to be mounted from Mount Scopus as well as from across the Kidron valley.

Had the Israelis known it, such frenzied preparations were hardly necessary. Far from being able to bring up substantial armoured reinforcements, Brigadier Ata Ali had been completely cut off by the success of Israeli moves to north and south, and by the Israeli Air Force's devastating attacks on Jordanian road convoys. His troops began a skilful withdrawal in the early hours of 7 June.

At 0804, just before his attacks were to start, Gur was at last given the order that he was so anxious to receive: he was told to take the Old City. Immediately after the air attacks on the Augusta Victoria Ridge, his men stormed over it, and at 0930 he was able to give the historic order to his brigade that the time for waiting was past.

The entry into the Old City was to be via the Lion's Gate, which was the only one able to take tanks, and as the armoured support of the paratroopers approached this point of entry, there was some sporadic defensive fire. Gur himself led the entry into the Old City, and his troops met only light resistance from isolated snipers. At about 1000, he reached the Wailing Wall. The brigade's ordnance officer produced a bottle of whisky, and passed it round. The 55th Brigade had won a victory that no one in Israel would ever forget.

9
The Falklands War

Wireless Ridge (1982)

John Frost

The British Army's Second Battalion of the Parachute Regiment fought in all the major battles of the 1982 land war between Britain and Argentina for the Falkland Islands (Malvinas). After spearheading the landings at San Carlos on 21 May, the battalion fought its way to Port Stanley against determined Argentinian resistance, via Bluff Cove, Goose Green and Wireless Ridge. The most famous of these battles is undoubtedly Goose Green (where 2 Para commander, Lieutenant-Colonel "H" Jones, won a posthumous Victoria Cross for his charge against an enemy position), but the engagement at Wireless Ridge on 13–14 June was no less dramatic and arguably more decisive. The Ridge, a spur on the north side of Port Stanley, was heavily defended by troops from the Argentine 7th Infantry Regiment and the Argentine 1st Parachute Regiment.

The origins of the Parachute Regiment lie with an initiative of Winston Churchill who, after noting the success of German paratroop operations during Germany's invasion of Holland and Belgium, suggested the formation of a British airborne elite force. The first units began training in June 1940, with volunteers from the units forming the Parachute Regiment in August 1942.

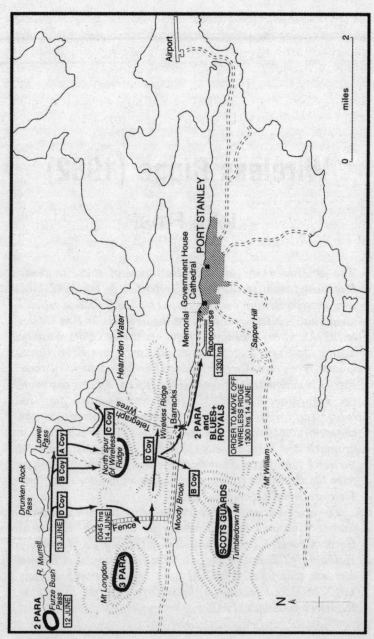

9.1 The Capture of Wireless Ridge and Port Stanley, June 1982

2 Para's task was to capture the Wireless Ridge features, keeping west of the telegraph wires, and Colonel Chaundler's plan called for a two-phase noisy night attack. In Phase 1, A Company would take the northern spur where the ponds were, C Company having secured the start-line. Once this was secure Phase 2 would come into operation, and B and D Companies would pass through from the north to attack the main Wireless Ridge feature itself. B Company would go to the right (the western end of the ridge), while D Company attacked the rocky ridge-line east of the track.

The mortars would move forward from Mount Kent to a position in the lee of the hillside south of Drunken Rock Pass, and this would also be the site for a static Battalion Headquarters during the attack. H-hour was to be at about 0030. The importance of digging in on the objectives was emphasized once more, since Wireless Ridge was dominated by both Tumbledown and Sapper Hill, and if enemy troops should still be there at dawn they could make 2 Para's positions untenable.

The orders were straightforward, and the plan simple, involving the maximum use of darkness. As the "O" Group ended the company commanders were told that they would now fly up to Mount Longdon to look at the ground over which they would operate.

The CO went on ahead with the Battery Commander to meet Lieutenant-Colonel Hew Pike, CO of 3 Para, and Major William McCracken, RA, who controlled the artillery "anchor" OP on Mount Longdon. They discussed and arranged for co-ordinated fire support, with 3 Para's mortars, Milan teams and machine-guns all ready to fire from the flank, and Major Martin Osborne's C Company, 3 Para, in reserve.

Back at the gully all was peaceful in the bright sunshine. Suddenly this was shattered as nine Skyhawks appeared further to the north, flying very low in formation and heading due west towards Mount Kent. The effect was electric, for no one expected that the Argentines could still flaunt their air power in this way.

At "A" Echelon, behind Mount Kent, there was no doubt as to who the jets were aiming for. As they came screaming up over the col and rose to attacking height, the formation split: three went for the area where the artillery gun-line had recently been, three went for 3 Commando Brigade HQ, and three attacked "A" Echelon. All the machine-guns opened up, claiming one possible hit as the bombs rained down. Amazingly, there were no casualties from this minor blitzkrieg. But the accuracy of the attack, and its obvious definiteness of purpose, left people wondering if the enemy had left concealed OPs behind, watching Mount Kent, or if satellite photography had shown up the various targets or, possibly, if Argentine electronic-warfare equipment had picked up radio signals from Brigade HQ.

The air raid created delays to all helicopter movement, but eventually the CO was able to fly on to Brigade HQ, while the company commanders were dropped on to Mount Longdon for their own recces. Colonel Chaundler had already been updated on the actual strength of the enemy, which was greater than had been thought, and a new Argentine position had been detected to the east of the pond-covered spur, on a knoll overlooking Hearnden Water and the mouth of the Murrell River.

While the CO was at Brigade HQ, the company commanders were able to study Wireless Ridge in detail from the commanding position on Longdon. It at once became obvious that much of the information so far given to them was inaccurate. What was thought to be C Company of 3 Para proved to be nothing of the sort: Major Dair Farrar-Hockley noticed that it was an *enemy* position of about company strength, situated dangerously on the flank of the 2 Para axis of attack, west of the northern spur. It was also clear that Wireless Ridge proper was heavily defended, with positions which stretched a long way to the east beyond the line of telegraph poles that marked the 2 Para boundary. Strangely, no harassing fire was being brought to bear during the day on any of the Argentine positions, and their soldiers were free to stand about in the open.

The company commanders flew back to Furze Bush Pass, but clearly a major change in plan was necessary. The CO returned from Brigade HQ as evening approached and was told of the situation. "Go away and have your supper. Come back in 45 minutes and you will have a new set of orders," he said. Meanwhile the move-up of mortars and the adjustment of artillery had been delayed, and as a result the changes to the fire-plan had to continue into the night, directed by the OP on Longdon and using illuminating rounds.

Unfortunately for the company commanders, normal battle procedure had already ensured that relevant details of the first plan had permeated to the lowest level. Platoon and section commanders had had time to issue clear and well-constructed orders to their subordinates, but now their efforts were all useless, for by the time the company commanders returned with the CO's revised plan, it was too late to go into new details. Such a sudden last-minute change did little for the men's faith in the system, but it was unavoidable and, in any case, the soldiers had by now become stoical, while the cynics among them were not disappointed by this evidence of fallibility at higher levels. Nevertheless, the battalion was able to adapt and change its plans and moved off on time. But Phil Neame had his misgivings about what the SAS to the east of his line of advance was *meant* to be doing, and there was no knowledge of what the SAS was actually *going* to do. Furthermore, no one really knew what was beyond Wireless Ridge to the south, in the Moody Brook area, and everyone would have liked to have known exactly when the 5 Brigade attack on Tumbledown was timed to begin.

The battalion's new plan was for a four-phase noisy night attack. In Phase 1 D Company would capture the newly dis-covered enemy position west of the northern spur; A and B Companies would then assault the pond-covered hilltop; Phase 3 called for C Company to take the knoll to the east; and finally D Company would roll up the enemy on Wireless Ridge itself, with fire support from A and B Companies, starting in the west and finishing at the telegraph poles.

Fire support was to be lavish in comparison to Goose Green: two batteries of 105 mm guns, HMS *Ambuscade* with her one 4.5-inch gun offshore, and the mortars of both 2 and 3 Para, totalling 16 tubes. Ammunition was plentiful, and the batta-lion's mortars had been moved complete from Mount Kent by helicopter, and were thus fresh for action. The Machine-Gun Platoon had also been flown forward. Between the six guns they had enough ammunition to provide a massive weight of fire, and the men were fresh and rather proud of their earlier achieve-

ment behind Mount Kent against the Skyhawks. The Milan
Platoon was already forward with the battalion – the experience
of Goose Green had demonstrated the capability of this precision guided missile against static defences. Finally the light
tanks of the Blues and Royals would be there, Scimitars with
their 30 mm automatic cannon and Scorpions with 76 mm guns,
and both equipped with very high quality night-vision equipment and having superb cross-country performance. All available support was allotted first to D Company, then to A and B in
their assault, and finally to D Company again as it traversed the
ridge.

As night closed in the tanks, the mortars and the Recce
Platoon, which was to secure the start-line, moved up. By
now the promise of the day had vanished and snow and sleet
were falling, considerably limiting the effectiveness of all the
gun-sighting equipment, and reducing visibility.

At about 0015 a storm of fire from the supporting artillery
and mortars was unleashed upon the Argentine positions. A and
B Companies passed by, led by C Company patrols to the new
start-line secured by Corporal Bishop's patrol in the relatively
safe ground overlooking Lower Pass. At 0045 hours on Monday
14 June, D Company moved over its own start-line further to
the west, and headed towards the identified enemy position.

As the company moved forward, the tanks of the Blues and
Royals and the machine-guns provided fire support while the
artillery increased its rate of fire. Enemy mortar fire in retaliation became heavy. In the rear of the company, Private Godfrey
of 12 Platoon had a near miss as a piece of shrapnel cut through
his windproof and dug into his boot. He dived for cover –
straight into an Argentine latrine!

The weight of supporting artillery and mortar fire was
singularly effective, for the enemy on the D Company objective
could be seen running away as the company pushed forward,
although 155 mm air-burst shelling increased as the Paras
began to clear the Argentine trenches, now abandoned except
for a few enemy killed by the barrage. The darkness of the night
and the extent of the enemy position caused the company to
spread out, creating problems of control. Lieutenant Webster of
10 Platoon counted up to 20 trenches on his right, with more

over to the left, where 2nd Lieutenant Waddington's 11 Platoon found the other half of the assault formation.

Occasionally as they moved forward, men would suddenly disappear into the freezing water of an ice-covered pond. Privates Dean and Creasey of 11 Platoon went in up to their necks, and had to tread water to stay afloat until their platoon sergeant, Sergeant Light, dragged them out.

Fire support for the company was immaculate. The tanks used their powerful image-intensifier night-sights to pinpoint targets. Once enemy positions were identified, they fired. As soon as the battalion's machine-gunners saw the strike they, too, opened up. Occasionally the machine-gun fire was too close for comfort, even for D Company, and in the end 10 Platoon Commander called for it to stop.

The opposition had fled, and D Company took its first objective in record time, remaining *in situ* while A and B Companies began their part of the battle. Enemy artillery fire was increasing, however, and Neame therefore decided to push forward for another 300 m into relative safety, to avoid the worst of the barrage.

Several of those waiting to move on the A and B Company start-lines were reminded of scenes they had seen from films of the First and Second World Wars. As shells landed all around, men lay huddled against the peat, with bayonets fixed. There could be no denying that, for the soldiers, fear of the known was in this case worse than blissful ignorance of the unknown. In the shelter of the peat bogs some smoked, watching the display of illuminants above.

Just as the time came to move, the shelling claimed its first victim, for Colour Sergeant "Doc" Findlay was killed in the rear of A Company, and soldiers from Support and HQ Companies were also wounded. The advance began, the two companies moving southwards parallel to each other, on either side of the track. The men crossed the stream in the valley north of their objective with the tanks firing over their heads. The effect upon the enemy was devastating. In their night-sights the tank crews could see Argentine soldiers running or falling as the accurate fire took effect. The boost to morale that this form of suppressive fire gave was considerable; fundamentally, the battle was being won by supporting arms, the infantry being free to do their own job, which is actually clearing and securing the ground.

On the left, all was going well with A Company. Command and control had been well practised back at Goose Green and now the junior officers and section commanders were quite expert in maintaining direction. Silence was unnecessary and orders were shouted backwards and forwards. The enemy were still shelling as the companies advanced, but now counter-battery fire was being provided by our own artillery. From his own position the CO could see the two companies in extended formation, moving quickly up the hill, the whole battlefield brightly lit by starshell.

Co-ordinating the two assaulting companies' advances was difficult, however. The track provided a boundary of sorts, but controlling upwards of 200 men during a noisy battle over difficult terrain is not easy. Colonel Chaundler had another worry. Earlier, before the battalion had moved up, he had been shown a captured Argentine map which indicated a minefield directly in the path of the assaulting companies. There was only 15 minutes to go before 2 Para set off – far too late for a change of plan. The CO only had time to brief OC B Company, while John Crosland had none in which to warn his men, and in any case was told to push on regardless, since there would be no time to clear the mines. Only afterwards did Major Crosland tell his men that they had actually moved directly through the minefield without knowing it. Miraculously, no one was blown up on the way.

The ponds on the spur claimed a victim, however, when Private Philpott of 5 Platoon suddenly plunged into over 6 ft of water. He was dragged out and his section commander, Corporal Curtis, immediately organized a complete change of clothing from the other men in the section, which probably saved Philpott's life.

The two companies consolidated on the objective. There was some firing from the trenches, swiftly silenced as the men of both companies ran in to clear them. Once more the enemy had fled, leaving only 20 or so of their number behind, quickly taken prisoner as they were winkled out of their holes. Radios were still switched on, and several dead lay around the positions. As the men dug in, the enemy shelling increased and it was to continue for the rest of the night at the same level of intensity. Most thought it was worse than Goose Green, but fortunately the abandoned enemy bunkers provided reasonable shelter, although a number of casualties occurred in A Company.

It was now C Company's turn. Already they had had a minor scare on the A and B Company start-line when a Scorpion tank had careered towards Company Headquarters in the darkness. It was hopelessly lost and its commander had to be evacuated after a dose of "hatch rash" – the effect of placing the head in the path of a rapidly closing hatch. The confused vehicle was soon heading in the right direction, but now under the command of Captain Roger Field, who had seized this opportunity to revert to a more honourable role than foot-slogging.

With A and B Companies now firm, C Company was ordered to check out the Argentine position further to the east that had been spotted from Mount Longdon on the previous day. Major Roger Jenner was glad to be moving again, for it seemed that the supporting artillery battery had developed a "rogue gun" and every sixth round meant for the enemy was coming in uncomfortably close to his company. He and his men set off, taking cover occasionally on the way as shells fell close by. There had been no firing from the company objective during the battle, and soon the platoons were pushing round the side of a minefield on to the knoll.

As the Recce Platoon advanced, they could hear noises of weapons being cocked. The bright moonlight left them uncomfortably exposed on the hillside. On the forward edge of the slope were two parallel lines of rock, and on the second line the platoon found a series of shell scrapes, suggesting recent occupation by a body of troops. Once again it seemed that the enemy had left hurriedly, leaving tents and bits of equipment behind in the process. Away over to the east Jenner's men could see the bright lights of Stanley airfield, and could hear a C-130 landing. The company was ordered to dig in, but since an enemy attack on this feature was extremely unlikely the CO changed the orders, and C Company moved up to the pond-covered hill.

If any particular group deserves special praise for what was done that night, then it must be the tanks of the Blues and Royals. Their mere presence had been a remarkable boost to morale during all the attacks that had taken place, and the speed and accuracy of their fire, matched by their ability to keep up with the advancing Paras, had been a severe shock to the enemy. Lance-Corporal Dunkeley's tank, which Captain Field had taken over following the injury to its commander, had alone fired 40 rounds from its 76 mm gun.

2 Para was performing superbly, its three first objectives taken with great speed and a minimum of casualties, despite heavy and accurate enemy artillery fire. Whenever the enemy in trenches had sought to return fire they had been met by a withering concentration of fire from the rifle companies' weapons which, coupled with very heavy support, had proved devastating. It is not known whether the Argentines had gathered that they were facing the men from Goose Green, but there can be no question that 2 Para knew.

D Company was now ready to go into the final phase of the attack and began moving forward again to the west end of Wireless Ridge. The tanks and support weapons moved up to join A and B Companies on the hilltop overlooking the D Company objective, and endured the artillery fire as well as anti-tank fire from Wireless Ridge to the south.

12 Platoon was now in the lead. Lieutenant John Page, who had taken over from the tragically killed Jim Barry, looked for the fence, running at right-angles to the ridge, that would guide him to the correct start-line for the assault. Unfortunately there was little left of the fence marked on the maps, and Corporal Barton's section, at the point of the platoon, could only find a few strands of wire to follow. The number of ice-covered ponds added to the difficulty and the intense cold was beginning to affect men's reactions, as they worked their way south to the western end of Wireless Ridge.

Once more, massive fire-power began to soften up the enemy, who apparently still had no intimation that they were about to be rolled up from a flank. The initial idea had been for D Company simply to sweep eastwards along the ridge without stopping, with 11 Platoon on the left, 12 Platoon on the right and 10 Platoon in reserve. There was still uncertainty as to whether Tumbledown to the south had been taken or not, and clearly a battle was still in progress on that mountain as the Scots Guards fought to drive out the Argentines on its summit. But Neame and his D Company had no intention other than to push on regardless, although they knew that if Tumbledown was still in enemy hands by daylight then 2 Para would be extremely vulnerable.

The bombardment of the western end of the Wireless Ridge continued as the platoons advanced. It seemed to have been effective, since no enemy were encountered at all, although, to be certain, 11 Platoon cleared any bunkers they came across on the reverse slope with grenades.

The first part of Wireless Ridge was now clear and across the dip, where the track came up, lay the narrower rocky outcrops of the remainder of the objective. Fire was concentrated on these areas from A and B Companies as tanks, Milans and machine-guns provided an intense concentration on to three enemy machine-gun posts that remained.

Efforts to switch artillery support further forward and on to the area of Moody Brook had unfortunate results. Five rounds of high explosive crashed on to the ridge around and very near the leading D Company platoons. 3 Section of 11 Platoon was caught in the open and, despite screams to stop the firing, it was too late. Private Parr was killed instantly, and Corporal McAuley was somersaulted into some rocks, completely dazed, and had to be picked up by a stretcher party.

There was a considerable delay while a livid Major Neame tried to get the gunners to sort themselves out. It seemed that one gun was off target, as C Company had noted, but at the gun-lines they did not know which, since in the dark it was impossible to note the fall of shot, even if there had been time, and the other battery was not available owing to shortage of ammunition. In the meantime the CO was growing increasingly impatient, urging the D Company commander to press on.

As soon as the gunners could guarantee reasonable support, and with increased efforts from the Blues and Royals, Neame was off again. All through the wait constant harassing fire from the enemy had been landing around the company, so none were sorry to move. Despite the fire pouring on to the ridge-line ahead, enemy machine-gunners continued firing from well-sited bunkers, and were still staunchly in action as the platoons advanced.

They moved with 11 Platoon on the left, 12 Platoon ahead on the ridge itself, with the company commander immediately behind and, in the rear, 10 Platoon. 12 Platoon came across an abandoned Argentine recoilless rifle, an anti-tank weapon, as they crossed the start-line, which may well have been the weapon that had earlier been engaging the tanks on the A and B Company positions. The platoon moved down into the gap between the two parts of the ridge line, but as the soldiers passed by some ponds, very heavy machine-gun fire began from their front and illumination was called for as the platoon answered the firing. Corporal Barton came across some orange string, possibly indicating a minefield, but his platoon commander urged him on regardless.

The enemy appeared to be surprised by the direction of the assault, and as the Paras advanced, they could hear an Argentine voice calling out, possibly to give warning of this sudden attack from the west. 10 Platoon came across a lone enemy machine-gunner who lay wounded in both legs, his weapon lying abandoned beside him.

Corporal Harley of 11 Platoon caught his foot in a wire, which may have been part of a minefield, and, fearing that it might be an Argentine jumping mine, unravelled himself with some care. The platoon pushed on, skirmishing by sections until they met a concertina of wire. Fearing mines, Sappers were called for from Company Headquarters, but these could do little in the darkness except tape off the suspect area. In fact channels could be discerned between the concertinas, and these were assumed, correctly, as it turned out, to be safe lanes.

While 11 Platoon was extricating itself from the minefield, Neame pushed 12 Platoon on and brought 10 Platoon out to the left to maintain the momentum. Suddenly an intense burst of firing brought the company to a halt. It was a critical moment. For a short time, *all* commanders had to do everything in their power to get things going again, with platoon commanders and sergeants and section commanders all urging their men on. It was a real test of leadership as several soldiers understandably went to ground.

A brief fire-fight ensued, with 12 Platoon engaging the enemy as they pushed forward on the right overlooking Moody Brook below, where lights could be seen. The moment of doubt had passed, however, and once more the men were clearing bunkers and mopping up with gusto. 10 and 12 Platoons now moved on either side of the company commander. Maximum speed was needed to keep the enemy off balance as they fell back, conducting a fighting withdrawal along the ridge. The tanks continued to fire, directed by the company commander. Unfortunately his signaller had fallen into a shell-hole and become separated, thus creating considerable frustration for the CO, who wanted to talk to Neame about the progress of his battle.

During 12 Platoon's brief fight Private Slough had been hit and died later in hospital, and another soldier was wounded.

Enemy artillery fire continued to make life uncomfortable. Fortunately D Company's task was no longer difficult, as most of the enemy bunkers had now been abandoned. 12 Platoon reached the telegraph wires and consolidated there, while the other platoons reorganized further back along the ridge. Shellfire intensified and snipers began to engage from enemy positions further to the east along the ridge.

Neame went up to see the platoon commander, Lieutenant Page. Snipers in the rocks were still firing on the platoon and it seemed that the enemy might be about to counter-attack from the direction of Moody Brook, to the right.

On several occasions the company commander was nearly hit, and his perambulations began to be the cause of some comment. Sergeant Meredith shouted to him, "For God's sake push off, Sir – you're attracting bullets everywhere you go!"

A hundred metres or so to the east, Argentines could be heard shouting to each other, as though rallying for a counter-attack. John Page called for fire support, and then ordered his own men to stop firing, for by so doing they were merely identifying their positions. They felt very isolated and vulnerable.

For two very long and uncomfortable hours the company remained under pressure. Small-arms fire mingled with all types of HE fell in and around 12 Platoon's position as the men crouched in the abandoned enemy sangars and in shell-holes. John Page continued to move around his platoon, organizing its defences, and suffering a near-miss in the process. He was hit by a bullet, which passed between two grenades hanging on his webbing and landed in a full magazine in his pouch. He was blown off his feet by the shock. "It was like being hit by a sledge-hammer and having an electric shock at the same time," he later described the moment. As he lay there a round exploded in the magazine, but fortunately the grenades remained intact, and he was soon on his feet.

Meanwhile the CO was still trying to get in touch with Neame to know the form. Lieutenant Webster, OC 10 Platoon, was momentarily elevated to commanding the company since he was the only officer left near Company Headquarters. As he talked to the CO, voices could be heard below in the direction of Moody Brook. Corporal Elliot's section opened up and automatic fire was returned by perhaps ten to fifteen men. 11 Platoon moved forward to join 10 Platoon in a long extended line along the ridge, the men firing downhill towards the enemy position. Eventually the CO got through to the company commander, who had had a hair-raising time walking along the ridge to discover what was happening. He now informed the CO of his fears of imminent attack.

Sporadic enemy fire from Tumbledown added to D Company's danger, and all the earlier fears of the consequences of delay to the 5 Brigade attack came to the fore. The CO offered to send tanks up but Neame declined, since they would be very exposed on the forward slope fire positions they would be forced to adopt. He would have preferred another company to hold the first part of Wireless Ridge, which as yet remained undefended.

The company reorganized, leaving Corporal Owen's section forward as a standing patrol while 10 and 11 Platoons found dug-outs on the reverse slope. 12 Platoon stayed in its positions near the telegraph poles.

There was little more that the Companies on the northern spur could now do to support D Company. Two of A Company's trained medical orderlies had been wounded by the shelling that still continued, so the platoons had to look after their own casualties – once again the value of the medical training for all ranks was vindicated. Fortunately the helicopters in support that night were fully effective, evacuating casualties with minimum delay, and other casualties were taken back to the RAP on one of the tanks. The enemy artillery fire gave the remainder every incentive to dig, and the possibility of being overlooked by Mount Tumbledown in the morning was an additional spur.

For A and B Companies it was now a matter of lasting the cold night out, which was not without incident. Privates "Jud" Brookes and Gormley of A Company's 1 Platoon had been hit by shrapnel. The rule was to switch on the injured man's easco light, normally used for night parachute descents, to ensure that he would not be missed in the dark. Sergeant Barrett went back to look for Brookes, whose light was smashed.

"All right, Brookes – me and the Boss will be back to pick you up later."

"Ee, Sarge," he replied in a thick Northern accent, "Ah knows tha f—— will."

Unknown to them, the men of 3 Platoon were actually sitting next door to 13 Argentine soldiers, who were taking cover from their own shellfire. Only later in the morning were they found and taken prisoner.

In B Company, the state of Privates Carroll and Philpott of 5 Platoon was a cause for concern, since both were now suffering from hypothermia after being immersed in one of the ponds. Their section commander, Corporal Steve Curtis, decided to tell the platoon commander. As he ran out into the shelling, a round exploded close by, shredding his clothes almost completely yet, amazingly, leaving him unharmed.

The mortar teams had been busy all night. By now they had moved on to the side of the A and B Company hill to avoid shelling, which had been uncomfortably close at their first position in the bottom of the valley to the north. Improvised bins had helped to reduce the tendency of the mortar tubes to bed into the soft peat, although not completely, and another problem was that tubes would at times actually slip out of their base-plates under recoil. To prevent this, mortarmen took turns to stand on the base-plates as the tubes were fired, and by the end of the night four men had suffered broken ankles for their efforts. The fire they had been able to provide was very effective, however, and all concerned had been determined that, this time, there would be no question of running short of ammunition or of being out of range. The 3 Para mortars on Longdon did sterling work providing illumination.

The Machine-Gun Platoons, too, had been hard at work, their six guns providing intense heavy fire throughout the night. Re-supplied by the tanks and by the splendid work of WO2 Grace's Pioneer Platoon, they had had no worries about ammunition. But gradually the guns broke down, and by dawn only two of the six were still in action.

In Battalion Headquarters the second-in-command, the Operations Officer and Captain David Constance had taken turns at duty officer. At one point the second-in-command, Major Keeble, had been able to see the flashes of the enemy 155 mm guns as they fired, but no amount of reporting back produced any counter-measures. Once the drone of a low-flying Argentine Canberra jet was heard, and amidst the din of artillery even larger thuds reverberated as the aircraft dropped its bombs. Private Steele of the Defence Platoon was unlucky: as he lay on the ground a piece of shrapnel caught him in the back. He hardly felt it, thinking that it was only a piece of turf from the explosion – only later did he discover a rather nasty wound where the metal had penetrated.

The CO's party had not escaped either. A stray round hit Private McLoughlin, a member of the Battery Commander's group, and actually penetrated his helmet at the front. The helmet deflected the round, however, and McLoughlin walked away unharmed.

The snipers were in great demand. Their night-sights enabled them to identify the enemy infra-red sights and to use the signature that then appeared in the image intensifier as an aiming-mark. The Commando Sappers had had a relatively minor role to play in the battle, since there were no mines that it was imperative to clear. But, as at Goose Green, they provided a very useful addition when acting as infantry.

On Wireless Ridge at first light, 12 Platoon was still being sniped at from behind and to the right. Further back along the ridge, Corporal Owen had searched a command post. While rummaging in the bunker, he found a map showing all the details of the Argentine positions, as well as some patrol reports. These were quickly dispatched to Company Headquarters and on to Brigade.

Private Ferguson, in Owen's section, suddenly noticed four or five men below them. The corporal was uncertain as to who they could be – possibly 12 Platoon – and told Ferguson to challenge. The latter yelled "Who's there!" and was instantly greeted with a burst of fire that left them in no doubt. Grenades started to explode around Owen and his men as the enemy counter-attacked. The section opened fire, and Corporal Owen shouted for the machine-guns to engage.

10 Platoon meanwhile were firing on either side of the section, and Owen himself blasted away with eight M-79 rounds. The section was soon short of ammunition, and the men began to ferret for abandoned Argentine supplies. Just then the remainder of the platoon moved up to join the section; though uncertain as to exactly where the enemy were, they were determined to prevent the Argentines from regaining the ridge.

Private Lambert heard an Argentine, close in, shouting, "Grenado, grenado!"

"What a good idea," he thought, and lobbed one of his own in the direction of the voice. There were no more shouts.

11 Platoon also saw a group of four men to its front. 2nd Lieutenant Chris Waddington was unable to make out who they were and, thinking they might be 10 Platoon, shouted to them to stop. The four men took no notice, so he ordered a flare to be put up – the figures ran off as the platoon engaged with small arms and grenades. The orders not to exploit beyond the ridge-line meant that not all the enemy positions had been cleared during the night, and it seemed that some stay-behind snipers had been left there, and it was probably these that had given 12 Platoon so much trouble. But the counter-attack, such as it was, had fizzled out. Artillery fire was called down on Moody Brook to break up any further efforts at dislodging D Company. Down below the ridge a Landrover could be seen trying to get away. Lance-Corporal Walker fired at it and it crashed.

11 Platoon now came under extremely accurate enemy artil- lery fire, possibly registered on the flashes of their weapons.

Major Neame therefore ordered them to cease firing with small arms, intending to continue the battle with artillery alone. Moody Brook was deserted, however. In the distance the men of D Company noticed two Argentine soldiers walking off down the track as if at the end of an exercise.

In the light of dawn it appeared to the Paras on the ridge that a large number of enemy troops were moving up to reinforce Sapper Hill to the south-east. Neame called for artillery with great urgency, but no guns were available. After a further 20 minutes or so, by which time the enemy had reached the top, the target was engaged. Meanwhile other Argentines could be seen streaming off Tumbledown and Harriet – 5 Brigade had won its battles.

As D Company began to engage this new target the CO arrived. He confirmed Neame's orders to fire on the enemy retiring towards Stanley, and the company now joined in with machine-guns in a "turkey shoot". John Greenhalgh's helicopters swept in and fired SS-11 rockets and, together with two other Scouts, attacked an Argentine battery. The enemy AA was still active, however, and all the helicopters withdrew.

The retiring Argentines on Tumbledown had made no reply to the helicopters, and their artillery had stopped. It was obvious that a major change had occurred. The news was relayed to the Brigadier, who found it difficult to believe what was happening. But the CO realized how vital it was to get the battalion moving into Stanley before the enemy could rally, and A and B Companies, together with the Blues and Royals, were ordered to move as fast as possible up on to Wireless Ridge. The Brigadier arrived, still disbelieving until Colonel Chaundler said, "It's OK, Brigadier, it's all over." Together they conferred as to what to do next. D Company ceased firing on the fleeing enemy on the far hillside, and the order was given that men were only to fire if fired upon first. Permission was then given for the battalion to move on.

B Company, by now on the ridge, was ordered down into Moody Brook. Corporal Connors's section of 5 Platoon led the way, still expecting to come under fire from the "Triple As" on the race-course. The other two sections covered him forward. He cleared the flattened buildings of the old barracks and

Curtis's section took over, clearing the bridge over the Murrell River and the building on the other side, while all the time their platoon commander was exhorted, "Push on, push on!" They remained cautious, fearing booby traps or a sudden burst of fire.

A Company now took the lead as B Company, covering A's advance, moved south on to the high ground on the far side of the valley, above the road, passing through three abandoned gun positions on the way. The tanks of the Blues and Royals moved east along Wireless Ridge to give support if it should be necessary. A Company was well on the way down the road into Stanley, with C and D Companies following, when Brigade announced a cease-fire. Cheers went up, and red berets quickly replaced steel helmets. Bottles of alcohol miraculously appeared to celebrate with. Relief, elation, disbelief – all in turn had their effect.

Major Dair Farrar-Hockley led his men towards the race-course, past the abandoned guns that had been spotted so many hours earlier yet had remained operational in spite of requests for artillery fire. According to civilians afterwards, the Argentines still on the outskirts of Stanley simply broke and ran when they heard that "the Paras" were coming. The leading elements of the battalion arrived in Stanley at 1330 hours, on Monday, 14 June some five hours before the official cease-fire, with 2nd Lieutenant Mark Coe's 2 Platoon the first into the town. They were the first British troops into the capital.

Eventually all the companies were brought into the western outskirts, finding shelter amongst the deserted houses, a few of which had suffered from stray shells. One or two dead Argentine soldiers still lay in the street where they had been caught by shellfire. On the race-course the Argentine flag was pulled down and Sergeant-Major Fenwick's Union Jack once more served its purpose.

10
The Persian Gulf War

Desert Storm (1991)

Jon E. Lewis

In the vast winter silence of the desert night the ominous keening of aircraft high overhead could be heard. Everywhere along the Saudi–Kuwaiti border troops looked anxiously sky-wards from their foxholes. The jets were flying east, and mud soldiers of the Coalition shivered a sigh of relief. Ours. At the wet, temporary HQ of Britain's First Armoured Division a single voice rang out clear into the sandy darkness: "Yellow Alert. We are at war."

It was 11.30 p.m. on the evening of 16 January 1991. Operation Desert Storm, the effort to remove Saddam Hussein from his occupation of Kuwait, and the biggest concerted military action since the Second World War, had begun – just five months and 13 days after the Iraqi dictator had sent his tanks rolling across the Kuwaiti border. If the invasion of Kuwait had been a military success, it had also proved to be the biggest political mistake of Saddam's career.

No sooner had Saddam ordered his 500,000 victorious inva-sion troops to dig-in along the Kuwaiti–Saudi Arabian border, than the Americans had, under the flag of the United Nations, garnered together a considerable Coalition of anti-Saddam forces dedicated to ejecting him from Kuwait. Wars are seldom fought for moral principle, and the war which would be fought in the Persian Gulf was no exception. Though politicians would

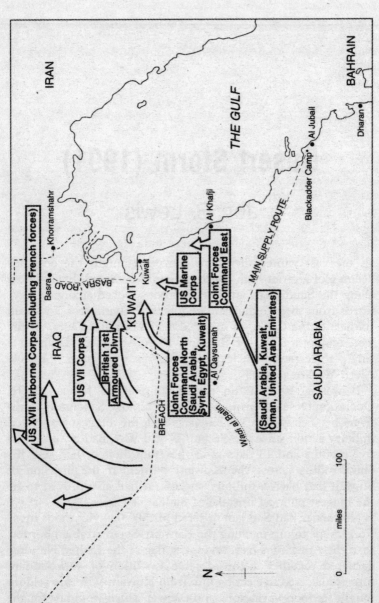

10.1 The Liberation of Kuwait, February 1991

declare that force was necessary to deal with the "bully" Saddam (while ignoring similar illegal occupations of smaller neighbours by Israel and Turkey, among other nations) the truth was always more prosaic: Saddam's occupation of Kuwait threatened to restrict the free access of the major economic nations to its huge subterranean seas of oil, as well as upsetting the area's fragile Arab balances of power.

As the US had taken the diplomatic lead against Iraq, so the US provided the overwhelming bulk of men, women and arms which would fight Operation Desert Storm; nearly 450,000 troops. In recognition of this, an American, General H. Norman Schwarzkopf, was appointed Commander-in-Chief of Coalition forces in the Gulf. (As a courtesy to the host country, Schwarzkopf was officially subordinated to the Saudi defence Minister, General Prince Khalid, but in practice operational command remained wholly with Schwarzkopf and his US CENTCOM; the only non-American on Schwarzkopf's central planning staff was Britain's Lieutenant-General Sir Peter de la Billiere, an acknowledgement of the fact that Britain provided the second largest troop contingent, 40,000 soldiers.) "Stormin' Norman", as he became dubbed, was a 56-year-old Vietnam veteran, of some irascibility. Whether by luck or design, in him the Americans had appointed a commander who was a canny user of the media – many American officers still blamed TV for defeat in Vietnam – and a master of the soundbite. At the end of the campaign, Schwarzkopf was asked by a journalist what he thought of Saddam Hussein as a military strategist. Using the fingers of his left hand to count off Saddam's "attributes", Schwarzkopf replied: "As far as Saddam Hussein being a great military strategist, he is neither a strategist, nor is he schooled in the operational arts, nor is he a tactician, nor is he a general, nor is he a soldier. Other than that, he is a great military man. I want you to know that."

Schwarzkopf himself, however, was all the above. A near-genius at battlefield strategy and tactics, his Operation Desert Storm would draw comparisons with Cannae and El Alamein.

Following his arrival in Saudi Arabia in August 1990, Schwarzkopf had initially been concerned only to secure the east Saudi border (Operation Desert Shield) against Iraqi

incursions. Two months later Washington, mindful that economic and diplomatic sanctions might well fail to persuade
Saddam to withdraw his forces from Kuwait, directed the
general to prepare contingency plans for an offensive.

On paper, at least, the Iraqi Army was a formidable
opponent and CENTCOM planned for the worst. Intelligence suggested that the Iraqi Army was as big and as
dangerous as Saddam Hussein himself claimed. It contained
over a million men, and possessed a devil's feast of modern
weaponry: around 6,000 tanks (including a number of Soviet
T-72s), 4,000 armoured personnel carriers, between 800 and
1,000 combat aircraft and 3,200 artillery pieces, including
some which could outgun those of the Coalition. Moreover,
the Iraqi Army was reputed to be battle-hardened after its
grinding 1980–8 war with Iran, and extremely adept at
defence. It had already fortified the border with Saudi Arabia
with a continuous belt of obstacles, including sand berms and
oil-filled trenches which could, with the touch of a torch, be
turned into a wall of fire. Most dangerous of all the Iraqi
forces were the armoured divisions of the "elite" Republican
Guard, held as a theatre reserve in southern Iraq and northern Kuwait. Uncomfortable at not having the classic three to
one ratio of advantage that military wisdom says an attacker
should have in order to guarantee victory, and worried that an
offensive might break down into an attrition battle or *slugfest*,
Schwarzkopf decided to exploit the Coalition's huge air force
to reduce Saddam's military capability, especially in the
Kuwaiti Theatre of Operations (KTO). This would be the
preliminary to a ground offensive with air support (in line
with the AirLand Battle Doctrine adopted by the Pentagon in
1982) which would outflank the main Iraqi defences in the
west beyond the point at which the Iraqi, Saudi and Kuwaiti
borders meet – and where the Iraqis had failed inexplicably to
build fortifications. This massive outflanking drive into the
KTO from the west would be accompanied by direct attacks
from the south and a feint amphibious landing from the east,
where 17,000 US Marines were waiting offshore. The Iraqis
would be crushed and caught in a massive envelopment.
Though it was apparently bitterly contested by some of his

staff, Schwarzkopf stuck to the essentials of his plan, finally getting it approved in mid-January 1991.

The plan was no sooner approved than it was called into use. The deadline for the implementation of United Nations Resolution 660 (Iraqi withdrawal from Kuwait) expired on midnight 15 January. The first Coalition aircraft were in the air twenty-four hours later, flying the first of a total of 110,000 sorties against targets across Iraq and Kuwait. Radar-guided American Stealth bombers executed pinpoint attacks with so-called smart bombs, accurate enough to be deposited down the airshafts of Iraqi bunkers. Other planes, wave after wave of them, F-15Es, F-A18 Hornets, A-6E Intruders and RAF Tornadoes bombed Iraqi military and communications targets and destroyed much of Saddam's air force before it could leave the runway. In the first day of the air campaign, US warships in the Gulf launched more than 100 Tomahawk Cruise missiles (each armed with half a ton of high explosive); observers in the Iraqi capital, Baghdad, watched in wonder as the Cruise missiles flew between buildings and turned corners before hitting their targets. Baghdad shook under the weight of the bombardment. Iraqi anti-aircraft fire turned the sky white.

Over the following weeks the air campaign drastically degraded Saddam's ability to fight a battle, destroying his highly centralized communications and command system, his arms and his army's morale. The Coalition achieved complete air supremacy. In Schwarzkopf's phrase, the removal of the Iraqis from the skies "blinded" Saddam. For this, the Allies were to lose a total of 67 aircraft.

The one black cloud in the Coalition's silver-lined air campaign was Iraq's Scud missile capability. Saddam began firing his Soviet-built Scud missiles on the second night of the air war, the first targets being Tel Aviv and Haifa in Israel. Although the six missiles which landed in Israel killed no one, and did not contain the feared chemical or nuclear warheads, the impact was psychologically and politically explosive. Israel threatened to take unilateral retaliatory action, something which would have wrecked the anti-Iraqi alliance, even perhaps starting a new Arab–Israeli war. Frantic diplomacy by the Americans, together with the dispatch of Patriot ground-to-air missile systems to shoot down Scuds, managed to persuade Israel from immediate punitive measures. The Patriots, though, were only of minimal effectiveness, failing even when they intercepted incoming Scuds always to destroy the warhead. Covert operations by British SAS and US Special Forces teams, dropped behind Iraqi lines, and the hunting of mobile Scud launchers by the Coalition air force did better. In the end, the Israelis suffered only 13 fatalities from Scuds. The Iraqis' most effective Scud launch was one of those aimed at Saudi Arabia. In the dying hours of the war a Scud landed on a US barracks in Dhahran, killing 28.

Such was the effectiveness of the air campaign that senior Coalition air force officers began to question whether a ground offensive was necessary. Schwarzkopf, however, along with the army and the Marines, was mindful that a war has never been won by airpower alone. Consequently, as the air campaign continued its attrition of enemy units, Schwarzkopf continued the deployment of the coalition army, most crucially of all the move west of the bulk of his forces: the US XVIII Airborne Corps, including the French Light Armoured *Division Daguet*, farthest west, its task a lightning drive to the Euphrates which would simultaneously protect the left flank of the invasion and cut off an Iraqi escape; then, to the right of XVIII Airborne, VII Corps, including British 1st Armoured Division, the steel *schwerpunkt* of the offensive which would smash north and then north-east towards Kuwait, hitting the Republican Guard in the flank. This remarkable movement of XVIII Airborne and VII Corps to their start positions was accomplished across several hundred miles of desert by thousands of tanks, trucks and other support vehicles. In order both to tie down Iraqi troops and confirm Iraqi expectations of a frontal attack on Kuwait City, Coalition Arab forces and the US 1st and 2nd Marines, together with the 1st (Tiger) Brigade of the US 2nd Armoured Division were deployed in the south of the battlefield, along the Kuwaiti–Saudi border.

While Schwarzkopf made ready, time was trickling away for Saddam Hussein. If the air war had degraded his military capacity it had done nothing to diminish his rhetoric or his will to hold onto Kuwait, promising the Coalition "the Mother of All Battles" should it try to force him out. A Soviet attempt to broker talks failed. On 22 February US President Bush gave Saddam the ultimatum to withdraw from Kuwait or face the consequences. In the best fashion of the Western, Bush's deadline expired at noon – noon (EST) on Saturday 23 February. Saddam refused to blink. That night, with singular appropriateness, American Forces network radio in the Gulf played "Saturday Night's All Right (For Fighting)". As Elton John sang, soldiers along the front line were making ready for combat, Marine bulldozers breaching Iraqi defences. Sand berms were demolished, trenches filled with oil burned off, and minefields cleared.

As Saturday night edged into Sunday morning, Coalition air force and navy began a massive bombardment of the Iraqi lines. It started raining. And then at 4 a.m., US and Saudi Marines in the coastal area that was the easternmost point of the battlefield began moving forward through the Iraqi defences, the vaunted "Saddam Line". The ground war had begun.

The Marines breached the Iraqi barriers with relative ease, the minefields posing fewer problems than expected: many mines had become exposed by shifting sand, while some Marines crossed the minefields by walking on anti-tank mines, knowing that they could not be detonated by the weight of a man. By the end of the first day of the ground war (G-Day) the 1st Marine Division had secured Al-Jaber airfield, halfway to Kuwait City, having bypassed some Iraqi units who were poised to fight but failed to counter-attack. The battlefield, eerily quiet and shrouded in acrid smoke from the Kuwaiti oil wells set on fire by the Iraqis on 22 February, was littered with burnt-out wrecks of Iraqi trucks and tanks, victims of the Coalition air force.

At the opposite end of the Allied line, the French *Division Daguet* and its attached US 82nd Airborne Division (the Screaming Eagles), given the task of sweeping around the Saddam Line and securing the offensive's left flank, penetrated rapidly into Iraq, brusquely subduing the Iraqi 45th Infantry Division with artillery and HOT anti-tank missiles from French-built Gazelle helicopters. The 101st Airborne Division, immediately to the east, after a hold-up due to poor weather, mounted one of the biggest airmobile operations in history with some 300 Chinook helicopters ferrying troops to establish an advance position, FOB Cobra, 70 miles inside Iraqi territory.

Iraqi resistance to the Coalition incursions was everywhere so minimal that by late morning Schwarzkopf decided to deal the enemy a further reeling blow, bringing the second phase of the offensive forward to the afternoon of G-Day instead of the morning of G + 1. The US 24th Mechanized Infantry Division – Schwarzkopf's old division – along with the 3rd Armoured Cavalry began rolling forward at midday, its mission to cross nearly 250 miles of Iraqi rock and sand and establish itself near the town of Basra, where it would cut off Iraqi forces and engage the Republican Guards. As the 24th roared across the desert it passed weary US Long Range Surveillance Detachments, who had been in Iraq for weeks sending back HUMINT (human intelligence). Also at midday, VII Corps – with 1,300 tanks the biggest armoured corps in history – led by the "Big Red One", the US 1st Infantry Division (Mechanized), began its breach of the Iraqi line, with the divisions of the Corps following through over the next 24 hours. The British 1st Armoured Division went through the breach in the morning of G + 1, the "anvil" on which the rest of the Corps would hammer the Republican Guards.

To the right of VII Corps, east of Wadi al-Batin, Arab forces from Egypt, Syria, Saudi Arabia and Kuwait began their advance in the afternoon of G-Day, proceeding more circumspectly than their neighbours, the US Marines, in part because they faced one of the most fortified sections of the Saddam Line. The Egyptians found themselves in front of walls of burning oil, but managed the breach in less than five hours after pushing sand into the trenches with their tanks and bulldozers.

By evening all Coalition forces had advanced well beyond their schedule, progress only improved by the Coalition's continuing deception operation, with thousands of Marines – apparently set for a seaborne invasion – waiting off Kuwait's shore, and a highly visible demonstration by the famous 1st Armoured Cavalry Division (the Air Cav) in the Wadi al-Batin. Casualties had been minimal. Among the worst losses of the day were those suffered by the British in a "friendly fire" incident, when an American A-10 "Tankbuster" mistakenly eliminated a British Warrior Armoured Vehicle; nine soldiers died.

As dawn broke on 25 February, G + 1, the scale of the Iraqi rout and disorientation became more apparent. The fast-moving *Division Daguet* had hardly encountered a living soul and continued its spectacular dash throughout the day, reaching As-Salman airfield, 70 miles inside Iraq, by evening, where it had to be ordered to pause. Eastward down the line the 24th Infantry Division (the Victory Division) rolled ever onwards, also without opposition, while the British 1st Armoured Division engaged and defeated the Iraqi 12th Armoured Division before becoming delayed by the throngs of Iraqi soldiers eager to surrender. Elsewhere over the battlefield it was the same story of Iraqis throwing down their weapons. The crush of POWs, indeed, posed more of a problem than the Iraqis who tried to fight; 25,000 prisoners were captured during the day. Only in a handful of places did the Iraqis put up serious resistance. An armoured division counter-attacked the US 2nd Marine Division near Al-Jaber but was heavily repulsed. Iraqi armour which tried to block the path of the 2nd Marine Division and the Tiger Brigade also fared badly. Perhaps the fiercest encounter of the day was at the Burgan oil field near Kuwait International Airport, where the 1st Marine Division met with well-entrenched Iraqi units. These were flushed out by a massive "time on time" artillery bombardment and then decimated by USMC tanks and Cobra attack helicopters. The Iraqis lost 50 tanks for no USMC loss.

If the Coalition needed any proof that things were going well, it came on the morning of the next day, Tuesday 26 February (G + 2), when Baghdad Radio announced that Iraq was prepared to withdraw from Kuwait. Washington's response was brusque: "The war goes on." In Kuwait City itself, panic-stricken Iraqis began to commandeer vehicles and flee northwards on the road to the Mutla Gap causing, as one commentator quipped, "the mother of all traffic jams". A dozen Coalition F-15s bombed the front of a 1,000-vehicle Iraqi convoy, and then bombed its rear. Coalition aircraft then swarmed down on the luckless trapped Iraqis in a turkey-shoot reminiscent of the destruction of the Wehrmacht as it tried to escape through the Falaise Gap in 1944.

The reason for the Iraqi haste in quitting Kuwait City was that the Coalition's southern groupings were now only miles from the suburbs, although the US 1st Marine Division had run into a sizeable formation of Iraqi armour determined to make a fight for the International Airport. The battle would last throughout the day and into the next, the sky so dark with smoke from oil well fires that flashlights had to be used to read charts. The Tiger Brigade and 2nd Marine Division also met opposition as they curled north around Kuwait City to prevent any retreat.

Meanwhile, far to the west, with the *Division Daguet* holding the left flank secure against Iraqi reinforcements, the XVIII Airborne Corps had consolidated its hold on the Euphrates valley, with the 24th Infantry Division reaching Highway 8 and then surging eastwards down it towards Basra, its helicopter attack regiment in the van. The 24th had the smell of success in its nostrils and was now riding towards the Republican Guard. A brigade of 57 Iraqi T-72 tanks unlucky enough to cross the 24th's path was decimated, the T-72s no match for the 24th's M1A1s and Apache attack helicopters.

Likewise closing on the Republican Guards was VII Corps, with the 2nd Armoured Cavalry making contact with the Guard late in the evening. After completing its rout of the 12th Iraqi Armoured Division, the British 1st Armoured Division had overrun the 17th and 52nd Armoured Divisions, eliminating 300 enemy tanks and armoured vehicles in the process. At midnight the British division reached its main objective, code-named Waterloo, at the south end of Phase Line Smash. Caught between an anvil and a descending hammer, the Republican Guard realized too late that the target of XVIII Airborne and VII Corps was not Kuwait but the Guard itself.

Over the next 32 hours, by 8 a.m. Thursday 28 February (G + 4), the Iraqi Army disintegrated. They surrendered in their thousands, waving anything white they could find. The Iraqi force at Kuwait International Airport was finally over-come, with the triumphant Marines opening their lines to give the honour of liberating Kuwait City to the Kuwaiti 35th

Mechanized Brigade, who entered the city at 9 a.m. on 27 February to an ecstatic welcome. Much of the city was anyway already in the control of Kuwaiti resistance fighters.

Along the Iraq–Kuwait border, meanwhile, XVIII Airborne and VII Corps engaged the Republican Guard in what would be the classic tank battle of the campaign, lasting into the morning of G + 4. Although some of the Iraqi units in the Basra Pocket put up a brave fight, especially those from the Guard's best-equipped divisions (Tawakalna, Medina and Hammurabi), it was always a one-sided contest. The Iraqis had no air cover and very poor communications, while the attack–attack tactic of the US forces never allowed them time to consolidate. The Coalition was fighting a multi-dimensional modern war while the Iraqis wanted a static war of First World War vintage. The Republican Guard left the field with its pretensions to military elitism in tatters. In truth the Guard was never the force Saddam claimed it to be, or the Coalition feared it to be. Its experience fighting the Iranians had left it not so much combat-ready as combat-fatigued. Moreover, the Guard – its primary function being the protection of Saddam's Ba'athist dictatorship – selected most of its officers for political reliability, not military ability. What was arguably the best Guard unit, *Amn al-Khas* (special security), was judged too important by Saddam to fight in the war, and was kept in Baghdad. Other Iraqi units, made up overwhelmingly of conscripts, had second-rate equipment and little desire to die for Saddam's lost cause. Nor were there as many Iraqi soldiers in the KTO as the Coalition had estimated (500,000); in all probability they numbered fewer than 300,000 – 200,000 fewer than the Coalition.

With the Iraqi Army almost completely encircled, Schwarzkopf would have liked to have continued the war to ensure its destruction. As it was, 700 Iraqi tanks escaped the net. The Coalition's Arab members had no wish to see the complete disintegration of Iraq – which would have unleashed a wave of protest in their countries, where support for Saddam was sizeable – and at 9 p.m. (EST), in a televised address, President Bush announced a ceasefire from midnight – 8 a.m. on 28 February in the Gulf. By the close of the ground war the Iraqis had suffered around 8,000 casualties; another 86,000 Iraqis had surrendered to the Coalition. The Iraqi Army had not only been driven from Kuwait, it had been routed. Coalition casualties during the ground war were minimal: 150 KIA, a quarter of these victims in "friendly fire" incidents. The Mother of All Battles had taken exactly 100 hours.

11
Afghanistan

Tora Bora (2001)

Johnny Verey

When you're wounded and left on Afghanistan's plains
And the women come out to cut up what remains
Just roll to your rifle and blow out your brains
An' go to your Gawd like a soldier.

Rudyard Kipling

The long fuse leading to the War on Terror was ignited in 1989 when an obscure Saudi millionaire, Osama bin Laden, formed a terrorist group to wage a holy war against the West. Al-Qaeda ("The Base"), as bin Laden dubbed his organization, supervised the 1993 attack on the World Trade Center, together with sporadic bombings of US embassies and military facilities, including the *USS Cole*, across the globe in the years that followed. These attacks, however, were but pin-pricks on the buffalo hide of the USA and few counter-terrorist measures against al-Qaeda were undertaken by the US authorities, save for the demanding of bin Laden's removal from Sudan and the placing of him on the FBI's "Ten Most Wanted" list. Only in 2001, when al-Qaeda turned airliners into bombers in its September 11 attack on the World Trade Center and the Pentagon, did the USA and the West wake to the systematic war being waged against them.

US retribution for "9/11" was swift. On 7 October 2001 President George Bush launched "Operation Enduring Free-

dom – Afghanistan", a massive offensive against al-Qaeda
training bases in Afghanistan. Since the Taliban rulers of
Afghanistan were supportive of al-Qaeda, they too found themselves in the cross-hairs of Coalition forces, principally raised
from the US and UK. The initial phase of Enduring Freedom
took the shape of a devastating aerial bombing campaign, in
which Taliban and al-Qaeda front-line positions were subjected
to constant poundings by B-1 Lancer, B-2 Spirit and B-52
Stratofortress bombers, ship/submarine launched Tomahawk
cruise missiles, AC-130 gunships and carrier-based F-14 Tom-
cat and F/A-18 Hornet fighters. Bombed by an enemy they
could not see or fight, the Taliban were soon in disarray. By
early November, even the most limited Allied special forces
operations on the ground, together with attacks by anti-Taliban
Afghan fighters, were enough for city after city to surrender. On
13 November the Taliban fled the Afghan capital, Kabul, to
ecstatic celebrations by its citizens.

Al-Qaeda proved to be made of sterner stuff than the Taliban, fanatically resisting all attacks by Allied units. As one of
the first US Special Operations Forces (SOF) officers flown
into Afghanistan, Colonel John Mulholland, observed: "Al-
Qaeda wasn't interested in surrendering, by and large." In the
last days of November some 2000 al-Qaeda fighters – principally highly experienced and well-equipped Arabs, Chechens
and Iranians – massed at Tora Bora in the White Mountains,
near the Pakistan border. Human intelligence (HUMINT)
from captured Taliban, local villagers and Afghan militias
indicated that bin Laden himself was holed up in Tora Bora,
along with his elite 055 bodyguard unit.

Tora Bora was an area bin Laden knew well. A complex of
caves, some stretching 60 feet into the granite mountainside,
Tora Bora had been built by the mujahadeen in the 1980s
during their war against the Soviet occupation of Afghanistan.
One of those lending a hand in the caves' construction was bin
Laden himself, who reputedly flew in bulldozers from his Saudi
family's gigantic construction firm. In one of the grimmest
ironies of modern history, a considerable tranche of the cost of
constructing the Tora Bora complex was financed by the CIA as
part of Operation Cyclone.

In line with its belief that the War on Terror in the Afghanistan theatre could be decided by airpower and suitcases full of dollar bills, US strategy at Tora Bora was to pound al-Qaeda positions from the air and hire a proxy army, in the shape of 2,500 Afghan militiamen from the "Northern Alliance" to fight the ground war. After intermittent air strikes, al-Qaeda positions at Tora Bora were subjected to saturation bombing on 30 November, included the dropping of devastating 15,0000-pound BLU-82 ("Big Blue" or "daisy cutter") ordnance. Three days later, the ground offensive began.

Tora Bora was never going to be an easy battle for the US-led Coalition. Much of the battlefield was near vertical, and thick with pine trees and snow. Colonel John Mulholland noted of Tora Bora: "This is incredible terrain, incredible elevations, and truthfully, very difficult with the force available to decisively search every nook and cranny, because there are no shortages of caves in Afghanistan. They probably number in the hundreds of thousands . . ." For the "Anti Taliban Forces", as the US military termed the Northern Alliance militias, grouped at the bottom of the mountains, it was a three-hour climb to reach the first tier of al-Qaeda caves. Unlike the ATF, al-Qaeda forces in the caves – which enjoyed electricity, courtesy of generators – were warm and well-provisioned with food. A pattern quickly became set: al-Qaeda withdrew into the caves during bombing raids, and then reassumed their positions while ATF forces climbed upwards towards them. When the ATF came within range, al-Qaeda soldiers ambushed them.

Allied problems at Tora Bora were not limited to the nature of the terrain. The ATF forces gathered for the ground campaign were a heterogeneous mixture of tribes, whose interests were far from identical. (Such, indeed, was the loathing between the two ATF leaders Hazarat Ali and Hajji Zaman that their followers opened fire on each on one occasion.) Few of the ATF forces were properly equipped or trained, and the only armour they could bring to the battlefield was a squadron of battered Russian tanks left over from the war against the Kremlin two decades before.

The inferior nature of the ATF soldier was mirrored by his commander. Ali and Zaman had come of age fighting skirmishes in the anti-Soviet war. A full-scale battle involving the deployment of thousands of troops and the co-ordination of air and land offensives was beyond their ken. Communication between the ATF leaders was sometimes non-existent: ludicrously, Ali failed to inform one key ATF commander, Zahir, that the ground offensive would commence on 3 December, leaving the latter to find out by watching CNN.

The absence of command was found at higher levels, too. The war in Afghanistan was overseen by the US's Central Command (CENTCOM), based in Tampa, Florida. Crucially, CENTCOM failed to realize that the ATF had only surrounded the Tora Bora complex on three sides, leaving the south unguarded. Although 4,000 US Marines, commanded by US Brig. James N. Mattis now arrived in theatre, Franks and the Bush administration refused to allow Mattis to deploy to Tora Bora, despite Mattis' protestations that the Tora Bora complex and the border to Pakistan needed to be sealed. According to leaks from US intelligence, the Bush administration would later concede that the failure to deploy Mattis and the Marines was a grave strategic error. CENTCOM, at this stage of the war, was notably "risk averse", remembering how TV pictures of US body bags being flown home from the Battle of Mogadishu had turned public opinion off interventions abroad. Although Franks did allow the insertion by helicopter of around ninety Allied special forces soldiers, principally elements of the US 1st Special Forces Operational Detachment-Delta, the Green Berets, the British 22 Special Air Service Regiment (22 SAS), the British Special Boat Service (SBS) and the German KSK, he initially restricted their tasks to advice-giving and the calling-in of air strikes.

Despite all the difficulties, the ATF, after a week of heavy skirmishing, succeeded in securing one of the main ridge lines in Tora Bora, from which Allied Special Forces advisors were able to direct more accurate air strikes on al-Qaeda positions, which were also now subjected to constant sniper fire. Sensing defeat, al-Qaeda began to plan a withdrawal from the complex of caves. They were inadvertently abetted in this withdrawal on

12 December, by the ATF commander Hajji Zaman who, concerned at the high rate of casualties amongst his men and the superior armaments of al-Qaeda, made radio contact with bin Laden's commanders and offered a cease-fire. Al-Qaeda accepted. Over the night of 12 December American intelligence officials believe that 800 al-Qaeda fighters escaped from Tora Bora through the unguarded southern slopes.

On the following day, an al-Qaeda rearguard, possibly seeking to buy time for the escape of the 800, resumed hostilities at Tora Bora. Into this tail-end of the battle were deployed two squadrons of 22 SAS, the regiment's largest single-battle deployment since the 1970s, which joined the ATF in the close-combat fighting required to clear the caves. (Reputedly, the SAS forces were led by the regiment's colonel, who won a Military Cross for his actions). By 17 December, the last caves had been overrun and the defenders eliminated or captured.

A search of the area by US forces revealed no trace of Osama bin Laden himself. American intelligence later indicated that he left Tora Bora on the evening of the 16th, riding south on horseback. This accords with reports from 22 SAS that they sighted bin Laden at this time, but were forbidden to eliminate him for political reasons: the Pentagon insisted that the honour of the kill be undertaken by US special forces. They arrived too late to intercept him.

The engagement at Tora Bora was a victory for the Coalition, but like King Pyrrhus of Epirus' victory over the Romans at Heracleia and Asculum, it was more costly to the winner than the vanquished. Certainly, the Coalition secured an al-Qaeda redoubt, killing or capturing over 300 terrorist fighters and driving the remainder from Afghanistan – yet the Coalition, crucially, allowed the bulk of the enemy to withdraw from the battlefield in good order. In particular, the Coalition allowed bin Laden to escape. Bin Laden was more than a political or military leader: he was a symbol. Bin Laden's capture or death would have been a massive blow to the morale of al-Qaeda and to those who looked towards it for inspiration.

In a political damage-limitation exercise, the Bush administration – including the president and Gen. Tommy Franks – insisted after the battle that there was no definitive information that bin Laden was even in Tora Bora in December 2001. Bin Laden was "never within our grasp" Franks informed the *New York Times*. Pentagon documents released in 2005 after a Freedom of Information Act request, however, show that government officials did, at the time, believe categorically that bin Laden was at Tora Bora in December 2001 and that he escaped alive.

The price of the Coalition's failure to deal al-Qaeda and Osama bin Laden a knock-out blow at Tora Bora was quickly apparent. The hunt for bin Laden no longer focused on an area of a few miles square but one of 40,000 square miles, the Pakistan-Afghanistan borderland. Not only was this borderland remote and mountainous, but its Muslim tribes tended to be supportive of bin Laden. There was widespread sympathy for bin Laden in Pakistan too, which prevented President Musharaf from resolute action against possible local sanctuaries for the terrorist.

If bin Laden, as most intelligence operatives conclude, holed up in the Afghanistan-Pakistan borderland, the same cannot be said of his commanders, who travelled to Iraq and other places to continue their "jihad" against the West. Inside Afghanistan, meanwhile, al-Qaeda regrouped sufficiently by February 2002 to establish a battle force of up to a 1,000 fighters in the Shahi-Kot Valley southeast of Zormat.

The consequences of Coalition failure at Tora Bora escalated. Elements of the Taliban, inspired by al-Qaeda's resilience, re-formed; operations against the insurgent Taliban and al-Qaeda, who frequently sheltered in civilian sites, caused high numbers of civilian Afghan casualties ("collateral damage" in modern military speak'); in turn the civilian casualties caused even sympathetic Afghans to oppose the Coalition. Soon the Coalition's "Operation Enduring Freedom – Afghanistan" (OEF-A) needed 20,000 troops in theatre – but still no end to the war came. To stabilize the country the UN dispatched the International Security Assistance Force (ISAF) which, by 2008, was 50,000-strong in Afghanistan. But still no stability came. Few noticed, for the War on Terror's Iraq theatre took the main headlines.

The war in Afghanistan, like Vietnam, may prove unwinnable. It is salutary to note that the Soviets – who were far from "risk averse" – preferred to bid Afghanistan *Do svidaniya* in 1989 rather than be bled to death by a running sore. More than a century and half before, the British too had been obliged to evacuate Afghanistan, a rare rebuff for Victoria's redcoats.

Looking back on the Tora Bora battle, Colonel John Mulholland US Special Operations Commander, Afghanistan, commented:

> Was it perfect? No, it wasn't perfect . . . In hindsight maybe would we have liked to have done more? Absolutely, we would like to walk out of the mountains with bin Laden and his cronies in hand, certainly, but it didn't happen. I think it's a mistake for people to cast too glaring an indictment of that operation not understanding fully the context of what was going on with the battlefield at the time, what was available, and the urgency of when people wanted to see things happen.

"The urgency of when people wanted to see things happen" – Afghanistan was the proof positive of the adage "Act in haste, Repent at leisure". There was no invasion plan ready in a filing cabinet before 9/11. Operation Enduring Freedom – Afghanistan was conceived, planned and put into effect within four weeks, chiefly because public opinion and the political inclination of the Bush administration was to do something – anything – to strike back at al-Qaeda.

In contrast, Operation Desert Storm in the Persian Gulf War was six months in the planning. In contrast it, unlike Operation Enduring Freedom – Afghanistan, was an unmitigated success.